Levon Aharonian

STORMY DAYS
Memoirs of an Iranian-Armenian Businessman

Gomidas Institute
London

This book was originally published in Persian (2008) and Armenian (2010). The English translation is from the Armenian.

© Copyright 2016 Gomidas Institute

ISBN 978-1-909382-32-9

05 04 03 02 01

Gomidas Institute
42 Blythe Rd.
London W14 0HA
United Kingdom
www.gomidas.org
info@gomidas.org

*To the memory of my wife and my faith
in the new generation, including my own grandchildren,
Andrei and Badrik. I hope my memoir, and others like it,
provide a truthful and worthy guide in their lives.*

Acknowledgements

This publication would not have been possible without the help of others. I would like to thank my translators, Mrs. Talin Voskeritchian and Mr. Asbed Kochikian. They did a wonderful job and it was my pleasure to work with them. I would also like to thank Mrs. Diane James, who edited the translation so well. And I owe a special thanks to Ara Sarafian and the Gomidas Institute for publishing this work.

Contents

	Map	11
1.	My Ancestral Roots and Early Childhood	13

Salmas – My Earliest Memories – Moving to Tehran – My First Encounter with Mohammad Reza Pahlavi – Elementary School – Middle and High School – Teen Pranks

2.	The Second World War Comes to Iran	37

The Rise and Fall of Reza Shah – Wartime Conditions in Tehran – The Emergence of Tudeh – The Crisis in Azarbayjan – André Shop – Dangerous Activities – The Movies – Sports – Summertime – The Soviet Repatriation Drive – An Attempt on the Shah's Life

3.	The Struggle to Nationalize the Oil	59

Coup d'état – The Charm of Democracy and Free Speech – The Polytechnic Institute – The Crackdown

4.	Young Manhood	69

How I Met Bella – Internship in Shazand – Starting a Career and a Family – Postgraduate Study Abroad – Encounters with the Shah – Expanding the Family Business

5.	Starting at Sati	83

Tavanir – The First Iranian Gas Trunkline – A Family Home in Farmaniyeh – The Manjil Power Plant – Pandemonium at the Port – Expanding Sati – A New Investor

6.	Doing Business with the Soviet Union	95

A Warning from SAVAK – Negotiating with a Soviet Armenian – Round Two – My First Visit to My Historic Homeland – Ramin Power Plant – Political Problems – Practical Problems – Russian Manners – The Heaviest Lift in Iranian History – Sati's Second Big Contract with the USSR – My Last Encounter with the Shah

7.	Before the Revolution	109

The ARF versus the Tudeh – The Golden Age – The Ararat Center – Ararat FC – Hunting – Looking for Boars, Finding Gazelles – Ibex and Bears in Varvash – Leopards in Marakan – The Anguran Reserve – Siah Kuh – The Hunter's Code – Cheating Death in Firuz Kuh – Fish and Fowl – André Safarian – Ara Vartanian

8. The Coming of the Revolution ... 131

Petrodollars – Opposition to the Shah – The Shah and the USA – The Gathering Revolution – Transitional Government – Ayatollah Khomeini

9. Consequences of the Iranian Islamic Revolution ... 147

The First Few Weeks – Law and Order – The Provisional Government and the Revolutionary Council – The Clerics Take Over the Government – Nationalizations, Expropriations and Bonyads – Revolutionary Guards Raid Sati – My Business Interests

10. The Islamic Government and the Hostage Crisis ... 163

The New Constitution – Regional Uprisings – The Armenian Community – A Sectarian Attack – The Hostage Crisis – The Failed American Rescue Attempt

11. The Struggle over the Schools, 1980–81 ... 179

The New Diocesan Council – The Beginning of Trouble for Armenian Schools – Meeting with Chief Justice Ayatollah Beheshti – Restructuring the Schools – Meeting with Education Minister Ayatollah Bahonar – Responding to Challenges from the Armenian Left – Trouble with the IAMM – My Relationship with the ARF – Fending Off Gender Segregation

12. The Iran-Iraq War and Civil Society ... 205

The Armenian Community's Contribution to the War Effort – Sati's Contribution to the Defense of Iran – Religious and Cultural Sensitivities – The Third Annual Commemoration of the Armenian Genocide – Back-to-Back Interviews on National TV – Incident at Bagh-e Keshmesh

13. Social and Political Turmoil ... 225

Destruction of the Mojahedin Khalq – Destruction of the Tudeh – The Monkerat – Ershad

14. The Struggle Over the Schools, 1981–82 ... 238

The Twenty-Point Circular – The Community's Response – High-Level Meetings – Victory at Last – Meeting with Education Minister Parvaresh – Meeting with President Khamenei – Prime Minister Mousavi's Circular

15. **The Struggle Over the Schools, 1982–83**   253

The Diocesan Council's Response – Ratcheting Up the Pressure – The New School Year – An Exchange of Views with Minister Parvaresh – Meeting with Prime Minister Mousavi – Final Exams – An Invitation to Convert

16. **The Struggle Over the Schools, 1983–84**   270

Persian-Language Religion Textbook Supplements – Problem Principal – Armenian Schools Closed – Final Exams – Surveillance and Entrapment – The Masks Are Finally Off

17. **Armenian Members of Parliament**   279

Vartan Vartanian – Ardavazd Baghoumian – Dr. Levon Davidian – George Abrahamian – Gevorg Vardan – Robert Beglarian – Some Notable Prerevolutionary MPs

18. **The Structure and Functions of the Diocesan Council**   287

Administration and Funding – Provincial Tours of Armenian Communities – Assistance to Emigrants – The Avedissian Community Clinic – Excess Alcohol and X-Ray Film – The New Avedissian Community Clinic

19. **Ecclesiastical Affairs**   297

General Assembly Meeting at Antelias – A Meeting of the Three Iranian Dioceses – Building New Churches and Renovating Old Ones – Celebrating Archbishop Manoukian – Raffi's Travel Memoirs

20. **Life-Changing Events**   305

My Mother's Last Years – My Open-Heart Surgery – The Eleventh Diocesan Assembly of Representatives – Learning to Read and Write in Armenian – The End of the War – The Spitak Earthquake

21. **Extortion by Obscure Government Agents**   315

Getting to Know Colonel X – Colonel X and the Interior Minister – Thus Began the Most Unpleasant Period of My Life – Midnight Forays with Farrokh – Prescription Opiates – Legal Advice – I Shut My Eyes and Open My Mouth

22. **Imprisoned, Interrogated and Exonerated**   329

Interrogation – A "Historic" Trial – The Chain Murder Scandal – Self-Financing Government Agencies

23. **The André and Almast Aharonian Kindergarten**   338

Construction – Opening Day – The Tenth Anniversary Celebration

24. Moscow and Armenia — 342
My Third Visit to Armenia – Journey to Meghri – Back in Yerevan – Easter Sunday at Echmiadzin – Back in Tehran

25. The First Diaspora Business Conference in the Last Days of Soviet Armenia — 355
Saturday, May 25, 1991 – Armenian Airlines – Conflict between the ARF and the ANM – Sunday – Monday – Tuesday

26. Post-Conference Developments — 366
Armenian Airlines – The Iran-Armenia Chamber of Commerce – Meghri Bridge Site Visit

27. President Ter-Petrosyan Visits Iran — 374
The Liberation of Shushi – Mission to Armenia – Made in Tabriz – Aid to Armenia – How the Permanent Meghri Bridge Was Built

28. The ARF and Community Business in Tehran — 389
An Off-the-Books Loan – Mrs. Ferahian's Will – The Gabrielian Building – The Property Committee – The Shishmanian Property

29. The Armenian Business Forum — 400
The Third Annual Conference – Remarks by President Ter-Petrosyan – A Private Meeting – Remarks by Vice President Harutyunyan – A Dinner Party – The Armenian Business Forum Company – The Faucet Factory in Ghapan – ABFCo and the Privatization of Armenian State Enterprises – Famous Armenians I Have Known – The Ani String Quartet

30. Diplomatic Overtures and Contretemps — 419
Commercial and Cultural Exchanges – Economic and Political Exchanges – Incident in Isfahan – Media Campaign – The New Iranian Ambassador to Armenia – Persistent Partisan Sniping – Alik's Role – Alik's Publisher Arrested

31. An Unexpected Request — 434
The Asia Hotel – Family Financial Crisis – Armenia's 1996 Presidential Election – The Two Holy Sees

32. Dual Mission to Armenia — 444
Mission to Echmiadzin – Mission to Yerevan – Back in Tehran – A Meeting with President Ter-Petrosyan's Emissary – Unauthorized Fundraising

Contents

33. **A Series of Historic Meetings** — 454

    Foreign Minister Arzoumanyan Visits Iran – Speaker Araktsyan Visits Tehran – Logistics for a Meeting with the Supreme Patriarch – The Meeting in Geneva – Second Meeting with President's Ter-Petrosyan's Emissary

34. **Reflections on Politics and Diplomacy** — 471

    Ambassador Bayburdyan – Ambassador Gharibjanyan – Ambassador Nazaryan

35. **Business and Philanthropy in Armenia** — 477

    Second IACOC Trade Fair – Third IACOC Trade Fair – School No. 136 Destroyed by Fire – Fourth IACOC Trade Fair – Rebuilding School No. 136 – Reopening School No. 136 – Construction Boom in Yerevan – The Armenia School Foundation – My Personal Investments in Armenia – The Masisavan Condominium Complex

36. **The 1700th Anniversary of Armenian Christianity** — 490

    Archbishop Sebouh Sarkissian – 1700th Anniversary Celebrations – Pilgrimage to St. Thaddeus Monastery – Touring Salmas with Raffi Hovannisian

37. ***Louys, Houys,* and the Diocesan Assembly Elections** — 498

    Launching Louys *– Assessment of the Eleventh Diocesan Assembly – Campaign for the Twelfth Diocesan Assembly – The Controversy over Aid to Armenia – Election of the Twelfth Diocesan Assembly – Election of the Thirteenth Diocesan Assembly – The End of* Louys *– Launching* Houys

38. **Sati's Fiftieth Anniversary** — 519

39. **Three Deaths in the Family** — 523

    Far Away in Fars Province – Funerary Rites – Remembering Annette – African Safari – Our Fiftieth Wedding Anniversary

40. **The Iran-Armenia Friendship Society** — 535

41. **The Establishment of the "Hay Dbrotz" (Armenian School) Foundation** — 536

    The First Delivery – My Investments in Armenia – Personal Investments in Armenia – Large Construction Plans in Armenia

42. The Role of Iranian Armenian Organizations After the Islamic Revolution   545

Ararat Armenian Cultural and Sport Organization (AACO) – The Armenian Association of Tehran Senior Citizens – The Tehran Chapter of the Armenian General Benevolent Union (AGBU) – Iranian Armenian National and Cultural Union (IANCU) – Iranian-Armenian Craftsmen's Association – Iranian-Armenian Writers' Union – Iranian-Armenian Engineers' and Architects' Union – Armenian Women's Benevolent Union of Tehran – Hay Agoomb (Armenian Club) – Church Ladies' Union of Tehran – Hay Geen (Armenian Woman) Organization – Nairi Armenian Cultural Association – "Charmahal" Armenian Sport and Educational Association – "Sipan" Armenian Sport and Cultural Organization – "Raffi" Sports and Cultural Organization – Iranian-Armenian Physicians' Association – "Sardarabad" Armenian Cultural and Sport Organization – "Sosse Mayrik" Seniors' Home – A Brief Glance at the Hay Dad (Armenian Cause) Committee of Tehran.

Index of Personal and Place Names   571

Chapter 1

My Ancestral Roots and Early Childhood

Haftvan is a village in Salmast (Salmas), the county west of Lake Urumia in Iran's West Azarbayjan Province (ancient Roman Atropatene, Eastern Armenian *Adrbadagan*). My ancestors on both sides were originally from Haftvan and I was born in the village on November 17, 1930.

My mother Almast was born in Haftvan in 1908. Her mother was the daughter of Melik Harutiun from the neighboring village of Mahlam, which was a source of great pride to my mother. My father sometimes jokingly called her "Melik's granddaughter." Her father, Abraham Babloyan, was known as Mghdsi Abro. He was a very rich man, thanks to the orchards he owned and the loans he made to merchants and migrant workers. It was said that he mocked his provincial compatriots because they went to Russia and labored under harsh conditions and came back to Haftvan in clean clothes and new scarves, and then asked for a loan to go back to Russia! Abraham was also a very true-believer and had managed to go barefoot for pilgrim from Salmas to Jerusalem via Iraq. After this trip, he received the title "Mghdessi" which is the Armenian for the Farsi word "Moghaddas," meaning "Holy". So Mghdsi is not his name but his title.

Anticipating an Ottoman invasion in the winter of 1914, Mghdsi Abro arranged for his family to escape north under the protection of his son, my maternal Uncle Mnatsakan Babloyan. The party of five – Uncle Mnatsakan, my mother, their sister Mahi, their mother Aslikhan and my uncle's wife Hayganoush Avakian – left Salmas by sled. Braving sleet and snow, they reached Khoy and stayed there for two nights. The next leg of the journey took them to the Arax River where they were ferried across on goatskin rafts. They eventually reached Tiflis where my mother completed her education at Hovnanian Girls School. Then they moved to Krasnodar on the Kuban River, north of the Great Caucasus Range. Krasnodar had then and still has a large Armenian population. My Uncle Mnatsakan started a business and my mother taught arithmetic in the Armenian school. She also assisted orphans who survived *Mets Yeghern* (the Great Crime), the term Armenians use to refer to the genocidal catastrophe that befell them during the First World War.

Mghdsi Abro never heard from his family again. He and seven paternal cousins along with some 800 other Armenians were killed in a single night by Ottoman soldiers on the grounds of a house near the water mill in Haftvan. Ashot Allahverdian has recorded this atrocity in his book, *Salmast*.

My paternal grandparents, Gevorg and Dilbar Madteosian, had migrated to Krasnodar before the Bolshevik Revolution. Back then, it was known as Ekaterinodar and that's where my father André was born. His family managed the restaurant at the railway station. It was in Krasnodar that my father became friends with my Uncle Mnatsakan and married his sister, Almast. Their first child was a beautiful baby girl named Rita, but she suffered a fatal brain hemorrhage when she fell from the nurse's arms. My mother was haunted by Rita's death for the rest of her life. My elder brother Henrik was born in Krasnodar in 1927. Around the same time, my maternal Aunt Mahi and her husband Budagh Budaghian died of tuberculosis. Life in Bolshevik Russia was becoming more difficult for Persian citizens, and the whole family – my paternal grandparents, my maternal grandmother Aslikhan, Uncle Mnatsakan and Aunt Haiganoush, my father, mother and brother – returned to Persia in 1929. They weren't permitted to enter under the name Madteosian, so they took the name of a family friend, Aharonian.

Uncle Mnatsakan bought a fabric shop in the central Salmas town of Dilman and looked after the properties he had inherited from his father, Mghdsi Abro. My father didn't speak Persian but he was fluent in Russian and Armenian. He went to Shahsavar (Tonekabon) on the Caspian coast and found a job as an accountant with Persazneft, a Russo-Persian joint venture marketing kerosene from Baku in Persia. A few years later, he moved his family back to Haftvan and he and a relative went down to Andimeshk where he got a job with one of the European contractors building the Trans-Iranian Railway.

Salmas

On May 6, 1930, the year of my birth, there was a terrible earthquake in Salmas. It flattened scores of towns and villages and took the lives of 4,000 people, both Muslims and Armenians. The central town of Dilman was completely destroyed. The Armenian villages lost schools, churches and monuments. My parents must have been going through unimaginable trauma and hardship when I was born six months after the quake.

But the hard-working people of Salmas had experienced such difficulties before and they began to rebuild. The Avakians, a merchant family that traded with Europe, built a school in Haftvan and my mother taught there. It had six classrooms and an auditorium. Similar development took place in other villages. Thanks to funds from the state and the people, the town of Shahpur rose on the ruins of Dilman.

The historian Vahid Maremati described Salmas as "history's mirror" in an article published in the Tehran daily *Hamshahri* (September 1, 2000). According to him, Salmas was built by Babylonians during the Third Assyrian Kingdom, some 3000 years ago. We know from ancient stelae that its original name was Salmanasar. At one time, it was part of the old Armenian province of Zarewand. After the Battle of Avarayr in 451 CE, it became part of Persia. According to Arshak Atayan's history of *Salmast* (Armenian Prelacy of New Julfa, 1906), the name of the town and the district is of Persian origin, from *salem* (healthy) and *ast* (being), referring to the area's healthy climate. He says the Ottomans called it Saghmasd but the original Armenians of Salmas called it Salmastepos. With its relatively mild climate and fertile soil, it is one of the world's oldest settled regions.

Salmas stretches from Khoy in the north to the town of Urumia on the western shore of the lake. Snow lies on the mountains in the west until midsummer and farmers irrigate their fields and orchards from the streams and rivers of snowmelt. In winter it is very cold but spring is cool and pleasant, especially when the fruit trees blossom and the foothills are covered with wild flowers. Summer is temperate and the gentle afternoon breeze is followed by the evening cool. Most people work in the orchards and vineyards. The local apricots, apples and grapes are known for their superior quality. Dried apricot (*chir*) is exported to many countries. The peasants of Salmas also raise sheep and cows; the sheep for meat and the cows for milk which is used to produce several kinds of delicious cheeses.

The people of Salmas have always placed a high value on education. Today, the great majority of Salmas Armenians, from Iran to Europe to the USA, enjoy the benefits of higher education. Men and women from Salmas are also known for their hard work and resilience. For centuries, Salmas Armenians have left their native land for seasonal work abroad, especially in Russia, where they would earn some money and return to their homeland. Accounts suggest that in the nineteenth century, Salmas men seeking work traveled as far as Japan and the USA. In their daily lives and customs, the people of Salmas are very similar to the Armenians of Armenia. Among the region's most notable sons are two giants of Armenian literature, the nineteenth-century novelist Raffi and the twentieth-century poet Paruyr Sevak who wrote the words of the patriotic anthem, *Sardarabad*.

The Armenians of Salmas also took part in the Armenian national liberation struggle, and they have always sought to safeguard the integrity of the Armenian family. I do not know of a single person from Salmas who has married a non-Armenian. Every Salmas village had its own church, even if some of these villages were quite close to one another. In the nineteenth century, there were 50,000 Armenians living in twenty-three villages in Salmas. Five of those villages – Haftvan, Payajuk, Mahlam, Ghalasar and Sarna – were populated entirely by Armenians, while the others had a mixed population of Armenians, Azeris, Assyrians and Kurds.

After the Bolshevik Revolution, many Armenians living in Russia returned to Persia, and some resettled in Salmas, including my family. Those who did not know how to till the land or tend the orchards soon moved on to Tabriz or Tehran. Persia threw off the yoke of reactionary Qajar rule and the returning Armenians, with their diverse skills and expertise, played a significant role in the country's development. They were innovators: the Budaghians in banking, the Avakian brothers in the export of carpets, the Sarkissians and the Sahakians in the franchised production of Coca Cola and Canada Dry and the export of beer, soap and other products. The Arakelians specialized in flour milling, the Khudikians in preserved foods, the Ghazarians in ice and halva, Grigor Kholian in fruit juices and *kvas* (a beer made from bread). The Avedissians and the Mikaelians started factories to produce *yershig* (spicy Armenian sausage). They were the first Iranians to produce such items commercially and they were also known for importing high-quality foodstuffs.

Benefactors from Salmas funded a number of institutions in Tehran to serve the Armenian nation: Markar Sarkissian built the Mariamian School for Girls in memory of his daughter; his sons Gurgen and Vazgen Sarkissian built St. Sarkis Church and the new Prelacy in memory of their parents; the Sahakian siblings, Daniel (Dodig), Henrik and Anahid, built the Sahakian School in memory of their father Israel; Gevorg Avedissian built the Avedissian Community Clinic in memory of his brother Avedis; and I myself built the Aharonian Kindergarten in memory of my parents. People from

Salmas have always been proud of their homeland and that pride was passed on to future generations.

My Earliest Memories

Our house in Haftvan was in an orchard next to Uncle Mnatsakan's house. It was relatively spacious and comfortable, a villa with several bedrooms, a dining room and a kitchen with a *tonir* (clay oven) where bread was baked and butter was churned. Aslikhan *Mayrik* (Maternal Grandmother) was a taciturn woman of medium height with red cheeks that radiated good health. I remember how she would open the churn, take some fresh butter and spread it on hot bread straight from the oven. Only three of her fourteen children survived beyond childhood, and after the forced emigration of 1914, she never saw her husband again.

We followed her "hunting" expeditions with great interest and pleasure. In the hayloft where grains of wheat lay scattered about, she would prop up a large sieve on a piece of wood with a string tied to it, and holding the other end of the string, she would sit on the stairs and watch the wild birds peck the grain. When a sufficient number of birds were gathered under the sieve, she would pull the string and trap them. Then she made *khorovats* (barbecue) for us.

Sitting on the same stairs one day, Aslikhan noticed a line of ants moving back and forth beneath her feet. She pointed to the yellow ants with longer legs and said,

"Look, *bales* (my dear child), the yellow ones are like the Ottoman soldiers: they swallow the smaller ones."

That was the first time I became aware of hatred for the Ottoman criminals.

Aslikhan was very careful about her health. Every summer, *Dashgachi* (Coachman) Avak drove her to Lake Urumia. There she stayed on her own for two weeks, daily immersing herself in the lake's therapeutic mud, and returned home rejuvenated and happy.

In 1935, when Reza Shah passed through Salmas on his way to meet Atatürk in Turkey, he stopped for lunch in Shahpur. Aunt Hayganoush lent her dinner table for the banquet and my cousin Ashot recorded the date on the underside of the table. Women were told they must wear a hat to welcome Reza Shah. The following year, he ordered the closing of Armenian schools, most likely in accordance with an agreement he had reached with Atatürk.

My mother had no choice but to gather all the students in our house and teach them Armenian. I vividly remember the boys and girls throwing snowballs during recess.

My mother would catch fish from the nearby Abra River and fry it for us, and sometimes she climbed the mulberry tree and shook it clean of berries for us to eat.

I also remember the death of Dilbar *Dadig* (Paternal Grandmother). She began to complain of pain in her stomach and the village elders told my Grandfather Gevorg that she should eat walnuts, both ripe and green. She took their advice and her abdomen swelled up and she died.

Other events are fresh in my memory. Picnics were regular events in the local villages. People called these outings *jujna*. I remember in particular the pilgrimage to Prashat to celebrate the Virgin Mary. Families gathered in a large orchard, men and women together, sheep were sacrificed and the *dhol* (drums) and *zourna* (woodwind instrument) accompanied the celebration.

I was a well-fed, red-cheeked little boy with a smile always on my face. I was sent to school before I turned seven. Since there was no kindergarten in Haftvan, I was placed in the first grade. One day my first-grade teacher (who was not an Armenian) whacked me over the head with his cane for no apparent reason. Considering my age, it was out of place and uncalled for. I was frightened and I decided not to tell anyone what happened, but when my mother was bathing me she noticed the lump on my head and made me tell. Of course, Uncle Mnatsakan and my mother as well as the school principal reprimanded the teacher, but the damage was done. It was the first time I ever experienced physical violence and it came at the hand of my teacher.

Moving to Tehran

After saving enough money from his job in Andimeshk, my father went to Tehran and bought a grocery store on Pahlavi Street in one of the city's most prestigious neighborhoods. Pahlavi Street – now known as Vali Asr – was and still is a main thoroughfare from the railway station in south Tehran to the foothills in the north. André Shop came to be known for its great variety of high-quality foods. My father rented an apartment on Kakh (now Felesteen) Street and we joined him in October 1937. Uncle Mnatsakan rented a car and drove us to Tabriz. There we stopped over with my mother's paternal Aunt Voski and her husband Khosrow Avakian. Everything was new to me. I had my first taste of the delicious peach there. A few days later, we were driven to Qazvin in a hired car. It was a rough trip, nearly 300 miles of unpaved road.

We arrived exhausted and covered in dust. I don't remember what we ate for dinner but I do remember the ice cream I had that night. Early the next morning we pushed on to Tehran, another ninety miles or so. My father was waiting to pick us up and we rode to our new home in two horse-drawn carriages. For a boy like me who had lived his whole life in a village, Tehran was a miracle. I was overcome with amazement. André Shop was a ten-minute walk from home and we spent all our free time there. Henrik and I would play out front while my mother helped my father inside. She continued to help out in the shop until the end of her life.

My younger brother George was born on October 26, 1938, and named after our paternal Grandfather Gevorg. He and his brother Gaspar, whom we called Gago, were still living at the time. They were elegant, attractive old men. I can still hear my grandfather's prayer-like words: "*Havadam, khosdovanem tser surp atchkerin yev yeresin*" (To your blessed eyes, to your saintly faces, I confess, I believe). A few years later, he went to Armenia with my paternal uncle. He died in Dushanbe, Tajikistan, at the age of 102.

My father enrolled Henrik and me in Irandokht School. Neither of us spoke Persian but we quickly picked it up. Soon I was singing songs and reciting poems to my family, though none of us knew what the words meant. I couldn't get used to the taste of the bread in Tehran and I longed for Haftvan bread. It wasn't long before my personality began to change and I started getting into mischief – lots of mischief – so much that my father's friends used to give me one toman for every hour I behaved myself. That was enough to buy a few *ponchik* (doughnuts), my favorite pastry.

One day I came home from school feeling extremely ill. My mother took my temperature and said I had a fever. When home remedies failed to lower my temperature, my parents called a doctor. Four prominent Armenian physicians came in succession. Each examined me thoroughly and prescribed medications, but after ten days my temperature remained high and I was also suffering from daily nose-bleeds. Then my father invited all four of them back and asked them to confer with each other. They concluded that I was suffering from a disease of the lungs and there wasn't much they could do.

My father took me straight to the Russian Hospital in Tehran. A young surgeon named Dr. Novikov examined me and decided to operate the next day. When he opened the right side of my lower torso, so much pus came out that it filled a large bucket. I felt better immediately and my temperature went down in a few hours. The operation was successful but I had to stay in the hospital for four months, during which time my lungs were regularly drained through a rubber tube. I learned some Russian from the doctors and nurses and to this day I haven't forgotten what I learned. My illness cost my father dearly and he had to borrow to pay the bills. One day when I was feeling better and walking along the corridor, I overheard my mother ask Dr. Novikov how long he thought I would live.

"To the age of eighteen or twenty," he replied.

It is thanks to my strong constitution and my lifelong attention to physical fitness that I am able to write these words today. I have never suffered any illness related to my lungs since then.

My illness deferred my schooling for a whole year. Instead of sending Henrik and me back to Irandokht, my father enrolled us in Tamaddon Elementary School. Persian was the mandatory language of instruction even though the entire student body was Armenian. The classrooms were dark and humid and the atmosphere unpleasant. I made a few friends and learned some new games and some new curse words. Now I was stepping into the real world.

One of the games we played was *lakhd* which called for speed and flexibility. One player would stand inside a circle and the others laid their belts on the ground at his feet. His job was to defend the circle with his own belt and prevent the others from retrieving theirs. If someone managed to grab his belt, he would hit the defender with it and take his place. In *klor mekhak*, we divided into two teams. One team would stand in a circle with their hands on each other's shoulders, protected by a few defenders, while the other team tried to jump on their backs. When everyone on the outside team had jumped on someone's back, they won. In *machalots*, one team would stand inside a circle while the other team, one boy at a time and hopping on one leg, tried to catch an insider and push him out of the circle. When they had pushed everyone out of the circle, victory was theirs and the teams changed roles. Another game we liked was *nizdi zadi* (leapfrog). Outside of school and especially in the summer, we would place *tashtaks* (bottle caps) on a chalk line and throw small stones at them. Whoever knocked the most caps off the line was the winner. Both boys and girls played *blan budik* (hopscotch) at home in their yards, using a flat stone as a marker.

When we were a little older, we would roll bicycle wheels with a stick. When we were even older, we built a scooter by nailing two boards together and attaching a small wheel. We put one foot on the floorboard and pushed the contraption around with the other foot. Sometimes we played cops and robbers on our "bikes." When I was going on eleven, my father let me ride the shop's delivery bicycle. I learned quickly, first with one foot on the ground and then with both feet on the pedals. I was practicing outside our shop in August 1941 when the Allies dropped leaflets over Tehran announcing the occupation of Iran.

Fist fights between older boys were common and everybody knew who was going to fight whom and when and where the fight would take place. At least once a week after school, a crowd of kids would gather on a certain side street to watch the fight.

Our crowd would meet in the courtyard of St. Mary's Church (*Surp Asdvadzadzin*) near the intersection of Qavam ol-Saltaneh and Naderi Streets in the Sheikh Hadi neighborhood. (After the Islamic Revolution, Qavam was renamed Mirza Kuchek Khan, and Shah, Naderi and Istanbul were stretches of the same street now known as *Jomhouri-ye Eslami* or Islamic Republic Street.) We often played *chan* (knucklebones) beside the wall and sometimes that led to fights. There was a small chapel on the east side of the yard. Construction of the main church began in 1938, and until it was consecrated in 1945, most of the congregation would stand outside in the yard when high holy days were celebrated in the chapel. I couldn't wait for Easter when boys and girls would hunt for eggs in the yard.

My First Encounter with Mohammad Reza Pahlavi

Not far from my father's shop, there was a public park called *Café Shahrdari* (City Café). Now the site of the City Theater Complex, during my youth it was the best and most affordable place for a stroll. Families would promenade in the park or relax over ice cream and coffee. Many brought picnic lunches. A singer and his band entertained the crowd. Every year on a Friday in the late fall, there was a festival called the Garden Party, the only time when an entrance fee was charged. One day, some of the organizers came to my father's shop to buy provisions for the festival. They said the Crown Prince, Mohammad Reza Pahlavi, was expected to attend and my father should send us there to meet him.

On Friday, I was there an hour before the Crown Prince was supposed to arrive. As soon as I spotted his entourage, I approached and fell into step beside them. The Prince went up to various booths and played the games on offer. One featured targets superimposed over pictures of game animals. The

Prince paid the price of a round, selected his targets and hit them all. The spectators applauded loud and long when he was given a prize. The atmosphere that day was quite positive. No one thought to question the young boy strolling along with the Prince the whole time. This is one of the most pleasant memories of my life. Now I ponder how the nation transformed that liberally educated Prince into a great King, then deified him, and then....

Elementary School

Henrik and I only spent one year at Tamaddon Elementary School. Students from various backgrounds were thrown together and the principal could never keep order. Now I realize there were just too many students. Nevertheless, community leaders were alert to our needs. Satenik Asrian, chair of the Church Ladies Union of Tehran, used to visit around the holidays and take note of the children for whom new clothes needed to be purchased. Originally formed to support the board of trustees of St. Mary's Church, the Church Ladies Union was led by Mrs. Asrian for twenty-five years, and she was the first woman ever elected to serve on the Diocesan Council of Tehran. The Council of the day was solicitous toward us and it is the duty of my generation to gratefully acknowledge their hard work and dedication.

When I was in third grade, my father enrolled us in the new mixed-gender Sepehr Elementary School on Qavam-ol Saltaneh Street. Tuition was slightly higher than at Tamaddon but the rooms were well lit and the classes were smaller. Overall, the students were better behaved and I never heard them curse or use vulgar expressions about parents. I made good friends at Sepehr School and still maintain contact with some of them.

The Armenian school board was very attentive to the students' needs. Hakob Hovanissian, the father of my close friend Felix, was a member of the board. They visited the school several times a year. I'm not sure whether it was the school board or the Church Ladies Union that organized extracurricular Armenian lessons, but a group of us studied with the poet Vosdanik at his home. We were also taught our mother tongue by Father Emmanuel Poladian. He had come from Beirut in 1938 to serve as the spiritual leader of the Armenian Catholic Church in Tehran. He was known as the "Red Priest" because of his reddish beard. Father Poladian was an extraordinary person, patriotic and spiritual, completely detached from the material world. He gave us each a white shirt, and on Sundays, we would put on our shirt and go to church with him. At that age, we didn't know the difference between the Catholic and the Apostolic Church.

We met children from other schools only once a year on New Year's Day at the Armenian Club (*Hay Agoomb*) on Naderi Street, where we sang and danced around the Christmas tree and always left with a small bag of *chir chamitch* (dried apricots and raisins). Perhaps the most meaningful holiday celebrations were associated with Christmas when we always went to church. Christmas was followed by *Diyarnendaraj* (the Feast of the Presentation) in February, and like many Christian holidays, this one incorporates a more ancient custom. In the courtyard of St. Mary's Church, a bonfire was lit and young people, especially newly married couples, would take a running leap over it and then light a candle from its flames. I too lit a candle and was very careful to keep it burning as I brought it home to my mother so that she could light our kerosene lamp with it. Persians have a similar fire-jumping festival, *Chaharshanbeh Souri*, which is celebrated on the Wednesday night before *Nowruz*, the Persian New Year, which coincides with the vernal equinox.

After Diyarnendaraj comes St. Vartanants which marks the martyrdom of Vartan Mamikonian and his companions in the Battle of Avarayr, near modern Khoy, in 451 CE when they defended Armenian Christians from forced conversion to the Zoroastrian faith but lost the province of Zarewand to the Sasanids.

Two weeks before Easter, we began preparations to dye the eggs, selecting the hardest ones with the thickest shells so they wouldn't be cracked by our opponents. After Easter came *Hambardzum* (the Feast of the Ascension). Then in mid-summer came *Vardavar* (the Feast of the Transfiguration). The custom of splashing each other with water or sprinkling rosewater that day harks back to purification rituals related to the ancient Armenian goddesses Asdghig and Anahit. Most Armenians in Tehran celebrated Vardavar in the picnic grounds of Vanak, which was then a village on the northwestern outskirts of the city. Hundreds of families would congregate under the shady trees to enjoy barbecue and other delicious foods. Unfortunately, some quarrelsome person always managed to spoil the fun.

In October, we celebrated the Feast of the Holy Translators (*Surp Tarkmanchats*) in honor of St. Mesrop Mashtots, who invented the Armenian alphabet at the beginning of the fifth century, and his collaborators who translated the Holy Scriptures, the liturgy and many other writings into Armenian.

When we were a little older, we always hosted a New Year's party at the home of our friend Felix Hovanissian. His parents, Baron Hakop and Madame Arpik, welcomed us with open arms. Much of the responsibility for organizing the party fell to me. We charged the boys admission but not the girls – they were our guests.

Middle and High School

In order to clear up the debts incurred during my illness, my father formed a partnership that enabled him to buy both premises on either side of André Shop and expand the business. After his partner married, however, the income was insufficient to support both families, so my father left the shop in the care of his partner and went up to Mianeh, about two-thirds of the way from Tehran to Tabriz, and bought the Pars Hotel. This was just before the Second World War and the Tehran-Tabriz branch of the Trans-Iranian Railway was under construction. Mianeh was full of foreign engineers and technicians, and once the war started, there were plenty of Russians too.

When I visited my father during the summer, he bought various creatures to keep me happy, including a pigeon, a hawk, a piglet, a rabbit, a hedgehog and a tortoise, and they kept me entertained all day long. Once or twice a week, a Yugoslav mining engineer named Efimov rode his horse into town and stayed at the Pars Hotel, and while he was there, he let me ride the horse around the grounds. With the help of another engineer named Fitisov, my father acquired a contractor's license which allowed him to supervise the construction of several bridges. After he had completed those projects, he sold the hotel and moved further west to Maragheh where he set up a bottling factory named *Sharq* (East).

My father's paternal cousin's son was a carpenter and he took me on as an unpaid assistant. One summer day, our Assyrian neighbor, who had a friend who worked with the British, suggested that we could both get paid work with a British company that employed hundreds of local workers. We took the tip and started work together. When our boss found out that we could read and write, he gave us the job of distributing tea and sugar to the workers. When I got my first wages at the end of the month, I was so happy that I bought my mother a present on the way home. When school started in the fall, I decided to keep working and attend night school. My mother was adamantly opposed but I carried on like that for a couple of months until my father came home from Maragheh.

"As long as I'm alive," he said, "you are going to school!"

And he took me by the ear, dragged me to school and re-enrolled me in Sepehr School.

After I finished fifth grade, I left Sepehr. My father rushed down from Maragheh again and enrolled me in Jamshid Jam School which was owned by the Zoroastrian community and was considered one of the best schools in Tehran. The students were drawn from affluent families – the upper echelons of the military and other social elites. There were a few Armenians in every class and I knew them all. I became close friends with some of them and have kept those friendships to this day.

Jamshid Jam School cultivated a rigorous discipline. When the first bell rang in the morning, we lined up in formation and sang the national anthem which was primarily a song in praise of the Shah. Punishment for misbehavior was unavoidable. Miscreants were called in to the principal's office. Wearing a wet smile, he would strike their palms with his cane. That brutal experience killed my spirit. I was always trying to thicken the skin of my palms in order not to feel the pain!

An unpleasant incident occurred a few days after the Christmas holidays. We Armenians came to school in new clothes and high spirits. Awaiting the arrival of our first-period geography teacher, we congregated in the middle of the room, talking and laughing. Mr. Vesali was a tall, thin Zoroastrian. When he came in and saw us standing there, chatting and smiling, he was enraged. He passed among the students and confronted me. I was taller and more energetic than many of my classmates. He gave me a resounding slap in the face. I felt that he was trampling on my self-worth, punishing me for nothing. I couldn't control myself and I slapped him back. A commotion broke out and I was taken to the principal's office where I was told to go home and come back with my parents. They would be given my report card and I would be expelled. There was no way out. I went home and told my parents what had happened. My father had a friend at the school, a math teacher named Mr. Mortazi, and he appealed to this friend. Mortazi then spoke with my classmates and they told him how severely Vesali had provoked me. He promised to resolve the situation, and after a long conversation with the principal, he told me that I would have to apologize to Vesali in front of the whole class. At that point, my father left.

The next day I apologized to Vesali, but having tasted the indignity of being slapped by a student, he demanded that I kiss his feet. I was under tremendous psychological pressure. My classmates urged me to comply but I categorically refused. The standoff lasted ten minutes but it seemed like a century. Finally, Mortazi intervened and asked Vesali to accept my apology. He did so and the matter was closed.

At the end of sixth grade, the Ministry of Education offered an examination called the *nhai* at designated schools. It was an important milestone. Passing it meant that you had left childhood behind and were entering adolescence. I passed it with flying colors and in the fall I enrolled in Alborz High School, which my brother Henrik had attended before me.

I was thirteen years old at the time, red-cheeked, mischievous and always smiling. Our Persian language teacher was the poet Mehdi Hamidi. He was originally from Shiraz and he spoke in his native dialect which we greatly enjoyed, but my ever-smiling face often confused him and he thought I was making fun of him. Sometimes we laughed at his dialect but it was never my intention to mock him.

Easter arrived and it happened to coincide with the day of our Persian language exam. There were only four Armenians in the class and we decided to observe the holiday. Mr. Hamidi declined to give us the exam on an alternate day, and since we were absent, he gave us a grade of zero. In those days, you couldn't move up to the next grade with a zero in any subject, no matter how well you did in the other subjects. That was our situation, and I was so discouraged that I decided to leave school altogether. Once again, my father intervened and persuaded me to change schools.

I registered at Tamaddon High School on Shirvani Street off Naderi. The principal was a strict but intelligent man known for his psychological insight. He appointed me class monitor and that had a profound influence on my life. I became a diligent and obedient student. As liaison between the students and the administrators, I had to earn the trust of both sides. I learned the true meaning of taking responsibility for something and seeing it through to completion. I was in charge of class activities and I solved whatever problems came up. My classmates were fond of me but that didn't influence the performance of my duties. I was kind and fair in my dealings with them and impartial in marking absences. I was in charge of collecting tuition, recording payments and turning over the money and the accounts to the administration. I also collected the fees for special classes in mathematics, engineering and physics, and distributed the money to the relevant teachers.

I held the position of class monitor until I finished high school. Whenever we had individual oral exams, I would take up my position at the door and usher in the students, one by one. Observing each exam, I would mentally correct my mistakes and memorize the answer to each question, and when my turn came, I got them all right.

My chosen major was natural science, but it wasn't taught at Tamaddon, so after completing eleventh grade, I left to enroll at Firouz Bahram, another Zoroastrian school. The boys at Tamaddon were happy, energetic, hard-working and mutually supportive, and I don't recall anyone in our group ever using alcohol or narcotics, though a few smoked cigarettes. But the students at Firouz Bahram were like the walking dead, indifferent and uninvolved, and that affected me deeply. I left after a month. Then I heard that Tamaddon had started teaching natural science, so I went straight back to the old school I loved so much. The students urged the principal to reappoint me as class monitor but he had already appointed another student. When they boycotted class, however, he gave in.

Some 70 percent of the students at Tamaddon High were Armenian, 25 percent Muslim, and 5 percent Jewish. The school had its own soccer team and I played right fullback. Soccer consumed a great deal of my time, and I also liked bicycle riding.

The Shah's birthday was celebrated on October 26, which was also the birthday of my younger brother George. Every year on that day, students representing schools from all over the country marched down Roosevelt Avenue (now Shahid Hojjatoleslam Dr. Mofatteh Street) and into Amjadieh Stadium (now Shahid Shiroudi Stadium), where the Shah and his wife observed the proceedings. I led our school's contingent twice, proudly holding the Iranian flag aloft.

Teen Pranks

There was a boy in our class named Tajbakhsh whose father was wealthy. He was often absent from school and when present he often behaved badly. As class monitor, I duly recorded his absences and he didn't like that. One day when he was absent again for no good reason, his parents were notified and asked to come in for a meeting. A few days later, two strangers appeared on the school grounds and asked for me. I approached them directly, followed by my friends. Some older boys noticed what was happening and they came over and asked the strangers what they were there for. When the latter started obfuscating, my defenders told them that if anybody even so much as touched a hair on my head, Tajbakhsh would never set foot in Tamaddon again. Realizing they were at a disadvantage, the strangers left and were never seen again.

Another boy named Jean Asatorian was full of energy and ingenuity. He contrived funny scenes to make us laugh. For instance, one day he raised his hand as if to ask a question. When the teacher called on him and everyone turned to look, they burst out laughing. Jean was wearing a dozen watches from his shoulder to his wrist. Another time, he hailed a horse-driven carriage on Naderi Street and stepped in along with five accomplices. As the carriage approached Tamaddon, the five accomplices hopped off, one at a time, without being seen and without paying the fare, and this was all orchestrated by Jean. Only when he hopped off in front of our school did the driver realize what was happening. He stopped the carriage and chased after Jean, whip in hand. It was a truly comic scene. Needless to say, Jean was much loved by all of us. Sadly, this joyous, dynamic friend died of a heart attack at a young age.

Leon Zohrabekian was even more mischievous. One day on his way to school, he saw a donkey in a side street, loaded with cucumbers. It was standing unattended so he brought it to school and forced it down the stairs and onto the playground. Students rushed to the scene and all the cucumbers disappeared within minutes. In the middle of the commotion, the donkey's owner arrived and started shouting. That drew the principal who lined up the students he thought might be involved and asked each one in turn if he knew how the donkey got there. As each answered no, he gave him a slap on the cheek. When it was Leon's turn, he confessed. He said he had seen the donkey standing all alone and felt sorry for the creature, so he brought it to school. Because Leon was honest, the principal didn't slap him. Instead, he ordered him to pay for the stolen cucumbers. The students quickly mustered the money and the problem was solved, but then another problem arose that was harder to solve: how to get the donkey back up the stairs!

Every day the blackboard eraser disappeared and I had to ask the custodian for a new one. One day the blackboard fell off the wall and what did we see? Twenty erasers hanging on the wall like criminals on the gallows. One of our classmates was the perpetrator of that mischief.

One time in the eleventh grade, our geography teacher made a casual anti-Armenian remark. One of our classmates was so incensed that, before the start of our next geography class, he removed the hinges from the door and left it standing in place. When our teacher went to open the door, it fell down flat and took him with it. He stood up and let out a loud scream. The principal came in and questioned us one by one. Everyone knew who was responsible but no one told and finally he left, none the wiser.

One day, the Ministry of Education put out a circular ordering students to keep their hair cut very short. When we resisted, the assistant principal singled out a few boys and cut the hair hanging down the back of their neck. But the resistance was so widespread that the Ministry relented and repealed the rule. Then several students came to school with their hair cut exceedingly short in the back. The assistant principal was outraged by their disobedience and rebellion.

My parents André and Almast in Russia.

My grandfather, Gevorg holding my younger brother, George.

With my younger brother, George.

My father in Russia.

A family picture taken while my father was away.

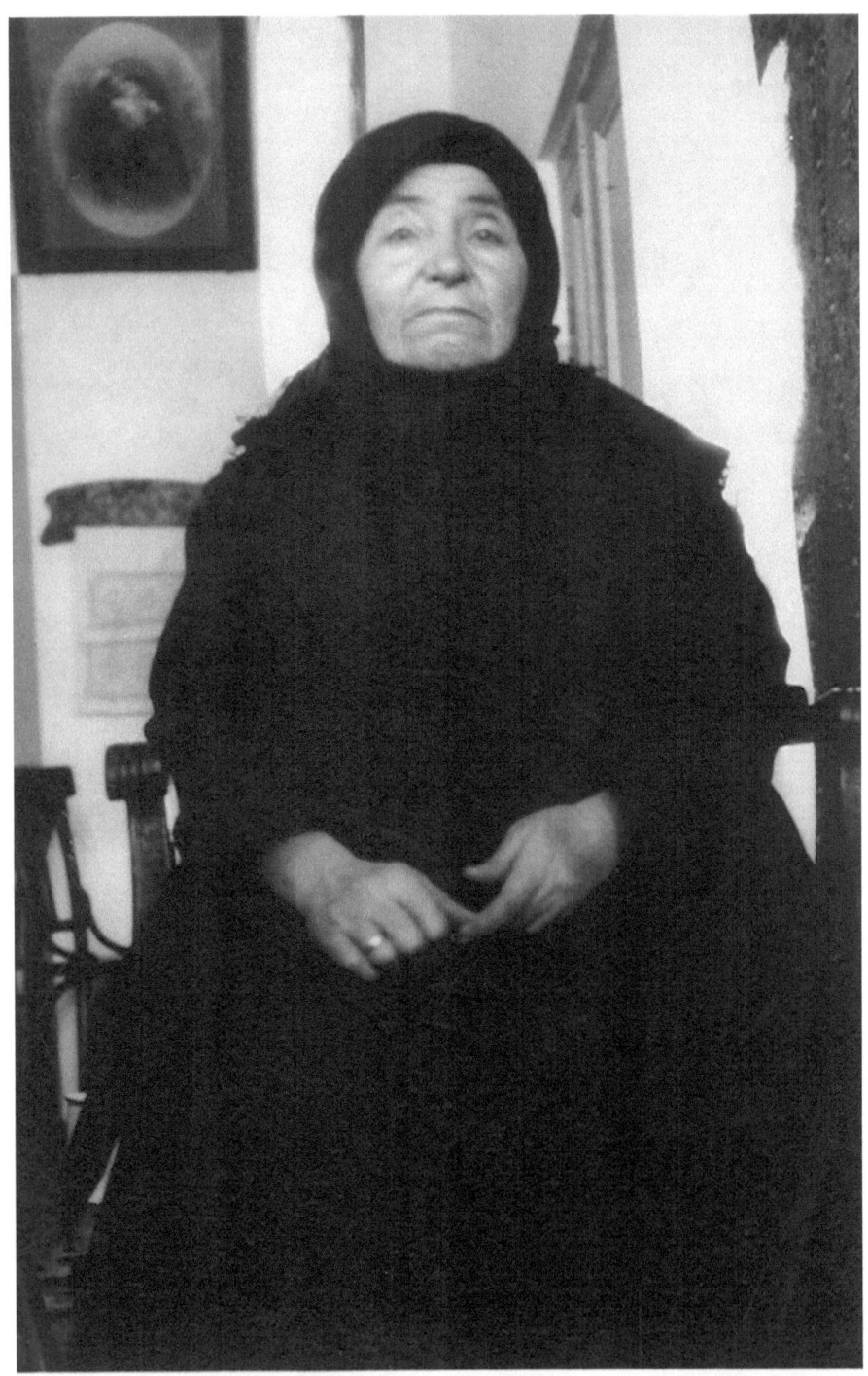

My grandmother Aslikhan.

A family picture.

With my brother Henry.

My mother Almast Aharonian.

My cousin Khachik Babloyan.

Author in his younger days.

My brother Henry.

Chapter 2

The Second World War Comes to Iran

One afternoon in late August 1941, I was riding my bike in front of my father's shop when suddenly I heard the sound of airplanes. Looking up, I saw five or six bombers flying low, dropping thousands of leaflets over the city. They announced that the armies of Great Britain and the Soviet Union had entered Iran that morning but they meant no harm to the country or its people. They warned of potential sabotage and called for the expulsion of all Germans. German companies had major business interests in the country and German nationals held key positions in the national infrastructure, including highways and the railway, the post, telegraph and telephone systems, and even Radio Tehran. In fact, several hundred Germans were wanted by name and some of them lived in our neighborhood!

But Reza Shah temporized about handing them over, while the two Allied armies advanced on Tehran. Over the next few weeks, the Iranian Army melted away as officers deserted and enlisted men headed for home. On September 17, 1941, as the British took over Doshan Tappeh airbase on the east side of town and the Soviets occupied Qaleh Morgheh on the west side, Reza Shah's eldest son, Mohammad Reza Pahlavi, aged twenty-one, took the oath of office as the new Shah. People were terribly sad and many were openly crying as word spread that Reza Shah had abdicated and left for Isfahan. A month later, we heard that he had been taken to the British-held island of Mauritius in the Indian Ocean. Later still, he was transferred to Johannesburg in South Africa, and he died there on July 26, 1944.

The Rise and Fall of Reza Shah

Reza Shah founded the modern Iranian state and ruled it with an iron hand for sixteen years. He was a deeply anti-clerical, fanatically nationalist dictator, yet at the same time he was the architect of the country's development and modernization. When he took power in 1925, Persia was a patchwork of tribal fiefdoms and principalities. Reza Shah created a modern national army, tried to bring the various provinces under his authority, and centralized administration under the palace bureaucracy. He gave himself the title of

Shahanshah (King of Kings) and renamed the country Iran, Persia being an Anglicized derivative of Pars or Fars, the historic heartland, while Iran referring to people of the Aryan race. Reza Shah oversaw the construction of many roads and a national railway connecting the Persian Gulf to the Caspian Sea. It was during his reign that the first modern university was founded in Tehran and hundreds of students were sent to European universities on government scholarships. Reza Shah introduced modern headgear and banned the chador. Although he owed his position to the British, he tried to counter their influence by developing extensive diplomatic and commercial ties with Germany and that led to his downfall.

Reza Shah was a martial man of humble origins. He attempted to elevate his status by infusing his line with nobility, taking a Qajar princess as his fourth wife, marrying his eldest son to a sister of Egypt's King Farouk, and marrying one of his daughters to the son of a Shirazi tribal chieftain and millionaire politician. I saw him several times when I was a boy. Our home overlooked a busy intersection and we could watch his motorcade when he left town on Thursday for his summer palace at Saadabad in the northern foothills and when he came back on Friday evening. And when the Crown Prince married Princess Fawzia in 1939, our father took us to Toupkhaneh Square to see Reza Shah with the newly-weds. Soldiers stood at respectful attention, but then, that was their duty.

Wartime Conditions in Tehran

During the war, Tehran grew more lively and beautiful every day, especially in 1943 when the Americans took over running the Soviet supply line up to Qazvin. The Soviets took delivery from there, but in the vicinity of the capital, they were generally confined to their base, while British and American soldiers could be seen loitering in the streets, behaving in all sorts of unbecoming ways conducive to immorality.

In the spring of 1942, over 100,000 Poles made their way southwest to Iran from Soviet prisons and internment camps in Siberia and Central Asia. Many were soldiers who transited the country to join the Allied forces, but some 50,000 women and children remained in Iran as refugees. They brought various contagious diseases, the most dangerous of which were typhus and typhoid fever. My brother George was infected with the former and my brother Henrik with the latter. The methods of treatment were elementary, but with the help of a friend, an Armenian physician trained in Russia, my mother managed to save their lives.

Polluted water was a major factor in the spread of typhoid. In those days, water was distributed via open channels (*jube*) through a system of shunts. It was directed to various neighborhoods on scheduled days when people filled their cisterns, but they only used it for laundry. For bathing, they went to a public bath once or twice a week. There were one or two baths in every neighborhood and people had to wait in line for a long time to get in. Drinking water was sold by the bucket and drawn at several centers that were supplied by *ghanats* (*qanats*, underground canals), but there was still no guarantee that it was safe to drink. It wasn't until the 1950s when pipes were laid and purified mountain snowmelt was brought from nearby Karaj that people had access to clean water.

Food became scarce over time and I saw men and women starving on the streets. I was responsible for buying bread for our family and I had to wait in line for hours just to buy a few pieces of poor-quality *lavash* (flat bread). Fortunately, our father sent us a big bundle of food whenever he could entrust it with someone traveling to Tehran, and every summer he brought us up to Maragheh where he had his bottling factory. I made friends with the local boys and we went fishing or swam in the river. At night, we caught crows and starlings by the light of kerosene lanterns. I also helped out at the factory by standing in for my father so that he could take a break for lunch and rest.

One day when I was alone on duty, I drank a small glass of cherry wine from an open amphora. I liked the taste, so I followed up with a second glass, and then a third.... I don't know how many glasses I drank, but I was completely drunk. After my father found out, I avoided him for several weeks and I stayed away from alcohol for a long time. But something similar happened two years later. We had an Italian neighbor whose wife was Russian and our families were on very good terms. My mother was anemic and our neighbor was concerned about her health, so he advised my father to bring her a bottle of Fernet Branca and make her drink a glass every day. I watched her take the bottle from the cupboard, pour a shot glass, drink it up, and put the bottle back. One day when she wasn't home, I took the bottle from the cupboard, filled a large glass and drank it down to the last drop. My gorge rose with a bitter taste and I began to vomit. My mother had a good laugh when she found out what I had done!

The Emergence of Tudeh

In the face of foreign occupation and the young Shah's weakness during the war and its aftermath, there was greater freedom of the press and more open debate in the Majles, and that gave rise to political parties. The Marxist *Tudeh* (Masses) Party was founded within weeks if not days of Reza Shah's abdication. Some of its leaders were members of the so-called Group of Fifty-Three, communist intellectuals who had been jailed in the 1930s and were amnestied by the new Shah, and one of them was an Armenian from Gilan named Ardeshir (Ardashes) Ovanessian. Among the Tudeh's opponents was the nationalist New Iran Party (*Hezb-e Iran Novin*) which emerged from the Engineers Association and became a pillar of Mosadegh's National Front in 1949. The Toilers Party (*Hezb-e Zahmatkeshan*) attracted Tudeh dissidents led by Khalil Maleki, but when the Toilers turned against Mosadegh in 1952, Maleki left to establish the pro-Mosadegh Third Force (*Niru-ye Sevvom*).

All these parties were active in the schools and the universities, but Tudeh was the most active and the most well organized, claiming 60,000 members at its peak. It systematically and aggressively propagated its ideas in its daily and weekly newspapers and through several student organizations. Many Armenians, both male and female, were active in those student organizations, and this gender-mixing was a new phenomenon in Iranian society.

Iran made significant social progress because of Tudeh, not as a direct result of the party's activities, but rather from the government's efforts to neutralize its ability to mount labor strikes and other disruptions. Government-mandated reforms included workers' insurance, a minimum wage and a forty-eight-hour, six-day work week.

In the Armenian community there were only two political options, the Tudeh or the Armenian Revolutionary Federation (*Hay Heghapokhakan Dashnaktsutiun*), known as the ARF or the Dashnaks. A third option was to stay out of politics altogether. The Armenian Tudehists managed to send Ardashes Ovanessian to the Fourteenth Majles in 1944, while the leaders of the ARF were elderly men who had headed the first Armenian Republic in 1918–20, had been exiled to Iran, were not fluent in Persian, and therefore could not play any significant role in Iranian politics. A few years later, however, a new generation of ARF cadres entered the political arena and fought back against the Tudeh.

That political division played out among students and occasionally there were violent physical confrontations. At Tamaddon High, some of my friends were politically active and most of them belonged to the Tudeh. Likewise, during my first year at the Polytechnic Institute, many students were pro-Tudeh and so were the teachers. One of our teachers at Tamaddon invited his students to a lecture at party headquarters and I went with my friend Jean Asatorian. The room wasn't big enough to hold everyone who came – students and teachers, workers and intellectuals, and people from various ethno-national groups such as Fars, Gilacs and Turkmens, each speaking his own dialect or language. I found the atmosphere inauthentic and unpleasant. What did I have in common with these people? What did their dreams have to do with my family's future? Jean and I left before the lecture was over and that was the first and last time I attended such an event.

The Crisis in Azarbayjan

Iran suffered four years of political and economic instability during the war, at the end of which the young and vulnerable Mohammad Reza Shah was left with a ruined country and a non-functioning army. When Churchill, Roosevelt and Stalin met in Tehran in December 1943, they thanked him for Iran's crucial contribution to the war effort. The UK and the USA delivered more than five million metric tons of war supplies to the USSR via Iran and that was a significant factor in the Soviet victory on the Eastern Front. Churchill called Iran the "Bridge of Victory" while the Americans called it the "Persian Corridor."

One of Iran's most intractable problems was the status of Azarbayjan Province which consisted of the southern area of historic Azerbaijan and shared a border with the Soviet Socialist Republic of Azerbaijan (SSRAz). Most people on both sides of the border shared the same ethno-national origins, which is why the idea of autonomy took hold. Ardashes Ovanessian, an ethnic Armenian, and Jafar Pishevari, an ethnic Azeri, represented the antagonism between the new Tudehists and the veteran Persian Communists.

In his memoirs, Ovanessian describes how the Central Committee of the SSRAz Communist Party, without consulting the Tudeh Central Committee, backed Pishevari and his comrades when they resurrected the Azeri Democratic Party (*Firqeh-i Demokrat-i Azerbaijan*) in Tabriz in August 1945. In December, the ADP declared the National Autonomous State of Azerbaijan (*Azerbaijan Milli Mokhtar Dowlati*) and appointed Pishevari Prime Minister. In effect, they were attempting to separate Azarbayjan Province from Iran. According to Ovanessian, backing the Azeri Democrats was one of Stalin's worst mistakes and Tudeh protested but to no avail.

The secession of Azarbayjan became an increasingly serious possibility over the winter, as US and UK forces withdrew from the south while the Red Army remained in the north, where the USSR was competing with American companies for an oil concession. It was during that period that MP (Member of Parliament) Mohammed Mosadegh came to national prominence with a proposal to ban all foreign oil concessions. But Prime Minister Ahmad Ghavam (Qavam) ol-Saltaneh, a veteran politician known as the "Old Fox," went to Moscow and reached an agreement with Stalin: if he withdrew his army, he would get the northern concession, pending Majles approval, of course.

The Red Army finally evacuated Azarbayjan and the Iranian Army recaptured Tabriz in December 1946. Zolfaghari (Zolfaqari) tribesmen crushed the Azeri Democrats in Zanjan and the Shahsavans finished them off in Ardebil. Pishevari and his comrades fled to Baku and the Armenian Tudehists escaped to Yerevan. A paternal uncle of mine was among the latter. He took his wife and his only son with him, but because of the youth's heedless extremism, they were expelled to Dushanbe, Tajikistan, where they spent the rest of their days.

In the fall of 1947, when the Fifteenth Majles rejected the Soviet oil concession, the people rejoiced, shouting "The Old Fox tricked Stalin!" But the real victor was the USA, because now Qavam began quietly renegotiating the terms of agreement with the UK's Anglo-Iranian Oil Company.

André Shop

When the Azeri Democrats occupied Maragheh in 1945, manufacturing came to a halt. My father's Sharq bottling factory shut down and he almost went bankrupt. He turned the entire operation over to a friend without compensation and rejoined us in Tehran. He still owned a half-interest in André Shop, and through the mediation of friends and with the aid of private loans, he regained full ownership, but now he was in debt again. With the evacuation of the Western Allies, business took a dive, but our family never gave up hope. We all supported my father by helping out with day-to-day operations and he paid off his debts within a year and put André Shop back on solid ground.

I was now fifteen years old and I took my responsibilities seriously. For many years without fail, I took my bike at 6:00 AM, picked up fresh baked bread and delivered it to the shop, a two-mile run. On his way to work, my father bought fresh produce from the wholesale markets on Istanbul Street. As soon as he arrived, I left my bike at the shop and walked to school. All that daily exercise was very beneficial to my health.

During the summer, my mother prepared ten or twelve containers of various fruit-flavored ice creams at home and our workers brought it to the shop. Her ice cream had no equal and people stood in line to buy it. The shop had no stove at that time, so all the cooking rested on her shoulders too. With the help of two workers, she would boil at least fifty chickens a day and make soup from the broth. Our situation improved because of our unity and cooperation and we three brothers never had any financial difficulties. My father never gave us an allowance but he always left the cash box unlocked and allowed us to take whatever we needed. His attitude had a strong influence on us. It made us think of ourselves as co-workers. We learned how to spend wisely and waste not.

Dangerous Activities

As young teenagers, we had few options for diversion or self-improvement. We would get together with friends and ride our bikes out to local villages to eat fresh mulberries or watermelon. On Sundays we would put on a white shirt and stroll down Naderi Street. We were starting to take an interest in girls but social convention prevented us from approaching them, and besides, we were all quite shy. Soon we began to learn European dances – waltz, foxtrot, tango, swing and samba – and on birthdays and other festive occasions, we danced with girls and had a good time.

Sometimes we got involved in dangerous activities. For instance, we secretly saved up money over a period of months and bought pistols. Then we went out to the countryside and practiced target shooting, but we always hid our pistols before we came back to the city, because if we had been stopped and searched, we would have been thrown in jail.

One day we were shooting at "Indian Camp," a site that had been occupied by the British during the war (most of the UK's occupation force consisted of British-officered Indian Army troops). We found some landmines there and started to dismantle them. When I went home for lunch, my mother told me about a man we knew who had injured himself and his friends fiddling around with mines. The next day, we dropped our mines into a deep well!

Opposite our shop, there was a palatial house owned by an Armenian millionaire who rented it to the British during the war. The custodians sold many things out of the house and I was one of their customers by way of Ali, one of our workers. He procured my pistol and some ammunition but I asked him to get me some more bullets. One day at the shop, Ali handed me a box of fifty. I couldn't leave it there because my father didn't know about our dealings, so I took it to my friend Gurgen's house on Naderi Street. It was a Friday night and the street was deserted. Gurgen wasn't home so I waited outside until he arrived a few minutes later. I had stuffed the box into my back pocket, and when I made a careless move, it fell out and hit the ground. There was a huge explosion. As soon as we realized that we were both unhurt, Gurgen went into his house and I went back to the shop. I returned a few hours later, hoping to collect any unexploded bullets, but when I saw a few policemen, I fled. The next day on my way to school, I saw the damage done to the metal door of a bookshop. We were lucky we weren't killed.

My obsession with guns was gradually reoriented toward hunting, thanks to my Uncle Mnatsakan. When Gurgen and I visited him in Salmas in the summer of 1946, he took us bird-hunting in the orchards around Haftvan. I came to love hunting and I asked my father to buy me a shotgun when I reached the age of seventeen. Seeing that nothing else would make me happy, he bought me one. He knew I wasn't looking for trouble and he always tried to meet my requests. He and my mother paid close attention to our moral education. Having been raised in Russia which they considered a civilized country, they took a rather dim view of their present surroundings and encouraged us to choose or create our own environment based on our values and goals.

Some of the most cherished memories of my youth involve family get-togethers. My father was an accomplished mandolin player and we would gather around while he played Armenian and Russian melodies. Then he would read aloud from the epic stories of *Sassountsi David* and *Mkhitar Sparaped*. He deeply loved and respected his family and his ancestral homeland. I never heard my parents arguing and their conduct toward each other was always courteous.

As I began to mature, I started reading more, first Persian and then Armenian books. I wasn't fluent in Armenian but I was a voracious reader of the great novelist Raffi. Everything I read was informed by themes of patriotism and love of nation. During that period, I made friends with some youths whose thinking was similar to mine and we started a collective. We often met at someone's house on a Friday, the weekly Muslim holiday. The leader was a skilled artisan named Vanik, and one Friday, he announced that in order to prove our courage and loyalty, we had to perform an act of bravery. When he ordered us to rob a bank, my enthusiasm quickly drained away. What if I were caught? How would I face my loving parents? I severed all contact with Vanik. Later, I found out that he wasn't really serious, he was just testing us.

The Movies

Cultural life was pretty vacuous during my youth. Only in 1944 did we begin to see organized community activities for young people. Nevertheless, everyone had their own favorite diversion and ours was the movies. My parents took me, my older brother and our maternal cousin Agnes Babloyan to the movies almost every Friday. We usually went to the Palace Cinema which showcased Russian films during the war.

When I was in fifth grade at Sepehr School, we went to the movies in groups to see American (but not Russian) films. I well remember Flash Gordon voyaging to the planet Mars, and Charlie Chaplin, Tarzan, Jane, Boy and Cheeta the Chimpanzee, but also Errol Flynn and Clark Gable. Tickets for *Gone with the Wind* had to be purchased in advance from agents who charged twice the price for an ordinary film which was 12 riyals (about 15 cents). But the price was irrelevant because we were learning about different countries, peoples and customs. Half a century has passed since then, but when I recall the films I saw as a youth, I realize their educational value in exposing me to the wider world. Music and art have no borders and film has become a unifying international art form.

In those early days, some in the audience couldn't read the subtitles and the film would roll for fifteen minutes, then pause for one of the house staff to summarize the dialogue. He didn't use a microphone and if people couldn't hear him, they would shout their questions from the corners of the house. In later days, they would ask us students to tell them what was said.

When I was at Tamaddon High School, the whole class would go to the movies whenever the teacher was absent, twenty or thirty of us at a time. Many Indian melodramas had musical scenes and some of my classmates would break into song and dance right there in the theater. No one ever complained or tried to stop them.

American and European films had a profound impact on young Iranians. When a good film opened in Tehran, Polytech students talked about it all week long, evaluating its artistry and interpreting its message. I should note that Italian films in the realist mode were the most popular with our crowd. In later years, I was fortunate to see Tolstoy's *War and Peace* and Dostoevsky's *Brothers Karamazov*. After seeing such powerful films, those novelists seemed like gods to me.

I was addicted to the movies and tried to see as many as I could. As soon as I finished my homework, I would rush off to see a 10:00 PM show. Most of the theaters were located on Lalehzar Avenue and tram service stopped at 11:00 PM, so I had to return home on foot. I would quietly open the front door but my mother was always waiting up for me. "Levon? Is that you?"

An Armenian named Ovanes Ohanian (or Oganiants) wrote and directed the first feature-length Iranian film in 1930, the silent comedy *Abi ve Rabi*. Only a dozen Iranian films were produced between 1930 and 1949, but the industry ramped up during the 1950s and took off in earnest in the 1960s. Over a period of fifty-four years, from 1930 to 1983, a total of 1,159 films were produced in Iran – an average of twenty-one films a year.

Under the Shah, films were subject to censorship and clerics warned that they were destroying the nation's religious and cultural traditions. That mindset was responsible for the burning down of Cinema Aria in Tabriz in 1976. In Tehran, the Bakri went up in flames in 1978. The worst fire was the one at the Rex in Abadan in August 1978, when some 400 patrons died because the exits were locked from the outside.

Armenians were involved in all phases of the industry from its earliest days as producers, directors, writers, composers, cinematographers, actors, editors and subtitlists. Sanasar Khachaturian, the proprietor of Cinema Diana, co-founded Diana Film Studio in 1950, Samvel Khachikian and Joseph Vaezian co-founded Azhir Film Studio in 1957, and Babken Avedissian founded Shahrestan Film Studio in 1958. From 1930 to 1983, Iranian Armenians produced fifty-one films, which was 4.4 percent of all the films produced in Iran. During the same period, they directed fifty-five films, which was 4.75 percent of total production. Considering the size of the Armenian community, which was approximately one half of one percent of the country's population, Armenians made a significant contribution to Iranian cinema.

Sports

In 1944, on the initiative of producer and director Samvel Khachikian, a number of talented young men and women from Tabriz formed the Armenian Youth Association and I became a member. The AYA offered salutary group activities such as athletics, including soccer, boxing, biking and gymnastics, scouting, a drama group and a choir, and I wanted to join them all. When I auditioned for the choir, I was asked to produce certain musical notes, but after several tries, I was told that, because of my "ear," I would never achieve anything in music. But I did play small roles in *The Capture of Tamkabert*, adapted from Tumanyan's poem of the same name, and Shakespeare's *Othello*, as well as several comedies directed by Tony Amatouni. (Amatouni went on to found the Charmahal Association's Geghard Theater Group in 1981.) My first ever mountaineering expedition was organized by Khachikian. We climbed Pasghaleh north of Tehran. Khachikian also organized a commemoration for the victims of the 1915 Genocide at Cinema Diana. It was the first event of its kind, if memory serves me well, and it left a deep impression on me and my friends. Unfortunately, I don't recall why the AYA ceased functioning. Perhaps it was the tight financial situation, or perhaps it was folded into the Ararat Armenian Sports and Cultural Association (also known simply as the Ararat Association) which, according to the late Sevag Saginian (1922–2003), he cofounded in 1946 with several others, including future *Alik* editor-in-chief Norair Pahlavouni (1924–2011) and future ARF Bureau chief Hrair Maroukhian (1928–98).

Lacking resources and training facilities, the Armenian athletic organizations of my youth could barely maintain visibility in the wider world of Iranian sports. Nevertheless, they trained many excellent sportsmen. Babken Mgrdichian was a talented athlete who taught physical education at the American College (later Alborz High School) where he trained hundreds of students, Armenian and non-Armenian alike. The school auditorium was named in his memory.

The first Armenian soccer team, dubbed "Sport," was formed even before the AYA came into being. The players were exceedingly well trained and some of them joined the Iranian national team. Soccer stars in my early youth included George Markarian, Artoush Asatourian and Hovsep Stepanian. Among the next generation, Garnik Mehrabian went on to become one of Iran's best coaches. He worked with the Ararat Association for many years.

Ashot Avedissian, known as Ashot Black, was a soccer star who also excelled in cycling and tennis, and he later headed the National Tennis Federation. It was after his unprecedented 1947 solo cycling trip from Tehran to Rome, Paris and London that two team-mates and I rode our modest machines to Bandar (Port) Enzeli and back.

Perino Mesropian was another soccer star and all-around athlete whose family lived near our shop. His grandmother had been a great help to my parents at the time of my childhood lung infection. One day, Perino was standing near our shop as usual, and his maternal aunt was crossing the street.

There was a gang of dagger-toting thugs in the area who had been holding up shopkeepers and one of them made a vulgar comment about Perino's aunt. He walked right up to the leader of the gang, a tall, thick-set man named Seyyed Abbas, and punched him in the forehead. Abbas collapsed in a faint. When he came to, he and his gang left in a hurry and were never seen again. Tall, well-built and handsome, Perino always symbolized the authentic athlete for me.

Iranian Armenians (and Assyrians) made important contributions to the success of national boxing teams and many of them later worked as trainers. Seroj Safarian taught physical education in Armenian schools for many years. Emmanuel Aghassian (Manuel "Mike" Agassi), a classmate of mine at Tamaddon, competed in the 1948 and 1952 Summer Olympics. His son André became an international tennis champion.

Among weightlifting champions, the most famous were Levon and Hakob (Yasha) Kurkjian. Levon (as Leon Kurukchian) won the heavyweight gold medal in the 1951 Asian Games. Both brothers later became referees with the International Weightlifting Federation. Levon was the father of the well-known poet Varand.

Iranian Armenian gymnastic champions included Vazgen Amirkhanian, Avres Melkonian and Garnik Nalbandian. Vazgen, another Tamaddon classmate of mine, was a versatile athlete who clinched his first bodybuilding title at the age of sixteen and was the reigning swimming champion for years.

Mountaineering has always appealed to Armenians. Emil Markarian, Felix Mnatsakanian and Norair Minassian were the best known climbers in my youth. Unfortunately, Felix fell to his death on Alam Kuh in 1954, and within two years Norair fell from the same peak.

Summertime

I was an avid athlete in my late teens. Even after I stopped delivering bread to our shop, I still awoke at the crack of dawn and rode a twenty-mile circuit up to Niavaran and back. Before heading off to school, I made myself an omelet of a dozen eggs. When lunchtime came around four hours later, I was so hungry that my hands were shaking. For years, my weight was stuck at 168 pounds.

After Ashot Black's historic European cycling tour, I started contemplating a long-distance trip myself, and in 1949, with the co-sponsorship of the Ararat Association and the Iranian Physical Culture Association, Rudolf Lazar, Grish Shahoumian and I toured Karaj, Chalus, Ramsar, Lahijan, Rasht and its port at Enzeli (then known as Bandar Pahlavi), returning by way of Rudbar, Manjil and Qazvin. Tehran's mass circulation daily *Ettelaat* covered our nine-day trip and we were welcomed with the respect and enthusiasm accorded to champions in every town along the way, but the trip wasn't all that easy.

The hard part began at Gachsar, a resort town about forty-five miles north of Karaj. We had to climb six miles of mountain road to reach Kandovan Pass. In places, the ascent was so steep that instead of riding we carried our bikes on our backs. Kandovan Tunnel was pitch black inside with water pouring down from the ceiling. Standing at the entrance, we hailed a truck driver and asked him to let us follow his lights. At the other end of the tunnel, a new world was revealed: fog, pouring rain and thickly forested mountains. We endured these conditions for another forty-four miles to Chalus on the coast. The next day we introduced ourselves to the director of the local athletic organization who was also the manager of the local silk factory.

By the time we reached Rasht, we were covered in mud from head to toe. We found a public bath where we bathed and washed our clothes, and only after they had dried were we able to get dressed and walk around town. At Bandar Pahlavi, the naval commander had his photograph taken with us. On the return trip, we had to be frugal with our money. We stopped at every teahouse and ordered three glasses of tea, and while waiting for it to be served, we finished off the sugar bowl, replenishing the calories we had burned.

The funniest part of our trip involved my costume. About ten miles before Qazvin, I realized that the trousers I had packed on the back of my bike had slipped out and got lost, so I had to get by with one pair of short pants for the duration of the trip. When we stopped off at city hall in Qazvin, it was the first time the authorities there had ever seen a young man in short pants enter the premises, and every one of them had something to say about it. People were still talking about it two months later when I went back to Qazvin with my friend Grigor. We paid a visit to his aunt, and his cousin and her girlfriends recognized me as the young man in short pants. They told him all about it, laughing and eyeing one another.

After our trip to Bandar Pahlavi, we returned every summer and stayed at the modest Tehran Hotel. We always got Room 10 which cost four tomans per night and slept fourteen, but we never slept at night. We met our local friends at the seawall and hung out on the sand. They brought songbooks and the girls often joined us. We sang and danced until sunrise. After breakfast, we swam in the sea until midday and then went back to the hotel for lunch. Toward the end of our holiday, we only ordered *borsch* which allowed us to stretch our money and stay for a few more days. After lunch we went back to our room to rest but that didn't last long. We started throwing pillows and pandemonium ensued, forcing the manager to come to our room and issue a stern warning. After that, we entertained ourselves by telling jokes.

Our father was dead set against the idea of his sons wasting the summer loitering in the streets, but his workload was such that he could never get away long enough to take us anywhere. There were some good summer resorts in the mountains north of Tehran, and after some investigating, he decided to open a seasonal restaurant in Ushan, a village twenty miles northeast of the capital. He put my brother Henrik and me in charge of managing the business with the assistance of our little brother George. The cook was a man named Hovannes, and he was assisted by two waiters. We addressed him as Baron Hovannes, *Baron* being the equivalent of Mister or Monsieur and a term of respect. Lots of people came up on weekends and we did our best to satisfy our guests.

For the rest of the week, we were swatting flies, as they say. When business was slow, my friends and I had picnics and parties where boys and girls sang and danced, talked and laughed and had a great time. Sometimes our friends rode their bikes or took the bus up to see us. When I was by myself, I went hunting. I climbed to the top of Mount Tochal twice, once solo and once with my friend Emil Markarian. The north side of the 13,000-foot peak is covered with snow year-round.

The Soviet Repatriation Drive

In late 1945, when the Soviets still occupied northern Iran, they started a campaign to encourage "repatriation" to the Soviet Socialist Republic of Armenia. That campaign had a profound impact on the Iranian Armenian community. Committees were set up to register prospective emigrants in towns and villages with large numbers of Armenians, and the Soviet Consulate in Tehran started processing applications. Thousands of Armenians whose ancestors had lived in Tabriz, Arak, Isfahan, Chahar Mahall and nearby villages for three centuries sold up and came to Tehran in the expectation of immediate transportation to Armenia. Yet the intake was restricted by area quotas, and while their applications were being processed, they were directed to Behjatabad which was then a village on the northern outskirts of the old city. More than two decades later, Behjatabad became the site of St. Sarkis Mother Cathedral and the new Prelacy.

While waiting their turn to leave, the migrants built temporary shelters from scrap wood and metal, their wives and children found work in homes, shops and factories, and they all went about their business in village garb. The Diocesan Council was completely unprepared for such an influx of people, but it worked with various Armenian organizations to assist these families. Armenian doctors and medical students provided free medical care, sponsored by the Armenian Alumni Association which later helped to establish the Avedissian Community Clinic.

I remember when the first group left for Armenia. Thousands congregated at the main railway station to bid farewell to their friends and relatives. Our family was directly affected by the repatriation drive. My brother Henrik was nineteen years old and full of patriotism. He earnestly desired to move to Armenia and continue his education there. In view of his determination, my father finally acquiesced, but the quota for Tehran was already filled. With the help of some friends, my father then acquired a new identity card for Henrik showing his birthplace as Arak, but the move never materialized and he remained in Iran.

The displaced Armenians in Behjatabad weren't allowed to remain there. With the help of the Diocesan Council and their own resources, they were relocated to more sparsely populated areas further northeast, and those with the means to do so started building permanent homes and eventually the Armenian neighborhoods of Heshmatiyeh, Majidiyeh, Vahidiyeh, Narmak and Zarkesh came into being. Over time, they built churches and schools and community organizations proliferated. Many of their sons and daughters became outstanding teachers, professors, intellectuals, physicians, engineers, architects and artisans.

Meanwhile, the economic situation became increasingly difficult and several times my father considered selling everything and moving to America, but because he was born in Russia, the American Consulate categorized his family as citizens of the Soviet Union and we had to wait years for our turn. When we finally got permission in 1949, I was already eighteen years old, which meant that I wouldn't be allowed to go with them. Since my father could never reconcile himself to leaving me behind, the question of emigration was closed.

An Attempt on the Shah's Life

Gabriel (Joseph) Kanon was an Assyrian whose father was a respected physician in Khosrova, the village next to Haftvan. I met him at our shop in Tehran and learned that he loved hunting. He told me that whenever he was free, he went out in the countryside to hunt small game. This was before I had my own gun, but I said I'd like to go with him sometime. He told me he had been looking for a hunting buddy and he welcomed my company, even though he was ten years older than me.

After tagging along with Joseph a few times, I persuaded my father to help me buy a 32-gauge shotgun. It was hard to find cartridges but I finally found some used copper ones. Now all I needed was a permit. I appealed to Baron Ohanik Mesropian, a community member with government connections, including a security chief who was said to be the Shah's cousin. Baron Mesropian told me to consider the problem solved and it was. Now I began hunting in earnest. I paid close attention to Joseph's instructions – how to arrange the pellets in the cartridge, how much powder to put in and how to load it.

On Friday, February 4, 1949, Joseph and I went hunting as we usually did on Fridays. That morning, we took the 7:00 AM train for Saveh and hopped off a few stops down the line near a hunting ground we knew. When we came back that night, the station was unusually still. Nothing was moving except for travelers alighting from the train. Since we were carrying our shotguns, we were stopped and searched right away. We showed our papers and permits, and after close questioning, we were told to go straight home and make it quick.

My parents were worried sick when I finally got home. They told me there had been an assassination attempt on the Shah. It happened outside Tehran University Law School where he had gone to pay a formal visit. The would-be assassin, posing as a press photographer, got off five shots, wounding him in the shoulder and the face, before he himself was shot dead by the Shah's bodyguards. Credentials from an Islamist paper were found in his pocket, but Army Intelligence later implicated the Tudeh. The Shah reinstated martial law and banned the Tudeh, but it remained active underground and party stalwarts carried on with the same energy as before, even if the scope of their activities was curtailed.

Now the country entered a new political phase. The economy was bad and getting worse. The government was operating on a month-to-month basis because, for six years straight, the Majles refused to approve an annual budget. The Shah never trusted his loyal prime ministers and he and his courtiers constantly meddled in government affairs. According to the Constitution, the Shah was supposed to reign, not rule, but after the attempt on his life, he tried to concentrate all power in his own hands. He forced constitutional revisions that gave him the right to dissolve the Majles at will, and he convoked the Senate for the first time, exercising his royal prerogative to appoint half its members.

The young men of Haftvan, including my father and uncle.

Haftvan, Feast Day of the Assumption of the Holy Mother of God. This gathering of Salmast Armenians was called Joujna.

Construction workers at the central railway station of Tehran. Second from the left on the first row was my uncle Abgar.

With my friend Gourgen on our way to Lake Urumia.

School life with my classmates at Tamadon high school.

Tamadon students at parade held at "Anjadiye" stadium, now called Shahid Shiroudi statium.

Visit to Pas Ghale heights.

Cyclists welcomed by officials from Routbar.

Author at the entrance to his uncle's house in Haftvan.

Chapter 3

The Struggle to Nationalize the Oil

Iran was only getting 10 percent of the proceeds from the operations of the Anglo-Iranian Oil Company (AIOC) in southern Iran, and the company's exclusive concession still had another forty-five years to run when Prime Minister Qavam started to negotiate for better terms. Saudi Arabia's 50-50 profit-sharing agreement with ARAMCO provided a strong incentive to keep up the pressure. Negotiations with the AIOC continued for seven years under a dozen successive prime ministers, but the issue became the focus of heated public debate in 1949, during the contentious Sixteenth Majles elections, when a coalition known as the National Front (*Jebheh Melli*), led by Dr. Mohammad Mosadegh, emerged as the most prominent advocate of outright nationalization of Iran's petroleum industry.

The Shah spent the last six weeks of 1949 in America where he traveled widely and met with President Harry Truman at the White House. The two heads of state confirmed a Mutual Defense Assistance Agreement and initialed the Point 4 Program which would provide American advisors and technical training in public health, education and agriculture. These two agreements together generated approximately $500 million in grants over the next decade and won the good will of Iran's educated classes. That was the beginning of American penetration of Iranian society. Hundreds of technicians and administrators were hired at impressive salaries, new businesses began to flourish and many young people were sent to the USA for study and training. Because Iranian Armenians' knowledge of English was generally superior to that of their Muslim compatriots, they were given priority in hiring. We envied the young Armenian men driving around in jeeps flying the Point 4 pennant whose insignia of two clasped hands symbolized Iranian-American friendship.

In March 1951, there was a crisis in the southwestern province of Khuzestan, the center of petroleum production. More than 50,000 Iranians from all over the country worked in its far-flung oilfields and the huge refinery complex at Abadan. When the AIOC laid off 800 workers and cut benefits for the rest, local strikes developed into a massive general strike organized by the Tudeh and supported by the National Front, whose demand to nationalize the oil industry became a strike slogan. Prime Minister Hossein Ala declared martial law and sent 20,000 troops to the province. It was a bloody affair: a dozen Iranians were killed by troops and three British nationals were lynched by an angry mob. The UK deployed three warships to the northern Gulf but the strike came to an end when the AIOC rescinded the cuts and raised the minimum wage. That set a powerful precedent in the struggle for nationalization.

Prime Minister Ala was forced to resign and Dr. Mosadegh was appointed to replace him. The Sixteenth Majles passed the Nationalization Act and the Shah signed it into law on May 1, 1951. The National Iranian Oil Company (NIOC) was established and soon took over AIOC headquarters at Khorramshahr. By October, all the expatriate managers and technicians had left the country. It seemed that the people's will had been achieved and a new horizon was opening before the nation.

But control of Iran's primary natural resource quickly became an international issue. As the AIOC's major shareholder, the British government lodged a complaint with the International Court of Justice at The Hague. The Court issued a preliminary injunction but Mosadegh rejected its jurisdiction and the Court eventually upheld his position. The UK then turned to the UN Security Council. Mosadegh, a Swiss-trained lawyer and a sophisticated politician, went to New York to argue the case for Iran. The question of just compensation for the AIOC was raised but no action was taken. At that point, the AIOC impounded Iran's royalty payments, the Bank of England froze Iranian assets, the UK instituted an international blockade of Iranian oil, and the industry was reduced to producing solely for domestic consumption. The economic crunch in Iran was severe.

Meanwhile, the outside powers were competing for influence, each one backing Iranian factions and individuals who were willing to further their interests. The Tudeh stood with Mosadegh against the AIOC concession but accused him of conniving to hand it over to the USA, whereas the party wanted to preserve the option for a Soviet concession. In the Majles, the clerical faction alternately supported and attacked Mosadegh, while out in the streets, the Islamic Fedayeen (*Feda'iyan-e Eslam*) were assassinating journalists and politicians. The USA sent Averell Harriman to mediate but his visit coincided with a Tudeh-led demonstration against Mosadegh. Police fired on the crowd and some twenty people were killed and more than 250 injured. The Interior Minister, General (ret.) Fazlollah Zahedi, was forced to resign.

Those were tense days. The instability and insecurity were approaching a critical point. Street fights and terrorists attacks were almost daily fare. Every day on our way home from school, we pricked up our ears for the newshawker's cry, eager to hear the latest developments.

After Mosadegh's triumphant return from New York, he seemed to lose his grip on power. Facing death threats, he conducted business from his home on Kakh Street. Dr. Hossein Fatemi, his parliamentary secretary and later his Foreign Minister, was attacked and seriously wounded by the Islamic Fedayeen. When the Seventeenth Majles convened in April 1952, the National Front had fewer votes than before. In an attempt to deal with the crisis, Mosadegh asked for plenary powers and demanded his constitutional right as Prime Minister to nominate the Minister of War, but the Shah refused to concede control of the Army. Mosadegh was forced to resign on July 16, 1952. He was replaced by the "Old Fox," Qavam ol-Saltaneh. At the Shah's behest, Qavam stationed tanks in front of the Majles in Baharestan Square. He warned the public that "the days of defiance" were over and it was time to "obey the will of the government." But Qavam only lasted five days, because now the people united behind the National Front's call for a general strike and there were mass demonstrations across the country. The biggest demonstration took place in Tehran on July 21 (*30 Tir*). Scores were killed and hundreds injured. The Shah was forced to restore Mosadegh as Prime Minister and concede control of the War Ministry.

But Mosadegh's supporters continued to defect, the National Front fractured and the Tudeh intensified its activities in response to the new balance of forces. The country was in a state of complete anarchy. Fearing a communist takeover, the UK and the USA began planning to overthrow Mosadegh in the name of the Shah. Their "Prime Minister designate" was the former Interior Minister, Fazlollah Zahedi. His son Ardeshir, who was then serving as chief aide to the head of the Point 4 program, was enlisted as CIA liaison to his father, while Colonel Hassan Akhavi was General Zahedi's liaison to the Shah.

Coup d'état

August 1953 was a historic juncture in Iranian politics. Tudeh, the National Front and the leading clerics were all planning mass actions. Student activists were writing articles and organizing demonstrations. There were internal conflicts in the Army, among the religious leaders and within Mosadegh's own cabinet. Those who identified with the British were terrified, knowing that Tudeh was better organized than any other party and fearing that a Tudeh victory would draw Iran into the Soviet Communist sphere of influence.

On Saturday night, August 15, 1953, Imperial Guard Commander Colonel Nematollah Nasiri delivered a *farman* (royal decree) to Prime Minister Mosadegh that relieved him of his duties. He also informed Mosadegh of another farman appointing General Zahedi to replace him. But Mosadegh knew that the Shah and his wife Soraya had left Tehran four days earlier for their summer retreat at Kelardasht near the Caspian coast. He dismissed the farman as a forgery and had Colonel Nasiri arrested.

Early Sunday morning, we were shocked to hear the radio broadcast that Mosadegh had foiled a military coup, that he had issued a warrant for General Zahedi's arrest and that he was already purging his enemies from the Army officer corps and the civil service.

Later that day, when the radio announced that the royal couple had left Iran and flown to Baghdad, Tehran was utterly transformed. Our apartment was located at the busy intersection of Shah Reza and Vali Asr Streets and my brothers and I watched the commotion from a second-floor window. Thousands of people, men and women of all classes, started toppling statues and tearing down symbols of the Pahlavis. Tudeh supporters were singing and dancing in the street, shouting, "*Be khaste mardom, Shah farari shodeh!*" (The people got fed up and the Shah fled). It seemed like the entire city was celebrating. I saw some of my classmates in the joyous throng.

It all lasted barely 48 hours. While the Shah and Soraya moved on to Rome and General Zahedi remained in hiding, the conspirators were busy distributing photostats of the Shah's farmans. On Wednesday, August 19, loyal troops and monarchists took control of the streets. They attacked anyone who was pro-Tudeh or pro-Mosadegh. Some 300 people were killed that day. The Army captured the radio transmission building and started broadcasting the royal decrees, interspersed with anti-communist diatribes.

The entire political situation was up-ended in a single day. Hundreds of soldiers and civilians were driving around, waving flags and shouting, "Death to Tudeh!" and "Down with Communism!" The civilians were generally older and upper-class compared with the demonstrators of the day before. I saw several Armenian youths whom I knew in the crowd.

At 4:00 in the afternoon, General Zahedi came out of hiding and spoke live on the radio. The Shah's brothers chimed in to ease the way for his peaceful return. Tanks and mobs descended on Mosadegh's home and his supporters rushed to his defense. He and his advisors escaped but gave themselves up a day or two later. When the Shah returned on Saturday, he was welcomed with elaborate demonstrations of obeisance. Once again, Iran entered a new political era.

Nearly half a century later, in April 2000, the *New York Times* published the CIA's secret history of TP-AJAX, written by Donald Wilber, the operation's principal planner, describing how the agency had collaborated with Britain's Secret Intelligence Service (MI6) to carry out the coup at the cost of little more than a million dollars which they secretly distributed to their agents. Some Iranian intellectuals had swallowed the story that a crowd of knife-wielding thugs and loose women toppled Mosadegh, but as he told the military tribunal that sentenced him to three years in solitary confinement followed by life under house arrest:

"It was the imperialists who forced me to resign…. You couldn't arrest a mouse!"

Kermit Roosevelt, the CIA officer who supervised the ground operation, later boasted in his book, *Countercoup*, that the Shah said to him,

"I owe my throne to God, my people, my army – and to you!"

Despite Anglo-American collaboration in the coup, a deep rivalry underlay their approach to Iran. When negotiations over the concession resumed in December, Iran's interlocutor was Iranian Oil Participants (IOP) Ltd., a new international consortium whose shareholders were the following:

Iranian Oil Participants Ltd.	Share
British Petroleum (formerly AIOC)	40%
Royal Dutch Shell	14%
Gulf Oil	8%
Mobil Oil	8%
Standard Oil of California	8%
Standard Oil of New Jersey (Exxon)	8%
Texas Oil Company	8%
Compagnie Française des Pétroles (Total)	6%

In the fall of 1954, Iran signed a complex 50-50 profit-sharing agreement with IOP Ltd., granting the consortium a twenty-five–year concession for the exploration, extraction, refinement and export of Iranian oil. The British, having previously enjoyed full control of the industry, had effectively ceded 60 percent of a reduced share of the profits to other (mostly American) companies. And to their displeasure, the Shah and his court obeyed the dictates of successive US administrations for the next quarter of a century.

Prime Minister Zahedi was forced to resign a year later, but his son continued to support American policies to the hilt. Ardeshir Zahedi married the Shah's daughter Shahnaz in 1957, was appointed Ambassador to the USA in 1960, Ambassador to the UK in 1962, Foreign Minister in 1967–71, and Ambassador to the USA again, from 1973 until the Islamic Revolution.

Prior to 1957, Iran's only intelligence service was *Rokn-e Do* or R–2 (Column Two), similar to the American G–2, i.e. Army Intelligence. When General Teymour Bakhtiar was appointed Military Governor of Tehran in the fall of 1953, this unit came under his authority. Thereafter he worked closely with US Army and CIA officers, the UK's MI6 and Israel's Mossad to organize and train what became the State Intelligence and Security Organization (*Sazman-e Ettelaat ve Amniyat-e Keshvar*) or SAVAK, and he was put in charge of the new service. SAVAK became very powerful, penetrating every branch of government and spying on the people. No one dared to say or publish anything critical of the Shah. People wouldn't even discuss politics on the phone. After General Nematollah Nasiri took charge of the organization in 1965, SAVAK perfected its control while continuing to maintain close relations with the CIA and Mossad. By the time of the Islamic Revolution, SAVAK was said to have over 5,000 employees and 50–100,000 informants, depending on the source.

The Charm of Democracy and Free Speech

Mosadegh's tenure, which barely amounted to twenty-eight months, was characterized by an unprecedented degree of freedom of the press. Indeed, it was one of the most liberated periods in Iranian history. We avidly followed the muckraking stories of courtiers' follies and ministers' misdeeds. The first thing I did on my way to school every morning was to stop at the local kiosk and scan the headlines. The most important establishment papers were *Ettelaat* (Information) and *Kayhan* (The World) and both are still published today. Tudeh's *Mardom* (The Masses) came out daily, despite being banned. Another Tudeh paper, *Besu-ye Ayandeh* (Toward the Future), reflected the views of leftist intellectuals in rich and complex language. *Bakhtar-e Emruz* (Today's West), an anti-royalist paper with an extreme nationalist perspective, was published by Dr. Hossein Fatemi. After the fall of Mosadegh, Dr. Fatemi went into hiding, only to be captured six months later. During his arrest, he was severely injured in a knife attack, allegedly by the ruffian Shaban Jafari, and despite his condition, he was court-martialed and executed by firing squad. *Shoresh* (Rebellion) was another nationalist, anti-royalist paper whose editor, Karimpour Shirazi, was arrested in October 1953 and deliberately burned alive in his cell five months later.

The most important of several Armenian papers was *Alik* (The Wave), launched by the ARF in 1931. It was invaluable for Armenians like my parents who were not fluent in Persian. My father impatiently awaited his copy every day, and when it arrived, he would say, "*Aha yegav* Alik *baydzar!*" (*Alik* is here, all bright and shiny!)

The Polytechnic Institute

In 1951, when I was in my last year of high school and trying to decide what to study in college, the Army was recruiting students to continue their education at the Military Institute. I decided to enroll but older friends and acquaintances advised me not to, especially being an Armenian. Since I was interested in industrial chemicals – how they were produced and what they were used for – I applied to the Chemistry Department at the Polytechnic Institute. I didn't ace the entrance exam but I was placed on a waiting list of three. I was confident that I would get in because slots always opened up when the top candidates accepted admission to other schools, which is exactly what happened.

My Polytech education lasted four years, the first three of which were devoted to classroom instruction and laboratory experimentation. We worked in the lab every day. Four students were assigned to a table and the group collaboration generated strong personal relationships. Sometimes we spent all night in the lab, chatting and laughing while we worked. Those days and nights were most enjoyable.

Student life was intensely political during my first year at the Institute. I was surrounded by young men and women with various political opinions. But after the coup, political activity was banned and an unusual silence prevailed on campus. I was suspicious of all ideologies and was never politically active, except for the day when we heard that the Army was going to arrest Prime Minister Mosadegh at his home. Everyone rushed to Kakh Street, perhaps to protect him, but he evaded capture by climbing over the garden wall.

In December 1953, when US Vice President Richard Nixon paid a visit to the Shah, students in the engineering department at Tehran University organized a protest. Troops appeared instantly and ordered them back to class. That had the opposite effect and things took a turn for the worse. They fired on the unarmed demonstrators and killed three. Students went on strike for a month, and I took the opportunity to go hunting for wild goats up in the mountains. Now, more than sixty years later, December 7 is still observed as Student Day in Iran.

Masht Hossein guarded the gate at the Institute and nothing escaped his eye. He was called "Masht" because he had made a pilgrimage to the shrine of Imam Reza in Mashhad. He was also a respected *pahlavan*, that is, a champion of *varzesh-e bastani*, the traditional Iranian athletic discipline. One day, word spread that Shaban Jafari was at the campus gate. Known as Shaban *Bimokh* (Brainless), he was a notorious brawler who had supported the overthrow of Mosadegh. He was also an adept of varzesh-e bastani. When students gathered around and showered him with insults, he said some ungracious things in reply. At that point, Masht Hossein came out of his guardroom. Shaban Bimokh approached the older athlete and kissed his shoulders as a sign of respect, following pahlavan custom. Masht Hossein told him that the young men and women present were like his own children, and if anyone were to offend them, he would take it personally. Shaban Bimokh signaled his men and they left without another word.

The Crackdown

One day in the fall of 1954, we were carrying out an experiment in the lab when one of the students cursed the Shah. Another student named Salehi, an Army officer with the rank of major, took offense. I intervened and asked the first student to apologize and that was the end the matter. Two weeks later, as we were walking home from school, we saw a crowd surrounding a news kiosk. Approaching under the pretense of buying a paper, we heard the shocking story that a Tudeh cabal had been discovered in the Army! Some 400 officers had been arrested, and to our great surprise, Major Salehi was one of those arrested.

Over the next few years, General Bakhtiar's R–2 captured over 4,000 so-called traitors, meaning supporters of Mosadegh or the Tudeh, women as well as men. Some were held in city jails around the country while others were banished to Kharg (Khark) Island in the Persian Gulf. Suspects were pressured to name their comrades and publicly recant; those who resisted were tortured. I had a Muslim friend from Rasht named Amin – we used to study together – and he spent two years on Kharg Island. When he came back, he said he was proud that he had stuck to his principles, but he soon emigrated to the German Democratic Republic (East Germany).

Two of my classmates who supported Tudeh were horrifically violated. For instance, horsetail hairs were inserted into their penises. After they were finally released, they suffered from bleeding for many years.

An Armenian youth named Vartan Salakhanian was arrested for distributing *Mardom*. I heard that he refused to reveal where he got the paper and that his nails were pulled out one by one, but he never broke his silence. Ultimately he died in prison. I'm told that Ahmad Shamlu honored Vartan's silence in one of his poems.

General Bakhtiar also arranged for the extrajudicial execution of fugitives. Jahangir Baghdanian was a brilliant student who always left his books at home and never took notes in class, but got the highest scores on exams. An R–2 operative tracked and murdered him on a street north of the Soviet Embassy. Another Armenian named Aramayis, a talented poet and actor from Tabriz, was killed in the same way.

One morning, several secret service men stormed into our second-floor classroom at Polytech. Ignoring the instructor, they brought in the janitor and ordered him to point out the student they were looking for. The janitor eyed us one by one but said nothing. Suddenly a window flew open and one of our classmates jumped down to the street and disappeared. A secret service man turned to the janitor and slapped him hard across the face.

I had a friend named Sako Babayan whose father was originally from Yerevan and a member of the ARF. His tanning business wasn't doing well and the family had fallen on hard times, so Sako did odd jobs to meet his expenses. For example, on test days at Tamaddon High School, he used to buy a quantity of cheap exam paper in the Bazaar and sell it to his classmates by the sheet. Later he set up a small commercial photography studio at home. At night, he distributed newspapers for Tudeh. Sako was ideologically 100-percent communist, and after *28 Mordad* (August 19), his father's friends urged him to flee the country. I was one of those who lent him some money for the trip. He escaped to West Germany where he worked as a longshoreman in Hamburg for a few months, and repaid me by sending the hunting rifle I had asked for. Then he went to California where he started out washing car windshields at Jack London Square in Oakland. He moved up to retailing doughnuts, then became a wholesale baker, and ultimately a millionaire dealing in Bay Area real estate. I visited him in San Francisco in 1964. He had three children and he took them to church every Sunday.

Chapter 4

Young Manhood

Our shop was doing quite well financially during my college years. We had enough workers so that I no longer had to deliver the bread, but there was nothing to keep me from getting up early. On some spring mornings I awoke at dawn and rode my bicycle. Every night I went to the shop at 8:00 PM to relieve my father. As my studies became more demanding, I got up earlier and did more homework. During exam weeks I hardly left the house for days at a time. I wasn't one of the top students – I was in the middle of the pack. My final year was devoted to research on a chemical of my choice and writing a thesis based on my research, and that was capped with a three-month internship.

As my friends and I began to take greater interest in girls, we organized parties where we could sing and dance and have a good time until midnight. Two dates had special meaning for me. One was my birthday, November 17, when my friends traditionally came to our home to celebrate. No formal invitation was required and we usually had about forty guests. My mother would start cooking two days ahead of time. My father's paternal cousin's son would bring over five-liter bottles of his home-made wine which our guests drank with great relish. The other special occasion was St. Sarkis Night. My friend Sako's father, a kind and gracious man, asked me to celebrate his son's namesake every year for as long as he lived. I organized the annual feast and Sako's father spared nothing to make it a festive event. My friends always chose me as *tamada* (toastmaster).

Over time, the camaraderie at our parties grew into something more serious and everyone seemed to find a partner. That became obvious when they danced cheek-to-cheek, European-style, and the same couples danced every dance together. There was a striking girl in our group with green eyes and a well-developed figure. All the young men wanted to dance with her and I was no exception. One day, I picked her up at her house and took her to a party. Naturally, I assumed that I would take her home at the end of the evening and I made up my mind to kiss her at that point. The moment arrived and I expressed my wish. She moved her head closer and my kiss landed on her forehead. The next day, I told a friend what happened and he laughed.

"Who told you a man is supposed to ask a girl's permission? What you need to do is put your hand on her neck and kiss her on the lips. That's how you prove you're a man!"

That was useful information.

How I Met Bella

I had made up my mind to choose a girlfriend but I still hadn't found one I fancied. I don't mean to sound conceited, but I was popular with the girls. New faces appeared and new relationships developed as various groups mixed and mingled at our parties, and that was how I met the girl who later became my life partner. Her name was Yolanda Bellardina Muratori. I called her Bella.

It was the birthday of one of our friends and she had invited her neighbor's daughter to the party. As usual, the boys jostled one another to dance with the new girl. I, on the other hand, took my time and waited for the opportune moment to ask her to dance. Afterwards, we talked for a long time and I could tell that she had developed a particular interest in me too. After that night, we saw each other a few more times. Then one day, she invited our group to her house for her birthday party. Later on, I learned that her father was an Italian contractor who had come to Iran before the war to help build the Trans-Iranian Railway. He married an Iranian Armenian woman named Regine and Bella was their only child. He died barely four years after Bella was born. Madame Regine remarried, this time to a Frenchman named Monsieur Roumestan, and they had a daughter named Jacqueline. The family was Catholic and Madame Regine taught French at Jeanne d'Arc School in Tehran. I had found the person I wanted to spend my life with.

Internship in Shazand

The last stage of my education at the Polytechnic Institute involved practical training at an industrial concern. Our group of six friends did a three-month internship at a sugar refinery in Shazand where the manager was a Polytech alumnus. Armed with his invitation and our dean's recommendation, we boarded the train for Arak, the station nearest to Shazand. We were introduced to the manager as soon as we arrived. Then we were settled in a furnished apartment with a cook on the second floor of a company-owned building. We started work the next day.

I had brought along my hunting gear and I immediately started looking for a hunting buddy. We worked in various sections of the factory in order to familiarize ourselves with every phase of production, and I soon learned that the head mechanic, Andranik, was a hunter. I introduced myself and we went hunting two days later. I gave the rabbits, ducks and partridges I bagged to our cook, and through Andranik's connections, we bought wine in the nearby Armenian village of Abbasabad.

My friends put me in charge of provisions and one day when I was shopping at the market in Shazand, I noticed an open barrel of honey. It appeared to be of good quality so I asked the price. As is customary, the shopkeeper invited me to taste it first, so I did. Just then, Andranik joined me and we started speaking in Armenian. The shopkeeper asked us what language we were speaking and I naively told him that we were Armenians.

"Unfortunately," he said, "now that you touched the honey, I have to throw it all away."

"If that's the case, why don't you sell it to me for half price?"

"With God's blessing. I hope you're a Muslim and not an Armenian."

Shazand's head accountant, who wasn't very well liked by the workers, lived on the first floor of our building and he raised chickens and turkeys in the courtyard. On several occasions, one of my flatmates praised the distinctive flavor of turkey. One day, he came in with a turkey under his arm, went into the kitchen, plucked and gutted the gobbler and handed it over to the cook. We invited the factory manager and the head accountant to dinner that night. Everyone loved the turkey, but when they credited me, I felt obliged to say I had bought it in Abbasabad. As for the accountant, when he realized that one of his turkeys was missing, he searched high and low for days.

When our three-month internship came to an end, we hosted a farewell party the night before we left Shazand. Everybody got drunk except Ali, a devout Muslim, a hard worker and the best student in our group of six, and the writer of these lines who always maintained a sense of his limits. The next morning, we managed to get ourselves to Arak on time and boarded the train for Tehran. Thus I completed my degree from the Polytechnic Institute with high marks in 1955. We were each given a small honorarium for our work at the factory. That was really my first salary and I bought Bella a present with it.

Starting a Career and a Family

Now I faced two problems. First I had to complete my military service and then I had to get a job. But because my older brother Henrik was then serving in the military, I was granted a one-year exemption. By the end of that year, the rules had changed and my service was no longer required.

Tehran's newly established Municipal Water Department was building reservoirs and laying pipe to distribute chlorinated water, and Sir Alexander Gibb and Partners, the British civil engineering firm, was managing the project. One of the engineers was a regular customer at my father's shop and he told us that the city needed chemists to analyze the water. He encouraged me to apply for a job in the Purification Division and he even took me to meet the director. I was asked to wait outside while they conferred in the director's office. A few minutes later, the engineer emerged looking quite disturbed. All he said was, "What a shame." Evidently, I wasn't going to be offered a job because I wasn't a Muslim.

There were two other possibilities, the sugar refinery in Shazand and the National Iranian Oil Company in Abadan, but I was reluctant to leave my father on his own. Henrik had married and was studying at Tehran University and my younger brother George was studying in the USA, so neither one of them was in a position to help him. What to do? Then I heard about a new soil analysis laboratory that was being set up by the Ministry of Agriculture with the assistance of the UN Food and Agriculture Organization (FAO). I was hired to start work on April 5, 1956.

In the meantime, I kept myself occupied in the private laboratory of the maternal uncle of a friend of mine, a retired scientist from the Ministry of Agriculture. Bella's stepfather, Mr. Roumestan, owned a lead mine in Savad Kuh County, over the mountains in Mazandaran Province, and one day he had a Russian chemist bring a sample of ore to the lab. The Russian asked for a beaker of water and a one-liter glass measuring bowl. He poured the water into the bowl, marked the level, put the ore in the water, marked the rise in the water level, and then he did some calculations. I realized that he was trying to assay the ore on the basis of its specific gravity rather than its chemical composition, so I tested it with chemical methods and got numbers that were 50 percent lower than his. When I told Mr. Roumestan what happened and suggested the Russian chemist was inflating the numbers, he was skeptical, but then he began to have his doubts. We decided to send a few specimens for testing in Switzerland. When the results came back, we compared them with my results and found only a small deviation which is normal in any experiment. Mr. Roumestan realized that extracting ore from the mine was costing him more than it was worth.

"You saved me," he said. "I'm indebted to you."

Bella and I were married on July 11, 1956. I rented a five-room apartment down the street from my parents' home. The rent was 400 tomans. My monthly salary was 480 tomans and Bella was earning 250 tomans working at her stepfather's company. We furnished our new home with her dowry and with my parents' gift of a table and twelve chairs. My father also gave us 400 tomans which we spent on a week-long honeymoon at Bandar Pahlavi (Enzeli). When we got back, we heard that the daughter of a friend of a friend was looking for a room to rent. Since our apartment was too big for us, we rented a room to her which considerably improved our financial situation.

That gave me the idea of turning another room into a lab, and I started doing chemical tests and experiments on minerals and gemstones at home. Sometimes a disagreement would arise between a buyer and a seller of precious stones and they would seek out my services in order to establish certain facts. A few times I was offered a bribe but I never accepted and I tried to avoid such offers. As a result, I won a reputation for honesty and fairness which in the long run brought me more rewards than I might have gained by taking a bribe. My work progressed so well that my clients came to include some prominent people and some big mine owners. The income from my private lab was five times my salary at the Ministry of Agriculture.

On May 2, 1957, our first child was born. Annette was a pretty and energetic little girl. Henrik's first son had been born the year before and two years later he and his wife were blessed with their second son. Our son Vahe was born exactly forty-five days after Henrik's second son. The Aharonians were multiplying! Henrik and his family lived with my parents and we lived two doors away. We shared every meal at my parents' table, enjoying my mother's delicious cooking.

I worked at the Ministry of Agriculture until 2:00 PM every day, and after a two-hour break for lunch and a rest, I went to work in my private lab. At 8:00 PM, I went to André Shop so that my father could go home early. I closed the shop at 10:00 PM and went home to continue work in my lab.

I liked my job at the Ministry and I applied myself with energy and dedication, but my older Iranian colleagues often asked me why I worked so hard for the government. There were eight FAO experts working in the lab with us, including Dr. Gracey, an elderly Scotsman who had worked for twenty-seven years as a soil chemist in Egypt. Despite his advanced age, he came to the lab early in the morning and worked all day without stopping. We conversed in English which I had studied in school, and he taught me a lot about soil analysis and interpretation. I owe him a great deal.

Another FAO expert was Dr. Divan, an Indian gentleman who showed me a great deal of respect. One day, he called me into his office and told me about an opportunity to pursue my specialization abroad. The FAO was offering one-year scholarships for junior engineers to study in the USA or The Netherlands. I was elated! I took an English exam at the Dutch Embassy and passed it with flying colors. When it was over, the examiner stood up, shook my hand and wished me a pleasant stay in his country. I was on my way to the University of Wageningen, a leading center of agricultural research.

Postgraduate Study Abroad

In September 1960, I flew to Rome where the FAO had its headquarters. I spent a few days in that beautiful city and then flew to Amsterdam on a Friday. At the hotel, a maid joyfully told me that tomorrow was going to be sunny. I secretly derided her enthusiasm, but after I had spent a year in The Netherlands where it rains ten months out of twelve, I fully understood what sunshine means to the Dutch. I spent Saturday in Amsterdam and on Sunday I took the train to Wageningen.

Everything was in place when I arrived. I was met at the station and accompanied to a pension where eight other students were staying. The next day, I was picked up and taken to the Soil Survey Institute where I was introduced to the director, Professor Edelmann, and the lecturer and lab supervisor, Professor Van Skarenburg, who became my mentor. I was assigned a desk and I started working immediately. Before leaving Iran, I had arranged to have some soil samples sent to me at Wageningen and I tested them in the new lab. I often discussed my findings and my interpretations with Professor Van Skarenburg. He soon came to the conclusion that I was an accomplished expert in my field and he complimented me in the presence of other instructors several times.

There were four Iranian students in the postgraduate program and we each received a monthly stipend of 500 florins from the Dutch Foreign Ministry. That was enough to cover the expenses of an entire family, and after two months without my wife and children, I arranged for them to join me. I rented a furnished apartment in Heelsum, a village near the university, and finally we were reunited. Annette and Vahe, who was just learning to speak, played in the street with the local children all day long. Annette started nursery school and learned to speak Dutch as well as her playmates.

I wanted to see more of Europe and for that I needed a car. Heelsum was twenty miles from the German border and Cologne was the nearest big city, so I went to Cologne and bought a used Opel, a year or two old. I had learned to drive in Tehran but had never driven in Europe and I was unnerved by the speed of the traffic, especially when I came to the on-ramp for the autobahn. As I hesitated, an elderly woman passed me and merged into the stream. Was I less capable than she was? Of course not! I accelerated and two hours later I reached home, safe and sound. The Opel was our first car and the children were overjoyed when they saw me drive up. I must confess that Bella and I were happy too. While I was based in Heelsum, I made trips with my family and friends to Paris, London, Brussels, and all the major Dutch cities.

We had a number of visitors while we were living in Holland. Mr. Roumestan and Bella's sister Jacqueline, who was studying in Paris, visited us three times. Each time he came, Mr. Roumestan encouraged me to join Sati, his transport and tourism company. Sati is a shortened form of SATTI, the acronym for the company's original name, *Société Anonyme de Transport et Tourisme International*. Mr. Roumestan didn't speak Persian and he needed someone he could rely on. I resisted because I was on the threshold of a most enjoyable scientific career, preparing to take a doctoral degree, but ultimately I gave in. My parents missed us terribly and I needed a job in order to take care of my family. I promised Mr. Roumestan that when I came home, I would give up working in my lab in the afternoons and help him at Sati.

When my year-long fellowship came to an end, the Dutch Foreign Ministry presented me with a certificate acknowledging my work and the favorable impression I had left on my colleagues. I recall that day with a sense of pride. I had left Iran with excellent recommendations and now I was returning home with equally strong endorsements of my research achievements. Bella and I sent the children ahead to Tehran and drove to Munich where we stayed with a friend of ours for a few days. Then we sold the Opel and flew back to Tehran by way of Beirut. A few days after I returned to work, I presented a report to the director of our Soil Survey Institute and he complimented me on my research. Within a year, I was put in charge of all twelve soil survey labs nationwide.

Encounters with the Shah

I met Mohammad Reza Shah twice while I was working in the Ministry of Agriculture. The first time was during the formal opening of the Soil Survey Institute in 1957. The building and its grounds were under SAVAK surveillance for the entire week preceding the royal visit and the staff was monitored too. The day before the opening, a security squad checked every room, drawer and fixture, and the staff spent the night in the building.

On opening day, the Shah came into the courtyard with an entourage of ministers and courtiers. He was welcomed by the Minister of Agriculture, General Hassan Akhavi (the Shah's liaison to General Zahedi back in 1953). After the speeches, General Akhavi handed the Shah a pair of scissors. The Shah cut the symbolic ribbon and entered the building, followed by his entourage. First they visited the section devoted to the study and cultivation of soils, then they moved on to the lab where I was working with several colleagues. As was his wont, the Shah asked each of us about our work. When my turn came, he indicated the scales on my lab table and asked me how accurate they were.

"They are accurate to one one-thousandth of one gram," I replied.

He turned to his entourage and said, "Ala could be weighed on those scales."

Former Prime Minister Hossein Ala, a slight and somewhat feeble man in his mid-seventies, was then serving as Minister of Court. Everyone laughed at the Shah's joke. What stands out in my memory of that day, aside from the Shah's quip, is the color of his eyes which gave his face its distinctive beauty.

The second time I met the Shah was after the Buyin Zahra earthquake in September 1962. Centered in a rural area west of Tehran, the horrific temblor claimed over 12,000 lives. When the Shah announced his intention to tour the region, the Ministry of Agriculture was tasked with setting up temporary service centers. The Soil Survey Institute erected a tent and we set up our equipment to make it look like a real laboratory. When the Shah and and his wife Farah stopped by our tent, he shook hands with my supervisor and struck up a conversation. As I stood by, listening attentively, I noticed again the distinctive glow and color of his expressive eyes. When he asked my supervisor a technical question that I knew he couldn't answer, I spoke up and answered in his place. Apparently the Shah took no offense because he left visibly pleased. I have a single photograph of that meeting which I have kept to this day.

I worried that my unsanctioned interjection might have annoyed my supervisor, but a week later, I received a certificate of appreciation from his superior, Dr. Iraj Vahidi, which put my mind at rest. Dr. Vahidi was appointed Deputy Minister of Agriculture shortly after the Shah's visit and he later rose to head both the Ministry of Agriculture and the Ministry of Water and Power and its successor Ministry of Energy.

Expanding the Family Business

I continued to help my father in the shop, relieving him every night at 8:00 so that he could go home and get some rest. We all helped out because we wanted to spare his health. André Shop stood on a 4,000-square-foot corner lot along with four other shops, an upstairs workshop, and a large courtyard. The workshop and the courtyard were owned by Baron George, an Arabic-speaking Armenian immigrant who used the space to produce and exhibit his finely crafted furniture. His wife, a Christian Arab, had no other family in Iran, and when he died, she decided to leave the country. We paid her the key money which allowed us to buy the workshop and the courtyard and we incorporated them into André Shop. I took charge of the remodeling and with the help of our carpenter friends and with loans from two other friends, it was completed in a few months. Now we now had a primary kitchen, a prep kitchen and cold storage on the ground floor and an office and dry storage upstairs.

André Shop was unique in all of Iran. Our clientele was mostly upper-class – high-ranking military officers, government ministers, physicians, engineers and the like. Dr. Mosadegh's sons, Dr. Gholam Hossein Mosadegh and Ahmad Mosadegh, were both loyal customers. The Shah's elder sister, Princess Shams, dispatched a servant several times a month with her hand-written shopping list.

At lunchtime, scores of teenage girls from Nourbakhsh and Anoushirvan Dadgar High Schools came to the shop for yershig. One day, my father got the idea of adding a few slices of tomato and pickle and wrapping the whole thing in lavash. They loved his sandwiches and we could hardly keep pace with the orders. We had three workers: Mikael who did the cooking, Abel who made the sandwiches and Johnny who worked the counter and charmed the young ladies. Abel and Johnny later immigrated to Armenia. I met Johnny there in 1990 and 1992 but lost track of him after that.

Every night before locking up the shop, I would take 500 to 1,000 tomans, depending on the day's business, and deposit it in the bank the next morning.

One day, my father asked me in a worried tone when I was going to repay Gougoush, one of the lenders who had helped finance the renovation of the shop. I told him that I had been putting money aside and that I had already repaid Gougoush in full. That was a huge weight off his mind and he was very happy. Meeting our obligations exemplified our honesty and cooperative spirit, qualities to be found in all Armenian families with a strong foundation.

With my university friends. Future general Moini, Afkhami and Jalil Vafayi, who was martyred during the revolution.

At the university.

University classroom.

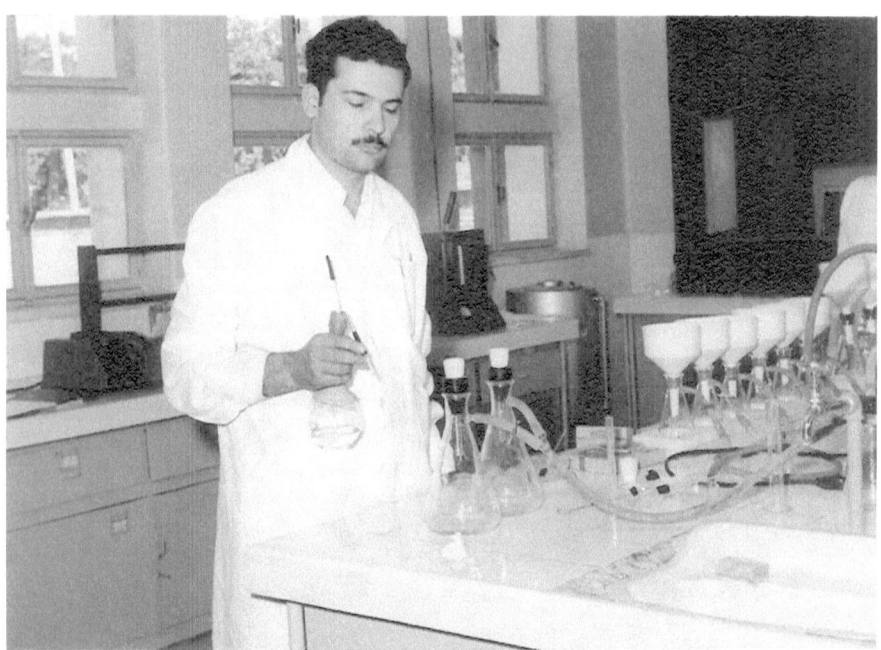
Chemistry laboratory.

My in-laws Abel Roumstian and Rejina Hovsepian.

My wife Bella in her wedding dress.

With my wife and friend.

Bella with our children Anet and Vahe.

Chapter 5

Starting at Sati

I started working part-time for my father-in-law's company in 1962, as promised, spending the afternoons from 4:00 to 8:00 PM at Sati. I knew nothing about the travel business or freight forwarding when I started, but I knew the difference between good and bad business practices, and after a few months, I realized there was considerable waste and even fraud among some of the top-echelon staff.

Mr. Roumestan had put a friend of his named Ketabchi in charge of billing. Ketabchi had been raised in Switzerland and his real name was Ketabchian but he denied his Armenian heritage. Sati had a contract with a French company that was building Iran's first big petrochemical plant near Shiraz. Most of the materials and equipment for the project came from France and the UK, arriving at Khorramshahr and Bushehr on container ships, and Sati's job was to load the containers onto flatbed trailers and move them to the staging area. The weight of these many containers varied considerably and Ketabchi was holed up in his office six days a week, using paper and pencil to calculate the cost of hauling each container. I was used to using a Swedish Facit calculator in my day job at the Ministry of Agriculture, so I ordered a Facit for Sati and did the same calculations in an hour. When I showed Ketabchi my results, he was quite taken aback. He complained to Mr. Roumestan that I was wasting money (by purchasing the Facit), but he ultimately conceded that my method was faster and more reliable. When he left the company a few months later, his responsibilities fell to me.

Mr. Roumestan had put another friend, a former village postal worker, in charge of accounts payable and had also made him a partner, hoping thereby to secure his loyalty. When the man bought himself a magnificent house, I started checking the accounts in earnest and found that instead of making a profit, Sati was actually losing money. I brought in an outside accountant who helped to uncover the partner's scheme. He was paying each invoice twice and pocketing the duplicate. I put the evidence together and took it to Mr. Roumestan at the Ritz Hotel where he and Madame Regine lived (she was the owner and manager of the Ritz). I told him what I had found and began to present the evidence, item by item. At first, he didn't believe me, but as I continued, he finally interrupted to say that he had heard enough and now he realized what a fool he had been. When we asked the partner for an explanation, he tried to pass it off as a tax-avoidance scheme. Eventually he left on his own steam and responsibility for accounts payable fell to me. By that time, I had gained sufficient skill and experience to finish the work in half a day.

I was doing two radically different jobs, immersing myself in technical-scientific work in the mornings and dealing with billing, accounts payable and freight forwarding in the afternoons, and I was exhausted. In 1968, I took unpaid leave from my government job, and while I was on leave, I was told that unless I returned to work immediately, I would be fired. I chose to resign and move fully into the private sector. The experience I had gained during twelve years of government service was worth ten times what I was taught in college. I would never have learned so much about diplomacy, intrigue and subterfuge if I had been working for a private concern or an Armenian community organization.

Mr. Roumestan's Iranian partner had recruited the manager of our Khorramshahr office, but he was a spendthrift and a womanizer who neglected his family, and fortunately, when the Iranian left, he too went quietly. We found a trustworthy replacement in a young man named Mardiros Keshishian. He had previously worked for the Customs Service but he had been fired because of his political views. When Mr. Roumestan asked him what salary he desired, he suggested 2,000 tomans. He was offered 3,000 tomans on condition that he demonstrate outstanding job performance. He accepted the offer with pleasure.

Mardiros Keshishian was an exceptional employee. His work ethic was exemplary. The words "no" and "impossible" were simply not part of his vocabulary. Clearing cargo through customs was a complicated and difficult business in those days, but for Mardiros, it was the easiest part of his job.

Tavanir

Up until the 1960s, water and power in Iran were the business of private concerns and local public agencies, but industrialization called for greater capacity and wider distribution, which in turn required central planning and funding. The Ministry of Energy, originally established in 1936 to provide Tehran with electricity, created Tavanir in 1969 to oversee the development of Iran's power infrastructure, including the planning, construction and coordination of new dams and central and regional power plants as well as the bulk transmission systems that would vastly increase the availability of electricity all over the country. TAVANIR stands for *Sherkat-e Sahami-ye Towleed ve Entiqal-e Niru* (Electric Power Generation and Transmission Company), and Sati would do a lot of business with the company in coming years.

One evening, Bella met me at the office so that we could go to a party together. It was around 8:00 PM and we were the only people there. Just as we were about to leave, the custodian came in and said that three Japanese gentlemen wished to see me. They introduced themselves as representatives of Mitsubishi Heavy Industries and said they had come on the advice of Mr. Rahmani, the general manager of Tavanir, with whom they were about to sign a contract to supply some turbines. Their primary concern was clearing customs by a date certain. Relying on Mardiros Keshishian's proven competence, I signed a contract guaranteeing clearance by their deadline. Keshishian had all the paperwork pre-approved before the cargo arrived in port. His excellent work was highly appreciated and Sati owes him a great deal.

When Nowruz came around, I bought a pair of carpets and had them delivered to Mr. Rahmani as a gesture of appreciation. He called me the next day and thanked me, but asked me to take them back, which I did.

The First Iranian Gas Trunkline (IGAT-1)

In January 1966, we heard a piece of resounding good news. Iran had reached a complex agreement with the Soviet Union whereby the Soviets would build a steel mill at Isfahan – Iran's first – in exchange for Iranian natural gas. The Soviets would also provide the financing and transfer the technology for both projects. The prospect of a steel mill had immense political significance. Before the war, Reza Shah had signed a contract with Germany to build a steel mill in Karaj, west of Tehran. Politics put an end to that but the people hadn't forgotten, and now it almost seemed like we were getting a steel mill for free. Iran's natural gas reserves are second only to those of Russia, but commercial exploitation was then in its infancy. The delivery of Iranian natural gas to Transcaucasia would allow the USSR to shift some of its own product to Europe, and the Iranian Gas Trunkline (IGAT-1) would encourage domestic consumption through the follow-on development of branch distribution networks.

A year after the agreement was signed, the 680-mile, 42-inch gas trunkline was already being laid from Bid Boland in the oil and gas fields of Khuzestan to Astara, a town on the Soviet-Iranian border where it meets the Caspian Sea. Williams Brothers, the American contractor, built the first section; Entrepose, the French contractor, built the central section; and a Soviet-Iranian joint venture built the last section. Entrepose needed 120,000 tons of pipes and equipment delivered to various sites along the route from south of Isfahan to Saveh, and Sati won a contract to move one-third of those pipes and some of the equipment, for a total shipment of 62,000 tons.

A Family Home in Farmaniyeh

Sati made a substantial profit on the Entrepose contract and my share was 20 percent. Several years earlier, I had purchased a quarter-acre lot in Farmaniyeh, then a rural area in the foothills above Tehran where many foreign embassies maintained summer residences. Now I built a beautiful, spacious summer home of my own with all the amenities. Our family enjoyed that house for many years, and as teenagers, our children and their friends held many parties there.

While my house was being built, my father often visited the site to check on the progress of construction. One day, he remarked how pleasant it was going be for my family, living there amidst the lush green trees, and he said that he too would like to settle nearby when he retired. The next day, I called a realtor who recommended that we look at several contiguous lots, each about an eighth of an acre in size, located two blocks north of my house. My father and I went and took a look and he liked them very much. When the realtor told us that each lot was priced at 40,000 tomans, he said he would take four, amounting to just under half an acre, for a total cost of approximately $25,000. I wondered how he would come up with the money.

The day before the transaction was slated to be finalized, I visited my parents at their apartment. After drinking a glass of tea, I reminded my father that we had to see a notary public the next day to complete the purchase.

"No problem, just give me a moment to get the money."

"Shall we go to the bank and get a cashier's check?"

"This has nothing to do with checks."

With that, he went into the bedroom and came back out holding a purse in each hand.

"Here's the money," he said, and he put both purses on the table.

I was astounded when I opened them and saw that they were filled with gold coins. Then my mother went into the bedroom and came back out holding a small wooden casket.

"Here's my share," she said.

The casket was filled with banknotes. My father was as incredulous as I was. My mother explained that she had saved the money from the sale of all the chicken soup she had made for the shop. Their combined savings were more than enough to buy the lots and the remainder would cover half the cost of building their home.

My father told me that he had lived through the Bolshevik Revolution, and whenever he bought inventory for the shop, he always put away a gold coin for the "black days." I was so moved by my parents' wisdom and sense of sacrifice that I couldn't control my tears. I bowed down and began to cry, and with my heart full of emotion, I kissed them both.

By this time, my brother George had returned from San Francisco with an engineering degree. He took charge of building a beautiful one-story home for our parents that included two bedrooms for their four grandchildren.

My father fell ill with heart disease in 1972 and he died on December 5. Archbishop Ardak Manoukian conducted the funeral service at St. Mary's Church. Hundreds of people attended, people of all different classes, Armenians and non-Armenians alike, including many local shopkeepers and neighborhood residents. The line of mourners was so long that we stood there shaking their hands for more than an hour. It all made me wonder how he had come to Iran as a middle-aged man with so few connections, without speaking Persian, and had managed to garner the friendship and respect of all the people who came to bid him farewell. I could only conclude that his kindness and his work ethic were the source of his success and the reason for the sincere outpouring of grief I witnessed that day.

The next day, *Ettelaat* published a photograph of my father with the caption, "The man who introduced the sandwich to Iran has died."

My mother didn't want to live by herself in Farmaniyeh, so we rented the house to an American oil company executive. In 1978, she asked us to sell the house, which we did, and she divided the money equally among her three sons.

The Manjil Power Plant

In the late 1960s, Siemens and AEG joined forces to form Kraftwerk Union (KWU) which built a number of power transmission stations in western Iran. There was fierce competition for the related transport business, and signing a contract with KWU was a major achievement for Sati. That was our entrée into the German market. I supervised that project with particular care, and six months after it was completed, we were invited to compete for another contract related to the construction of a new power plant at Manjil, located northwest of Tehran in the Alborz range where the Qezel Owzan and the Shahrud (Royal River) join to form the Sepidrud (White River) which flows north to the Caspian Sea.

When I had started working for Sati, the company had a contract with Saser, the French company that built an irrigation dam at Manjil as well as a small 87.5-megawatt (MW) hydroelectric power plant that was inaugurated in 1968. Now KWU and Brown Boveri, the Swiss electrical engineering company, formed a consortium to build a 240-MW thermal-electric (steam) power plant at the site.

I was given a list of the equipment to be hauled. It included four heavy-lift items: two 140-ton generators and two 110-ton transformers. That required a bogie which is a trailer with a subassembly of axles and wheels that facilitates turning. Neither Sati nor any other Iranian company owned one at the time, but Entrepose, the contractor with whom we had worked on the IGAT-1 project, had imported a bogie and I knew it was still in country. I did my calculations and submitted my bid.

Two weeks later, I was invited to Siemens headquarters in Erlangen, West Germany. A committee of fifteen interviewed the representatives of the bidding companies. They looked like a panel of magistrates interrogating suspects, and the "suspects" seemed unable to answer most of the questions. They kept saying they had to check with Tehran first. When my turn came, I felt a rush of self-confidence. I answered every question like a student fully prepared for an exam and my interview went on the longest. The committee's primary concerns were clearing Iranian customs and hauling the heavy loads. I assured them that I would take personal responsibility for solving all the problems we discussed. After everyone had been interviewed, we were told that we would be notified of the committee's decision in a week. At that moment, I felt like a gambler who had played his last card.

Before the week was out, I got word that we had won the competition. Mr. Roumestan was stunned at my daring. Now we needed to line up the bogie and I suggested that he contact Mr. Guilleau, the head of Entrepose, and ask about renting it. As it turned out, Guilleau had been planning to relocate to Madagascar, but when he found out what it would cost to ship his equipment, he decided to sell everything. His asking price for the bogie and two heavy-duty Mack trucks was 800,000 tomans ($120,000), and he offered us a transport project that would cover half the cost of the purchase. I urged my father-in-law to take out a loan for the other half from the Bank of Tehran where the manager was a friend of his. When the bank turned him down, he took it so hard that he got sick, but I never lost hope.

My brother Henrik was working at Bank Etebarat at the time, and one evening, the bank's manager came in to André Shop. Overcoming a slight hesitation, I told him about Sati's new project and asked for his assistance. He suggested we meet the next day and discuss it further. After hearing me out, and learning that Sati's fee for the Manjil project far exceeded the amount of the loan I was requesting, he asked me to provide him with a letter from the KWU–Brown Boveri consortium. The letter was in his hands within twenty-four hours. He approved the loan, I paid Guilleau, and that's how Sati became the first Iranian company to own a ten-axle, eighty-wheel bogie. Of course, we paid off the loan punctually.

Khorramshahr was the most important port on the Gulf at the time and that was where the consortium's heavy-lift items would enter Iran. The distance from Khorramshahr to Manjil is about 800 miles, most of it winding banked roads crossing scores of rivers and streams. We did a lot of preparatory work on bridges and bypasses and each one of those projects presented its own challenges. Sometimes our trucks had to exit the main road and travel on secondary roads for two or three days.

The biggest challenge was building a bypass bridge over the Shahrud whose wild gushing waters often forced us to stop work. Under pressure to deliver the equipment on time, I contracted to temporarily divert the river using a series of water pipes one yard in diameter, lined up side by side and fortified with concrete. The entire structure was eight yards wide and eighty yards across, and this arrangement allowed us to complete the bypass bridge.

When the first generator arrived, about thirty people had gathered to witness the delivery. The Germans were so happy that they showered me with kisses and the celebrants put away four cases of beer. The press had been invited too, and the next day, several papers reported our success. We also received a certificate of appreciation from Tavanir.

Pandemonium at the Port

After that, we successfully delivered the two transformers, but our final megahaul ran into a problem at the port. The second generator came in on a vessel owned by the Bremen-based Hansa Line. This was the captain's final voyage before his retirement and he had invited some 500 people to a party aboard ship that night. The off-loading would take place the following morning. I was staying at the International Hotel in Abadan, along with the project's chief engineer and his wife, and we were planning to drive back to Khorramshahr for the party. At 7:00 PM, Mardiros Keshishian called me to say that the captain had decided to off-load the generator that very night in the presence of his guests.

We raced to port, parked near the ship's berth and got out to see what would happen next. A band was playing and everyone on board was having a good time, dancing on the deck or climbing up and down the stairs. The first mate signaled to open the hatch and the cranes went into action. The heavy cables were let down into the hold. It took half an hour to hoist the generator. Soon it was swinging in mid-air and gaining momentum. Suddenly Mardiros rushed over and pushed me back. Then the ship began to rock and the hawsers came loose. The generator dropped and snagged some power lines before it hit the rear end of our bogie. Sparks jumped and the lights went out all over the port. Pandemonium broke out as the ship rocked back and forth like a pendulum. People lost their balance and some were injured. All this lasted only ten minutes but the anxiety was indescribable. We stayed on the scene until dawn. Mardiros subsequently submitted a claim to the ship's insurer for the damage to our bogie, and when we received the pay-out a year later, we bought another one.

Expanding Sati

The volume of commercial ties between Iran and the West was increasing and the transportation business was booming. Sati's reputation was growing steadily and we came to be known as experts in our field. Our work began at the ports and with the Customs Service and our job was to bring thousands of tons of equipment and materials to the construction sites of dams, power stations, oil and gas refineries and petrochemical plants. We received several queries a week from French, Italian, German and other European companies doing business in Iran, but we only took on projects that would contribute to the country's progress. Most of these companies had permanent representatives in Tehran and some of them worked closely with bilingual Iranian agents. The Germans were the most dynamic but we did the most business with French companies, probably because Mr. Roumestan was French.

Sati was growing and we were adding staff, and soon we had to rent a couple of nearby apartments for the overflow. One floor of our three-story office building was set aside for our travel business and the other two floors were devoted to our transport business. The man who originally sold us the building had built another one next door for his son, a medical doctor, to use as a clinic. After his son decided to move his practice to north Tehran, our space problem was solved. It took a lot of doing, but I finally persuaded Mr. Roumestan to buy the building, and thereafter our business continued to grow.

A conflict was brewing between my father-in-law and myself because he was reluctant to expand the business whereas I believed that we needed to expand or else we would fail. Not long after we acquired the building next door, I noticed several Frenchmen coming in to meet with him behind closed doors. Since he had turned day-to-day operations over to me, I assumed these meetings were personal in nature and I didn't pay them much attention. Then one day, I ran into Ruben Grigorian, the manager of the Levant Express Company, and he asked me if Sati was up for sale. I was completely taken aback but he was sure of his information. In fact, he said, the prospective buyer was Fueltrans. Now I realized that the Frenchmen meeting with my father-in-law were Fueltrans staff members and I recalled that they always came with the company's Iranian representative whose mother was French. I also recalled that the general manager of Fueltrans had asked us to rent a small plane to fly him to Julfa where he wanted to visit our branch office, but that foray had fallen through.

I began to worry and then I got angry. When Mr. Roumestan came into the office at 11:00 the next morning, I confronted him with what I had been told and asked for an explanation. He confirmed the gist of the story and said that he was getting old and he wanted to retire to France. I told him that I respected his wishes but that didn't justify the destruction of our mutual trust and friendship, which the sale of Sati would bring about. If that was his plan, why hadn't he told me earlier? I would never have given up my career in scientific research.

It turned out that his decision to sell was based in part on a financial report that Fueltrans had commissioned. It included some negative forecasts and Fueltrans backed off. Of course, those predictions were wrong and the whole thing was forgotten.

A New Investor

The late 1960s was a time of relative political stability and the government was promoting the development of local industry in order to move Iran toward self-sufficiency. Iran National, founded in 1967, was the country's first automobile assembly plant. Using knocked down units from Chrysler UK, it produced the five-seat *Paykan* (Arrow), an Iranian version of the Hillman Hunter. Then Citroën entered the market in partnership with SAIPA (*Société Anonyme Iranienne de Production Automobile*) which was controlled by the Aysseh family. In 1968, SAIPA began producing a version of the Deux Chevaux (2CV) called the *Jiyan* (Formidable), and later it partnered with Renault to produce a version of the Dauphine known as the *Saipa 5*.

Alfred Aysseh ran SAIPA's local 2CV assembly plant. I had known his family since childhood when their Armenian driver used to bring them to André Shop for sandwiches and ice cream. His father was a Lebanese Christian and his mother was an Armenian who spoke the language fluently. Her mother was a survivor of the Genocide. I was thinking about buying a 2CV as a surprise for Bella, so I dropped in on Alfred at his office and he welcomed me with the utmost respect. He showed me some catalogs and promised to give me a good discount, but I wasn't ready to make the purchase since I didn't know whether Bella liked the 2CV. A few days later, we were out driving and I saw one on the street. Pointing it out to her, I said,

"Isn't that a beautiful car?!"

"That is the ugliest car I have ever seen."

I forgot about the 2CV and eventually bought her a little Renault Dauphine.

The next time I met with Alfred, he didn't say anything about the 2CV. Instead, he started talking about the cost of importing and shipping the steel sheets and the engines and all the other parts to SAIPA's assembly plants. He said he was thinking about setting up his own transport firm or else buying shares in an existing company. Then he asked me point-blank if he could buy shares in Sati. I replied that even if we had any shares for sale, I wouldn't be willing to sell to him because I was looking for a partner to take on some of the responsibility of running the company, whereas he was only offering financial involvement. He said he knew the ideal candidate but would have to check with the man before giving me his name. I was in a similar position since I hadn't discussed any of this with Mr. Roumestan. We decided to meet again a few days later.

When I told Mr. Roumestan about my conversation with Alfred, he welcomed the idea. After the collapse of his negotiations with Fueltrans, he had asked me several times if I were interested in buying him out over a number of years. I wasn't open to the idea because he had three heirs in France and I knew that whatever I paid for his stake, they would think I had snatched their inheritance for a song.

Alfred introduced me to his brother-in-law, Goriun Nersissian, as a potential business partner. Goriun was an old Tamaddon classmate of mine and I knew him to be a man of impeccable character. He did take an interest in Sati at a later point. In the meantime, however, we continued our negotiations with Alfred and ultimately he bought a 33-percent share of Sati for $500,000. I held an 11-percent share and Mr. Roumestan now offered me the remaining 56 percent for $100,000. I discussed it with my brothers, hoping the three of us could go in together, but they declined. Instead, I bought 22 percent, bringing my stake up to 33 percent, and Bella's mother retained a 34-percent share. By that time I knew that Fueltrans had suggested a price of $100,000 for the entire company. It was because of my determination to make Sati known for its excellence in international business circles that Mr. Roumestan was able to sell his interest for a very good price.

Alfred had an excellent relationship with COFACE (*Compagnie Française d'Assurance pour le Commerce Extérieur*), the respected French export insurance organization. He was already using Sati's services to move automobile components from port to factory. We owned twenty trucks at the time and we took advantage of his connections to buy another twenty over a period of two years. Alfred himself purchased forty trucks which he leased to Sati at rates based on the number of trips they made. In effect, we now had a fleet of eighty trucks.

The expansion of SATI once again presented us with new challenges. We were adding staff which in turn required more space. There was a vacant 4,000-square-foot lot on the east side of our building. We located the owner, bought the lot and built a new four-story structure.

Chapter 6

Doing Business with the Soviet Union

One day in 1974, the chief engineer at Tavanir, the state electricity company, called me in for a meeting. He told me the company was planning to import two 350-ton transformers and he asked me to look into the technical requirements and the cost of moving such heavy loads from Bandar Emam Khomeini to a site in Khuzestan. I contacted Nicolas, the French manufacturer of heavy load transporters, and they sent me a list of what was required along with the prices which were quite high. The most important element was a bridge system which was very expensive. I prepared a detailed report and gave it to the chief engineer.

Two months later, he called me back to his office and told me about TechnoPromExport (TPE), the Soviet foreign trade organization that was building turn-key power infrastructure projects in several dozen countries around the world. TPE was going to build a 700-MW natural gas–fired, thermal-electric power plant near Ahvaz, and I had been chosen to go to Moscow and negotiate a contract for the in-country transportation of equipment and materials. I was shocked, because up to that point, all of Iran's modern power plants had been built by Western contractors. I confess that I was pleased at the prospect of visiting Moscow.

A Warning from SAVAK

A week later, I got a call instructing me to come for a meeting in a certain office building which I gathered belonged to SAVAK. There I was welcomed with the utmost respect by a man in a well-cut business suit, though his bearing suggested military training. He escorted me to the second floor where a high-ranking military officer awaited me. After the usual exchange of pleasantries, the officer said that he understood I would soon be traveling to Moscow and he warned me not to meet with any Tudeh fugitives there. He asked me whether I had any friends in the Soviet Union and I replied that I did not. Then he asked about my Uncle Abgar. I explained that he was a family friend and that we Armenians customarily addressed respected elder gentlemen as "uncle." The officer dropped that line of questioning, but I wondered how he knew about my father's brother, given the fact that they had different surnames. Later I realized that SAVAK must have intercepted their correspondence.

The officer proceeded to warn me to avoid beautiful women, not to accept drinks from a stranger, and not to buy rubles in Iran or take any with me to Moscow. In conclusion, he told me that I would be traveling with two other Iranian businessmen and advised me to stick with them.

I met my colleagues at Mehrabad Airport on the day of our departure. Mr. Behbahani and Mr. Ardalan, both engineers by profession, were the directors of the General Mechanic Company and the Melli Sakhteman Company, respectively, both of which would eventually be involved in the expansion of the new power plant under discussion. At Sheremetyevo Airport, we were met by three English-speaking Soviets who quickly cleared us through Customs and Passport Control and drove us to the Hotel Berlin. By now it was 3:00 AM and we were told that negotiations would begin at 3:00 PM.

That afternoon, we were fetched by Mr. Gabrielov, a Russian who was fluent in French and English, and taken to a large building in central Moscow where a guard was standing at the entrance. At the reception desk, Gabrielov introduced us to an officer who checked our names against a register, pinned name-cards to our lapels and asked a young woman standing by to escort us up to the logistics department.

Negotiating with a Soviet Armenian

The head of logistics was a gray-haired man named Sergeyev. He had an uncanny resemblance to Aram Khatchaturian, the Armenian composer. He told me that he was Armenian too but that he didn't speak the language. Our interpreter was a beautiful young woman whose English was perfect – I asked her about her education and she told me that she had studied English at the Institute of Foreign Languages in Moscow. I had brought a few gifts from Iran which I offered to our Soviet counterparts. Actual negotiations would begin the next day. What a strange world we live in – the lead negotiators on both sides were Armenians!

Our talks went on for a few days but we failed to reach an agreement. Sergeyev repeatedly told us that our figures were too high, even though he had no basis in fact for saying so. One evening, we were invited to dinner at the Iranian Embassy. Told of our lack of progress, the Ambassador said this was an ordinary Soviet tactic. They had no idea what it cost to move freight in Iran and their starting position was always half what the other side put forward. If that didn't work, they would add a few percentage points. He said it was impossible to conclude an agreement with them in the first round, and of course he was right.

In that era, there was only one flight a week between Moscow and Tehran and we took first available flight home. It was the end of the first week in December. On landing at Mehrabad, we learned that the roof of the main terminal had caved in under the weight of snow and caused a large number of casualties. Two days later, I was called in for another interview with the same SAVAK officer. He questioned me about every person I had encountered, even the Iranian students who came back on the same flight. He told me they were studying steel production in Moscow and he wanted to know what they thought of the Soviet Union. I responded that openness was essential: people, especially students, should be free to go and see for themselves.

Round Two

In April 1975, I was invited back to Moscow for a second round of negotiations. I sensed that TechnoProm was looking for positive results. This time, I stayed at the big Intourist Hotel. Gabrielov came every morning and took me to the now-familiar foreign trade center where I was escorted up to the conference room by the interpreter.

On the penultimate day, Sergeyev met me in the lobby and greeted me with a few words of broken Armenian. At that moment, they were the most beautiful poetry in the world. I replied in broken Russian, although I preferred not to speak the language at all. We entered the crowded elevator and he smiled at me as he pressed the button for the eighth floor. I returned his smile. The elevator stopped at the sixth floor and everyone else got out. After the door slid shut, he took a scrap of paper from his pocket and handed it to me, making it clear that I should put it away immediately. When we entered the eighth-floor conference room, he told the others that he had chanced to meet me downstairs.

I was in an agony of impatience for the session to break so that I could read his message. Finally, I excused myself and went to the bathroom, locked the door and took out the scrap of paper. The first line said, "No concessions." The second line said, "I am Armenian, you are Armenian, I help you, you help me." I was deeply moved. At that moment, I knew the true meaning of being Armenian. Sergeyev was risking his position to help a fellow Armenian. I decided to keep his words alive forever in a corner of my mind.

Things turned out the way he wanted. My terms were accepted and we signed a contract. Afterwards, I asked to meet with the chairman of TechnoPromExport in order to personally offer him the gift I had brought from Iran. Alexander Sergeyevich Maklakov was an energetic and gregarious man of sixty. He welcomed me cordially, and when I told him that I wanted very much to visit Armenia, he picked up the phone and arranged for my trip on the spot.

As we left the building, I decided to invite TechnoProm's top executives to dinner that night. I asked Gabrielov to draw up the guest list and make the arrangements. The dinner was held in the sumptuous banquet hall of the Hotel Berlin where I had stayed on my previous visit to Moscow. Gathered around a table for twelve, our party of eleven ordered the best drinks and the most delicious dishes. I do not exaggerate when I say that we put away ten bottles of vodka, five or six bottles of champagne, a dozen bottles of beer and a few bottles of Armenian cognac. Of course, we Iranians can't drink like the Russians do and when they weren't looking I tipped my glass under the table.

A band played the latest European hit songs. They were supposed to knock off at 11:00 PM, but as long as I continued paying them ten bucks a tune, they kept going. I began to notice that my guests were excusing themselves, one by one, for the restroom. Finally, I was the only one left sitting at the table. At that point, the band stopped playing, the waiters disappeared, and I left the Berlin and went back to the Intourist.

My First Visit to My Historic Homeland

The next day, Gabrielov told me that my ticket was ready and I could fly to Yerevan that very evening. I was elated. My childhood dream of seeing Armenia at least once in my life was coming true. As soon as the plane took off, I observed that the passengers were flouting every rule of air travel. They hung their packages from the armrests and nobody stopped smoking or sat in their assigned seat or even buckled their seatbelt. I had never experienced anything like this. It felt like the whole cabin was the scene of a lively party. Everyone was speaking Armenian. It was a truly Armenian milieu, a most pleasant atmosphere. I was barely able to contain my emotions. The young man sitting next to me said,

"Look at the way they shop! That's something the Russians can never do."

I asked why not. He laughed and said things were different in the Caucasus. The standard of living was higher there and people were skilled at *papakh* (bribes).

"An Armenian can offer a Russian ten bottles of cognac, but not even ten Russians have the wherewithal to offer an Armenian a bottle of vodka."

A few hours later, the plane landed at Zvartnots which was then just a small local airfield. An Intourist rep was waiting to escort me to the Armenia Hotel. I had a light supper at the hotel restaurant and then went straight to bed.

After a good night's sleep, I awoke in the morning and went down for breakfast. I asked the waiter what was on the menu and he ticked off the ordinary fare – *tsvadzegh* (omelet with parsley), bread, butter, cheese, pastries and so on. I asked if they served a traditional Armenian breakfast and he asked if I meant *harissa* (shredded chicken with hulled wheat).

"Bless you, young man, that's exactly what I want."

I ate harissa for breakfast every morning for the next five days.

My time in Yerevan was precious to me and I didn't want to waste a minute. Intourist had assigned me a car, a driver and a guide who took me to Garni Temple, Geghard Monastery and Lake Sevan with its unique climate and mysterious beauty. Then we visited Echmiadzin and its majestic cathedral, the spiritual center of the Catholicosate of All Armenians.

I didn't know anyone in Yerevan but a good friend of mine in Tehran, a lawyer named Yervand Papazian, had given me the phone number of his brother Hagop. When I called him, he came to the hotel immediately and I gave him the letter and gifts his brother had sent. Professor Hagop Papazyan was a lecturer at Yerevan State University and a director of the Matenadaran, the national repository of ancient manuscripts. He gave me a tour of the archives and took me to see other cultural sites.

I knew that the father of Professor Papazyan's son-in-law was the writer Vakhtang Ananyan and I told him that I wanted very much to meet the man. Ananyan had written hundreds of hunting stories, and being an avid hunter myself, I was keen to learn more about the wild animals in Armenia's mountains. Professor Papazyan set up an appointment at the author's home. He was seventy years old at the time. After the initial exchange of pleasantries, I sensed that he was in a bad mood, but I started talking about the various fauna found in Iran and I managed to kindle his interest. He was surprised when I told him that I had seen the Armenian mouflon (*Ovis orientalis gmelini*) as far south as central Iran where I had hunted them myself. He thought their size and their long, back-sweeping, curved horns made them the most beautiful sheep in the world. I asked him about the Sevan trout known as *ishkhan* (*Salmo ischchan*) and he told me how it had evolved from the *garmrakhayd* (salmon-trout), a local cold-water fish with red spots on its skin. He said it had undergone genetic changes while confined to Lake Sevan over eons of time. We went on talking like this for two hours. It was a very enjoyable evening for both of us.

Ramin Power Plant

Back in Tehran, my work commenced almost immediately. The site of the new power plant was the village of Vis (Veys) on the Karun River some twenty miles north of Ahvaz. The plant was dubbed "Ramin" in memory of an ancient Persian romance in which the hero and heroine, Ramin and Vis, are reunited after a series of trials and tribulations. The name was a conceit to permanently reunite the two lovers.

All of the materials and equipment – except the huge transformers – would come by rail from the USSR to Julfa on the Soviet-Iranian border. In August, I hired new staff for our branch office in Julfa. Our biggest challenge, however, was the transformers. We lacked the equipment to haul these 350-ton, forty-foot–long payloads. Alfred and I went to Paris and discussed our requirements with Nicolas, a manufacturer of heavy-lift equipment. What we needed was a twenty-axle, 160-wheel bogie with a built-in hydraulic bridge system. The "bridge" is a beam gantry mounted on ten axles at each end, thus evenly distributing the load on all twenty axles. The projected cost was one million US dollars. Alfred soon secured a loan and we put in our order. A year later, we took delivery at Bandar Shahpur (now Bandar Emam Khomeini), and Sati became the first and only Iranian company possessing its own very-heavy-lift equipment.

Political Problems

Working with the Soviets had its difficulties, some related to the work itself and others involving political considerations. After my second trip to Moscow, SAVAK invited me back for another interview. This time, I acted with foresight and volunteered that I had gone to Yerevan. Asked if I had met any Tudehists there, whether Iranian or Armenian, I told the officer that I had run into the brother of my friend Yervand Papazian on the street, as well as the son of another friend, both of whom were legal immigrants to Armenia.

"You will have quite a few such meetings in the future," he said. "You must report every detail to us."

Sensing that he was nudging me toward espionage, I told him that I was a very busy man and could not report to him on a regular basis. He considered that in silence for a moment, then said we would discuss it later.

I had a friend named Esmail Atabaki whom I had known since we were teenagers. He had pursued a military career and attained the rank of general, and now he was the executive officer for General Manuchehr Khosrowdad, commander of the Army's paratroop division and its fleet of helicopters. Atabaki and I were still close friends but we rarely met because we were both very busy.

A week after my interview with SAVAK, Atabaki called and said he wanted to take a break from work. Could we meet for a meal someplace where we could relax and chat for a few hours? We met the next day at the Indian restaurant across from my office. After the usual pleasantries, he asked me about my trip to Moscow, whom I had met and so forth. I stopped him right there and said I had already answered those questions when they were put to me by SAVAK. Disarmed, he said,

"Now that you know where I'm coming from, let me give you some brotherly advice. Even if you only drink a glass of water with the Russians, don't try to hide it from SAVAK."

After we parted, I became pensive and anxious. How did SAVAK know about my friendship with Atabaki? Then I remembered that I had used his name as one of the references on my application for a hunting permit. Of course, I had asked his permission to use his name. Back then it was Colonel Atabaki.

During the boom years, I was constantly receiving guests from all over the world and I always invited them out for a meal. Sometimes I didn't get home for lunch even one day a week. TechnoProm's chief Iranian agent was Rahim Irevani, a wealthy businessman who owned dozens of factories and hundreds of shops (he had founded the National Shoe Company in the 1950s). One of his associates was Edic Khachaturian, the son of Sanasar Khachaturian, the producer and director who had built the Cinema Diana. Edic was very wealthy too. One day he conveyed the message that a delegation of Soviet officials was in town and wanted to meet with me. I called Mr. Loukinov, a Georgian engineer who managed TPE's Tehran office, and asked him to arrange the meeting. When I met the Russians, I invited them to dinner, but since they were pressed for time, we had lunch instead. Afterwards, I dropped them off at the Soviet Foreign Trade Mission on the north side of the Embassy.

A few days later, a tall man in his forties turned up at my office and introduced himself as Mr. Shahbazi from SAVAK. He told me that from now on he would be visiting me once a week. Dear man, I thought to myself, what kind of *khata bala* (trouble) have you gotten yourself into now? SAVAK was ubiquitous yet invisible, feared and hated by all. Mr. Shahbazi proceeded to question me about any interaction on the part of my branch office staff with TPE technicians stationed in Julfa and Ahvaz, and about my own meetings with any Russians. General Atabaki's words came back to me: "Even if you only drink a glass of water with the Russians, don't try to hide it from SAVAK." So I told Shahbazi about the lunch I had hosted for the delegation from Moscow earlier that week and he replied in the calm, confident tone of the thoroughly well-informed that I should definitely keep him posted about any such meetings. Later, I realized that SAVAK spies positioned around the Soviet Embassy must have taken down my license plate number when I had dropped the Russians off there after lunch.

Shahbazi dropped in almost every Wednesday evening. On one occasion, he criticized our branch office people, saying they had practically no contact with the Russian technicians who were handling the incoming freight. He sounded frustrated. I replied that I didn't know what he wanted from us – we had leased housing for the Russians and their families and we had done everything we could think of to avoid interaction with our staff.

"That's where you're wrong," he said. "We *want* your people to interact with the Russians."

"If you insist," I replied, "I will call them here from Ahvaz and Julfa and you can train them yourself. *You* tell them what to do because I have neither the time nor the expertise for such things."

He agreed to that, so I invited a few of our employees to Tehran and explained what the agency wanted. They stayed in town for a week, during which time I never inquired about the specific responsibilities they were asked to take on, and at the end of the week they went back to work.

Sometime later, General Atabaki dropped by my office at around 5:00 in the afternoon and we chatted for a while, as usual. We left the office together at 7:00, since I was going out that evening and his home was on the way. When we reached his home, he invited me in, but I said I had to rush off because I was late for a reception. He asked me who was hosting it.

"The Soviet Embassy," I replied. "It's their annual celebration of the October Revolution. I've been on their guest list for years."

He blanched and nearly fainted. In a barely audible voice, he asked why I had never told him that. He knew he was being watched, he knew his watchers would attend the reception, they would see me there, and because they had seen him with me, they would associate him with the Soviets and that would cost him dearly. He was so frightened that I told him I would skip the reception. As we parted company, I thought about the tight security environment in which high-ranking military officers like Atabaki had to function.

Practical Problems

We ran into all kinds of administrative problems as soon as we started working with the Soviet cadres. Obviously they had little experience in dealing with the Iranian bureaucracy. The Soviet specialist responsible for commercial transportation was a thin, good-natured fellow named Alyokhin. I had told him everything he needed to know in order to clear customs but he hadn't paid much attention and his assistant kept repeating,

"*Yesli nagladkay yest, fsio*" (If there's a waybill, that's enough).

But the Customs Service also required an invoice and a bill of lading, and it wasn't long before the freight started piling up at Julfa. Alyokhin asked me to intervene personally. The only way I could see to move forward was to ask the local customs official to clear the freight on the basis of Sati's guarantee that the Russians would produce the required documentation within three months.

"I don't want to hear anything about the Russians," the official told me. "If you guarantee it, I'll see that it's cleared."

And it cleared without a hitch.

A few months later, a Tavanir administrator asked me to accompany him to Julfa for a meeting with the local customs chief. We sat down with the chief and he produced a file that contained documentation supporting the clearance of all our freight thus far. It was nearly eight inches thick and every document bore Sati's stamp with the signature of our authorized representative. Paging through the file, the man from Tavanir was aghast.

"How dare you sign off on all these documents? Who gave you the authority?"

I told him that we were responsible for everything we signed for, and every single item in that file had reached its destination, as evidenced by the receipts. Furthermore, I told him,

"If you want to wait for Russian guarantees, the plant will never be built."

Back in Tehran the next day, I received written notification from Tavanir that Sati was not authorized to clear anything through customs without proper paperwork from the contracting entity. I passed the word to our Julfa office.

One night two weeks later, I got a call at home. A woman announced that General Fazeli was on the line. I was dumbfounded. General Mohammad Fazeli was Special Inspector for National Security in the Prime Minister's office. He spoke up immediately.

"Who gave you the right to block deliveries to Ramin?!"

I replied that we were following Tavanir's instructions to the letter, even though I had warned them that it would only create problems. His tone softened a bit. He told me that freight was piling up at Julfa and it had to be moved at once. The next day I learned that 20,000 tons of cargo was sitting in customs at Julfa. I laid out my terms and conditions and they were accepted by the responsible parties. We cleared the backlog in less than three weeks, during which time General Fazeli called me every night for an update and the head of Tavanir called me every day.

Russian Manners

It would have been absurd to offer a Russian guest a glass of tea or coffee, which is why I always kept a bottle of whiskey in my office and a small refrigerator stocked with beer and soda. Whenever Alyokhin dropped by, I asked him what he would like to drink and he always replied,

"*Abejo* (beer), of course."

I developed good friendships with people from the Soviet foreign trade organizations. Practically every week, one Russian or another would drop by my office and he always left with a gift. The most valuable gift was a roll of fabric that was long enough to be made into two suits for my guest or his wife. Once I was asked if a roll like that could be purchased in the Bazaar. I replied that there was no limit to how much fabric one could buy in Iran, and that if the customer bought enough for a hundred suits, the merchant would probably throw in a bonus.

I began to notice that our Ahvaz office was filing extremely high expense claims on the TechnoProm account, and I asked our branch accountant for an explanation. He told me that Loukinov, the manager of TPE's office in Tehran, often brought clients down to Ahvaz and took them out to nightclubs. The bulk of these high claims represented what he spent on beautiful women. From what the accountant told me, I could tell that he had been coached by SAVAK.

Some months later, I ran into Loukinov at the Soviet Embassy – it was another annual celebration of the October Revolution. He buttonholed me and started raving that he was still a true communist even though the communist system was rotten to the core. I became alarmed and moved away to circulate in the crowd while he was still haranguing me.

Cement was in short supply in those days and one day Loukinov told me that he appreciated everything I had done for TechnoProm and he wanted to do me a favor since he happened to be in a position to send me some extra cement via Julfa. I told him in no uncertain terms that I wasn't the kind of person he thought I was. A year later, Loukinov was recalled to the Soviet Union, and some time after that, I heard that he was being "cured" in a Moscow psychiatric clinic.

When we originally ordered the bridge system from Nicolas, they told us they wanted to closely monitor the transshipment of the transformers from their point of origin. I conveyed the request to TechnoProm and the Soviets made no objection, so when the equipment was ready to leave the factory, Nicolas arranged to send a consulting engineer from Paris to meet me in Moscow. The factory was located in Tolyatti, an industrial town on the Volga, and we planned to travel there together. I arrived in Moscow a day ahead of schedule, only to find that the engineer was under arrest, having entered the Soviet Union without a visa. It took TPE nearly six hours to get him out of jail. We finally met that night at the Intourist Hotel.

The next morning, he told me he hadn't slept a wink. His baggage had been thoroughly taken apart and inspected before he even got to his room, and three or four times during the night, silent figures had entered his room and looked around, apparently just to make sure he was still there. The same thing happened the following night.

On the third day, we were told we would have to wait ten days for permission to travel to Tolyatti, which in effect meant that permission was denied. When my French colleague heard that, he said he hadn't slept for three nights in a row and if things went on like this he was going to lose his mind. On that note, we parted. He flew back to Paris and I flew back to Tehran.

The Heaviest Lift in Iranian History

The transformers finally began their voyage from Tolyatti to the Black Sea port of Illichivs'k, bound for Bandar Shahpour (Bandar Imam Khomeini). At our end, I had sent the talented and resourceful Mihran Keshishian to Nicolas in France for a month-long training in the operation of the bridge system, and I had arranged with the German-Dutch firm Smith to have their specialized cranes on-site when the transformers arrived at Bandar Shahpour (Bandar Imam Khomeini). Two technicians had come back from France with Mihran and together they finalized the arrangements to take delivery. When the big day came, hundreds of dignitaries gathered to watch the discharge of the heaviest load ever in an Iranian port. The French technicians complained about the heat and asked for two six-packs of beer. It took two days to clear customs, but everything went according to plan and on time.

Finally, the huge rig was loaded with the first transformer and left the port with a police escort. Safe passage over the Khalafabad bypass was our main concern. Williams Brothers had built a temporary bypass bridge for the IGAT-1 project a few years earlier and we had reinforced it with concrete. Our bogie descended into the valley with the assistance of three huge vehicles, crossed the bypass, rejoined the main road and drove on without any problems. In Ahvaz, thousands of people came out to watch this phenomenal caravan pass through the city to the construction site where the transformer was delivered safe and sound.

When it came time to move the second transformer, Mardiros assured me that our chief mechanic "Mihran" was fully capable of supervising the operation and we no longer needed the French techs. The only difference was that he didn't need a six-pack of beer to do the job! And indeed, he was as good as his word.

Our work with Soviet foreign trade organizations and with American, British and European firms rapidly increased, and within a few years, Sati became one of Iran's premier transportation companies in terms of both volume of business and quality of service.

Sati's Second Big Contract with the USSR

In early 1976, I got word from the Soviet Embassy that representatives of SelkhozPromExport (SPE), the Soviet agro-industrial foreign trade organization, were in town and wanted to meet with me. SPE had a contract to build grain elevators at seven different locations in Iran. They would be importing 60,000 tons of rebar, cement and other materials via Julfa and they wanted Sati to take charge of getting it all through customs and forwarding it to the various construction sites. I was asked to submit a detailed proposal including quotes for our fees, which I did shortly after our meeting. A month later, I was invited to Moscow to sign the contract.

Bella and I arrived in Moscow in May 1976. As before, the chief Soviet negotiator was an Armenian, Mr. Ter Minassov. Unfortunately, he spoke not a word of Armenian. When he introduced me to the chair of SelkhozProm, General Vladimir Alekseyevich Medvedev, the latter told me that he had close ties with Marshal Ivan (Hovhannes) Baghramyan. They had fought the enemy side by side during the Second World War, he told me, and Marshal Baghramyan had been decorated as a Hero of the Soviet Union. General Medvedev boasted that he himself had commanded a tank battalion when the Soviets entered Bucharest in August 1944.

During our stay in Moscow, Ter Minassov placed his car and chauffeur at my wife's disposal and his secretary was her companion. That week, Ararat, the Armenian soccer team, was playing Russia's famous Dinamo FC. Ter Minassov was rooting for Ararat.

It didn't take long to sign the contract and I invited Medvedev and Ter Minassov to dinner that evening. Then I went to Intourist and applied for a permit to visit Armenia, but I was told that it would take two weeks. At dinner that night, Bella told General Medvedev how much we wanted to visit Armenia. He said he would do his best to smooth the way. The next day, our paperwork was ready and hotel reservations had already been made for us. We flew to Yerevan.

As we were settling into our room at the Armenia Hotel, we heard shouting and cursing in the corridor just outside our door. I called the manager and he told me that a couple had been forced to vacate the room we were now occupying because Marshal Baghramyan had insisted that the hotel accommodate us, even though they were full up. It wasn't what we had been hoping for but we couldn't intervene.

We spent a week in Yerevan. A Volga GAZ-24 and a good-natured driver were placed at our disposal and our minder was a beautiful young Armenian woman. We visited all the important historical sites but what we enjoyed the most was a soccer match at Hrazdan Stadium. Ararat FC was playing against another team from Moscow. The home-team crowd loudly cheered their side even for minor successful plays and jeered and cursed them for the most insignificant errors. When Ararat won, their joyous enthusiasm was absolutely unrestrained. We left Yerevan with fond memories. This time, SAVAK didn't call me when I got back and Shahbazi's visits tapered off. Later, I saw him once at the airport when I was on my way to welcome a Soviet delegation. He was standing in a corner, just watching. I pretended not to see him and continued on my way.

My Last Encounter with the Shah

A dedication ceremony was held at Ramin Power Plant in August 1977, and as one of the contractors, I was given to understand that my attendance was mandatory. With only twenty-four hours' notice, I somehow managed to get there on time. After presenting my ID and my invitation to the security staff, I was directed to a huge open plaza where scores of people were standing in a line. An hour later, there was a roar in the sky and four US-made Cobra helicopters put down in the landing zone. The Shah emerged from one of them and stepped onto a red carpet that ran all the way to the main hall. A military band struck up a slow march, creating a beautiful solemn atmosphere. The Shah passed along the receiving line, shaking hands, occasionally saying a few words, and he shook my hand too. I used to have a photograph of that brief encounter. I had it framed and hung it on the wall of my office, but after the Islamic Revolution, I took it down and burned it for reasons of personal security.

Persistent power outages were contributing to a growing political crisis and the Shah had just appointed a new Minister of Energy. The Minister stood at the head of the receiving line along with the general manager of Tavanir, the Soviet Ambassador, the new chairman of TechnoPromExport and several top Soviet engineers. The Shah led this elite group into the hall and left the rest of us standing outside. I noticed something in his expression that day – the glow in his eyes had faded and their color had turned greyish. He looked ill and tired.

Chapter 7

Before the Revolution

The Armenian Apostolic Church in Iran had been governed by the Mother See of Holy Echmiadzin for centuries, but after the Bolsheviks took over Armenia in 1920, Echmiadzin was prevented from independently administering its Iranian prelacies. The last Echmiadzin-appointed Prelate of Tehran abandoned his post shortly after the end of the Second World War, leaving Father Hovannes Hajian and Father Mesrop Shirvanian to serve as the community's spiritual leaders until 1958, when the Iranian dioceses transferred their allegiance to the Catholicosate of Cilicia which is based in Antelias, a suburb of Beirut. The Iranian authorities supported the new arrangement, hoping it would break the ties between Iranian and Soviet Armenians, and they welcomed young Bishop Ardak Manoukian when he arrived from Antelias in 1959 to take up his post as the Prelate of Tehran.

He was born Mgrditch Manoukian on January 21, 1931, in Beirut. The Cilician See had been established in Antelias the year before, several years after losing its historic seat in southeastern Anatolia. Young Manoukian was educated at the Armenian Theological Seminary in Bikfaya, situated in the hills above Beirut. He was subsequently sent to the University of Lausanne to study theology. After completing his studies, he returned to Beirut and took on a series of important positions in the Cilician Catholicosate. Later he completed a two-year course of postgraduate theological studies in Lyon, France.

Archbishop Manoukian was a man of great energy and administrative abilities. During his first years as Prelate, he established the Diocesan accounting office and oversaw the drafting and ratification of a new Diocesan charter which laid the foundation for the Diocesan Assembly of Representatives, the community's highest elected body. The Assembly elects the Diocesan Council and its finance committee.

Thanks to his eloquence and his connections, Archbishop Manoukian was able to enlist the support of Armenian philanthropists and community leaders in building schools, churches and cultural centers in Armenian neighborhoods. He played a key role in founding the Armenian studies program at Tehran University and he taught Armenian in the program for many years. He was instrumental in the construction of Holy Translators Church (*Surp Tarkmanchats*) in Narmak, consecrated in 1968, and St. Sarkis Church in the Behjatabad neighborhood, consecrated in 1970, as well as the adjacent Prelacy offices.

The ARF versus the Tudeh

The Armenian Revolutionary Federation (ARF) has experienced many upheavals since its founding in 1890. After the first Armenian Republic became the Soviet Socialist Republic of Armenia in 1922, many party activists moved south to Iran. Most of them settled in Tabriz, but significant numbers came to Tehran, and during and after the Second World War, many more moved to the capital.

From the time of the founding of the Tudeh Party in 1941 until its suppression after the 1953 coup, its membership included Armenians who shared in its very active political struggle. Armenian Tudehists and Dashnaks both had supporters in the community and there were frequent conflicts and even violent clashes between the two factions. After the fall of Mosadegh, when the Tudeh and its activists were brutally suppressed, Armenian former Tudehists were shunned by the community and prevented from working within its structures. By the 1960s, a number of ARF intellectuals had risen to prominence and the party effectively controlled community affairs, even though its presence wasn't necessarily apparent to outsiders. But it would be wrong to attribute ARF predominance to the party's efforts alone. For one thing, SAVAK imposed its own demands on the Armenian community, which often put individuals in a false position. Meanwhile, as ex-Tudehists joined other leftist movements in opposition to the monarchy, false bourgeois nationalist leaders were able to influence the ARF and turn community structures into instruments of their whims, greed and ostentation. With the ARF in control of community structures, and with a few wealthy members and their retainers rising to the top of those structures, some Armenians became alienated and began to distance themselves from community affairs.

Iranian Armenian students who went abroad for higher education were strongly influenced by the ideas and attitudes they encountered in the West and many forgot their Armenian heritage. Some married non-Armenians and that worried us a lot. Increasing numbers were attracted to the communist underground and that worried us too. In those critical times, it was imperative that the community rally around its collective patriotic identity.

Younger ARF activists realized that national preservation entails more than nationalist slogans. They had to be effectively nationalist *and* socialist, which was the aim of the ARF in the first place.

One initiative was a youth journalism project. The itinerant ARF propagandist Jirair Gharibian was invited to Tehran to join *Alik* as an assistant editor and coordinate *Alik Nobavegan* (Juniors), a biweekly youth magazine produced by a volunteer staff of aspiring young journalists. But some of Gharibian's interns were already quite sophisticated and they reacted negatively to his preaching. Some left the country and joined communist parties abroad. Others joined leftist parties in Iran, only to be shunned by the community and further alienated. One such young man, the son of a friend of mine, was executed after the Islamic Revolution.

"I sent him to *Alik* to become an upstanding ARF nationalist," he told me. "Instead, he became a communist."

When he protested to *Alik*'s management, they blamed Jirair Gharibian, but Gharibian had already left Iran and moved on to Boston. There he cofounded the Armenian Independent Radio Hour in 1979 with Norair Pahlavouni, a former editor of *Alik*. Gharibian died in Watertown in 1991, while Pahlavouni had a twenty-year career with the Armenian section of the Voice of America. He died in Boston in 2011.

The Golden Age

Thanks to the oil revenues pouring into the country, the prosperity of the Armenian community increased dramatically during the mid-1970s, but it was a false prosperity to the extent that, rather than educating their children or even themselves, many wealthy Armenians wasted their money on fine dining and expensive vacations, trying to outdo each other in conspicuous consumption. Only the middle class seemed capable of understanding the importance of real values and standards. The children of the Armenian villagers who had migrated to Tehran after the war became very good and sometimes exceptional professionals, technicians and craftsmen. Aside from the community institutions he helped to build, Archbishop Manoukian played an important role in establishing charitable organizations, although it must be said that few Armenians were poor and sometimes it was hard to find indigent Armenian families to assist in Tehran or anywhere else in Iran.

My family life was peaceful and harmonious. My son Vahe was a student at Alishan School for Boys and Girls which was owned and run by the Armenian Catholic Church in Tehran. The Alishan School had been built by

Catholic benefactors in 1962, largely through the efforts of Father Emmanuel Poladian, a man of true piety in spirit and action. Most of my friends' children attended Alishan School and my wife Bella was a member of the Parents and Teachers Association.

When my daughter Annette finished sixth grade at Alishan, she and some of her friends went on to *Hadaf* (Purpose) School for Girls. We parents didn't want our girls to lose touch with their culture so we registered them with the Armenian Sports and Cultural Organization and its Girl Scout troop. Annette also volunteered to work on *Alik*'s youth supplement. We were pleased with that project because we thought she and her fellow interns were getting a firm grounding in national values by working on an Armenian newspaper.

The years from 1976 to 1978 were the golden age for the Iranian Armenian community. Armenians all had good jobs and were doing well financially. I and many of my friends owned cars, which made it possible to take long trips to far-flung destinations. Our family's favorite get-away was the Caspian coast where the children could enjoy themselves in the water. In the early years, we vacationed in the least expensive coastal towns where the accommodations consisted of straw beach huts open to the sky, and Annette and Vahe could run down to the shore right after breakfast. When our financial situation improved, we stayed at the new Motel Ghou, about twenty miles up the coast from Chalus.

A few years later, I and some of my friends bought summer homes in Darya Kenar, not far from of Babolsar. It was the only majority-Armenian town in Iran and it was a very pleasant environment for our children. Scores of Armenian boys and girls of all ages would ride their bikes or walk to the beach. The older kids would meet at their favorite spot on the shore and sing and dance and have a good time until midnight. Sometimes our wives and children would spend the whole summer in Darya Kenar and we husbands and fathers would join them on weekends. I spent many a pleasant weekend in Darya Kenar.

One summer, my wife and children set out for Darya Kenar with our driver. Bella took over the driving and at some point she lost control of the wheel and the car hit a boulder. They were all taken to the hospital with injuries. I raced to the hospital and I was slightly relieved when I saw they were all alive. Everyone urged me to offer an *oukhd* (sacrifice) in gratitude, but I was against such practices. Instead, I made a commitment to cover the tuition of needy students at Alishan School. That was more than four decades ago and since then, I have subsidized from four to ten students annually. Many have become doctors, lawyers, engineers and teachers. After Armenia gained its independence, I made the same commitment to students there, because I believe that no Armenian child should be denied an education for lack of means.

The Ararat Center

The Armenian community had good relations with the Shah and his government. Shahen and Emma Aghayan knew Prime Minister Amir-Abbas Hoveyda socially, which made it possible for Emma to be elected to the last prerevolutionary Majles as MP for the Armenians of northern Iran. Her predecessor MPs Dr. Gaguik Hovakimian, Sevag Saginian and Felix Aghayan also enjoyed the government's respect.

Felix Aghayan was a personal friend of the Shah and also his business manager. In the latter role he handled huge sums of money, especially in the sugar trade in which he was personally interested and which earned him a certain amount of enmity. The Shah made him a senator and appointed him to head the National Ski Federation. He was largely responsible for building the Dizin Ski Resort in the mountains above Tehran.

Prominent community members made good use of propitious conditions and good connections to advance the community's interests, and one of their greatest accomplishments was the Ararat Center in Vanak. The village had long since been absorbed into Tehran when Shahbanou Farah ordered its disused cemetery transferred to the Diocesan Council in 1971 for the purpose of building a community sports complex. My brother George and his father-in-law Hratch Msrian had the eighteen-acre property cleared and leveled within a few months. That operation cost an estimated 500,000 tomans (about $75,000), which was the largest in-kind contribution to the project, and we three brothers later donated 120,000 tomans which was used to build dressing cabins next to the swimming pool.

The architect Rostom Voskanian, a close friend of mine, was a member of the organizing committee. He designed some of Iran's most beautiful civic buildings. He renovated the former Swedish Embassy building on Khark Street for the Armenian Club and added an underground auditorium for large gatherings. With his brother Rubik, he also designed one private house for me in Farmaniyeh. And in 1971, he won the competition to design the Ararat Center and its 10,000-seat stadium.

I remember the people's enthusiasm at the groundbreaking ceremony. The evening event was a triumph for the community. Thousands of Armenians attended and Archbishop Manoukian blessed the project with a prayer. Members of the organizing committee emphasized that they were starting the project with empty hands, relying on the community's moral and financial support to carry it through. I recall the contribution of a young lottery-ticket seller, one of very few Armenians in that occupation. The price of a ticket was two tomans and ticket sellers kept 10 percent of their sales. This young man pledged to donate the price of one lottery ticket which was a disproportionate share of his income compared to the contributions of wealthy donors. People cheered him on with wild applause. Afterwards, they held hands and danced and sang, strangers kissed and congratulated one another, and then, in a solemn moment, everyone formed a vast circle around the soccer field and sang the patriotic song, *Erebouni*, which is the ancient name for Yerevan according to Urartian cuneiform inscriptions. Four years later, the complex was ready for use.

At the center of the triangular campus is the magnificent soccer stadium with its bright green field. It was built to meet international standards and 25,000 tons of concrete went into the seating. There are two swimming pools in the northwest corner of the campus, along with a playground and plenty of tables and benches. People often picnic there in the evenings, especially during the hot summer months. There are four tennis courts and related facilities in the south corner of the campus.

A gate on the north side is only used on ceremonial occasions. The ordinary entrance on the west side leads to the main building and several parking lots that can accommodate a hundred cars. The main building has two large halls on the ground floor for national feasts and other events. A large hall on the second floor is used for athletic training and competitions. Additional facilities include a kitchen, office space and meeting rooms. A smaller building houses training facilities and guest quarters. A small chapel, also designed by Rostom Voskanian, was built in 1987.

Ararat FC

In 1977, I got a call at my office from Vachik Gharabegian, a prominent community leader and a founding member of the Ararat Association. I had known him since childhood – he was the older brother of my friend Grigor (Gougoush) – and he was already an ARF activist then. He asked for a meeting, so we made an appointment and he came to my office with the engineer Hrand Movsisian. After the usual greetings and chit chat, Gharabegian told me that the Ararat Football (Soccer) Club was bankrupt and the Ararat Association had racked up 800,000 tomans in debt to cover the players' pay. That was equivalent to more than $100,000.

"We can't move forward and we can't turn back," he said. "We thought it would be appropriate to appeal to you for help in seeking a solution."

I promised to do whatever I could and I started thinking about how to mobilize 100,000 Tehrani Armenians. I made a list of my friends and business associates, including a few millionaires, and within a week I raised 1.4 million tomans ($200,000). Next, Gharabegian asked me to form and head up a board of trustees. I drafted Shora (Alexander) Aftandalian, Shahen Haroutunian, Mardik Hovsepian and Edward Sahakian, and the board appointed an executive committee headed by Hrand Movsisian.

Our first move was to recruit an experienced coach. A Serbian named Zdravko Rajkov was the manager of Taj FC (the predecessor of today's Esteghlal FC) and his contract was about to end. We hired him at a salary of 16,000 tomans (about $2300) and we set the players' salary at 2–3,000 tomans per month. We continued to meet weekly and develop a strategy for financing the club. Since the government had forbidden the importation of athletic uniforms, we asked well-to-do community members traveling to Europe to bring back Adidas athletic shoes and high-quality uniforms and donate them to the team. We bought 200 chairs and placed them along the sidelines of the soccer field. The sale of those seats netted 40,000 tomans.

One day, Coach Rajkov came to see me. He complained that we were spending too much money on non-essentials and that more money could be spent on nutrition, for example. He said the players weren't eating the right foods and they didn't have the energy to win. We addressed the problem immediately. Rubina Shahverdian (Begoumian) was a professional nutritionist who catered receptions at the Ararat Center and she always served delicious, high-quality food. We asked her to oversee the preparation of meals for Ararat FC, using the best meat available, and the team was fed after every training session. Now they were getting paid and fed. Of course, Ararat athletes and coaches in other sports complained of special treatment, but that couldn't be helped.

Ararat FC started playing in the A-League and racking up wins, yet the community remained oblivious to their success. Only Manook Khodabakhshian, the best soccer announcer and possibly the greatest Iranian sportscaster ever, acknowledged the team's achievements on his TV show. But that wasn't enough, so I proposed to Norair Pahlavouni that he allocate one page of *Alik* to sports coverage. I promised to take responsibility for the sports page, including the cost of high-quality, four-color photo reproduction, and to encourage my friends and business associates to advertise in the paper. He accepted my proposal. Now I had to find a qualified editor and produce a regular page that would capture the community's attention. Razmik Boghosian, a veteran journalist who covered provincial news for *Kayhan*, introduced me to Hrair Roustamian, and for the next two years Hrair and I spent three afternoons a week in my office putting the sports page together.

Hunting

In my late teens, I often hunted small game with my friend Joseph Kanon. During duck-hunting season, we would bicycle out to the countryside almost every Friday and come back loaded with ducks and rabbits. Our families never lacked for meat and sometimes we had to distribute the excess among friends and relatives. A few years later, I met a group of hunters who were after bigger game, animals with horns, and for that I needed a proper long-range rifle. When my friend Sako Babayan sent me one from Hamburg, I was ready to hunt with my new friends.

In my half-century of hunting, I sometimes came face to face with death. Once when I was stuck in a snow storm, I took shelter in a cave, only to realize that I was being stalked. I stood perfectly still on the border between life and death. Another time, I drove through a river in spate and got stuck in the middle, only to be saved from drowning by fellow hunters.

Most of my hunting companions were men who worked with their hands. A *nouveau riche* like myself, living the good life in the city, would never survive the hardships of the hunt if it weren't for the wisdom and experience of his friends. Stalking big game, climbing mountains and scaling ravines is not only good physical training, it shapes a man's character and prepares him for whatever life throws at him. The energy and *joie de vivre* that I have at my advanced age I owe to my deep love of hunting and my attachment to nature. When a person communes with nature, nature itself surely leaves its mark on his spirit and character. It makes him patient and strong and nurtures foresight and endurance.

My fifty years of hunting gave me the kind of rich and varied experience unavailable to the man who doesn't hunt. In my quest for game I penetrated the far corners of Iran's vast landscape and reaped benefits that no ordinary traveler could even imagine. I wandered through many of Iran's villages and spent summer and winter nights with their inhabitants. Iran's population was still largely rural and peasants were the foundation of Iranian society. Their simple way of life represented the true image of the Iranian. Many a winter night I sat with a village family around their *kursi* – a table-shaped contraption covered with a *lahaf* (a kind of comforter stuffed with cotton or wool) – warming my feet by the small brazier under the table.

When I went hunting with these decent folk, I drank the sweet waters of the mountain springs whose taste was far superior to that of the city water I was used to. I drank tea prepared with spring water boiled over an open fire. From the same fire I ate *khorovats* (barbecue) of the hearts, kidneys and lungs of the animals we caught. As for the red-spotted trout, when cooked on the open fire immediately after it's caught, its taste is heavenly.

I deeply love the land and the people of Iran. I often wondered what it was that nurtured my love for Iran, given the fact that we Armenians are different in religion, culture and way of life. I concluded that my love is grounded in the people, especially the rural people, with whom I developed genuine and intense relationships. I could not have achieved this degree of authenticity and satisfaction in any other country in the world.

When we were young, my hunting buddies and I used to boast of how many creatures we shot. When we grew older, we boasted of the quality, not the quantity of what we caught, because we understood that hunters must protect nature and its creatures. We tried to hunt old animals, estimating their age from the number of ridges on their horns. We often ran across immature animals but we never shot them. If we didn't find any old ones, we went home empty-handed.

I had the heads of the animals I shot stuffed and mounted by a professional taxidermist. They graced the walls of my home for many years until I donated them to the Armenian State Nature Museum in 2004. Whenever I looked at them, I could relive the hunt and I always enjoyed telling my hunting stories to interested listeners.

Looking for Boars, Finding Gazelles

Nowruz is the most important national holiday in Iran. The old year ends and the new year begins at the vernal equinox. During my student years, schools and government offices observed a week-long holiday that many people extended to thirteen days. On the thirteenth day, Iranians traditionally leave the comfort of their home and give themselves over to nature, and while they are outdoors, any evil residing in their home is expelled.

One year, my friend Felix Hovanissian told me that he had access to a Willys Jeep during Nowruz. This was excellent news. We decided to go hunting along with Jora, an old friend of ours though not a hunter, and my Assyrian friend Albert. We headed for a location about 200 miles northwest of Tehran on the Qazvin-Rasht route. Finding no game there, we decided to continue on to Rasht and hunt for boars. It was raining hard in Rasht so we drove east along the coast to Chalus, planning to take the Karaj route back to Tehran, but heavy snowfall had closed the road. So we continued further east to Babolsar, hoping to get back by way of Shahi (Qaem Shahr) and Firuz Kuh. The road was rough and the tires on the Willys were old and worn and we knew we had to do something about that. Somehow we got to Shahi, but when we counted the money between us, it wasn't enough to buy food and fuel and change the tires.

Jora's father owned a hotel in Shahrud, southeast of Gorgan. Since we were already half-way there, he suggested we go and borrow some money from his father. So we agreed, and the next day we reached Gorgan where we learned that a hunter in the nearby village of Ramian had very good hunting hounds. We looked him up and went boar hunting, then got back on the road for Shahrud. After driving for about a hundred miles, we reached Jora's father's hotel at 8:00 PM. He was very happy to see us. We regaled him with our stories and he offered us a delicious shish kebab. Later that night, we left with the money he gave us.

It was 250 miles to Tehran. We stopped at the teahouse in Semnan where the proprietor told us that gazelles came to graze nearby every night and he offered to show us where. We went out with flashlights and shot three. Then we got back on the road and reached Tehran at noon. The next day, Felix gave us the bad news: he had been fired for taking the company jeep without permission.

Ibex and Bears in Varvash

The Shah's younger brother Ali Reza Pahlavi was one of Iran's most famous hunters. He owned all the prime hunting grounds and forbade anyone else from using them. When he died in an airplane crash in 1954, those previously closed areas opened up, and one such area was Varvash, named for the 13,222-foot peak (known to Western climbers as Varavasht) east of the Karaj-

Chalus road in the central Alborz. From early spring to late autumn, grass sprouts at the foot of the mountain which makes it ideal for grazing animals.

A few miles north of Kandovan Pass, my friends and I reached Pol-e Zanguleh. We stopped at a teahouse and waited until lunchtime when a mule train came by en route to the Ilika coal mine. We paid the mule-drivers to carry us as far as the mine, and from there we went on foot to the village of Kamarbon at the base of the mountain. We knew who to contact: Baba Ali, the *katkhoda* (village headman) and Ali Reza's former hunting guide.

Baba Ali welcomed us warmly and took us to the guest room reserved for hunters where we bedded down for the night. In the morning, we mounted three mules and began our ascent with Baba Ali leading the way. When we came to a place where he thought we might find game, he stopped, raised his binoculars to his eyes and surveyed the cliffs and ravines before us. Hunters call this "scouring the mountain."

That day we saw some mountain goats (Persian ibex) but they were way beyond our range. At sunset, Baba Ali led us to a cave with a semi-circular lip that gave some protection from wild animals and the bitterly cold wind. He fetched water from a nearby spring and brewed some tea. We ate the food we had brought and bedded down. A few hours later, the troubled braying of the mules woke us up. Stones were coming down outside the cave. Baba Ali quickly pulled the mules inside. He said the bears were throwing stones at us. Somehow we got through the night and in the morning we continued our ascent. Less than an hour had passed when Baba Ali stopped and pointed out the bears. There were five of them, walking along and playing. A flock of sheep was grazing a short distance away from them. Suddenly they attacked the flock, grabbed two and carried them off. Baba Ali said he would show us the "sacrificed" sheep when we came back that way in the evening. He told us that bears take out the heart and eat it, then hide the remains and come back a few days later to eat the rest. Toward evening, we passed the same spot and saw the two carcasses covered with stones, just as he had said. We didn't find what we were looking for that day, but on another day I shot the biggest ibex I ever hunted. It was an eleven-year-old animal with fifty-inch horns.

Leopards in Marakan

One of the areas where we liked to go hunting was Marakan which is on the way to St. Thaddeus (*Surp Tadevos*) Monastery in West Azarbayjan Province. There are many Armenian churches in the area and scores of *khatchkar* (carved tombstones) in the hills. In winter, Armenian mouflon migrate south from Mount Ararat and cross the Arax River to Marakan and beyond. There are two statues of male mouflon carved from tuff rock in Marakan village. Since there's no tuff in the area, people say the statues must have been brought from historic Armenia.

Marakan was a protected zone: a special permit was required to hunt and government guides accompanied hunters, so the hunting was safe and relatively easy. The local village hunters had no guns and they relied on hounds to track their quarry, bring it down and turn it over to their master. I never saw this way of hunting anywhere else and it fascinated me.

One day we were hunting for ibex up among the cliffs and big boulders. Unlike the mouflon which live on decomposing slopes and sandy hills, the ibex favor rocky terrain at high altitude. We climbed to the top of a ridge and scoured the rocks on the opposite slope. Suddenly the guide drew our attention to two leopards down in the ravine. One was resting under a rock overhang and the other was poised above a herd of ibex grazing below. It attacked and brought one down in an instant, and both leopards began to consume the poor creature's flesh. Hunters very rarely witness such a scene.

Now I felt a compulsion to shoot one of those beautiful cats. Back in Tehran, I applied for a permit, and as soon as I got it, I set out for Marakan with my good friend, Boris Papanian. It was a winter day and the mountains were covered with a foot and a half of snow. We spent the night in the village and the next morning we headed up to the mountains accompanied by Ali, our friend from the village, and a government guide named Zolfaghari. Boris didn't have a permit to hunt leopards so he turned back before we reached the peak. Ali went with him while Zolfaghari and I kept climbing. As soon as we made it to the top, it started snowing. The mountain was enveloped in fog and we could barely see more than thirty yards ahead.

Suddenly we saw drops of fresh blood on the snow. Moving forward, we saw the half-eaten hind legs of an ibex in a small clearing. A leopard had eaten there and left the legs behind. We followed its tracks to a great rock where they disappeared, which meant the leopard was hiding nearby. Zolfaghari pointed to a cave. I moved in closer and saw the leopard's tail. The two of us climbed to the top of the rock. I was carrying my Czech-made Brno rifle and he was carrying my short-range five-cartridge shotgun. I placed both guns beside me and told Zolfaghari to throw some stones into the cave. He threw about a dozen but the beast wouldn't come out. I had given up when suddenly it was standing in front of me. I took aim and fired. The leopard roared and disappeared into the fog. I was sure I had hit it but I was afraid it would attack us in a rage. Zolfaghari had told me that a hunter from Urumia had been wounded that way a month earlier.

We cautiously followed the leopard's tracks to a large boulder stained with gouts of blood. Now we knew it was wounded. Its tracks became increasingly bloody and soon we saw puddles of blood where it had paused to gather its strength. A little further on, we saw it lying motionless, spread out on the snow-covered slope. We approached it, trembling with fear, but the creature had exhaled its last breath.

Ali had heard the shot and he soon caught up with us. Standing beside the prey, I handed Zolfaghari a gratuity. We took several photos with the leopard at our feet, and then Ali hoisted it onto his shoulders and took it down to the car. They say that hunting a leopard brings honor to the hunter. That leopard honored our home for nearly three decades.

The Anguran Reserve

I often went hunting with my friend Boris Papanian and my wife Bella frequently came with us. She even helped with the driving. While he and I climbed a mountain, she would drive around to the other side and pick us up at the bottom.

I had a Chevrolet Blazer and one winter day, the three of us – Bella, Boris and I – decided to go hunting in the Anguran Reserve southwest of Zanjan. After purchasing a permit at Zanjan, we entered the reserve and drove up and down the gently rolling hills. At sunset, we stopped at the top of a high hill and got out to scour the mountain. We didn't see any game so we decided to drive on, but the car wouldn't start. We tried hard but couldn't get it started. Finally we looked at a map and located the Anguran zinc mine not too far away. We walked up and down hills in the dark for three hours until we finally reached the mine. The manager turned out to be an old Tamaddon schoolmate of mine and he gave us a warm welcome, offered us a delicious meal and put us up in three clean, well appointed rooms. The next day he sent us back with a car and a mechanic. The mechanic said the Blazer's battery was dead but he managed to start it anyway. The day ended well: we shot an Armenian mouflon, one of those migrants from Mount Ararat.

Siah Kuh

Iran has a total area of over 636,000 square miles. More than half the country consists of mountainous terrain and a vast central desert that begins some sixty miles southeast of Tehran and stretches all the way to the south. We had heard that Siah Kuh (Black Mountain), a range near the northwestern edge of the desert, was a prime hunting location, but we needed a reliable vehicle that could stand up to conditions there. When my friend Albert bought an old Dodge Command car and fixed it up, a hunting trip to Siah Kuh became feasible.

We passed through Varamin and stopped at the village of Qaleh Boland where we made the acquaintance of the katkhoda, Agha Ali Naghavi, and he agreed to be our guide. The next day we reached the foot of Siah Kuh. We left the Dodge near the only spring in the vicinity and began to climb. We saw some ibex before we even reached the top of the first hill and shot two within a few minutes.

We liked these hunting grounds very much. There was a decrepit caravansary not far from the spring known to local people as the Khan of Shah Abbas. In fact, it used to be a stopping place for pilgrims en route to Mashhad from Isfahan and Yazd. We cleaned out a small room and leveled the floor, and whenever we went hunting in Siah Kuh, we spent the night there. I can't recall a single trip when we came back empty-handed.

One time we went to Siah Kuh over a long holiday weekend. After two days of looking for game, we found nothing. On the third day, we stumbled across the shredded carcass of an ibex. Half an hour further on, we saw a leopard on the opposite hill, slipping around to the other side. Albert and I followed it, he going one way and I the other. Suddenly, I heard two shots and then silence. When I reached the other side, I found Albert standing beside it. He had killed the enormous creature and he was elated.

The Hunter's Code

One day, Ali, our former worker, came to André Shop and told me that he was now working at an American military club in Tehran. Ali was the one who had gotten me a pistol and supplied me with bullets when I was a teenager. He told me there was a junior officer at the club named Jimmy who wanted to go hunting and he asked me to take him along at least once. I asked Ali to introduce us and he brought him to the shop, and Jimmy and I went hunting a few times.

Like every other field of activity, hunting has its unwritten rules, the cardinal rule being that novice hunters learn the ropes and the rules from experienced hunters. Another rule is that when a group goes hunting together, if one of them runs into trouble, the solution has to be based on a collective decision. Another is that if one shoots an animal, the meat is shared with the others. The same applies to fishing.

One day, I suggested to Jimmy that we go hunting in Siah Kuh. He was all for it and he asked if he could bring along two friends. We stocked up on supplies and headed out in two cars. Agha Ali Naghavi and his paternal cousin were waiting for us at Qaleh Boland. We filled the jerry cans with water and drove on to the caravansary where we spent the night.

When we began our ascent the next morning, Jimmy and his two friends decided to climb the mountain from the other side. Over the next couple of hours, the weather changed and a violent storm erupted. Visibility was barely six feet. Somehow we managed to get back down the mountain to where the cars were parked, but Jimmy's car was gone and the storm had wiped away its tracks. As soon as I got back to Tehran, I called Jimmy. He told me they had left early because they had to attend a birthday party. I tried to explain to him that when you go to a distant and dangerous place with a group of hunters, you have to abide by the hunter's code and meet your obligation to the group, but it seems my words fell on deaf ears.

One year during Nowruz, Albert, Jimmy and I decided to go hunting in Shish Rudbar (Six Brooks), a canyon in Savad Kuh near my father-in-law's lead mine. We set out by way of Firuz Kuh. Night fell before we reached our destination, so we bedded down in our sleeping bags and slept warm through the night. When we awoke in the morning, the ground was covered with a foot of snow. Since our plan was doomed, we decided to head back immediately. Jimmy went first in his US Army jeep. He had hardly gone a hundred yards when we saw it skid and drift toward a deep ravine, stopping short of the edge. We got out and tied branches to the rear wheels, but when Jimmy restarted the jeep, it slid closer to the edge. At that point, he completely lost his composure. He got out of the jeep, got down on his knees and begged God to save the jeep. He kept asking us where he was going to get $10,000 to reimburse the US government. This was at the height of the Cold War and we were pretty shocked. We asked him,

"How do you expect to fight the Russians with an attitude like that?"

Jimmy said he had a desk job and he had no intention of fighting the Russians himself.

So I drove to my father-in-law's mine and asked the manager for help. He dispatched twenty workers with picks and shovels. They cleaned the wet clay off the jeep's undercarriage and pushed it to the middle of the road, then they cleared the way a few hundred yards ahead. Albert and I offered them a gratuity while Jimmy drove off and never looked back.

Cheating Death in Firuz Kuh

My work at the office was varied and exhausting, and sleeping in on the weekend didn't relieve my fatigue. I needed to escape the city. I often took my family on outings where the children could play and have fun. If they couldn't join me, I went hunting with my friends, and if my friends couldn't join me, I took my gear and headed out alone.

One winter day, I drove out east in my Vauxhall. It was a hundred miles to Firuz Kuh and I was headed for a hunting ground some twenty miles beyond that, near the pass at Gaduk. Firuz Kuh is one of the coldest parts of Iran and in the winter the temperature can hit 20 degrees below zero (Fahrenheit). The road to Gaduk is a steep incline exposed to wind and fog all the way. As I left Firuz Kuh, it began to snow, small flakes falling slowly at first, then big flakes coming down fast. The windshield wipers couldn't keep up and I had to stop and clear the snow by hand. The ferocity of the wind was terrifying. I couldn't turn back – I was afraid that if I tried to turn around, I would lose control of the car and be buried in a snowdrift. Somehow I made it to the pass and descended two and a half miles in relative ease to Heydar's teashop. It was packed with stranded travelers and they all asked about the condition of the road. I told them to stay put until the storm was over.

I used to hunt with Heydar's uncle, but after he died, I began hunting with his son, Mirza Gholi. I asked Heydar to send a messenger to Mirza Gholi to come early the next morning so that we could go hunting. After making further arrangements, I went to the guest room behind the teahouse and got ready for bed. Heydar brought in a kerosene heater and I tucked into my sleeping bag. Around midnight, I became dimly aware that I could hardly breathe and my body felt very heavy. The room was full of smoke and the air was poisoned with carbon monoxide. Somehow I found my way out. Once again, I cheated death.

Mirza Gholi was a kind-hearted man who worked in construction for the Trans-Iranian Railway (the track cuts through the Alborz at Gaduk en route to the Caspian coast) and I had found jobs for four members of his extended family at Sati and with a business associate of mine. He came to the teahouse with one of his brothers before sunrise and the three of us set out for our destination, a two-hour hike. The ground was covered with snow which made hiking difficult but we persevered. We saw some mouflon grazing on the grass that was sprouting through the snow. I shot one, then we collected firewood and roasted the heart, kidneys and lungs. We ate sitting on the snow and then had some tea. Afterwards, we loaded the carcass onto the shoulders of Mirza Gholi's brother and secured it with rope. We hiked back to the teahouse and from there I drove straight home to Tehran.

Fish and Fowl

Trout fishing permits were issued from May 20 through September 30, and after that, it was the season for hunting four-legged creatures. We usually went fishing on the nearby Karaj River or else on the Lar, about fifty miles northeast of Tehran. The Lar Plain, which is one of the most beautiful areas in the country, lies at the foot of Mount Damavand, Iran's highest peak. In my youth, there were thousands of trout in the Lar and we caught forty or fifty, sometimes even a hundred whenever we went fishing there. For two months in the spring, the Lar overflows with gushing waters from the snowmelt. On one such day, I was walking along the riverbank with my son who was eight years old at the time. Suddenly, and for no good reason, I decided to cross the river. I hoisted Vahe onto my shoulders and waded in. I hadn't gone very far when I began to feel that I might lose my balance. My son sensed the danger and started to panic. As if to convince myself, I told him there was no reason to be afraid, he must trust my strength and skill. Somehow we made it to the other side. I still get a chill whenever I recall that terrible crossing.

In winter, the northern Caspian grows bitter cold and countless fowl migrate to the southern shore which then becomes a prime area for bird hunting. One winter, five of us headed out from Darya Kenar in two cars. My partner and I drove ahead. When we spotted some geese and ducks on a rainwater lake about 200 yards from the road, we stopped and got out. Quietly we crept closer. Now the moment was at hand. We each fired several shots, killing two geese and four large ducks, but none of the other fowl took flight. I realized these were domestic fowl but it was too late. We collected the birds and agreed to tell the other three hunters that the birds were wild. That went down well at first, but as we told our story, one of them said they looked like domestic fowl to him. We pretended to take offense and another one tried to make peace:

"What difference does it make? They're ducks and geese! Let's go home. Our wives will roast them and we'll have a feast."

We did have a feast and our friends made no derisive allusions in front of our womenfolk.

André Safarian

Whenever I recall my hunting experiences, the memory of André Safarian is always fresh in my mind. He was my closest friend and my best hunting and fishing partner. He was born in Syria – his mother was a Christian Arab and his father was Armenian. He had three brothers and one sister, all well-educated with good jobs. André was the regional sales manager for Gruppo Lepetit, the Italian pharmaceutical firm. He was fifteen years older than me, and when I first met him, he lived with his mother in an apartment next to our shop. I often saw him loading his hunting gear into his car or unloading it after a trip. One day I told him that I too loved to hunt and he asked me how come I'd never gone hunting with him. I said he might not want me along because of my age. With a kindly smile, he told me that my supposition was unfounded, and from that day forward, we became fast friends.

André and I hunted in the best locations over the course of many years, but our relationship wasn't confined to hunting. His wife, Francesca Laghi, who was Swiss, was Shahbanou Farah's personal dressmaker and she had permission to enter the palace whenever she wished. André and Francesca were a happy couple. The six of us – he and his wife, Bella and I and our two children – often went fishing or bird hunting together, camping out and sleeping in tents. There were few fishermen who had never heard of André. His skill took on a mythological dimension.

"If there's only one fish in the river, it won't get away from André!"

Francesca introduced André to a group of Swiss snipe hunters. The snipe, which they called the *bécasse*, is a long-billed shorebird that winters on the southern shores of the Caspian. It was greatly prized but increasingly rare in Europe, yet still plentiful in Iran. The Swiss came every December and we would spend a week hunting on the coast near Babolsar. We enlisted local villagers to beat the vegetation and we shot the snipe as they broke cover and took flight. The Swiss always went home with 200–300 birds each.

André and his wife were forced to emigrate after the Islamic Revolution. They settled in Francesca's hometown of Lugano, and he died there in 1998.

Ara Vartanian

The market for hunting and fishing gear was controlled by Muslims but there were a few Armenians in the business. Ara Vartanian and his younger brother Sebouh sold sporting gear at their shop on Lalehzar Avenue. Ara managed the business side while Sebouh handled the equipment. Ara was kind, modest and wise, and because of his character, he had an impeccable reputation in the international light arms trade. He imported two rifles for me from Belgium and Czechoslovakia in 1962 and I still have them. He was known throughout Iran and even the Shah relied on him to outfit his foreign guests for hunting expeditions. His office was a meeting place for courtiers who would drop in on a Saturday or a Sunday and share stories from their weekend hunting trips.

I had the good fortune to hunt with Ara a few times. He had a beautiful and deeply humane habit. When he spotted game, he didn't shoot it himself but offered his partner the opportunity. He would lower his rifle and coolly gesture to me, even though he was in an excellent position to take a shot. That rare manner of his made an indelible impression on me. As hunters know, when three spot the same animal, all three shoot at once.

One day we went to Khosh Yeylagh which is north of the town of Shahrud on the way to Gorgan. It was considered one of the prime muflon hunting grounds. André Safarian joined us on that trip. We drove almost 300 miles to Shahrud and then another hundred miles to Khosh Yeylagh. We spent the night in the accommodations provided for hunters, and in the morning we drove into the mountains. About fifteen minutes in, we came upon a mountainside that appeared to be painted light brown from base to peak. It was covered with thousands of mouflon. This was what we had come for, but we decided not to disturb them. Instead, we left the car and hiked into a ravine where we sat on a big rock and contemplated the beautiful scene before us. Soon, a mouflon came and stood atop another rock not six feet away from us. Ara whispered, "Go, *hayvan* (animal)," but it didn't move. Either it hadn't noticed us or it had never seen human beings before. While we were debating this question, our guide pointed out a few ibex grazing deep in the ravine. We studied them through our binoculars and ascertained that they were quite large. André and I moved in closer and shot two ibex with very big horns, only to realize that we couldn't possibly carry them out of the ravine. We went to a nearby village and asked for help. A few men went in and brought out them out, but we were six miles from our car. We ended up giving them to the villagers. The next day, we brought down four big male mouflon.

Another time I went hunting with André and Ara on Sutak Kuh, one of the lesser peaks in the central Alborz. We took the Karaj-Chalus road to the village of Valangerud where we rented seven mules and set out with two state gamekeepers. On the way up the mountain, we came to a stream and stopped for an hour while André caught more than a hundred trout, even though fishing was prohibited in the area.

When we reached the summit, we pitched our tents and made a delicious meal of trout grilled over an open fire, followed by drinks to help us withstand the cold. It was July 20, 1969, and we were following the coverage of Apollo 11 on a transistor radio. It was almost midnight when the lunar module touched down. By the time the astronauts set foot on the moon, it was past dawn in Iran and we were already scouring the mountain. We shot three magnificent long-horned mouflon that day. Back in Tehran, I heard that one of the Shah's half-brothers had gone to the same place the day after we were there and found nothing but a shepherd grazing a flock of domestic sheep, and he shot quite a few out of spite.

The last time I saw Ara was in 2001. He was in his late eighties and he had lost some of his mental acuity. I had gone to renew my rifle permit, and when I mentioned that I was going to see Ara Vartanian, a high-ranking official named Haj Agha Nateghi overheard me and said that he had heard so many good things about him that he would be honored to meet the man, so I brought him along. I was quite moved by the encounter. Ara regaled us with stories of his dealings with the late Shah, apparently oblivious to the fact his guest, being highly placed in the Islamic government, was a dyed-in-the-wool anti-royalist, but Haj Agha took no offense. My dear friend and venerable hunting buddy died on June 4, 2003. He was almost ninety years old.

My daughter's kindergarten class photographs with Mrs. Elbis Ferahian.

My daughter's class with the founder of Alishan School, Father Manouel Poladian, and the school principal, Tamara Brambila.

On a hunting trip with my friends Gourgen Hovsepian and Felix Hovhannisian.

With local hunters in Abbas Abad village.

Chapter 8

The Coming of the Revolution

In 1968, the Shah challenged the production quotas set by Iranian Oil Participants, Ltd., arguing that Iran needed more foreign exchange for development. Over the next five years, Iranian crude oil production more than doubled and oil export revenues more than quadrupled. After the Arab-Israeli War in 1973, the international price per barrel nearly tripled and Iranian oil revenues quadrupled again, surpassing $20 billion in 1974. The Shah doubled public sector investment, but with the lack of skilled manpower, the shortage of raw materials, poor infrastructure and inadequate port facilities, the economy was unable to efficiently absorb the influx.

By mid-1975, the ports were jammed. At Khorramshahr, over 200 ships were waiting for a berth. The demurrage costs and other damages caused by such delays were absorbed by the government. Additionally, the government had lifted the ban on importing certain goods. As a result, new jobs were created and there was nearly full employment. In fact, there was a labor shortage and thousands of workers were brought in from Turkey, Afghanistan, Pakistan, South Korea, the Philippines and elsewhere. Farmworkers were leaving the countryside and migrating to cities for better-paid assembly-line work. This led to a shortage of agricultural labor, and tomatoes were rotting in the field while the country was importing tons of canned tomatoes.

Sati had a contract with the Spanish branch of Westinghouse to deliver a number of transformers to various sites in Iran. They came in to Khorramshahr on a ship that was also carrying a consignment of canned tomatoes. The ship had to wait three months before it was given a berth, and when the hatch was opened, the stench was so horrible that no one wanted to go near the hold. The cans had burst from the heat and their contents had soiled the transformers. The ship was forced to put out to sea and dump the rotten tomatoes, and only after it had been thoroughly scrubbed clean was it allowed back in port. Because of complications like that, cargo owners increasingly relied on transport companies to facilitate storage and forwarding, and our industry grew accordingly. Sati devised a strategy using

1,000- and 2,000-ton–capacity barges to move cargo from ship to shore, and together with two partners, we bought a thirty-seven–acre lot in Khorramshahr. It was covered with palm trees but Mardiros Keshishian, our local manager, supervised the clearance of the lot and we soon had a serviceable storage depot.

Petrodollars

Foreign investment in various sectors of the economy ramped up and scores of assembly plants were set up. More refineries and power plants were built to produce more oil, gas and electricity. Transportation and distribution systems multiplied. In addition to thermal electric and gas turbine power generation plants built by companies such as General Electric, Westinghouse, Brown Boveri and TechnoPromExport, the Shah signed agreements with Germany's Kraftwerk Union to build two nuclear reactors near Bushehr on the Persian Gulf, and with France's Framatome to build another two on the Karun River south of Ahvaz and a nuclear research center in Isfahan. The Shah also negotiated with the USA to purchase nuclear reactors, but all these projects were put on hold by the Islamic Revolution.

Oil revenues also generated a building boom and many new buildings went up, especially in big cities like Tehran, but the construction was often shoddy. The country was awash in billions of dollars and this was harmful in ways the government hadn't foreseen and couldn't control. There was rapid inflation and the cost of food and housing rose dramatically. By 1977, rents were ten times what they had been a decade earlier. Iran was in the grip of so much change that the people couldn't keep up with the pace. Change was imposed wholesale rather than introduced gradually and people weren't adequately prepared to accept it.

Large numbers of students had the opportunity to study in the West where they saw first-hand what life was like in a free country and came to realize how precious was the right to freedom of speech and political activity. When they came home with their foreign degrees, they were monitored by SAVAK, and the more intrusive the surveillance, the more rebellious they became. Seeing the children of the elite immediately being offered high-paying jobs, many of them joined the anti-royalist movement. In those turbulent years, when one section of the population was visibly growing wealthier by the day, many Iranians believed the country was run by the so-called Thousand Families who were also the primary beneficiaries of its wealth and development. The

Iranian Armenian community benefited from the economic boom and its overall situation improved dramatically.

But American dollars hadn't reached the hinterland and the vast majority plodded along under difficult conditions. Most of the country lacked piped water and electricity. Most of the roads were unpaved. Most village homes were built of mud brick or rammed earth and villagers lacked access to basic health care. There was a shortage of schools and teachers. The country was like a parched garden with only one area being watered and showing its bloom. And because of such deficiencies and limitations, Iran was a largely consuming society, and even the productive sectors, such as automobile assembly, were almost entirely dependent on foreign input. Whenever components were stalled at the port, production came to a halt. Clearly, the country was heading toward a crisis.

As for the Shah, his arrogance reached its apotheosis in 1971 when he spent millions of dollars to celebrate 2,500 years of Persian monarchy. More than sixty heads of state were invited to attend the party. A French-made tent city was set up near the ruins of Persepolis where the guests were feasted and entertained. The opulence of the week-long celebration acquired legendary dimensions. It began on October 12 at the tomb of Cyrus the Great in nearby Pasargadae and ended on October 16 with the dedication of the Shahyad Tower in Tehran, now known as Azadi (Freedom) Tower. The Shah delivered a speech at the tomb of Cyrus that later became the object of popular scorn and mockery:

> O Cyrus, great King, King of Kings, Achaemenian King, King of the land of Iran. I, the Shahanshah of Iran, offer thee salutations from myself and from my nation. Rest in peace, for we are awake, and we will always stay awake.

After the Islamic Revolution, people joked that the Shah blinked and the 2,500-year-old Persian kingdom came tumbling down.

Cavalier toward the Constitution and contemptuous of the demands placed upon him by the changing times, the Shah governed as he imagined his royal predecessors had done centuries earlier. For nearly two decades, he managed political activity under successive state-sponsored parties. In 1975, when he announced the dissolution of *Hezb-e Iran Novin* (the New Iran Party) and the formation of *Hezb-e Rastakhiz* (the Renaissance or Resurgence

Party), he said that anyone who didn't like the system could get a passport and leave the country. And after the first local uprisings that would ultimately lead to his overthrow, he said,

"Let the dogs bark, the moon shines on."

Such vulgar remarks only provoked more anger and discontent.

One of the Shah's most provocative moves was the introduction of a new *shahanshahi* calendar in 1976. Like the lunar *hijri* calendar that prevails in the Sunni Muslim world, Iran's traditional solar calendar begins with the year of the Prophet's migration (Arabic *hijra*) from Mecca to Medina in 622 CE. The shahanshahi calendar was pegged to the coronation of King Cyrus nearly two millennia earlier. The *olema* (learned men), already negatively predisposed toward the Shah, vigorously resisted the new calendar and used it as a focus for popular discontent in their struggle against the monarchy.

Opposition to the Shah

In fact, a revolution was already underway, secret and systematic in its planning. One of my employees was a very devout man who made two or three trips a year to the Shiite shrine city of Najaf in southern Iraq, where Ayatollah Khomeini was living in exile. I knew the man's financial situation wasn't very good, so one day I asked him why he kept making these trips. He told me that Bazaari merchants wanted their *khoms* (religious dues) to go directly to Khomeini and that dozens of volunteer couriers regularly delivered millions of tomans to their *marja-e taqlid* (source of emulation).

Clerics across the country were preparing the youth to join the revolution. Later, I was told by a member of the National Front that key government positions were already being allocated to young clerics while the NF leadership was asleep at the wheel. A year before the revolution, several friends advised me to take all my liquid assets out of the country, using bank loans to effect the transfer, but I was always of the opinion that Iran would remain stable and that our safety would never be compromised.

The Liberation Movement of Iran (*Nehzat-e Azadi-ye Iran*), known as the LMI, had emerged from Mosadegh's more secular National Front in 1961 and was subsequently involved in all the country's religious and nationalist movements, whether openly or underground. The movement was led by Mehdi Bazargan (1907–95), a devout Muslim from a Bazaari family, educated in Paris on a scholarship from Reza Shah. Bazargan headed the engineering department at Tehran University in the late 1940s and was appointed managing director of the NIOC when it took over operations from the AIOC in 1951. He served time in prison after the 1953 coup and the 1963 uprising. After the Islamic Revolution, he would be appointed Prime Minister in the short-lived Provisional Government.

The Organization of the People's Holy Warriors (*Sazman-e Mojahedin-e Khalq*) was an off-shoot of the LMI's youth wing. Founded in 1965, it focused on armed struggle for political change. After their initial political indoctrination, young recruits were sent to PLO camps in Jordan for paramilitary training. The Maoist Peykar group (*Sazman-e Peykar dar Rah-e Azadi-ye Tabagheh Kargar*, i.e. Struggle for Workers' Liberation Organization) was a later off-shoot of the Mojahedin Khalq.

The Mojahedin Khalq were inspired by Dr. Ali Shariati (b. 1933). A native of Khorasan Province, Shariati enrolled in Mashhad's Teacher Training College while still in high school and taught in local high schools while studying for a degree in modern languages at Mashhad University. He graduated with flying colors in 1958, but the award of a government scholarship for graduate study abroad was delayed because of his nationalist political activities. When he finally went to Paris in 1960 to study at the Sorbonne, the Algerian struggle for independence was entering its climactic phase. Shariati became a student of the Algerian Revolution and then an active supporter, and while in Paris he cofounded the overseas branch of the LMI with Ebrahim Yazdi, Sadegh Ghotbzadeh and other young activists. On his return to Iran in 1964, he was jailed on account of his political activity. After his release, he taught elementary school until he was appointed as a lecturer at Mashhad University. There he lectured on the state of contemporary Islam and its historical accumulation of polluting superstitions and prejudices. His unorthodox approach was not well received by the authorities and his courses were cancelled. In 1969, he moved to Tehran and began lecturing on religion and ideology at the Hosseiniyeh Ershad.

The Hosseiniyeh Ershad was a new community research and educational institute in the Shemiran district of north Tehran, built by members of the LMI with Bazaari funding and headed by Ayatollah Morteza Motahhari. Dr. Shariati's lectures drew thousands of listeners, both young and old. They were taped and transcribed and widely shared. He was also a prolific writer. Traditional clerics disapproved of his interpretations but softened their criticism since he was helping to inspire renewed interest in Islam. SAVAK, however, saw his message as a potential threat to the monarchy and shut the institute down in 1972. Arrested the following year, Shariati spent eighteen months in prison. On his release, he was banned from teaching and public speaking and harassed by SAVAK. He eventually left Iran for the UK, but within a month of his arrival, he died under mysterious circumstances on June 19, 1977.

The Organization of the People's Guerrilla Commandos (*Sazman-e Cherik'ha-ye Feda'iyan Khalq*) was another leftist group. Formed by students and intellectuals in the mid-1960s, the Fedayeen Khalq or FK trained in the Caspian forests and carried out their first action on February 8, 1971, when a dozen members attacked the police station at Siahkal in Gilan Province.

The Tudeh Party was also active among Iranian students abroad and in clandestine anti-government activities in Iran, initially cooperating with the Mojahedin Khalq.

There were repeated assassination attempts on the Shah in 1965, 1967, 1973 and 1976. Other targets included SAVAK officers and American business and military personnel. The Mojahedin Khalq carried out a number of these attacks, one of which was the attempt on the life of US Ambassador Douglas MacArthur II in 1971. He escaped death thanks to the Embassy's resourceful Armenian driver, Haikaz Ter Hovenissian.

The Shah and the USA

The Shah's most consequential mistake was placing Iran at the disposal of the USA. Thousands of American military officers were cycled in and out of the country under the pretext of training and supply-chain management, and the Imperial Iranian Army chafed at the relationship. The Pentagon largely dictated decisions about which American weapons systems Iran should buy. The Shah purchased nearly nine billion dollars worth of American arms during the 1970s, and that was less than a quarter of his total arms purchases worldwide. American weaponry worth another twelve billion dollars was on order at the time of the revolution. Even though the Army had doubled in size since the early 1960s, it couldn't absorb such a massive infusion of sophisticated equipment.

A key locus of disaffection was found among the *homafaran*, avionics technicians who maintained the complex electronic systems of the military's fixed-wing and rotary aircraft. Homafars were high school graduates, for the most part from the lower middle class, generally religious, not culturally Westernized, and technically highly educated to the requirements of their specialization. Posted to every airbase in the country, they far outnumbered flight officers. Some homafars took advanced coursework at local universities which brought them into contact with student revolutionaries.

By the mid-1970s, the USA had become known the world over for courting war and supporting dictatorships, and President Richard Nixon and his successor Gerald Ford backed the Shah as the "Policeman of the Gulf." But as the Cold War began to thaw, US and European attitudes toward their authoritarian allies began to change. During America's 1976 presidential election, the Democratic Party challenger put human rights at the top of his foreign policy agenda. Of course, Jimmy Carter was targeting the Soviet Union and its East European satellites, but conditions in Iran were not all that different. The Shah had made cash contributions to Nixon's presidential campaigns and he likewise backed Ford, but Carter won.

At the beginning of his term in office, President Carter pledged to link human rights and arms sales. The Shah responded by promising Iranians a more free and open political life, hoping thereby to maintain his unhindered access to American arms, and for the first time ever, he allowed the International Red Cross to visit Evin and Qasr Prisons in Tehran where many political prisoners were held.

Emboldened by this opening, three veteran National Front activists signed an open letter to the Shah in July 1977, demanding that he

> end despotic government, observe the principles of the Constitution and the Universal Declaration of Human Rights, forego the one-party system, allow freedom of the press and of association, release political prisoners, permit exiles to return, and establish a government based on majority representation.

The signatories were Karim Sanjabi (1904–96) who had been Minister of Education under Mosadegh and would briefly serve as Foreign Minister in the postrevolutionary Provisional Government; Shapour Bakhtiar (1915–91) who had been a Deputy Minister of Labor under Mosadegh and would become the Shah's last Prime Minister; and Dariush Forouhar (1928–98) who, like Sanjabi, would briefly serve in the Provisional Government. Their appeal was ignored by the Shah.

A month later, however, the Shah dismissed his long-serving Prime Minister, Amir-Abbas Hoveyda, and reassigned him to the position of Court Minister, and replaced him with Jamshid Amouzegar, an American-educated economist and technocrat. In his first public speech, the new Prime Minister said that all factions must cooperate with the state, and that people could demonstrate their cooperation by eschewing luxury and embracing thrift, which was the reverse of Hoveyda's message.

When the Shah went to Washington, DC, to meet President Carter on November 15, 1977, the security precautions were grossly inadequate and the result spelled trouble for His Imperial Majesty. The welcoming ceremony was held on the White House lawn, facing the press corps. A large crowd gathered across the street and 70 percent of them were opponents of the Shah. The rest were pro-Shah demonstrators recruited by SAVAK. A fight broke out and police used tear gas to stop the brawl. Over one hundred people were injured, including some two dozen officers. As the gas drifted across the street, the President spoke with tears running down his face and the Shah mopped his eyes with a handkerchief. This unpleasant scene was broadcast around the world and the people of Iran saw it too.

Six weeks later, President Carter and the First Lady undertook a nine-day world tour, stopping off in Tehran to spend New Year's Eve with the Shah and the Shahbanou and their guests. During the banquet at Niavaran Palace, Carter toasted his host in the following terms:

> Iran under the great leadership of the Shah is an island of stability in one of the more troubled areas of the world. This is a great tribute to you, Your Majesty, and to your leadership, and to the respect, admiration and love which your people give to you.

The Gathering Revolution

On January 7, 1978, *Ettelaat* published an article attacking the clerics and defaming Ayatollah Khomeini personally. The pseudonymous author was rumored to be close to the Shah and the article provoked the first in a series of clashes between civilians and security forces that broke out in one city after another, increasing in frequency and intensity until the climax of the revolution thirteen months later.

The first major clash occurred on January 8–9 in Qom where a mass meeting was called to protest the offending article. A number of people were killed and hundreds were wounded. On February 18, at the end of the forty-day mourning period, there were peaceful demonstrations in a dozen cities, but in Tabriz, demonstrators took over the city center and destroyed cars, banks, cinemas, police stations and the headquarters of the Rastakhiz Party. The Army put down the revolt and again there were hundreds of casualties.

Forty days later, in late March, mourning processions took place in scores of cities and towns and some turned violent. Another forty days later, in early May, there was rioting in dozens of towns and more deaths and injuries. And on June 5, a general strike was called to mark the fifteenth anniversary of the 1963 revolt. At that point, the Shah fired General Nasiri as head of SAVAK and sent him to Islamabad as Ambassador to Pakistan.

On August 5, which was Constitution Day, the Shah announced that in response to the people's desire, he would reform the censorship law, allow greater freedom of expression and hold free elections the following year. But the people no longer believed him. On the contrary, they were listening to the opposition and anticipating the return of Ayatollah Khomeini from his exile in Najaf, where he was predicting an imminent "explosion." Two weeks later, on August 19, one of the most tragic incidents of those days occurred in Abadan, when a fire broke out in the Rex Cinema but the exits were locked and hundreds of people were killed. Over the next few days, there were reports of theaters being set on fire in some thirty other locations.

Prime Minister Amouzegar resigned under extreme pressure, having served barely a year. He was replaced by the loyal technocrat, Jafar Sharif-Emami, a former Prime Minister and Senate President and the leading Freemason in Iran. Sharif-Emami urged the people to work for national reconciliation, and as a sop to the clerics, he annulled the dynastic shahanshahi calendar and restored the traditional solar-hijri calendar.

During the first week of September, I noticed youthful demonstrators placing flowers in the barrels of the rifles held by soldiers on duty in Tehran. Then on Friday, September 8, my family and I were driving to the Armenian Club for lunch when we turned onto Shah Reza Street and encountered a caravan of cars carrying hundreds of injured people. Some of the injured were sitting on top of the cars in their blood-stained clothing, shouting, "Death to the Shah!" It was like a siren going off, a call to get ready for the revolution that was surely coming. According to the government, eighty-six people were killed and 205 injured that day at Jaleh Square, which has since been renamed Martyrs Square (*Maidan-e Shohada*).

In October, the Shah granted amnesty to over a thousand political prisoners. They joined the increasingly united front against him. Among those released was Ayatollah Seyyed Mahmoud Taleghani, a cofounder of the Liberation Movement of Iran. He was one of the most popular and most respected figures of the revolution. Younger revolutionaries were inspired by his return to the political arena, especially the Mojahedin Khalq who believed he was sympathetic to their cause. Ayatollah Khomeini, only recently arrived in Paris, sent Ayatollah Taleghani a telegram inviting him to join his movement. Unfortunately, Ayatollah Taleghani died less than a year later at the age of sixty-nine.

On November 5, my elder brother Henrik called me from André Shop to say that a crowd of club-carrying vigilantes was smashing up shops along Vali Asr Street. I told him to leave the area immediately but he stayed to watch from across the street as they reached our shop and destroyed or looted everything in sight. That night, the central business district was devastated. When I went to the shop the next day, the only thing left was the safe – it was too heavy to carry. Unfortunately, some of our neighbors were among the looters. We submitted a formal complaint but to no avail. Who would listen to us in times like that?

A story made the rounds that the Shah asked Court Minister Hoveyda what was going on outside that day.

"Nothing important," Hoveyda replied, "just a bunch of hooligans demonstrating."

But the Shah decided to see for himself, and he flew over the city in his helicopter and surveyed the scene below. On his return, he summoned Hoveyda and slapped him across the face.

"How dare you deceive me?"

So the story went, but there's no proof it was true. In any case, Hoveyda resigned as Court Minister. Two months later, he was arrested and sent to Evin Prison.

Prime Minister Sharif-Emami resigned on November 6 and the Shah replaced him with Army Chief of Staff General Gholam-Reza Azhari. The print press went out on strike and stayed out for two months, but National Iranian Radio and Television (NIRT) remained on the air. Azhari regularly appeared on TV, fulminating against the revolutionaries. Hoping to placate the public, he announced the arrests of Hoveyda, General Nasiri and Gholam-Reza Nikpay, a former mayor of Tehran, which failed to mollify anyone and further demoralized the Shah's supporters. Business was paralyzed by the strikes and demonstrations. I went to work every day but did little other than get together with friends and talk about the political situation.

One evening I invited my friend General Atabaki to dinner at the Armenian Club, and over the course of the evening, I sought his views on the current situation. His last word on the subject surprised me:

"Everything will calm down once he leaves the country."

Of course he was referring to the Shah. Then he gave me an anguished look and said he was under constant surveillance. It wasn't his own safety he was worried about – he was afraid his only son might be kidnapped. I had a Chevy Blazer that I used for hunting, but with the fuel shortage and all the instability, hunting was out of the question. I offered to lend him the Blazer so that he could drive his son to and from school. He declined my offer that night, but two days later he sent a driver to pick up the car.

The biggest demonstrations took place on Tasua and Ashura, the ninth and tenth days of Moharram (December 10–11, 1978), when the Shia traditionally commemorate the martyrdom of Emam Hossein. Upwards of two million people marched in the streets of Tehran as helicopters circled overhead.

Transitional Government

Ten days later, Prime Minister Azhari was incapacitated by a mild heart attack and the Shah was forced to parlay with members of the opposition. After several others refused the job, Dr. Shapour Bakhtiar accepted and was promptly expelled by the National Front. He had trouble forming a cabinet since no one was willing to work with him.

It was during those dark days that I got a call at the office one morning. An aggressive male voice informed me that anti-Shah flyers duplicated at Sati were being handed out on the street. He ordered me to find out who was responsible and put a stop to it immediately. Otherwise, he said, our buildings would go up in flames. Furthermore, a spy on my staff would report on my actions. I was shaken. After some difficulty, I reached Shahbazi. He swore that SAVAK had nothing to do with it. We soon found out that our night watchman was using the company photocopier for his political work. The spy turned out to be an Armenian woman who had worked in our office for years. After the revolution, she and her brother were both exposed as SAVAK agents.

At the end of the year, Bella and I escaped for a short holiday. We stayed with her mother and stepfather in Paris and visited with our children. Annette was studying in Brussels and Vahe was attending the Kiski School in Lugano, since education had become impossible in Iran. After the holidays, I returned to Tehran but Bella stayed in Paris with her parents. Now I was alone, except for my domestic servant and his family. Sometimes my friend André Safarian came over and spent the night. Whenever the power was out, which was often, we would sit by the fire and listen to the BBC and the VOA on a transistor radio. Their reports were surprisingly detailed.

One of Bakhtiar's conditions for accepting the post of Prime Minister was the Shah's temporary absence from the country. He was still present when the leaders of the USA, the UK, France and West Germany met on the Caribbean island of Guadeloupe on January 4, 1979, and concluded that the Shah had lost control and had to go. That same day, American Air Force General Robert Haiser arrived in Tehran. Some believed his mission was to guarantee the Shah's peaceful departure, while others said he came to provoke a coup.

On January 6, the Majles approved Bakhtiar's appointment and the Shah announced his pending departure, but it was another ten days before Bakhtiar was able to name his cabinet. On January 16, the royal couple finally left Iran. In a brief interview at the airport, his eyes brimming with tears, the Shah said he was exhausted and he was going to the upper Egyptian town of Aswan for some rest and relaxation. He said nothing about returning to Iran but he wished the Prime Minister success. When NIRT reported the news of his departure, a million people took to the streets. Their joyous celebration turned into a national holiday that went on until midnight.

Tehran was still under martial law and General Atabaki had command of the northwest sector. His office wasn't far from mine and he often stopped by during those tense days. We would drink coffee and discuss the political situation. He told me the Army was in crisis, unable to tell friend from foe. Troops in Tabriz had refused orders to shoot. Homafars at airbases in Isfahan, Shiraz and Mashhad had defied their officers. There had been a mutiny at Lavizan Barracks in the northeast sector and a dozen Imperial Guards had been killed. There were a thousand desertions a day and fraternization with the public was on the rise.

Ayatollah Khomeini

Ruhollah Mousavi Khomeini was born in 1902 in the village of Khomein near Sultanabad (now Arak). His father was killed a few months after his birth and the future Ayatollah was brought up by his mother and an aunt. He began his religious studies at the age of nineteen under Sheikh Abdol-Karim Haeri in Sultanabad, and followed him to Qom where he completed his studies at the Faiziyeh Seminary. During the 1930s, he taught classes in

Islamic philosophy at Qom, and after Haeri died in 1937, he became a deputy to *Ayatollah ol-Ozma* (Grand Ayatollah) Mohammad Hossein Borujerdi, Haeri's successor as spiritual leader of Iran's Shia. Although both of his mentors were quietists, Khomeini fervently believed that Iran should be governed by Islamic law, but it was only after the death of Ayatollah Borujerdi in 1961 that he became an outspoken critic of the monarchy. These are the broad outlines of the early years of the cleric who would lead the Islamic Revolution in Iran.

In 1963, Khomeini spoke out against the Shah's "White Revolution" – or the "Shah and People Revolution" as it was later dubbed – a modernization program widely believed to have been forced on Iran by the Kennedy administration. His particular targets were the provisions for the redistribution of land to the peasants and the female vote. When a referendum showed that 99.9 percent of the voters approved the program, Khomeini denounced the vote as fraudulent and continued attacking the Shah as a tyrant subservient to the USA. On June 3, which coincided with Ashura, the tenth day of Moharram, in an act of extraordinary bravery, he warned the Shah to reverse course or suffer the fate of Reza Shah:

> Let me give you some advice, Mr. Shah! I advise you to desist in this policy. I don't want people to give thanks if your masters decide one day that you must go. I don't want you to become like your father! Iranian nation! Those of you who are older than thirty or forty will remember how three foreign countries attacked us during the Second World War. The Soviet Union, Britain and America invaded and occupied our country. The people's property was threatened and their honor was imperiled, but God knows they were happy because the Pahlavi was gone!

In those days, merely to hear such words, let alone speak them, wrought fear and terror among the people. Before dawn the next day, Khomeini was arrested and brought to Tehran. Popular protests led by clerics broke out in Qom, Tehran, Isfahan, Shiraz, Tabriz, Mashhad and elsewhere. The three-day uprising was brutally crushed. Informed sources estimate that as many as 10,000 people were killed. Khomeini was condemned to death, but Grand

Ayatollah Kazem Shariatmadari promoted him to Ayatollah in order to save his life, since clerics of that rank enjoyed immunity from the penalty of death.

After eight months under house arrest in Tehran, Ayatollah Khomeini was allowed to return to Qom, but in the fall of 1964, a controversy arose over "capitulations," that is, the Status of Forces Agreement (SOFA) according to which US military personnel and their dependents stationed in Iran would be immune from prosecution under Iranian law. A huge American loan was contingent upon the SOFA guarantee, and Ayatollah Khomeini was outraged when the Twenty-First Majles pass the implementing legislation:

> They have reduced the Iranian people to a status lower than that of an American dog! If someone runs over a dog that belongs to an American, he will be prosecuted. If the Shah himself runs over a dog that belongs to an American, he will be prosecuted. But if an American cook runs over the Shah, no one has the right to interfere with him.... Of course, taking the money means that someone has to become a slave. *You* take the money and *we* become the slaves!

Within twenty-four hours of that speech, Khomeini was deported to Turkey. The following year, he was allowed to move to Najaf where he was reunited with his family, and there he remained until October 1978 when he left Iraq under pressure and was granted asylum in France. Since then, he had been staying at Neauphle-le-Château, a village outside of Paris, receiving visitors, giving interviews, sending messages to Iran.

During a press conference he gave at Neauphle-le-Château on January 6, 1979, French Armenian journalists posed several questions about the prospects for Armenians in a future Islamic Republic of Iran. Khomeini replied that the Armenian presence in Iranian society was manifest in architecture, commerce and the skilled trades, and furthermore, he said,

"They will continue to enjoy all their freedoms and be treated with the utmost fairness."

Pressed on the issues of practicing the Armenian Christian faith and teaching students the Armenian language, Khomeini assured the reporters that Armenian rights would be guaranteed.

Armenian community leaders in Iran heard that conference and disseminated the Ayatollah's remarks by publishing them in *Alik* and reprinting them on leaflets distributed to the community. That information campaign went a long way to alleviate the community's fears.

On Thursday, February 1, 1979, after fourteen years in exile, Ayatollah Khomeini, who was already being referred to as Emam, came home to Iran, accompanied by a planeload of exiled Iranian revolutionaries and Western journalists. Two million people lined the six-mile stretch from the airport to the center of town. The Armenian community also sent a delegation of high-ranking clerics and community leaders to welcome him.

When the chartered Air France jumbo jet landed, his bodyguards were the first to emerge. After a twenty-minute delay, he came down the steps followed by his retinue, most of whom were turbaned clerics. He was driven to the airport VIP lounge where he made a brief statement denouncing the Shah. Then he left the airport in a Chevy Blazer driven by Mohsen Rafigh-Doust, en route to Behesht-e Zahra, the great cemetery on the southern edge of the capital. There the crush of people was so great that he had to be picked up by an Air Force helicopter and flown to the site where he delivered a historic speech lambasting the entire monarchical tradition and the unrepresentative Majles. He also attacked Prime Minister Bakhtiar and said he would appoint a new government. Afterwards, he was helicoptered to central Tehran where he set up temporary headquarters at the Refah School. On Sunday, he appointed Mehdi Bazargan as Interim Prime Minister and ordered him to present his cabinet as soon as possible.

The following Thursday, *Kayhan* published a photograph of junior Air Force officers saluting Khomeini at the Refah School. The next day, a firefight broke out in the Air Force Training School at Doshan Tappeh in east Tehran, pitting pro-Khomeini homafars and cadets against their royalist officers. The Imperial Guard was called in and open warfare spread across the base. Civilians rushed to the scene, revolutionaries raided the arsenals and distributed weapons, and over the next forty-eight hours, armed insurrection engulfed the city.

At 2 PM on Sunday, February 11, NIRT broadcast a statement from the Supreme Council of the Armed Forces, declaring the Army's "neutrality in the present political conflict." Prime Minister Bakhtiar resigned and went into hiding. Revolutionaries took over NIRT and broadcast the national anthem, followed by continuous revolutionary songs.

Later that day, I got a call from General Atabaki.

"The past is over," he said. "My future looks very bleak."

A tradition of monarchical rule stretching back 2,500 years had come to an end and anew and uncertain horizon opened before Iran.

Chapter 9

Consequences of the Iranian Islamic Revolution

Curious to see for myself what was going on, I started driving around alone in my car. There was a whole new atmosphere in town. The police were nowhere to be seen and armed youths were patrolling the streets. The police stations were occupied by crowds of people. The gates of Evin Prison had been thrown open and prisoners were pouring out, including some of the courtiers and high-ranking military officers arrested on the orders of three different Prime Ministers over the previous three months. A caravan of revolutionaries drove by, shouting that they had taken control of Eshratabad Garrison. I drove over there and saw men, women and children carrying away guns, blankets and other gear.

After things calmed down, it appeared that no major thefts had taken place other than the pillaging of the Shah's palaces. Thieves were out in the streets flogging stolen paintings by world-famous artists at ridiculous prices. In our Farmaniyeh neighborhood, Shapour Bakhtiar's abandoned home had been ransacked.

Sheikh Mohammad Montazeri, the madcap son of Ayatollah Montazeri, soon turned up at Mehrabad Airport with a posse of sixty armed men and hundreds of pieces of luggage, all packed with propaganda for the Islamic Revolution, or so they said. In fact, they were packed with plundered treasures. The Sheikh and his men tried to board an Iran Air flight for Libya, but since none of them had any proper documents, airport security refused to let them on the plane, so they occupied the runway for several hours until they were finally allowed to board – without their "literature." That wasn't the Sheikh's only notorious escapade. People called him "Ayatollah Ringo" after the gun-slinging hero of a series of spaghetti Westerns popular in the late 1960s.

On Tuesday, February 13, General Atabaki called to say he wanted to return my Chevy Blazer. We agreed to meet at my office the next morning. On Wednesday, I was sitting around the office with several employees, waiting for Atabaki, when suddenly we heard sporadic gunfire. It sounded like it was coming from the US Embassy which was in our neighborhood. We ran up to the roof and saw revolutionaries attacking several buildings in the compound as guards tried to hold them off with teargas. When a volley of shots rang over our heads, we fled the roof and went back inside. The shooting kept up for over an hour until one of Emam Khomeini's aides arrived with another group of revolutionaries and persuaded the first group to leave.

I waited all day but Atabaki never showed up. The next day my brother Henrik called and told me that Atabaki had been arrested, along with some two dozen other high-ranking officers, and that he had already been executed. On Saturday, the press reported the execution of several top generals, including Nematollah Nasiri, the former head of SAVAK, and Manuchehr Khosrowdad, the former commander of Army Aviation and Atabaki's boss. A few days later, Atabaki's wife called and told me he was still alive.

About a month later, she came to our office with a letter she had written to Emam Khomeini. It said that her husband had never taken part in any anti-Islamic or anti-democratic activity and had always acted within the strict limits of his military responsibilities. I and some of our employees added our signatures to the letter. Six months later, I got a note from Atabaki himself. He said I could pick up the Blazer at Colonel Khalatbari's house. I sent a driver to Khalatbari with a message and he came back with the Blazer. It was in exactly the same condition as when I had lent it, immaculate.

Atabaki served two years in prison. Afterwards, he told me how close he had come to being executed. For the first few days, he was held in a big room at the Refah School with some generals and former officials, including Court Minister Hoveyda. One night, Atabaki was blindfolded and taken up to the roof. He heard the executioners loading their weapons. He expected to be shot at any moment, but the execution was called off and he was taken back downstairs. The next night, he was blindfolded again and taken up to the roof. This time, the man standing next to him was shot. The third and last time he was blindfolded and taken up to the roof, Atabaki's guard whispered that he wasn't actually going to be killed, he had been saved.

Later, he found out that his life had been spared for two reasons. The first was that once when he was flying over the city in a helicopter gunship, he had refused orders to fire on a group of revolutionaries down in the street, saying he wouldn't shoot innocent, unarmed civilians. The second was related to a request from General Abdol-Ali Badrei, commander of the Army's ground forces. After the Army had declared its neutrality on Sunday, February 11,

Badrei called Atabaki and asked for a helicopter to fly him out of the country. Atabaki said he could only do so on direct orders from General Khosrowdad or from the Shah himself. General Badrei rang off and within twenty-four hours he was dead. In both cases, Atabaki's response was captured on tape by the Shah's communications monitoring system which had been penetrated by the revolutionaries. After they heard the tapes, they appealed to Emam Khomeini to pardon Atabaki. A year after he was released from prison, he moved to California.

The First Few Weeks

For a brief period after the Revolution, there was a pleasant atmosphere in Tehran. People were in high spirits. They addressed each other as "Brother" and "Sister." Government bureaucrats treated ordinary citizens with respect. There was little crime, and lying and bribery were virtually non-existent. The press published uncensored news and feature articles, something that was virtually unprecedented. Radio and television offered new programming, though it was devoid of music other than revolutionary songs. Emam Khomeini was heard on the air every day, sometimes several times a day. He always began his remarks with a Koranic verse, and people began following his example. It was so common that even I, as a Christian, felt the need to invoke the Koran whenever I spoke.

Scores of cinemas, nightclubs and casinos were shut down. Music was prohibited and women were explicitly forbidden to sing. *Shahr-e Now* (New Town), the red-light district in southeast Tehran, had been burned to the ground, and revolutionaries were setting up a training center where former prostitutes could learn an honorable trade.

Most men stopped shaving and women covered their heads, some as a voluntary gesture of modesty, others as a matter of social conformity. Emam Khomeini decreed that women must wear *hejab* in the workplace, and before long, Islamic garb in public became mandatory for all women without exception. A chador and dark socks were required to conceal those parts of the body that arouse desire. The chador is an all-enveloping sheet of cloth, usually black, that has to be held in place with one hand. Sometimes only the eyes are visible. At first, there was general dissatisfaction among Armenian women, but they gradually came to terms with it. They joked about the word *chador* which derives from *chadra* (tent). Mispronouncing it, they told the Prelate they wouldn't wear a tent on their head under any circumstances, which provoked indulgent laughter.

Law and Order

The country was still in the grip of a general strike. Banks and the Customs Service were closed and business was practically at a standstill. Emam Khomeini appealed to workers to call off the strike and go back to work. Law and order were in the hands of young revolutionaries. Thousands of students who had been studying abroad were coming home to join them. In Tehran alone, some 300,000 weapons stolen from the armories were still in the hands of the people. Large caches were being stored away by private citizens and political groups who feared for their future. Khomeini asked the people to go to the mosques and surrender their arms to designated officials and allow newly trained security cadres to reestablish order. The US government issued a public statement about the potential danger of Iran's advanced American-made weaponry falling into the hands of opportunists.

The Armenian community had played an active role in the revolutionary struggle, especially the young men, and some of them had lost their lives. During the takeover of the garrisons, Armenian youths had captured two armored vehicles and stationed them near Armenian neighborhoods in the northeast quarter. They had joined the *komitehs* (security committees) set up by local people for neighborhood self-defense. After the Revolution, komitehs replaced the Shah's police and the Armenian community began to feel safer.

But that stability was quickly eroded. The komitehs were penetrated by unsavory characters who used their authority to invade homes, steal property, rape women and sometimes even commit murder. Every day, they arrested scores of people on real or trumped-up charges, which made people anxious and frightened. Before the Revolution, even the lowliest beat cop had carried identification papers, but now there was no such thing. Anybody who hadn't shaved for two weeks and sported a prayer mark on his forehead could join a komiteh and do as he pleased. That dark spot supposedly came from praying several times a day, bowing and pressing one's forehead on a *mohr-e namaz* (a small cake of sanctified earth), but these opportunists got their prayer mark from the touch of a hot iron. I attended the funeral of a Muslim acquaintance where the presiding mollah alluded to this in his sermon:

"I'm sixty years old and for sixty years I sat on my rear end for hours every day, so how come there's no black mark on my rear end?"

That reinforced my belief that opportunists were exploiting the situation. Others used the komitehs to settle personal accounts. We had an employee at Sati who drove a small delivery van, and at one point, he took the van and disappeared for an entire week. I sent someone to his house to find out where he was. His family said he had left town but would be back soon. When he returned to work, I fired him on the spot. He went straight to the local komiteh and complained that I had treated him unfairly. The next day, two armed komiteh members came looking for me at the office. As soon as I introduced myself, they asked me why I had fired the driver. After I explained the situation, one of them countered that the man had been ill and it was incumbent upon me to take him back. While he was telling me this, his partner fiddled with his pistol and he meant it as a threat.

"First," I replied, "your friend would be well advised to put that pistol away. I've known how to use those things since before you two were born. Second, are you sure the driver was ill? If you have proof, let's see it! Third, and more important, I suspect he was using our van to move contraband. He may even be dealing in stolen goods. The point is that Sati employs more than 200 people, and as the managing director, I must act decisively in a case like this. Even if you were to put me up against the wall and shoot me, it wouldn't make any difference because I'm not taking him back."

A few days later, some twenty armed militants invaded our building and started searching the offices and questioning the staff. I went down and introduced myself to their commander and asked him what they were looking for. He said he had information that Sati's employees were dissatisfied, that more than 2,000 people hadn't been paid, that the company had secretly transferred money abroad, that the Shah was a major investor and I had been photographed with him many times. I knew immediately where all those lies were coming from. Fortunately, I had taken down the framed photos of myself with the Shah a few days earlier. I told him he was wrong on every count:

"First of all, the Shah was never an investor in Sati. Our entire staff does not exceed 200 and all of our employees are satisfied with their working conditions. As a matter of fact, every one of them was paid for the six months during which nobody did any work. As for the transfer of funds abroad, you're welcome to review our bank statements as long as you're properly authorized to do so."

"I heard just the opposite," he replied. "I heard that Sati wasn't paying its employees."

"Ask them yourself, please, be my guest."

He hesitated for a moment, then said that his orders were to occupy the building and keep an eye on everyone. It seemed pointless to continue the conversation. Instead, I sent a letter to Hojjatoleslam Khamenei, Tehran's Friday prayer leader (*Emam Jomeh*), asking him to have the militants withdrawn from our building as soon as possible.

The next morning, four elderly revolutionaries arrived and asked who wrote that letter. Having ascertained that I was the one they were looking for, they came up to my office on the fourth floor and asked me a few questions. Satisfied with my answers, they went back down by way of the stairs, collecting all the young militants floor by floor, and mustered them in the forecourt. After a brief exchange with the militants' commander, they oversaw their speedy departure. Afterwards, they told me the militants belonged to the Mojahedin Khalq and they confirmed that our former driver was the source of their false information.

People appealed to Emam Khomeini to dismantle the hundreds of komitehs, but he refused, saying only that criminal elements must be caught and punished. Yet who would dare to expose such people in times like that? Instead, he ordered the creation of the *Sepah-e Pasdaran-e Enqelab-e Eslami* (Islamic Revolutionary Guards Corps or IRGC), also known as the *Sepah* or the pasdars, which absorbed various paramilitary groups and komiteh toughs. The new force existed alongside the traditional Army (*Artesh*) which was purged but not dissolved, and the revolutionary leadership spared no effort to build up and equip the IRGC.

The Provisional Government and the Revolutionary Council

Interim Prime Minister Mehdi Bazargan had announced the members of his cabinet during the first week after the Revolution. They were all nationalists, veteran activists, experienced technocrats and devout Muslims like Bazargan himself. But real power was now in the hands of the clerics on Khomeini's Revolutionary Council (*Showra-ye Enqelabi*). Very little was known about the leading clerics because the Shah had made sure they kept a low profile, but there were quietists who rejected clerical governance and only spoke out on rare occasions, like Grand Ayatollah Shariatmadari, and there were hard-line activists whose ideology was Islamic internationalism in which there was no place for Iranian nationalism. These latter strove to establish Islamic governing structures as quickly as possible.

The older generation of clerical activists who drove the Revolution, born in the 1920s or earlier, included Ayatollah Dr. Mohammad Hossein

Beheshti who was appointed head of the Judiciary in June; Ayatollah Mohammad-Reza Mahdavi-Kani, a former student of Ayatollah Khomeini who was appointed to centralize the komitehs; Ayatollah Hossein-Ali Montazeri, also a former student of Khomeini who was put in charge of the Friday prayer leaders; Ayatollah Morteza Motahhari, another former student who had headed the Hosseiniyeh Ershad and who taught theology at Tehran University; Hojjatoleslam Dr. Mohammad Mofatteh, Dean of the Divinity School at the university; and Ayatollah Seyyed Abdol-Karim Mousavi-Ardebili who was appointed the first postrevolutionary Civil Attorney General.

The younger activists who ultimately replaced their elders included Hojjatoleslams Dr. Mohammad Javad Bahonar (1933–81), Ali-Akbar Hashemi-Rafsanjani (1934–), Seyyed Ali Khamenei (1939–), Seyyed Mohammad Mousavi-Khoeiniha (1942–), and Ali-Akbar Nategh-Nuri (1944–). There were three young laymen as well who had advised Khomeini in Paris and returned to Iran with him: Dr. Ebrahim Yazdi (1931–), Dr. Abolhassan Bani-Sadr (1933–), and Sadeq Qotbzadeh (1937–82), all activists in exile since their student days abroad.

It became obvious who was in control when the clerics took over the legal system and set up Revolutionary Tribunals while they went about reforming the traditional courts. The worst possible charges that could be laid in a Revolutionary Tribunal were *moharebeh ba khoda* (enmity against God) and *mofsed fel arz* (sowing corruption on earth). In all such cases, a *hakem shar* (Islamic religious judge) was the final arbiter.

Hojjatoleslam Sadegh (Sadeq) Khalkhali was appointed Chief Judge of the Revolutionary Tribunal in Tehran. His first order of business was to try former members of the Shah's government. His trials were short, his verdicts were severe, and in many cases the punishment was immediate execution by firing squad. Every day, we heard about the arrest and execution of another general, minister or SAVAK officer and the appropriation of their assets.

The televised interrogation of Amir-Abbas Hoveyda, the Shah's longest-serving Prime Minister, compelled the attention of Europe and the United Nations. France in particular pressured Prime Minister Bazargan to intercede and spare Hoveyda's life. Bazargan promised to do what he could, but Judge Khalkhali went ahead and tried Hoveyda in secret and had him shot in the middle of the night. Some say Khalkhali pulled the trigger himself.

Judge Khalkhali's uncompromising decisions horrified and frightened the public. For example, he threatened to turn the monumental tomb of Reza Shah into a toilet. Instead, he had it blown up. Worse, he threatened to raze Persepolis to the ground in order to obliterate any trace of Iran's monarchical past, but the majestic ruin was nominated and adopted as a UNESCO World Heritage Site before the year was out, and he was prevented from carrying out his threat.

The Clerics Take Over the Government

Barely two months after the triumph of the Revolution, conflicts emerged among its leadership. Foreign Minister Karim Sanjabi resigned in mid-April because, he said, a group of totally unknown individuals was interfering and preventing the government from carrying out its duties. Dr. Sanjabi was considered one of the most outstanding leaders of the Revolution. He had struggled against the monarchy for decades. Emam Khomeini appointed Dr. Ebrahim Yazdi to replace him as Foreign Minister. That was the beginning of the Revolutionary Council's takeover of the Provisional Government. In July, the Council created deputy ministerial positions for its own people: Hojjatoleslam Khamenei in the Ministry of Defense; Hojjatoleslam Hashemi-Rafsanjani and Ayatollah Mahdavi-Kani in the Interior Ministry; Hojjatoleslam (later Ayatollah) Bahonar and his protégé, a former school teacher named Mohammad Ali Rajai, in the Ministry of Education; and Dr. Bani-Sadr in the Ministry of Finance. In effect, these shadow ministers took control of the Ministries they were assigned to.

As a result of the conflict between technocrats and clerics, the latter ultimately took complete control of the government. Dr. Hassan Nazih (b. 1921) was a prominent civil rights attorney, a former chair of the Iranian Bar Association and an active revolutionary. He was openly secular but he was not an opponent of Islam. I knew him because he had served as Sati's legal counsel. Prime Minister Bazargan appointed him to head the National Iranian Oil Company, but the clerics were incensed when Dr. Nazih spoke out against Islamic rule, saying it couldn't solve the country's problems and it would even be detrimental. Emam Khomeini fired him and called for a criminal investigation. After that, he fled to France and joined the secular opposition.

They say the revolution devours its children and that was certainly true of the Islamic Revolution. A mysterious terrorist group emerged under the name *Forghan*, an ancient term meaning "the true word of God," i.e. the Koran. Its members were extreme fundamentalists who opposed both government by technocrats and government by clerics. Their first victim was General Valiollah Gharanei, who had briefly served in the Provisional Government as Army Chief of Staff. He was assassinated on April 23. Ayatollah Motahhari was assassinated a week later. He was the chair of the Revolutionary Council and one of Khomeini's closest collaborators, "the fruit of my own life," as he said in mourning. Three weeks later, Hojjatoleslam Hashemi-Rafsanjani escaped an attempt on his life, and in December, Hojjatoleslam Dr. Mofatteh was murdered in his office at Tehran University. Not much more was heard of Forqan after a dozen or so members were arrested in January 1980. The following year, it would be the turn of the Mojahedin Khalq and the Fedayeen Khalq, and after that, it would be the Tudeh's turn.

Nationalizations, Expropriations and *Bonyads*

It took a while for some of the millionaires and big landowners to come to grips with the fact that a revolution had taken place. They were expecting a replay of 1953 and thought the Shah would soon return. My friend Daniel (Dodig) Sahakian – whose family, together with the Sarkissian family, owned scores of food and beverage companies – had originally intended to keep the factories running, but two months on, seeing how workers' councils were taking over the management of factories like his, he packed up and left the country.

But we shared some memorable times during those two months, hiking on the weekends, fishing in the Lar and relaxing at Darya Kenar. One day, we were hiking in the mountains when the snow was beginning to melt and the *jashir* (wild asparagus) were starting to sprout. Cooked with a little vinegar, they are delicious. We met a villager carrying a large sack of these delicacies on his back and we bought whole sack. Only when we picked it up did we realize how heavy it was. We decided to take turns carrying it, and when it was Dodig's turn, he quipped,

"If only my workers could see me now!"

Another friend of mine was the manager of the local office of Entrepose, the French construction company. After the Revolution, his employees locked him in the bathroom for a day and a half. Two days after that, he crossed the mountains into Turkey with the help of Kurds and made his way to France.

The reader may recall Mr. Rahmani, the general manager of Tavanir who had recommended Sati to Mitsubishi for assistance in clearing customs back in the late 1960s. One day, Rahmani came to see me at my office. I was quite surprised but I welcomed him respectfully. We talked for a while and then he came to the point of his visit. He said he wanted to make a special request, one that he couldn't trust with anyone else. His family was already in America and he wanted to join them. Could I help him leave Iran? I knew a royalist who had turned into a revolutionary but still had good connections at the airport. I introduced the two and Rahmani soon left the country.

On March 6, the government announced plans to try the Shah in absentia. On the same day, the Revolutionary Council established the *Bonyad-e Mostazafan* (Foundation for the Oppressed) to take control of the Shah's assets as well as those of the executed and the exiled. The Bonyad Mostazafan was the first and most powerful of several tax-free parastatal organizations whose charters make them unaccountable to any government agency. It soon controlled hundreds of factories, farms and commercial and residential properties, all shielded from accountability, and employed tens of thousands of people. The extent of its present holdings is unknown since it remains accountable only to the Supreme Leader.

A friend of mine owned several factories that were expropriated by the Bonyad Mostazafan. One day, he asked me to see what I could find out from another friend of mine who was well connected, regarding his prospects for repossessing his factories. My friend came back in a week with an answer of sorts. He said my other friend would never get his factories back because they were now supporting three different revolutionary institutions, and furthermore, if he were to pursue the matter, his life could be in danger.

In May, Prime Minister Bazargan announced that all private banks would be nationalized. A process of mergers and regroupings was carried out over the next month, at the end of which some fifty banks were reduced to six: Banks Mellat, Melli, Refah Kargaran, Saderat, Sepah and Tejarat (Republic, National, Workers Welfare, Export, Army and Commercial Banks), all of which continued to operate under the supervision of Iran's Central Bank. The same process was applied to private insurance companies. In July, it was the turn of large-scale industrial concerns such as automobile manufacturing, aircraft-and ship-building, and mining and metallurgical companies. In August, some two dozen agro-industrial firms were nationalized. The Tudeh Party was behind this trend – they wanted Iran to follow the example of Algeria and eliminate private enterprise altogether.

Sensing a threat to our businesses, a group of us met with various influential people and tried to explain the dangers of nationalizing certain firms. But we lacked clout as mere citizens, so we decided to revive the International Transport Companies Syndicate (ITCS), which had been founded a decade earlier but had never been very active. We called for a new governing board and the election was held in the great hall of the Iranian Chamber of Commerce, Industries and Mines. Fifty-five representatives of various transport companies took part. I ran for a seat and won the votes of everyone except the chairman of the outgoing board. After the new board chose me as president, the ex-president wrote to the Minister of Labor and asked him to annul the election, citing a Koranic verse in support of his argument that a non-Muslim cannot be the leader of Muslims. Nothing came of it and I served two two-year terms as president of ITCS, during which period the board's achievements were substantial. We kept our industry from being nationalized, and with the onset of the Iran-Iraq War in September 1980, freight shipping became even more important. After four years in office, I declined to seek re-election because by then, I was chairman of the Tehran Diocesan Council which entailed very heavy responsibilities, but the ITCS board honored me with a special citation for my service.

Revolutionary Guards Raid Sati

One morning I was at the ITCS office, having just returned with a group of my colleagues from a meeting at the Ministry of Labor, when I got an urgent call from my secretary. She told me that Sati was being raided by some thirty pasdars and that there were several men in my office, threatening to break open my desk unless somebody gave them a key to the drawers. I asked her to pass the phone to their leader. I identified myself and said I would be there in fifteen minutes. When I arrived, the foyer was crowded with pasdars. I made my way through and took the elevator to the fourth floor where two armed pasdars were standing guard at the door to my office. Without acknowledging them, I entered and found two more inside, but they were unarmed. I greeted them in their own vernacular:

"May God keep His watchful eye upon you and grant you the strength and energy to accomplish your mission. How can I be of help?"

"Our orders are to search every desk and drawer, and unless you have the keys...."

I took out my keys and unlocked the drawers. They made a thorough search but found nothing of interest to them. When they were finished, I asked,

"Could you please tell me what has prompted this search?"

"We found espionage equipment in your warehouse."

"Is it possible that you have the wrong address?"

One of them reeled off the address of our warehouse out in District 18.

"Yes, that's our facility, but kindly tell me exactly what you found, because to my knowledge there's nothing there but vehicles and spare parts."

"We have the evidence! And you still deny your crime?"

"Kindly tell me what crime I have committed."

"You're using radios to communicate with Israel and the USA!"

As soon as I heard the word "radios," I knew what he was talking about. I explained that Sati was in charge of transport for Entrepose, the French contractor that was laying a natural gas pipeline from Sarakhs in the far northeast to towns on the Caspian coast, and we were storing some of their equipment. Those radio transceivers were used on construction sites and their range was only a mile, if that. Entrepose had brought them into Iran with permission from the Ministry of Communications and was awaiting permission to ship them back to France.

"We also found crates packed with paintings. Are you planning to ship those to France too?"

"Those belong to a friend of mine. He asked me to store them while he was away on business. He said his house wasn't secure, and since we have room, I was happy to do so."

At that point, he said they were taking me to central komiteh headquarters. I asked to see a warrant for my arrest but he didn't have one. Instead, he said I was invited to meet with a revolutionary judge and answer some questions. I said I preferred to appear on my own steam, since it would reflect poorly on me if my employees saw me being taken away under guard. He took my point and told me to be there in half an hour. I asked my colleague, Ardashes Zomorodian, to accompany me. When we reached the central komiteh headquarters, the same pasdar was waiting for me at the entrance. I asked Ardashes to wait outside and told him that if I wasn't back within two hours, it would mean I was under arrest.

I was taken to a large hall. The only person there was a man sitting at a desk. He asked me to sit down and tell him the whole story, which I did.

Then he asked me to write it all down and sign my account. His straightforward manner suggested that he wasn't an extremist. I sensed that he was satisfied with my story. He made me promise to let him know when the owner of the paintings returned. After three hours, he finally let me go. Ardashes was still waiting outside.

The paintings actually belonged to the former local manager for Entrepose who had fled the country after his staff turned against him. I called him in Paris and told him what happened. He asked me to contact the company's Iranian attorney, which I did, and they undertook to retrieve the radio transceivers, but they were never seen again. In time, the paintings were forgotten. When my friend's wife came back a few years later, I gave her the paintings without informing the komiteh.

My Business Interests

In 1978, Alfred Aysseh still held a 33-percent share in Sati, but he saw the Revolution coming, so he transferred his share to his brother-in-law, Goriun Nersissian, and left the country. After the Revolution, Goriun emigrated too. When new regulations required that a company's registered capital reflect its actual capitalization, we were twice forced to increase our capital investments in order to avoid having Sati's operations frozen. Both times, we notified Goriun, but he declined in writing to increase his own investment, and as a result, his share shrank from 33 to 8 percent.

One day, Sati's bank accounts were all frozen at once. I made some inquiries and found out that the *Bonyad-e Shahid* (Martyrs Foundation) was responsible. When I contacted the director and asked him for an explanation, he told me that Goriun's share was now owned by the Martyrs Foundation and that all of our banking transactions required its countersignature. He wasn't satisfied with my explanation but I did get him to unfreeze our accounts. He sent an accountant to review our books, and after further inquiries, the foundation lost interest and left us alone. Goriun's share was later transferred to the Office of the Prime Minister, but after that office was eliminated in the 1989 constitutional revision, the 8-percent share was sold to my business partner, Alfred Mehrabian.

Sati's business activities had ground to a halt in the immediate postrevolutionary chaos, and for a while, the company survived on its capital alone, but fortunately, business soon picked up. We got contracts with ACEC Belgium (Alstom) and the Spanish branch of Westinghouse, but our most important client was TechnoPromExport (TPE). The Soviet foreign trade organization was building another unit at the Ramin Power Plant in Khuzestan and starting a new plant in Isfahan. Over the next twenty years, TPE built eight 200-megawatt units at Isfahan and Sati got transport contracts for all of those projects.

One day, the manager of TechnoProm's office in Tehran, Mr. Sayenkov, invited me to meet with him. After the usual exchange of pleasantries, he told me that Tavanir had asked TPE to appoint a permanent Iranian representative in order to ensure continuity. He said that I was the only reliable person he knew in Iran, and the fact that I hadn't left the country after the Revolution was an indication that I had never been under SAVAK's thumb. I explained that Sati couldn't represent TPE because our business focus was quite different. I said we would have to create a new company for that and I asked him specifically what kinds of services were required.

Sayenkov offered the example of a long-term project involving twenty Soviet technicians. They and their families needed a place to live, but since local landlords were unwilling to rent to foreigners, their housing had to be arranged, and he wanted them all in the same location in order to simplify transportation. That had to be provided too, i.e. hiring and scheduling a crew of drivers and maintaining a fleet of vehicles. It would be a complicated operation and they wanted a reliable local company to handle it. I countered that a project like that would require a substantial initial capital outlay. He told me not to worry, TPE would provide the capital, all they needed was my agreement in principle. Once he had that, he would itemize the requirements and ask me to draft a budget on that basis.

I told Sayenkov I needed a few days to make a decision and I began considering possible business partners. I didn't want to start a company like that on my own and I knew I needed to involve some non-Armenians. I contacted Mr. Goya, an old colleague in the Ministry of Agriculture – we had worked together in the soil lab for twelve years – and I explained the nature and scope of the new company. He enthusiastically agreed to become a partner. He was planning to retire from the Ministry soon and then he would be able to devote his full attention to the new company. Moreover, he needed the income to send his son to university abroad.

The second partner I chose was Mr. Zandi, a young man recommended by my younger brother. Zandi had graduated from an American university and his English was good enough, which was an important qualification. He would manage the enterprise. The third partner was Alfred Mehrabian, a Sati shareholder and one of my closest friends. Alfred would supervise the accounting. Because Zandi refused to accept anything less than 25 percent, the shares were divided in such a way that I held 55 percent, Zandi held 25 percent, and Alfred and Mr. Goya each held 10 percent. We named the company Tabarzin after the traditional Persian battle axe that modern dervishes still carried as a symbolic weapon.

We set up an office and applied for and received permission to represent TechnoPromExport. Sayenkov laid out our responsibilities and we provided a breakdown of our fee, requesting a total of 5 million tomans (approximately $720,000). That amount was transferred to Tabarzin at a time when our own investment was no more than 100,000 tomans (approximately $15,000). We immediately rented a ten-story, twenty-unit apartment building in one of the most prestigious areas of Tehran, purchased a dozen or so vehicles and hired a team of skilled drivers. Tabarzin and its successor Tavanza continued to meet TPE's various requirements over the years and made quite a bit of money. Mr. Goya was able to send his son and his daughter to top-notch American universities and buy a home in California.

Because of my business contacts, we also secured administrative contracts from European companies. The longer the Iran-Iraq War went on, the more reluctant they became to send their nationals to represent their interests in Iran, and because they knew and trusted me, our clientele grew, our income was substantial and it was paid in foreign currencies.

Given my other responsibilities, I had little time to devote to Tabarzin, but after a while, I heard that Zandi was abusing his position. He bought himself a Cadillac with company funds. He came to work late and left early. He kept visitors waiting while he attended to personal business. He gave the same treatment to people from TechnoProm, even though TPE was our most important client. At one point, he went to Europe to take delivery of substantial payments to Tabarzin and he leased a plane to fly from capital to capital. Then, instead of depositing the money in the company's account, he deposited it all in his own account. At that point, I asked him to resign. He refused, so I asked Alfred and Mr. Goya to join me in removing him from his position, and Mr. Goya took over as manager.

Zandi turned around and filed a complaint with the Ministry of Labor. The Ministry ordered Tabarzin to pay him a certain sum in compensation, which we did, but he wasn't satisfied with that and he cooked up another scheme. When his machinations began to interfere with the company's operations, we set up a new company named Tavanza, and once Tavanza was established, we dissolved Tabarzin. Alfred handled the liquidation and paid all the debts, taxes and penalties. Zandi then set up his own company, which he named Tabarzand, and contacted former clients of Tabarzin, but he failed to get a single contract.

One day Afo, one of SATI's employees who was helping un in Tabarzin, was arrested and taken to the local komiteh. Our consulting attorney, Dr. Jaleh Shambayati, learned that Zandi had filed a complaint with the Revolutionary Tribunal, making false and highly inflammatory allegations about Tabarzin's foreign currency accounts. Because Zandi was well informed about the company's business dealings, and even more so because of the strict currency control regime, his accusations could not be lightly dismissed. However, Dr. Shambayati managed to have the case transferred to the Civil Court.

All four former shareholders were summoned to the first hearing, at the conclusion of which the court ordered an audit of Tabarzin's books. We asked to have it done at Sati and placed an office at the auditor's disposal. At first, he tried to frighten Afo with financial horror stories, but when he learned that Alfred had been trained at the Petroleum Ministry's School of Accounting and Finance, he showed him more respect. And when he finished comparing Alfred's ledgers with the documentation provided by Tabarzin's former clients, he conceded that they were immaculate and that Zandi's complaints were groundless.

Nevertheless, Zandi appealed and the case dragged on for years. He ultimately lost the case and was ordered to reimburse his former partners for the funds he had transferred to his personal account *and* to cover our legal expenses, even at the cost of his home.

Chapter 10

The Islamic Government and the Hostage Crisis

After the triumph of the Revolution, everyone was debating the future direction of the country. The press was full of ideas. Some people wanted a democratic republic, others wanted a democratic Islamic republic, still others envisioned a communist regime. Emam Khomeini said the only question was whether Iran would be an Islamic republic, yes or no. A national referendum on that question was held on March 30–31, 1979, coinciding with the last days of Nowruz. Archbishop Manoukian and Dr. Vartkes Nahabedian, who chaired the Diocesan Council, urged the Armenian community to cast their votes. People were very enthusiastic about it. The "yes" vote was 98 percent. Afterwards, my wife and I went to the mosque near our home and joined in the celebration.

The New Constitution

Later in the spring, a draft Constitution was published and the imminent election of a large Constituent Assembly was announced. Instead, a smaller Assembly of Constitutional Experts was elected in August. Hrair Khalatian was elected to the seat allocated to the Armenians. He worked hard to affirm the rights of minorities and to make sure the new Constitution clearly defined those rights. The Assembly concluded its deliberations in October and a referendum on the Constitution was held on December 2–3, 1979.

For the first time in Iranian history, the new Constitution recognized Jews, Christians and Zoroastrians as religious minorities, "free to carry out their religious rites and practice their religion in personal status and religious education" (Article 13), and free to use "local and ethnic languages in the press and mass media or the teaching of their literatures in schools, along with Persian" (Article 15). Other provisions extended protection through inclusive language, as in Article 19: "The people of Iran, of whatever tribe and clan, shall enjoy equal rights, and color, race, language and the like shall not be a privilege."

According to the Constitution, the Supreme Leader (*Rahbar*) is the most powerful position in government. He holds supreme command of the Armed

Forces and he can declare war or peace and appoint or dismiss the service chiefs. Likewise, he can appoint or dismiss the heads of the Judiciary and the state broadcasting network, known as the Voice and Vision of the Islamic Republic of Iran (*Seda ve Sima-ye Jomhouri-ye Eslami Iran*). He also confirms the election of the President and may dismiss the President for cause (Article 110).

The President is elected by popular vote but his powers are relatively circumscribed. He cannot veto legislation passed by the Majles (Article 123), his cabinet ministers must be approved and may be dismissed by the Majles (Articles 89, 133, 135), and he or any of his ministers may be called before the Majles to defend their actions (Article 88). The Constitution of 1979 also outlined the responsibilities of the Prime Minister, but that office was abolished in the 1989 revision.

The Supreme Leader (subsequent to Emam Khomeini) is chosen by the Assembly of Leadership Experts (*Majles-e Khobregan-e Rahbari*), a body of eighty-six senior clerics popularly elected every eight years. Candidates for the Assembly, as well as for the Majles and the Presidency, are screened by the Guardian Council which supervises elections.

The Guardian Council (*Showra-ye Negahban*) reviews all legislation passed by the Majles to ensure its conformity with the precepts of Islam and the provisions of the Constitution (Article 96). The Council consists of twelve members who serve six-year terms. Six are appointed by the Supreme Leader and six are elected by the Majles from a list provided by the head of the Judiciary (Article 91).

The Majles (*Majles-e Showra-ye Eslami*, or the Islamic Consultative Assembly) is elected every four years and currently has 290 members. Article 64 specifies the representation of the minority communities:

> The Zoroastrians and Jews shall have one representative each; Assyrian and Chaldean Christians collectively shall have one representative, and the Armenian Christians of the south and the north shall each have one representative.

The Constitution also provides for the local election of town councils. Tehran's first municipal elections were held in 1999.

Because the Majles and the Guardian Council often deadlocked over legislation, Emam Khomeini created a new body to settle such disputes. The Council for the Discernment of the Interest of the Islamic Order (*Majma-e Tashkhis-e Maslahat-e Nezam-e Eslami*), known as the Expediency Council, was incorporated into the revised Constitution in 1989. The Supreme Leader appoints its members to five-year terms and convokes it to meet. The Expediency Council makes its own procedural rules, subject to the Leader's approval (Article 112).

The Supreme Leader appoints the head of the Judiciary who in turn appoints the President of the Supreme Court and the Attorney General (Article 158), proposes candidates for the cabinet position of Minister of Justice (Article 160), and oversees the administration of justice in the Higher and Lower Criminal Courts, the Civil (General) and Special Civil (Family Law) Courts, and the Revolutionary Tribunals. Trial procedure resembles the French system of magisterial inquisition rather than the Anglo-American system of adversarial advocacy before a jury.

The new Constitution was approved by 99 percent of the voters. The first presidential election was held in January 1980. Emam Khomeini barred clerics from standing as candidates, and on his orders, Ayatollah Beheshti, the leader of the Islamic Republican Party and the head of the Judiciary, stayed out of the race. Khomeini also barred the leader of the Mojahedin Khalq, Masoud Rajavi, from running for President because his party had boycotted the referendum on the Constitution and rejected the concept of *velayat-e faqih* (rule of the jurisconsult). The Ayatollah backed his loyal technocrat, Dr. Abolhassan Bani-Sadr, and indirectly encouraged people to vote for him. Bani-Sadr won with 75 percent of the vote, but from the first day, the clerics and the opportunists who supported velayat-e faqih actively opposed Bani-Sadr and eventually ran him out of the country. In June 1981, after less than eighteen months in office, he was impeached by the Majles. He went underground, only to emerge in Paris a month later with Masoud Rajavi.

Elections for the First Islamic Majles were held in May 1980. Hrair Khalatian, backed by the ARF, was elected to represent the Armenians of northern Iran. An accountant by profession, he was a revolutionary intellectual, the editor of *Alik* for many years, and the author or translator of more than twenty books. It was a different picture for the Armenians of southern Iran who were concentrated in Isfahan and Shahin Shahr and nearby Armenian villages, and in Shiraz, Ahvaz and Abadan. They were represented by the leftist physician, Dr. Hratch Khachaturian. The Islamic Republican Party won a majority of seats, and in July, Hojjatoleslam

Hashemi-Rafsanjani and Hojjatoleslam Mousavi-Khoeiniha were elected Speaker and Deputy Speaker respectively.

Regional Uprisings

The Islamic government was assailed by regional revolts practically from the moment it took power. With the gathering Revolution, ethnic groups in outlying provinces began to think about self-government, then talk about it, then take up arms in pursuit of their own cause. Azeris in the north, Kurds in the northwest, Turkmens in the northeast, Baluchis in the southeast and Arabs in the southwest all demanded autonomy in the first few months after the victory of the Revolution.

In Tabriz, the capital of East Azarbayjan Province, the Muslim People's Republican Party (MPRP) was founded two weeks after the Revolution. The party was endorsed by Grand Ayatollah Shariatmadari, a native of Tabriz and a much loved and respected *marja-e taqlid* (source of emulation). Both the Provisional Government and the Revolutionary Council opposed the MPRP's demand for local autonomy. They didn't want to see a regional power base established in Azarbayjan, especially one identified with Ayatollah Shariatmadari who was already at odds with Emam Khomeini over the direction he was taking the country.

Shariatmadari had been the leading cleric in Qom before Khomeini's return, and in terms of rank he was above him, since he had issued the fatwa declaring Khomeini an Ayatollah in order to save his life back in 1963. Shariatmadari questioned the principle of velayat-e faqih, and he and the MPRP boycotted the referendum on the Constitution in December. After his residence in Qom was attacked, his supporters in Tabriz rose up in protest. Emam Khomeini gave the young prosecutor Hossein Mousavi-Tabrizi full powers to settle the problem and he brutally crushed the revolt. That widened the rift between the Emam and the Grand Ayatollah and Khomeini subsequently stripped Shariatmadari of his religious title and placed him under house arrest. Deprived of his religious mission, he died in 1986 at the age of 81.

Even though the Kurdish Democratic Party and the Komeleh Party held divergent political views, both were adamant in their demand for Kurdish autonomy. The first clashes occurred in March in Mahabad, West Azarbayjan Province, and Sanandaj, the capital of Kordestan Province. The government fought the Kurds with extra zeal, knowing that Turkey and Iraq were backing them. Scores of people were killed and hundreds injured. Unfortunately,

Kordestan was in a state of war for the next ten years, and while government troops kept watch by day, the rebels were in control at night. It was only after the end of the Iran-Iraq War in 1988 that the government was able to focus on the region and put an end to Kurdish aspirations for autonomy.

In Gonbad-e Kavous, Turkmen allied with the Fedayeen Khalq seized the police station in late March 1979, and scores of people were killed in the clashes that followed. Ayatollah Taleghani was sent to mediate but the unrest continued until early the following year when Judge Khalkhali and the Sepah undertook to end the movement by executing scores of Turkmen.

Clashes between Baluch tribesmen and Iranian revolutionaries broke out at the same time as the Turkmen revolt, and the Revolutionary Council was concerned that neighboring Afghanistan and Pakistan would exploit the situation, so they dispatched Hojatoleslam Khamenei on a peace mission. Having been internally exiled in Sistan-ve-Baluchestan Province himself, Khamenei had friends there and he was instructed to do whatever was necessary to pacify the Baluchis. He accomplished his mission in the best possible way.

On the other hand, when Iranian Arabs in oil-rich Khuzestan demanded autonomy, the insurgency was quickly crushed by traditional Army and Navy forces under the command of the provincial governor, Admiral Ahmad Madani.

The Armenian Community

One of the most important events for Iranian Armenians during the early postrevolutionary period was when Archbishop Manoukian led a delegation of community leaders to visit Emam Khomeini in Qom on March 29, 1979. That historic meeting played a defining role in community life and was widely covered in the media. *Kayhan*, the highest-circulation Tehran daily, reported as follows:

> Archbishop Manoukian congratulated Emam Khomeini and the Iranian people on the victory of the Islamic Revolution and said Armenians were prepared to continue the struggle.
>
> "Islam is tolerant toward other religions," the Emam replied. "The achievements of this Revolution will undoubtedly have a positive influence on minorities too."

As their meeting concluded, the Prelate handed the Emam a letter saying that Iran's enemies had not only stolen the country's wealth and spread evil across the land, but they had diverted her people and especially the youth from faith in their religion, and that the struggle against the monarchy and imperialism was a deep-rooted struggle against corruption and the forces of injustice.

"Under the guise of protecting the wealth and property of the Christians," the Prelate's letter continued, "those who may be misinformed about the essence of the Islamic movement are trying to create a rift between Christians and Muslims, but the Armenians of Iran are alert to this danger and will neutralize all such devious manipulations. Since the very first days of the Revolution, Armenians have joined their Muslim brothers in strikes, marches and national rallies. The Armenian daily *Alik* has covered the Revolution in full, reporting on the part Armenians have played in the great national liberation struggle. They too were martyred for the cause, and together with their Muslim brothers, they will continue the struggle until injustice and oppression are utterly uprooted from Iran."

Dr. Albert Bernardi, a prominent Iranian Armenian attorney, served as interpreter between the two religious leaders. Of course, *Alik* carried full coverage of the meeting.

The first tangible benefit of the Revolution for our community was the right to demonstrate in memory of the victims of the Genocide. Public commemoration had always been strictly forbidden by SAVAK, although the Diocesan Council had managed to get permission to erect a modest monument in the courtyard of St. Sarkis Church and the Prelacy. The march held on April 24, 1979, was the realization of the community's sixty-four-year-long aspiration. The next day, it was front-page news in *Kayhan*:

> **Mass Demonstration on the Anniversary of the Armenian Massacres**
>
> Thousands of Armenians took part in a march in Tehran yesterday that was organized by various Armenian organizations to protest the 1915 Ottoman Genocide of 1.5 million Armenians. Men and women, young and old, and many students gathered at St. Sarkis Church at 9:00 AM, where they

listened to a speech by Archbishop Manoukian and then marched to the Turkish Embassy.

The Archbishop told the rally that some nations of the world had condemned the mass killings even as they were taking place, but unfortunately, other world powers that were aware of the atrocities remained silent, which made them complicit in the Genocide. According to the Archbishop, the purpose of the demonstration was to raise the level of community awareness.

The march began at St. Sarkis Church on Villa [now Ostad Nejatollahi] and Karim Khan Zand Streets, proceeded south to Islamic Revolution Street [*Enqelab-e Eslami*, formerly Shah Reza Street], turned east to Ferdowsi Square, then south on Ferdowsi Street to the intersection with Istanbul Street, where it stopped across from the Turkish Embassy. A four-point declaration was read out, recalling the massacres perpetrated in 1915 and in earlier years. The demonstrators cheered the declaration and demanded the return of Western Armenian lands to their rightful owners. Then they marched west on Naderi Street to St. Mary's Church. In the courtyard, they sang revolutionary songs and heard speeches about the Genocide. The tolling of the church bells at 2:00 PM brought the demonstration to a close.

Some demonstrators held up pictures of Emam Khomeini and Ayatollah Taleghani, while others carried pictures of Yasser Arafat. They made statements in support of the Palestinians and their just cause and chanted anti-imperialist slogans. Those slogans made it clear that the Armenian nation fully supports Iran's Islamic Revolution.

Messages on their placards included "The UN covers for imperialist states," "Salute to Khomeini, greetings to Taleghani," "We support the struggle of oppressed peoples," "Death to imperialism and its allies," "Liberate Armenian lands stolen by Turkey," "NATO get off our land," "Imperialism is destroyed when oppressed nations struggle together," and "Steadfast cooperation between the Armenians and the Iranian Islamic Revolution." Other slogans were "Armenian fedayeen, continue on your path," "The supporters of Turkey are the enemy of the Armenian people," and "America is the enemy." At Ferdowsi Square, Muslims joined the demonstration carrying placards that read "We too condemn the 1915 massacres of the Armenians."

I saw some of those slogans displayed, but the ones with a leftist slant reminiscent of Tudeh's ideology were simply invented by the reporter. Yet that was tolerable for a people who had waited for more than half a century to bring their protest to the world.

A Sectarian Attack

As in the course of every revolution, the settling of accounts began soon after the victory and no one had any qualms about taking long-delayed revenge on individuals and institutions. In September 1979, a university professor named Shapour Bastani targeted Armenians and Jews in an opinion piece published in *Kayhan*:

Religious Minorities and Their Leadership in Today's Iran

The historical record shows that Jews and other minorities living as guests and refugees in Iran have enjoyed great respect, thanks to the hospitality of our ancestors. When the Ottoman Turks planned and carried out the Armenian massacres, killing hundreds of people a day, Iran was their sole refuge in the Middle East. It is well known that Iran has always been the best country for religious minorities. There have been a few insignificant exceptions, as when certain fanatics made offensive remarks about Jews and Armenians at various times. Setting those incidents aside, it must be acknowledged that people in neighboring countries or even in Europe have never been as welcoming toward minorities as they have been in Iran. Unfortunately, some of our minorities, particularly our beloved Jewish community, have not always responded to our hospitality with honor and respect.

A careful study of their conduct shows that they have enjoyed the blessings Iran has long extended to them even as they exhibit the attitudes of new immigrants. They avoid integrating with the majority and sometimes they show indifference to our traditions, our way of life and our family conventions, as if they were entirely separate from the Iranian people. It is painful to describe the behavior of some in these communities. During the Second World War, for example, when the Soviet army ignored Iranian neutrality and attacked our country, some Armenians welcomed their tanks with flowers. Many Iranians found that disturbing. It is important to remember individuals such as Yeprem Khan and others like him who also belong to this religious minority and who have nobly served the nation. Their service must always be acknowledged....

These people have taken the economic reins of the country into their hands, used every form of deceit, trafficked in illegal drugs and artificially inflated the market in order to accumulate their wealth on the backs of the impoverished majority. They pollute the minds of the people. They sponsor international symposia at Tehran University with budgets rivaling those of an oil company. They facilitate the infiltration of world Zionism into every stratum of our society. They have set up bank accounts to support Israel. We know that some of them consider Israel their homeland. They use the excuse of medical treatment to go there.

What is surprising today, when the light of Islamic justice has replaced the dark and despised justice of the former regime, is that numerous Jewish groups have sold their possessions and moved to Israel. They have transferred the wealth of the Iranian people to another country. But what is even more surprising is that the government has taken the stance of a neutral observer, watching the flight of millions of dollars a day at the hands of these rich Jews. The government has done nothing to stop this transfer. If all the rich Jews leave and only the poor Jews remain, Iran's economic future will be quite uncertain. The government must look into how much money these people have amassed and how they got it. The government must protect Iran's wealth and stop this transfer....

Inspired by the Koran and the true teachings of Islam, the Emam has chosen to overlook the dark past of the Jews and to keep them under Muslim protection. Perhaps they are unaware of the blessings of the current leadership in terms of reconstructing the country. If the minorities fail to take an active part in this reconstruction as faithful and obedient individuals of the Islamic Republic of Iran, I advise them to take the following precepts to heart, lest they become the target of vengeance on the part of the majority:

1. Follow our national and religious traditions more carefully and respectfully. Do not shun national celebrations merely because you are not Muslims.

2. Think of yourselves as true Iranians. Take pride in being Iranian instead of being part of a separate national group.

3. Be goodwill ambassadors of Iranian culture and civilization. Behave properly outside the country instead of exploiting its benevolence. Whenever Jews achieve fame and success, they identify with their own community. Whenever Armenians, God forbid, do something wrong abroad, they flash their Iranian passport. Instead of building private schools to avoid learning Persian, instead of widening the gap between yourselves and the Muslim majority, use your culture and traditions to further enrich Iranian culture.

5. Accept the limits established by the Islamic Republic for the people's well-being and do not characterize them as the precursors to dictatorship.

6. Cease making money through exploitation and illegality. Work honestly and faithfully for the betterment of the Islamic Republic of Iran. Always bear in mind the words of the Supreme Leader: "If the Islamic Revolution is stabilized and an Islamic Republic is established, God willing, the people at every level of society will achieve their aims and live a comfortable and happy life."

Professor Bastani's article provoked considerable anxiety in the Armenian community but no one spoke up. That concerned me, so I penned a response that was also published in *Kayhan*:

Most Respected Professor, Why Sow Discord between Muslims and Minorities?

The first qualification of a university professor is that his conclusions must be based on evidence produced by research and analysis. Unfortunately, your article contains no such thing. The issues you raise only escalate conflict and thereby contradict the teachings of Emam Khomeini who has always called for the unity and cooperation of the people.

You refer to minorities as "guests" and "refugees." This is unacceptable to Armenians. You emphasize Armenian immigration as a result of the Ottoman attempt to exterminate them, but you don't mention the fact that Armenians were living in Iran long before the massacres and that is why survivors chose Iran as a place of refuge. Armenians have always been grateful for Iranian hospitality.

You must admit that an entire nation cannot be cast in a single ideological mold. If a few Armenians welcomed Soviet tanks with flowers during the Second World War, that cannot be generalized to all Armenians.

Yeprem Khan was not the only Armenian who fought for freedom. If you study the history of earlier Iranian constitutional struggles and liberation movements, you will encounter many Armenian names. They fought to free Iran from the yoke of the Great Powers. After the events of August 19, 1953, many young Armenian men died on the street or in prison for the cause of freedom. In the past year alone, Armenians have taken an active part in the revolutionary struggle and given a disproportionate number of martyrs.

Wherever Armenians have lived, they have used their knowledge and faith to work for the country's progress and freedom. The monuments they have raised in Iran can be seen from the Arax River to the Persian Gulf. The names of Armenian engineers, architects, physicians and revolutionary leaders are well known to all Iranians.

You threaten minorities "lest they become the target of vengeance on the part of the majority." That suggests that Armenians are a useless minority and others should tell them how to behave. We consider that an insult to our community.

Dear Professor, Armenians have lived in Iran with their Muslim brothers for centuries and continue to do so today. We do not need your advice about respect for Iranian customs and traditions. We have always been with our Muslim brothers in times of sadness and in times of joy. I have to wonder where you got your information. Have Armenians ever trampled on the rights of Muslims? Have they ever given offense to the feelings of the majority? If you were in Tehran during the euphoric days of the Revolution, you must have seen young Armenian men taking part in the struggle, joining demonstrations, disabling tanks and losing their lives in the process. And still you threaten us with the vengeance of the majority? That threat comes from a minority and you are part of that minority.

Your second "precept" is that we Armenians must consider ourselves Iranians. That is already the case and we don't need an invitation to do so. We call ourselves Iranian Armenians and our attitudes and way of life are living proof of this.

Dear Professor, if you had bothered to study history, you would have known that some 350 years ago, thousands of Armenians were expelled from their homes and forced to immigrate to Isfahan. In the face of adversity, they played an important role in economic and cultural development during that era and since then they have helped defend the country's borders. If you had known these facts, you would not have laid such false charges against the Armenians.

You say that when minorities achieve success they do not identify as Iranians, and that when Armenians make a mistake they display their Iranian passport, yet you offer no evidence for this absurd slander. On the contrary, Armenians are known throughout the world for their honesty and loyalty. Armenians have been subjected to oppression and extermination for centuries and that is why they have developed an attitude of reverence.

You made certain statements about schools. I want to draw your attention to the fact that teaching and speaking the Armenian language is our most important and fundamental right, one that we can never give up. Our mother tongue is an important factor in our national existence, survival and unity. The Armenian language is essential to our religious life and to any attempt to understand the nature of our faith. A few hours of instruction in the mother tongue should not be such an annoyance to you, especially considering the fact that

Armenian students study Persian beginning in kindergarten and continuing through university. This right is specified in the draft Constitution and your comments stand in opposition to that principle.

You state that Armenians gain their income through illicit and illegal means. On the contrary, Armenians are known as hard-working, tough, correct and loyal individuals and it is obvious that honorable people do not earn a living by illegal means.

Dear Professor, I do not blame you for what you have written. We Armenians are to blame, because as a community with a 2000-year history in Iran, we have failed to make our culture and history known to our Muslim brothers. Because of extraordinary pressures and censorship in recent years, we have not had the opportunity to work seriously in this direction.

I hope that this succinct explanation will motivate you and other Muslim compatriots to adopt a better attitude toward the Armenian community. Respecting the words of Emam Khomeini who always emphasizes the unity of the Iranian people, together we can work to reconstruct a free and independent Iran.

If Bastani's article had gone unanswered, it would have given others license to cast aspersions on our nation. The Armenian community applauded my initiative and scores of people called to congratulate me. That was a turning point for me. Many of the people I know today had never heard of me before they read my letter in *Kayhan*. The most tangible result came the following spring when I ran for a seat in the Tenth Diocesan Assembly of Representatives and was elected with the highest number of votes.

The Hostage Crisis

Barely a week after the Shah arrived in Egypt in January 1979, he flew to Morocco, anticipating an official invitation to come to the United States, but after the brief occupation of the US Embassy in Tehran on February 14, no such invitation was forthcoming. The Shah moved on to the Bahamas and then Mexico. Unknown to the public, he was suffering from lymphatic cancer. When his health sharply deteriorated, President Carter relented and allowed him to enter the USA for surgery on October 22.

The Bazargan government was somewhat pro-American, but Iranian nationalists had not forgotten how America had forced the resignation of their beloved Prime Minister Mosadegh a quarter of a century earlier and solidly backed the Shah ever since. The clerics thought America would never accept an Islamic regime in Iran. Ayatollah Khomeini lambasted the USA, urging student activists to increase their attacks on American symbols in order to force the government to return the Shah to Iran.

"America is the source of all our problems," he railed. "Let the pen that defends the USA anywhere in the world be broken. Let the tongue that speaks for the USA be silenced!"

On November 4, my friend Shahen Haroutunian came to my office at around 11:00 AM and told me that crowds of young people were converging on the US Embassy. They appeared to be students but there were a few clerics among them. Several youths had climbed over the wall and opened the main gate. Hundreds had rushed in and now they were holding the staff hostage. The news spread rapidly throughout the world and all eyes were on Tehran.

Two days later, Emam Khomeini accepted Prime Minister Bazargan's resignation. The Provisional Government was dissolved and the Revolutionary Council took over the functions of government.

The hostage-takers called themselves Muslim Students Following the Line of the Emam (*Daneshjuyan-e Mosalman-e Peyrow-e Khatt-e Emam*). They had planned their action to mark the first anniversary of a military crackdown at Tehran University in which some three students had been killed. They issued a communiqué informing Emam Khomeini that after the Shah's army, with US support, had killed so many students, their patience was exhausted and they could no longer tolerate American scheming. Various political groups and Islamic organizations chimed in to support their just cause.

At first, they held more than a hundred captives, including a number of Iranian Armenians on the Embassy staff, but the locals were quickly released. Two weeks later, thirteen African American and white American female personnel were sent home. Six months later, a seriously ill vice-consul was sent home. That left fifty-two hostages for what turned out to be a very long haul.

Trawling through Embassy files and reconstituting piles of shredded documents, the students found evidence that some of their hostages were spies. They also found records of CIA contacts with current Iranian politicians which were selectively leaked to the press. Eventually they published over eighty volumes of these materials under the series title, *Asnad-e Laneh-ye Jasusi* (Documents from the Den of Espionage).

The Shah, after recuperating somewhat in the USA, was flown to Panama in December. There he remained for three months, still very ill, until the threat of extradition to Iran caused him to accept President Sadat's invitation to return to Egypt, and he flew to Cairo on March 23, 1980.

The Failed American Rescue Attempt

At dusk on April 24, six C-130 Hercules transport aircraft took off from Oman's Masira Island airbase. The passengers included over one hundred commandos from America's new Delta Force unit. Two hours later, eight Sea Stallion helicopters lifted off from the USS *Nimitz* in the Arabian Sea. Phase One of the operation called for all fourteen aircraft to fly under the radar and rendezvous before dawn at a landing site near Tabas in Iran's vast central desert. Phase Two called for the helicopters to fly the commandos to a hideout near Garmsar, some fifty miles southeast of Tehran, where they would lie low until sunset when local collaborators would drive them to the Embassy. The plan was to extract the hostages and herd them across the street to Amjadieh (now Shahid Shiroudi) Stadium, where the choppers would pick them up and ferry them to an airstrip about fifty miles south of Tehran. From there they would all be airlifted out of the country in huge C-141s.

En route to the desert landing site, however, two helicopters experienced technical difficulties. One was abandoned and the other flew back to the *Nimitz*. When a third helicopter failed at the rendezvous, the mission was aborted and all hands prepared to return to base. But in the process of refueling, two of the aircraft collided and burst into flames. Eight US servicemen lost their lives in the conflagration. If the operation had proceeded as planned, there surely would have been many more casualties on both sides.

After the failure of the rescue mission, the students dispersed the hostages to various locations. Archbishop Hilarion Capucci, formerly of Jerusalem, facilitated the return of the bodies of the dead to the USA. President Carter scaled back his re-election campaign. The Shah died in Cairo on July 27, and in September, Iran and the USA finally began secret negotiations. On November 4, Carter lost to the Republican challenger. The hostages were released immediately after the inauguration of President Ronald Reagan on January 20, 1981. They had been held for 444 days.

Chapter 11

The Struggle Over the Schools, 1980–81

After the Revolution, new political groups emerged within the Armenian community, most of them extreme leftists. They opposed the Prelate, the Diocesan Council, the Diocesan Assembly of Representatives, in short, they opposed the whole system of community administration, but first and foremost, they opposed the Armenian Revolutionary Federation which had dominated the community unchallenged for years. The ARF pervaded every aspect of Armenian life, including the schools, the grassroots organizations and the athletic and cultural centers, overshadowed only by SAVAK which had the community in such a stranglehold that it was impossible for any leftist groups to function. And the ARF more than any other organization was pleased with that state of affairs, but other organizations were not displeased. The Revolution had broken that stranglehold and now the opposition was growing by the day.

An ex-ARF member named Souren led the most extreme leftist group which was known as the *Sourenagans* (Souren's Followers). On November 26, 1979, the Diocesan Council was about to start its regular Monday night meeting when Souren asked the chairman, Dr. Vartkes Nahabedian, if his group could sit in on the meeting, and Dr. Nahabedian gave his consent. I wasn't a member of the Council at that time but Vigen Gevorkian, an engineer and a Council member who witnessed the scene, told me what happened. Souren brought in several hundred followers and took the floor before anyone could say a word. He accused the Council and its various committees of stealing the people's property, living off their wealth and ignoring their needs. Then he paused and respectfully suggested that Archbishop Manoukian retire to his office. Once the Prelate had left the room, Souren announced that the Council members were being held hostage. Then he paused again and ordered sandwiches brought in for the hostages. After that, he singled out each one of them for a barrage of vulgar accusations.

Meanwhile, the Prelate alerted the churches to what was happening and their bells started tolling the alarm. Around 1:00 AM, thousands of armed and anxious Armenians converged on the Prelacy, men and women, young and old. When some pasdars showed up, they were told that this was an internal matter and the community would settle it. People crowded into the main hall and filled it to overflowing. A young man came forward and announced that he and his group from *Alik* and the Ararat and Sipan Associations had come to rescue the hostages. Now the tables were turned. Souren tried to flee but he was caught and given a severe beating. Some people were ready to kill him but the Prelate came to the rescue and had him spirited out the back door and the confrontation came to an end.

Of course, the Sourenagans were aping the US Embassy operation three weeks earlier, but their action threw the entire community into crisis. Rumors started flying and many young people came out against the ARF and Antelias. They blamed the party for splitting the Iranian dioceses from Echmiadzin and attaching them to the Cilician See back in the 1950s. Leftist and other anti-ARF forces relentlessly attacked the party, the church and the community leadership. In this way, they were instrumental in bringing new blood into the community's elected bodies. The members of the Diocesan Council and the Diocesan Assembly were physically and emotionally drained. Accused of collaborating with the *ancien régime*, they were suspect in the eyes of the community, which was to be expected since the entire country was undergoing a transformation and the Armenian community was no exception. The Council applied to the Interior Ministry for permission to hold elections for the Tenth Diocesan Assembly and it was scheduled for the spring of 1980.

A friend of mine named Vachik Khachaturian, a well-known ARF partisan, came to my office and urged me to run for a seat. We talked it over and came to the conclusion that since we had not left the country and we had no intention of doing so, it was up to us to take charge. I declared myself a candidate from the St. Sarkis–Vanak electoral district where I was now living. The architect Dr. Armen Hakhnazarian and I got the most votes. At the first meeting of the new Assembly, Dr. Tadevos Karapetian and the architect Seroj Soukiassian, both prominent ARF members, were elected chair and vice-chair, respectively. Dr. Karapetian presided over our meetings with great skill, and Soukiassian, despite his youth, proved to be an able administrator.

Unlike its predecessors, the Tenth Diocesan Assembly included people with diverse political ideologies as well as politically unaffiliated intellectuals. There was a sense of give-and-take and the community followed its deliberations with great interest. The Representatives thoroughly reviewed every item on the agenda and put it to a vote. They revised the diocesan bylaws, taking the new political realities into account and attending to the smallest details, and in July they sent the updated bylaws to Antelias for approval. In short, the atmosphere was most conducive to serious community work.

The New Diocesan Council

At the end of that first Diocesan Assembly meeting on May 20, 1980, the Diocesan Council presented a report on its activities during the previous term and tendered its resignation, as was customary. The Diocesan Assembly then elected a new Diocesan Council as well as a new finance committee. I stood for election to the Council and won by a large number of votes, and at its first meeting, I was elected chairman. Little did I realize what a huge responsibility I was taking on. For some reason that remains a mystery to me, that Council was declared an acting or temporary body. Nevertheless, it carried out its work for six years, until July 1986. Its members were as follows:

Name	Position	Profession
Archbishop Ardak Manoukian	Ex Officio Member	Prelate
Levon Aharonian	Chairman	Chemist
Torgom Der Hagopian	Vice-Chairman	Architect
Eskandar Eskandarian	Treasurer	Skilled Craftsman
Hovik Haroutunian	Recording Secretary	Staff Member
Rafik Der Petrossian	Recording Secretary	Architect
Armen Hakhnazarian	Schools Liaison	Architect
Vagrig Manoukian	Schools Liaison	Engineer
Shahen Aboulian	Member	Engineer
Dr. Ardavazd Melikian	Member	Lawyer
Yeznik Shahbazian	Member	Skilled Craftsman
Khoren Der Vrouyrian	Member	School Principal

The member of the Majles who represented the Armenians of northern Iran always attended Council meetings, first Hrair Khalatian (1980–84) and later Vartan Vartanian (1984–2000). The meetings were recorded by Andranik Baghoumian, an individual of great kindness, patriotism and energy who carried out his duties with devotion for many years.

Before the Revolution, the Diocesan Council had dealt with national and religious concerns such as marriage and divorce, birth and baptism, death and burial, and education and the community schools. After the Revolution, the

Council got involved in all kinds of internal and external political issues, willingly or of necessity. On one side, new groups and organizations were challenging the old structures. On the other side, the Islamic government had very little knowledge of our community and started promulgating all kinds of rules and regulations that conflicted with our constitutional rights. No one serving on the new Council had ever served on a previous Council, but we were like a ring under pressure. We became stable and resilient, we endured and we overcame many obstacles.

Command of Persian was essential for the Council's public relations and written correspondence, yet despite the fact that we Armenians have lived in Iran for centuries, few of us are completely fluent in the language. Of course, I don't mean ordinary conversational Persian, but in order to write well, one must love the language and be steeped in its literature. Within the relatively small Armenian community, those attributes are found mostly among lawyers. In the beginning, Dr. Ardavazd Melikian was responsible for drafting all of our letters, but when he emigrated, he left a gaping hole in our work. We searched for quite some time before we found an accomplished young lawyer endowed with many talents.

Aida Avanessian (Hovhannisian) had studied law at Tehran University and was fluent in Persian, Armenian and English. Her direct and witty approach won the respect of everyone she met. She worked with the well-known attorney, Dr. Jaleh Shambayati. Her extraordinary abilities became fully evident following the resolution of the hostage crisis when she served as one of the advocates for the Iranian side in the litigation of commercial claims at The Hague. She later earned a doctoral degree in international law from King's College, University of London, based on her study, *The Iran–United States Claims Tribunal in Action*, published in 1993. She also oversaw the posthumous publication of a treatise by her late mentor and colleague, Dr. Parviz Owsia, titled *Formation of Contract: A Comparative Study under English, Islamic and Iranian Law*, in 1994. She began work with the Council in an official capacity in April 1981 and has continued to play an important role in Armenian community life in Iran. As of this writing, she was serving as chair of the Diocesan Council and her term has been characterized by professionalism and competence.

The first item on new Diocesan Council's agenda was to ask the government to let the Ararat Association's scout groups visit Armenia. Permission was granted and as a result, hundreds of Iranian Armenian youths would visit Armenia in the coming years. Next, we decided to send a letter of protest to President Bani-Sadr on behalf of a youth from Darya Kenar who had been whipped for drinking alcohol. Our third decision was to place an announcement in *Alik*, inviting all those who were interested to apply for membership on the Council's various committees. Fourthly, we discussed the situation at Soukerian Hall in Majidiyeh, where the newly established Hrazdan Association had set up an office and seemed to consider the hall its exclusive domain. We decided to solicit proposals from Majidiyeh's neighborhood committee for the best uses of the hall. Finally, we decided to invite the Chief Superintendent of Schools, Mr. Khoshnevisan, to the Prelacy to discuss the situation of the Armenian schools.

The Council's work moved along at a steady pace for two months until July when we learned that a group of students had vandalized Ararat Boys School in Majidiyeh and destroyed the electrical system. Four of us including Archbishop Manoukian went to assess the damage. I was shocked by what I saw. How could students desecrate a holy site where the Armenian language was taught, one of the founts of our people's endurance?

From Ararat School we went to Soukerian Hall where we were received by local residents. The Prelate introduced us and expressed his deep sorrow at the damage done to the school. Our hosts had set out a light repast of pastries and sliced watermelon. At the end of the table sat the remaining half-watermelon. We were invited to partake, and afterwards, as we were leaving, we heard a loud smash. We turned around and saw a young man glaring at us. He had pushed the half-melon off the table, and having grabbed our attention, he told us in a voice full of rage that it had been purchased with stolen funds and should not be eaten. I sensed what poisonous attitudes were at work in our neighborhoods and wondered how an Armenian youth could bring such grief to the Prelate who was such a source of stability in those trying times. Unfortunately, we struggled for years against such misguided and ill-informed elements.

The Beginning of Trouble for Armenian Schools

When Chief Superintendent Khoshnevisan arrived at the Prelacy, Archbishop Manoukian welcomed him on behalf of the Diocesan Council and began our discussion by explaining that the Armenian Church and Armenian schools are independent of the Vatican. This was important because the government had recently shut down the Vatican-sponsored Andishe School for "preaching Christianity" to its students. We covered all the issues that would roil our schools for the next four years and more: ownership and control, hiring and firing, Armenian language instruction and religious education, student access to the school of their choice, and the use of school facilities for extracurricular activities.

When the Prelate mentioned that the Armenian Church was tolerant of co-educational schooling and that the community was disturbed by the prospect of segregating their schools, the Chief Superintendent responded that all Iranian students must attend gender-segregated schools. A Council member remarked that that would certainly cause a shortage of qualified teachers. Khoshnevisan replied,

"If you teach Armenian six hours per week instead of twelve, you'll have a surplus!"

When the Prelate told him that our schools had all been built with funds donated by private benefactors or by the community as a whole, Khoshnevisan said the very idea of separate minority schools was irrelevant now and we should sell or donate our schools to the Ministry of Education. Besides, he said, they should teach the "language of religion" (by which he meant Arabic) rather than Armenian. He reiterated that the government would never allow co-ed schooling, but he also said we were welcome to visit him at the Ministry for further discussion. The meeting lasted two hours. Its tone and content portended great challenges to come.

Subsequently, the Diocesan Council sent a delegation to meet with Khoshnevisan in his office and they worked out a draft agreement to the following terms:

- The Armenian community would retain ownership of its schools while the government would take financial responsibility for repairs.
- The Council would appoint school principals and vice-principals and oversee instruction in language and religion.
- There would be twelve hours of Armenian language instruction per week in elementary school, ten in middle school, and six in high school, and grades in these classes would carry the same weight as grades in any other course.
- Students would not be required to enroll in the school nearest their home, and only Armenian students would be allowed to enroll in Armenian schools.

- The Islamic dress code was not a problem since our girls had always worn modest clothing in accordance with Armenian tradition.
- The Council's right to organize extracurricular activities for students and their parents was recognized.
- And finally, the Council was given until the start of the new school year to reorganize co-educational Armenian schools as gender-segregated institutions.

We were satisfied with these terms and awaited confirmation from Khoshnevisan, but two weeks went by and we heard nothing, so we wrote him a fifteen-page letter reiterating the details of our agreement. Still we had no response.

Thus we were taken aback when Khoshnevisan sent us an official Ministry of Education circular rolling back key provisions in our draft agreement. Effective immediately, all privately owned schools were to be sold or donated to the Ministry. Religion could be taught in the Armenian language in Armenian schools, but the Armenian language itself could not! Students were required to enroll in the school nearest their home, and most worrisome of all, if enrollment in a particular class failed to reach one-third of capacity, that class would be canceled. The implications of all this were very serious indeed. Armenian neighborhoods were scattered across the city and our schools did not have the capacity to accommodate every student in their particular vicinity. In Majidiyeh, for example, there was a large Armenian population but no high school for girls, so they went to the Mariamian School for Girls on Sheikh Hadi Street downtown, which was three miles away. And if classes were canceled due to low enrollment, students would walk away from our schools, and in one generation our community would be Armenian in name only.

Word of these new policies spread quickly and threw the community into a major crisis. Scores of Armenians called the Prelacy every day and they all asked the same question: What will become of our schools?

Meeting with Chief Justice Ayatollah Beheshti

Motivated by this question, the Diocesan Council asked for a meeting with Chief Justice Ayatollah Beheshti. He gave us an appointment for July 30, 1980. Our delegation consisted of Archbishop Manoukian, Bishop Goriun Papian, the Prelate of Isfahan, MP Khalatian and MP Khachaturian, and several Council members including myself. Dr. Beheshti gave us a warm welcome and was especially cordial toward the Archbishop. He told us that he was quite well informed about Christians, having spent six years in Hamburg where he had headed the Emam Ali Mosque and Islamic Center. The Archbishop described the new restrictions on our schools and asked the Chief Justice to help lift them. Dr. Beheshti turned to an aide and instructed him to place a call. After a ten-minute phone conversation, he hung up and thanked us for our patience. He assured us that the Armenian community would retain ownership of its schools, that they were free to teach the Armenian language and Armenian religious studies, that the requirement that students enroll in the school nearest their home was void, and that Islamic dress would not be mandatory in our schools. The only issue on which we failed to persuade him to our view was gender-segregation. That policy was mandatory nationwide and there would be no exceptions. He brought the meeting to a close by asking Archbishop Manoukian to convey his best wishes to his Armenian brothers and sisters and added,

"Let us work hand in hand to support our country's development and prosperity."

Although it wasn't an unqualified success, at least the meeting put an end to uncertainty and minimized the harm our community would have suffered if Khoshnevisan's directives had been implemented. We immediately sent an announcement to *Alik* and distributed thousands of leaflets in the community. Council members made frequent visits to the schools to keep the students and their parents informed. But because we remained skeptical of government promises, we sent the minutes of our meeting with Chief Justice Beheshti to *Alik* and to Chief Superintendent Khoshnevisan.

Restructuring the Schools

Two-thirds of some thirty Armenian community schools were financially administered by the Diocesan Council. Each school was supervised by a Parents Council whose members had children attending the school. Their work was coordinated by the Central Board of School Trustees, all of whom were dedicated, hard-working community members.

At that time, our schools employed 455 people, including 178 regular faculty, 110 adjunct teachers, 99 support staff and 68 maintenance workers. The preponderance of elementary school teachers were women, but the faculty was more nearly gender-balanced in the middle and high schools. Persian was the primary medium of instruction, but for religious education classes, our schools all used the same Armenian-language textbooks published by the Diocese.

During this period of crisis, private schools that were not owned by the Prelacy, such as the Armenian Catholic Alishan School and the Armenian Protestant Gohar School, agreed to join the network of schools under Diocesan Council administration. The Council immediately set about reorganizing the network according to the new mandate. We formed a committee to prepare the staffs for the great upheaval and restructured twenty-three co-ed schools as gender-segregated institutions, and all this was accomplished before the start of the 1980–81 school year.

In 1980, there were nearly 16,000 Armenian students in Tehran: 14,577 in our community schools, 320 in our kindergartens and 1100 in government-run schools. In 2005, I asked Edward Babakhanian, then-chairman of the Diocesan Council's education committee, for the most recent data on student numbers. Oddly enough, there were more children in our pre-schools and kindergartens, but the number of students in our middle and high schools was half the number in 1980–81, which suggested that the size of the community was decreasing as well. That was a worrying trend: it meant that future generations would face increasing difficulty in protecting our community's rights, especially in the area of education.

In this uncertain environment, a number of unpleasant incidents further soured the situation. The supervisor of schools in the third district decided to prevent Armenians from enrolling in Aram School which the community had built and maintained. The Council lodged a formal complaint with the Ministry of Education, without result. We were forced to file suit and Bayar and Aida Hovhannisian vigorously argued our case. The supervisor alleged that Armenian students were scheming to sell *aragh* (araq) on campus. We lost the case and we lost the school, and to this day, the government has not paid the community one cent in compensation.

Meeting with Education Minister Ayatollah Bahonar

After the resignation of the Provisional Government the previous November, Deputy Minister of Education Mohammad Ali Rajai (a protégé of Ayatollah Bahonar, as mentioned earlier) had stepped into the position of Minister of Education, and after Dr. Bani-Sadr was elected President in January, he struggled with the Majles over the composition of his cabinet until he was ultimately forced to accept Rajai as his Prime Minister. Rajai in turn appointed his mentor, Ayatollah Bahonar, as Minister of Education. The

Diocesan Council already had an appointment to meet with Ayatollah Bahonar in November 1980 when we learned that students at Koushesh High School for Girls had gone on strike to demand the resignation of their Ministry-appointed principal for making derogatory comments about Armenians. Our delegation was headed by Archbishop Manoukian and included Vahik Khachaturian, the chairman of the Central Board of School Trustees, Vagrig Manoukian, the Council's liaison to the schools, and myself. Ayatollah Bahonar was an erudite and gracious *mojtahed* (trained theologian) who welcomed us warmly. The first thing he said was that he was aware of the conflict at Koushesh School and that he had already fired the principal. Then he patiently heard us out. Finally, he wrote "Armenian schools" on a piece of paper, circled the words and said we were free to administer our schools as we wished. Very much impressed by his attitude, we left the meeting in high spirits. Unfortunately, his assassination nine months later put paid to our hopes.

We continued to seek meetings with the highest government officials in an effort to resolve the situation of our schools. We were given an appointment with President Bani-Sadr but were met instead by his chief of staff, Mr. Zanjani, the thirty-five-year-old son of a well-known cleric. Having been raised in the West, Zanjani was surprised to hear about our problems and promised to discuss the situation with the President. Then he asked how our neighborhoods were protected and whether we had our own police force.

"Armenians are protected by the municipal police, like other citizens," I replied, "but we aren't allowed to serve on the force."

That surprised him too and he told his aide to take a note. To us he said he would recommend that the President allow the Armenian community to have its own police force. After we left the meeting, we started laughing. The naïveté of this well-intentioned young man exemplified the gulf between the technocratic President and his clerical opposition. Twenty years later, Zanjani called me out of the blue. He wanted a refrigerated truck to haul apples to Russia! Yesterday's technocrat was today's international trader.

Responding to Challenges from the Armenian Left

The Diocesan Council met at the Prelacy twice a week, on Mondays and Wednesdays, and every time we met, the Sourenagans demonstrated outside in the courtyard, shouting slogans against the ARF and the community leadership. We sent representatives out to try and start a dialogue but they responded with insults and blew them off. After that, we stopped trying to negotiate with Souren and his group.

The Council's most urgent problem was our community schools and the right to teach the Armenian language. The Ministry of Education had left us in suspense and we were told that the government was developing a minorities policy. We had no choice but to wait and carry on with our work. We undertook a round of regular visits to the schools in order to keep the teachers, parents and students abreast of developments. Archbishop Manoukian headed our delegations which often included MP Khalatian. The first time I spoke publicly was at the Sahakian School in Heshmatiyeh. Afterwards, as we were driving back to the Prelacy in my car, the Prelate said my talk was very effective. I didn't take him too seriously. I felt he was trying to encourage me. He was a very generous and capable religious leader.

These community meetings were always attended by generally left-leaning groups who were opposed to the ARF, the Cilician See, the Diocesan Council and community structures across the board. In Heshmatiyeh, a community organization called Erebouni (formerly the Shah Aziz Sports and Culture Association) took a milder and more intelligent position and the Council tried hard not to antagonize them. They lacked a meeting place of their own and former MP Emma Aghayan was instrumental in providing them with a community center.

In 1983, another group of young people in Heshmatiyeh started the Sardarabad Association. Later, they renamed their neighborhood Sardarabad. At first, they met in private homes, but a couple years later, the Diocesan Council and the Alik Foundation, with the assistance of Minas Hovannissian, bought a property for the organization and helped develop it into a vibrant center of cultural and athletic activity used by residents of both Heshmatiyeh and Vahidiyeh.

In Majidiyeh, the Hrazdan Association continued to monopolize Soukerian Hall. An Armenian philanthropist had set up a trust fund to build the hall and the terms of the trust stipulated that it was for the use of all the Armenians in the neighborhood, yet Hrazdan never missed an opportunity to assert its ownership. They distributed Persian-language leaflets in which they claimed to be the sole champion of Armenian students' rights, and they put up bilingual posters vilifying the members of the Diocesan Council. For example, they said I was a capitalist who knew nothing about democracy and was incapable of understanding the people's just demands.

Another organization in Majidiyeh was the Abovian Association set up by Souren of Sourenagan fame. He never missed an opportunity to attack the Diocesan Council or any other Armenian organization. Of course, his main target was the ARF, but he did a lot of damage to the community as a whole. When the Council was negotiating with Chief Superintendent Khoshnevisan, the Abovian Association distributed Persian-language leaflets in which they accused the Council of diverting 15 million tomans (approximately $2 million) in school funds to the ARF. Much worse was their proposal to replace the Central Board of School Trustees with local governing committees, which would have meant dismantling the financial and administrative structures that our community had built up over many years of hard work and hard-earned experience.

In Narmak, the Sipan Sports and Cultural Association had been founded in 1963 by a group of ARF members led by Norair Elsaian. With funds from the Alik and the Gulbenkian Foundations, they had purchased a vacant lot and built a one-story building which they later expanded into an all-purpose community center. In addition to athletics, Sipan sponsored scout troops, a theatrical division, two choirs and the Paruyr Sevak Library.

One day, the Diocesan Council was invited to Holy Translators Church in Narmak to update the community on the situation of our schools. When I arrived with several other Council members at 5:00 PM, there was already a large crowd in the courtyard, and the leaders of Sipan were there too. I gave a detailed report on the work we were doing and then took questions from the audience. A number of young men repeatedly asked for clarifications on my report, compelling me to dig deep into my personal experience for answers. The discussion was gradually politicized and derailed as they pressed me on Council activities going way back before my tenure. I felt they were trying to intimidate me and undermine the very purpose of the meeting. It went on for three hours and I answered every question put to me, until finally the leaders of Sipan brought the meeting to a close.

There were two brothers who had left the pro-ARF Sipan Association to establish their own organization that was known as the *Agnotsavor* (Those Who Wear Spectacles) because they both wore glasses, but they quickly disappeared from the scene and did no harm to the Council.

Another organization in Narmak was the Sanahin Association. It joined forces with several smaller groups to pressure the Diocesan Council to lean on the Ararat Association to let them use the athletic facilities at the Ararat

Center in Vanak, but that was impossible. Ararat was a well-run organization and it was under no obligation to allow access to any other community organization. In September 1980, certain people affiliated with Sanahin raised questions about the income generated by the Pan-Armenian Games, a nationwide event organized by the Ararat Association every year since 1967. The issue became so complicated that the Council reluctantly decided to suspend the games that year and Ararat complied with our decision.

A third sports and cultural association in Narmak was the Raffi Union, founded in 1979 and inspired by the great novelist's observation that "community is the essence of all things." Characterizing itself as an independent organization that kept out of party politics and relied solely on its members and supporters for funding, the group developed a wonderful community center on an acre-and-a-half property that now has all the facilities and equipment for soccer, basketball, volleyball, gymnastics and other sports, as well as conferences, cultural activities and administrative office space. I only got to know the organization years later when the president of Raffi's board, Petros Abcarian, gave me a tour of the complex. I was very impressed.

Trouble with the IAMM

The community organization that posed the most serious challenge to the Diocesan Council was the Iranian-Armenian National and Cultural Association (*Iranahay Azgayin yev Mshagutayin Miutune*), known by its acronym, IAMM. *Mshaguyt* (Culture), its predecessor organization, was originally founded in 1944 and used to work out of the Sepehr School building near St. Mary's Church. One of its supporters was the much-loved singer Hovannes Badalian who still lived in Tehran in those days. The organization folded within a few years for political and other reasons, but after the Islamic Revolution, its supporters revived it with a host of new activities that attracted left-wing and communist artists and intellectuals and significantly increased its membership. The IAMM had ample resources, with offices adjacent to the left-wing weekly *Pyunik* (Phoenix) in a building owned by Vardan Aloumian, a wealthy Armenian leftist, on Somayyeh (formerly Soraya) Street, a few blocks northeast of its original downtown location.

Several impartial and well-meaning Diocesan Council supporters – including Tomas (Babig) Tomassian and Janet Lazarian – knew some of the people on the IAMM's executive board and they offered to arrange a meeting where we could iron out our misunderstandings. The Council agreed to meet without preconditions and we met in my office. Torgom Der Hagopian and I represented the Council while the IAMM sent two representatives, one of whom was a tall, handsome young man named Vahag. Babig and Janet attended the first meeting and made the introductions. After the usual exchange of pleasantries, as we were about to get down to business, I asked Vahag if he liked dolma. He was taken aback – perhaps he thought I was hallucinating – but he quickly recovered his composure and politely replied,

"Yes, I like dolma very much."

"So do I," I said, stretching out my hand in a gesture of friendship. "That means we're both imbued with the Armenian spirit and we share the same tastes. Thus we agree on the first issue raised between us."

Over the next two days, we spent six hours together, from 9:00 AM to noon, working behind closed doors with the phone off the hook. We analyzed the social, educational and cultural structures of our community and reached agreement on some issues but agreed to disagree on others. Finally, we drafted a memorandum of understanding. When it came to signing the final draft, however, Vahag said he had to get his party's approval. I asked him which party he belonged to, and he replied,

"The Tudeh."

"The two parties engaged here are the IAMM and the National Prelacy," I told him. "We cannot sign an agreement with a political party that advocates internationalism."

That put an end to our dialogue and we parted with nothing to show for it. I later learned that Vahag was a KGB officer based in East Germany who was sent wherever there was political turmoil that had a direct bearing on the interests of the Soviet Union. That explained why he had suddenly turned up in our community and disappeared just as quickly and mysteriously as he had come.

Other than those mentioned above, the Diocesan Council had no problems with Armenian community organizations and we did our best not to rock the boat.

My Relationship with the ARF

Meanwhile, significant internal changes were taking place in the Armenian Revolutionary Federation. Most of the previous leadership had either left the country or soon would, leaving the party in a state of uncertainty. As younger members rose to replace them, they rejuvenated the party and brought it out of its inertia and confusion. I kept my distance from the party and its internal problems, but once in a while a veteran activist would confide in me that the younger generation was not only taking over the reins of leadership but had it in for the old guard.

Nationwide, the left was in the ascendancy and leftists were filling important positions in key government ministries. Armenian leftists were gaining ground too, and although their struggle was mainly against the ARF, those with government jobs never missed an opportunity to cast aspersions on the party. It got so bad that party members took to concealing their affiliation. Whenever the Diocesan Council contacted officials in the Interior Ministry's Department of Minority Affairs, they would brazenly refer to so-and-so as an ARF member or sympathizer which, in their view, was code for American agent. The Council's situation was complicated by the fact that whenever we met with government officials, our delegation usually included at least one party member.

One time when we met with Mr. Giveian, an official in the Minority Affairs Department, our delegation included Vagrig Manoukian and myself from the Diocesan Council and Seroj Soukiassian, the vice-chairman of the Diocesan Assembly. Giveian made a derogatory comment about the ARF which provoked Soukiassian to say that he was proud to be a member. Giveian upped the ante by saying the ARF was blowing the Genocide out of all proportion. Soukiassian responded with an Iranian proverb: *Mar gazideh az risman siyah ow sefid mitarsid* (A man who has been bitten by a snake is afraid of a black and white rope). His remark was unseemly and later I asked Archbishop Manoukian not to include such bold characters in future meetings with government officials.

As a member of the Diocesan Council, I was on very good terms with the leaders of the ARF and with individual members, which was as it should be since we needed their support. Our purpose was to serve the community and protect and sustain our religious, educational and cultural institutions and we knew the ARF shared the same purpose. Of course there were disagreements, but these were motivated by personal differences.

Many of my childhood friends were party activists and I often ran into them at social gatherings, but we never discussed political affiliations. Naturally, I had friends on the left as well as on the right, but we all respected each other, regardless of ideology. My own ideology is based on love of nation. Service to culture is one of the most sacred of national duties. One of the ways to serve the nation is to help preserve its national and community systems and institutions. That was why I joined the Diocesan Council, and as a member of the Council I found a labor of love. My character is such that I must love what I am doing, otherwise it is of no interest to me, even though it may bring prestige or financial gain.

When I was a boy, I had a good friend named Grigor (Gougoush) Gharabegian. Gougoush had injured his knee and he couldn't walk. He was ultimately cured with fish oil by a folk osteopath from Salmas, but while he was incapacitated, we never left him alone. His older brother Vachik would occasionally drop in to say hello and exchange a few words with us kids. In those days, Vachik was already an ARF activist. Many years later when we were both living in Farmaniyeh, our children became friends and we got to know each other better. By then, the difference in our ages didn't matter and we became good friends. It was because of our friendship that he had asked me to lend a hand in 1977 when Ararat FC was in financial crisis.

After the Revolution, social interaction among Armenian families intensified. I often met Vachik Gharabegian at gatherings hosted by our mutual friend, Vachik Khachaturian. Gharabegian praised the Diocesan Council's work and told me privately that I should let him know if the Council ever wanted to deal directly with the ARF. In time, we began to meet monthly. Dr. Sampson Stepanian later joined our meetings and Dr. Vartkes Nahabedian came twice. By then, my family was living abroad because of the Iran-Iraq War and I was usually alone. I started cooking for myself, and at the risk of sounding immodest, I became an excellent chef. I would invite my friends over for dinner and we would share a few drinks, conversation and laughs. We also discussed whatever community problems cropped up. Thanks to their vast experience in community organizing, our discussions had a very positive impact on relations between the ARF and the Diocesan Council.

For example, I asked Dr. Nahabedian how come his party couldn't preempt the Hrazdan Association in Majidiyeh. He confessed that the ARF had a weak presence in the neighborhood but said they were thinking about starting a new community organization there. Not long afterwards, the Nayiri Armenian Cultural Association came into being. The Diocesan Council granted it free use of a property with a large hall and a basketball court. As for the Hrazdan Association, it didn't survive very long because it lacked a firm organizational footing.

Vartan Kamalian was an extreme nationalist member of the ARF who had braved the party line by declaring himself a candidate for the northern Armenian seat in the First Islamic Majles, and for that the party expelled him. The ARF backed Hrair Khalatian and of course he won. Kamalian ran a cooperative in Narmak that sold cheap goods and made small loans. When he asked the Diocesan Council for a personal loan, we turned him down, but the next time I saw Vachik Gharabegian, he urged me to reconsider. In the end, the Council lent Kamalian 200,000 tomans (about $25,000), which he soon paid back.

In 1982, Gharabegian told me that the ARF wanted to establish the Armenian Research Center in Tehran. This organization, known by its Armenian acronym, HOOSK, was a branch of the Armenian Cause (*Hay Dad*) which was devoted to research and documentation on the Genocide. HOOSK needed a place to work and Gharabegian asked me to allocate some office space in the Gabrielian Building on old Takht-e Tavous Street (now Ostad Motahhari Avenue), which the Diocesan Council had recently acquired from an expatriate Armenian millionaire. I took his proposal to the Council and they examined it and accepted my recommendation to accommodate the organization.

Fending Off Gender Segregation

The Diocesan Council always paid particular attention to Armenian sports organizations and the most important ones were Ararat in Vanak, Erebouni (Shah Aziz) in Heshmatiyeh, Hrazdan in Majidiyeh (for a while), Sardarabad in Vahidiyeh, Sipan and Raffi in Narmak, and the IAMM downtown. Not all of them had their own community centers and the Council allowed them to use the athletic facilities of local Armenian schools during off-hours whenever possible.

In the fall of 1981, the Majles passed a series of laws ordering gender segregation in public places, from swimming pools to wedding halls. Even public transportation was segregated and women were obliged to sit in the back. This caused great consternation in our community. Not only was the separation of the sexes alien to our traditions and conventions, but we lacked the resources to fully segregate our facilities. Moreover, it would have isolated our young men and women from each other and that would have had dire consequences.

Ararat and Sipan were the only legally registered Armenian sports organizations at the time and they were asked by the Department of Physical Education to propose language for new legislation ordering gender segregation in sports. On November 3, 1981, the Diocesan Council sent a deputation of five to meet with the director and his deputy: Albert Bernardi and myself represented the Council, Norair Melkonian and Golia Jaghabegian represented Ararat, and Seroj Soukiassian represented Sipan. We presented a detailed picture of the social and cultural attributes of our community and asked that the legislation make specific allowances for Armenian sports organizations. We also hand-delivered a letter asking that the status of religious minorities be clearly defined and emphasizing the fact that the land on which the facilities of Ararat and Sipan were located belonged to and was legitimately administered by the Armenian community's legal religious authority. I followed up with another letter and we also met with the Prime Minister's chief of staff on November 29. Because of our united stand and timely appeals, our efforts were successful in that the internal operations of Armenian as well as non-Armenian community organizations were minimally affected by the new laws.

Tehran Armenian Diocesan Council, including Archbishop Ardak Manoukian and the representative of Armenians in northern Iran, Vartan Vartanian.

The consecration of the site for a new church at Ali Abad village in Gorgan.

With Archbishop Goriun Papian, Der Bagrad Melkonian, Head of Azerbaijan province and me at the cemetery of Salmas, Payajuk on renown Armenian writer, Raffi's mother's grave.

Author with member of parliament from northern Iran, Vartan Vartanian.

With Archbishop Ardak Manoukian, Lar.

Greeting ARF Bureau Member Hrair Maroukhian.

In Beirut with Dr. Dasnabedian and Samuel Saroukhanian.

(Sitting right to left) The publisher of the daily Alik, Albert Ajemian; Hrair Maroukhian; Archbishop Ardak Manoukian; Member of Parliament Vartan Vartanian; and editor of Alik Norair Elsaian.

Four delegates at the National Council, Antelias (Lebanon).

With the president of the Islamic Republic of Iran, Ayatollah Khamenei. Hrair Khalatian *(left)*, Archbishop Ardak Manoukian *(second from left)*, author *(right)*.

With the speaker of the Speaker of the Iranian Parliament Hashemi-Rafsanjani, Archbishop Ardak Manoukian, and Hrair Khalatian.

With Armenian soldiers conscripted during the Iran-Iraq War.

A group of Armenian craftsmen preparing to leave for the front during the Iran-Iraq War.

Hojatoleslam Karroubi, Archbishop Ardak Manoukian, MP Vartan Vartanian and author at a remembrance ceremony dedicated to Armenian martyrs in the Iran-Iraq War.

My contribution at the memorial.

Chapter 12

The Iran-Iraq War and Civil Society

In September 1980, Sati was getting ready to pick up a 140-ton transformer and a 240-ton generator at Khorramshahr port. They were destined for Ahvaz No. II Power Plant. The situation was shaky because clashes along the border with Iraq had been escalating all summer and everyone was waiting for the big war to start. Our bogies were still on the way to the port when the ship came in two days ahead of schedule. On September 22, when Iraqi forces crossed the border at Schalamche, only ten miles upriver from Khorramshahr, the captain told us that unless we took delivery immediately, he would put out to sea and discharge our cargo in a neutral port, which he had a right to do under the laws of war. We couldn't allow such expensive equipment to be diverted, so I called Tavanir and they advised us to ask the Customs Service to embargo the ship. We did and it worked. Our bogies arrived the next day, took delivery and headed out.

Two days later, the Iraqis launched their attack on Khorramshahr. Mardiros Keshishian, the manager of our local office, called to tell me the city was being shelled and people were fleeing. I told him to take his family and leave immediately. Khorramshahr was only occupied after four weeks of street fighting, but it was almost completely destroyed. Meanwhile, Iraq was preparing the siege of Abadan a few miles downriver. There they met with stiff resistance from the Army, the Navy, the Sepah and the residents, and they never did succeed in occupying the island oil town.

Iranian military capabilities had been considerably weakened since the Revolution. Hundreds of professional officers had been retired or executed. The traditional Army had been reduced to half its prerevolutionary strength, while the Islamic Revolutionary Guards Corps was still only a small force of 30,000 or so. In July 1980, a conspiracy of royalist Air Force officers had nearly pulled off a coup d'état. The so-called Nojeh Uprising was reportedly uncovered after a tip-off from Tudeh infiltrators. Some 600 officers were court-martialed and 150 were executed. Iraq took advantage of the disarray in the Air Force to hit western Iranian cities with its long-range missiles.

As soon as the invasion began, Emam Khomeini addressed the nation. The war was a "blessing" (*barakat*) in his eyes. He called it an "imposed war" (*jang-e tahmili*) and urged the people to wage a "just war" (*jang-e haq*) in defense of the country. Thousands of men of all ages volunteered to fight. Khomeini initially entrusted President Bani-Sadr with the defense portfolio, but as Supreme Leader, he himself was still Commander-in-Chief.

The Diocesan Council set up emergency medical clinics in Armenian neighborhoods and distributed information about safety precautions. The government advised the public on how to take shelter from bombs and told them, above all, to keep the lights off at night. Oftentimes a blackout was ensured by a power cut. As a result, Iranian cities lay in total darkness at night for eight long years.

At first, people were in the grip of confusion, but they gradually got used to the war. Thousands spent the night on the street or camped out in the big *maidans* (squares). Many people slept huddled against the walls of the Soviet Embassy, hoping that it was safe because Saddam Hussein was a Soviet client.

When we went to bed at night, we often wondered whether we would wake up in the morning, and when we woke up and were getting ready for work, we wondered whether we would make it home that night. One morning, I was looking out the window and suddenly I saw a row of buildings disappear one by one in a cloud of dust. The blast was so powerful that my bedroom rocked and shuddered. Fifteen minutes later, when I opened my eyes, I was devastated by what I saw outside. One afternoon when I was driving home from work, a rocket fell near my car. I saw a young woman running here and there, madly screaming. I quickly made her get into my car and drove her to her home. Another day, I was driving to work when I saw two Armenian priests waiting for a taxi near my office. I stopped and asked them to get in, saying I would take them wherever they wanted to go. There was no need to introduce myself since all the priests in Tehran knew me. We chatted as I drove toward Maidan-e Emam Hossein. They said I could drop them off at the square since they didn't want to take any more of my time. I stopped, they got out, and I turned around to head back to the office. I hadn't finished turning when I heard a powerful blast and my car bucked so wildly that I lost control of the wheel. I looked back and saw how close the explosion had been. Fortunately, the priests were unhurt.

The Armenian Community's Contribution to the War Effort

The Iranian Armenians of Khuzestan were a generally prosperous community, but everything they had worked for all their lives was destroyed in a matter of days. Two Armenian churches were bombed in Abadan and Ahvaz, several Armenians were killed, scores were injured and the rest ran for their lives. They had to leave their homes and their hometowns and seek refuge with relatives and community organizations far from the front line. The Diocesan Council used every resource at its disposal to help them. Our food and medical aid committees were on call twenty-four hours a day, ready to assist the needy and treat the wounded.

The Council saw three ways to encourage the community to support the troops. First, we set up a special account at a bank near the Prelacy and placed the following notice in *Alik*:

> Dear Compatriots: As you all know, Iran is facing an imposed war. In this critical period, all Iranians are united in defense of the motherland. As citizens of Iran, we too must take responsibility for the noble task of defending the country's unity. We plan to contribute generously to these aims and therefore we ask you, respected compatriots, to respond wholeheartedly to our appeal. Contributions can be made to the account opened by the Diocesan Council at the Villa Street branch of Saderat Bank. A committee composed of representatives of all community organizations has been created in order to expedite this fundraising effort. We are confident that you will make great sacrifices to support the soldiers who are fighting for the security and the territorial integrity of Iran. We urge you to contribute as generously as you can to the defense of the Iranian homeland.
>
> Archbishop Ardak Manoukian, Prelate of the Tehran Diocese
> Levon Aharonian, Chairman of the Diocesan Council of Tehran

That campaign raised a substantial sum in little over a year. Second, we purchased machinery and equipment at cost-price and delivered it free of charge. Third, we appealed to Armenian mechanics and technicians and arranged for them to set up workshops behind the lines where they repaired damaged aircraft, vehicles and other equipment free of charge. It was during this period that the Iranian-Armenian Craftsmen's Association was founded to train young technicians. Council treasurer Eskandar Eskandarian oversaw the complex logistics of this volunteer operation and wrote a memoir about his experience. Unfortunately, he died before it could be published.

Scores of Armenian doctors and nurses joined the government medical teams that were sent to the front. They also treated casualties that were brought back to hospitals in Tehran. One morning at about 2:00 AM, I got a call from Andranik Baghoumian, the Diocesan Council secretary, who told me that an Armenian soldier in critical condition had just arrived at Sajjad Hospital in Behjatabad and he needed our help immediately. I called Dr. Oshin Hagopian, a surgeon endowed with a spirit of service and dedication. Ten minutes later, he was on his way. Afterwards, he told me the hospital had been overwhelmed with incoming casualties that night and the young man would not have made it through the night if he hadn't received immediate attention. We later learned that he was the son of a dry goods dealer who owned a shop in Gonbad-e Kavoush.

Sati's Contribution to the Defense of Iran

The government often called on Sati in emergency situations. Abadan Island lies between the Arvanderud (Arvand River, *Arabic* Shatt al-Arab) and the Bahmanshir Channel, and we were asked to block the channel to prevent Iraqi naval vessels from reaching Abadan from the rear. We hauled decommissioned locomotives and dismantled wharves to the site and maneuvered them into position. The area was shelled while the operation was underway, but fortunately, there were no casualties except for one of our drivers who was temporarily deafened by the explosions. It was many months before he regained his hearing.

At one point when the aerial bombardment was intensifying, Tavanir asked Sati to help carry out a secret operation. Two generators and a transformer were coming into port in three days time. Could we take delivery? Our bogies were on-site when the cargo arrived. Since the equipment was destined for Ramin Power Plant, we were counting on the Soviets to prevent Iraq from attacking the convoy and we counted right. Moving only at night, we completed delivery in forty-eight hours without incident.

Power outages were a constant problem. The authorities did everything they could to repair damaged power stations and transmission lines while they carefully and persistently pushed for completion of the new power plant at Isfahan. Again, because it was a Soviet project, they were reasonably certain that it was safe from Iraqi attack. As mentioned, Sati had a transport contract for the Isfahan project, and the heavy-lift items came in at Bandar Abbas on the Straits of Hormoz in the far south. A dozen 240-ton transformers arrived there in the spring of 1982, but there was a major hurdle on the road to Isfahan. Tangeh Zar is a treacherous gorge about seventy miles from the port. The gorge is bypassed by a tunnel named *17 Shahrivar* (i.e. September 8, named after Black Friday in 1978). The standard vertical clearance for tunnels in Iran is a minimum of twenty-one feet, but here it was reduced to less than eighteen feet by a massive immovable boulder sticking out from the ceiling. The transformers alone were over fifteen feet high. Put one on a bogie and the total height exceeded eighteen feet. But our bridge system provided the solution. With a transformer suspended from the bridge, the total height gave us a four-inch clearance.

The bridge system had been stored at Khorramshahr throughout the Iraqi occupation. We had no idea what shape it was in, but shortly after the city was liberated in May 1982, we got permission to send in two of our people. They found the components intact, with only minor damage from machinegun fire. Mihran had the system ready within a month.

Scores of high-level officials from Tavanir and the Ministry of Roads and Transportation came down from Tehran to watch the first pass. The governor of Hormozgan Province ordered traffic halted in both directions and lines of cars and trucks were idling at both ends. Starting at 9:00 AM, Heros Azizian, a very skillful and resourceful driver, negotiated the rig through the mile-and-a-quarter–long tunnel and then down the daunting seven-and-a-half–mile descent. He was truly the hero of the day. Over the next two weeks, while we moved the rest of the transformers, I was on the road day and night between port and tunnel, supervising the operation with Mr. Koloushani, the chief engineer and general manager of construction at Isfahan. The success of this operation had a very positive impact on Sati's future.

The largest item we moved was the 100-ton, 80- by 40-foot hovercraft used for troop transport in the marsh areas of southern Iraq. In early 1984, for example, we were given two days' notice to move these flying ships to the Hawiza (Howaizeh) Marsh, which was how we knew about the planned attack on Majnoun Island two days in advance. One of our bogies was harried by Iraqi helicopter gunships during the transport operation, but fortunately, our driver wasn't hurt and the bogie wasn't damaged.

After the "War of the Cities" began in earnest, we were asked to remove two 150-ton transformers from a power plant near Tehran and store them off-site until further notice. A couple months later when it seemed like the bombing had stopped, we hauled them back to the plant.

When Iranian forces captured Iraq's Fave Peninsula in February 1986, they took over a vast quantity of arms and equipment along with the abandoned military installations. That was a boon, since unlike Iraq which was backed by the Arab countries, Iran was suffering from shortages of all kinds. Two years later, we were asked to transfer some tanks from Fave to the recently captured Iraqi Kurdish village of Halabcheh – about 350 miles north as the crow flies and some ten miles inside the Iraqi border. We sent two Armenian drivers to pick up the tanks, but the pasdars occupying Fave refused to give them up. They said they needed them for their own defense, but word came down from higher up and the next day they were forced to release them. Our drivers had the tanks loaded onto their low-bed trailer trucks and drove up to Halabja where they came upon a horrific scene. Iraqi aircraft had gassed the village the day before they arrived. If the pasdars had given up those tanks one day earlier, our drivers would have been gassed too. They completed delivery and left as fast as they could. That massacre claimed 10–15,000 casualties, including some Iranians. A month later, Iraq recaptured Fave.

All throughout the war, we transported huge quantities of equipment and ammunition to the front, free of charge. If company vehicles were unavailable, we rented whatever we needed from other firms, again without charge to the government. Our contribution to the war effort also included bottled water and field toilets for the troops and office supplies for the field stations, all of which we donated and delivered free of charge. In return, we received scores of letters from the military thanking us for our work, and many official acknowledgements from the government.

One day, the Transport Syndicate got an urgent request for ten refrigerated trucks to bring up the war dead from Ahvaz. We quickly marshaled a fleet and sent it south. A few days later, when the drivers turned in their paperwork, some of the receipts didn't match the manifests: there were more corpses listed for pick-up than the number actually delivered. The explanation was heart-wrenching: some of the corpses turned out to be alive.

Religious and Cultural Sensitivities

Since the Diocesan Council was the link between our community and the government, it was imperative that we be sensitive to anything that might affect that relationship. On election days and national and Muslim religious holidays, Archbishop Manoukian always sent good wishes in telegrams and letters to government officials. During Ramadan when Muslims fast all day, and especially during Moharram, the Shia month of mourning, we customarily published announcements in *Alik*, asking the community to refrain from holding banquets or public celebrations out of respect for our Muslim compatriots.

Three months after the war began, instead of planning celebrations of the New Year and Christmas holidays, we distributed an appeal signed by the Prelate and myself, asking community centers and organizations to refrain from hosting festive gatherings out of respect for the victims of the war. We repeated this appeal throughout the season and our compatriots complied.

The Diocesan Council paid close attention to the annual observance of *Merelots* (Day of Mourning) which, during the war, was held on the day after Christmas. Fallen Armenian soldiers were honored with a special mass led by Archbishop Manoukian at the graves of the martyred soldiers in Nor Bourastan, the Armenian cemetery, and high-ranking government officials and military officers were invited to attend. It was an opportunity for the community to pay its respects to the martyrs and to show the Iranian leadership that our small community had suffered a disproportionately large number of losses in the collective effort to defend the country. Hojjatoleslam Mehdi Karroubi, the head of the Martyrs Foundation, and Hojjatoleslam

Gholam-Reza Safai, the head of the military's Political-Ideological Directorate, attended the Merelots ceremony every year throughout the war.

We also took part in *Dahe-ye Fajr* (Ten-Day Dawn), the annual celebration of the Revolution starting on February 1. With the Diocesan Council's encouragement, large numbers of Armenians throughout the country attended government-sponsored festivities, including international sports and cultural events. On the final day, the Council organized a celebration at the Ararat Association's Gomidas Hall on Now Bahar Street, featuring talks by prominent personalities, lectures by intellectuals and cultural presentations by various community organizations. High-ranking government officials were always invited to this event. They enjoyed the show and congratulated us on the high caliber of the programs.

The Diocesan Council was never indifferent to the natural disasters that often befall our country. Whenever there was an earthquake or a fire or a flood, the Prelate appealed to the community to contribute funds and foodstuffs. In tandem with these appeals, he sent his condolences to the Supreme Leader, the President, the Prime Minister, the Speaker of the Majles, the head of the Supreme Judiciary Council and other officials and religious leaders, always emphasizing the community's willingness to help the victims.

The Diocesan Council also made sure that Armenian traditional and religious holidays were observed with the solemnity and pride they deserved. One of the most important days was the Feast of the Holy Translators in October, when Armenian schools were closed and community organizations observed Armenian Culture Day with events of the highest artistic standards. St. Vartanants Day was celebrated in February with religious services and cultural and artistic events. Other important holidays were the Feasts of the Holy Cross, the New Year, Christmas and Easter. On Christmas and Easter, Archbishop Manoukian received good wishes from the Council members, the leaders of the Armenian Protestant Church and the Armenian Catholic Church, the religious leader of the Assyrian community, the Iranian Ambassador to the Vatican and other personalities.

The Third Annual Commemoration of the Armenian Genocide

The Diocesan Council's first meeting in March 1981 was devoted to organizing the upcoming commemoration of *Mets Yeghern* (the Great Crime). Our aim was to inform Iran's revolutionaries, and especially the young people, about the Ottoman Genocide of 1.5 million innocent and unarmed Armenians that began on April 24, 1915.

With two years' experience under our belt, we began planning an entire week of cultural and artistic events utilizing the full resources of the community. We set up a main organizing committee, which I chaired, and several subcommittees. We asked all Armenian organizations to appoint a representative to the law-and-order subcommittee which was tasked with deciding on the slogans to be used. The ARF was quite flexible but the IAMM haggled over every word, which led to protracted discussions, not to say arguments.

In early April, we applied to the Interior Ministry for permission to hold the march, which was granted on April 22. On the evening of April 23, we performed the traditional wreath-laying ceremony in the courtyard of St. Sarkis Church, with every Armenian organization in Tehran placing flowers at the Genocide memorial.

On Friday morning, April 24, Archbishop Manoukian led the holy mass at St. Sarkis while the marchers gathered outside. After the mass, they left St. Sarkis over 40,000 strong and headed south on old Arteshbod Zahedi Street (now Sepahbod Qarani), crossed Islamic Revolution Street and continued south on Ferdowsi to old Winston Churchill Street (now Neauphle-le-Château), where they turned right and passed between the Embassies of the UK and the USSR, marched several blocks west to old Qavam ol-Saltaneh (now Mirza Kuchek Khan), and finally turned left to reach St. Mary's Church, the traditional destination.

The day's slogans expressed the views of a cross-section of the community. They were blasted out from loudspeakers mounted on vehicles that were stationed along the route, and the marchers chanted back: "Greetings to Emam Khomeini!" "Death to the fascist Turkish regime!" "Liberate the lands of Western Armenia!" "Death to NATO, imperialist sponsor of military bases on Armenian lands!"

Headed by the Prelate, a group of Diocesan Council members along with a few priests and prominent community members left St. Sarkis by car and took an alternate route to St. Mary's. There we made our way to the head of the march as it reached the church, and when people filled the courtyard, a declaration was read out. The crowd's response was loud and clear, and then it slowly dispersed.

About a thousand people remained in the courtyard when suddenly forty or fifty revolutionary volunteers in black shirts waded in among them. When they started arresting Armenian youths, the atmosphere changed in a split second. People watched in horror as they corralled the boys in a corner and struck anyone who got in their way. I noticed they were taking orders from a man in civilian clothes who looked to be about forty years old. I approached him and introduced myself and asked what was going on. I told him we had a permit from the Interior Ministry and we had observed every condition. He identified himself as an Interior Ministry official and said it was a mistake to burn the Turkish flag in the street. I was shocked.

"Whoever did that must belong to some other organization!"

"You're wrong," he shot back. "They were part of your march. They broke off and went down Ferdowsi to the Turkish Embassy."

I pointed out that the youths they were holding in the courtyard had nothing to do with whatever happened at the Turkish Embassy. He moved in closer and whispered that he knew our march was purely political and that he himself wouldn't trade a single hair from the head of an Armenian for ten Turks, but he advised me to disperse the crowd and he promised to release the detainees, which he did. Later we found out that a group of nationalists had climbed up on the roof of the Turkish Embassy with the connivance of the local police and taken the flag down.

Back-to-Back Interviews on National TV

That same evening, a beautiful exhibition opened at the City Theater. Sponsored by *Alik*, it included photographs, documents and memorabilia related to the Turkish attempt to exterminate the Armenians. Thousands of Iranians saw the show and I was struck by the interest of the younger generation. Vagrig Manoukian and I attended as part of a Diocesan Council delegation headed by Archbishop Manoukian, and Hrair Khalatian came with us. While we were there, I got a message from the Prelacy, asking me to call immediately. *Seda ve Sima* (Voice and Vision), the state broadcasting network, had called twice, asking for a spokesman to do an interview on Sunday. Obviously, it would deal with the march and the meaning of April 24. We consulted with the Prelate and decided that Vagrig and I would go.

Arriving at the Voice and Vision complex, we were told where to park and given directions to the studio. A Mercedes flying the Turkish flag flashed by with a passenger in the front and one in the back. When we reached the studio, the Mercedes was parked out front. We surmised that I would be debating Ambassador Tanşuğ Bleda or his representative. Instead, I was taken directly into a recording booth and the interview began. While it was going on, I was unaware that Ambassador Bleda was being interviewed at the same time next door. Both interviews were broadcast later that night, back to back, right after the evening news. The news hook was the flag-burning incident which the anchor said was bound to have a negative impact on relations between Iran and Turkey. The interviews were presented as an effort to clarify the issue. Ambassador Bleda's interview went first, with simultaneous translation into Persian:

> *Voice and Vision:* As you know, our Armenian compatriots held a march last Friday to commemorate their martyrs and a group split off to attack the Turkish Embassy. What is your view of those events?
>
> *Ambassador Bleda:* What that group did was against Islamic principles. But first, I want to thank Voice and Vision for the opportunity to communicate with our Iranian brothers. I am also grateful to the Iranian people for their concern about the heinous attack that took place on April 24. I agree with the Iranian authorities that not all those who took part in it were Armenians. It was not an expression of the Armenians' true feelings.
>
> The source of the problem is the historical conditions created by imperialism, and this is what has hurt relations between Turkey and Iran. The individuals who carried out that attack failed to achieve their aim and they never will achieve it. Friendly relations between Turkey and Iran span the history of our two peoples. Our relationship belongs to both peoples and that is why it cannot be spoiled by such incidents, nor will we allow it to be spoiled, just as the Iranian authorities will not allow such incidents to recur in a land where Islamic values prevail. They will arrest and prosecute such groups if they dare to do anything like that again, which is what my government expects from the Iranian leadership with whom we have friendly relations.
>
> Let me take this opportunity to also thank the Iranian police, the Islamic Revolutionary Guards Corps and all the forces of law and order that defended our Embassy with the

highest sense of self-sacrifice. I wish a speedy recovery and good health to those who were injured during the incident. [Here it must be noted that no one was actually injured.]

Voice and Vision: How do you view the issues the Armenians raised regarding April 24?

Ambassador Bleda: In my view, this is more a matter of historical events that are part of the history of the Iranian and the Turkish peoples. The history of the so-called Armenian genocide was written by a few high-ranking military officers and Christian missionaries who were living in the Ottoman Empire but were actually working for the imperialist countries. They are the ones who talk about genocide, but is what they say true? If you consult any modern dictionary, the word "genocide" has only one definition: it means the extermination of an ethnic group, and in order for such an extermination to be carried out, orders must be issued.

Voice and Vision: Were such orders issued?

Ambassador Bleda: On our way over here, my assistant and I leafed through all the history books because I wanted to find out what kinds of orders were issued.

(The Ambassador's inadvertently comic remark did not go unnoticed by Iranian viewers. As everyone knows, it's only a half-hour drive from the Turkish Embassy to the Voice and Vision complex. One wonders how he managed to review all the history books in thirty minutes!)

Ambassador Bleda (continuing): The orders emphasized that whatever property the Armenians left behind, it had to be protected until the owners' return. The orders insisted that Armenian caravans had to be safeguarded. The Armenians were supposed to gather at the train stations whence they would be transported by rail and their food would be paid for. The orders emphasized that anyone who failed to carry out those provisions would be subject to severe punishment. These facts can be found in the history books. So, what is the truth? As you know, the Ottoman Empire stood against the armies of all the imperialist powers during the First World War. The Armenians had been living in peace, but urged on by the imperialist powers, nationalist groups began to arm themselves and plan attacks against Turkey in eastern Anatolia. Therefore, the Armenians living in that region became refugees.

Unfortunately, there were victims on both sides. The authors who write books on behalf of the Armenians do not speak the truth. They consider the punishment of those nationalist groups to be genocide. Compare the situation of Iran which is now in a state of war. If an opportunistic group were to attack your country, it would be the duty of your government to resist the attack with decisive action. How can such decisive actions be called genocide?

I would like to seize this opportunity to make a few general observations: It is time for us to forget these matters. Let us leave it to the history books. That is the way to neutralize imperialist provocations. Today, some 80,000 Armenians live side by side with their Turkish brothers, enjoying full and equal rights. We know that Armenians in Iran enjoy full rights too. The leaders of Turkey and other countries are appealing for peace and brotherly relations with the Armenians. I hope these appeals are made, not in the spirit of vengeance, but rather as invitations to the peace and stability the nations of the world desire. Why shouldn't we cooperate and choose the path of peace rather than terrorism?

Ambassador Bleda went on to discuss relations between Iran and Turkey at greater length. At the end of his interview, the anchor introduced my interview, saying that as a representative of the Tehran Diocesan Council, I would clarify the incident in which a group of young Armenians attacked the Embassy and burned the Turkish flag:

Voice and Vision: First, please tell us briefly about the Armenian Genocide and then we will discuss the incident at the Turkish Embassy.

Aharonian: In the name of God. First, I would like to express my gratitude to the Interior Ministry which gave us permission to publicize and discuss our just cause after so many years of silence. My thanks also go to the producers at Voice and Vision for inviting me to speak. These things have convinced us that the Islamic Republic of Iran fully abides by the Articles of the Constitution that defend those whose rights have been trampled upon.

Allow me to offer an example related to the Armenian Genocide. Ashura [the date of the martyrdom of Emam Hossein] has great significance for Shia Muslims all over the world, as we all know. I believe that when a Shia mother gives birth to a child, Ashura is born in that child, and the feelings and beliefs of Ashura are what gave rise to the Islamic Revolution, as we have seen. Therefore, Ashura will be eternally present for the world's Muslims, and especially for the Shia.

Likewise, the Armenian Genocide was not a minor event that can be easily forgotten. It was the one of the twentieth century's most horrific and inhumane crimes. That atrocity was the work of Ottoman Turks imbued with the expansionist chauvinism of Pan-Turkism. They wanted to integrate the Turks of Asia Minor with the Turks of Central Asia and they saw the Armenians as an obstacle. They decided to solve the problem by exterminating the Armenians.

When an Armenian mother gives birth, she is under the influence of those horrific events. When she nurses her newborn child, she is under the influence of the horrors committed against her people. And that child is imbued with the memory of those horrors. Because of the Genocide, Armenians are dispersed all over the world. It is deeply rooted in the historical consciousness of all Armenians. Naturally, they cannot forget the atrocities.

What does an Armenian youth see upon reaching maturity? He or she sees that 80 percent of Armenia's ancestral lands are occupied. That youth's forefathers were subjected to mass murder after having lived on these land for 3000 years. In 1915 and earlier, criminal Turks expelled them from their homes. The deserts and mountains of Syria and the Euphrates and Tigris Rivers became their graveyards.

Voice and Vision: April 24 is the Armenian national day of mourning for the victims of the Genocide. Is it honored and commemorated by all Armenians around the world?

Aharonian: Yes. I was surprised to hear that the Voice of

America tried to muddy the waters and trivialize the Genocide by saying that we Armenians organized the march and other events because we wanted to derail an economic treaty that Iran and Turkey were about to sign. The VOA had a parallel aim which was to cast Armenians as opponents of the Islamic Republic. As soon as the Diocesan Council heard about that broadcast, we telexed a letter of protest to the Voice of America and that letter was read twice on the VOA this morning.

Today, Armenians are dispersed in fifty-four countries, and in many places they are threatened with assimilation. Add to that the fact that the current Turkish government is methodically destroying historic Armenian sites and monuments in the occupied lands. Witnessing all this, how is it possible to bury history? The Armenian people are the dynamic, living heirs of a rich culture. Demonstrations are a principal element of the struggle through which the Armenian people are trying to achieve their legitimate aims.

Voice and Vision: How do you explain the incident on April 24?

Aharonian: If you mean the attack on the Turkish Embassy, I must emphasize that the Diocesan Council had no foreknowledge of that whatsoever. We organized and carried out our march according to the terms of the permit that was issued to us. As for what those young men did, one must accept the fact that they acted out of emotion. It is impossible to stifle that emotion. Those young men are endowed with humane principles and the spirit of struggle, therefore it is impossible to restrain them.

Voice and Vision: But you should have foreseen the possibility that they might be overcome with emotion and do something like that. Why didn't you take steps to preempt their action?

Aharonian: First, I must tell you that every Armenian wanted this march to happen. We invited thirty-two organizations to assist in planning it and their assistance was essential. It has to be emphasized that we have no policemen or security forces who could have helped us in this area. Security was provided by a group of participating scouts and students. They did a superb job. There wasn't a single incident of disorderly conduct along the route of the march. We also published an appeal in *Alik*, asking participants to maintain order and not to disturb the peace. We certainly do not wish to bring about any conflict with the authorities of the Islamic Republic of Iran.

Voice and Vision: We know that our Armenian compatriots struggled against the monarchy during the Revolution and that some Armenians were martyred in that struggle. Can you tell us more about the role Armenians played in the Revolution?

Aharonian: As you noted, the Armenians unconditionally joined in the revolutionary struggle and some died in that struggle. One result is that the new Constitution includes several Articles devoted to minority rights, which is the first time that has ever happened in the entire history of Iran, and today we are the beneficiaries of that Constitution.

Regarding the current war, Armenians have never stood apart and it would be unfair to separate us from our Muslim compatriots. A few days ago, there was a show on TV about the families of Armenian war martyrs. I personally visited several of those families here in Tehran to offer my condolences. There are bereaved Armenian families in Ahvaz, Isfahan and Tabriz whose sons fought and died alongside their Muslim brothers. But it isn't only our soldiers and their families who have been hurt by this war. We are caring for homeless Armenian families who fled the battle zones. The Diocesan Council, with its limited means, is providing them with food, shelter, employment and so on. We are always looking for ways to assist the government and lighten its load. We know the reasons for this war and we condemn those who imposed it upon Iran.

We Iranian Armenians have been living in this country for centuries, at least since Shah Abbas ordered our migration almost 400 years ago, and there is evidence that Armenians have been living here for 2000 years. So we consider Iran our homeland and we are loyal patriots. We believe it is our duty to defend every inch of Iranian territory.

As soon as the broadcast ended, I had scores of people calling me from all over the country. I was on the phone for hours. An Azeri acquaintance from Tabriz called to say that the comparison with Ashura was correct and very apt. *Alik* published complete transcripts of both interviews along with its own analysis, as well as a screen shot from the broadcast.

Incident at Bagh-e Keshmesh

On April 26, 1981, the same day the two interviews were broadcast, a dangerous confrontation occurred in *Nor Jugha* (New Julfa), the Armenian section of Isfahan, but it was peacefully resolved through the government's intervention and the wise and intelligent mediation of community leaders.

After the Revolution, the Southern Diocesan Council had divided up a property known as *Bagh-e Keshmesh* (Raisin Orchard, i.e. Vineyard) and distributed the lots among local Armenians who had no land of their own. Some of them started to build homes on the land, and when they raised a few glasses to celebrate the start of construction, some Muslim youths who were present took offense. The Armenians in turn took offense and told them to leave, which they did, but they came back an hour later, cursing and throwing stones. Then another group arrived carrying their *kafans* (shrouds). In a crisis, when Muslims come with their kafans, it means they are ready to die for their cause.

Realizing the situation was getting out of hand, the Armenians called on nearby residents for help. The neighbors went up on their roofs and stood guard with shotguns and stones. An hour later, a unit of armed pasdars showed up. The Armenians said they were only defending themselves but the pasdars promised to protect them, and with that assurance, they handed over their shotguns. Within minutes, the number of attackers doubled, then tripled. The crowd beat them with sticks and stabbed them with knives. About 150 Armenians were injured before another law enforcement unit arrived and put an end to the carnage. Three Armenians were shot, but they survived. There were rumors that some Muslims were shot too.

As soon as we heard about the incident, the Tehran Diocesan Council decided to seek consultation with the top Muslim religious leaders. We wanted them to spread the message in Friday sermons that religious minorities must be treated with tolerance and respect. MP Hrair Khalatian arranged for us to meet with Ayatollah Hossein-Ali Montazeri who was the highest ranking cleric after Ayatollah Khomeini. He lived in the shrine city of Qom, about a hundred miles south of Tehran. Archbishop Manoukian headed our delegation which included Bishop Goriun Papian of Isfahan and Dr. Albert Bernardi who would serve as interpreter. Sheikh Mohammed Montazeri, the Ayatollah's son so-called Ayatollah Ringo, came with us.

I drove one car and Archbishop Manoukian sat beside me in the front. Sheikh Montazeri sat in the back between Bishop Papian and Dr. Bernardi. MP Khalatian drove the second car, taking along Father Aharon Galoustian from Narmak and a reporter for *Alik*. I drove as conscientiously as I could, never exceeding eighty miles an hour. Sheikh Montazeri remarked that I drove like a European. He said that his bodyguards (who were bringing up the rear) usually took this road at 110–125 miles an hour. I replied that since I had three important religious leaders on board, it was incumbent upon me to follow the rules of the road. Privately, I thought his sobriquet suited him well!

Bishop Papian lit a cigarette and stretched his arm out across the Sheikh's shoulders. The Sheikh seemed to savor the smoke drifting under his nose. That surprised me, because whenever Muslim dignitaries visited the Prelacy, they always declined the tea and cigarettes we offered, excusing themselves on religious grounds. Of course, Sheikh Montazeri had spent twenty years in Lebanon.

In Qom, he escorted us to his father's home. It was an old traditional house with the *birouni* (exterior) in front where guests were entertained and the *andarouni* (interior) in back where the Ayatollah's family lived. The Ayatollah was born in Najafabad near Isfahan and he welcomed us very warmly. Following his custom, we all sat down on the carpet. Next to where he sat, there was a Koran on a small table called a *rahl-e Koran*. The walls were lined with modest bookshelves completely packed with books. Archbishop Manoukian began by thanking him for his warm reception. Then he broached the incident at Bagh-e Keshmesh and asked him to counsel the people against persecuting minorities. Ayatollah Montazeri responded that the country was in a revolutionary ferment and Armenians must be careful not to inadvertently offend Muslim religious sensitivities, but he promised to mention it in general terms during his next sermon. Their conversation then turned to their respective holy books. The Archbishop said it was his understanding that the Koran had been compiled during the reign of Abu Bakr, but the Ayatollah contradicted him and explained the history. Then he in turn asked which direction Christians face when they pray and how they bury their dead. The Archbishop explained that Armenians build their churches on an east-west axis and bury their dead with the head to the west. The Ayatollah couldn't quite visualize that, so his assistant demonstrated by lying on the floor in the direction described.

Our next meeting was with Hojjatoleslam Seyyed Ali Khamenei who was the Emam Jomeh of Tehran, as mentioned earlier. The Prelate had sent him a letter explaining the incident at Bagh-e Keshmesh and was given an appointment right away. I accompanied him as interpreter, and we arrived at Khamenei's office at 5:00 PM on Thursday evening, May 14, 1981. Two mollahs were waiting to see him, and after they went in and came one after the other, we were ushered in only fifteen minutes after the appointed time.

Hojjatoleslam Khamenei stood to welcome the Prelate very warmly and bade us both sit down. He asked about the Armenian community's well-being and praised its contributions to the country's development. He said he was well aware of the role Iranian Armenians had played in the triumph of the Revolution. Finally, the conversation focused on Bagh-e Keshmesh. The Prelate mentioned his explanatory letter and the Hojjatoleslam said that he had read it carefully and that he was planning to tackle similar problems occurring elsewhere, as well as the broader issue of minority rights. He said the judiciary had been instructed to pursue the case with diligence and arrest the real criminals. Any conspiracy against the Armenians was not only an insult to them, he said, but a threat to the very foundations of the Islamic state. He promised to provide the necessary guidance in his Friday sermons.

That was the first time I met Hojjatoleslam Khamenei. I had imagined him to be an extremist, but he showed himself to be cultivated, even erudite, and well versed in Western philosophy. He said he had visited All-Savior's Cathedral (*Surp Amenaprgitch*) in New Julfa, and he asked about the Armenian Church which he said was a subject of particular interest to him. The Prelate responded in succinct and appropriate terms. When the Hojjatoleslam mentioned Iranian Armenian contributions to the war effort, I asked him whether he thought there would soon be peace. He replied that Iran must prosecute the war until the enemy was defeated – that was the only way to guarantee that an adversary wouldn't start another war with the Islamic Republic.

Our meeting was pleasant and satisfactory for both parties. It lasted for more than three hours and we left at 8:30 PM.

Chief Justice Ayatollah Beheshti was the third high-ranking religious leader we met regarding the incident at Bagh-e Keshmesh. Unfortunately, two members of our delegation had drunk a considerable quantity of liquor the night before. When we picked them up, the car was pervaded with alcoholic fumes, and as we took the elevator up to Dr. Beheshti's office, the odor was still noticeable. In fact, our escort turned his face away. When we reached the office, I insisted they remain outside but they promised not to open their mouths, so we let them come in with us. Dr. Beheshti welcomed us cordially and Archbishop Manoukian began to explain our purpose. Suddenly, the Chief Justice interrupted the Prelate and said it would be best for us to make it clear to the Armenian community that liquor was strictly forbidden in the Islamic Republic of Iran. With that, the meeting came to an end. We had met with Dr. Beheshti on three previous occasions and he had never been as dry and brusque as he was that day.

Chapter 13

Social and Political Turmoil

A key to Emam Khomeini's popularity was his homespun style when addressing the public. He used simple language and he often spoke in parables, as in this one from a speech broadcast on the radio:

> A farmer goes out to his orchard and sees three men filling their sacks with fruit. He ambles over and strikes up a conversation. He finds out that the first one is a mollah, the second is a shopkeeper and the third is a tailor. He takes the first two aside and tells them how much he respects men of their class. "Help me tie up the tailor and you two can divide his sack." So they lend the farmer a hand and that's how he gets rid of the tailor. Next he takes the mollah aside. "You're a servant of God, right? You can't be mixed up with those thieves. Help me tie up the shopkeeper." So the mollah pitches in and helps the farmer tie up the shopkeeper. They give him a few punches and toss him aside. That leaves the mollah. The farmer shouts "Thief!" and knocks him out cold. That's how the savvy farmer deals with thieves.

Khomeini was signaling to the public how his government would go about defeating the opposition, one group after another – the Mojahedin Khalq, the Fedayeen Khalq, the Tudeh and the rest – and that's exactly what happened.

Destruction of the Mojahedin Khalq

The Mojahedin Khalq had battled against the monarchy before and during the Revolution, and it still had a large following, both men and women, as well as an active military wing. As students of the late Dr. Shariati, the Mojahedin had their own distinctive interpretation of Islam and they generally rejected the version preached by the mollahs. They were considered the Islamic left wing, though it would be more accurate to call them Islamic socialists. They were excluded from power practically from the beginning. Emam Khomeini barred their leader from running for President and the ruling clerics harassed them and drove them underground.

In June 1980, the Mojahedin Khalq mounted a huge rally and military display at Amjadieh Stadium. They had a permit to hold the event, but police stood by while participants were attacked by paramilitary *Hezbollahis* (members of *Hezb-e Allah*, i.e. the Party of God). Thousands of people were beaten up and hundreds sustained serious injuries.

A friend of my daughter's named Vahig Hovnatanian was arrested by Muslim extremists during a Mojahedin Khalq demonstration. They were about to execute him right there in the street when someone recognized him and said he was an Armenian, thus he couldn't be a Mojahed. They grabbed him by the hair, called him a *kafar* (heathen) and told him to get lost. It was a miracle that he escaped.

Some communist groups like the Peykar allied with the Mojahedin Khalq. Robert was the son of a friend of mine who had disavowed his father's wealth and joined this extremist group. After he was arrested during a demonstration, he refused the order to publicly recant and identify his comrades. Even when the judge invited Archbishop Manoukian to intervene, Robert still stood firm. I was in New York at the time and his father asked for my help, but by the time I got back, Robert had already been executed. His aunt came to see me and told me that his body had been buried in the Baha'i cemetery which was next to the Armenian cemetery. She said she had asked the person in charge there to release the body to his family at night, and now she requested permission to have it passed over the wall and buried in Nor Bourastan. I talked to the Holy Father and he gave his consent, but it turned out to be impossible. The revolutionaries buried the bodies of their victims in large common graves and covered them with caustic lime, making it difficult to dig out an identifiable corpse.

Another Armenian who met the same fate as Robert was Vazrig Mansourian. He had been a journalism trainee with Jerair Gharibian when the latter ran the youth project at *Alik* in the early 1970s. Vazrig left the ARF to join Peykar.

After the Majles impeached President Bani-Sadr on June 21, 1981, the struggle for power led to a paroxysm of violence. On June 27, there was an attempt to assassinate Hojjatoleslam Khamenei: his right hand remains withered from the attack. The next day, a massive explosion destroyed the headquarters of the Islamic Republican Party (IRP). The blast was attributed to the Mojahedin Khalq. Over one hundred people were killed, including Ayatollah Beheshti and our erstwhile friend, Sheikh Montazeri.

A snap election was held in July to replace Bani-Sadr as well as the several dozen MPs killed in the bombing of the IRP. Bani-Sadr's Prime Minister, Mohammad Ali Rajai, was elected President. He appointed Ayatollah Bahonar as his Prime Minister, but they didn't serve for very long. On August 30, when they were both meeting with the head of the national police to discuss the terrorist threat, all three were killed by a bomb in a briefcase left in the room. In October, the third presidential election in two years brought Hojjatoleslam Khamenei to power. He held that office for two terms, nearly coinciding with the war, and after the death of Ayatollah Khomeini in 1989, he would be elected Supreme Leader by the Assembly of Experts and acquire the rank of Ayatollah in the eyes of the public.

The Mojahedin Khalq assassinated many other leading revolutionary clerics, including Chief Revolutionary Prosecutor Ayatollah Ghoddousi and the Friday prayer leaders of Tabriz, Shiraz and Yazd, Ayatollahs Madani, Dastgheib and Saddoughi (Sadduqi) respectively, as well as the IRP ideologue Hassan Ayat.

The government went after the Mojahedin Khalq with a vengeance. Some 12,000 were executed over the next few years. I had a friend who lived near Evin Prison and he finally had to move. Every night starting at 1:00 AM, he would hear shouting that went on for a long time, and then a series of single shots. On some nights, there were more than fifty "salvation shots," so-called because they put an end to the victims' suffering. Before a virgin girl could be executed, she was handed over to a Revolutionary Guard as a temporary wife (*sigheh*), which was justified by the religious injunction against killing a virgin. By the end of 1982, the Mojahedin Khalq was destroyed as an organization in Iran.

While all this was going on, the Fedayeen Khalq (FK) split into two wings. The FK-Majority gave up its opposition to the government and tried to become a legal political party, while the FK-Minority carried on the armed struggle. Both were destroyed in the end. But the pro-Soviet Tudeh Party and its military wing continued to support the government with all its considerable political and organizing skills.

Destruction of the Tudeh

Tudeh Secretary-General Nureddin Kianuri was taken completely by surprise when the party was outlawed in the spring of 1983. After all, Dr. Kianuri had preached communist ideology at universities in Moscow and Prague and debated Ayatollah Beheshti on Iranian state TV. Now he was recanting on television. Apparently, he became a fanatical Muslim practically overnight. Months later, he and other party leaders engaged in a "roundtable discussion" that was videotaped at Evin Prison and widely distributed. Gagik Hovanissian, an Armenian Tudehist who had spent a decade in prison after the post-Mosadegh crackdown, was one of the discussants in that staged group recantation.

A few years later, I got a call from someone at Evin who told me that an Armenian prisoner had died and asked for someone to pick up the body. He suggested that no funeral be held and no obituary published either. I arranged for Andranik Baghoumian to take care of it. The deceased turned out to be Gagik Hovanissian.

One afternoon during a meeting of the Diocesan Council, the door opened and in walked Dr. Hratch Khachaturian, MP for the Armenians of southern Iran. He asked for a private word with me so we went outside. He said he had been elected by leftists and he asked me what to do now. I told him he had nothing to worry about. The people had elected him and the government was well aware of that. Sensing he needed further reassurance, I said the Council never gave up names, which was true. What's more, I said, we never even talked about Armenian leftists in our meetings.

The Monkerat

In September 1981, the Deputy Transportation Minister called me to his office and told me that FIATA, the International Federation of Freight Forwarders Associations, would soon be meeting in Dublin to set new international standards. The government wanted to send a delegation but had no budget for it. Since I was president of the Iranian Transport Syndicate, I rounded up a few of my colleagues and we attended the five-day conference on our own tab.

On my return, I was surprised to find Bella waiting for me at the airport, since my driver, Eskandar, usually picked me up when I arrived late at night. As we drove home, Bella gently said it was useless for us to stay in Iran. That surprised me because she ordinarily took the opposite view. Then she told me that Revolutionary Guards had raided our home the day before and confiscated Annette's piano, our family photographs, films and videotapes from community events, and my three hunting rifles and ammunition. They also took more than one hundred airline mini-bottles of various wines and liquors that I had collected on my travels abroad. They even tried to take our billiard table but it was too heavy so they left it.

The next morning, I reported the confiscation of my rifles and ammunition to the authorities, as required by law, and was asked to turn in my hunting license, which I did. When I got to the office, I found that our staff had already heard about the raid, so I sent one of our employees, a devout Muslim whose forehead bore the mark of his daily prayers, to the Committee to Combat Immorality (*Komiteh Mobarez-e ba Monkerat*), known as the Monkerat, to find out what had become of our belongings. He came back two hours later and advised me to wait a few days before taking any action, otherwise I would be met with disrespect.

That afternoon, the Diocesan Council had an appointment with the Deputy Minister of Islamic Guidance regarding an unrelated community problem, and as the meeting came to an end, he said to us, seemingly out of the blue,

"You Armenians don't seem to realize that this is an Islamic Republic and alcohol is forbidden. Only two days ago, a hundred bottles of liquor were found in the home of a prominent member of your community."

I knew he was referring to me so I spoke up and said that was my home and those bottles were airline favors whose total contents wouldn't fill a single standard bottle. His only response was to warn us all not to keep alcohol in our homes.

That evening at the Council's regular meeting, I brought up the raid on my home. Another concern we had was the imminent expropriation of Babig Tomassian's home by the Foundation for the Oppressed (*Bonyad-e Mostazafan*). This organization had been set up to take over the Pahlavi Foundation and now it was taking over the assets of wealthy civilians. We decided to request an appointment with the Interim Prime Minister and it was granted almost immediately. Ayatollah Mohammad-Reza Mahdavi-Kani had been appointed to replace the late Ayatollah Bahonar and would only serve as Prime Minister until the newly elected President Khamenei appointed Mir-Hossein Mousavi to the position a few weeks later.

Ayatollah Mahdavi-Kani welcomed us warmly. We began by talking about the ongoing war and the recent terrorist attacks in Tehran. Archbishop Manoukian expressed his condolences, especially for the loss of life in the bombing of the President's office. Then he outlined Tomassian's situation. Babig was a well-known community benefactor who was getting on in years and was about to be evicted from his own home by the Foundation for the Oppressed. The Ayatollah turned to an aide and asked him to get the head of the foundation on the line. When the connection was established, he spoke to the man in a low voice, then hung up and turned back to the Prelate.

"Rest assured," he said, "Mr. Tomassian won't be bothered anymore."

"Something happened to Mr. Aharonian too," the Prelate replied. "He'll tell you about it."

So I related what had happened, and when I told him how the pasdars had berated my family for possessing pornography – which is what they labeled the photos of my wife and daughter at the beach – the Ayatollah covered his face with his hands. Then he looked up and said,

"Emam Khomeini would disapprove of their conduct and I consider it unacceptable."

He acknowledged that Christians were free to drink alcohol at home so long as they didn't sell it to Muslims, and he assured us that we would be left alone so long as we abided by this rule. Then he called the head of the Monkerat, a Mr. Sajjadi, and while he was on the phone, he asked me to repeat my name. Afterwards, he told me that Sajjadi would be happy to see me and take the appropriate measures.

The next day, I sent our devout employee back to the Monkerat to size up the situation. He reported that the atmosphere had improved: he hadn't heard a single bad word said about me.

I went to the Monkerat the following day and was told that my case had already been settled. I was directed to the office of Judge Tabatabai. He was busy with a trial so I sat down to wait. Opposite me sat a beautiful young girl with delicate features, perhaps eighteen years old, guarded by a pasdar. She was telling him that her sentence was 270 lashes, that she had already taken seventy and was prepared for the rest but she was praying not to be sent to prison where she would be housed with "immoral women." Her tone was so full of pathos that I still can't forget her.

Finally, I was called in to see the judge. He welcomed me warmly while he shuffled through the piles of paper on his desk. When he found my file, he read through it quickly and set it aside.

At that moment, a young pasdar came in with an update on the case of an adulterous woman who had been arrested *in flagrante*. Judge Tabatabai asked the youth whether he himself had seen the blood-soaked cotton wadding, the point being that if the accused were having her menstrual period, she couldn't possibly have committed the alleged act and would therefore be exculpated. The young man confirmed that he had seen the evidence and the judge dismissed him. I was amazed at this extraordinary intrusion into someone's private life.

Judge Tabatabai returned his attention to me and said the substance of my case was of no interest to him. Then he started talking about all the beautiful young women who needed husbands. He elaborated on their virtues at such length that I began to worry he was trying to persuade me to marry one of them, but his intentions soon became clear.

"They all need dowries," he said. "How much do you think you can donate?"

I asked about the range of donations and he mentioned an Armenian who had recently given 10,000 tomans (more than $1,000 at the official exchange rate).

"I'm prepared to give 20,000 tomans," I said.

He thanked me profusely and wrote an account number on a scrap of paper.

"You can deposit your donation here and bring me back the receipt."

When I brought him the receipt the next day, Judge Tabatabai thanked me again and handed me a letter addressed to the manager of the Monkerat's warehouse complex. There I was told that the manager was busy and I would have to wait. Wandering around, I noticed an open warehouse with several pianos. A bearded young man approached me and politely asked what I was looking for. When I said I was looking for my daughter's Schimmel piano, he took me inside and pointed it out.

"They left it out in the rain but I had it moved inside," he said. Evidently he was a music-lover. "Follow me if you want to see something incredible."

He took me to another warehouse that was filled from top to bottom with hundreds of tars, guitars and violins. He told me sadly how "those brutes" had burned a famous tar player's precious instrument right in front of him. Then he excused himself and said I could find the manager in the courtyard.

As I neared the courtyard, I heard wailing and sobbing and soon I came upon a horrific scene. Several boys were standing in line, waiting to take their punishment, a whipping imposed by the Revolutionary Tribunal. One boy lay face-down on the ground, his mouth stuffed with a handkerchief to muffle his screams. A man was sitting on his feet, another was delivering the strokes, and a third, a handicapped man sitting in a wheelchair, was counting them. If for any reason he wasn't satisfied – if a stroke was too weak or it missed its mark – that stroke was repeated. At the other end of the courtyard, the same pain was being inflicted on a line of girls.

I finally located the manager and gave him Judge Tabatabai's letter. He read it, then went off and left me there to wait. I suspect he wanted me to hear the torture of those teenagers whose only "crime" was attending a birthday party together. It was psychologically very stressful for me. When he returned an hour and a half later, he told me he was "worn out" and asked me to come back tomorrow.

I came back the next with a rented truck, and after my driver and I had loaded Annette's piano into it, I started searching for our family photographs. I ran into the same bearded young man again and he told me that confiscated photographs were burned immediately. I eventually got my rifles back after a great deal of aggravation, but with substantially less ammunition.

My friend Vahik Khachaturian later told me how my case had come about. He had heard the details from a friend of his who had access to the file. The raid on my home was instigated by a former guard at St. Mary's Church who had been fired for selling spirits from the sacramental store.

After Muslims were prohibited from producing or consuming alcoholic beverages, some Armenians started to home-brew araq and sell it privately. Since the profit margin was good, some Muslims did the same. This business became a headache for the Diocesan Council. Practically every day, we heard about a constituent who had been whipped for drinking, or jailed for possession of one bottle of araq, or merely fined for possession of ten bottles. We wanted to put out a clear statement of how the law applied to Armenians, and in order to make sure that our information was correct, we took up the issue with the head of the Monkerat.

A delegation consisting of Dr. Albert Bernardi, Father Varazdad Derderian and I met with Mr. Sajjadi at 8:00 AM on October 7, 1981. Dr. Bernardi explained that the Prelacy was seeking clarification of the rules and regulations concerning alcohol and I cited the confusing examples mentioned above. Sajjadi merely replied that as long as we obeyed the law, our honor would be respected, but selling araq to Muslims was a clear violation of the law. He gestured to a stack of files on his desk and said that 80 percent of them involved Armenians selling home-made araq to Muslims. Dr. Bernardi assured him that the Prelacy and the Diocesan Council were categorically opposed to selling alcohol to Muslims and that the Prelate had repeatedly warned the community against doing so. Sajjadi brought the meeting to a close by telling us to watch for a circular that would soon make the rules perfectly clear.

Ershad (Guidance)

After the Revolution, the old Ministry of Information and Tourism was turned into the new Ministry of National Guidance. Then it was renamed the Ministry of Islamic Guidance (*Vezarat-e Ershad Eslami*), or Ershad for short. Ershad expanded by absorbing departments from the prerevolutionary Ministry of Culture and Art and the Ministry of Science and Higher Education. A few years later, it was renamed the Ministry of Culture and Islamic Guidance, but it was still known as Ershad. It oversaw all aspects of daily life and culture. For example, the contents of all media had to be pre-approved by Ershad, whether film, book, magazine or newspaper. Likewise, no conference or seminar could take place without Ershad's written approval.

On June 18, 1983, Ershad sent the Diocesan Council a letter claiming that certain community members had contacted the Ministry about the rules governing weddings and banquets. Ershad cited that query as its rationale for asking the Council to disseminate the following directives to everyone involved in catering such events: Armenians must respect the Islamic dress code and women must wear head scarves. Alcoholic beverages were strictly prohibited and anyone who got drunk must be expelled. Live music was forbidden but taped music was permissible. The only permissible instruments were the traditional dhol and zourna, but the music must not be audible beyond the walls of the banqueting hall. No Muslim guests were allowed to attend an Armenian wedding, nor could Muslims be employed to serve the guests. Finally, any community center that disobeyed these rules would be shut down.

Ershad added a new condition in a letter dated April 10, 1985. Restaurants, banquet halls and community centers must apply to the Ministry for a permit well in advance of any social event they were planning to host. An application form was enclosed with the letter. It required the applicant to agree in writing to Ershad's rules and regulations, or else forfeit the right to host such events. Less than a week later, the Council received another letter reiterating the previous directives, especially the prohibition against alcohol, and adding that the neighborhood komiteh must approve the scheduling of events too.

We wrote back that the Diocesan Council lacked the capacity to supervise all these social events. We could carry out Ershad's directives with respect to the Ararat Center, the Armenian Club and the Chahar Mahall Sports and Educational Association, but we suggested that the police be responsible for enforcing the rules at other sites. We followed up with another letter explaining our communal festivities and enclosing a booklet of Armenian folk and revolutionary songs and dances, all of which, we said, are imbued with the spirit of our Christian faith. We argued that the Armenian Apostolic Church and Armenian traditions do not restrict the use of musical instruments, that it is the nature of the music rather than the type of instrument that can arouse the emotions, and that the interrelation between Armenian music and dance is so vast and diverse that it is virtually impossible to define them as separate cultural expressions. We said that we were satisfied with the Ministry's ban on vulgar, inauthentic Western music and expressed the hope that Armenian traditional music could replace it. In conclusion, we said that if Ershad wanted Armenian bands to perform purely Armenian music, the Prelacy would provide all the necessary support.

Less than ten days later, Ershad tersely responded by referring us to its earlier directives, which meant that the Prelacy had to meet the burden of applying for permits and supervising wedding parties for more than a decade, until the rules were finally changed in 1997.

We sent scores of letters to the relevant Ministries in an attempt to stave off the enforcement of gender segregation at our community events. It would be a crushing blow to community life, especially to our young men and women. How was it possible that they could be prevented from meeting each other in the natural environment of our community centers? That was a most unpleasant prospect, but at least it encouraged many young people to attend church where they could meet within the confines of the courtyard.

Scores of disturbing incidents took place during private family banquets. Whenever a party was in progress, pasdars would barge in and take the young people away for interrogation at the local komiteh. The task of securing their release became a constant preoccupation for MP Vartan Vartanian who succeeded Hrair Khalatian in 1984.

Ershad was particularly concerned about the slogans proposed for the annual commemoration of the Armenian Genocide. We exchanged some correspondence over this issue but it really fell within the purview of the Ministry of the Interior, which is why we always applied to the latter for permission to organize the marches, seminars and cultural programs surrounding April 24. In short, our relations with the state were thoroughly tied up with the Ministry of Islamic Guidance, the Ministry of the Interior and the Ministry of Education.

A meeting between Armenian Prelacy Committee (Temakan), the Armenian Archbishop and then Iranian Prime Minister Mir Hossein Moosavi.

(right to left) Iranian Prime Minister Mir-Hossein Mousavi, Hrair Khalatian, author and Vagrig Manoukian.

My brothers and I at a ceremony blessing the site where "A. A. Aharonian" kindergarten would be built.

His Holiness Karekin I's visit to A. A. Aharonian kindergarten.

Chapter 14

The Struggle Over the Schools, 1981–82

All the bombings and assassinations in the summer of 1981 led to personnel changes in the higher echelons of government, and in many cases, the new officials were more fanatical than their predecessors, which is what happened in the Ministry of Education. Ayatollah Bahonar had left the Ministry to replace the late Ayatollah Beheshti as head the Islamic Republican Party. When he was appointed Prime Minister, he appointed the extremist Ali-Akbar Parvaresh as Minister of Education. Mr. Parvaresh in turn appointed Mr. Mozaffar as Chief Superintendent of Schools, replacing Mr. Khoshnevisan with whom we had, after all, developed a good working relationship.

The Twenty-Point Circular

Six weeks into the new school year, on October 12, 1981, we received a twenty-point circular from the Ministry of Education. The cover page was signed by Chief Superintendent Mozaffar. The most salient points were the following:

- The appointment of principals was subject to the tenets of Islamic law; teachers would be assigned and supervised by the Ministry's district-level superintendents; there would be no discrimination in hiring; and teachers adhering to a minority faith could teach Muslim students and vice versa.

- Religious education would be supervised by a special director assigned to each school by the Ministry's Bureau of Education (*Omur-e Tarbiyati*).

- Schools were to teach the curriculum authorized by the Ministry, including the religious education curriculum, in the official language of Iran (Persian), and religious minorities were prohibited from teaching their language at school, even as an extracurricular activity.

- Students must enroll in the school nearest their home; there would be no objection if the entire student body of a particular school belonged to the same religious minority as an effect of residential concentration.

- All extracurricular activities during recess and lunch periods must be pre-approved by the principal or the district-level superintendent; no extracurricular activities were permitted on campus outside of the official school day.

- Wherever a school was located on the grounds of a church or a synagogue, the house of worship must be enclosed by a wall in order to prevent religious ceremonies from disrupting classroom instruction.

If our schools were to be nationalized, which is what these conditions amounted to, all of these institutions, 90 percent of which had been built by Armenian benefactors or their estates, would be lost and we would be forced to abandon the centuries-old struggle to preserve our language.

Although the twenty-point circular repeatedly referred to "religious minorities," it was clearly aimed at the Armenian community. The constitutionally recognized religious minorities, whose parliamentary representation is specified in Article 64, are the Jews, the Zoroastrians and the Christians, with the latter being explicitly identified as Assyrians, Chaldeans and Armenians. Persian is the lingua franca of Iranian Jews and Zoroastrians. Some Iranian Jews don't even speak Hebrew. Historically, they have not resisted temporary conversion in times of repression. The Zoroastrian holy book, the *Avesta*, is written in Old Pahlavi and very few modern Zoroastrians read this forgotten language. Thus, the problem of language was not a priority for Jews and Zoroastrians. The Assyrians are a very small minority divided into several sects. They speak a dialect of Assyrian among themselves but few know its alphabet and very few are conversant with its literature; they read and write in Persian. The issue of language instruction was therefore of concern solely to the Armenians.

Perhaps the cruelest provision was the unequivocal prohibition of extracurricular activities on campus. That would make it impossible for us to celebrate our national and religious feasts in the schools, and then where would our students learn to read and write in their mother tongue?

The appointment of religion teachers was a serious concern because these positions were usually filled by fanatical Shia clerics whose real task was to indoctrinate the students and convert them to Islam. These "spiritual advisors" had already persuaded scores of boys to drop out of school and volunteer for the war.

For example, the business manager of our Transport Syndicate urgently requested my help when he learned that his twelve-year-old son had been recruited. His religion teacher had arranged to send him to the front the very next day, but his father got an extension and took him to Behesht-e Zahra, the vast graveyard on the southern outskirts of Tehran, and tried to explain to him the true meaning of martyrdom. The boy agreed to a two-week postponement during which my colleague took his family to Turkey on the pretext of a holiday. From there they immigrated to the United States.

Sati had a mailroom worker whose fourteen-year-old son was persuaded that martyrdom would lead straight to Paradise. He volunteered for the front and was given a plastic Key to Paradise that he wore on a chain around his neck. It wasn't long before he went missing. Fourteen years later, his father was presented with a casket containing the boy's remains. Inside, there were four bones. His heart was broken and he passed away shortly thereafter.

The Community's Response

Mozaffar's twenty-point circular provoked a major crisis. The community simply could not implement its strict and shocking directives. Primary- and middle-school students went out on strike and the movement quickly spread to the high schools. Students organized a demonstration at the Prelacy to demand its immediate cancellation. Some revolutionaries intervened and tried to chase them out of the courtyard, but Diocesan Council members stood with the students and expelled the interlopers. We promised to spare no effort to have the circular annulled and our rights restored.

We set up an advisory committee headed by Archbishop Manoukian and consisting of MPs Khalatian and Khachaturian, attorneys Albert Bernardi and Aida Hovhannisian, psychologist Dr. Haroutiun Davitian, former Council chairman Dr. Vartkes Nahabedian, Soghomonian School principal Norair Elsaian, Central Board of School Trustees chairman Vahik Khachaturian and myself. We met nearly every day. We wrote dozens of letters to the highest authorities: President Khamenei, Prime Minister Mousavi, Interior Minister Nateq-Nuri, Education Minister Parvaresh, Speaker Hashemi-Rafsanjani and the new head of the Supreme Judicial Council, Ayatollah Seyyed Abdol-Karim Mousavi-Ardebili. We also requested an appointment with Chief Superintendent Mozaffar, but he declined to meet with us, saying he had nothing to add to the twenty-point circular.

In the meantime, the Iranian-Armenian National and Cultural Association (IAMM) and the Abovian Association distributed their own "seven-point plan" in leaflets printed in both Armenian and Persian. Their three key demands were that Armenian language, literature, history and religion be required subjects for all Armenian students, irrespective of which school they attended; that the government establish a teacher-training program and provide funding to support instruction in these subjects; and that the Ministry of Education set up a permanent committee representing the religious minorities to hire teachers, develop curriculum and revise the religion textbooks for minority students.

Required subjects? Teacher training? Revised religion textbooks? Had they just dropped in from another planet? Were they completely unaware of the plan already underway to Islamize our schools? Here, a Persian proverb is apropos: "He wasn't allowed to enter the village but he still wanted to know where the *katkhoda* (headman) lived." A Western approximation might be: "That train has already left the station!" Nevertheless, we couldn't ignore the potential dangers of such political adventurism. The Ministry of Education might adopt the IAMM–Abovian proposal for a committee of minority representatives in order to get rid of its Diocesan Council headache.

The IAMM followed up with flyers and articles in *Pyunik* attacking the Diocesan Council and "the political party that sponsors it." They accused us of exploiting the crisis and provoking the student strike in order to reinforce the Council's "monopoly" on community structures and to "drive progressive groups out of the political arena." In reality, their campaign was a manifestation of the struggle between the ARF and the parties on its left. Instead of confronting the ARF directly, they attacked the Prelacy and the Diocesan Council as ARF front organizations and refused to recognize them as national institutions. Where were these people when we published an open invitation to join the various Council committees that administer community affairs? And had they forgotten that the Prelacy was their only option for weddings, baptisms and funerals?

High-Level Meetings

Ayatollah Mousavi-Ardebili agreed to meet with us on November 16, 1981. As Attorney General for the civil court system, he had been a member of the five-man Supreme Judicial Council headed by Dr. Beheshti, and after the latter's death, had succeeded him as the highest judge in the land. He graciously welcomed our delegation which was led by Archbishop Manoukian and included MP Khalatian, Father Derderian and myself. The Prelate began by thanking the Ayatollah for his warm welcome and then focused on the twenty-point circular and the deep concern it had raised among the Armenians of Iran.

"People who hold such orthodox views believe they are serving Islam," he replied, "whereas the opposite is true: they are harming Islam and its legal structures."

Then he turned to an aide and instructed him to take the circular along with the documentary evidence we had assembled and get a legal opinion from the Supreme Judicial Council's internal law office.

Because of the ongoing student strike, we were invited to meet with Mr. Mortazavi, Director of the Interior Ministry's Department of Minority Affairs. I had met Mortazavi before, and since he obviously knew nothing about the Iranian Armenian community, I had given him the two-volume *History of the Armenian People* translated by Edic Baghdasarian under his pen name, Germanik, and published by the Soviet Armenian Academy of Sciences.

When we arrived at Mortazavi's office at 9:00 AM on November 18, he poked his head out and asked us to wait a bit. We waited for a long time and I grew impatient. Finally, I stood up and walked right into his office. A man stood there haranguing him. He had his back to me but I immediately recognized him as the president of the IAMM. He was telling Mortazavi that the ARF wouldn't allow the students to end their strike and go back to school. He carried on in this vein until he became aware of my presence, at which point he controlled himself, bid Mortazavi goodbye and left the room. I was outraged. When thousands of our students were out on strike, I found it extremely painful that the head of an Armenian organization, a man who considered himself a nationalist and an intellectual, would express such anti-nationalist views to a government official. I told Mortazavi he would do better to get the facts from me than from that unsavory character.

Ironically, when I got back to the Prelacy, Archbishop Manoukian was counseling the distraught wife of the same character. He later told me she was worried that her grandchild might not be able to study Armenian in school.

A week later, on Wednesday, November 25, I was leafing through *Alik* when a bold headline caught my eye: "Friday at the Sports Stadium."

According to the story, Diocesan Council chair Levon Aharonian had asked the students to end their strike and go back to school and they had agreed to do so, but the community was invited to one last rally at the Ararat Center on Friday, November 27, when the Council would explain its position.

The Interior Ministry had warned us more than once that the strike must end, but this story was an irresponsible ARF provocation that placed the Diocesan Council in an extremely false position. If we were expected to present a report to the public, shouldn't we have been notified in advance? Moreover, the rally would predictably end with political sloganeering, and when that happened, the government could very well use it as a pretext to shut down the Ararat Center.

I was supposed to leave town for a hunting trip the next day but I had to cancel it. Instead, I called a meeting of the education committee and strongly protested the rally announcement. Our discussion went on at great length. Finally, I proposed to let the rally go forward as planned, on condition that everyone present sign off on the minutes of our deliberations. At that point, Dr. Nahabedian asked for a recess. He and his ARF cohorts went outside for a private palaver. Fifteen minutes later, they came back in and said they had decided to cancel the rally. Dr. Nahabedian whispered to me that this reversal was a first for the ARF. Thursday's *Alik* headlined the rally's last-minute postponement.

Victory at Last

On Saturday, November 28, Ayatollah Mousavi-Ardebili's office phoned the Prelacy at 4:00 PM to say that the Supreme Judicial Council's legal office had studied the twenty-point circular and found it impractical and it was therefore canceled. I was there with several other Diocesan Council members when the call came in. We held a brief meeting and decided that I would deliver the good news to the students who were demonstrating outside in the courtyard at that very moment. I climbed up on a chair to get their attention and began by commending them for defending our golden alphabet. Then I announced the news they were secretly hoping to hear. There was an explosion of joy. Everybody was hugging and kissing like one big family. People shed tears of happiness. My eyes welled up too and I felt a heady sense of lightness. Everyone was relieved, and most importantly, the community's faith in the Council's work was strengthened and that encouraged us to carry on.

At our next Council meeting on Monday, we decided to send letters of gratitude to Judge Mousavi-Ardebili, Speaker Hashemi-Rafsanjani, Minister Parvaresh and even Chief Superintendent Mozaffar for their good will and support in resolving the problems surrounding our schools.

Meeting with Education Minister Parvaresh

Although Chief Superintendent Mozaffar's infamous twenty-point circular had been scrapped, the fate of our schools remained uncertain. The IAMM and the Abovian Association were still pushing their seven-point plan while Dr. Bernardi, at the Diocesan Council's behest, was hard at work drafting a new agreement that we hoped the Ministry of Education would accept. Council members Armen Hakhnazarian and Vagrig Manoukian were in continuous negotiations with various Ministry officials, demonstrating that we Armenians approached the issue of our schools with great sensitivity and meticulous attention to detail. As a result, they secured an interim agreement that allowed us to appoint Armenian vice-principals to serve with Muslim principals in our schools. In the new year, we asked MP Hrair Khalatian to set up a meeting with Minister Parvaresh himself, and Parvaresh invited us to lunch in the Majles dining room. Our delegation consisted of Central Board of School Trustees chair Vahik Khachaturian, Council schools liaison Vagrig Manoukian and myself.

Minister Parvaresh was there to welcome us when we arrived and Hrair Khalatian soon joined us. He made the formal introductions and we all sat down around a table. Since I wanted to steer the conversation in the direction of our main purpose, I found an opportune moment to convey the Archbishop's good wishes, and then I brought up the idea of an agreement regarding our schools. The Minister smiled mysteriously and said that might be useful, but with whom should he sign an agreement? After all, two other Armenian organizations were claiming to represent the community. We Armenians should first settle the matter among ourselves and then address the Ministry in a single coherent voice. Khalatian and I countered by outlining the structure of the Prelacy and summarizing its traditional activities. We emphasized the fact that the Diocesan Council and its auxiliary bodies had been sanctioned by the Interior Ministry. Parvaresh said he was aware of all that, but because these other organizations had lodged formal complaints, he was obliged to review the issue and determine which body legitimately spoke for the community.

We subsequently learned that Souren had met with Ministry officials on behalf of the Abovian Association and challenged the Diocesan Council's legitimacy, and we were shown a copy of a letter the IAMM had sent the Ministry in which they actually proposed to dissolve the Council and the Prelacy and turn over control of our schools to a parliamentary committee of minority representatives. We were worried about the effect these disturbing representations might have, and as a countermove, we invited the community to a meeting in the courtyard of St. Sarkis Church on February 23, 1982, for an update on the situation of our schools. Some 10,000 people turned out. The Prelate opened the meeting and then I spoke. *Alik* published my speech in full:

> I must note at the outset that my remarks on behalf of the Diocesan Council are not motivated by malice toward any particular individual or community organization. We do not condemn the organization but rather those executive committee members who have taken counterproductive actions.
>
> The organization as such cannot be condemned because, for us Armenians, the three pillars of community life are the church, the schools and the sports and cultural organizations. The Diocesan Council does not wish to see any organization destroyed, whatever its ideology may be. Our sole aim is to make sure that young Armenians, men and women alike, have a place to meet in an Armenian environment.
>
> Let me take you back to the time almost two years ago when our school problems were just beginning. At that time, the situation was even more grave than it is now because a new government had taken power and the situation was unclear. New directives were issued and new problems emerged. We could not implement those directives because they would have harmed our schools. We spent countless hours on those problems until, weeks later, we were able to solve them. And here I must acknowledge the late Ayatollah Beheshti who played an important role in that process.
>
> Yet during that difficult period when we were caught up in the struggle to save our schools, a certain Armenian organization distributed a leaflet in Persian accusing the Diocesan Council of stealing 15 million tomans a year, even

though the Council's annual income is less than that. Our income is derived from weddings, baptisms and funerals. Some 1200–1300 people get married every year, there are 500–600 baptisms, and 400–500 people pass away. Clearly, financial gain is out of the question. It is possible to review the Prelacy's accounts and the Prelacy will soon make those figures public.

The Diocesan Council did not react to those accusations nor did it engage in battle with its accusers. Then fresh problems arose. At the start of the school year last fall, the Ministry of Education sent the schools a twenty-point circular. This was a very dangerous development and it became the focus of our concern. Again, we appealed to the authorities and we were able to prevent its implementation.

Our community was in a constant state of tension all throughout that period. We constantly received calls from community members, offering their help and support in whatever way necessary, and that was tremendously encouraging.

At the same time, certain organizations distributed flyers saying that point number ten of the Ministry's twenty-point circular [the prohibition against Armenian language instruction in school] had been amended and that the problem was solved. The individuals who distributed those flyers should be asked why they were spreading false information and why they said the Diocesan Council was making an unnecessary fuss when it took a stand for the community.

Those problems also passed. We began negotiating with the Ministry of Education and we had many meetings with various officials. Here I wish to thank Minister Parvaresh, Speaker Hojjatoleslam Hashemi-Rafsanjani and Judge Ayatollah Mousavi-Ardebili for their help in this matter. Our aim was to clarify the status of our original agreement, since we were never told whether or not it was actually in force. We were seeking a permanent written agreement.

It was then that the Ministry of Education asked us to clarify who we were. We were told that a group of Armenians had presented the Ministry with a letter stating that the Diocesan Council had no jurisdiction over Armenian schools and that they themselves were supposed to be in charge. Then we found out that the IAMM and the Abovian Association were making these claims. That was a shock because the Diocesan Council has a long-standing agreement with the government regarding our schools. This brings up an important question: If every organization assumes the right to meddle in educational matters and propound its opinions about our schools, what will become of our community rights? If the Ararat Association with its membership of more than 2000, for example, or Hrazdan or Sipan or Sanahin were to interfere in these matters, what would become of us as a community?

What are these gentlemen proposing? Their ideas are deceptive. They say they want a teacher-training program, which is an excellent idea on the face of it. But when we were waging a struggle against the twenty-point circular and every one of those points created a host of new problems, could we go and ask the government to institute a training program for our staff? And why didn't these gentlemen propose that idea to the Diocesan Council first?

When they say our schools should be governed by a parliamentary committee of religious minorities, they are hiding their real aims. Who are these religious minorities? The Zoroastrians, the Jews, the Assyrians and the Armenians. If a person's head doesn't hurt, he won't know what a headache is. The Zoroastrians have no language issues, nor do the Jews. The Assyrians belong to three or four different churches. They admit they have but one school with no more than 500 students. But we Armenians have more than thirty schools. Our problem is different. Our language problem is completely different, so how can we govern our schools in collaboration with the representatives of other religious minorities?

Suppose we agree to this system of administering our schools. Why do we elect our representatives and send them to the Majles? So they can devote their time to governing our schools? We often have business with our Member of Parliament and he is invited to Diocesan Council meetings. He promises to arrive at 5:00 but he rarely makes it by 6:00 because he's very busy. With all the responsibilities they have, how can they take charge of our schools?

No, the real aim here is something else: it is to remove Diocesan Council control over our schools. That is the reason for all these different moves by the opposition. They talk big about removing this or that principal because he or she belongs to such-and-such a party. Fine. Let us assume that a principal takes a political position and is then fired because of complaints from the community and replaced by a very competent, non-Armenian principal. The new principal has never had a single Armenian friend. He or she knows nothing about our culture, our religion or our schools. How can this person instill the Armenian spirit in our students? This person may very well be a good principal – for a non-Armenian school.

These people and their organizations are interpreting a particular provision in the Constitution to mean that the Diocesan Council has no right to interfere with our schools because that provision only refers to cultural, benevolent and public functions and does not mention education. These people are unwilling or incapable of seeing that their interpretation is wrong because the government controls education in this country. That is the law. But minorities have been given the right to preserve their language and culture and the Prelacy has been designated as the entity through which our community's cultural heritage can be preserved, therefore our schools fall within the sphere of the Prelacy's responsibilities.

Considering all these factors, I ask why some Armenians want to interpret the law in a way that harms rather than benefits our community? What would they gain if the Prelacy were to disappear from the scene?

The Diocesan Council is sometimes criticized for not talking to these people or taking their views into consideration. On the contrary, we have talked to them several times. We have told them that this is not the way to struggle. We have invited them to run for election to the Diocesan Assembly and the Diocesan Council.

No doubt you are wondering about the status of Armenian schools. At present, our schools are not in danger, but our original agreement with the government must be reinstated. Your presence here today is evidence that our community is deeply interested in the status of its schools. That is our greatest success, because indifference would be destructive. Our community has never been indifferent. We have survived for centuries because we have cherished and protected our language, our religion and our culture, and I have no doubt that we will continue to do so.

We are doing everything we possibly can. We will continue our discussions with high-ranking officials and we will resolve this crisis. The purpose of this meeting is to keep you informed so that in the very unlikely event that our efforts are not successful and the existence of our schools is threatened, it cannot be said that we have not kept our community abreast of developments.

We hope that with the support of the community we can sustain our unity, which is essential to solving our problems.

Finally, on behalf of the Diocesan Council, I want to thank all of you for being here today, for your deep concern and dedication to the well-being of our schools and the education of your children.

Meeting with President Khamenei

President Khamenei had agreed to receive Archbishop Manoukian on the very next day. Hrair Khalatian and I accompanied him and we were given a very warm welcome. Earlier, I mentioned our appeal for monetary contributions to aid the soldiers fighting in the Iran-Iraq War. Now the Prelate presented the President with a check for the entire sum the community had raised which was the equivalent of more than $90,000. Their remarks were reported in *Alik* the following day (February 25, 1982):

Archbishop Manoukian congratulated the President on the third anniversary of the Islamic Revolution and said that the Iranian-Armenian community had stood with their Muslim brothers since the early days of the Revolution. Now, in the imposed war, he continued, Armenian soldiers are fighting alongside Muslim soldiers to defend the country on the path to victory.

His Holiness continued by saying that when Emam Khomeini asked the churches to toll their bells for the oppressed and the dispossessed, the Armenian Church was the first to toll the bell, because the Armenian Church is a national church that is administratively independent of Europe or the USA. The Armenian Church and the Armenian nation have suffered tremendously under the yoke of the great powers and that is why Armenians understand what it means to be an oppressed people who have been denied their rights. Armenians also know from historical experience that a Genocide took the lives of 1.5 million Armenians during the Ottoman period. Armenians have confirmed many times over the past three years that they have the freedom to worship in Iran, that the Armenian Church is free, and that the community has been free to teach the Armenian language and religion in accordance with the Constitution.

Archbishop Manoukian concluded his speech by saying that Armenian students had refrained from celebrating the New Year. Instead, they and the community at large collected money for the victims of the war. He then presented the President with a check in the amount of 6,421,000 riyals.

The President thanked the Prelate and responded as follows:

"I am very happy that we meet again. Our last meeting left a good impression on me and I have fond memories of our productive conversation. It was an honest dialogue that intimated unity and cooperation.

"As you noted, the Armenians as well as other religious minorities have supported the Islamic Republic of Iran. Even before the Revolution, our struggle was backed by our dear Armenian compatriots. I personally know the Armenians who struggled with us in the political arena. After the triumph of the Revolution, I witnessed the extraordinary assistance the Armenians extended to us.

"I will never forget one particular soldier in Ahvaz. I was there talking to the troops and asking about their conditions. A soldier spoke up and said that he was Armenian. I felt great joy to see this Armenian among Muslims. They were fighting side by side like brothers. This Armenian was not conscious of being a fighter among Muslims, and the Muslims were not thinking of their brother-in-arms as an Armenian. They were all engaged in the struggle for a single cause.

"At the beginning of the war, a few Armenians contacted me and offered assistance in repairing the machines and missiles used in the war. I thanked them and that collaboration has continued and we are very happy with the results.

"Of course, the solidarity you have shown in presenting this check from our Armenian brothers for the victims of the war has great significance for us. They will be informed of your gesture so that everyone – particularly our enemies who cannot witness it – will know that Iran is blessed with national unity and solidarity.

"You are also aware of the fact that our enemies, both the external superpowers and the internal enemies under their influence, pretend that there is no such unity in Iran, that there is in fact religious and national strife. Glory be to God, because I have felt this overwhelming unity since the day the Republic was established.

"Today I am sitting beside a Christian religious leader and there is no conflict between us. I am a Muslim, you are a Christian cleric, and we are walking on the same path toward a shared victory.

"Clearly, we must beware of our enemies. They never stop fanning the flames of conflict among our people. Even among Muslims they try to promote the differences between the Shia and the Sunnis.

"It is certain, most respected Holy Father, that there are enemies among our Armenian compatriots too, working to provoke tensions which must be neutralized by the wise and careful leadership of the Armenian community.

"We have seen dark forces lurking in the shadows, using the community, trying to harm its unity through groups and movements they have sponsored and supported under various pretexts.

"We are happy and hopeful that the presence of individuals such as yourself in the Armenian community will result in the strengthening of our national unity."

After this exchange, Khalatian outlined our community institutions, emphasizing that the Armenian Apostolic Church is an independent national church. He explained that when Armenia lost its independence in the fourteenth century, all state functions were transferred to religious leaders, and thus Archbishop Manoukian was a national as well as a religious leader. Then we laid out the problems our community was facing, the most pressing of which was of course the situation of our schools in the aftermath of the twenty-point circular. The President promised to discuss the issue with Minister Parvaresh and said he would speak with the relevant officials about the other issues we raised.

Khalatian also briefed the President on the annual commemoration of the Armenian Genocide. He said that we had more freedom to commemorate that tragic event since the Islamic Revolution and this reflected positively on Iran and was hugely beneficial to its international interests. President Khamenei asked us to convey his best wishes to his Armenian compatriots and tell them that he knew Iran had always had and would continue to have their support. Finally, we were photographed with the President.

On April 10, Archbishop Manoukian met with Interior Minister Hojjatoleslam Ali-Akbar Nateq-Nuri to request permission to mount our fourth annual commemorative march and demonstration. Hrair Khalatian, Council vice-chair Torgom Der Hagopian and I accompanied the Prelate. Minister Nateq-Nuri received us very respectfully. I translated the Prelate's remarks about the Genocide and our wish to express our just grievances. The Minister promised to review the matter, and soon enough, permission was granted. On April 24, tens of thousands of Armenians gathered once again in and around the courtyard of St. Sarkis Church. The event began with a memorial service for the victims of the Genocide, followed by a number of speeches. Then the marchers took the traditional route from St. Sarkis to St. Mary's Church. It turned out to be one of the most successful demonstrations our community ever organized.

Chapter 15

The Struggle Over the Schools, 1982–83

On April 25, 1982, the Ministry of Education put out a new directive reinstating and reinforcing point number ten of Mozaffar's twenty-point circular: Religious education must be conducted in Persian. All religious education textbooks must be written in Persian and approved by the Ministry. Armenian students must take their final religion exam in Persian, like their Muslim counterparts, and they could not advance to the next grade or graduate from school without a passing grade in the subject.

By way of example, the directive discussed the Ministry's authorized high school textbook, *Binesh-e Dini* (Religious Worldviews), dividing it into Parts A and B. According to the directive, there was no disagreement among monotheistic religions over the content of Part A, theological issues: the acceptance of God and belief in the existence of the prophets and their resurrection. Part B, on the other hand, concerned issues specific to each religion: the prophecies, the commands and guidance of the prophets, religious rites and ceremonies, morality and prayer. The religious minorities were responsible for preparing textbook supplements covering Part B. If it were necessary to cite evidence from their holy books, it was permissible to include a sentence in the ancestral language on condition that it be directly followed by a Persian translation. These draft textbooks supplements would have to be approved by the Ministry's Department of Instruction and Curriculum Development, after which they would be published at the expense of the minority communities and distributed to schools by the Ministry. The new directive cited Article 15 of the Constitution as its rationale. It was signed by Minister Parvaresh and issued by the Department of Instruction and Curriculum Development.

The Diocesan Council's Response

The religion textbook supplements became the point at issue in a kind of cold war between the Armenian community and the Minister of Education, and from that day forward, there was a constant struggle between extremist clerics and progressive reformers. Minister Parvaresh was backed by powerful clerics from the Hojjatiyeh Society who now took complete control of educational policy. While the new directive was superficially accommodating, its true aim was different. Indeed, it was designed to prevent the teaching of Armenian and in that way to gradually bring about the end of our ancestral language and culture in Iran.

In all our contacts with the government, we had always highlighted the fact that knowledge of the Armenian language is essential to the understanding and practice of our religion. Our emphasis on religious instruction in our mother tongue was based on our awareness that the authorities were deeply committed to the inculcation of religion, but this new directive cut the ground from under our feet. Our students would have to study Christianity from an Islamic point of view that was quite different from our ancient beliefs and practices. If we were to implement the new directive, we would have to disavow our faith and convert to Islam. The community still hadn't recovered from the shock of the twenty-point circular and this put an end to their patience. The resort to Article 15 was particularly perverse and insidious. It states in full:

> Persian is the common and official language and script of the people of Iran. Official documents, correspondence and texts as well as textbooks must be in this language and script. However, the use of local and ethnic languages in the press and mass media or the teaching of their literatures in schools, along with Persian, shall be free.

Furthermore, Article 13 states that Zoroastrians, Jews and Christians are free to "practice their religion in personal status and *religious education*" (emphasis added). A correct reading of the Constitution would therefore find the requirement to teach our religion in Persian unconstitutional. After all, the Muslim holy book was written in Arabic and some people even believe that translating the Koran is against their religion.

We forwarded a copy of the new directive to the education committee and the Central Board of School Trustees and requested their comments. Then we met with the Board and with Bishop Papian of Isfahan and Father Bagrad Melkonian of Tabriz. We decided to send Minister Parvaresh a response over the signature of all three religious leaders. Dated June 4, 1982, It began as follows:

> Dear Minister Parvaresh,
> We were informed that your Ministry wishes to sign an agreement with the minority communities regarding school

issues, but we were surprised to receive the directive dated April 25, 1982. It contradicts the views of the Leader of the Revolution and it even contradicts the Constitution. As everyone knows, Emam Khomeini and other religious leaders have said that the government must respect the rights of religious minorities. We wish to inform you that ever since the creation of the Armenian alphabet sixteen centuries ago, the Armenian nation has performed all its rites and ceremonies in Armenian. Therefore, Armenian students must be competent in the language in order to understand the teachings and sermons of our church leaders. That is why, throughout the centuries, religious education textbooks used by the Iranian Armenian community and by other Armenian communities in the Muslim world have always been written in Armenian and instruction has always been carried out in our ancestral language.

The signatories explained their interpretation of Articles 13 and 15 and requested that the new directive be annulled and the issue reviewed. And finally, they asked that the Ministry come to a formal written agreement on the issue with the Diocesan Council. Based on our previous experience, we didn't expect to receive a reply, but this time we did:

His Holiness Archbishop Ardak Manoukian, Esteemed Religious Leaders,

Warm salutations. We are in receipt of your letter. We thank you for the spirit of cooperation you have shown and for what you have told us about your educational difficulties. We appreciate the information you have provided about Armenian Christian traditions and the points you have emphasized. We ask God to grant the Islamic Republic of Iran with the blessing of progress. The Constitution of the Islamic Republic of Iran clearly and unequivocally respects the rights, traditions and languages of the country's minorities. Article 15 in particular emphasizes these rights. Our brothers in the Armenian community are therefore free to organize and articulate their demands within the framework of the Constitution.

The Minister concluded by paraphrasing Article 15:

Persian is the common, written language of the Iranian nation. Therefore, all correspondence, documentation, official texts and textbooks must be in Persian. The use of the local ancestral language in the press and other publications, as well as the teaching of this language and its literature alongside Persian are permitted.

With best wishes for your success,

Ali-Akbar Parvaresh, Minister of Education

The emphasis in his last paragraph was an advance over Mozaffar's twenty-point circular which had explicitly banned Armenian language instruction on campus, but the Minister remained immovable on the textbook issue. Once again, we sent a barrage of letters to the authorities. Every official who replied supported the Minister's position.

Hrair Khalatian urged us to restart direct negotiations. He facilitated a meeting with Minister Parvaresh on July 6, and a separate meeting on the same day with Speaker Hashemi-Rafsanjani. The Minister invoked Article 15 and the Speaker promised to review the matter and help if he could. Two weeks later, Albert Bernardi, Aida Hovhannisian and I met with Ayatollah Ahmad Jannati of the Guardian Council. He too supported the Minister's interpretation of Article 15. Not one of them was willing to consider the validity of our concerns.

Meanwhile, the Prelate had asked the Diocesan Council to discreetly advise our students to cut their Persian-language religion classes, which we did, and they did. At the end of the school year, he arranged for them to take their final religion exam *in Armenian* under the supervision of the Central Board of School Trustees. Students enrolled in non-Armenian schools took the same exam at the Prelacy.

Ratcheting Up the Pressure

One day I was told that officers from the National Intelligence and Security Organization (*Sazman-e Ettelaat ve Amniyat Melli*, or SAVAMA) wanted to sit in on a Diocesan Council meeting in order to "dialogue with the community." SAVAMA was the interim successor to SAVAK and would in turn be superseded by the Ministry of Intelligence and State Security (*Vezarat-e Ettelaat ve Amniyat Keshvar*), known to some as VEVAK and to others as MOIS.

At the appointed hour on the appointed day, five intelligence officers showed up at the Prelacy. Archbishop Manoukian knew two of them: both were former SAVAK officers. The other three were young staffers who took notes but said nothing. When the meeting started, the two senior officers made it clear to the Prelate that he would be exiled if he didn't cooperate. He in turn made it clear to them that he would never sanction religious instruction in Persian, even if they threatened to kill him. Furthermore, he said,

"*Binesh-e Dini* has nothing to do with Christianity."

A few days later, three men made an unannounced visit to my office at Sati. They declined to identify themselves but said they wanted to discuss religion textbooks. I tried to explain to them why it was absolutely essential to our community that religious instruction be conducted in Armenian. In the end, all I could say to them was that it was not in my hands to solve this problem.

Next, I was summoned to a meeting with Ershad. Council schools liaison Vagrig Manoukian came with me. The meeting went on for three hours. When they finally realized that they couldn't persuade us to change our position, they threatened to accuse us of rebellion. They also told us that the Armenian Catholics had accepted the government's position and that Bishop Vartan Tekeyan, Prelate of the Armenian Catholic Church, had done so in writing. That was extremely disturbing. As soon as we left, I told Archbishop Manoukian what I had heard. He was quite taken aback. The news spread like wildfire. At 4:00 PM, someone from Majidiyeh called me at home and asked me to tell the Bishop that unless he reversed course within twenty-four hours, he would be killed. I called a Catholic acquaintance and asked him to pass the message along. Bishop Tekeyan withdrew his statement the next day.

The New School Year

On September 25, 1982, which was the first Saturday after the start of the new school year, the Diocesan Council held an open meeting in the Prelacy courtyard to update the community on our efforts to cancel the new directive. Again, more than 10,000 people showed up. I commended them for standing shoulder to shoulder with us as we negotiated with the government. I said there were two issues on which we were unwilling to compromise: religion and language. That drew loud applause. I also told them that the Interior Ministry had warned us about "external and internal forces scheming against the Islamic Revolution," and in that context, I asked them to refrain from demonstrating and to let the schools resume regular instruction: this would generate a calmer atmosphere that would be more conducive to negotiations. Recognizing the difficulties we were facing, a student spokesman promised to support our efforts.

"As of today," he announced, "there will be no more rallies at school, but we will gather in our churches. The people's demands will not be denied!"

A week later on Sunday evening, October 3, I was at the Prelacy when the guard came in and said there was a police action at an Armenian school, though he didn't know which one. I drove straight to the central police station where I was told that a disturbance had been reported in Heshmatiyeh two hours earlier. When I reached Dah Metri Aramaneh Street in Heshmatiyeh, it was crowded with thousands of Armenians of all ages. There were so many people that I barely got through to the gates of Sahakian School. A few policemen were standing guard and inside the gates there were more police and some pasdars in the yard. I went up to the second floor and found the principal with a man who introduced himself as Colonel Moazzemi. The principal was relieved to see me. He took me aside and said that Moazzemi had ordered the pasdars to do whatever it took to disperse the crowd.

Down in the yard, a pasdar was shouting through a bullhorn, ordering people to leave, but they were completely oblivious. The thought crossed my mind that a spontaneous gesture could spark a violent clash at any moment. With Colonel Moazzemi's consent, I went down and borrowed the bullhorn, then I walked through the crowd, identifying myself and asking people to leave, but they kept shouting that they wanted their children back! I finally gathered that there were dozens of students locked inside the classrooms. As soon as I understood that, I promised they would soon be freed. In the meantime, the Parents Council had alerted Archbishop Manoukian, and as soon as he arrived, people felt reassured and began to disperse.

Then the students started pouring out of the classrooms and mingling with the few hundred people still in the yard. Suddenly, a few clean-shaven young men in jeans appeared out of nowhere. They pointed out certain students and the pasdars herded them into a corner. I recognized their leader immediately – he was the same Interior Ministry official I had met at St. Mary's Church more than a year before, when he had ordered the release of the youths detained at the end of our march on April 24. Now I realized that his men were secret police attached to the Interior Ministry. Unlike all the other security forces, whether Police, Artesh, Sepah, SAVAMA or Hezbollah, and aside from anti-revolutionaries, they were the only clean-shaven men in jeans one ever saw in those days.

I signaled to the man and he recognized me. After we talked for a few minutes, I began to feel better. I asked him what would happen to the boys and girls they were rounding up and he said they had incriminated themselves by their actions and they would have to be interrogated.

"What about the girls? Do they have to be interrogated too?"

He answered in the affirmative.

"I assume you have children," I said. "You must be sensitive to a father's concerns. Please understand that Armenian tradition won't tolerate young girls spending the night away from home. I hope you'll take that into account and let them go."

He considered that for a moment, then stepped away and spoke with someone on his walkie-talkie. When he came back, he said he would release the girls but he couldn't make any promises for the boys. I was satisfied.

Thirty girls were led out through the gates and boarded a bus that was standing by. I asked a few people from the Parents Council to ride along and see that they all arrived safely at home. Twenty-one boys were loaded onto another bus and taken to the police station where Colonel Moazzemi was in charge. Finally, the yard was empty. I went back inside to update the principal and the Prelate. We stayed there until after midnight when the chaperones returned to report that all the girls were safe at home.

We were about to head for the police station when we learned that the boys had been diverted to the komiteh headquartered at Maidan-e Eshratabad. There, an elderly armed guard confirmed that the boys had been brought in, so we crossed the street and stood around waiting for them to come out. An hour later, the guard asked us what we were waiting for. When we told him, he laughed.

"Everyone brought in here goes to Evin – that's where they interrogate them."

By now, it was 3:00 AM. There was nothing more we could do, so we went home.

Over the next two months, the Diocesan Council mobilized every resource to free the students. Hrair Khalatian and his secretary, Anoush Hovian, were key to this effort. Archbishop Manoukian repeatedly met with the interrogators. They were trying to force the students to reveal who was behind their protests, but the Prelate told them over and over, the students were motivated solely by their religious faith. They were finally released in

December, but it was nine months before their teacher, Seroj Tilimian, was freed.

An Exchange of Views with Minister Parvaresh

Less than three weeks after the incident at Sahakian School, *Ettelaat* published an interview with Minister Parvaresh about "the controversy surrounding the Armenian schools." The Minister restated his policy that all textbooks, including religious education textbooks, must be written in Persian. He briefly mentioned the appointment of school principals, stating that "priority will be given to qualified individuals from the community," and then he reverted to the subject of religious education:

> Mr. Parvaresh noted that the Supreme Council of the Ministry of Education has offered another option regarding minority religious instruction in the schools, especially the Armenian schools, namely that religious minorities can draft a textbook supplement and submit it to the Ministry of Education. "If we approve the contents of the draft," he said, "then surely it can be put into circulation. Furthermore, if some students choose not to attend religious education classes, they are free not to do so."

That was not what the community wanted to hear. The Diocesan Council immediately responded in a letter over the signatures of the Prelate and myself:

> In the Name of God
>
> 3 Aban 1361 [October 25, 1982]
>
> Most Respected Mr. Parvaresh,
>
> Minister of Education of the Islamic Republic of Iran
>
> Secularists have no better means of suppressing disenfranchised peoples than to penetrate their culture. Emam Khomeini
>
> We thank you for your explanations regarding Armenian schools in *Ettelaat*, 29 Mehr 1361 [October 21, 1982]. They demonstrate the special consideration the authorities have shown concerning the difficulties our schools are experiencing. While we hope these difficulties will soon be removed, we find it necessary to bring the following points to your attention.
>
> The Diocesan Council is pleased with the importance you have placed, both in writing and in practice, on safeguarding the status and operations of Armenian schools. We have

communicated to you and to other officials on several occasions, both in face-to-face meetings and in written correspondence, that the preservation of the Armenian school system is the only guarantee of the survival of the Armenian community with its religion and its distinctive culture. These two interrelated factors form the individual and ancestral profile of the community and protect our far-flung people from being penetrated by other cultures which, according to Emam Khomeini, is the only way disenfranchised peoples can be suppressed by secular forces. This principle accords with Article 14 of the Constitution of the Islamic Republic of Iran.

If the Constitution recognizes Iranian Zoroastrians, Jews and Christians and grants them rights, then the survival of these communities must also be guaranteed. Any circumstance that endangers the survival of these communities undoubtedly contradicts the noble principles of Islam as well as the letter and the spirit of the Constitution.

Armenian schools, with their dedication to the teaching of religion, language and culture, are the most important safeguards of the survival of the Armenian people. These schools must support the education of a new generation of faithful and pious Armenians. In order to attain these goals, a number of factors must be taken into account, but in recent months, some of them have been compromised:

1. The Diocesan Council is pleased to note your statement that, whenever possible, Armenian school principals must be appointed from among qualified candidates within the community, since the application of this principle would resolve one of the greatest difficulties our schools have encountered. But we are saddened to note that the Ministry has disregarded its own principle in replacing a number of principals in Armenian schools. Candidates with religious credentials who meet the Ministry's requirements have applied for these positions, but the Ministry has chosen instead to appoint individuals with little knowledge of the specific religious and traditional attributes of the Armenian people, and this has created complications and tensions among students and their parents.

2. The directive that religion must be taught in Persian is one of the major threats facing the normal functioning of Armenian schools. It goes without saying that all citizens must abide by the principles of the Constitution. In affirming the necessity of teaching our religion in Armenian, the community has relied on Article 13 of the Constitution which states that religious minorities are "free to carry out their religious rites and practice their religion in personal status and religious education." The invention of the Armenian alphabet and the translation of the Bible into Armenian, which is the basis of our church traditions, requires the teaching of religion in the Armenian language.

In addition to these points, interpretation of the law requires attention to the spirit and the purpose of the law. Moreover, if the implementation of one principle threatens that of another, ways must be found to remove the causes of the contradiction. As explained above, the rights of religious minorities lose their meaning if the practical means of their survival are not guaranteed. The teaching of religion in their native tongue, which determines the performance of religious rites and makes them accessible to Armenian congregations, has been an essential factor for the Armenian people throughout their history. Thus, the insistence of the Iranian-Armenian community and the Diocesan Council that religion must be taught in Armenian reflects the tenets of the Constitution.

It is clear that no law, and even more so, no constitution can foresee all the practical problems that may arise in the future. Practical details are defined in the process of implementation which must take into consideration both the letter and the spirit of the law. For instance, Article 15 of the Constitution states that textbooks must be in Persian, but in practice, foreign languages are taught in schools and foreign-language textbooks are prepared and used for such instruction.

3. It is surprising that, in the interview published in *Ettelaat*, you stated that Armenian students have the right to decide whether or not to attend religious education classes. The Armenian people have always insisted on the importance of the correct teaching of religion. The Islamic Republic was founded on the noble principles of Islam and has promoted religion as

the way for pious generations to be educated. It is odd, therefore, that the Islamic Republic, whose highest aim is to halt the spread of atheism and solidify religious faith at all levels of society, has chosen to solve the problems related to religious instruction in Armenian schools by promoting the idea of the students' freedom of choice in this matter. The Iranian-Armenian community and the Diocesan Council insist that religious instruction be mandatory in our schools. And in order to reap the best results, the language of instruction should be Armenian. Armenian students will study their religion. In its attempt to solve a problem that need not have been raised in the first place, the Ministry of Education ought not propose steps that would lead to the spread of godlessness among our youth.

We believe the controversy surrounding the difficulties of the Armenian schools is neither ideological nor insoluble. It can easily be resolved by adhering to the noble principles of Islam and the letter and the spirit of the Constitution. The solution will reinstate the conditions under which the Armenian schools previously operated. We hope the authorities will approach this matter with good will, which is in keeping with the principles of the Constitution.

In closing, we ask God Almighty to grant long life to Emam Khomeini, the Leader of the Islamic Revolution and the Founder of the Republic, and ultimate victory in war to the heroic Iranian nation.

Because many people had read the Minister's interview in *Ettelaat*, we sent copies of this letter to *Ettelaat* as well as to *Jomhuri Eslami* (the organ of the Islamic Republican Party), to the offices of Emam Khomeini and Ayatollah Montazeri, and to the President, the Prime Minister, the Interior Minister, the Ministry of Islamic Guidance, the Guardian Council, the head of the Supreme Judicial Council and the Speaker of the Majles. *Alik* translated the exchange and published it on October 29 and 30, 1982.

Parallel to our interaction with the Ministry of Education, the Diocesan Council, together with the Central Board of School Trustees, organized a series of extracurricular activities intended to boost our students' national and religious spirit. Archbishop Manoukian regularly visited the schools in company with members of the Council and the Board. For instance, Vahik Khachaturian and I went to Rostam Elementary School with the Prelate on February 15, 1983, during the stormiest days of our struggle. His presence lifted everyone's spirits: students, teachers, staff and parents alike. The principal gave a welcoming speech and the students sang a resounding *Sardarabad*. The Prelate then spoke about the importance of teaching religion in Armenian and the harm that would befall our community if religion were taught in Persian. Then he took questions from teachers and parents. This was followed by a reception hosted by the Parents Council. These visits had a positive impact on the schools and the community at large. They were also intended to show the authorities that the survival of Armenian schools and religious instruction in Armenian were of the utmost importance to the community.

Meeting with Prime Minister Mousavi

On May 9, 1983, Prime Minister Mir-Hossein Mousavi received Archbishop Manoukian in company with Hrair Khalatian, Vagrig Manoukian and myself. The meeting was covered by local radio and television, and when we arrived at 10:00 AM, the Prime Minister welcomed us with open arms. The Prelate thanked him for receiving us while I simultaneously translated his speech into Persian. He acknowledged the government's condolences on the passing of Catholicos Khoren I at Antelias in February, and alluded to the prospect of a visit by Garegin II, the new Cilician Catholicos. Then he talked about the triumph of the Islamic Revolution and the Armenian community's contributions to the defense of Iran in the imposed war:

> It is true that we are different in matters of religious faith, but the Armenian community of Iran is an inseparable part of the Iranian nation. As you know, young Armenians have fought with all their might to preserve Iran's integrity and sovereignty during this war. Today, the blood of Armenian youths mixes with that of their Muslim brothers to protect the country.

The Prelate went on to say that the Armenian Church is independent, oriented neither toward East nor West, as he himself had made clear from the beginning of the Revolution. He affirmed the Armenian community's loyalty to the political path charted by the authorities and added that the community had publicly confirmed its freedom to practice its religion, culture, language and traditions. The Prelate asked only that government officials exercise wisdom and show respect for the community's legitimate rights. Our difficulties in the area of education were being fomented by a group of civil servants who knew nothing about the issues.

"We want to maintain the distinctive character of our schools," he said. "The Constitution grants us that right."

He concluded by thanking the Prime Minister for once again permitting our April 24 march, and asked God to protect Emam Khomeini.

Prime Minister Mousavi responded by saying that the government considered the Armenian community an integral part of the Iranian nation. He acknowledged that young Armenians had sacrificed their lives for the same high principles shared by Muslims and Christians alike. Though different religions may have different views on how the country should be governed, he said, they all shared the same authentic values, and Muslims and Christians alike must be willing to make sacrifices in order to uphold those values. After the Revolution, which was the triumph of mankind's most noble values, he said, the people of Iran had shown a very positive attitude toward the Armenians. He said it would be truly dangerous if the majority suppressed the minorities and he thanked Almighty God that Iranian Muslims had no intention of doing that. On the contrary, he said, the majority of the people were positively predisposed toward the Armenians and this collective disposition flowed from their revolutionary faith.

> Referring to the Armenians' historic contributions in the fields of science and technology, he said they could play a creative, constructive and dynamic role in the Islamic Republic. The right conditions must be created for them to continue their innovations and inventions, and as revolutionary structures solidified, Armenians could increasingly take up their proper roles in Iranian public life.
>
> Regarding the issue of Armenian schools, the Prime Minister promised to see that negotiations were restarted. If any government official had erred in judgment or in law, he said, they must be held accountable. He urged us to contact his office whenever a problem arose and his office would try to solve it. Even the most intractable issue could be settled through negotiations. In closing, he expressed his hope that Armenians would remain diligent and constructive. And

finally, he asked us to convey his greetings to Albert Ajemian, his university classmate and fellow architect.

Prime Minister Mousavi was an educated and gracious man, worthy of his position, as evidenced by the sound logic of his comments. He saw all social strata as part of a unified entity, but he was unaware of the despicable actions of lower-level bureaucrats.

Prime Minister Mousavi's Circular

Two weeks later, Minister Parvaresh forwarded a new circular from Prime Minister Mousavi ordering the following arrangements for minority schools:

- Community ownership of minority schools established by beneficial trusts was confirmed, with the caveat that during school hours, they were under the authority of the Ministry of Education.
- The Ministry was responsible for hiring principals, teachers and religious instructors through the mechanism of district supervisory councils that must include representatives from the Ministry of Education, the Ministry of Islamic Guidance (Ershad), the Ministry of the Interior and the Ministry of the Islamic Revolutionary Guards Corps.
- A minority-appointed educational advisory committee would have input on the criteria for professional appointments.
- Minority students would be allowed six hours of language instruction per week in lieu of Koranic study.
- Extracurricular activities outside of school hours would be permitted with the prior approval of both the principal and the religious leader of the minority community, and in the case of political events, with the prior approval of the Interior Ministry.

The Diocesan Council was extremely worried by the tone and content of this new circular. After careful consideration, we responded point by point in a letter dated June 15, 1983:

- Although the Prime Minister's circular confirmed our community's ownership of its trust-funded schools, that left out the schools built with community-wide donations.
- There was no provision for minority representation on the hiring councils.

- The hiring process itself was disadvantageous, since there was no guarantee that minority candidates would be hired.
- Nowhere in the Constitution was there any mention of substituting Armenian language study for Koranic study.
- The circular politicized school issues by allowing the arbitrary designation of extracurricular activities as political and therefore subject to prior restraint.

The scheme involving multiple Ministries in the hiring process was worrisome too, but since it also called for a "minority-appointed educational advisory committee," we invited representatives of the other religious minorities to meet at the Prelacy and work out a collective response. They came to several meetings and brought along their MPs, but everyone was playing his own tune, as they say. The Assyrians tended to agree with the Armenians, the Jews said they didn't dare make a move against the government and the Zoroastrians were indifferent to the whole issue. Nobody was happy with how things were going, but neither did they have any answers, and as a result, nothing positive emerged. On the other hand, a few weeks later when I met with Mr. Mortazavi at the Interior Ministry on an unrelated matter, he said to me,

"So, Mr. Aharonian, I hear you've been meeting at the Prelacy with representatives of the other minorities, and it has been proposed that you get together and wage *armed struggle* against the Islamic Republic!"

I was shocked. Had he merely said "struggle," that would have been acceptable, but when he said "*armed* struggle," I knew there was conspiracy afoot.

Leery of being labeled anti-government, which of course were not, we wrote to Mr. Safizadeh, the Director of Minority Affairs in the Ministry of Education, about forming the mandated minority educational advisory committee. We didn't expect to hear anymore about it and we never did.

Final Exams, Spring 1983

Although the Armenian students had refused to be taught their religion in Persian, when it came time for final exams, the Ministry of Education faxed the Diocesan Council that they would have to take the religion exam *in Persian*. The Prelate insisted by return fax that the questions had to be written *in Armenian*. He asked the Ministry to send the questions to the Prelacy so that they could be translated into Armenian, but that never came to pass and the students were given the questions in Persian. When the fifth-grade and eleventh-grade students turned in blank sheets, that hurt them: they were held back and forced to repeat the entire year.

Mr. Safizadeh later told *Kayhan* (October 9, 1983) that "the Armenian religious leader personally wrote the religion exam questions and distributed them to the Armenian schools." Archbishop Manoukian was asked about this by *Alik* (August 20, 1984) and he replied,

> That is simply laughable. We immediately denied that story in a press release that was published in *Alik*. The official who was quoted did not name the Armenian religious leader, nor was it clear why he even made that statement. I must say that the idea that an Armenian religious leader wrote the exam questions in Persian is quite far-fetched. If by "religious leader" he meant the Prelate of the Tehran Diocese, his statement bears no resemblance to reality.... We also sent an emissary to that official on the day that story appeared, to ask which religious personality he was referring to. Unfortunately, he was unable to answer the question. All he said was that we Armenians must reach an agreement with the authorities and that will solve all our problems. As you can see, contradictory statements are being made. We unequivocally state that no Armenian religious leader, including myself, wrote the questions in Persian and sent them to the schools. Which cleric is sufficiently well versed in Persian to even write them?

An Invitation to Convert

The Ministry of Education assigned Dr. Gholam-Ali Haddad-Adel to write the Persian-language religion textbook supplements for minority students. On the pretext that he needed a Persian translation of the New Testament in order to write the texts, Dr. Haddad-Adel asked the Diocesan Council to provide the translation, but the Prelate advised us to say it would be against our religion. Dr. Haddad-Adel even asked the chairman of the Central Board of School Trustees to intervene, but our answer was always a resounding no. Yet he still kept pestering us to assist him.

Dr. Haddad-Adel came from a very devout family. His younger brother had been martyred in the war, and one day I saw an item in the paper announcing a commemoration of his death at the family's private mosque. I knew their father, Haj Agha Haddad-Adel – he had the been the president of the truck owners syndicate before the Revolution – and since this was an open invitation to the public, it occurred to me that I could see him there and ask him to use his influence on his elder son to ease the pressure.

After some difficulty, I found the family estate. When I entered the small mosque called Hossieniyeh and sat down on the carpet, a servant brought me a Koran so that I could read from it, as per tradition, but I didn't open the Muslim holy book. After a few minutes, I looked around but didn't see Haj Agha. I called the servant back and asked if I could speak with the patriarch, but the servant said he was away on business. Realizing that my presence served no purpose, I gave him my card and asked him to give it to Haj Agha when he returned, and then I left.

A few days later, Haj Agha called me at work to thank me for coming to pay my respects to his younger son. I told him that I had an important matter to discuss with him and he suggested we meet that afternoon in his office, so I went. We had both been involved in resisting the leftist project to nationalize the transport industry which, thankfully, had been scuttled. After we had spent some time reminiscing about our common struggle, I mentioned the trouble we were having over the religious education textbook issue. I asked if he could persuade his elder son to deal with us in a more kindly way. He responded graciously, saying that it wasn't solely up to his son, he was only carrying out the Ministry's policy, but he promised to ask him to handle the issue with more sensitivity. Suddenly, he said something utterly unpleasant.

"Mr. Aharonian, what is this Armani Parmani stuff that's bothering you so much? Forget about it. Let me arrange for you to become a Muslim. Then you'll be one of the happiest men in this world and the next!"

I was laughing inside but I smiled and said, "Haj Agha, I'm fifty-two years old and I've been a Christian for fifty-two years. At my age, it would be silly to change my religion."

With that, I took my leave. The following spring, his son was elected to the Majles, and twenty years later, he was elected Speaker of the Majles. If such people were unwilling to let go of me, what chance did our children have to be free of their grip?

Chapter 16

The Struggle Over the Schools, 1983–84

Our students were terribly upset by the lack of extracurricular activity at their schools. They had always observed important days in Armenian history like St. Vartanants, Mets Yeghern and First Republic Day, but now no principal would dare defy the Ministry of Education, which meant that our children were deprived of a key component of their education. Even scouting activities were banned. The Ararat Association's program was a thing of the past. The Armenian General Benevolent Union was the only organization that still sponsored a scouting program, thanks to the efforts of Shavarsh Barkhoudarian. He devoted his life to scouting and he inspired a new generation.

The Diocesan Council decided to organize a scout camp in collaboration with the Parents Councils in the summer of 1983. The safest location for this was the Monastery of St. Thaddeus, about 150 miles northwest of Tabriz and ten miles south of Maku. *Avak Kahana* (Archpriest) Bagrad Melkonian, the Deputy Prelate of Azarbayjan, worked with community organizations in Tabriz to ready the site and provide the camping gear. The scout camp lasted for the entire month of August. A group of Barkhoudarian's scouts came up to direct activities, parents volunteered as cooks and chaperones, and the Avedissian Clinic sent a doctor and a nurse.

Archbishop Manoukian and I drove up on August 7, stopping off in Tabriz to pick up Father Melkonian. The students gave us a rousing welcome, and the Archbishop and I each gave a short speech about the importance of our schools, our language and our religion. We spent two days and two nights camping out with the kids. In the mornings, we took part in scouting activities and toured a display of student artwork and handicrafts. In the afternoons, we attended the tricolor flag ceremony. And in the evenings, we gathered around the campfire and listened to the kids sing patriotic songs and recite classic poems. On the second day, we were drenched by a sudden rainstorm. The tents were flooded but the kids were in such high spirits that it did nothing to dampen their enthusiasm. Soon the bright August sun reappeared and they opened up the tents and laid out their things to dry. When we left, they were getting ready to go home and another group had already arrived.

Persian-Language Religion Textbook Supplements

After the Ministry of Education published its religious education textbook supplements for religious minorities, people from all walks of life wrote to the Diocesan Council, urging us to be careful but not to give in. One such letter came from Reverend Tadevos Mikaelian, a leader of the Armenian Protestant Church in Iran. I had known him since we were teenagers. He was born in Tehran in 1932 and educated at Sepehr School. An intelligent and diligent student, he had studied law at Tehran University, then theology at the Near East School of Theology (NEST) in Beirut. When he returned to Tehran, he helped found the Gohar School. He started teaching there and ultimately became the principal. Like Father Poladian with the Alishan School, Reverend Mikaelian had voluntarily committed the Gohar School to the Diocesan Council's administrative supervision at the beginning of the schools crisis. Now he was the Pastor of St. John Armenian Evangelical (Presbyterian) Church in Tehran. He was a respected patriot and a devout Christian, but unlike clerics in the Armenian Apostolic Church, he tended to proselytize, and in fact, he managed to convert a few Muslims. We were amazed at how freely and courageously he expressed himself, for example, in an interview with the BBC on the textbook issue.

In his open letter to the Council, Reverend Mikaelian presented a detailed analysis of the textbook supplements, pointing out misinterpretations of Christian doctrine and contents borrowed from Islam, including Koranic quotations in the elementary-level supplements. He himself quoted the Koran – *La ikraha fi'd din* (There shall be no compulsion in religion) – in order to make the point that people should not be forced to study their religion in a language other than their own. His letter was written in Persian so that we could submit it to the Ministry of Education should the need arise. Ten months later, he wrote another open letter:

> In God's Name, Most Respected Principals, Dear Brothers and Sisters, Salutations.
>
> Now that our children, as members of religious minorities, have been told that they must use Persian-language religion textbooks in the classroom, I wish to draw your attention to my previous commentary on this subject.
>
> National and religious sensitivities have been offended by

the preparation of these textbook supplements without the consent of Christian leaders, and by the insistence that they be used in schools, and this has unfortunately had negative repercussions. We have information that some high-ranking Islamic officials agree with us.

Sadly, misinformed and misguided officials in the Ministry of Education have interpreted student protests against these textbooks as politically motivated acts, and they have sent the Sepah into our schools and forcibly shut them down.

This is a religious issue involving the preservation of our mother tongue. Therefore, I pray to the Almighty to keep our children safe from harm and help us reach a solution in the spirit of cooperation. We must also take care that the solution does no harm to the honor and integrity of the Islamic Republic of Iran.

In prayer,

Reverend Tadevos Mikaelian

Pastor of St. John Armenian Evangelical Church of Tehran

Like his earlier letter, this one was written in Persian. It was also distributed as a flyer so that it came to the notice of ordinary people, both Armenians and non-Armenians. Copies were sent to the Armenian MPs, the leaders of all the Christian communities in Tehran and Ershad's Department of Minority Affairs.

Ten years later, Father Mikaelian was brutally murdered. Three young Mojahedin were shown on television describing his murder in grisly detail, but other reports contradicted their story. Ultimately, his death was seen as one of scores of killings known as the Chain Murders that began in the late 1980s and continued for a decade under the authority the Ministry of Intelligence and Security, until they were exposed by President Khatami at a critical moment in 1999.

Problem Principal

Fatemeh Moghaddam was a zealot who fervently believed she was serving Islam. After the Revolution, she had been appointed principal of the Jewish high school for girls in the *Ettefaq* (Alliance) complex. Her outrageous actions caused such an uproar that the Jewish community temporarily closed the school in order to get rid of her. Next, she was appointed principal of Anoushirvan Dadgar High School for Girls, a Zoroastrian institution. This was at the height of the war on the Mojahedin Khalq when thousands of young people were condemned to death, including twelve girls from Anoushirvan Dadgar. Mrs. Moghaddam herself turned them in. She even accused several girls of being communists and they served two or three years in prison. The Zoroastrian community somehow got rid of her, but unfortunately, Minister Parvaresh appointed her as principal of Mary Manoukian High School for Girls.

The first thing Mrs. Moghaddam did was to force the students to wear a *maghnaeh* (headscarf) in class, even though women were only required to cover in the presence of unrelated men. She actually gave the teachers needle and thread and ordered them to sew headscarves to the heads of students who were not wearing them. It wasn't long before the students went on strike.

I met a young teacher from Mary Manoukian High School at the Prelacy and I asked her why Mrs. Moghaddam was hated so much. She told me the staff had worked with bad principals before, but never as bad as this. Their hatred congealed when she asked them during a staff meeting whether it was true that on their wedding night, Armenian girls were required to offer their virginity to their father. The outraged teachers walked out of the room, and word of the incident reached the students.

One day Mrs. Moghaddam sent Archbishop Manoukian a note proposing that Mary Manoukian High School be renamed after Saint Mary. Of course, he rejected the idea, but Mrs. Moghaddam was undeterred. She made an appointment with him and repeated her proposal in person. That made him so angry that he told her to mind her own business. I had to explain to her that our schools are named by their benefactors as a condition of their support.

The tension increased to such a degree that the Diocesan Council asked the Ministry of Education to remove Mrs. Moghaddam from her post. Eventually we were given an appointment with Chief Superintendent Mozaffar. The Prelate, Vagrig Manoukian and I arrived at the appointed time and, after a brief wait, we were ushered into his office by Mozaffar himself. His feet were bare, which was his way of telling us that he had just finished his prayers. After we introduced ourselves, he sat down and put his socks on. I asked myself what I was doing there. What could we expect from an official who puts on his socks in the presence of our community's religious leader? He would never understand how deeply Mrs. Moghaddam had offended our students.

The problem continued to fester until the spring of 1984 when Mrs. Moghaddam decided to run for a seat in the Majles. I suspect the Ministry of

Education facilitated the opportunity as a way of getting rid of her. She won a seat, but her new career was cut short by her death in a car crash at the age of fifty-three.

Vartan Vartanian also won a seat in those elections as the MP for the Armenians of northern Iran, and he would go on to serve four terms. One day, I asked him how he managed to work with these people.

"The mollahs are decent folk," he said. "Their sole aim is to propagate and perpetuate Islam. Our problems are with the former servants of the monarchy who switched sides and now think they have to prove their piety at every turn."

Armenian Schools Closed

By the spring of 1984, some seventeen schools had been shut down and the administrative staff in most of the others had been completely replaced. The Tomassian Girls School in Narmak posed a special problem. The Interior Ministry had long coveted its large, beautiful grounds. We feared it would be seized and turned over to a non-Armenian school with a much larger student body, which would be a real tragedy for the local Armenian students, so we asked Father Aharon Galoustian, the neighborhood priest, to rally as many people as possible to occupy the campus. Two days later, Mr. Giveian from the Interior Ministry's Department of Minority Affairs called me on the phone. Before I could even say hello, he asked in a sour tone,

"Mr. Aharonian, why are you sending old men and women to fight with us?"

"What in the world are you talking about?"

"I mean the Tomassian School and all the old people camping out there!"

"Well, since the government closed the school, the community has to protect it."

"The government is not about to start a fight with old men and women!"

With that, he hung up, and the old folks stayed where they were until the Tomassian School was reopened.

In April, when Nor Ani School was closed, the Parents Council appealed to Mr. Safizadeh at the Ministry of Education, but since he had moved to the Department of Legal and Parliamentary Affairs, he referred them to Mr. Madani who had replaced Mr. Mozaffar as Chief Superintendent of Schools. When Madani found out who sent them, he started cursing Safizadeh up and down:

"Why did he send you to me? What do you want? Now you're wasting my time instead of his! You caused a sensation in Israel. You must be working for Mossad. You probably work for the CIA too. Are you the ones who keep calling my office and threatening my family with death? Terrorists! You have no scruples, no principles, no honor! I'm the one who shut your school down and I'll shut the rest of them down too. And you can tell whoever you like what I said because I'm not afraid of anybody!"

Afterwards, the Nor Ani parents wrote to Safizadeh, saying it was never their intention to anger the Chief Superintendent of Schools. If their visit had been misinterpreted, they were prepared to apologize. Their sole request was that he reopen their school and save their children from wandering around in the streets. The problems related to Armenian schools could not be solved by closing them. The Diocesan Council followed up with letters to the national leadership and to Chief Superintendent Madani himself protesting his rude behavior.

Final Exams, Spring 1984

With most of our schools closed and our students boycotting religion class in those schools that were still open, the Ministry of Education magnanimously decided to allow all of our students to take their final religion exam in Persian on a single day. When an estimated 3,000 students turned in completely blank exam papers, it caused a sensation in the national press. The Diocesan Council leadership was summoned to the office of President Khamenei where we were met by his advisor, Mostafa Mir-Salim. After the usual pleasantries, Mir-Salim launched his attack:

"The President wants to know who told the Armenian students to blank their religion exams. This is pure subversion! We know this was organized by a political party and you need to identify the conspirators, otherwise the government will take severe measures."

When he had finished saying his piece, I calmly replied,

"Has the government forgotten that Iran is a pious nation? That the Islamic Republic was founded on the principle of piety which is shared by Armenians and Muslims alike? That piety compels us to demand that our students receive their religious education in Armenian. Why would the government want to lend a political coloration to our pious motivation?"

Mir-Salim hastened to assure us that the government was positively disposed toward the Armenians and had no intention of creating conflict with the community, but he urged us to settle the problem quickly before it got completely out of hand.

Surveillance and Entrapment

In fact, the school closings and the blanked exams were attracting unwelcome attention from abroad. Journalists now regularly called on the Prelacy to get the latest news and local reactions, and whenever an Armenian organization or individual anywhere in the world said something about the crisis in our schools, we were accused of leaking information, whether we knew anything about it or not.

One journalist in particular, a non-Armenian who worked for IRNA (the Islamic Republic News Agency), dropped by almost daily. Before long, he befriended some of the Council members. Then one day, he came to see me at my office. We had a glass of tea and talked about this and that. After about ten minutes, he leaned in closer and whispered that he had a personal and confidential proposal. I said go ahead, present your proposal. He swore me to secrecy and I nodded my head. Then he started talking about how important the news was, how crucial it was to get the information first, before anyone else got it. I kept nodding, wondering where this was going. Then he switched gears and started talking about how expensive everything was and how meager his salary was. Finally he came right out with it. For a monthly stipend, he was prepared to deliver information on government machinations regarding our community issues. He said he owned his own car and we would go for a drive and that's when he would hand over the documents. I was dumbfounded. I didn't know what to say. After thinking about it for a while, I told him, first, that the Prelacy didn't have the budget for such an undertaking, and second, that such an offer required a collective decision. I would discuss it in confidence with the Diocesan Council and let him know what they decided. He would have an answer in two days. Before he left, he repeated several times that it had to be handled with the utmost secrecy.

I was left pensive and uncertain. How useful would his information be? And how reliable? How much would he ask in return? And most important, how could it possibly be kept secret? I contacted Archbishop Manoukian and asked for his advice. He suggested I discuss it with several prominent community leaders. I contacted one of those individuals whom I knew personally. He told me to give it a try and see what happened. But I kept mulling it over, reviewing the journalist's behavior. A man who worked for the state making a pass like that.... He must be a provocateur. He was probably under surveillance himself. Suppose I were arrested for buying state secrets. Not one of those prominent community leaders would bother to visit me in prison, much less work for my release. The next time I saw the journalist, I told him the Council had unanimously declined his offer and that was the end of a dubious proposal.

Another regular visitor at the Prelacy was an Armenian named Hovannes, a police informant. Although illiterate, he was intelligent and willful, but flexible too. During the Shah's era, he had worked as a waiter at Chetnik, an American-owned restaurant in north Tehran, and that's where he was recruited. Back then, he was known as General Jafari's man. He had been tasked by the Deputy Chief of Police with spying on the workers at factories owned by the Sahakian and the Sarkissian families. When Police Chief General Samadianpour had suddenly retired and left the country a month before the Revolution, General Jafari had replaced him, but after the Revolution, he too retired yet remained in Iran. Two months later, he was convicted of sowing corruption on earth and executed. Other high-ranking police officers had been allowed to keep their jobs (as long as they hadn't been involved in any killings) while the new government trained up its own people. One of those officers was General Jafari's former aide, Colonel X, General, an extremely shrewd man in a powerful position. His department monitored political activity. He knew the Armenian community very well and Hovannes became one of his agents.

Hovannes would drop by the Prelacy several times a week. Occasionally his roots got the better of him and he would do us a favor, such as giving us a heads up when one of our schools was about to be shut down. These tips, though not always reliable, gave Hovannes entrée. He would try to pump the Prelate for scraps of information. Archbishop Manoukian never hid anything from the Diocesan Council and he always told me whenever Hovannes had been around. He would smile and say his information wasn't that important:

"He exaggerates his role."

The Masks Are Finally Off

We heard unpleasant rumors concerning intentions about our schools, but they were not rumors but very real. During those critical years, the Diocesan Council was like a drowning man flailing his arms and gasping for air. We were open to the advice and counsel of all our friends in the community, and when a prominent Iranian Armenian lawyer offered to set up a meeting between Archbishop Manoukian and the head of the Court of Administrative Justice (*Divan-e Edalat-e Edari*), we agreed to it, since the latter had the authority to arraign any government official for dereliction of duty or misuse of office.

Vagrig Manoukian and I accompanied the Archbishop. We waited outside the Ayatollah's office for a few minutes until two armed pasdars told us to enter. Inside, two more armed pasdars stood at attention. The Ayatollah sat at the head of a long table. Without rising, he gestured for us to sit. That was not how traditional leaders greeted visitors. Ayatollah Montazeri, Dr. Beheshti, Speaker Hashemi-Rafsanjani, President Khamenei and others had all risen to welcome the Archbishop whenever they met. Some had even embraced him. But no mollah had ever received him with armed guards in the room.

The Ayatollah came straight to the point and asked him what he wanted. The Archbishop thanked him for agreeing to see us and then outlined the problems surrounding our schools. After I had finished translating his remarks, the Ayatollah looked at him and said,

"You should know that this is a Muslim country. It would be against the spirit of our laws to waste time and money helping minority communities. Sooner or later, the whole world must accept Islam. If we were to help you, it would only delay the inevitable."

Suppressing my fury, I said, "Most respected Ayatollah, there are two billion Christians in the world. How do you intend to make them change their religion?"

"It may take a thousand years but it will come to pass."

"But according to the Constitution, which was drafted by clerics, religious minorities have the right to teach their religion and their national literature."

The Archbishop urgently interjected, "We don't know what will happen in a thousand years. We want to exercise our constitutional rights now. That's why we came to you."

In response, the Ayatollah spun out a constitutional argument. We had heard much the same in less dogmatic terms from Khoshnevisan, Mozaffar, Madani and other bureaucrats. Either they didn't know what was going on or they were simply being tactful. How was it possible to reach agreement with people who wanted to forcibly convert everyone to Islam? The meeting had one positive outcome, however. The masks were off and the ruling clerics' real intentions could no longer be disguised.

Chapter 17

Armenian Members of Parliament

The atmosphere was tense in the spring of 1984 when elections were held for the Second Islamic Majles. Hrair Khalatian had declined to seek reelection and the ARF was backing Norair Elsaian, the principal of Soghomonian School. His campaign posters were plastered all over the Armenian neighborhoods. Three days before the first round, I drove down to Qom with a Diocesan Council delegation to meet with Ayatollah Montazeri about our schools. When we got back to Tehran in the afternoon, we were surprised to see that Elsaian's posters had been replaced by posters for Vartan Vartanian. Apparently, Elsaian had been disqualified by the Guardian Council which not only supervises elections but vets the candidates under the principle of "approbatory supervision" (*nazarat-e estesvabi*), so the ARF came up with Vartanian as a replacement candidate. Vartanian was not very well known but he was the president of the Armenian Association of University Graduates and that was where I had met him. The leftist candidate was Dr. Vigen Zargarian, a pediatrician who ran his own clinic in Narmak. The Diocesan Council expected even worse problems with our schools if he won, so we decided to go all-out for Vartanian. For example, I spoke in his favor at a meeting of the Chahar Mahall Sports and Education Association. A united front was quickly formed and Vartanian won by a solid two-thirds majority.

Likewise in the south, Hratch Khachaturian decided not run for reelection. The leftist candidate was Azad Matian, a poet and lecturer in Armenian language and literature at the University of Isfahan. The ARF candidate was Ardavazd Baghoumian, but the party lacked a strong following in Isfahan and Baghoumian's win would have been much more difficult if the ARF hadn't sent help from Tehran. Georgik Aghazarian took busloads of Armenians down to Isfahan and Shahin Shahr to vote for him and the party carried the day.

Vartan Vartanian (North, 1984–2000)

Vartan Vartanian was born in Isfahan in 1943. His mother was a kindergarten teacher in New Julfa and his father was a builder, originally from Salmas. He earned a degree in mechanical engineering at Tehran University and continued his training in Germany where he specialized in building materials.

Vartanian was considered one of the best Armenian MPs ever and he was highly respected by his colleagues in the Majles. I supported him in all his election campaigns. He had a strong command of the English language, and for this reason, and in his capacity as a member of the parliamentary committee on mining and productivity, he was often sent abroad with official delegations. He was sought after by the media and his analyses of issues related to productivity were often heard on radio and television. He addressed the Majles on April 24 several times and informed his listeners about Mets Yeghern.

Vartanian never hesitated to help an Armenian in need and he was always involved in the issues that were important to the community. He worked the phone, lobbying officials to attend to problems his constituents brought to him. When fanatics at certain universities tried to force Armenian students to wear the chador, he negotiated their transfer to other universities where milder policies were in force. When Armenian students were arrested for dancing together at private parties, he followed their case and strove to convince the judge that it was natural and normal for Christian men and women to dance together and therefore it was not prohibited. He always attended Diocesan Council meetings and provided us with invaluable information about government policies and advance notice of pending changes. Whenever the Council wanted to meet with a particular government official, he spared no effort to facilitate the meeting.

Vartanian's home was near my office and he usually dropped by on a weekly basis. Sipping coffee, we would discuss matters of mutual interest. One day, we decided that our mothers should get to know each other. They were close in age and had both been teachers. We thought it would be a source of friendship and intimacy for them and we were not wrong. After we introduced them, my mother spoke highly of Digin Vartouhi and Vartan told me that his mother was very pleased with Digin Almast. We arranged for them to meet at least once a month. Sadly, death came too soon for both of them and they passed away within a few days of each other. Their friendship made me think how useful it would be to have a place where elderly Armenians, both men and women, could meet and create new friendships.

Vartanian had little interest in material things. His mother once invited me to her house without his knowledge. She had cancer and she told me that she had asked Vartan many times to allow the family home to be transferred to his name. She asked for my help in effecting the transfer as quickly as possible. I carried out her wish and she signed the paperwork ten days before she died. Vartan's attitude toward the transfer wasn't a matter of indifference but rather a reflection of his devotion to his mother. He didn't want her to feel that her end was near. His modest and humane disposition made people love and respect him.

Ardavazd Baghoumian (South, 1984–2000)

Ardavazd Baghoumian was born in 1954 in the village of Sangbaran in Isfahan Province. His family was imbued with national traditions. He attended an Armenian primary school in New Julfa and continued his secondary education in state schools. He graduated from the University of Isfahan with a degree in accounting and went on to study political science at the National University in Tehran (now Shahid Beheshti University).

For a brief period, Baghoumian taught in Armenian schools in New Julfa, and after the Islamic Revolution, he was active in community organizations in Isfahan. Elected to represent the Armenians of southern Iran in the Majles in 1984, he too went on to serve four terms. He fought for Armenian constitutional rights, and in particular, he worked diligently with *Hay Dad* (the Armenian Cause) to promote recognition of the Genocide. As a member of the parliamentary oil committee, he frequently attended OPEC meetings. In 2000, he was elected to Tehran's Twelfth Diocesan Assembly of Representatives and he served as vice-chairman of the Assembly for two years.

Dr. Levon Davidian (North, 2000–2004)

Dr. Levon Davidian was a psychiatrist by training. He was born in 1944 in the western Iranian city of Hamadan and attended Koushesh School in Tehran. He completed his premedical studies at the National University (Beheshti University) and took his doctorate in London. He directed the psychiatric division of Mehregan Hospital for many years.

Dr. Davidian was a very active member of the community. He served as the chairman of Tehran's Diocesan Council and Diocesan Assembly of Representatives, and in 1997 he was a delegate to the General Assembly of the Catholicosate of the Holy See of Cilicia.

During his term in the Majles, Dr. Davidian was a member of the parliamentary health committee. He delivered numerous speeches about Mets Yeghern and other Armenian issues. He and MP George Abrahamian spared no effort to persuade the government to recognize the Armenian Genocide, but eventually they had to stop. I believe they were told that the time was not right for a debate over the issue.

George Abrahamian (South, 2000–2004)

George (Georgik) Abrahamian was born in Tehran in 1952. He attended the Arax and the Koushesh-Davidian Schools in Tehran and studied Armenian language and literature at the University of Isfahan. He served two years in the Army, after which he married and settled in Isfahan with his Armenian wife. A kind man with a pleasant disposition, he was much loved by the community.

Abrahamian was very active in community organizations. He served as the chairman of Isfahan's Diocesan Council and as a member of the southern Diocesan Assembly of Representatives. He taught Armenian language and literature at the Kananian School in Isfahan for many years. Like Dr. Davidian, he was supported by the ARF. During his term in the Majles, he was a member of the parliamentary public relations committee where he provided great service to the country. His speech about Mets Yeghern was an impressive event.

Gevorg Vardan (North, 2004-2012)

Gevorg Vardan was born in Tehran in 1969. He attended Alishan Middle School for Boys and graduated from Koushesh-Mariamian High School in 1987. He received his Bachelor's and Doctoral degrees in engineering from Elm ve Sanaat (Science and Technology) University in Tehran. As a graduate research student, he was awarded patent rights for his discoveries which came to be used as practical guidelines in the field of engineering. He also conducted research on the mining, extraction and refining of aluminum, cadmium, nickel, gold and other precious metals.

Before his election to the Majles, Vardan worked for Iran Khodro, the Industrial Precision Automobile Company (IPACO), and SAIPA (*Société Anonyme Iranienne de Production Automobile*), where he oversaw processing, production, quality control and technology transfer.

Vardan has been active in community life since his youth. He joined the Ararat Association's athletics committee at the age of thirteen or fourteen and took on various leadership positions. For many years he was a member of the board of HOOSK, the Armenian Research Center, having been an activist in

Hay Dad since his youth. He worked in the community and in non-Armenian circles for recognition of the Genocide and its imperative in Armenian national life. He attended the Armenia-Diaspora Conferences in Yerevan, and in 1999, he traveled to Nagorni Gharabagh (Nagorno Karabakh) to mark the tenth anniversary of the Gharabagh liberation struggle.

Vardan was elected to the Twelfth Diocesan Assembly of Representatives in 2000 and elected vice-chair of the Assembly in 2003. After he joined the Majles in 2004, he served on various parliamentary committees tasked with investigating issues related to industry and production, as well as with developing good relations between Iran and Armenia. As an MP, he represented and defended the national, legal, and community interests of his constituency. As a professional, he contributed significantly to many projects related to the growth of Iranian production. In addition to meeting with members of his constituency in his office, he regularly reported on his activities in various neighborhoods of Tehran and nearby towns. He was active in community organizations and paid special attention to the families of war martyrs and the indigent. He offered legal support to citizens of the Republic of Armenia residing in Iran on questions of citizenship, court procedures, and most important, taxation. Gevorg Vardan's dedicated, specialized and life-long service to the community and to the Islamic Republic of Iran earned him trust and respect at the highest levels.

Robert Beglarian (South, 2004-2012)

Robert Beglarian was born in 1961 in Tehran. His family moved to New Julfa when he was a child and he formed strong ties to the region. As a youth, he was active in sports, especially soccer. He was a member of Sevan FC, the soccer team sponsored by the New Julfa branch of the Ararat Association, and later, he joined the association's cultural committee. He had a deep interest in art and literature and he served on the editorial board of the quarterly journal *Payman*.

Beglarian earned his graduate and postgraduate degrees in economics at the University of Isfahan and joined the Ministry of Finance and Economic Affairs in 1993, first as a tax assessor, then as a senior economist, and then as deputy director of communications, based in Tehran. From 2000 until he was elected to the Majles in 2004, he was director of the Ministry's library and archives and was also involved in retraining Ministry employees.

In the Majles, Beglarian was a member of the parliamentary economic committee and various subcommittees involved in drafting laws against money laundering and exploring the possibilities of tax-free zones.

Some Notable Prerevolutionary MPs

Earlier, I discussed the career of Ardeshir Ovanessian (Ardashes Hovanissian), one of the founders of the Tudeh Party. He represented the Armenians of northern Iran (1944–46) in the Fourteenth National Consultative Assembly (*Majles-e Showra-ye Melli*), as it was called during the reign of the Shah.

Vahram Khan Zohrabian (d. 1975) was employed in the financial department of the National Bank of Iran. During his two-year term representing the Armenians of southern Iran (1954–56), he succeeded in having confiscated properties returned to the Armenian community.

Sevag Saginian (d. 2003) was the Armenian MP with the longest political career, serving in the Majles for twenty-two years (1956–78). With ARF support, he was first elected to represent the Armenians of northern Iran, and then from 1960 on, he represented the Armenians of southern Iran. He was instrumental in building the Ararat Center in Vanak and establishing Armenian studies programs at the University of Isfahan in the late 1960s and at Tehran University in 1971. After the Revolution, he immigrated to the USA and settled in Glendale, California, where he was a founding member of the local Ararat Association.

Dr. Gaguik Hovakimian, a biochemist, was born in Tehran in 1912. He served two terms as the MP for the Armenians of northern Iran in the late 1960s and mid-1970s.

He had received his university education in Paris and Brussels and for many years he taught biochemistry at Tehran University where he founded a successful research lab. He and his colleague Alexander Baghdikian co-authored twenty-four books on biochemistry. He often lectured abroad and he attended yearly scientific conferences in the West, by means of which he kept himself and his students abreast of the latest developments in their field. He founded the Iranian Biochemical Society in 1955, and in 1962, he was the founding editor of *Acta Biochimica Iranica*, an annual research journal publishing papers in Persian, English and French.

Dr. Hovakimian was a sincere patriot. He was the founding editor of *Hoor*, a bilingual monthly literary journal in Armenian and Persian. He was a close friend of Dr. Manucher Eqbal, a confidant of the Shah and the managing director of NIOC (1963–77) who was helpful, through their friendship, in resolving some of the problems then facing the community.

After the Islamic Revolution, Dr. Hovakimian settled in Paris, and whenever I visited him there, he was eager to hear news of developments in Iran and Armenia. He died in Paris in 2004.

Emma Aghayan was the first and still the only woman ever elected to represent the Armenians in an Iranian parliament. She was MP for the Armenians of northern Iran in the last prevolutionary Majles (1977–79), and afterwards she continued to work hard for the betterment of the community. One of her most important projects was supporting the Erebouni (Shah Aziz) Association in Heshmatiyeh.

Armenian MPs, 1980–2016

(Region) MP	Majles	Term	% of	Votes	Total
(N) Hrair Khalatian	1	1980–184	54	11,064	20,532
(S) Hratch Khatchadrian			53	2,494	4,706
(N) Vartan Vartanian	2	1984–1988	66	20,628	31,464
(S) Ardavazd Baghoumian			61	2,622	4,335
(N) Vartan Vartanian	3	1988–1992	85	16,226	19,165
(S) Ardavazd Baghoumian			58	3,458	6,014
(N) Vartan Vartanian	4	1992–1996	84	19,064	22,889
(S) Ardavazd Baghoumian			53	2,829	5,369
(N) Vartan Vartanian	5	1996–2000	75	20,341	26,957
(S) Ardavazd Baghoumian			59	2,998	6,105
(N) Levon Davidian	6	2000–2004	70	16,062	23,108
(S) George Abrahamian			65	2,821	4,317
(N) Gevorg Vardan	7	2004–2008	88	11,862	13,489
(S) Robert Beglarian			95	2,731	2,880
(N) Gevorg Vardan	8	2008–2012	81	11,311	14,000
(S) Robert Beglarian			97	2,504	2,588
(N) Karen Khanlari	9	2012–2016			
(S) Robert Beglarian					

Chapter 18

The Structure and Functions of the Diocesan Council

During my chairmanship, the Diocesan Council oversaw the work of the following bodies:

Church Councils: Each church has its own council of clerical and lay members that deals with issues of particular concern to it.

Legal Council: Deals with family issues and divorce.

Office of the Notary: Maintains records of marriage, divorce, baptism and death, staffed entirely by Armenians, subject to the Ministry of Justice.

Education Committee: Administers schools under the Diocesan Council's jurisdiction and extracurricular activities therein, hires teachers of Armenian subjects, determines their salaries, supervises the preparation and publication of textbooks in Armenian subjects.

Property Committee: Oversees the acquisition, maintenance and sale of properties owned by the Diocesan Council.

Building Committee: Oversees the restoration of properties owned by the Prelacy, especially schools and churches.

Dzkhagan Tax Board: Collects a modest annual levy from members of the Armenian Apostolic Church which is passed on to the Diocesan Council.

Auxiliary Committee for the Indigent: Reviews the situation of indigent Armenian families and provides assistance in cases of need.

Avedissian Community Clinic: Governed by a board of trustees appointed by the Diocesan Council.

Diocesan Council Library: Housed in the offices of the Prelacy, managed by a Council-appointed employee.

Finance Committee: Supervises the Diocesan Council's financial affairs and serves a consultative function.

Administration and Funding

The Prelacy employed a manager and an assistant manager who coordinated the Prelate's schedule as well as meetings between members of the Legal Council and its clients, such as couples seeking a divorce. The Diocesan Council employed a staff of seventeen to coordinate the work of its numerous councils and committees and to answer the scores of inquiries that came in every day from individuals and organizations all over the country. The Council reviewed every request and conveyed its decision to the staff who drafted the response in Persian, as required by law.

According to the Diocesan Council's reports to the Diocesan Assembly, the Council collected a total of 546,800 tomans (approximately $80,000) in *dzkhagan* taxes from 3,978 parish families (an average of $15–20 each) in 1979. In 1980, the number of parish families who paid their taxes increased to 5,184, and in 1981, to 6,295, which shows that the community was beginning to have more faith in the Council's work. Nevertheless, the sums collected hardly covered staff salaries and administrative expenses.

The Diocesan Council controlled three major trust funds established by community benefactors for specific purposes. The Shahverdian Fund guaranteed the educational expenses of a few Armenian students. The Jenishian Fund was set up by a Western Armenian philanthropist to help low-income Armenians secure gainful employment and take care of their family's needs, and the Council disbursed monies as dictated by the fund's terms and conditions. The Yeghia Baghoumian Fund was established to support a publishing program and it had its own council which identified worthy projects.

Other funds under the Diocesan Council's jurisdiction included the Berjouhi Arakelian, Arzoumanian, Isahak Derderian, Ferahian, Sahakian, Soukerian, and Souren Voskanian Trust Funds, and various other smaller bequests and legacies whose owners had assigned the conditional right of disbursement to the Council. Each of these benefactors had donated a valuable building to the Prelacy.

The Diocesan Council administered two nursing homes. One was located downtown next to the Church of St. George (*Surp Gevorg*). It was founded in 1971 and housed both men and women. Expenses were paid from community funds raised for this purpose. The other home, named after the Armenian *feda'i* Sosse Mayrik (1868–1953), served women only and was founded in 1978 by the Women's Auxiliary of the Armenian General

Benevolent Union (AGBU), thanks to the generosity of Mrs. Shushanik Hordananian. Room and board were covered by the residents or their guardians with supplements from municipal and government agencies. The Council used the interest on a dedicated community fund to maintain the facility. The AGBU managed both homes in consultation with the Diocesan Council.

Provincial Tours of Armenian Communities

The jurisdiction of the Diocese of Northern Iran includes Qazvin, the gateway to the northwest; the Caspian coastal towns of Rasht, Enzeli, Babolsar and Sari; Gorgan, Ghorogh and Mashhad in the northeast; and Arak, Hamadan and Kermanshah in the west. One of the Diocesan Council's major undertakings during my chairmanship was to visit each of these cities and towns.

We set out for Qazvin on January 14, 1981. Archbishop Manoukian headed the Council delegation which consisted of treasurer Eskandar Eskandarian, Yeznik Shahbazian who was an expert in building construction and renovation, and myself. Since we would be dealing with various legal conundrums, we also brought along Mr. Khayyatzadeh, a Muslim Iranian lawyer.

Qazvin had once been home to a large Armenian community with a church and a school and associated councils, but now only thirty families remained. Sunday mass was conducted by a visiting priest, and only twenty of the 200 students enrolled at Raffi School were Armenian. The rental income from a few shops adjoining the church and school helped to support their operations but it wasn't enough. There was a large Armenian cemetery and we decided to sell part of it in order to cover the church and school councils' expenses.

Armenians had a long history in Rasht and Bandar Enzeli – the heart of Gilan Province and Iran's gateway to Russia and Europe – but now there were only sixty Armenian families left. Their most intractable problem was an old caravansary left to the local council by a merchant without heirs. The local council had leased the land and its shops to a Muslim who, after the Revolution, insisted they belonged to him. Mr. Khayyatzadeh looked into the matter, and a few years later, the property was returned to the community.

Things had changed in Enzeli too. There were only forty Armenian families and little sign of the pensions and restaurants that my pals and I had patronized as teenagers during our summer holidays. We visited Digin Arax

Limontian, a woman of advanced age who had played a role in the national liberation struggles and was still active in community affairs. She owned a coffee shop on one of the best streets in town, with a loyal clientele. Her customers would present her with their empty demitasse and ask to have their fortune read and she never refused their request. We also visited Madame Arpik, the manager of Agha Jan's Pension. She was the mother of my childhood friend, Felix Hovanissian, and she had married Agha Jan after the death of Baron Hovanissian. Agha Jan's will specified that after her death, the pension should be given to the Tehran Diocesan Council, and some years later, his wish was carried out.

There were almost no Armenians left in Babolsar. A property bequeathed to the Diocesan Council by the late Mr. Panyants which was claimed by his former employee, the non-Armenian mother of his daughter, was and remained the object of litigation between the Council and the woman.

In Sari, the center of Mazandaran Province, there were sixty Armenian families. They had no church and the only property they owned was the Armenian cemetery. They needed help documenting their ownership, after which they planned to sell part of the land and use the income for community purposes.

Armenian refugees from the Bolshevik Revolution had settled around Gorgan and Ghorogh near the southeastern point of the Caspian Sea. There they had prospered as farmers, but emigration had depleted their ranks. Only fifty-nine families remained in 1981. They were very well off and they had strong community loyalty but no community structures. We were able to form the Ghorogh Armenian Community and Church Council as a branch of the Tehran Diocesan Council. When they decided to build a small church, fifteen sponsors (of whom I was one) each donated 50,000 tomans. I attended the consecration of the Church of the Blessed Virgin Mary (*Surp Mariam Asdvadzadzin*) which was conducted by Father Aharon Galoustian. Unfortunately, when I last visited the area in 2003, only seven Armenians remained.

Further east in Khorasan Province, no more than 200 Armenians remained in Mashhad after the Revolution. Given their small number, the local Chief Superintendent of Schools had ordered them to open their school to non-Armenian students who attended free of charge. The Havan brothers, local construction magnates, took care of community needs. Elsewhere in the province, in Neyshabour and Sabzevar, scores of Armenian families were involved in growing cotton and manufacturing cloth.

In 1982, we toured Armenian communities in the west. In Arak, there were 166 Armenian families (720 individuals). Some of them were descendants of the Armenians brought to Persia by Shah Abbas in the seventeenth century, others were the children and grandchildren of the many ARF intellectuals exiled to Arak after the fall of the first Armenian Republic in 1920. These latter had a strong influence on the community's development. The location of Arak on the main route from Tehran to Khuzestan attracted mechanics and other technicians, especially during the Second World War and the Iran-Iraq War when their skills were much in demand. Sati often used their services. The community was well organized, with schools, kindergartens and cultural centers, and its leaders had strong relations with Arak's municipal leaders, which enabled them to sell part of the Armenian cemetery and build a new school and other facilities. The Diocesan Council assisted in these arrangements.

Southwest of Arak near Shazand, where I had done my internship as a Polytech chemistry major, a few Armenian families still lived in the village of Kalava, and former residents who owned farms in the area returned for the harvest every summer. Armenians from Tehran helped restore the half-ruined Church of St. Hagop and I was present for its reconsecration by Archbishop Manoukian. Father Galoustian was there too, as well as the provincial governor and a large number of Muslim guests of both genders.

Hamadan (ancient Ecbatana) had been a British stronghold during the Second World War when there was a large Armenian community, some of whom were affiliated with the Anglican Church. Only five Armenian families remained in 1982, but the Diocesan Council assisted in repairing the church, whose caretakers were an Assyrian family. The Armenian Anglican community ran a clinic but ultimately could not sustain the operation.

Kermanshah was an important stage on the ancient trade route to Iraq, the Mediterranean Sea and Europe. More recently, its oil refinery had attracted a small Armenian community who established a school and community center. But the town's proximity to the border made it a target of daily bombardment during the war with Iraq. The Armenians fled and the school and the center were destroyed, and the Diocesan Council ended up selling the land where they once stood.

Assistance to Emigrants

As mentioned, there were very few Armenians in the Caspian coastal town of Babolsar and no Armenian school, so the nine-year-old daughter of an Armenian couple was forced to attend a state school. One day, the mother learned that her daughter was not only being taught Islamic prayers in school, but was being made to stand in front of the class and lead the students in prayer. When the child's father was told about this, he quit his job as a skilled refrigeration technician and brought his family to Tehran, and from there they immigrated to the USA.

One morning during the war, an Armenian man was taking his son and daughter to school when a bomb went off near Sepah Square. The man and his son were killed and his daughter sustained an injury to her leg. Archbishop Manoukian and I visited her in the hospital and offered our condolences to her mother. A few months later, the mother came to my office and told me that, as compensation for the loss of her husband and son, she had been offered a house in Tehran Pars, a neighborhood just northeast of Narmak. She asked whether she ought to accept the offer and I advised her to do so, thinking it would give her a modicum of security. Six months later, she came to see me again and told me that the local mollah had come to her new home and asked her to convert to Islam and become his wife. She and her daughter left the country shortly thereafter.

There was a talented young Muslim who played soccer for Ararat FC and later succeeded Zdravko Rajkov as coach. I knew him from my time on the club's board of trustees. He spent all his time with Armenians and he spoke the language perfectly. His friends had him baptized and gave him the name "Hamlet" and he married an Armenian girl. One day, he came to me for help. He said his paternal uncle was out to kill him as a *mortad* (apostate), and I advised him to leave the country. A year later, Hamlet sent me a note from America with a photo of his children.

Another day, I was with the Prelate in his office when we were told that a man was waiting downstairs with two children. He insisted on seeing the Holy Father, so we went down to meet him. We learned that he was a watch repairman, he was suffering from bone cancer, and his children were six and eight years old. His wife had converted to Islam and run off with a pasdar, taking their twelve-year-old daughter with her. Not long afterwards, we brought up this man's case during a meeting with Ayatollah Beheshti. He responded that the mother had accepted Islam and that, according to Islamic law, children must remain in their mother's custody until the age of eighteen. We were in contact with the Armenian College and Philanthropic Academy of Calcutta which had extended an open invitation to take any students we cared to send and give them a free education. We sent the watch repairman and his two kids to Calcutta.

The Avedissian Community Clinic

The Avedissian Community Clinic was originally established after the Second World War during the repatriation to Soviet Armenia, when thousands of Armenian peasants left their farms and came to Tehran in the expectation of expedited emigration. Arriving en masse with no place to stay and no prospect of work, they gradually dispersed from the Behjatabad collection area and settled on vacant land to the northeast which eventually became the neighborhoods of Heshmatiyeh, Majidiyeh and Narmak. Their living conditions were very bad and there were several outbreaks of contagious diseases. Physicians who had helped found the Armenian Association of University Graduates mobilized Armenian medical students from Tehran University to help treat the refugees free of charge. That led to the establishment of a clinic funded by Gevorg (Youra) Avedissian in memory of his brother Avedis. Over time, however, the clinic ran out of funding and suspended operations.

The Avedissian Community Clinic was reopened after the Islamic Revolution, largely through the efforts of the Diocesan Council and a group of physicians headed by Dr. Zaven Nersissian. It was staffed by very competent doctors and offered various specialized services including eye and dental clinics, ear, nose and throat specialists, an internal medicine section for cardiac, digestive and other ailments, a laboratory and X-rays. The clinic served the wider community without prejudice, and in fact, only 40 percent of its clientele was Armenian. When the clinic's board of trustees asked permission of the Diocesan Council to expand the facility by incorporating the courtyard into the existing building, the Council agreed and the renovation project was given to a contractor who had pretensions to being a community leader, though it later became clear that his only aim was to swindle the clinic.

One night when Archbishop Manoukian was experiencing an irregular heartbeat, we asked Dr. George, a young physician who worked in the clinic, to examine him. His treatment was very professional and the Prelate quickly regained his health. After *Alik* published our press release announcing his recovery and expressing our gratitude to Dr. George, the number of the doctor's clients increased and he started working late at the clinic to accommodate them all. Dr. Nersissian disapproved and complained that the extended hours were generating more expenses than income. That caused tension among Diocesan Council members and led to daily verbal clashes that threatened the clinic's viability.

During that period of extreme tension, Dr. George arranged an intravenous feeding for a patient in a private room, and after attending to his other patients, he left the clinic and forgot about the one with the tube in his arm. Hours later, a nurse noticed the patient and called around for Dr. George. She eventually located him and he arranged for the removal of the tube and had the patient sent home.

Dr. Nersissian, who chaired the clinic's board of trustees, was immediately informed of the contretemps. He had been waiting for such an opportunity. The next day, he wrote a letter to the Iranian Medical Association (*Nezam Pezeshki Iran*) on behalf of the board. Fortunately, the clinic's director knew that such a communication exceeded the board's authority and he sent the Diocesan Council a copy of the letter. We decided that the only way to avert a major crisis was to dissolve the board and take over the administration of the clinic. As Council chair, I was a member of the transitional leadership. Two years later, when a new board was elected, my tenure on the Council had come to an end and I was able to join the clinic's board as chairman, a position I held for ten years.

The clinic was in terrible condition when we took charge. The renovation was unfinished and the contractor had left the country. Conflicts between the medical staff and the previous board of trustees had negatively impacted daily operations. The new board brought the situation under control and in two years, the clinic was fully functioning again. Most important, there was harmony between the physicians and the board.

Excess Alcohol and X-Ray Film

After all these adjustments, the Avedissian Community Clinic became self-sufficient and even started to turn a profit. But in 1990, several unpleasant incidents cast a shadow over our achievements. All clinics were allocated a monthly supply of twenty bottles of alcohol by the Ministry of Health. Our clinic only used a few bottles a month, so twice a year we sold the excess to people we knew and used the proceeds to buy other supplies. Similarly, the clinic was a member of a government-supervised cooperative that purchased

X-ray film at a discount. Every two or three months, we sold the unused film on the open market and the profit enabled us to cover a gap in the clinic's budget.

One day, the director came to my office in a state of confusion and anxiety. According to his story, he had gone to the bank and withdrawn 400,000 tomans (about $4,000) to cover the clinic's payroll. On his return, as he was exiting a taxi near the clinic, a man rode up on a motorcycle and snatched the cash bag. I immediately informed the Prelate and the chair of the Diocesan Council so that they could contact the police.

Two months later, the board of trustees instructed the director to sell some more X-ray film, since we were planning to purchase a new piece of equipment for the clinic. The next morning, the director phoned to tell me that a burglar had entered the clinic the night before, broken the lock on the storage cabinet and taken all the film. I went straight there to see for myself what had actually happened. A window near the cabinet was broken and there was a broken lock on the floor, but it didn't fit the latch on the cabinet. I realized that the director had fabricated the story. The police were called in to investigate. They told us that even though the missing film had been recorded in our inventory, it had never actually been brought into the clinic. As a matter of fact, in order to save money, we had relied on the director's reputation and entrusted him with the job of receiving and selling the film.

This series of events created an uproar in the community. The director blamed an innocent young man who, he said, had been in the clinic until very late on the night of the burglary. But the security guard, who knew everything that went on in the building, said that all the doors had remained locked all night. There was another consideration that tended to exonerate the youth. The film weighed some 250 pounds and a car would have been necessary to carry it all away. In other words, the director's story just didn't hold water. The Prelate and the Diocesan Council chose not to pursue the matter any further, to just forget the whole thing. On the other hand, I came under pressure from the director's relatives. My response to them was that, in my position, it was my duty to protect the community's interests, not to help the guilty.

The New Avedissian Community Clinic

In the late 1990s, the Diocesan Council purchased a property in Narmak for the new Avedissian Community Clinic. Council chair Aida Hovhannisian oversaw the construction of a six-story building outfitted with the most up-to-date equipment. The clinic opened its doors on August 27, 2004. The new Prelate, Archbishop Sebouh Sarkissian, presided over the opening ceremony. My wife and I were among the invited guests, along with other community members, local and national government officials, and Muslim residents of Narmak who unreservedly expressed their appreciation of the new clinic.

Chapter 19

Ecclesiastical Affairs

In January 1983, the Diocesan Assembly was invited to send representatives to a meeting of the General Assembly of the Catholicosate of the Holy See of Cilicia at Antelias. Because of the ongoing civil war in Lebanon, it had been years since the General Assembly had convened. There were delegates from Cyprus, Greece, Syria, Kuwait, Abu Dhabi and the USA, but the Iranian delegation was the largest from any country. The Tehran contingent included Archbishop Manoukian, school board chairman Vahik Khachaturian, schools liaison Vagrig Manoukian (both members of the ARF), and myself. A few members of the ARF Bureau also attended, notably Bureau chief Hrair Maroukhian.

It being wartime in Iran, there was a general travel ban, but exceptions could be made. We quickly assembled the required documents and sent them to the Ministry of Islamic Guidance where they were verified and then sent on to the security section for further inspection and assessment of the purpose of the intended travel, and if approved, forwarded to the section that issued travel documents. The whole process took a few days. A week before our scheduled departure, I learned that travel documents had been issued to everyone except me. I appealed the decision and was given a hearing with a young judge in the Revolutionary Court. I told him that my position was such that if the Armenian community knew that I was forbidden to travel, they would assume either that I had done something wrong or that the government had it in for the whole community. There was another consideration as well: the Armenian left was opposed to Antelias, and if I were not allowed to attend the conference, the leftists would seize on that and make something out of it.

The judge told me that he personally considered the minorities, and especially the Christians, to be people of good will, but my travel ban was related to an investigation into the sale of forged airline tickets. Some months earlier, a squad of pasdars had raided Sati's ticketing office and confiscated the records of all our sales since the Revolution, but we had never been given an explanation. The judge told me that no evidence had been found that I or any other member of a religious minority caught up in the raid was guilty, but I was banned from travel because the matter was still under investigation. Nevertheless, he decided to lift the ban with the proviso that I furnish a guarantee of my return in the form of a real estate title, which I presented immediately and was then granted an exit permit.

Security at the airport was tight, and in our case, the pre-boarding search was meticulous. Archbishop Manoukian even had his robes searched. Since there was no direct flight to Beirut, we flew to Damascus where two cars were waiting to take us over the mountains. Arriving at Antelias in the afternoon, we paid a courtesy call on Catholicos Khoren I and his Coadjutor, Catholicos Garegin II. Catholicos Khoren had been in poor health for several years and this was the first time I met him. I found him rather downcast but I was deeply impressed by his spirituality. He invited us to stay for dinner, and afterwards I had the opportunity to play *nardi* (backgammon) with him.

General Assembly Meeting at Antelias

The next day, Catholicos Khoren made a brief appearance to deliver the opening speech, and Catholicos Garegin chaired the rest of the proceedings. The agenda included delegates' reports and local educational, cultural and religious issues. Each of our communities had similar concerns and difficulties and I stressed this point when I had a chance to speak. The atmosphere was such that we felt like the sons and daughters of one big family.

Toward the end of the third day, a draft resolution was read out, after which Hrair Maroukhian stood up and made a number of critical points. Everyone took them to heart, including Catholicos Garegin, and as a result, the resolution was completely revised. It was then that I realized how strong ARF influence was on policy made at Antelias.

Maroukhian invited the Iranian delegation to his home for dinner that evening. A sumptuous table was set with an abundance of food and drink of the best quality. His wife Anahid Sarkissian-Maroukhian was a childhood friend of mine and this was a pleasant occasion to renew acquaintance with someone I have always respected.

The Catholicosate arranged several tours for the delegates after the conference. In parts of Beirut, we saw the devastation of the civil war. Some neighborhoods were utterly deserted, with only hungry cats lurking in the streets. We visited a gym run by *Homenetmen*, the Armenian General Sports Association, where we watched young men training in the martial arts. Their trainer asked one youth what he was training for and he replied that he wanted to be strong so that the Turks wouldn't kill him. We also visited the Armenian village of Anjar. On our last evening, we were treated to a Lebanese-style dinner. In the middle of the night, we were all awoken by a huge explosion some distance away.

The next day, I flew to Paris on Middle East Airlines, the only carrier then flying that route. I was fortunate to be sitting in first class with Archbishop Garegin who was the focus of the crew's respectful attention. It was a most pleasant journey. A week later, I was deeply saddened to learn of Catholicos Khoren's death. His funeral took place at Antelias on February 15, 1983, and according to the Paris daily *Haratch*, 50,000 people attended. Archbishop Garegin succeeded him as Catholicos of the Great House of Cilicia. Twelve years later, Garegin would be elected Supreme Patriarch and Catholicos of All Armenians at Echmiadzin.

A Meeting of the Three Iranian Dioceses

The Tehran Diocese always maintained good relations with its sister dioceses. They function independently of one another and each deals with issues specific to its region and its internal organization, but all three share information and confront common problems as one. That unity was at work in their collective response to the Education Ministry's twenty-point circular and subsequent directives.

It was essential for the leaders of the three prelacies to meet regularly in order to strengthen the community as a whole and to safeguard its interests. The last time they had met was in May 1978. Their first postrevolutionary meeting took place in Tehran on May 18, 1983. The participants were Archbishop Manoukian of Tehran, Bishop Papian of Isfahan, the V. Rev. Father Melkonian of Tabriz, MP Khalatian, the chairs of the three regional Diocesan Councils, as well as Vagrig Manoukian, Dr. Armen Hakhnazarian and Dr. Aida Hovhannisian from Tehran's Diocesan Council.

Archbishop Manoukian began the meeting with a prayer and then welcomed everyone. He emphasized how important such meetings were and called for diocesan representatives to meet much more frequently. The agenda for the three-day meeting consisted of thirty-one items under five headings: organizational, diplomatic, community policy guidelines, religious, and miscellaneous.

The first item, which was unanimously approved, was the proposal to invite His Holiness Garegin II to visit Iran. I made a presentation about the importance of such a visit and suggested a schedule of meetings with various Iranian leaders.

Then the three spiritual leaders each presented a report on the activities of his diocese, with particular attention to issues and problems concerning the schools, especially the religion textbook supplements. A proposal to have the three Diocesan Councils meet more often regarding these issues was approved.

Discussion during the second day centered on mixed marriages, family law, individual rights, baptisms, the religious education of young people, the publishing program, the renovation of historic Armenian monasteries, and the estates of community members who passed away without heirs. Bishop Papian and Father Melkonian explained how they had transferred ownership of the assets of such decedents to their respective Diocesan Councils without any interference from the government. This was useful information for the Tehran Diocese and we subsequently followed their example in cases under our jurisdiction.

One of the most important decisions taken concerned St. Thaddeus Monastery in West Azarbayjan Province. Its walls were on the verge of collapse due to their age and a series of natural disasters. A committee was formed to restore the site and Dr. Hakhnazarian was elected chair. The Northern and the Southern Dioceses promised to support the effort which came under the jurisdiction of the Diocese of Azarbayjan, and when the actual work began, the Ministry of Culture and Islamic Guidance provided both technical and financial support.

Building New Churches and Renovating Old Ones

Earlier, I mentioned Archbishop Manoukian's role in building the Holy Translators Church in Narmak and St. Sarkis Church in Behjatabad, consecrated in 1968 and 1970 respectively. In January 1981, the Diocesan Council put the construction of a new church in Majidiyeh on its agenda. Had the project been postponed for a year or two, it would have been impossible to get a building permit. Community donations had already covered the purchase of the land where the church was going to be built, and the Council tasked a committee to implement the project. Jirair Simonian won the design competition. The estimated cost was 2 million tomans, not including auxiliary structures such as the office, reception area and restrooms, nor did it include paving the courtyard. *Alik* published a report on the project at the end of January.

On May 19, the Diocesan Council learned that Grigor and Hrachouhi Melikian had agreed to fund construction of the church in Majidiyeh as well a chapel at the Ararat Center. Certain considerations prompted the Council to accept their offer to fund the church but to seek other benefactors for the chapel. Archbishop Manoukian requested and the Council agreed to name the church after Mr. Melikian's namesake, St. Gregory the Illuminator (*Surp Grigor Lusavorich*).

The construction committee met with Mr. Melikian in June to present the plans and the budget. Levon Keshishian was put in charge of project oversight and Council members Armen Hakhnazarian, Rafik Der Petrossian and Yeznik Shahbazian were tasked with overseeing construction, which took two years. Due to unforeseen factors, the project ran over budget by 250,000 tomans, which was par for the course on a project of that scale, and which was graciously covered by the benefactors. The total cost of the church was approximately $300,000. Parishioners donated funds for the baptismal font, the altar curtain and other furnishings, as well as for construction of the office complex, while the Council underwrote the cost of heating and air-conditioning the church. Archbishop Manoukian presided over the consecration ceremony on January 8, 1984, with thousands of Armenians in attendance.

In Heshmatiyeh, where there was no church, the people asked to have the large hall on the first floor of the Sahakian School converted into a church. At peak enrollment, the school had had over 1,500 students, but emigration had reduced the Armenian population and the church was built partly to stave off expropriation. Archbishop Manoukian consecrated it as St. Vartanants Church in 1986.

The Ararat Center was the most important focus of community life, but many outsiders were envious of this beautiful community center and sports complex that was built and run by Armenians. As a protective measure, the Center's executive board decided to build a chapel on the grounds which could be considered a replacement for a ruined church in old Vanak village. As mentioned, Grigor and Hrachouhi Melikian were prepared to finance construction of the chapel, but the Diocesan Council advised Ararat's board to recruit multiple benefactors instead. They accepted the Council's advice and invited twelve benefactors, all of whom agreed to contribute to the project, and I was one of the twelve.

Rostom Voskanian, the architect who had laid out the original plan for the Ararat Center and designed its athletic stadium, now designed a modernist chapel in keeping with the existing structures. In the prevailing atmosphere of extreme Islamism, it would have been impossible to get a building permit, so it was decided to put up a screen around the southeast corner of the grounds where the chapel would be built. That way, nothing was visible from the outside and we didn't have any problems. The groundbreaking ceremony took place in the presence of the benefactors in 1986 and construction began immediately. Holy Cross (*Surp Khatch*) Chapel was consecrated one year later, and now the Ararat Center has a beautiful chapel where baptisms, weddings and other religious ceremonies can take place.

In addition to Archbishop Manoukian's role in building new churches, he was instrumental in the renovation of old ones. The Chapel of SS. Thaddeus and Bartholomew (*Surp Tadevos-Bartoghimevos*), built some 250 years ago near the Grand Bazaar, was in terrible disrepair due to years of neglect. The Prelate arranged for Dr. Hakhnazarian to oversee its restoration. That process revealed beautiful polychrome murals and Armenian script on the northern walls. Evidently the chapel was built by Armenian craftsmen who came from Constantinople to work on the mirrored halls of the Golestan Palace complex. Several tombstones in the courtyard mark the graves of Europeans.

The Prelate also initiated the renovation of the Church of St. Minas (built in 1854) in Vanak and St. George (1795) in Sheikh Hadi which is the oldest Armenian neighborhood in Tehran, though not a single Armenian lives there now. On the Prelate's advice, the Diocesan Council bought a small lot adjacent to St. George's Church and built a home for Armenian senior citizens who had no relatives to care for them. Deacon Zareh Ohanian played an important role in renovating the church and taking care of the elderly Armenians housed next door.

Celebrating Archbishop Manoukian

In late 1984, the Diocesan Council appointed Hovik Haroutunian to chair a committee charged with organizing a celebration of Archbishop Manoukian's twenty-five years of service to the community. The date was set for May 24, 1985, and as the day approached, the Prelacy was inundated with congratulatory cables, letters and phone calls. The celebration was held in the Ararat Center's Sassountsi David Hall which has a capacity of 2000, and the hall was filled to capacity. Representatives of all the Armenian organizations as well as the other Christian minorities took part. The stage was covered with wreaths. A group of artists created a souvenir symbolizing the Prelate's tenure and it was my great privilege as a member of the Diocesan Assembly of Representatives to present it to him. Other community leaders delivered speeches including Aida Hovhannisian who spoke on behalf of the Diocesan Council, gracious young people recited poems, and the Ararat Choir conducted by Gurgen Movsissian performed the musical interludes. After the public event, the Ararat Association hosted a private dinner for invited guests honoring the Holy Father.

Raffi's Travel Memoirs

One Monday afternoon that year, I went to the Prelacy an hour before the Diocesan Council meeting to discuss the agenda with the Holy Father, as I usually did. I asked him how he was feeling and he said he hadn't slept at all last night. What kept him awake was a long article by Bagour Garabedian in the Yerevan literary journal *Grakan Tert* titled "Dialogue of a Hundred Years," which outlined the history of the Armenian villages of Nagorni Gharabagh and provided ample evidence that those villages did in fact belong to Armenians. Garabedian's essay was by way of introducing the travel memoirs of the great novelist Raffi, which he maintained had great literary and historical value but had never been collected in a single volume. The Holy Father was so moved that he suggested we publish them. I agreed to finance publication on condition that I be allowed to dedicate the book to my mother. The first edition of 1,000 sold out quickly. Though it wasn't easy in those days, I sent ten copies to my daughter in Brussels to forward to Garabedian. I saved the first copy for my mother and presented it to her on New Years Day, 1986, in the company of friends.

Raffi, the pen name of Hakob Melik Hakobian (1835–88), was born in the Salmas village of Payajuk. There were nearly 50,000 Armenians in twenty-three villages in the Salmas region at the beginning of the twentieth century, but by 1985, only fifty Armenian families remained, almost all of them in the town of Salmas itself. The others had long since migrated to the cities, primarily Tabriz and Tehran, and only their churches and monuments remained. Many sold their fields and orchards to Kurdish and Azeri farmers through an Azeri go-between named Yousef Ali. He had grown up among Armenians and he spoke the Salmas dialect so well that you could hardly tell he wasn't an Armenian. He came to Tehran in 1984 and persuaded my maternal cousin Ashot Babloyan to sell Uncle Mnatsakan's farm in Haftvan. Likewise, he persuaded my mother to sell her father's land in the same village.

No one lived there anymore. She was crying as she signed the power-of-attorney, but what else could she do? Which Armenian could be persuaded to go back and till the soil?

Chapter 20

Life-Changing Events

After my father died, we expanded André Shop and my elder brother Henrik took over the management. As a combination grocery and delicatessen, it was practically the only store of its kind in Tehran and it became one of the best known shops in the city. When a new building went up across the street, Henrik bought the place and used part of the ground floor for storage, installing a sub-zero freezer and two commercial refrigeration units, which was a great help to our business. Soon, André Shop was preparing hot meals for scores of institutions on a daily basis, employing two cooks and a large staff of assistants to meet the demand.

The only one who could help my brother with this challenging job was my mother. She would go to the shop early in the morning, count the money in the cash register and straighten up the display items, and when the cashier came in at 9:00 AM, she would hand him the money and take a receipt. Only after Henrik arrived was she able to go home and rest a little before doing her housework. My cousin Ashot and I usually joined her for lunch which was sent over from André's, and sometimes Henrik joined us too. She would ask about my work on the Diocesan Council and she always read about our doings in *Alik*.

My Mother's Last Years

My mother had a distinctive personality. There were many women in her social circle, yet she socialized with very few. Her pastimes were limited. She did not like to play cards or get together for coffee. She was a woman of great humanity, and she was fearless. She often sheltered youthful demonstrators fleeing the police. At such times, her door was always open and she offered them not only shelter, but tea and pastries too.

My mother was never able to reconcile herself to the psychological emptiness that followed my father's death, but with the help of her grandchildren, she began learning to read and write in Persian. She also learned to crochet. I remember two beautiful bedspreads that she made for her grand-daughters. I once entered her work in an exhibition of Armenian women's handicrafts sponsored by the Chahar Mahall Association of Tehran and it won first prize in the competition.

After the Islamic Revolution, the families of my mother's three sons were all living abroad and her nest was completely empty. She and her grandchildren had been very attached to each other. They used to love eating the food she cooked for them and sharing it with their friends. But now that they were all in America, for whom could she cook? Anyone who is a grandparent will understand what I mean.

She was living alone in the four-room apartment she had shared with my father on old Shah Reza Street. We thought the upkeep was too much for her and we were afraid for her to live there by herself, but we couldn't persuade her to move in with Henrik or me (our younger brother George was living in the states at the time). Perhaps she thought she would be a burden. But she had spent half her life there and she was loath to leave its sweet memories behind. Besides, it was a cheerful place. She would sit on her balcony for hours, keeping herself occupied with reading or crochet. At one point, we decided to send her to Los Angeles to visit her grandchildren, but they had grown up by then, some were in college, others were working, and they had little time for her, so she asked George to send her home. We finally persuaded her to move into a small apartment in the building across the street. It had built-in heating and air-conditioning, but she still missed her old home.

One night in the summer of 1985, Henrik called me from the shop at around 8:00 PM. He said he had tried to call our mother several times but she hadn't answered, so he had sent one of the workers across the street to check and he found her lying on the floor. I rushed over and took her to Pars Hospital. Apparently she had fallen and broken her leg. The surgeon explained that her bones were fragile due to her advanced age. He operated that night and placed a platinum rod in her leg. We brought her home to recover and hired a kind Armenian woman to take care of her. After that, she was wheelchair-bound. She was very sad to have lost her mobility, especially since she could no longer help my brother in the shop. But she still crocheted, studied Persian, and read *Alik* every day.

On February 14, 1986, Henrik telephoned me to say that her health had deteriorated. I went to her apartment and found her lying on her bed. She didn't recognize me. I called the Avedissian Clinic and asked Dr. Vazrig Der

Petrossian to come right away. A few minutes later, this kind, hard-working woman passed away. Dr. Der Petrossian determined that she had died of a heart attack.

My mother's funeral took place in a somber atmosphere. Since most of my relatives were living abroad, my real friends were the grateful community members. A large congregation of mourners returned her to the earth, and for weeks afterward, *Alik* carried messages of condolence and testimonials to her memory.

My Open-Heart Surgery

One day in 1985, I was walking along the shore in Darya Kenar with the Holy Father when I felt an unusual pain in my chest. I consulted a cardiologist and he ordered several tests, all of which showed that I had a healthy heart, but I wasn't satisfied. I went to France and sought the advice of my brother-in-law, the cardiologist Dr. Yves Louvard. He had me admitted to a first-class hospital and subjected to various tests, including a bicycle test during which he checked my breathing and blood pressure. He too said my heart was healthy.

I was planning a trip to the states for my son's wedding in May and Archbishop Manoukian asked to join us, which was a great honor. We all flew to Los Angeles together. Vahe's bride was a young Iranian Armenian woman whom he had met at a chapter of the Ararat Association in Southern California. Her family had moved to Armenia when she was a child and subsequently moved to the USA.

While I was in Los Angeles, my friends suggested that I consult with a cardiologist at the UCLA Medical Center. An angiogram showed that three of my arteries blocked. I had stents inserted, but six months later, further tests showed that one of my arteries was 90-percent blocked. So I returned to the USA and underwent open-heart surgery on July 23, 1986. Over a three-month period of recovery, I gradually regained my health.

The Eleventh Diocesan Assembly of Representatives

With the Tenth Diocesan Assembly of Representatives approaching the end of its term, the Diocesan Council requested permission from the Interior Ministry to hold elections for a new Assembly. Within days, we received detailed instructions as to procedure and the Council appointed a committee to supervise the elections. After the candidates' names had been submitted to the Ministry and had been approved, the committee published an announcement in *Alik* laying out the rules and regulations, listing the candidates by district, and specifying the number of Representatives to be elected from each district:

St. Sarkis Church and Vanak (north of Taleghani Street)	12 representatives
St. Mary's Church (south of Taleghani Street)	6 representatives
Heshmatiyeh (Sardarabad)	3 representatives
Majidiyeh (Zeytoun)	5 representatives
Sassoun (Vahidiyeh, Zarkesh and Narmak)	12 representatives

The Prelate would appoint seven Representatives, for a total of forty-five. The Interior Ministry would post observers at the polling stations and at the counting of the ballots, and after verifying the tallies, certify the results.

Even though I was exhausted by my responsibilities on the Diocesan Council and I needed to rest, it would not have been in keeping with my character to suddenly withdraw from community life, and besides, it would have made a bad impression. So I ran for office in the St. Sarkis–Vanak district and again I was elected with the highest number of votes.

Unfortunately, compared to the Tenth Diocesan Assembly, the Eleventh evinced a retreat from the norms of civilized behavior. To this day, I have never understood the ARF's strategy for that election or for the election of the new Diocesan Council by the Assembly. The party diligently campaigned to have its members elected, yet some wise and well-known veterans were absent from the list of candidates. I suppose the ARF wanted to encourage the emergence of new faces and prove that there was real democracy in the community. Whatever the intention, the results were very bad indeed.

I do not wish to offend my former colleagues with whom I served for fourteen years, but because this concerns the Iranian Armenian community and ultimately our nation, I cannot refrain from speaking the truth. The Eleventh Diocesan Assembly could not be considered a superior body. As a whole, it lacked the knowledge and the ability to fully understand the country's politics, chart a course for the community and justify its demands on the basis of that understanding. The wise and well educated members of the Tenth Diocesan Assembly were replaced by a bunch of shopkeepers and semi-literate workers with almost zero understanding of community issues. Those types outweighed the few who were well informed and involved in community affairs. Only fourteen Representatives were university-educated and four of those never attended the meetings. All told, barely ten ever expressed an opinion or offered a motion. For the rest, "Present" was practically the only word they uttered during their fourteen-year tenure. Many were oblivious to the rules of order. When the topic of discussion was the critical situation of our schools, for example, they would raise their hands and talk about making shoes. When a vote was called, these pathetic characters would surreptitiously glance around and raise their hands or not, according to what their better informed colleagues did.

The only distinguishing accomplishment of the Eleventh Diocesan Assembly was that it formed a quorum every time it met, and chairman Dr. Haroutiun "Harmik" Davitian and Golia Jaghabegian conducted the meetings with patience and little controversy for fourteen years. Sebouh Amirkhanian, the director of Nayiri Publishing, and Hovannes Abrahamian served as recording secretaries.

The reason the Eleventh Diocesan Assembly lasted for fourteen years was because the Interior Ministry refused to allow the Diocese to hold another election until the year 2000. The Ministry's rationale was that the new laws regulating political parties and community organizations made no such provisions for the Diocesan Council and the Diocesan Assembly. Under the monarchy, the Diocesan Council had been registered and recognized as the Armenian Religious Council (*Showra-ye Khalifeqari Aramaneh*), but under the new regime it was deemed a "community organization." Its status was the subject of prolonged negotiations until finally, as a result of our diligent pursuit of the matter and the government softening its position, the Diocesan Council was recognized as the legitimate plenipotentiary body of the Armenians of Iran.

Learning to Read and Write in Armenian

For more than six years as chairman of the Diocesan Council after the Islamic Revolution, I had faced the struggle to preserve our rights as a community, and I had been present at practically every meeting between community representatives and the government. I didn't want those difficult days and horrific challenges to ever be forgotten. Indeed, I had a national duty to record my experience. Gradually, the idea took root in me to write a book about what had happened, but I was unable to realize my aim at that time because of my incomplete command of the Armenian language. If I had written the story in Persian and had it translated into Armenian, the spirit would have been lost and the authenticity compromised. I decided to postpone that project until I had perfected my Armenian.

I was approached by Albert Ajemian who was now *Alik*'s owner of record. He encouraged me to run for election to the new Diocesan Council. In return, he said, he would find someone with whom I could and would like to work on my book project. I declined his offer because I was beginning to feel that my health had weakened to such a degree that I couldn't carry on as before.

Yet my workload was now considerably lightened and this was unusual for me, so I decided to devote my energies to the study of my mother tongue. My deficiency in this area had never been an issue on the Diocesan Council where I was surrounded by Armenians with excellent command of the language. There were many others who could draft or parse letters and documents in Armenian, and I could understand any written Armenian text if I read it slowly. Still, as an Armenian, I felt the need to remedy this deficiency. I began to look for a teacher but no one wanted to teach me. They couldn't believe that a man my age, and one who had chaired the Diocesan Council for so many years, had only lately realized that he needed to learn Armenian. Some even doubted my sincerity. But I didn't give up and eventually I found Misha Hayrabedian, one of the best teachers in the community. He believed that I sincerely wanted to learn the language and he said he was ready to help me. Our sessions took place once a week in my office after work. I began like an elementary school student, diligently following his instructions and carefully completing my assignments. As I progressed, I began to feel the need to write, and after a few months, my tutor was already me assigning composition topics. When it came to a topic I did not particularly like, I could hardly bring myself to put pen to paper. At such times, I wrote against my will, purely out of a sense of duty.

I subscribed to *Time* magazine, and one day I read an article about the effects of alcohol on the fetus. I was very moved by that article and I asked my teacher if I might translate it into Armenian. He encouraged me to do so, and when he read my first draft, his expression was a mixture of surprise and admiration. Then he congratulated me. He made a few corrections and submitted it to *Alik*.

That was the first in a series of articles on health that I translated for *Alik*. I spent a great deal of time on those articles, sometimes spending an hour searching for the correct equivalent term. I was helped in these efforts by my old friend Dr. Razmik Sirakian who was very patient and generous. Dr. Harmik Davitian, who headed the Psychology Department at Tehran

University Medical School, appreciated my translations and always encouraged me to continue. Dr. Albert Bernardi and Dr. Galoust Galstian also encouraged me. There was a lot of interest in these articles, and in order to create more variety, I subscribed to *Reader's Digest* where I found material from all over the world. As time went on, I also wrote a number of original articles about post-independence Armenia.

When I began these translations, the much-loved teacher Norair Elsaian was *Alik*'s editor-in-chief. Norair was devoted to Armenian letters and I had a great deal of respect for him. But after he was succeeded by a new editor, I noticed that my articles were no longer being published. I didn't ask for an explanation, but I found out later that a group of Armenian doctors had complained that *Alik* shouldn't publish my translations because I wasn't a doctor, and that they promised to submit their own translations in lieu of mine.

In 1999, Nayiri Publishing brought out a collection of my translations under the title, *Live a Healthy Life*, in a limited edition of 2,000. I dedicated it to my teacher, Misha Hayrabedian. Of course, the book wasn't published for commercial gain. I gave hundreds of copies to students, intellectuals, doctors and officials in Armenia where it was greatly appreciated, especially by the doctors.

The End of the War

On July 3, 1988, a strange event happened over Iranian territorial waters in the Strait of Hormuz. At 9:54 AM local time, the American cruiser USS *Vincennes* fired two missiles at an Iranian government–owned jetliner that was flying its regular commercial route from Bandar Abbas to Dubai. Iran Air Flight 655 disintegrated in the air and all 290 on board perished, including sixty-six children.

Each side blamed the other for the incident, but it woke up the pro-war side from its deep slumber and played a decisive role in ending the Iran-Iraq War. Much of the blame for its prolongation has been placed on the shoulders of Speaker Hashemi-Rafsanjani whom Emam Khomeini had appointed acting commander-in-chief. After Iran liberated Khorramshahr in 1982, the Arab League offered Iran 40 billion dollars to end the war. A rift developed within the Iranian leadership. Some were in favor of a cease-fire but others wanted to carry on until Iran succeeded in occupying some part of Iraqi territory. There were repeated attempts to take Basra, and in the vicinity of

Kermanshah, there were road signs that said, "Only 300 km to Baghdad." Rafsanjani and his group were intent on fighting until Iran achieved outright victory, even when there were hints that Khomeini was willing to settle.

Less than two weeks after the downing of Iran Air 655, Khomeini sent the Supreme Defense Council a confidential message calling for an end to the war. The next day, President Khamenei wrote to the UN Secretary-General, accepting UN Security Council Resolution 598. Two days later, Imam Khomeini's confidential message was released to the public:

> This decision was as bitter to me as drinking a cup of poison. I submitted myself to God's will and drank this drink for the Almighty and for His satisfaction.... I had promised to fight to the last drop of my blood and my last breath.... Had it not been in the interests of Islam and the Muslims, I would never have accepted this, I would have preferred death and martyrdom.

The cease-fire formally came into effect on August 20, 1988, although skirmishes continued over border issues, the sequence of prisoner exchanges and navigation rights along the Avanderud (or the Shatt al-Arab).

This senseless, brutal war lasted eight long years and ended without victory or defeat. It brought only lost lives and immense economic damage to both sides. It was Iran's longest and most meaningless war. The economy was in a state of collapse. The people were exhausted and they were beginning to express a lack of trust in the government. Fewer men were willing to volunteer for the front. There was a shortage of arms and equipment, so much so that in the last year of the war, Sati was asked to move a few captured tanks from the FAV Peninsula all the way up to the northern front. Even the food supply was in jeopardy and some combatants died of hunger and thirst. Altogether, some 300,000 Iranians died, a million were injured, and 70,000 were taken prisoner. Millions more were left homeless. Scores of factories, oil refineries and petrochemical plants were destroyed. The total cost to Iran was estimated to be one trillion dollars.

There is no doubt that the war was encouraged and fed by the superpowers. Few if any advanced industrial nations did not sell arms to one side or the other or both. Yet Iraq was in a more advantageous position. It was able to continue pumping oil through pipelines to the northwest, while Iran could only ship through the Persian Gulf. The Arab states provided continuous support while the superpowers pressured Iran to accept a cease-fire. According to a friend of mine who worked in Saudi Arabia during the war, arms and ammunition were constantly coming in to a Red Sea port near Jeddah and being trucked to Iraq. Iran never received that kind of consistent support from any country, which is why Iranians justifiably called it the imposed war.

The Spitak Earthquake

On December 7, 1988, Armenia was hit by a terrible earthquake centered on Spitak. It shook the entire country and took some 25,000 lives. The greatest impact was felt in Gyumri, Armenia's second largest city. Iranian radio and TV provided around-the-clock coverage of the calamity. Every day brought news of more victims found under the rubble, of condolences being cabled to Secretary Gorbachev, of aid arriving from all over the world. The Armenian Diaspora was in a state of mourning. The pain was unbearable.

The Diocesan Council set up a relief committee and appointed me chairman. We set up subcommittees in towns with large Armenian populations and tasked different groups with collecting clothes, bedding, food staples and medical supplies, and the Prelacy set up an account to receive monetary donations. I was so busy organizing the work of the subcommittees that for a few days I didn't go to work at all. Volunteers put in the maximum effort from sunrise to sunset. Men and women, young and old worked together. People gave whatever they could – clothes, blankets, even cash. Many declined a receipt, saying it wasn't necessary. The important thing was that aid should reach the victims as quickly as possible. Those efforts continued for ten days. We separated the worn-out clothes and bedding and sent the rest to be washed and ironed, then we packed the clean clothes and bedding with the dry goods and medicines in special containers and sent them to Moscow and from there to Armenia.

Under my supervision, the monetary donations were pooled at the end of each day, counted and turned over to a Diocesan Council representative who deposited it all in the dedicated account the next morning. I wasn't interested in what the total was but a friend of mine on the Council later told me it was 70 million tomans, which in 1988 was equivalent to $650,000. Later, there was an announcement that Archbishop Manoukian and MP Vartanian had gone to Echmiadzin and given the Supreme Patriarch $100,000 for aid to the victims.

After Armenia became independent in 1991 and Armenians from all over the world could visit whenever they wanted, I often dropped by the Prelacy after work and saw various community activists in the first-floor meeting room, talking among themselves. Later, I found out that a decision had been taken there to use the rest of the community's earthquake relief donations to set up a faucet factory in Ghapan (Kapan), a small town in southern Armenia. Profits from the factory were supposed to be used to help the survivors. This was at a time when Azerbaijan had embargoed oil deliveries and a thousand factories were sitting idle in Armenia. It reminded me of a Persian saying: *Bozak namir bahar miyad, kombozeh ve khiyar miyad* (Don't die, little goat, spring will come, bringing cantaloupes and cucumbers).

Chapter 21

Extortion by Obscure Government Agents

In early 1988, when the War of the Cities heated up again and Tehran was the regular target of long-range missile attacks, the city practically emptied out. The Caspian coast was considered the safest refuge, and the Ministry of Education even set up classes for children staying there. My wife and children were living abroad at the time and I stayed at our home in Darya Kenar whenever I could. I had scores of Armenian visitors and my housekeeper, hired from Tehran, served my guests tea, pastries and fruit. We held backgammon (*nardi*) tournaments every night. Archbishop Manoukian took part in these games and he was a skillful player.

One Thursday night, I drove up for the weekend with the Archbishop and my friend, Dr. Razmik Sirakian. As soon as we arrived, we set up the board and started playing. At midnight, very unexpectedly, the phone rang. A Kurdish friend who lived one street over was calling to say that pasdars were raiding homes in the area and citing people they caught playing cards or nardi. By the time I got off the phone, they were pounding on the door. The first thing I did was to guide the Holy Father into the bedroom. Then I opened the door and in they came. When their leader spotted the board, he said,

"Don't you know nardi is forbidden by Islamic law?"

Dr. Sirakian started talking about how he had operated on a Sepah commander only a few hours earlier in Tehran.

"His liver was torn to pieces by an enemy bomb but I managed to save his life. And this is my reward? You want to deny me a few hours of rest and relaxation?"

The pasdar said he was only obeying orders, and he took out a sheet of paper, wrote down the charges and asked me to sign it. I refused, so he picked up the board, tucked it under his arm and told us to appear at the local komiteh before 10:00 AM the next day. He signaled his men to follow and they left.

In the morning, we went to the komiteh and found scores of people waiting around, all there for the same reason. When it was our turn, Dr.

Sirakian again brought up the fact that he had saved an officer's life the day before. After hearing him out, the komiteh chief told us to take our board and leave quietly. We went home, locked the doors, drew the curtains and continued to play.

Getting to Know Colonel X

A few weeks later, the Archbishop was again my guest at Darya Kenar when Hovannes, the police informant, dropped by. He said that his friend Colonel X, General was in town and would like to meet the Holy Father. Colonel X, General was the chief of police intelligence in Tehran. I had spoken with him on the phone about Diocesan Council business but I had never met him in person. We asked Hovannes to bring him over the next morning, and when they arrived at the appointed time, we received him with the utmost propriety. Hovannes did the introductions in his distinctive style, first introducing the high-ranking officer to us, and then vice versa. We honored our guests with tea and pastries and invited them to stay for lunch, but they expressed their regrets, saying they had to return to Tehran on important business. As they were leaving, the Colonel said I shouldn't hesitate to call on him if I ever had a problem.

Back in Tehran a few days later, Hovannes called and told me that Colonel X, General was taking *iftar* at his house in Majidiyeh that night, and he invited me over for some friendly after-dinner conversation. *Iftar* is the breaking of the daylight fast during the month of Ramadan, and since the Colonel had sent his family to Qazvin because of the missile attacks, he had asked Hovannes to have his mother prepare his evening meals. I subsequently met the Colonel several times at Hovannes's home.

During one of those meetings, he asked me whether I had any legal problems related to my investments. I assumed he meant the fraudulent suit brought against me and my partners in Tabarzin by our former partner, Mr. Zandi. I quickly answered yes, and asked the Colonel how he knew about the case. He said the judge had asked him to find out through Interpol how much income Tabarzin had received from European clients. He added that he couldn't help me in this particular case, since he was obliged to turn over whatever he found to the court, but he did tell me that Zandi had filed a number of affidavits from prominent clerics attesting to his good character. In any case, he promised to assign a fair and open-minded interrogator. A week later, my partners and I were called in for questioning, then repeatedly called back for further questioning over the next six months. Ultimately, our side was totally vindicated.

After the Colonel's wife and daughters returned to Tehran, he invited me to his home several times and I got to know his family. They were observant Muslims but far from fanatical. His wife was a gracious, university-educated lady. In general, Muslim women are only allowed to uncover their heads in the presence of men who are *mahram* (close, intimate), i.e. their father, husband, brothers, sons and maternal uncles, but the Colonel's wife and daughters did not cover their heads in my presence.

That summer, Colonel X, General told me he wanted to give his wife and daughters a European vacation, but he was worried about getting the visas, for two reasons: first, if he were seen entering a European embassy, it would get around and his enemies would exploit the information, and second, if a consular official were to ask him for a quid pro quo, it would expose the visa transactions and jeopardize his position. I said I could help in this matter, and I solicited personal invitations for his wife and daughters through West German friends. On that basis, we got their visas for Germany, and since having a visa for one European country facilitated getting a visa for another, we got their visas for France too, likewise with the aid of French friends. Mrs. X, General and her daughters flew to Frankfurt as the guests of their so-called friends and relatives, and a few days later, they moved on to Paris. I was there at the same time and I treated them as my guests. I arranged for an Iranian Armenian woman I knew to show them the sights, and I provided them with every opportunity to enjoy themselves in the French capital. When the cease-fire with Iraq was declared in July, I shared the good news with them, and before they returned to Tehran, I offered them gifts and asked them to take back some gifts from me to Hovannes's mother and sister too.

Colonel X and the Interior Minister

Interior Minister Nateq-Nuri had been succeeded by the fanatical Hojjatoleslam Ali-Akbar Mohtashamipour, the man behind the suicide truck bomb that had killed 241 innocent American servicemen in Beirut in 1983 when he was the Iranian Ambassador to Syria. Colonel X had very close relations with Mohtashamipour, and Hovannes was being "watered by the same water," as the Armenian saying goes. In fact, he was working directly for the Minister. He had secured a French residency permit and he would fly to Paris several times a year to look up exiled Armenian millionaires and offer his help in recovering their expropriated homes and factories in Iran.

Hovannes exaggerated his influence, as the Archbishop had observed, but in some cases he was able to deliver on what he promised, thanks to his influence with the Minister and the Colonel. The important thing is that Hovannes extracted a lot of money from his clients.

It was thanks to the Minister's recommendation that Colonel X was promoted, and we all congratulated him wholeheartedly. Hovannes hosted a lavish reception in his honor, which I attended (though the Holy Father declined his invitation), and I also attended a reception General X held at his own home to celebrate his promotion. He introduced me to his friends and colleagues and those social interactions continued for a few months.

One day, General X told me that he and Minister Mohtashamipour had just spent a few days in Chalus as the guests of a friend of Hovannes. The General said he was looking to buy a summer home in Chalus and he had found one that he liked, but the asking price was 2.1 million tomans and he was 300,000 tomans short (about $3,000). Afterwards, it occurred to me that perhaps he wanted to borrow the money but didn't want to come right out and say it. Acting on my hunch, I put 300,000 tomans in an envelope and went to his house. He wasn't home, so I left it with his wife without telling her what it was all about. Then I left Tehran for a holiday with my family in Darya Kenar. It was a few days before Nowruz, the Iranian New Year, which is officially a five-day holiday, but in practice, work stops for thirteen days. After five days on the coast, I returned to Tehran because I had to fly to Warsaw with my business partner.

Thus Began the Most Unpleasant Period of My Life

I returned to Tehran on the night of April 1, 1989. Early the next morning, a close friend called to say that General X had been arrested. My friend said his information came from a young intelligence officer who knew about my close relations with the General and he advised me to be careful if I had had any business dealings with him. At first, I felt sorry for the General, but then I remembered the 300,000 tomans I had given him and I wondered if that was going to be a problem. But I quickly convinced myself that it could be seen as a gift or a gesture of support and not as payment for anything he had done for me. Thus I tried to console myself.

On April 11, when I came home for lunch, my wife told me Hovannes had called and had asked that I call him back immediately. I knew the news wouldn't be good. I called him after lunch and his voice confirmed my fears.

He said there were two men at his house who wanted to see me there, right now.

When I rang the doorbell, Hovannes's sister opened the door. Her eyes were red and swollen. I entered the foyer and saw his mother sitting on a chair, crying. I went into the living room and found Hovannes collapsed in a chair. There were actually four men with him and they were all armed. They acknowledged my greeting with an air of arrogance and contempt. I later learned that the leader of the group was called Haj Agha Younesi and his second-in-command was Farrokh. Haj Agha Younesi asked me if I was Levon Aharonian. When I said yes, he flashed a sheet of paper before my eyes and I caught a glimpse of Muslim names and Armenian names, including my own.

"You're under arrest," he said.

He didn't look anything like an officer of the law. He seemed to be in a stupor. He could have been short on sleep, drunk or even stoned.

I asked, "Whatever for?"

"What do you think? Bribery."

I protested that I didn't know what this was all about. I asked him to let me read the document he was holding. I wanted to know which government agency he represented. He answered every question in curt, crude terms. Hovannes sat there mute with fear, and after more of this back-and-forth, he finally spoke up and asked permission to speak to me briefly in Armenian. Haj Agha Younesi nodded his consent.

"It's useless to argue with these people," said Hovannes. "They want money and they'll keep harassing you and your company until you give them what they want."

"But I paid my taxes! And I supported the government all throughout the war!"

"These people aren't interested in what you did. They're secret service agents and they want money for their agency."

"How much?"

"Five million tomans."

Five million tomans was the equivalent of $50,000. It was astronomical! I told Hovannes I didn't have that kind of money. I said I would rather surrender myself to the state and let the law sort it out, but he kept telling me they could really do me harm unless I coughed up. He impressed upon me the fact that they were very powerful people.

Having concluded our colloquy, we reverted to Persian and began to bargain with our tormentors. Eventually we agreed on 3 million tomans, but having agreed on that, they said it had to be delivered in US dollars, i.e. $30,000 cash. And finally, they demanded my passport and my wife's passport too. They sent the youngest member of their cohort home with me to pick up the passports.

A few days later, the phone rang in the middle of the night. In his gruff, thick voice, Haj Agha Younesi asked if the money was ready. I said that part of it was. It was difficult to put together that many US dollars because Iranian banks were only disbursing cash in small notes. He ordered me to get it together and take it to the northern entrance of the Ararat Center at a certain time a few days hence. He said he would be waiting there to pick it up and he warned me not to make any false moves or I would pay dearly.

After much difficulty, I managed to accumulate the required sum. I put it in a large envelope and drove to the Ararat Center in my wife's Peykan. Arriving at the northern entrance at the appointed time, I didn't see any other cars there, but not a minute had passed when a white Mercedes Benz drove by. The driver made a U-turn and came to a stop beside the Peykan. It was Farrokh. I got out and approached him. He opened the front passenger door and told me to get in. There was a Colt pistol lying on the seat beside him. When I was settled in, Haj Agha Younesi spoke up from the back seat and asked if I had the money. I handed him the envelope and when he opened it and saw the green one-hundred-dollar bills, he began to smile. Suddenly, six cars swarmed around us, creating the impression that a sting was underway. Instead, Haj Agha Younesi told me to get back in the Peykan and drive home. He said they would all follow me, but on the way, four cars peeled off and left the caravan.

When we reached my apartment building, I told the guard that the people in the cars behind me were friends and they could park in the lot. Six men came up in the elevator with me. They were armed and they had cameras too. Once inside my apartment, Haj Agha Younesi looked around and said,

"You rich people are all alike. You bribe our young officers and divert them from the straight and narrow path."

"I'd like to know whom I have bribed and what for," I said.

"Shut up."

He ordered his henchmen to search the rooms, collect any suspicious items, bring them into the dining room and put them on the table. In less than ten minutes, the table was covered with my three hunting rifles, boxes of ammunition, bottles of liquor and wine, jewelry that Bella had inherited from her mother, and various other things. I protested when they started photographing everything. Who were they taking these pictures for? I had permits for the rifles, and Ayatollah Mahdavi-Kani had told me personally that I as a Christian was allowed to keep liquor in my home. When they heard that, they let me to put the bottles away. Then they made a list of everything left on the table and had me sign it.

While they were making out the list, Haj Agha Younesi and Farrokh were nosing around in my study. When they came out, Farrokh approached me and whispered that he hadn't realized how prominent I was in the Armenian community. Apparently he drew this conclusion from the photographs on the wall, one of me with the Prelate at his Silver Jubilee and another of me with MP Vartan Vartanian.

"Haj Agha Younesi has decided not to arrest you," he said. "We'll only call on you in an emergency."

Haj Agha Younesi approached me and asked if I was angry.

"Not only am I angry, I'm utterly shocked. How can the supreme leadership of the Islamic Revolution wage a campaign for justice against all the superpowers in the world, and at the same time allow its officials to entrap an innocent, well-meaning citizen of Iran?"

He ignored me and ordered his men to bag the stuff on the table. On their way out the door, he turned back and said casually,

"We're taking the Mercedes and the Peykan, but you'll get the Peykan back tomorrow."

They kept both cars for five months.

Midnight Forays with Farrokh

Now my real troubles began. Two or three times a week, Farrokh would call me at 1:00 in the morning and ask me to meet him someplace. He would be waiting there in his car with a portable siren stuck on the roof. He would have me sit next to him, with his Colt pistol lying on the seat between us. He would drive around to places I had never been. Sometimes he would stop beside a pedestrian and ask me if I knew the man. If I did, I said so, and if not, I said no. A few times, I recognized one of these midnight ramblers and gave Farrokh the standard information, just basic things.

One night, Farrokh called and asked if I knew Koko Aghayan. I told him that I knew him well enough to exchange greetings but that was all. He asked me to describe Koko – his height, weight and so on. He told me that Koko was flying in to Tehran that night and they were planning to arrest him at the airport.

Koko's real name was Zareh. He was the youngest son of the attorney Dr. Alexander Aghayan (d. 1963), a pioneer in Iranian patent and trademark registration. Alec Aghayan's three sons had inherited an annual income stream of hundreds of thousands of dollars related to his legal work. Felix, the oldest son, had been an MP in the 1960s and then a senator. Shahen, the middle son, had managed the family firm before the Revolution and afterwards he ran the Paris office. Koko remained in Iran and ran the Tehran office. I first met him at the Prelacy when he paid a call on the Archbishop. Later, I met him a few times at receptions hosted by Babig Tomassian. Koko was short, morose and usually silent, a heavy drinker and a chain-smoker. He wasn't a lawyer and I don't know anything about his education, but Hovannes always made sure that he was referred to as Dr. Koko Aghayan. He was surrounded by freeloaders like Hovannes and military-intelligence types like Farrokh. As I eventually came to realize, Hovannes took protection money from wealthy men like Koko, while the intelligence types contrived to extract their entire fortune.

The day after Farrokh asked me about Koko, I phoned a mutual friend and asked if Koko had arrived home safely, putting the question in such a way as not to raise suspicion. He told me that Koko was safe at home and that he had driven him home from the airport himself.

My relationship with Farrokh was becoming increasingly familiar and that worried me. He often visited me at my office on old Roosevelt Avenue (now Mofatteh Street), which borders the east wall of the former US Embassy compound. It was a one-way street but Farrokh always drove up the wrong way. He asked me for airline tickets for his "friends" several times, and once he asked me to arrange for a German company to extend an invitation to an entire family. It wasn't easy to get that kind of cooperation and I would never allow myself to put forward such a request. I tried putting him off, saying the company was still reviewing the matter, but I finally told him that German companies could only invite two foreign guests at a time and they had to be company directors.

After that, the phone at home would ring at 7:00 AM, and when I picked it up, there was nothing on the other end but heavy breathing. For a time, I disconnected the phone.

One day, Farrokh came to my office asking for airline tickets again. The day before, I had received a form letter from the Islamic Revolutionary Guards Corps, requesting the full name, address and telephone number of each of our employees. I mentioned it to Farrokh and he seemed taken aback. He mulled it over for a while. Then he said his group had nothing to do with it but he wanted to know how I got the letter. I told him it was hand-delivered by a pasdar. That worried him and he asked whether I had told the man anything about him or his group. He seemed relieved when I said no. I learned something important that day: I had assumed that he worked for Sepah intelligence, but I was wrong.

A few days later, Farrokh informed me that his commanding officer had decided to move part of their agency into our building. I explained that if our clients found out about it, they would stop doing business with us. I also told him that it would take a court order to appropriate office space like that. In any case, it never happened.

One Thursday afternoon, Farrokh called me at work and said he was waiting for me in the parking lot of my apartment building. When I got there, he stepped out of the white Mercedes, formally greeted me and asked for a bottle of whisky. I was overcome with hesitation and confusion. Should I give it to a him or not? The idea of giving him what he wanted didn't bother me, but I was worried that it might be another trap, like the $30,000. He guessed the reason for my hesitation and swore that no harm would come to me if I granted his wish. I went up to the apartment, wrapped a bottle of whisky in paper and brought it back down to him.

Hours later, Farrokh called me in the middle of the night to tell me that they had gotten Koko drunk and made him divulge all kinds of family secrets, such as the relationship between his elder brother and the Shah's twin sister, and that they had it all on tape.

Prescription Opiates

Late one night, Farrokh called and told me where to meet him. He was waiting for me in the white Mercedes. I got in and he drove to a car rental agency near Ferdowsi Square, went in for ten minutes, came back out, drove north a few blocks to Apadana Hospital, parked and went inside. Thirty minutes later, he came back and handed me three prescriptions, saying they were for an old woman who was suffering from cancer. He asked me to have them filled by my business associates in Germany and he named an Iran Air pilot who would fly them back. I countered that German pharmacists might not be willing to fill prescriptions written by Iranian doctors, but I said I would do what I could.

I had never heard of these drugs, but with a little investigation, I found out that Iran's Red Crescent pharmacies stocked them. I told Farrokh there was no need to import them and he asked me to go ahead and buy them, which I did. They all came in medical syringes for hypodermic injection. After that, he repeatedly asked me to have the same prescriptions refilled. It got so that I kept a supply in a drawer in my office, ready for him to pick up.

One time, he forced me to go to the office in the middle of the night and pick some up, then drive him to a house in Zafaraniyeh, one of the most affluent areas of affluent Shemiran. Only millionaires lived there. He told me to wait outside, and if he wasn't back in fifteen minutes, I was free to leave. A few minutes later, a patrol car pulled up beside me and a police officer asked what I was doing there at that hour of the night. I pointed to the house and said I was waiting for a friend. A look of recognition crossed his face. He bid me goodnight and drove off.

Ten minutes later, I drove home. Bella was waiting for me. Her troubled expression affected me deeply. How could I explain these midnight forays? When would they ever end? After that night, I resolved to find out exactly what was going on. Through further investigation, I learned that Farrokh's drugs were very potent, highly addictive narcotics usually given to terminally ill patients as pain palliatives. I realized that I was an unwilling conspirator in a criminal network. I took the remaining syringes and crushed them under my feet. The next time he asked me to refill the prescriptions, I told him that the pharmacists had become suspicious and refused to sell me any more. After that, he never asked me again.

Legal Advice

Sati had developed a good relationship with a skilled and experienced lawyer, Mr. Sadr ol-Hefazi, whose wife was a cousin of Emam Khomeini's daughter-in-law. Sadr ol-Hefazi was steeped in the intricacies of the country's internal politics, both pre- and post-revolutionary. He no longer practiced law but we occasionally sought his advice, so I decided to consult with him. I made an appointment and went to his house, and after I told him the whole story, he said that my conduct was correct and appropriate. He mentioned the unsolved murders of journalists, political activists and businessmen and said that my tormentors could easily kill me and leave my corpse in the street, and no one would ever know what happened.

"All they want is money, but human life is more precious," he said. "Think of yourself as a twig on a stream and consign your fate to the currents. When the stream dries up, all these machinations will come to a stop. You must be patient."

I also consulted with Dr. Jaleh Shambayati. Apparently she had had a comparable experience and she urged me to throw myself on the mercy of Hojjatoleslam Ali Younesi, the head of the Armed Forces Judiciary. Ten years later, after the Chain Murder scandal broke and the head of the Ministry of Intelligence and Security was forced to resign, Justice Younesi would be appointed to replace him.

I confided in Vartan Vartanian too, and he was barely able to contain his anger. He wanted to bring my story to the Majles and demand action, but I persuaded him not to. What should I do? Complain to the government? I had no doubt that my tormentors were part of some secret government agency, and for that reason I never lodged a formal complaint.

I Shut My Eyes and Open My Mouth

One day, Farrokh told me that he and his men wanted to meet with Babig Tomassian and that the best place for them to meet was my office. Babig was eighty years old and blind. He was close to Hovannes who visited him twice a week and was paid a couple of million tomans a year in protection money.

A few days later, Farrokh showed up after hours with several other men and they waited for Babig to arrive. When he came in accompanied by Hovannes, they all went into a conference room, and half an hour later, they all came out and left. I wasn't told what it was about, nor did I ask Babig, but it was then that I realized Farrokh and his gang were preying on people connected to Hovannes.

Late one night, Farrokh called and told me where to meet him. I got in his car and sat beside him. His Colt lay on the seat between us, as usual. After driving around for a while, he told me that Hovannes had taken a beating. In fact, he said, Hovannes had been beaten so badly that he vomited blood, and after the assault, he divulged some secrets, including one about me. Farrokh declined to elaborate but I insisted, so he said Hovannes had heard that I was behind a clandestine group that was plotting to overthrow the government. When I heard that, I completely lost it. I shut my eyes and opened my mouth, as they say.

"Who are you? What do you want from me? You've been torturing me for months! You're destroying my wife's psychological balance. Every day, you want something else. You might as well pick up that Colt and shoot me! At least it would put an end to my suffering!"

I was hysterical. Everything I had been holding in erupted. I demanded that he return my wife's passport because I desperately wanted her to go abroad for some rest and calm. He told me to be quiet and warned me not to mention our conversation to anyone, or else he would turn me into "dust." Gradually, we both calmed down. By now it was 3:00 AM. He dropped me off in front of my apartment building and drove away.

A few days later, I was told to go to Vanak Square. Haj Agha Younesi was sitting there in a Nissan van. I hadn't seen him since he and his men had invaded our apartment months earlier. He stepped out and personally handed me Bella's passport.

A week after that, Farrokh called from Brussels and asked me to authorize two airline tickets from there to Geneva. I said it would be illegal and I couldn't do it. Later, I found out that he was traveling with Koko Aghayan and they went to a bank in Geneva where Koko withdrew $250,000 and handed it over to Farrokh.

He continued harassing me in the middle of the night. One night, he wanted a million tomans (about $10,000). I turned him down flat, but he insisted. He said he wanted to buy a house and he was short by that much. When I still refused, he offered to sign a promissory note and pay me back in a year. In the end, I was forced to give him the money, but I didn't get the note.

In late August, my wife and I decided to go to Darya Kenar for some much needed rest. We hadn't been out of Tehran in months. A pleasant feeling came over me as we drove north on a Wednesday afternoon. When we reached our summer home, I called a couple we knew and invited them over. He and I played nardi and our wives played Scrabble. It was a most pleasant evening whose effects, alas, were cut short in the morning when my secretary called from Tehran to say that Farrokh was trying to reach me. She said he was upset when he heard I was out of town. When I called Farrokh, he told me to pack a bag because he and I were going on a trip abroad. He would pick me up on Saturday and we would be gone for two months. My mood changed dramatically. Surely this meant prison. I tried hard not to let on that I was upset but Bella asked me why my spirits were down. I said that perhaps it was due to my losses at nardi, but she knew I was never upset when I lost a game. I finally had to tell her the truth.

We drove back to Tehran on Friday morning. I met with Alfred Mehrabian, my business partner, and explained how to manage in my absence. Then I went to see Vartan Vartanian and told him what was up. He said he could only track me if he knew where these people were taking me, so he would stay at home and await my call. On Saturday, I waited for Farrokh all day but he never came. A week later, he called to say the trip was off. He had kept me, my wife, Alfred and Vartan in a state of extreme nervous tension for an entire week. It was his way of reducing me to a state of abject submission.

In September, Farrokh came to my office and asked for a written statement to the effect that the $30,000 I had been forced to give him and Haj Agha Younesi five months earlier was a purely voluntary donation to his agency. He also said that his commanding officer would soon thank me in person. I wondered why he wanted such a statement at this late date, and I asked for his superior's name or at least the name of the agency, but he wouldn't tell me, so after some discussion, I produced three different statements addressed "to whom it may concern" and told him his boss could choose the one he liked.

Around that time, Farrokh's henchmen returned my Mercedes and Bella's Peykan. They were both in terrible shape, almost unrecognizable, but I thanked the drivers. What else could I do? I barely got the Mercedes to the nearest garage. Evidently it had been used as the family car because there were toys and children's socks and underwear in the trunk.

After I got the cars back, Haj Agha Younesi telephoned and said he was going to visit me at home on a certain day and return the items he had confiscated from our apartment. He also told me that General X had been released from prison. That was a pleasant surprise, but I didn't call the General because I knew there would be dire consequences if I did. Yet our acquaintance would prove helpful a few years later when Albert Ajemian was abducted.

Haj Agha Younesi came to my home and returned my passport, my wife's jewelry, and two of my rifles along with the ammunition, but not my .22 caliber Winchester. He promised I would have it in ten days. A month passed. Finally, he brought it to my office.

"Here, take your precious rifle," he said, and thrust it into my hands.

Early in November, Bella handed me a sealed envelope with my name on it. She told me a ten- or twelve-year-old boy had given it to her, saying it came from his father who was in prison. Inside was Farrokh's receipt for one million tomans. Apparently my loan was supposed to be written off as a gift. But the most important thing was that now I knew he was locked up.

Chapter 22

Imprisoned, Interrogated and Exonerated

Two years passed. Sunday, November 17, 1991, was my sixty-first birthday. I was at work in my office when the telephone rang at 4:00 PM. My secretary had already left so I picked up the call. A man identified himself as Heydari and said we had to meet right away. I explained that it was my birthday and I had to get home to receive my guests. Couldn't we meet the following day? He said he would take no more than ten minutes of my time and he would be at my office in fifteen minutes.

It was past 5:00 when Heydari arrived. He was wearing civilian clothes but his deportment indicated his military training. His approach was courteous and respectful. He told me that the Armed Forces Judiciary wanted to ask me some questions regarding a matter that was under investigation and an examiner was waiting for me at the courthouse. I called Bella and told her I would be late and asked her to convey my regrets to our friends.

At the military courthouse on Dr. Ali Shariati Street, Heydari asked me to wait while he went to alert the examiner. A few minutes later, he returned and said the man had gone out but would be back in an hour, and he left me there to wait. One hour became two, then three, until finally a sergeant approached and told me the examiner would not be coming back that night. My interrogation would take place in the morning, he said, and I would be held overnight at Evin.

I was taken to Evin Prison with several other detainees. Our guard handed a roster to a guard at the gate, and after a roll call, we were taken inside. Another guard led me to a cell and locked me in. The walls were covered with graffiti. There was a bed with a blanket and a small pillow, a bucket near the door, and two books in a niche in the wall. One of them was a Koran.

The admission process had taken a few hours and I was exhausted. As a hunter, I had spent many a night sleeping rough in the mountains. I put my head on the pillow and slept until I was awoken at dawn by the Muslim call to prayer. Since I had no connection with Islam, I went back to sleep. An hour later, the door opened and breakfast was brought in: a cup of tea, a few pieces of bread and a chunk of cheese. After breakfast, I couldn't go back to sleep, but I had decided to keep my spirits up, so I did my exercises. That took me an hour, and after that I occupied myself by reading the lines written on the walls by prisoners before me. Some of them were quite interesting, others were illegible.

Interrogation

The next morning at 8:00, a number of detainees were called and dispatched to various courthouses, depending on the type of crime they were accused of. Ten of us were sent to the military courthouse on Shariati Street. There was a roll call and the roster was given to a guard who sat next to the driver. Riding along and seeing people walking outside, I was deeply moved by the thought that nothing was more precious than freedom.

At the courthouse, there was another roll call and we were transferred to the custody of an officer of the court. I was taken to a large hall on the ground floor and told to wait until I was called for. Half an hour later, I was taken to the examiner's office. He was a kind-looking man around fifty years old. He was obviously not a zealous young revolutionary and he seemed to have some real life experience behind him, so I was happy to meet him. He accepted my greeting in a friendly way and asked my name and surname. Then he handed me a sheet of paper and asked me to write down my answers to each of his questions and initial each one.

The first question concerned my identity: my name, my parents' names, and the date and place of my birth. The second question was when and where I had first met Mohammad Afshar and Mohammad Nowruzi. I was nonplussed. I told the examiner I had never heard those names before. He began describing Mohammad Afshar and I said that sounded like someone I knew named Farrokh. He smiled and said Farrokh's real name was Mohammad Afshar, and Mohammad Nowruzi was his superior, the man who called himself Haj Agha Younesi.

Another question concerned the bribery of a military officer. I thought it must refer to the 300,000 tomans I had placed in an envelope and left with General X's wife. When I tried to explain the circumstances, the examiner cut me off and said the investigation had to do with Mohammad Afshar and Mohammad Nowruzi and no one else.

I wrote about all of my encounters with both of them, beginning with our first meeting at Hovannes's house and including my $30,000 donation to their agency, the confiscation and eventual return of my possessions, the airline tickets, the midnight forays with Farrokh, and the million-toman loan, or gift. The only things I left out were the prescription drugs and Farrokh's allegation that I was involved in a plot to overthrow the government. The examiner asked me why I had given Farrokh a million tomans and whether I had a receipt.

"I certainly do. It's stored in a safe at my home."

"If I send you home with a guard, can you produce it?"

"Of course, with pleasure."

He summoned a soldier and ordered him to escort me home. Before we left, he instructed me to take the receipt out of the safe in the presence of the soldier and hand it to him. Then he ordered a car and driver. I mentioned that I had had cardiac surgery and needed to take my medications. He said I could bring them back but warned me not to speak to anyone at home, and especially not in Armenian.

When I entered our apartment, Bella asked me where I had been all night. I put a finger to my lips, making it clear she was not to say a word. With the soldier following me closely, I went to the safe, dialed the combination, opened it, took out the receipt and handed it to him. Then I picked up my medications and silently followed him out of the apartment.

Back in the examiner's office, the soldier handed him the receipt. The expression on his face told me that he recognized Farrokh's handwriting. He attached the receipt to my answer sheet and picked up his questioning where he had left off. After another hour, he said he still had more questions which he would put to me in our next session. I was shocked. I had expected to be set free, but I was sent back to Evin.

According to regulations, anyone who was locked up for more than a day had to wear prison garb. I was given a blue and white striped outfit, and after I changed clothes, I was taken to my cell. An hour later, I was given supper. I hadn't eaten since early morning, so I ate voraciously without paying much attention to what I was eating. Afterwards, a guard came to retrieve the dish. From his accent, I gathered that he was Azeri so I spoke to him in *Türki*, the Turkic language spoken by Azeri Iranians. That surprised him. He told me he was from Julfa and I said my company had a branch office there. When he realized I was talking about Sati, he said a friend of his worked in our office. He went on talking at great length. Given the nature of their work, prison guards suffer from a lack of human interaction, and when they get a chance to converse, they tend to say everything stored up inside them. Before he left, he told me there was a canteen in the basement and if I wanted anything, he could get it for me.

On Tuesday, I was photographed and finger-printed. When the photographer learned that I was Armenian, he asked me why I was in prison. I said that I myself did not know why. They had extorted money from me and now they were asking me why I had given them money. He was visibly upset and he said he knew about the unjust and arbitrary goings on at Evin.

The time I spent in prison was very boring. I was so restless that I re-read the graffiti on the walls. Then I leafed through the Koran which was in Persian translation. I found much that was interesting and I read some more. The other book was about the invention of braille, the alphabet for the blind. That was interesting too. Of course, I did my exercises and that filled an hour. I had come to terms with my situation and I made every effort to keep my spirits up. I thought of myself as a solitary vacationer, devoid of companions. When the lights went out at 9:00 PM, the only thing left to do was sleep.

On Thursday morning, I was taken back to the military courthouse. About a dozen others were waiting in the large hall on the ground floor. Part of the hall was partitioned off by a wooden panel, creating a nook where Muslims could pray if they wished. Suddenly, a loud voice rose above the others, praying in Arabic. It held my attention because the others were praying very softly, almost whispering. The loud voice fell silent, and a few minutes later, a man came out from behind the panel. It was Farrokh, or rather, Mohammad Afshar. I was stunned. Who was he trying to deceive? God or the examiner?

Half an hour later, I was taken to the examiner's office and he resumed my interrogation. A guard came in and whispered in his ear. He nodded and the guard went out. Then Father Varazdad Keshishian from our Prelacy came in. He respectfully greeted both of us, but I was embarrassed at having to greet him in prison garb. Father Varazdad told the examiner he had a letter from our Prelate concerning my case. The examiner took the letter and said there was no reason to worry, it would certainly be taken into consideration, and Father Varazdad left the room.

Ten minutes later, Mohammad Afshar and Mohammad Nowruzi were brought in. The examiner asked them to sit down and then he read my answer sheet aloud. Those two men, who had tormented me so cruelly for so long, confirmed everything I had written without making a single objection. The examiner ordered the guards to take them away and when they were gone he resumed questioning me. The phone rang, he picked it up and his tone became ultra respectful. He said the order would certainly be carried out. Then he told whoever was on the line that he had received a letter from "their religious leader." When he hung up, he told me he would arrange to have me released the following day which was Friday, a holiday.

Back in my cell at Evin, I offered the Azeri guard a gift. I told him I was supposed to be released tomorrow and asked if prison officials worked on Friday. I wanted to make sure the arrangements for my release would go smoothly. He told me not to worry – there were no holidays in prison. Somehow I made it through the night.

On Friday, my clothes were brought to my cell at 10:00 AM. After I changed clothes, I was taken to the front office where my identity was verified and I was given a release slip which I presented at the main gate. Thus ended my week-long stay at Evin Prison.

Both of my brothers and one of my nephews were waiting outside with my Persian friend Mr. Goya. He had brought along the deed to one of his properties which he was prepared to put up as bail if necessary, but no bail had been set and I was free to go.

A "Historic" Trial

Another year passed, and I was summoned to appear as a witness in the trial of Mohammad Afshar and Mohammad Nowruzi on December 14, 1992, at 9:00 AM in the military courthouse on Shariati Street. When I entered the building, there was a huge crowd in the large hall on the ground floor. I had never seen so many people there, and this time the civilians outnumbered the soldiers. The courtroom was upstairs, so I made my way through the crowd and up to the second floor where more people were standing about. I found the office of the clerk and showed him my summons. He said the proceedings would begin in fifteen minutes and asked me to wait outside. When I came out, I saw Koko and Hovannes. I approached them, and after the usual pleasantries, I asked what all these people were doing here. Hovannes said that Farrokh and his people had extorted money from every one of them and they were all here for the trial.

Fifteen minutes later, we were called into the courtroom. Koko and Hovannes sat in the second row and I sat behind them. The judge declared the court in session. His assistant stood and recited some verses from the Koran, then his secretary read out the indictment of Mohammad Afshar aka "Farrokh" and Mohammad Nowruzi aka "Haj Agha Younesi." The judge asked them how they pled. Farrokh pled guilty to some of the charges but Haj Agha Younesi denied everything and said the chief witness against him was lying. The judge turned to Hovannes and asked him what he had to say in response to that. Hovannes stood up, took a small Koran from his pocket, kissed it and touched it to his eyes.

"I am a Christian," he said, "but I have great faith in the Koran. I swear on the Koran that everything I say is true."

He pointed to Farrokh and said that man had beaten him with an electric cable for a whole month. He asked the judge's permission to take off his coat and shirt in order to prove that he was telling the truth. The judge assented and Hovannes bared his back. It was coal-black from his shoulders to his waist. He turned around and showed this horrific sight to the judge who looked shocked. The courtroom was in an uproar. Hovannes said his wounds had taken months to heal. His mother had bathed and anointed them every day and she had cried so much that she lost her sight.

While Hovannes was speaking, Farrokh and Haj Agha Younesi never once looked at him, and when he was finished, the judge turned to Farrokh and asked him how he could explain his barbaric behavior. He replied that he was a major in the intelligence department of the Gendarmerie, and that after his office had received a tip that Hovannes was extorting wealthy Armenians, he had been ordered to exploit Hovannes's connections and even beat him if necessary. That was how he had extracted the names of Koko Aghayan, Babig Tomassian and myself. At that point, Hovannes lowered his head to show us that he was ashamed of having given up our names.

The judge then asked Koko and me to respond, and we each in turn told the court how Farrokh had harassed and tortured us and extorted large sums of money. Next, the judge asked Farrokh what he had done with the one million tomans he had borrowed from me. Without a trace of shame or contrition, he testified, "I spent a week in Isfahan with a beautiful woman. I thought I had a right, after collecting 700 million tomans and turning it over to my superiors, including a number of Ministers."

I wondered why his superiors weren't on trial if Farrokh was telling the truth, but the judge obviously didn't want their names mentioned in court. He quickly redirected his attention to Koko and me and asked whether we had anything else to say. Koko had nothing to add, but I said that my company had made significant contributions to the war effort, and as for the

$30,000 that was extorted from me, I offered it to the state as a gift, but I would like Farrokh to repay the million-toman loan.

The proceedings lasted for about two hours, at the conclusion of which the judge asked me to provide the court with a written statement of my testimony. I submitted the four-page document on December 23, 1992.

Four months later, I received written notice that I should contact the court within one week if I wanted to know what the judge had decided. I called the clerk the next day and was told that Mohammad Afshar and Mohammad Nowruzi had each been sentenced to thirty years in prison. No punishment or penalty was assigned to me but the court accepted my $30,000 gift on behalf of the state. The million-toman loan was deemed a personal matter, unrelated to the case. If I wished to contest the ruling, I must do so within a week. Considering the political situation, I wrote a letter stating that I was satisfied, and in this way I drew a line under the most torturous period in my life.

The Chain Murder Scandal

When I review that period, it occurs to me that my behavior could be seen as that of a weakling who timidly gave in to Farrokh's threats, but an important motivation for my seeming acquiescence was the precarious security situation. Iran had just emerged from eight years of war, and over the following decade, murder, kidnapping and other violent acts were rampant, if barely covered by the press. Many victims were abducted and their bodies were later found in the desert, on the street or in the morgue as happened to Reverend Tadevos Mikaelian and Bishop Haik Mehr Hovsepian of the Armenian Protestant Church, both murdered in 1994. Some died in prison under mysterious circumstances, like the poet and social critic Ali-Akbar Saeedi Sirjani. The names of the victims might be reported, but the perpetrators were never identified unless they themselves were slated for suicide or execution in prison.

The Chain or Serial Murder (*Ghatlha-ye Zanjirehi*) scandal broke in 1999 after five prominent intellectuals were murdered in Tehran. Among them were Dariush Forouhar, a seventy-year-old opposition activist who had served as Minister of Labor in Prime Minister Bazargan's government, and his wife Parvaneh Majd Eskandari, both brutally stabbed to death in their home. In January, a cleric who claimed to have worked for the Ministry of Intelligence and Security (MOIS) sought political asylum in Germany, offering in exchange sensitive documents that shed light on who was responsible for those heinous acts. These developments so shocked the public that President Khatami, elected in 1997, was able to force the head of the MOIS to admit that agents of his Ministry were responsible for the murder of Forouhar and his wife. The Minister resigned and Deputy Minister Saeed Emami (or Eslami) was personally accused of planning and overseeing the murders. Several months later, it was announced that Emami had committed suicide in prison by ingesting *vajebi*, a depilatory containing arsenic. In this way, the state attempted to placate the public and close the case.

But scores of dissidents had been murdered over the previous decade and the press began digging into the secrets of the respective presidencies of Seyyed Ali Khamenei (1981–89) and Ali-Akbar Hashemi-Rafsanjani (1989–97). Among the most astute investigative journalists were Emadeddin Baghi (Baqi) and Akbar Ganji, both of whom served time in prison as a result of their work. Ganji's research, for example, implicated Rafsanjani in the murders and raised questions about his and his family's business dealings.

Self-Financing Government Agencies

A few years after the war was over, President Hashemi-Rafsanjani claimed that it had left Iran debt-free, while others claimed the country owed upwards of 100 billion dollars. Whatever the case may be, the government was so financially strapped that the bureaucracy actually suffered a shortage of paper. Rafsanjani urged government agencies to become financially self-sufficient, and people like Farrokh were encouraged to set up free-wheeling units accountable to no one, which they funded by extorting well-to-do individuals.

Yet Farrokh's case continues to shock and baffle me, and this goes back to the day I learned that he worked for the Gendarmerie. In the old days under Reza Shah, the Gendarmerie (*Amniyeh*) was responsible for rural policing and its poorly educated officers were known to prey on powerless villagers. But under Mohammad Reza Shah, all the security forces – Army, Navy, Air Force, Police, Gendarmerie and SAVAK – were part of the Iranian Armed Forces: they all underwent military training, they all had their own intelligence units, and their officers were generally drawn from the educated middle class or had been educated at state expense. Through eight long years of war, the expanding Islamic Revolutionary Guards Corps had replicated these service arms and their intelligence units, but unlike officers in the prerevolutionary Artesh, Sepah commanders were not required to be university-educated and were appointed more on the basis of their experience and connections. Even so, as a major in the Gendarmerie, Farrokh would certainly have been university-educated, and in fact, I later learned that he came from a military family, yet he behaved like an old-fashioned gendarme, preying on the powerless, and I have no doubt that he was responsible for the death of many people. He was a sadist without a shred of humanity.

One day a few years later, the door to my office opened and there stood a thin, toothless, white-haired man.

"Do you remember me?"

It was Farrokh, or ex-Major Mohammad Afshar. Despite having been sentenced to thirty years in prison, he had just been released. He said he couldn't find his wife and children and he thought they might have gone to Sweden. He said he hadn't eaten in days and he asked me for some money. I warned him that if he ever came back again, I would turn him in to the police. He promised not to come back and I gave him 20,000 tomans. That was the last I saw of him, and with his disappearance, a most torturous part of my life definitively came to an end.

Years later I ran into General X on the street, and I saw him again at the funeral of Babig Tomassian's wife, Digin Jenik. As for Hovannes, the last time I saw him was at Babig's funeral.

Chapter 23

The André and Almast Aharonian Kindergarten

Back in 1982, the Diocesan Council had decided to build a high school for girls in Majidiyeh because there was none in the neighborhood and female students were forced to commute to the Mariamian School downtown. The project would require substantial funding but many of our community benefactors had left the country. Archbishop Manoukian thought we should wait until a new one stepped forward. I had always wanted to honor my parents by funding a worthy national cause, and I wanted to contribute to the growth and well-being of our community to the extent that I was able, so I decided to fund the construction of the school myself. When I informed the Prelate of my decision, he was very happy. He broke the news to the Council on April 2, and on May 1, the Council wrote to Education Minister Parvaresh, requesting permission to build the school and explaining in great detail why this was a necessity for our community. The Prelate wrote a press release that was published in *Alik* on May 8:

> We are pleased to announce that Baron Levon Aharonian, chairman of the Tehran Diocesan Council, and his family have graciously assumed responsibility for the construction of a girls' school in Majidiyeh. The school will be named the Almast and André Aharonian High School for Girls in honor of Baron Aharonian's parents.

Unfortunately, Minister Parvaresh ignored our request for permission to build the school. We sent another request on October 9, but the result was the same. MP Vartanian followed the matter closely for a few years, but in the end, all our efforts were fruitless.

The reader may wonder why the government would oppose the construction of a school. This was related to the influence of the Hojjatiyeh Society which was very powerful at the time. In their view, non-Muslim Iranians had no right to survive, much less prosper. That was why the Diocesan Council built the Holy Cross Chapel at the Ararat Center without permission: we knew it would never be granted.

But I still wanted to fund a community construction project, and when Catholicos Garegin II of Cilicia visited Iran in 1990, he proposed that instead of a girls' school, we build a kindergarten in Majidiyeh. I was aware of the fact that kindergartens were not regulated by the government and I accepted his suggestion immediately.

Construction

As the site of the André and Almast Aharonian Kindergarten, the Central Board of School Trustees designated a small lot owned by the Diocesan Council on the same street as Soukerian Hall and the Church of St. Gregory the Illuminator. The Council organized a design competition that was won by Hrair Aboulian. He drew up the plans for a building in the traditional Armenian style. My brother George, a civil engineer, supervised the project with the assistance of the architect Henrik Aghamalian. Construction went smoothly and took about two years. Rebar was in short supply on the open market, but the government was offering it at a discount to bona fide construction projects and we took full advantage of the opportunity. MP Vartanian was a great help in this connection.

With a footprint of 3,600 square feet, the three-story building provides students with over 10,000 square feet of indoor space, in addition to a 2,400-square–foot playground. It includes eight classrooms and a third-floor auditorium with a capacity of 300, furnished with a stage and other amenities. Offices for the director and the teaching staff and workspace for the cooks are located off the foyer on the ground floor. The basement contains the heating units and storage space, as well as separate living quarters with all the necessary facilities for the guard and his family. The school was equipped with all the modern conveniences, the systems were the most advanced and the materials and furnishings were of the highest quality. I spared no effort to make sure this institution would bring honor to our community.

I will never forget the day in 1992 when Catholicos Garegin II, on another visit to Iran, asked to see the kindergarten. It was a rainy day when he came to the site. He blessed the building and said he was pleased to see a project of such significance to the community.

Opening Day

Construction was completed in December 1993 and the furnishings were installed in January 1994. We decided to hold the opening ceremony on

February 3 during *Dahe-ye Fajr* (Ten-Day Dawn), when Iranians celebrate the triumph of the Revolution and there are large-scale events all over the country. That way, we were able to conduct the ceremony as we wished without drawing unwonted attention. Archbishop Manoukian presided and Silva Markarian was an admirable Mistress of Ceremonies. Some 300 people attended, including special guests Ambassador Vahan Bayburdyan and his wife and Professor Hagop Papazyan from Armenia. Of course, my wife Bella was present, along with our daughter Annette and my brothers Henrik and George and their wives.

The Holy Father gave his blessing at the doors to the building, then I cut the ribbon and everyone entered and went up to the auditorium on the third floor. A member of the education committee offered opening remarks and introduced a young child who expressed appreciation and gratitude on behalf of all the children who would attend the school. Then Diocesan Council chairman Dr. Levon Davidian saluted me and my family for the benevolent gesture that had made the construction of the school possible, and expressed his hope that it would be a place where generations would be educated to take up leadership positions in the future. After a program of songs and recitations by the children themselves, Archbishop Manoukian was invited to the stage. He too saluted the Aharonian family and talked about the significance of community responsibility and philanthropy. He concluded by reading out a decree from Catholicos Garegin II, honoring me and my wife with the Cilician Prince (*Ishkhan*) Medal, which he duly bestowed upon each of us.

Then it was my turn to address the gathering. I said that the idea of making this modest contribution to our community had come to me from earlier philanthropists. I recounted how the older generation had supported my generation and stood by us in steadfastness and strength. My task was to follow their example. It was a national duty to build this kindergarten, and the mission of educating the next generation was now entrusted to the teachers and their young students. MP Vartanian had the last word. He congratulated everyone on this important achievement and spoke at length about the mission of educating each new generation. I brought the ceremony to a close by presenting commemorative gifts to everyone who had helped to build the school.

The first director of the Aharonian Kindergarten was Angelle Tounayan, and she was succeeded by Annette Baghdassarian. Both worked closely with the teachers and the Parents Council. Everyone involved with the school worked with energy and selfless devotion.

The Tenth Anniversary Celebration

The tenth anniversary of the Aharonian Kindergarten was celebrated in February 2004 in the presence of Archbishop Sebouh Sarkissian. Scores of organizations sent congratulatory letters on the occasion. The students' presentations, their conduct, even their carefully fashioned costumes made a strong impression on me. I sensed the indelible mark of our cultural values on these young children. I could barely contain my emotions. In my speech that day, I expressed pride in having contributed to the creation of an institution that provides so many benefits to the community.

I said to myself, *Honor and glory to our people for whom culture is a pillar of endurance and progress.* We must kiss the hands of our cultural leaders through whom our religion, our language, our culture, and above all, our homeland are preserved. Among those torch-bearers are the teachers at the Aharonian Kindergarten. I repeat, *Honor and glory to their devotion and sacrifice for Armenian culture and education.*

Chapter 24

Moscow and Armenia

While momentous changes were underway in the Soviet Union, Sati continued to work with TechnoPromExport (TPE). Work on the first phase of the Shahid Mohammad Montazeri Power Plant in Isfahan had continued throughout the Iran-Iraq War and was completed in 1988. This involved four units, each of which produced 220 megawatts (MW) of power, and when all four units were operating, total output was 880 MW. Postwar Isfahan was experiencing growth in various sectors, and since adequate electricity was the key to development, the Ministry of Energy signed an agreement with TPE to build four more units at Isfahan. Naturally, this opened up new prospects for Sati, and I was invited to Moscow to negotiate a contract to transport materials and equipment for the new project.

My wife and I left for Moscow on Thursday, March 21, 1991. Our trip would coincide with the Iranian New Year holidays. The earlier restrictions at Sheremetyevo International Airport had been eased and we quickly cleared Customs and Passport Control. We were met by Gabrielov who was very happy to see us. Now he was able to speak freely and he even spoke French with my wife. He took us to the Rossiya Hotel where reservations had been made for us. I had been there once before. With 3,000 rooms, it was a small city unto itself. Since we were foreigners paying in US dollars, we were given one of the best rooms. Gabrielov said he would pick me up at 9:00 AM the next day and Bella arranged to take a tour of Moscow's cultural landmarks.

When we went down for breakfast in the morning, our table was already laid with a variety of foods, as is customary. There was a glass-fronted refrigerator near the entrance, displaying some expensive items that were not on the menu, and one of those items was a kind of compressed and somewhat soft caviar. The Russians call it *presni* (pressed). It is delicious and it was my daily breakfast at the Rossiya.

When Gabrielov arrived, he told me my first appointment was with Stanislav Bokov, TPE's new general director. I asked him to give me a few minutes to go back up to my room and get the gift I had brought for Bokov. I knew him from the 1970s when he was chief engineer on the first two units at the Ramin Power Plant. After I rejoined Gabrielov in the lobby, he went out to signal a company car that was waiting at a distance from the hotel. The driver brought it forward, and fifteen minutes later, he dropped us off in front of TPE's new headquarters in the Arbat district. Gabrielov showed his identification and we took the elevator to the seventh floor where Bokov had his office. He gave me a warm welcome and told me he was well aware of how helpful Sati had been to TPE, and he expanded on how much he trusted my company. He also said he hoped to visit Tehran again some day.

Unfortunately, Bokov fell ill with cancer some years later and he spent months undergoing treatment in Denmark. The last time I saw him was in Tehran in the late 1990s. He had told his colleagues that I was the only person in the city he wanted to see, and I invited him to dinner at the Armenian Club. I was stunned when I saw him. That horrible disease had so altered his appearance that he was unrecognizable. He had lost weight and his hair had fallen out. I was sad to see him in that condition. He was quite downcast and he didn't linger after our meal but went straight back to the Russian Embassy where he was staying. A month later, I heard that he had died.

In Moscow, our meeting only lasted fifteen minutes, after which Gabrielov accompanied me down to the fifth floor for discussions with Sayenkov. There I learned that dear Sergeyev, or Sergei, as I had come to know him – the Armenian logistics manager with whom I had negotiated our first contract with TPE in 1975 – had retired and died not long afterwards. I was very sad because I had been looking forward to seeing him again in the new political environment.

Sayenkov, whom I also knew from Tehran, was fluent in Persian. He had served in the Soviet Army and held the rank of colonel. One time when he was in Tehran, I learned that he was having trouble with the circulation in one of his legs and faced the prospect of having it amputated. I took him to consult with a friend of mine, the surgeon Dr. Oshin Hagopian, who referred him to another physician who saved his leg from amputation.

Sayenkov welcomed me warmly, and after the usual pleasantries, he suggested we start by going over each item in Sati's proposal. We came to an agreement on terms the next day. He could have settled in one day but he wanted to draw out the process in order to show his colleagues that he was being meticulous. I went up to Bokov's office to sign the contract, after which we congratulated each other and toasted our new collaboration with glasses of Armenian cognac. I took my leave and went back down to say goodbye to

Sayenkov. He told me that Bokov's deputy, Valentin Kuznetsov, whom I also knew, wanted to see me, so I went back up to the seventh floor where Kuznetsov had his office next to Bokov's.

When Kuznetsov learned that I was planning to go to Yerevan, he gave me the phone number of his friend, the engineer Ruben Hovsepyan, and asked me to convey his regards. Then he confided that the Soviet Union was on the verge of dissolution. When that happened, he said, the constituent republics would be in a terrible fix – except for Armenia, because its large Diaspora could lend it support. Kuznetsov was very fond of Armenians. When Bokov died, he succeeded him as general director of TPE, and the Soviet organization was subsumed by the Russian Federation and continued to function as part of Rostec.

I have worked with many Russian engineers and administrators over the years and found them to be gracious and highly professional. The problems and obstacles in my dealings with them were invariably rooted in their fear of the KGB. My father had grown up among Russians and he used to say that they were generally kind-hearted and hard-working people and that it was rare for them to be deceitful. Bokov and Kuznetsov belonged to that majority my father used to speak well of.

My Third Visit to Armenia

We left Moscow for Yerevan on Saturday, March 23, 1991. Kuznetsov had arranged for Ruben Hovsepyan to meet us at Zvartnots Airport. We were also met by a young man named Yuri Nshanian. Since not many Iranians flew in to Yerevan in those days, it was easy for them to find us.

Yuri Nshanian entrusted me with a letter and a gift for Prime Minister Vazgen Manukyan from Mohsen Rafigh-Doust, the head of Iran's *Bonyad-e Mostazafan ve Janbazan* (the Foundation for the Oppressed and Disabled, as it was renamed during the Iran-Iraq War.) A few weeks earlier, Rafigh-Doust had sent an emissary named Fariborz Shabanian to meet with Prime Minister Manukyan and other officials and explore the potential for commercial trade between Iran and Armenia. Shabanian had also brought Rafigh-Doust's offer to fund the renovation of the Blue Mosque in Yerevan. Although Armenia had declared its independence the previous summer, it had not yet been recognized as such by any other country and formal diplomatic contacts still went through Moscow. So when Shabanian returned to Tehran with an agreement in principle on the renovation of the mosque, Rafigh-Doust sent his letter and gift for Manukyan with a second emissary who conveyed them through a third party to Nshanian, who gave them to me so that I could deliver them to the Armenian Prime Minister without any diplomatic complications.

We were taken from the airport to the Ani Hotel. It was very late, we were very tired and we fell asleep immediately. The next morning, Ruben Hovsepyan came by after breakfast, wanting to make sure we were being well taken care of. Then Yuri Nshanian dropped by to ask if we needed anything. I asked him if he could arrange for us to meet the Prime Minister and he promised to do so in the next two days.

After Nshanian left, Dr. Vazrig Der Petrossian came to visit. He had already heard from his ARF friends that I was in town, even though we had been there barely half a day. Dr. Der Petrossian was a family friend and a former intern at the Avedissian Community Clinic. He had attended my mother's death in 1986. Since then, he and his family had immigrated to Armenia. I told him too that I wanted to meet the Prime Minister.

The next day, Der Petrossian took me to the Writers Union and introduced me to the poet and architect Ruben Hovanissian (pen name R.). I learned that he was a representative of the ARF Central Committee in Armenia. He too promised to help with my request to meet the Prime Minister. When we got back to the hotel, Professor Hagop Papazyan was there waiting to see me, and while the three of us were chatting in the lobby, a young man approached Der Petrossian and told him that the Prime Minister would see us at 2:00 PM that very day. I was pleased and surprised that the meeting had been arranged so quickly.

I was at the Prime Minister's office at 2:00 PM sharp, accompanied by my wife, Vazrig Der Petrossian and Ruben Hovsepyan. He welcomed us warmly and asked me about Iran. I gave him a brief overview of the political and economic situation, mentioning Iran's rich mineral resources and its production and export capacity. I told him that Iran wanted to establish good relations with Armenia. Then he asked for news of his friends and acquaintances in Iran. I mentioned that Mohsen Rafigh-Doust and Fariborz Shabanian sent their best regards, and I brought out Rafigh-Doust's letter and gift. At that point, a group photograph was taken, and then coffee was served.

The congenial atmosphere sparked an idea in my mind. I told the Prime Minister that we in Iran had little information about the towns and villages in Armenia's southern border region, particularly Meghri, and we were keen to know more. In fact, I had a friend named Varoujan Arakelian, an architect with a vast knowledge of Armenia, and I had asked him about Meghri, but all he knew was that it was connected to Yerevan by a mountainous road.

"The chances are that Armenia will soon become fully independent," I told the Prime Minister. "When that happens, a good road between Yerevan and Meghri will be very important for business. Why not consider that prospect now?"

Prime Minister Manukyan liked the idea and said he was grateful for the Diaspora's interest and involvement in Armenia's future development. I mentioned that Bella and I were planning to return to Tehran in a few days but we would gladly postpone our departure if his office could arrange a trip to Meghri. Three hours later, back at the hotel, I received a message saying that I should be ready and waiting to leave for Meghri on Wednesday, March 27, at 8:00 AM. I was incredulous that this historic trip could be organized so quickly. Vazrig Der Petrossian would join me, along with five officials from various Ministries, including Mr. Atabegian, a very knowledgeable engineer from the Ministry of Road Construction and Maintenance.

Journey to Meghri

Our party of seven plus the driver set off in an RAF (Riga Autobus Factory) minibus. I had visited Armenia twice before, but this was my first trip south. On our right, we saw Sis and Massis, the twin peaks of Mount Ararat. The scene was breathtaking and deeply moving and I asked our driver to stop for photographs. Further along, we passed Ardashad (Artashat) east of the highway, and a couple of miles in the distance, we saw gold refining and cement production factories. Atabegian pointed out unlined sections of the road which he said had been used as military airstrips. We continued southeast, parallel with the Arax River, for about twenty-five miles until we left the Ararat Plateau for the mountain road to Yeghernadsor (Yeghegnadzor) with its green landscapes, multifarious trees and cultivated fields. Yeghernadsor lies north of the Arpa River whose abundant waters flow west through the Azerbaijani province of Nakhichevan to join the Arax, but part of the water was being diverted to Lake Sevan via the Arpa-Sevan tunnel and aqueduct system.

From Yeghernadsor, we followed the Arpa River to Vayk where we met another group from the Ministry of Road Construction and Maintenance at a riverside restaurant. It was 10:00 AM and we were ostensibly meeting for breakfast, but we were served a sumptuous lunch of shishkebab. Our cups clicked as one toast followed another, until our hosts finally conceded that we had a long way to go and it was time for us to get back on the road. Our hospitable companions took care of all the expenses and wouldn't allow me or Dr. Der Petrossian to contribute in any way, and we felt very bad about that. Heading southeast from Vayk, we drove past Goris an hour later and reached Ghapan (Kapan) in another half-hour or so.

In Ghapan, we were greeted by a red-cheeked local policeman, and when Atabegian told him that we were looking into the feasibility of a bridge over the Arax River, he was so happy that he took up the stance of a traffic cop, one hand resting on his hip and the other pointing toward Kajaran, another fifteen miles to the southwest. From Kajaran down to the Meghri Valley, the road is extremely mountainous. It was late March and the land was still covered in snow, but our minibus navigated the many switchbacks without much difficulty. On the return trip, I remarked to Atabegian that big rigs carrying heavy loads could never navigate those turns. He said they couldn't be widened without permission from the central government, and one of his colleagues explained that the road had been built that way for tactical military reasons, so that tanks and trucks couldn't pass. Prime Minister Manukyan had told me that a Yugoslav company was going to build a tunnel from Kajaran to the valley, bypassing the mountain road. Years later, the governments of Iran and Armenia discussed a similar project, but eventually an alternate route was built further east, from Ghapan via Tsav to Shvanidzor and the border road.

The southern half of Syunik Province, dominated by the Zangezur Mountain Range, has the most diverse mineral and metallurgical deposits in the country. Copper and molybdenum, gold and silver are all mined in this area. I was very interested in Armenian mining and I was aided in my research by Professor Papazyan who introduced me to Azad Vhouni, also an immigrant from Iran. Vhouni was a lecturer in mineral sciences and the author of many books and articles on the subject, and he shared a great deal of information with me.

At the time of our visit, Meghri, along with nearby Agarag (Agarak) and surrounding villages, had a population of about 15,000, most of whom worked in mining and agriculture. The Meghri Valley is famous for its figs, mulberries and pomegranates, and the peasants are robust and extremely hard-working: they carry soil up to hillside terraces to make their land even more productive. With its proximity to the border, the area is also strategically important. The proposed bridge over the Arax would be built a few miles upriver from Meghri near Agarag, opposite the Iranian village of Nourdouz.

We checked into the only hotel in Meghri. It hadn't had any guests for a long time but it looked adequate. Once in our rooms, however, Dr. Der Petrossian and I were dismayed at the terrible conditions we found. Nevertheless, we were so tired that we fell asleep immediately. Later, when I woke up and turned on the light, huge cockroaches scuttled across the floor. As a hunter, I had slept in worse conditions many times, so I fell right back to sleep.

The next morning, we met Mayor Levon Abrahamyan and his deputy. When I told the Mayor we wanted to see the Arax River up close, he said we would have to get permission from the KGB. Fortunately, the local KGB chief was a young Armenian who escorted us to the river. First, we came to the railway station of the defunct Baku-Nakhichevan-Yerevan line, and a little distance beyond that, there were two parallel fences, each with a gate guarded by Russian soldiers with trained dogs. The young KGB officer took out a ring of keys and unlocked each gate in turn, and we approached the river and stood on the shore.

Streams of snowmelt were gushing into the river and the beauty of the Arax in spate was indescribable. An orchard on the Iranian shore was partially submerged – the treetops were barely visible. We stood there on the river bank for fifteen minutes, each forming his own impression of the view, but we all agreed that if a bridge were to be built, this would be the most suitable site.

Returning to Meghri, we encountered scores of people gathered around a huge, ancient tree in the center of town. They were all talking about our bridge project and the benefits they anticipated for themselves and for Armenia and Iran. They were so excited that one would have thought construction was starting tomorrow! Someone offered his land in Agarag as a potential parking area and repair station for commercial trucks. Another person thanked us for finally paying attention to their remote town. We had several photographs taken as we mingled with the peasants, and one of them invited us to lunch in Agarag at a very old restaurant built of stone. According to the manager, it was over a hundred years old and had only recently been renovated. After lunch, we returned to Meghri and had dinner with Mayor Abrahamyan and his deputy.

The next day, we left for Yerevan, a 250-mile drive. From Kajaran to Ghapan and from Goris to Sisian, we passed scores of deserted villages, abandoned by Azeris after the start of the conflict over Gharabagh. En route from Goris to Sisian, we took a side trip to the Shakeh Falls, a scene of distinctive beauty in those days when its abundant waters were allowed to flow freely. We stopped for lunch in Sisian where a friend of Atabegian's invited us to the best restaurant in town. From there, we drove straight on through to Yerevan, a distance of over 120 miles. We were all very tired and our companions fell silent.

Sitting next to each other, Dr. Der Petrossian and I quietly chatted about Armenian politics. He was a very idealistic member of the ARF. He said he had been doing political work in the villages around Yerevan and Armavir and he was pleased with the results. He was confident that when Armenia became independent, people would vote for the ARF, and in five years, the party would control the government. I told him the ARF would be lucky if it won power in fifteen years! As a matter of fact, it was eight years before the ARF met the 5-percent threshold to win party representation in the National Assembly. My friend's views were not news to me, though such blind faith may be surprising to some. Zealous partisans, no matter which party they belong to, follow the words of their leaders. Their field of vision is so restricted that they only see what is right in front of them.

Back in Yerevan

It was dark when we got back to Yerevan. The three-day journey was one of the happiest times of my life. Vazrig Der Petrossian and I were the first Iranian-born Armenians to travel the road from Yerevan to Meghri, and the first-hand information we gathered was invaluable.

While I was away, Bella had made friends with Yuri Nshanian's sister, Rima Bedesta, who was the general director of the state-owned Myasnikyan Clothing Factory in Yerevan. (A few years later, she privatized the factory and became its president and chairman of the board.) She invited us to her home for dinner and I met her father, a former Communist Party official in Meghri. He offered me a glass of araq distilled from mulberries, a very powerful drink. What surprised me the most about Mrs. Bedesta's home was how luxurious it was. I never imagined that anyone could live in such palatial surroundings in a communist country. A house like that in Iran would have cost a million dollars.

Our "foot was blessed," as the saying goes, because Yuri Nshanian's wife gave birth to a healthy boy that same day.

Mrs. Bedesta later showed us around her factory and there we met Khosrov Harutyunyan, a most pleasant and well informed man. Trained as an engineer, he too had once run a clothing factory in the industrial town of Charentsavan and had risen to chair the town council. At the time we met, he was a member of Armenia's Supreme Soviet. He later served as Prime Minister of the Republic and as Speaker of the National Assembly. Mrs. Bedesta also introduced us to Gohar Yenokyan, the director of another clothing factory. Mrs. Yenokyan was a daring and fearless character. She was then a member of the short-lived Congress of the People's Deputies to the Soviet Union, and I was told that she had wagged a finger in warning at Gorbachev.

We met many Iranian émigrés during our stay in Yerevan. The painter Arshaluys Aghayan took us to a meeting of the Iranian Armenian Association which was held in a classroom at the Raffi School. Twelve members came to see us, including Arshaluys's brother Arshavir. They all wanted news from Iran and I answered their questions to the best of my knowledge. The Iranian artist Lida Berberian had given me the address of her brother Arzrouni Berberian and asked me to bring back news of him. He wasn't hard to find. He had a studio and gallery next to the Ani Hotel where he exhibited traditional Armenian handicrafts and antique weapons and carpets, as well as some of his own creations. He still had friends among the community of jewelers in Tehran. He welcomed us warmly and we spent a few hours with him in his studio and had some photographs taken.

People we didn't even know came to our hotel room at all hours of the night, even though there was a guard stationed on every floor. There would be a knock on the door at 11:00 PM and I would open to find a man with some outlandish commercial proposition. I didn't want to be impolite, so I would invite him in, listen to what he had to say and then gently send him on his way. The most surprising thing about these visitors, who by their own admission were working people, was that they all carried what they called a "diplomatic" bag, in many cases stuffed with rubles which they called "black" money. Apparently they were hiding it from their own family for fear it might be stolen.

Interestingly, when Mayor Abrahamyan and his deputy came up to Yerevan from Meghri, I invited them to dinner at the hotel. The maître d' inquired as to which currency I would be using, and when I said rubles, he told me all the tables were full. When I asked whether a table could be made available if we were to pay in US dollars, he promised to solve the problem "somehow," and we were soon shown to a table. Bella and I had had a similar experience with rubles and dollars in Moscow.

One night very late, there was a knock on the door. Bella was in bed with the flu but I felt that I couldn't ignore the visitor so I opened the door to a gentleman who greeted me with the utmost respect and introduced himself as Jora Mirzabegian, a lecturer at the Polytechnic Institute in Yerevan. He said he was originally from Iran but had emigrated with his family when he was a child. After this introduction, he said he was disappointed that we had failed to consult with him on the Meghri Bridge project, since he had already designed a plan for the bridge. That meeting was the beginning of a relationship that resulted in a most fruitful collaboration.

The most enjoyable part of our stay in Yerevan was a concert by the Armenian Philharmonic Orchestra conducted by Loris Tjeknavorian. I am a great fan of his. He was born in Iran in 1937 and started composing as a child. He immersed himself in Iranian folk music traditions and later studied in Austria and the USA. He served as principal conductor at Tehran's Roudaki Hall in the early 1970s, and subsequently pursued an international touring and recording career with RCA. After the Spitak earthquake, he directed a benefit gala concert for the victims at Carnegie Hall in New York, and then he moved to Armenia to help restore cultural life in the devastated country. He was appointed artistic director and principal conductor of the Armenian Philharmonic Orchestra in 1989.

After the concert, as I was coming out of the hall, I heard people calling my name. I turned around but didn't see any familiar faces. A group of young people approached me and said they were Iranian Armenians studying in Yerevan. I asked how they knew me and they said they knew of my work on the Diocesan Council and our efforts to save Armenian language and religious instruction in Iran. I was very moved by their acknowledgment and gratitude for the modest work we had done for our nation and culture. They invited us to their dormitory and served us tea and pastries.

Easter Sunday at Echmiadzin

Professor Papazyan arranged for Bella and me to meet His Holiness Vazgen I, the Supreme Patriarch and Catholicos of All Armenians. I had seen photographs of him but had never met him in person. At Echmiadzin, he welcomed us warmly and asked me to give his regards to Archbishop Manoukian. When he learned that I had been a member of the Diocesan Council, he treated me like a member of his faithful flock. He invited us to have lunch with him the following Sunday, which was Easter Sunday. Bella and I accepted his invitation with gratitude and happiness.

We arrived early on Sunday morning and waited outside for the holy mass to start. When the Catholicos entered the cathedral at the head of a procession of religious personalities of various ranks, from archbishops to seminary students, we followed right behind. Just then, we noticed a camera crew filming the procession. Later, a friend of mine in Paris called to say that he had seen us in *Mayrik*, a film by the French Armenian director Henri Verneuil (Ashot Malakian). I eventually saw the film in Paris myself. The procession scene in which we appear is only ten seconds long, and we can also be seen as part of the congregation in a quick cut to the mass. It was against the law to import films into Iran and I went to a lot of trouble to bring back a copy so I could show it to my friends.

Among those attending church that day were the highest ranking officials in Armenia's transitional government, the Supreme Soviet (or Council) of the Armenian Soviet Socialist Republic which was in the process of turning itself into the National Assembly of the Republic of Armenia. After the mass, we were led into the dining room while His Holiness received some Western Armenians from the Diaspora and then changed his garments and joined his guests for lunch. Some two dozen officials had been invited and Bella was the only woman present. I was introduced to Levon Ter-Petrosyan, the president of the Supreme Council. When I asked him about the prospects for a resolution of the Gharabagh conflict, he said that if we could have 80,000 Armenians living in Gharabagh, then we could say that we were the rightful owners of the region. Otherwise, he said, things would get complicated.

As the day of our departure drew near, I invited our friends to a farewell dinner at a restaurant on top of Musa Ler, a hill west of Yerevan overlooking the Ararat Plain. Among my guests were Professor Papazyan and his wife, Khosrov Harutyunyan and his wife, Rima Bedesta, Gohar Yenokyan and Ruben Hovsepyan who had become my close friend.

On our last day in Yerevan, I was given a letter from Prime Minister Manukyan and a lovely wooden vase carved with Armenian motifs and asked to deliver them to Mohsen Rafigh-Doust. Since the letter was carelessly typed, I had it copied in beautiful Iranian script by a professional scribe. As a result of these contacts, Iran's Foundation of the Oppressed and Disabled funded the renovation of the Blue Mosque on Mashtots Avenue in central Yerevan, and today it is both a place of worship and an interesting tourist destination.

Back in Tehran

Bella and I returned to Tehran with fond memories of our trip to Armenia. It was completely different from my earlier visits when I was monitored by Intourist and Armenian citizens were never allowed to mix freely with foreigners. The effects of Gorbachev's glasnost policy were evident everywhere. People welcomed us enthusiastically and conversed without restraint. Our hosts expressed their political opinions without fear. The National Assembly had already changed the name of the country to the Republic of Armenia and everyone was talking about the upcoming referendum on secession from the Soviet Union.

That reminded me of a speech by ARF Bureau chief Hrair Maroukhian two years earlier. On his way home from a visit to Moscow in 1989, he had stopped off in Vienna and met with the Austrian Armenian community. A friend of mine had given me a cassette tape of the meeting and I had listened to it many times on my way to and from work. Maroukhian spoke highly of Gorbachev and advocated reconciliation and collaboration with the USSR, which for an ARF official was unprecedented. Ever since the Bolsheviks had overthrown the ARF-led First Republic in 1920, no party leader had ever publicly called for cooperation with the Soviet Union. The very idea was unthinkable. But here the party leader was urging Diaspora Armenians to lend their moral and financial support to the homeland. During the question-and-answer session, Maroukhian was asked about the prospects for Armenian independence. He replied that, under the terms of the Soviet Constitution, Armenia could conceivably apply for independent status sometime during the next decade, and might even achieve that status by the end of the twentieth century. As politically astute as Maroukhian was, he failed to anticipate Armenia's bid for freedom and the collapse of the Soviet Union.

The first thing I did after I returned to Tehran was to arrange an appointment with Mohsen Rafigh-Doust to deliver Prime Minister Manukyan's letter and gift. Ruben Karapetian and Fariborz Shabanian accompanied me to the meeting. I asked Rafigh-Doust if I could announce the news of Iranian-Armenian cooperation and he said that it would be fine. *Alik* reported on the bonyad's trade negotiations and its plans to renovate the Blue Mosque on May 14, 1991.

Next, I wrote a wide-ranging report in Persian on Armenia's political and economic situation. Before submitting my report to the Ministry of Foreign Affairs (and sending copies to the Ministry of Transportation and Road Construction and the Chamber of Commerce, Industry and Mining), I read it at a meeting of the Union of Iranian-Armenian Engineers and Architects, less formally known as the Garni Society. Most of my colleagues thought highly of the report, but some of the more conservative members were surprised at my frank assessment of conditions in one of the Soviet Republics. The Ministry of Transportation had the report published in *Kayhan*, and a condensed translation was published in *Alik* on May 20, 1991. Later, I wrote a long article for the ARF's monthly *Droshag*, an abridged version of which was read aloud on an Armenian radio program in Paris, all of which generated a great deal of interest among the Diaspora.

My reporting covered the residual effects of the Soviet economic system on labor and industry; Armenia's reliance on Soviet imports; the challenges of the new government's decision to promote private-sector commerce, industry and agriculture; the country's hydrological and mineral resources; the strong potential for a tourism industry; the high level of literacy; and the wealth of highly trained scientists, engineers, physicians, teachers and artists. I emphasized that Armenia could be a bridge between Iran and Europe, and I included a detailed map highlighting the potential transport route from Meghri to Yerevan and on to Tbilisi and the Black Sea ports of Batumi and Poti, and from there to Russia, Ukraine and Bulgaria and ultimately to the countries of western Europe. I concluded by saying that this international trade route could only be realized with the construction of a bridge over the Arax River.

Chapter 25

The First Diaspora Business Conference in the Last Days of Soviet Armenia

In April, I made a short trip to Paris, and while I was there, my wife called to say that Albert Ajemian, the publisher of *Alik*, was trying to reach me. I called him right away. He said the Armenian government was sponsoring an international conference of Diasporan business professionals in Yerevan at the end of May. He had put my name down as a member of the Iranian Armenian delegation and he was calling to ask for my consent. Even though I had just returned from Yerevan, I told him I would be happy to participate. I soon received a formal invitation from Yesayi Stepanyan, Armenia's Minister of Foreign Trade Relations. According to the invitation, the aim of the conference was to interest Diasporan investors in factories in Armenia. The government would cover all expenses, excluding travel to and from Yerevan.

The Iranian Armenian business delegation consisted of Rafik Gasparian, Ruben Karapetian, Norair Melkonian, Armen Moutafian, Tomas Saroukhanian and myself. Archbishop Ardak Manoukian, Archbishop Goriun Papian and Albert Ajemian were invited as honored guests. In order to get exit permits, we had to submit a certified translation of the invitation and other supporting documents to the Iranian government. Two months earlier, when my wife and I had applied for permission to travel on the basis of a letter from the Ministry of Energy, it had been quickly granted. This time, it was a different story. The same official, whom I knew personally, considered our applications on a case-by-case basis. He called each of us into his office individually, advised us to avoid contact with people we didn't know and warned us against making new friends, but we all got permission to go. Then, with our invitations in hand, we applied for visas at the Soviet Embassy where there had always been an Armenian on the consular staff to deal with Iranian Armenians, ever since the end of the first Armenian Republic. Our visas were issued without any problem.

There were still no direct flights to Yerevan, so on Thursday, May 23, we flew to Moscow via Aeroflot, spent the night there, and flew to Yerevan the next day. Representatives of the Catholicosate met us at Zvartnots and took the Archbishops to Echmiadzin, while government officials escorted the rest of us to the Dvin Hotel.

A special exhibition of domestic light industry had been organized that day for conference participants, but because our flight had been delayed, it looked like we were going to miss it. When we arrived at the hotel, however, we were met by Telman Ter-Petrosyan, a successful businessman and one of Levon Ter-Petrosyan's older brothers. When I told him how much I wanted to see the exhibition, he drove me and several of my colleagues there in his own car. We were impressed by what we saw. There was a display of textiles of good quality and design, and another display of shoes, a sector in which Armenia had made great progress, exporting 22 million a year. We saw various types of electronic equipment and power tools. They were attractive and tastefully designed, and I was told that Armenian computers were highly sought after in Soviet and East European markets. We also saw various types of medical equipment, medicines and chemical compounds. The exhibition was well worth our rush to see it.

When we got back to the hotel, we spent a couple of hours talking in the lobby, and then we finally went to our rooms to rest. We were exhausted.

Saturday, May 25, 1991

The conference was held in the Shahumyan Palace, a ten-minute walk from our hotel. It began at 10:00 AM on Saturday, May 25. Four hundred Armenian business professionals from thirty countries had been invited. Of those, 230 attended, as well as a large number of business professionals from Armenia. The conference was a historic event in the life of the Armenian nation. The main item on the agenda was the foundation of an international association of Armenian business professionals. As Article 2 of the draft bylaws stated:

> The purpose of the association will be to support the creation and strengthening of commercial-economic, scientific-technical and humanitarian ties between the members of the association and also between Armenia and other countries. By centralizing the economic, scientific and information resources of its members, the association will create more advantageous conditions for the development and expansion of business, encourage mutual support among its members, and support the implementation of humanitarian initiatives.

It was hoped that commercial agreements would be concluded on the sidelines of the conference, and the establishment of an international pan-Armenian bank was also in view.

The conference opened with the words of Supreme Council President Levon Ter-Petrosyan, read by a member of his staff. Prime Minister Manukyan then stepped up to the podium and welcomed everyone, after which he turned the proceedings over to Minister Stepanyan. The Minister saw to it that everyone who wanted to speak could do so in an orderly fashion. Some spoke in Eastern Armenian, others in Western Armenian, and still others in French or English because they were hesitant to speak in the mother tongue, but everyone spoke with great enthusiasm. Some told their life stories, sad tales of adversity and bad luck. For example, one man said that his father was born in Western Armenia and died in Beirut, while his mother was a native of Beirut. He himself was born in Brazil but was now living in India. He said that Armenians were tired of this wandering life and urged us all to come together in Armenia and build a free, independent and prosperous homeland. Everyone who spoke promised to support Armenia on the path to economic prosperity, and every speech ended with sustained applause for the speaker's heartfelt words.

Armenian Airlines

One speaker was a non-Armenian émigré who was married to an Armenian. Speaking in English, he announced that he was planning to start a company in Los Angeles to fly passengers between the USA and Armenia and he was going to call it Armenian Airlines. The entire hall resounded with wild applause, but I was deeply dismayed. First, because I had known this man quite well when he lived in Iran, and second, because I understood the implications of his choice of that particular name. Companies spend years promoting their name and making it internationally recognized. Under that name, he could register his company with the International Air Transport Association and proceed to create markets throughout the world. And when the day came that Armenia wanted to establish a national airline, as it surely would, and Armenia wanted to use the usurped name, which it had an inherent right to do, it would have to file a lawsuit in an international court to reclaim it.

I went straight to Vazgen Manukyan's aide and told him that I had something very important to discuss with the Prime Minister. I asked for a ten-minute appointment and he put me down for 10:00 AM the next morning.

I noticed that everyone who got up to speak was either European or North American, and they all focused on developing relations between Armenia and the West, whereas I found those prospects unrealistic. It seemed that no one from Armenia's neighbors in the East was willing to speak up. After discussing it with the other members of our delegation, I decided to say something. I raised my hand for permission to speak, and I sensed that the chairman must also have felt the lack of balance because he called on me right away.

I began by talking about the historical relations between Armenia and Iran which go back centuries. I said that Armenia has always been a bridge for both commercial and cultural exchange between Iran and the West, and that Armenia has the same geographic importance today and must develop that role. Then I gave a brief account of Iran's economic profile and potential and its many diverse natural resources.

As an Iranian Armenian, I went on, I believed that Armenia must have strong relations with Iran and its enterprising people. Armenia must become one of the connections between Iran and Europe, a role that promised many benefits for both countries. For example, product components could be imported from Iran and assembled in Armenia, and the finished products could be exported to the western republics of the Soviet Union (Georgia, Russia, Ukraine, Moldova and Belorussia), whose total population was 200 million, which was a huge market.

I said it would be unwise to attempt to export Armenian goods to the West at that time because Western markets were saturated with high-quality products produced by firms with significant capital investment. For example, if Armenia's profit from a ten-dollar investment were two dollars, the same profit could be made in the West from a five-dollar investment. On the other hand, Armenia could sell its products in the markets of its southern neighbors, including Iran, Iraq, the Gulf Emirates, Pakistan and India, where the high quality or luxury quotient of a product was perhaps not essential. These commercial ties could be developed with the help of Armenians in the West who could transfer the technology and equipment needed to improve the quality of goods manufactured in Armenia and could even set up assembly plants in Armenia, and I urged them to get involved in such projects. I also urged them to help develop packaging techniques which was crucial for Armenian products in today's market. I observed that pay was very low in

Armenia and that some profit might be gained from the wage differential between Armenian workers and their counterparts in other countries, but that wouldn't last long.

I concluded by saying that commercial success was based on three key factors: The first was Iran's demonstrated good will toward Armenia and the Armenian people. The second was technology transfer facilitated by Armenian business professionals in the West. And the third and most important factor was Armenia's hard-working people. They are by nature tough, skilled, innovative and resourceful and they should seize the initiative. These three factors would guarantee the prosperity of Armenia.

My speech was received with loud applause and expressions of appreciation. Before I left the podium, I mentioned that Prime Minister Manukyan had facilitated my recent trip to Meghri to investigate the feasibility of building a bridge across the Arax River. That brought a standing ovation.

At the end of the day, when everyone who wanted to speak had spoken, the conference ratified the bylaws of the new association by a unanimous vote.

Conflict between the ARF and the ANM

During breaks in the conference, participants met in the side rooms adjacent to the main hall for private conversations or business negotiations, and it was in one of those rooms that I witnessed a most interesting incident during the first break. Hrair Maroukhian was representing the ARF at the conference, and he was surrounded by people, all talking about the upcoming referendum on secession, which had been set for September 21. Suddenly, Maroukhian started attacking the leaders of *Hay Hamazgayin Sharjoum*, or the Armenian National Movement (ANM).

The ANM had emerged from the Gharabagh Committee in 1989 after its leaders, including Levon Ter-Petrosyan and Vazgen Manukyan, had spent six months in jail for their political activities. The movement had registered as a political party and won a plurality of seats in the 1990 elections for the Supreme Soviet. There was a peaceful transfer of power from the Communist Party to the ANM, and the Supreme Soviet transformed itself into a National Assembly, declared the Republic of Armenia a sovereign state, and announced its intention to secede from the Soviet Union through the legal process of a popular referendum.

But now Maroukhian was telling the people surrounding him that the ANM had to be defeated at all costs, which seemed at odds with his remarks two years earlier in Vienna. A group of Armenians in Armenia was struggling for Armenian independence and the liberation of Gharabagh. Why would the ARF oppose them?

In fact, the ARF could not tolerate the new political configuration in the Transcaucasus, where Abulfaz Elchibey was gaining power as the head of the ultranationalist Azerbaijani Popular Front (*Azerbaijan Xalq Cebhesi*), and the ultranationalist Zviad Gamsakhurdia was about to be elected President of Georgia. Apparently the Armenian National Movement, whose very name signified its aversion to fanaticism, was insufficiently nationalist for Maroukhian. The ARF, which had likely received promises from the Soviet leadership, considered itself the rightful heir to power in Armenia, and that is why it decided to oppose the ANM. Thus, the ARF and the ANM became not only political opponents but sworn enemies.

Sunday, May 26, 1991

When I met with Prime Minister Manukyan on Sunday morning, I asked him what he thought of the previous day's announcement about the formation of a company called Armenian Airlines, and he replied that he thought it would be of great benefit to Armenia. Then I asked him what would happen if the Republic of Armenia decided to create a national airline? What would it be called?

"Armenian Airlines is a brand name worth millions," I said, "and here it is being claimed by a man with dubious credentials cheered on by Armenian businessmen!"

He replied that he hadn't considered the potential value in the name. I cited the example of Siemens: the name itself symbolizes quality and that quality attaches to hundreds of products branded by the company. People see the Siemens name on something and they buy it out of loyalty and trust. I emphasized that "Armenian Airlines" symbolizes Armenia and its people and that can't be bought for any price.

It being Sunday, we were fortunate to attend mass at Echmiadzin. His Holiness Vazgen I officiated, with Archbishop Manoukian and Archbishop Papian participating. He concluded his sermon with a word about May 28, two days hence. Afterwards, conference participants were invited to the hall on the second floor of the patriarch's residence where they received his blessings and good wishes. There was a solemn atmosphere as he spoke about the current political situation and the upcoming referendum. We were enthralled by his imposing presence and his honest, hopeful words.

When the conference resumed in the afternoon, the atmosphere was more subdued, less enthusiastic than the previous day with its fiery speeches. There was some discussion of the project to create an Armenian international bank, and a number of people pledged donations toward the project. When the total reached $25,000, I pledged to match it.

Monday, May 27, 1991

On Monday, conference participants agreed that the pan-Armenian bank proposal was premature and dropped it from the agenda. They turned to the work of setting up a committee to develop and maintain networking ties among members of the new business association, and it was decided that the committee should include at least one person from each country that was represented at the conference. An ad hoc board of thirty-one was elected, with six from Armenia and twenty-five from the Diaspora. Armen Moutafian and I were chosen as the representatives from Iran.

The conference was brought to a close with speeches by Levon Ter-Petrosyan, Vazgen Manukyan and Yesayi Stepanyan. That evening, we were honored with a dinner hosted by Ter-Petrosyan, Manukyan and several other officials in the Armenia Hotel's banqueting hall. After the dinner and the speeches, Armenians from Armenia and Armenians from the Diaspora talked late into the night in a pleasant atmosphere.

Tuesday, May 28, 1991

May 28 is the date of the founding of the First Republic of Armenia in 1918, and that night there was going to be a big celebration in Yerevan's Lenin Square (now Republic Square). My friends Rima Bedesta and Gohar Yenokyan invited the Iranian delegation to lunch in an orchard out towards Garni. An entire family provided the excellent food and service. When we arrived at 2:00 PM, the table was already set and the toasts began with our local host serving as tamada. He raised one toast after another, and he even drank to the health of the leaves on the trees, as the saying goes. I never had such a long lunch in my life! After five hours around the table, we were keen to get back to Yerevan for the evening's festivities, but our host announced that he had just slaughtered a few more chickens for the barbecue. So we spent the entire day eating and drinking in an orchard!

The Diaspora Business Conference was a turning point in my future involvement with Armenia. When I got back to Tehran, I wrote another report in Persian and I also wrote an article in Armenian on economic conditions and prospects in the Republic of Armenia which was published in *Alik* on July 13, 1991. Diasporan Armenians knew very little about Armenia at that time, and my article attracted a good deal of attention and praise from the Iranian Armenian community.

With Armenian Prime Minister Vazken Manoukyan.

In the Armenian foothills of Mt. Ararat.

Armenian Prime Minister Vazken Manoukyan arranged for an Iranian delegation of seven (including author) to travel from Yerevan to the Iranian border.

The delegation at Shaki falls on the road to Meghri.

Looking for a suitable location for a new bridge over the Arax river. *(Right to left)* Author, engineer Abdollah Dast Gheyb, General Haj Addollah Roudaki, Prof. Mirzabegian, Telman Ter Petrosyan from Armenia...

Temporary, pontoon bridge near Meghri, in Nordouz, Iran.

Chapter 26

Post-Conference Developments

During the Soviet era, Iranians were rarely allowed to visit Armenia. The prohibition was even more strictly applied to Iranian Armenians, and it was enforced by both the Iranian and the Soviet security services. In order to get to Armenia, Iranians sometimes had to fly to a European capital first, and from there to Moscow and finally to Yerevan, an expensive and time-consuming trip. But under Gorbachev, the prospects for direct flights between Tehran and Yerevan improved, and after the Diaspora Business Conference, the Diocesan Council set up a cultural relations committee to bring this about. I was a member of that committee along with Norair Elsaian and Seroj Soukiassian.

Soukiassian and I met with the head of the newly established Iran Air Tours Company, Seyyed Mehdi Ghaffar, whom I knew well. He supported our proposal in principle and suggested that we contact Edward Bojolyan, the head of an Armenian tourist agency, whom I also knew. Bojolyan arranged for an Iranian delegation to come to Yerevan and start negotiations with Mr. Yeritsyan, the head of Aeroflot's Armenian regional service.

We flew to Yerevan in August 1991. Our delegation included Soukiassian and myself from the Diocesan Council's cultural relations committee, Seyyed Mehdi Ghaffar and his company's chief financial officer, and a man named Mozaffar. I don't know whom Mozaffar represented, since he played no role in the negotiations and merely took notes on occasion, but I assume he was from one of Iran's security services.

We were all staying at the Dvin Hotel, and one of the Muslims in our delegation asked me for the direction of the *ghebleh* (Arabic *qibla*, direction), i.e., the direction of the Kaaba in Mecca which Muslims face when they pray. I didn't know the answer so I asked Soukiassian and he didn't know either, so we took the question to an ARF official who was originally from Isfahan. He gave us a diagram showing the proper direction and I gave it to our Muslim colleagues. They were forbidden by their faith from eating non-*halal* meat, i.e., meat from an animal that was not slaughtered in the prescribed way. Perhaps they had anticipated that problem because they brought along canned fish and one even brought tomatoes and cucumbers.

We met with Bojolyan the day we arrived and he set up an appointment with Yeritsyan the next morning at the latter's office near the airport. Yeritsyan gave us a warm welcome and expressed his support for our proposal. Our discussion proceeded to practical questions and we were already on to fuel supply and ticketing, when a member of Yeritsyan's staff entered the conference room, whispered something in his ear and went back out. Yeritsyan followed him out and left us there to wait for his return. He came back half an hour later, visibly angry:

"If I could get my hands on that fat-bellied man, I'd cut his head off!"

Of course, we wanted to know who that fat-bellied man was, and Yeritsyan's deputy, Samuel Markaryan, told us that he was the same man who had announced at the Diaspora Business Conference that he was starting a company called Armenian Airlines. Apparently he had leased an aircraft and was already flying people in from America, but he had bribed Turkish officials in order to avoid paying the overflight fee, and when Soviet aviation authorities found out, they detained the plane in Yerevan. The crisis had just broken and our meeting was suspended, but we had already agreed that an Armenian delegation would come to Tehran to finalize arrangements.

Our return home via Moscow coincided with the August 19 putsch against Gorbachev which was resolved through Yeltsin's intervention, but we were stuck in Moscow for two days until regular flights resumed. A month later, the Armenian people voted for independence from the Soviet Union.

Armenia's first presidential election was scheduled for October 16. A few days before that, Soukiassian joined me for a game of tennis at the Ararat Center. He was one of the most prominent members of the ARF, and naturally we talked about the upcoming election. He was confident that the ARF candidate, an actor named Sos Sarkissian, would be elected with at least 50 percent of the vote. I told him,

"The ARF should thank God if their candidate gets even 5 percent of the vote!"

But Soukiassian was so confident that he bet me a case of beer. The results were plain for all to see. Levon Ter-Petrosyan won with over 80 percent of the vote, and the ARF candidate got 3 percent. Of course, Soukiassian didn't pay up. Instead, he invited me for a drink the next time we were both in Yerevan. He confided that he had told an ARF leader about our wager and the man had laughed in his face, saying it was a waste of time talking politics with me because I lacked political maturity and knowledge. But after the election, Soukiassian continued, he had told the same man that he was wrong to say hurtful things about me:

"You see? He was more realistic than we were!"

Armenian Airlines

Armenia's airline delegation arrived in Tehran on Thursday, November 21. On Saturday, they visited the Prelacy at the invitation of the Diocesan Council. Archbishop Manoukian welcomed them and talked about the historic significance of their mission. He also gave them a basic idea of how the Iranian Armenian community was organized through its various institutions. Afterwards, the group paid a visit to *Alik*'s editorial offices.

Negotiations began on Sunday at Iran Air Tours, where Seyyed Mehdi Ghaffar led the Iranian side while the Armenian side was led by Edward Bojolyan, who had been appointed chairman of the State Committee for External Tourism, and Samuel Markaryan, appointed vice-chairman of the State Aviation Committee. Soukiassian and I served as mediators.

After six months of hard work, our discussions produced positive results. The direct route was inaugurated on Thursday, January 30, 1992, when a Tupolev-134 landed at Mehrabad International Airport and seventy-six passengers boarded for the sold-out flight to Yerevan. Among the passengers were Archbishop Manoukian and other community leaders, ordinary Armenian families and individuals, and a reporter from *Alik*. The only Muslim was Seyyed Abdollah Dastgheib, an Iranian government researcher whom MP Vartan Vartanian had invited along.

Everyone stayed at the Armenia Hotel, but sadly, due to the Azerbaijani fuel embargo, there was no heat and the rooms were extremely cold. All the guests were aware of the situation and showed great patience. Being in the homeland meant so much to them that they easily overcame the otherwise unbearable conditions. They went to bed in their heavy overcoats, the men shaved with freezing cold water, and there were no complaints.

Our group included Vantsig Papazian, one of the best-known diamond merchants in Iran, and my close friend Lemuel Avedian, the renowned goldsmith and jewelry designer. They had both been purveyors of gems and jewelry to the late Shah and his courtiers. Lemuel was so highly respected that the Islamic government had given him the task of sorting out the jewels in the state treasury. Vantsig and Lemuel especially wanted to see Armenia's diamond cutting workshop which employed a thousand workers.

On Sunday, we attended holy mass at Echmiadzin. Afterwards, we were warmly received by His Holiness Vazgen I. When he learned that Dastgheib was not Armenian, he singled him out for attention and spoke of the centuries-old relationship between Iran and Armenia, and he emphasized the prospects for its future development. Sunday coincided with the start of Dahe-ye Fajr, Iran's annual festival commemorating the Islamic Revolution, and of course, Dastgheib's presence made it imperative that we organize a celebration. Had he not been with us in Yerevan, we might have overlooked it.

Dastgheib was researching Armenia's natural resources, manufacturing capacity and export-import activity. He asked me to introduce him to Ashot Safaryan, the Minister of Industry, whom I had met in Paris through Petros Terzian, the author of *OPEC: The Inside Story*. Safaryan welcomed my request and the three of us met late one night in his office, a big room with a small heater – he was wearing a Russian fur hat. Since he and Dastgheib spoke no common language, I served as interpreter. Dastgheib presented himself as a wholesale merchant interested in trade. During our week-long stay, he accepted every offer that came his way and signed contracts to buy goods worth two million dollars, but the only thing I saw him actually buy was a wool hat. Evidently his pose was a way of verifying commercial information.

Armenian Airlines, having reclaimed the national brand, operated the Yerevan-Tehran route until it went bankrupt in 2003. Armavia Airlines took over the route but went bankrupt in 2013. At present, the route is served by half a dozen airlines, none of them owned by Armenian nationals.

The Iran-Armenia Chamber of Commerce

My business friends and I had started thinking about how to alert investors and industrialists to the economic potential of bilateral trade between Iran and Armenia. We decided to establish the Iran-Armenia Chamber of Commerce (IACOC) as a non-profit information center dedicated to promoting commerce and trade between the two countries. We had to get over a few hurdles in order to gain permission from the Iranian government, but Armenia's decision to secede from the Soviet Union helped bring our plan to fruition. Iran was one of the first countries to recognize independent Armenia, making an official announcement to that effect on December 25, 1991. In February, the two governments signed a diplomatic protocol, and in

April, Iran opened its Embassy in temporary quarters at the Hrazdan Hotel on Proshyan Street in Yerevan.

We decided to apply for affiliate membership in the Iranian Chamber of Commerce, Industry and Mining (ICCIM). I knew Asadollah Asgar-Oladi, a member of the ICCIM's executive board who turned out to be the key to our success. Four of us met with Asgar-Oladi and presented our plan. He said he liked it and he took it to the board. A week later, he got back to us with the board's formal approval, subject to certain conditions: the ICCIM would appoint five of the IACOC's nine-member board, and the chairman had to be a Muslim.

We accepted those conditions and set to work. Albert Bernardi and Onnik Sahakian, two of the community's best-known lawyers, drafted the bylaws pro bono. The founding members each contributed 40,000 tomans and we opened an account for the organization's expenses under my name and that of Armen Moutafian. Once we completed those preparations, the IACOC was duly registered as a subsidiary of the ICCIM on April 21, 1993, by Iran's Department of Non-Trade Companies and Institutes.

The formation of the IACOC's executive board took place on December 14, 1993. Over a hundred people gathered in the large hall on the eighth floor of the ICCIM building. I had been told that Shahrokh Zahiri, a prominent businessman and factory owner, was slated to be the chairman. He came in about half an hour before the proceedings were supposed to begin, and when he saw that almost everyone in the room was Armenian, he approached me and said he was amazed at how many people there were, adding that it must be because of their confidence in me. He considered the precondition regarding the chairmanship outrageous and he said he wouldn't accept the appointment. He would persuade Asgar-Oladi to set it aside, adding that I ought to be the chairman and he could be vice-chairman, and off he went to see Asgar-Oladi. Half an hour later, he came back with a smile on his face. We proceeded to elect the four board members and the entire board then elected me chair and Zahiri vice-chair.

The forty-five founding members were the following:

Shahen Aboulian	Edward Davitian	Tadevos Mouradian
Leon Abrahamian	Yeprem Der Andonian	Vigen Mouradian
Robert Abrahamian	Rafik Der Petrossian	Armen Moutafian
Henrik Aharonian	Vigen Gevorkian	Vachik Pezeshkian
Levon Aharonian	Mardiros Grigorian	MehranBoghos Piroomian

Souren Allahyari	Vachik Grigorian	Morteza Sadeghi
Hratch Artchounian	Onnik Haroutunian	Leon Sarhadian
Golia Arzoumanian	Jorgig Hayrabedian	Edward Shahbazian
Grigor Tadevos Avakian	Vahe Injirgholli	Norair Shahbazian
Lemuel Avedian	Vahe Jovakim	Souren (Hrair) Shahbazian
Abraham Ayvazian	Ruben Karapetian	Yeznik Shahbazian
Vachik Babakhanian	Razmik Khoudabakhshian	Vahik Shahnazarian
Rozig Barkhan	Vahik Mansourian	Stepan Stepanian
Salman Barseghian	Rouzas Markarian	Tomas (Babig) Tomassian
Mihran Boukhanian	Mohammad-Ali Moayed	Shahrokh Zahiri

We had been promised an office in the ICCIM building but that didn't pan out, and we soon realized that rents downtown were much higher than we could afford. Sati stepped in and provided an office that we could use as our temporary headquarters, which included telephone, utilities and maintenance.

Our work was multifaceted, especially since the fledgling Armenian Embassy in Tehran had yet to establish a commercial section. We were contacted by countless individuals, private firms and government organizations – including scores of non-Armenian business interests in the former Soviet republics – for information on industrial productivity and business opportunities in both Armenia and Iran, and our board members were often asked to sit in on business-related negotiations between Iranians and Armenians.

Meghri Bridge Site Visit

On April 23, 1992, President Ter-Petrosyan's brother Telman and the architect Jora Mirzabegian came to Iran to discuss issues related to the construction of a temporary bridge over the Arax River and to visit the site at Nourdouz on the Iranian side. Joining us for the trip to Nourdouz were Seyyed Abdollah Dastgheib and his friend Commander Haj Abdollah Roudaki, an IRGC naval officer and war hero. Dastgheib brought Roudaki along because of his ability to gain access to restricted areas.

They day after my Armenian guests arrived, I picked them up at their hotel at 4:00 AM in order to make the 5:00 AM flight to Tabriz. Dastgheib and Roudaki met us at the airport. Our bags went through security check, first mine, then Dastgheib's, Roudaki's, Ter-Petrosyan's, and finally

Mirzabegian's bag. The airport security officers stopped him and told him to open his bag. Inside were three bottles of Armenian cognac. At that point, they told him he was under arrest. Our Muslim colleagues picked up their bags and moved on while I desperately tried to explain that Mirzabegian was visiting from Armenia, he didn't know the laws of Iran, and he had brought the cognac as gifts for Armenian friends in Tabriz. Somehow I convinced them to let us go, but they kept the cognac.

I had had my driver, Eskandar, take my car up to Tabriz the day before, and when we landed at the airport, he was there waiting for us, along with the manager of Sati's local office. Without wasting any time, we set off for Julfa, which is about seventy-five miles north of Tabriz. In Julfa, we stopped off at Sati's local office and were served breakfast by the staff.

Then we went to the regional border control office and met with the commandant. Colonel Taghavi, a native of Iran's Talesh region, was very kind and accommodating. After reviewing the documents that Commander Roudaki presented, he said he had no objection to our traveling in the border zone but we needed permission from the Julfa security office because only local residents had free access to the area. We proceeded to the Julfa security office where Dastgheib and Roudaki were both known to the staff. They welcomed us warmly, served us tea, and shortly produced a letter of permission which we took back to Colonel Taghavi. After reading it, he said he would personally accompany us to Nourdouz, which is a forty-mile drive from Julfa. The first part of the road was asphalted, the next part was under construction, and the last part was just a dirt road.

Nourdouz was then an uninhabited expanse of orchards and green pasture opposite the Armenian town of Agarag. We got out and walked to the riverbank. The Arax was in spate, looking strong and majestic. Ter-Petrosyan saw some compatriots he knew across the river and called to them by name. A few minutes later, a man approached and introduced himself. He owned the orchards there and Colonel Taghavi knew him well. He offered us tea brewed from the waters of the Arax which he boiled over an open fire. The exact location of the bridge had already been determined and Ter-Petrosyan had brought several long spikes. We drove them into the ground to symbolically start construction.

On the way back to Julfa, we stopped at a military garrison where we were given lunch. Two hours later, we were back on the road, and as we neared Julfa, Ter-Petrosyan asked if we could make a detour to look at a Russian-

Tsarist–era bridge over the Arax. It was already getting dark but he insisted on seeing it, so Colonel Taghavi drove us there himself. Ter-Petrosyan got out and studied the bridge for a few minutes, then returned to the car. Later when we were alone, he told me that after having seen the clearance under the old bridge, he was confident the Meghri Bridge would not be vulnerable if the Azeris were to open the upstream barrage.

We drove back to Tabriz and spent the night there, while Dastgheib and Roudaki flew back to Tehran. The next morning, we visited Jora's friend, the one for whom he had brought the cognac. His friend turned out to be the uncle of my colleague Ardashes Zomorodian. Jora stayed in Tabriz while Telman and I caught the 11:00 AM flight to Tehran. It was April 24 and a huge demonstration had taken place that morning. Thousands had marched north from St. Sarkis Church to Argentina Square where the UN was headquartered.

We went straight to my home, and after a light lunch, we discussed the construction of the bridge in greater detail. He told me that he had already purchased a ready-made temporary structure from the Russian Army. Then he told me in strict confidence, as he would tell his own brother, that Armenian fighters were going to liberate Shushi and Lachin in ten days. The Kurdish population of Lachin had agreed to evacuate peacefully but Shushi would have to be taken by force. That made me happy and I promised not to tell anyone. A few days later, my friend Armen Hakhnazarian called me from Germany. He said he had heard the same thing from an Armenian general.

Dastgheib asked me for a report on Armenia's history and geography, social make-up, economic productivity, etc. After consulting with some well-informed friends, I wrote up my notes in Persian and gave my report to Dastgheib who passed it along to President Hashemi-Rafsanjani. The Iranian President was preparing to receive the Armenian President in Tehran.

Chapter 27

President Ter-Petrosyan Visits Iran

President Levon Ter-Petrosyan began his first state visit to Iran on Wednesday, May 6, 1992. Members of his team had preceded him finalize the details of a series of bilateral agreements, and his advisor, Vahan Papazyan (Professor Hagop Papazyan's son), arrived on Monday to oversee final arrangements. On the day of his arrival, *Alik* carried a report from Armenia that a ceremony would be held in Meghri at 2:00 PM that very day to mark the opening of a temporary bridge over the Arax River.

President Ter-Petrosyan's flight touched down at 5:08 PM. His party included Foreign Minister Raffi Hovannisian, Energy Minister Sebouh Tashjiyan, National Assembly Vice President Ara Sahakyan, several members of the National Assembly including Khosrov Harutyunyan, and the director of the Armenpress News Agency, Gevorg Hovhannisyan. They were met at the airport at by President Hashemi-Rafsanjani, Foreign Minister Dr. Ali-Akbar Velayati and other high-ranking officials, along with representatives of the Iranian Armenian community. The flags of Iran and Armenia were flying and a band played their national anthems. In his welcoming remarks, President Hashemi-Rafsanjani emphasized the need to resolve the conflict in Nagorno Gharabagh:

> I expect this visit to contribute to a peaceful resolution of the Gharabagh conflict and to the development of relations between our two countries. Certain countries are trying to exploit the Gharabagh conflict in order to consolidate their influence in the region, and we must develop constructive bilateral relations in order to neutralize those efforts.

President Ter-Petrosyan thanked the Iranian President for his warm welcome and his mediation efforts and added,

> There is no need to demonstrate the strong relations between our two countries. Our thousand-year history testifies to that fact. Today, the Republic of Armenia is obligated to cooperate with the Islamic Republic of Iran.

The President and his party proceeded to St. Sarkis Church where more than 15,000 Armenians had gathered to pay their respects, despite a torrential rainstorm. A wave of joy overtook the crowd when the esteemed guests arrived, and when President Ter-Petrosyan spoke of the unprecedented development of relations between Iran and Armenia, the crowd was euphoric. The tolling of the bells mixed with a hail of applause as the presidential party entered the church where they stayed for the service and took communion. The service was performed by Archbishop Goriun Papian of Isfahan with the participation of the V. Rev. Father Nshan Topouzian, Pontifical Legate of the Diocese of Azarbayjan, and Father Emmanuel Poladian of the Armenian Catholic Church.

After the service, Archbishop Papian welcomed President Ter-Petrosyan on behalf of the community, and then the President addressed the following remarks to the congregation:

Dear Brothers and Sisters,

Under the sacred columns of this magnificent church, I salute you in the name of free and independent Armenia.

The centuries-old dream of the Armenian people throughout the world, in Armenia and in the Diaspora, has become a reality. Armenia has freed itself of the yoke of Communist oppression. At the price of a long struggle, Armenia has achieved freedom and independence.

Today, in this deeply moving atmosphere, Armenia and the Iranian Armenian community – two wings of the Armenian nation – have achieved unity. The President of Armenia is present among you at the official invitation and sponsorship of the Iranian government. I believe this visit will be a turning point in relations between Armenia and Iran and between the people of the two countries. I expect it to significantly strengthen our cooperative relationship.

I note with satisfaction that this development is multidimensional and evident at all levels – political as well as economic. What is most important is that our relationship has already reached the level of negotiations and is producing practical results. The most recent proof of this is the new bridge connecting Armenia and Iran across the Arax River.

Because I will have the opportunity to enjoy your presence tomorrow and communicate with you in a more comprehensive way, allow me to conclude tonight by wishing you all the best – happiness, peace and pride – from free and independent Armenia.

The President and his party then went out to the courtyard where he placed a wreath at the Monument to the Martyrs of the Genocide, and as they returned to the Prelacy building, still under pouring rain, the crowds waved placards and shouted, "Long live Iran," "Long live Armenia," and "The Islamic Republic, protector of the weak and vulnerable."

Direct negotiations between the two Presidents and their respective Ministers began later that night. As reported in *Alik* the next day, the Iranian Ministers of Foreign Affairs, Finance and Economic Affairs, Petroleum, and Energy took part in the talks. Their discussions covered bilateral relations in the areas of politics, communications, cultural issues, and commerce and trade, including oil and gas, as well as the prospect of resolving the Gharabagh conflict. According to President Hashemi-Rafsanjani's spokesperson,

> The longer the conflict goes on, the greater the losses for both peoples and the stronger the enmity between them, and if it gets any more complicated, it will stand in the way of the post-independence reconstruction of both Armenia and Azerbaijan.

The Armenian President was quoted as saying,

> The efforts of the Islamic Republic of Iran in the process of establishing peace between the warring factions in the Gharabagh conflict have convinced us that Iran is completely neutral in this matter and that its sole aim is humanitarian, motivated by the search for a just solution to a thorny issue. The international community also has a positive view of Iran's mediation, and the people of Armenia are grateful to Iran for its efforts.

On Thursday, May 7, the Armenian presidential party, accompanied by Archbishop Papian, MP Vartan Vartanian, MP Ardavazd Baghoumian and Diocesan Council chairman Serge Soukiassian, visited the shrine of the late founder of the Islamic Republic of Iran. There they were met by his son, Hojjatoleslam Seyyed Ahmad Khomeini. President Ter-Petrosyan laid a wreath at the shrine as a gesture of respect. Afterwards, he signed the visitors book and shared a cordial conversation with Hojjatoleslam Khomeini.

That evening, President Ter-Petrosyan and his entourage met the Armenian community at the Ararat Center, and the President delivered the following speech:

Dear Compatriots, Sisters and Brothers, Mothers and Fathers,
I am very happy that here, too, as in the homeland, people address me as Levon rather than Your Excellency.

Today, the Armenians of Iran are experiencing profound joy because, for the first time, they are welcoming the President of the sacred Armenian homeland, free and independent Armenia. I have seen the Armenian tricolor flying all over Tehran these last two days. I am doubly honored to be speaking to you in this community forum because I began my political life in public gatherings in Yerevan. That is why I am deeply moved by this meeting: your presence reminds me of the thousands of meetings we held in Yerevan.

Everything in Armenia began from such meetings, and within four years, our national struggle was crowned with the supreme achievement of freedom from the oppression of Communism and with the institution of independence and statehood.

Today, Armenia is an independent nation, recognized by more than a hundred countries. It has embassies in scores of capitals all over the world. In this regard, the development of relations between Armenia and Iran is very important. It is therefore significant that Iran is only the second country I have visited as the President of Armenia.

The Armenian nation's independence was not a gift or a heavenly blessing. It was acquired through the people's unrelenting struggle, and unfortunately at the cost of irreversible losses and a great deal of deprivation. Today, too, our brave sons are fighting in Gharabagh for their honor and dignity, for their ancestral land.

Our nation is a peace-loving nation. We value peace highly because we have suffered the most from wars. At the same time, we have demonstrated through the brave people of Gharabagh that, when necessary, we are able to protect our honor and dignity by military means.

While being ready for self-defense, we must also understand that the continuation of war will have no positive result for our nation or for the Azerbaijani nation. We must work for the peaceful resolution of the conflict. Such a resolution is in the best interests of Gharabagh as well as those of the newly independent Republic of Armenia. The efforts of the present Armenian leadership are all directed toward this end. It is gratifying that the Azerbaijani authorities are currently engaged in similar efforts aimed at resolving the Gharabagh conflict through negotiations mediated by the Islamic Republic of Iran.

Here I would like to acknowledge the efforts of the Islamic Republic and especially those of its honorable President Hashemi-Rafsanjani.

We are convinced that Iran is an honest mediator that espouses peace and security and seeks a just solution, one that respects the views of all sides to the conflict. This is the only kind of mediation we need, and tonight I can declare that Armenia has complete confidence in Iran's mediation efforts and in the success of those efforts.

The friendship between Iran and Armenia, between the peoples of Iran and Armenia, is centuries old. Our entire history is evidence of that friendship and of the cooperation between our two peoples. This gathering, too, is evidence of that friendship. Blessed be the country where, after 400 years, Armenians cannot separate themselves from the people of their motherland, neither in their joys nor in their passions, neither in their language nor in their way of thinking.

The friendship between Armenia and Iran, which has continued unabated over the centuries, is now being shaped at the state level according to bilateral principles. Here I must note with satisfaction that our bilateral relations are developing in a very natural and desirable way. Today, we can point to some concrete results of that relationship. The Embassy of the Islamic Republic of Iran opened in Yerevan a few days ago, and the Embassy of the Republic of Armenia will open in Tehran very soon. And yesterday, coincident with my visit to Iran, a temporary bridge was opened over the Arax River. It links our two countries which until yesterday were separated by the river.

This visit by the Armenian President has huge political and economic significance. It symbolizes the friendship between our two countries. Negotiations over a range of practical issues are now taking place. I must mention with satisfaction that members of the Armenian delegation who arrived in Tehran a few days before me have been engaged in serious negotiations with their counterparts in the Iranian government. No doubt, you are familiar with these individuals through the media, but tonight you have the opportunity to meet them in person.

President Ter-Petrosyan then introduced the members of his delegation, as well as his wife Lucia, to loud rounds of applause. He continued:

I must mention again that the Armenian delegation has been involved in very productive negotiations which have already resulted in the signing of several preliminary agreements that will be incorporated into the overall bilateral agreement.

I must also say that this visit has been extremely productive. It can be considered a turning point in relations between Armenia and Iran.

The Armenian delegation has received a very warm welcome from the Iranian authorities, and especially from President Hashemi-Rafsanjani.

I consider this to be evidence of the importance the Iranian authorities attach to the development of cooperative Armenian-Iranian relations, as well as the expression of their appreciation of the Armenian community of Iran for their contributions to the country's progress.

For 400 years, the Iranian Armenian community has dedicated all its resources to the progress of this country. They have been model citizens. But at the same time, they have maintained deep ties to their ancestral homeland. I am certain that the strengthening of ties between Armenia and Iran will contribute significantly to the efforts of this community.

> Long live free and independent Armenia!
>
> Long live the peoples of Iran and Armenia!
>
> Long live the Islamic Republic of Iran and the Republic of Armenia!
>
> Thank you.

On Friday, May 8, the presidential party flew to Isfahan with Archbishop Papian and MPs Vartanian and Baghoumian. At the airport they were met by Provincial Governor Vaghefi, a number of high-ranking military officers, and clerical and lay representatives of the local Armenian community. They were honored by a luncheon at the Shah Abbas Hotel (now the Abbasi), after which President Ter-Petrosyan took a stroll around the historic central maidan.

At 5:00 PM, he and his party entered the grounds of All-Savior's Cathedral (*Surp Amenaprgitch*) in New Julfa. The courtyard and the surrounding streets were teeming with Armenians who had been gathering there since morning. Thousands welcomed him with shouts of "Free and independent Armenia!" and "Long live Levon Ter-Petrosyan!" The President and his party entered the cathedral where Archbishop Papian presided over the holy mass. Afterwards, the Holy Father pronounced a short welcoming speech and then led the President outside to the Monument to the Martyrs where the latter laid a wreath. After observing a moment of silence, he delivered a speech that more or less followed the same trajectory as his remarks at the Ararat Center the night before, with a noteworthy addition on the theme of Gharabagh:

> In Gharabagh today, a war of life and death is being waged and grave events are taking place. But here again, I believe that the Iranian government's intervention, President Hashemi-Rafsanjani's intervention, has finally succeeded in bringing the warring sides closer. The Presidents of Armenia and Iran sat at the negotiating table, and after much effort, a document was signed. That raises hope that there will finally be peace on the border between Iran and Armenia [*sic*]. We believe that war is the greatest threat for any nation. Only under stable conditions of peace can a nation's potential be harnessed for the common good. Because the hostilities have greatly intensified, there are difficulties in resolving the Gharabagh conflict. A lack of trust has become deeply rooted in the two nations. But Iran's fair mediation, whose only purpose is the just resolution of the conflict on the basis of respect for the rights of both sides, is a very positive force for the overall success of negotiations.

The Liberation of Shushi

Alik provided extensive coverage of President Ter-Petrosyan's visit all week long. In addition to the transcripts of his speeches quoted above, the paper offered three front-page stories on Saturday, May 9. The first reported on the overall bilateral accord signed by the Presidents of Armenia and Iran based on agreements to expand exchanges in the areas of energy, communications, trade and politics previously signed by the relevant Ministers. The second story reported on an agreement between the Presidents of Armenia and Azerbaijan:

> President Levon Ter-Petrosyan of Armenia and Acting President Yakub Memmedov of Azerbaijan signed a declaration in Tehran instituting a ceasefire in Gharabagh and affirming the continuation of discussions to bring about the removal of the blockade of Armenia, with Iran playing the role of mediator. The two leaders were in Tehran at the invitation of President Hashemi-Rafsanjani who was present at the four-hour negotiations which resulted in the public statement. After the signing ceremony, President Hashemi-Rafsanjani thanked the Presidents of Armenia and Azerbaijan for the goodwill they have shown in the effort to resolve the Gharabagh conflict.

The third front-page story was datelined Saturday, May 9, Stepanakert, Gharabagh:

> **Shushi Liberated**
>
> Stepanakert, the capital of Nagorno Gharabagh, and surrounding areas have been living under horrific conditions, with the looming threat of starvation and disease, as a result of constant bombardment, the embargoes and the shortage of electricity and natural gas. The authorities in Gharabagh were forced to resort to extraordinary measures to silence the elements disrupting the stability of the Republic. The complex operations of the Armenian guerilla fighters were crowned with success in the liberation of the town of Shushi. By midnight, Shushi was completely under their control. Nearby military posts have also been silenced.

As soon as the Armenians of Tehran heard this promising news, they began quietly congratulating one another. They did not want to provoke the anger of Muslim Iranians, particularly the Azeris, but they saw the liberation of Shushi as an act of great heroism. I only realized the full significance of that victory a few years later when I visited Gharabagh and saw that high mountain plateau with my own eyes. Hardened Armenian troops had used ropes to climb a seemingly inaccessible slope and throw the Azerbaijani aggressors out of the land that belongs to Armenians. The Azerbaijanis never dreamed the Armenian fighters would climb that mountain and they didn't even have time to realize what was going on. They were simply forced to flee their positions, effectively restoring the land to its rightful owners.

The peace negotiations in Tehran were cut short and President Ter-Petrosyan and his party left the next day. This turn of events was a blot on the record of the Iranian Foreign Ministry and intelligence agencies and it left a negative impression on the country's leadership: they could not understand how the Armenian President could have been unaware of plans to attack and most likely occupy Shushi.

Mission to Armenia

The Iranian Foreign Ministry moved quickly to rectify the contretemps. Seyyed Abdollah Dastgheib called and told me that he was being sent on an urgent mission to Armenia and he needed my assistance as mediator and interpreter. We took the first available flight to Yerevan.

I was asked to restart negotiations by contacting presidential advisor Vahan Papazyan. Vahan and I decided to recommend that the Armenian government write explanatory letters to both President Hashemi-Rafsanjani and Supreme Leader Ayatollah Khamenei. Vahan took this plan to President Ter-Petrosyan. He agreed to write the letters himself, but he wanted them both hand-delivered. It was decided that Vahan would deliver the letter to the President of Iran, and his father, Professor Papazyan, would deliver the letter to the Supreme Leader.

Because we were carrying confidential state documents across the border, we sought help from the Iranian Embassy in its temporary quarters at the Hrazdan Hotel. The small staff had opened for business only days earlier. Chargé d'affaires Bahram Ghasemi, a man of impeccable character and impressive credentials, was on duty, along with First Secretary Mohammad Farhad Koleyni and two clerks.

We left Yerevan at 6:00 AM in two cars, Dastgheib and I riding with Bahram Ghasemi in the Iranian Embassy car, and Vahan and his father in a car provided by the Armenian government. When we reached Goris, we stopped for breakfast but we couldn't find an appropriate venue. Dastgheib said that he urgently needed to find a bathroom, so we knocked on the door of the nearest house. The proprietor took him in straightaway and we waited outside in the cars. And we waited. I began to worry. Finally, I went into the house and found the owner holding a tray with a bottle of cognac and two glasses, urging a drink on our Muslim colleague. The more Dastgheib refused, the more his host insisted. He couldn't imagine that anyone would refuse a glass of Armenian cognac. When Dastgheib saw me come in, he begged me to extricate him from this embarrassing situation. I stepped in between them and motioned for him to leave, then explained to the Armenian gentleman that alcohol was forbidden to my friend because he was a Muslim. Our host was quite bemused:

"But my Azeri neighbors are Muslims and they drink more than Armenians!"

I explained that my companion was an *Iranian* Muslim and that Iran was an Islamic Republic. At this, he cast a most dubious glance at me.

"Are you a Muslim too?"

"No, I'm an Armenian Christian."

"Come then, let us share a drink!"

I hadn't had a thing to eat but I couldn't refuse. The first glass burned all the way down. At that point, I was ready to say goodbye, but he refilled my glass, and again, I couldn't say no. Then he gave me a tour of his house whose several rooms were decorated with beautiful Armenian carpets, and he told me that he was a first-class mechanic with a good income. Somehow I managed to extricate myself from his sincere but compulsory hospitality, saying I would look him up again, but alas, the next time I was in Goris, I couldn't find his home.

We passed through Meghri and crossed the temporary bridge under the watchful eyes of the Russian border guards. On the Iranian side, we were met by Iranian border guards as well as by representatives of the Foreign Affairs Ministry and the Ministry of Intelligence and Security (MOIS) who had driven up from Tabriz to meet us. They escorted us to the customs post at Julfa, after which they took us to Tabriz and put us up in the Gostaresh Hotel. They were concerned that local Azeris might get wind of the presence of emissaries from Armenia and cause problems.

There was considerable animosity among Azeris in Tabriz as a result of the war over Gharabagh, exacerbated by the fact that they have ancestral and village ties with Azeris in Azerbaijan. Iran's Supreme Leader took a wise and well-considered step the following year when he went to Tabriz and delivered a speech in Türki, the Azeri Iranian language. It helped to alleviate the animosity and reduce the tension and soon the whole issue was forgotten. After the collapse of the Soviet Union, the Azeris of northwestern Iran had become more positively predisposed toward their compatriots in Azerbaijan, but over time they came to understand that it was easier to make friends with local Armenians than with Azeris across the river.

We had planned to fly to Tehran the next morning, but Professor Papazyan wanted to visit the graves of his parents before leaving Tabriz. The Iranian officials had been instructed to see that none of us left the hotel until we went to the airport, but the head of the MOIS group took personal responsibility for obliging the Professor. Since it was a holiday, it took several hours to arrange permission to visit the cemetery, but it finally came through and his wish was granted.

By the time we landed in Tehran, it was already dark, so we delivered the letters the following morning. They had a very positive impact, particularly given their timing.

Made in Tabriz

My elder brother Henrik had commissioned a weaver in Tabriz to make a carpet with our father's image and I was powerfully impressed by the portrait's resemblance. I decided to commission the weaving of a similar carpet with a portrait of President Ter-Petrosyan and present it to him as a gift. When it was finished, I had it framed, and I asked Berj Msrlian to make an appointment with the President. On the appointed day, Bella and I, along with Msrlian, brought it with us to the meeting. Two other couples, all American citizens, were waiting to see the President too. We were all shown into a large hall, and a few minutes later, President Ter-Petrosyan came in and welcomed us. After offering our expressions of respect, we unwrapped the carpet and presented it to him. He thanked us but I felt he wasn't that impressed. The Americans were very impressed, however, and when they asked how it was made, the President went over and took a closer look. He hadn't realized that it was a carpet, and when he examined the back and saw the fine craftsmanship, he pronounced it a fantastic work of art. My wife and I decided that for the rest of our lives we would make a similar gift to each successive President of Armenia.

Aid to Armenia

The two years that followed Armenia's declaration of independence and the collapse of the Soviet Union were by far the worst in its history. Armenia has very little arable land, and during the Soviet period, it had imported most of its grain from other Soviet Republics. On the other hand, Armenia had been known for its productivity during the same period when it accounted for three percent of Soviet production while its people constituted one percent of the Soviet population. Now, because of the war in Gharabagh, Azerbaijan and then Turkey imposed embargoes on Armenia, and the scarcity of basic commodities, from grains to gasoline, heating oil and electricity, made life unimaginably difficult. Factories ceased operating and there was massive unemployment. Armenia was forced, and as of this writing is still forced to import food and fuel through Iran and Georgia.

During that crucial period, the temporary bridge over the Arax River played an important role in the exchange of goods between Iran and Armenia. Thousands of tons of Iranian wheat and other grains were sent across the bridge, as well as cargo coming into Iran through Bandar Abbas from Dubai, India and elsewhere. Thanks to timely support from the Diaspora, the people of Armenia were able to stabilize their situation, and among all the humanitarian initiatives, I too had my modest part.

One day, Norair Elsaian, the editor of *Alik*, told me that he had been entrusted with funds from the Australian Armenian community to purchase food staples and ship them to Armenia. The scope of the project was quite large and he asked for my help. A staff was required to handle all the purchasing, packaging and shipping. Relying on the expertise of Sati's employees, I managed the entire project and dispatched everything to the address Elsaian gave me.

During the last months of 1992, I got a call from Vice President Gagik Harutyunyan. He said there was an emergency in Zangezur (Syunik) Province. People were on the brink of starvation and 500 tons of flour was urgently needed. I immediately called my friend Varoujan Arakelian who managed a large grain mill in Tabriz. In those days, Iran did not permit the export of flour, but Varoujan managed to secure a special permit. In less than a week, we shipped 500 tons of flour via Sati's fleet of trucks to the temporary bridge, where payment was collected and the freight was transferred to Armenian trucks.

Vice President Harutyunyan took the opportunity to thank me personally when he came to Tehran the following winter. He had just returned from an Iranian government–sponsored tour of Kish Island with a delegation of Armenian officials and they were staying at the Esteqlal Hotel (the former Royal Hilton) up in Shemiran. I visited him there and he told me the mayor of Kish had designated part of the island resort exclusively for tourists from

Armenia during the cold winter months. Then he recalled the previous winter's crisis and expressed his deep appreciation for the prompt delivery of the flour. I replied that the Armenian people had first and foremost the Iranian government to thank for its goodwill toward Armenia.

Another time, the Armenian community of Vienna provided funds to purchase food in Iran, particularly flour, and ship it to Armenia. Varoujan secured another special export permit and we shipped the flour to St. Sarkis Cathedral in Yerevan. We sent along a request that some of it be set aside for the Armenian Philharmonic Orchestra, because the concerts that Loris Tjeknavorian was presenting in those dark days were helping to lift people's spirits. But musicians do not live by bread alone, so Varoujan and I purchased 270 Valor-brand portable space heaters with our own money and sent them to Tjeknavorian to distribute to members of the orchestra.

Around the same time, I heard a TV news report in Yerevan that the children of Gharabagh were losing their teeth due to deficiencies in their diet, so I purchased two metric tons of Iranian foodstuffs and shipped the freight to Armen Darbinyan, then–Deputy Minister of the Economy, and asked him to forward it to child welfare organizations working in Gharabagh.

How the Permanent Meghri Bridge Was Built

It seemed that construction of the permanent Meghri Bridge was going to be jump-started when the Armenian government learned that a Russian foundry specializing in steel structural components already had three 200-foot steel beams in stock. They had been manufactured for a bridge in Sochi but that project had been cancelled for lack of funding after the USSR collapsed. The Armenian government negotiated to purchase the beams for 21 million rubles and paid over the first installment in May 1992.

Armenia's No. 107 Bridge Brigade was contracted to transport these and other Russian-made components to Meghri. They easily shipped a quantity of thirty- and sixty-foot–long components to Tbilisi via the western railway, but the 200-foot beams couldn't make the tunnels. The alternate route went through Azerbaijan where they would surely be confiscated because of the embargo. The Armenian government finally came up with a solution: documents were drawn up in cooperation with a Georgian firm claiming the latter had placed the order, and the 370-ton cargo was safely shipped to Tbilisi on Azerbaijani heavy-load wagons. Now a new problem arose. Since Georgia was not a member of the Commonwealth of Independent States at the time, Russia wanted to impose a tax amounting to the entire value of the bridge. But Armenia was a member and the government intervened to have the sum reduced. Finally, everything was shipped by rail from Tbilisi to Yerevan and from there trucked to Meghri.

Once all the components had arrived in Meghri, the Armenian government was faced with the cost of construction which was beyond its means in that first year of its independence, but this too was resolved in a positive way. The Armenian communities of New Zealand and Australia had set up a Fund for Assistance to Armenian Victims of the Earthquake (known as HAOF), which had raised a considerable sum to build housing in the devastated northwestern provinces. But again, because of the difficulty of importing construction materials due to the Azerbaijani embargo, construction of housing was frozen. When the chairman of HAOF, Bishop Aghan Baliozian, consulted with Vice President Harutyunyan as to the best way to allocate the money, the latter explained the vital role of the Meghri Bridge and suggested it be used for that project because it would guarantee the passage of goods and people between Armenia and Iran. Bishop Baliozian graciously offered 2 million Australian dollars for the project which also included construction of the highway leading to the bridge. HAOF approved the plan on July 6, 1992, and on July 28, the sum of 1.3 million Australian dollars (approximately 1 million US dollars) was made available to the Armenian government. Construction of the highway and preparation of the bridge site began soon thereafter. In May 1993, Bishop Baliozian visited the site with a delegation led by President Ter-Petrosyan and he was very enthusiastic about what he saw.

Detailed plans for the bridge were finalized in August 1993, and in November, Armenia and Iran signed a fifty-fifty cost-sharing agreement. Unfortunately, Iran failed to meet its obligations in a timely manner and actual construction of the bridge only began in 1995, but it was completed in December of that year. Once it was finished, scores of loaded trucks were sent across to test its strength and durability. The results confirmed the expertise of the Armenian architects and engineers responsible for the project. Jora Mirzabegian and I subsequently collaborated on a book underwritten by Sati titled *How the Meghri Bridge Was Built*.

It was officially opened on January 9, 1996, when Vice President Harutyunyan and Iranian Finance Minister Morteza Mohammadkhan and other officials from both countries walked across the bridge to congratulate each other. I had been invited to the opening by both sides but I was unable to attend because I was out of the country.

In 2003, Prime Minister Andranik Markaryan formally expressed his gratitude to a key group of individuals for their role in building the Meghri Bridge, including Telman Ter-Petrosyan, Professor Mirzabegian and former Transportation Minister Henrik Kochinyan from Armenia, and former MPs Vartan Vartanian and Ardavazd Baghoumian and myself from Iran. In a letter to me dated April 21, 2003, the Prime Minister wrote, "On the tenth anniversary of the construction of the bridge between the Republic of Armenia and the Islamic Republic of Iran, I offer my thanks for your active participation and support of this project."

Chapter 28

The ARF and Community Business in Tehran

On June 29, 1992, only two months after President Ter-Petrosyan's first state visit to Iran, he went on Armenian state television to attack the ARF and its leaders, accusing them of collusion with the KGB and misappropriation of funds raised for Armenia and Gharabagh. It was the eve of an international party conference that was supposed to be held in Yerevan, and he gave ARF Bureau chief Hrair Maroukhian forty-eight hours to leave the country.

Hrair Maroukhian was born in Iran in 1928. His father was the principal of the Armenian school in Rasht, but after Reza Shah closed Armenian schools in 1936, Maroukhian's family settled in Tehran. He belonged to my generation, and for us he represented the nationalist ideal. He cofounded the Ararat Sports and Cultural Association, as noted earlier, when he was still a teenager. He studied mechanical engineering at the National University and later established his own engineering firm. He was intelligent and well educated and he had an inborn talent for organization and administration. His wife, Anahid Sarkissian-Maroukhian, was a person of noble character and high national ideals. Our families had been neighbors and friends and I knew her people well. Maroukhian was elected chairman of the ARF Central Committee of Northern Iran, and in 1963, he was elected to the ARF Bureau, the party's highest international body. He moved his family to Beirut where the Bureau was based, and in 1972 he was elected chairman of the Bureau. Because of all these factors, Maroukhian was admired and respected by many in the Armenian community. He received countless invitations to speak whenever he came to Iran, and he tried to oblige as many organizations as he could.

Since the ARF dominated the Iranian Armenian political arena, the Iranian authorities invited Maroukhian to Tehran to discuss new cooperative relations in April 1993, and as a result of their negotiations, a number of problems our community had been facing since the Islamic Revolution were largely resolved. Maroukhian's week-long stay was a most memorable time. Everywhere he spoke, he stressed the need for a government of national unity in Armenia. He spoke at the Prelacy, at the Ararat Center and to *Alik*'s editorial staff. He spoke at public gatherings in Armenian neighborhoods and he met privately with the families of martyrs in the war for the liberation of Gharabagh. I was present at some of those events and I invited him to dinner along with a number of community leaders and we were able to honor him in my home.

The war in Gharabagh had reached a critical stage and Armenian freedom fighters from various countries were traveling there to join the struggle for national liberation, leaving behind their young wives and newborn babies, knowing they would probably never see them again. Armenians throughout the world were in the grip of passionate enthusiasm. Was it not our duty to do more than pride ourselves on their sacrifices? I considered it my national duty to make a financial contribution to the sacred struggle, within the limits of my ability, and when ARF representative Rafik Gasparian appealed to me, I made the largest contribution I possibly could.

But tensions between the ARF and the ANM continued to grow, especially after December 1994 when President Ter-Petrosyan suspended the party in Armenia. As a result, the ARF split and the pro-Maroukhian faction went all out to discredit the President and his party, and *Droshag*, the ARF mouthpiece, became a platform for harsh criticism of the Armenian government and its policies.

These developments had a very negative effect on the Armenian Diaspora, especially the Iranian Armenian community. Most Iranian Armenian intellectuals did not support the ARF and some ARF dissidents disagreed with their party's opposition to Ter-Petrosyan's government. The dissidents held their peace for a while, but when they saw that a large majority of Iranian Armenian intellectuals supported the Armenian government, they too began to voice their differences with the ARF.

This played out in the Eleventh Diocesan Assembly of Representatives in Tehran, which carried on year after year, electing a new Diocesan Council every four years, defining its responsibilities, guiding its activities and approving its budget, but never renewing its own mandate since the Interior Ministry refused to authorize the election of a new Diocesan Assembly. Thus the ARF's internal conflict was reflected in the Assembly's deliberations and it made for some lively sessions when dissenting party members spoke out against their leaders' motions. I myself never felt compelled to bow to any ideology. I held fast to my unchanging principles and always spoke my mind.

An Off-the-Books Loan

One day at a private reception, I was chatting with the chairman of a community organization and he asked me whether *Alik* had repaid the Diocesan Assembly. I didn't know what he was talking about, so he explained that the Assembly had lent the paper 30 million tomans to build a new office complex. It seems that *Alik* had outgrown its quarters on old Naderi Street and had purchased a small lot on Sohrevardi Street in the northeast-central business district. In fact, all three Iranian dioceses had pitched in to lend the paper a total of 90 million tomans for the new building. This was all news to me and my friend was surprised at my ignorance:

"What kind of Representative are you? How come you aren't up to speed on this?"

I figured the loan must have been approved during one of the rare meetings I had missed. The next day, I asked an Assembly colleague about the loan and he too was unaware of it. I became concerned about this shady transaction which showed disregard if not contempt for the forty-five lay and clerical Representatives. How could such a decision have been taken without a vote? By what right had the Assembly lent 30 million tomans to a newspaper that was owned by a political party? If the issue had been put on the Assembly's agenda, I would have been willing to make a personal donation to the project. But as for the Diocese lending *Alik* the money, that was a different matter. I should note that according to the bylaws, the Diocesan Council was allowed to spend up to 5 million tomans on its own authority, but any expenditure higher than that required the Assembly's authorization.

The annual review of the Diocesan Council's budget was on the agenda for the Assembly's next meeting. The Council's treasurer listed the major expenditures they anticipated and the cost of each one, and then the floor was opened for debate. I put my name down to speak, and when my turn came, I was overcome with indignation. I said the annual budgets for this year and last year were both made-up. Without mentioning where the money went, I said the Council had left out a 30-million–toman debit and was covering it up. I insisted that the Council make the true situation known to the Assembly. When I finished, Council chairman Dr. Levon Davidian asked the other Council members to leave the hall. True, I had spoken in anger, but I spoke the truth. The Council had to make the facts known to the Assembly. The Assembly chair cut off debate and the meeting broke up in disarray.

At the next meeting of the Diocesan Council, it was announced that the previous year's financial report had listed 30 million tomans as "receivable." That didn't satisfy me at all. The Council was not a business enterprise and it could not reasonably list such a large sum as a receivable. Its income came from the churches, from the sale of candles, from weddings, baptisms and other ceremonies. All those sums were paid in advance. There was no such category as receivables in the Prelacy's accounting system as I had known it.

Ultimately, the community was told there was an agreement which stipulated that the Diocesan Council had lent the money to *Alik* on condition that when the paper sold its old building, it would return one-third of the proceeds to the Council. Thus the matter was closed, but without a satisfactory explanation.

The groundbreaking for *Alik*'s new building was held on April 29, 1994. The ceremony was attended by Archbishop Manoukian, Archbishop Papian from Isfahan, the V. Rev. Father Topouzian from Tabriz, Bishop Aharon Galoustian, Bishop Varazdad Derderian, Reverend Tadevos Mikaelian, Diocesan Council chairman Dr. Davidian, MP Vartanian, MP Baghoumian, representatives of almost all the Armenian organizations and scores of community members, as well as Armenian Ambassador Vahan Bayburdyan. Publisher Albert Ajemian, educator Misha Hayrabedian and Archbishop Papian each spoke to the gathering, and after Archbishop Manoukian delivered the final speech, a spontaneous collection brought in scores of donations to the building fund.

Mrs. Ferahian's Will

I also had my disagreements with the Diocesan Council over the sale of community-owned property, and one such property was the home of the late Mrs. Elbis Kovanian Ferahian. When the Council sold it for far less than it was worth, my protests were forthright and vocal.

Mrs. Ferahian was born in Tehran in 1907. She attended Sarvarian Kindergarten and Koushesh-Davidian Elementary School until her family moved to Vienna during the First World War. They subsequently moved to Tiflis where she was trained as a teacher. When they returned to Tehran, she taught at the Iran Bethel School and she founded the Nobavegan Kindergarten. Then, at the request of the Community Educational Council of Tehran, she established the Koushesh-Davidian Kindergarten and she directed it with the utmost dedication for many years. She composed songs and poems for her students which are still taught in Armenian schools in Tehran. Both of my children attended her kindergarten. She and my wife were close and Bella was very fond of her. She enjoyed the love and respect of the entire community.

Mrs. Ferahian retired after thirty-five years as an educator, and after her husband's untimely death, she lived with Jean Marie Simonian, the daughter of her sister-in-law and her only close relative.

One day I received a call from a former (retired) employee who told me that Mrs. Ferahian wished to meet with me on a personal matter. I contacted her immediately and she asked me to be the executor of her will. Having no children, she wished to leave her estate to the Diocese and she wanted me to ensure that it was used for a project that would benefit the entire community. I asked her to write a letter to that effect. When I told the Holy Father about it, he wanted to meet the kind benefactor in person, so we visited her together at her home. It was a warm and honest meeting. The Prelate promised to see that her wishes were carried out, and she subsequently sent me the following letter:

> May 30, 1990
>
> Dear Mr. Aharonian,
>
> I would like to express my heartfelt thanks for the visit you and the Prelate paid me on April 28, 1990. I am a woman of advanced age and deteriorating health. I have no immediate family members in Tehran who could carry out my wishes. I appeal to you as a tireless community leader. I ask for your assistance and mediation in arranging that during my lifetime, my modest estate be donated toward the construction of a new kindergarten. I also ask that, after my death, the living expenses of my beloved Jean Marie Simonian be covered so that she can live in comfort. My estate consists of the following:
>
> 1. A house built on a 3600-square-foot lot.
>
> 2. An account with Bank Sepah on Qavam os-Saltaneh [Mirza
>   Kuchek Khan] Street with a balance of 2,225,872 tomans.
>
> 3. Jewelry and gems worth 1.5 million tomans.
>
> 4. Four large carpets, a piano and home furnishings.
>   Elbis Kovanian Ferahian
>   33 Ladan Street, off Enqelab Street

Miss Simonian, who was also quite elderly, had worked closely with Mrs. Ferahian at the Koushesh-Davidian Kindergarten. She requested that the Prelate and I serve as her co-executors and she wrote a letter to the Holy Father requesting that her savings in the amount of 2.5 million tomans be transferred to a Diocesan account in her name; that the interest on the principal be paid to her to cover her living expenses; that she retain the right to withdraw from the principal in the case of unforeseen medical or travel expenses; and that after her death, the balance in the account be applied toward the construction of a community kindergarten in accordance with Mrs. Ferahian's will. Unfortunately, not long after Miss Simonian gave us these instructions, she experienced heart problems and checked into the Avedissian Clinic. There she suffered a heart attack and passed away.

Now Mrs. Ferahian was completely alone and for that reason I visited her more often. In accordance with her living will, and in order to avoid any potential legal complications, she deeded her home and transferred her Bank Sepah account to the Diocese. One day, she told me she also had $250,000 in a bank account in Brussels that she wanted to donate to an apolitical organization for charitable work in Armenia. She asked me to recommend one and I suggested the All-Armenian Fund (*Hayastan Hamahaykakan Himnadram*), sponsored by the President of Armenia and the Supreme Patriarch and Catholicos of All Armenians. She liked that idea and she wrote to her fiduciary agent in Brussels, a gracious young man named Ara Vruyr, to introduce me to him and ask that after her death he arrange with me for the donation of $200,000 to the All-Armenian Fund, and that he transfer the balance to another legatee whom she named.

Mrs. Ferahian died at the beginning of 1994. Two weeks later, a Diocesan delegation consisting of two priests and a layman went to her house, took inventory of the contents and conveyed the valuable items to the Diocesan secretary.

I went to Yerevan and contacted the office of Vice President Harutyunyan. Since we knew each other well, I was given an appointment right away. I told him about Mrs. Ferahian's generous gift. Ara Vruyr and I had agreed that he should act upon written instructions from the All-Armenian Fund, so I asked the Vice President if he could arrange for this. A letter signed by President Ter-Petrosyan and His Holiness Vazgen I was promptly dispatched, and Mr. Vruyr completed the transaction. On June 21, 1994, I received a thank-you letter from Manoushag Petrossian, executive director of the All-Armenian Fund:

> With this letter we would like to inform you that on May 28 we received the sum of 200,000 US dollars, transferred through the All-Armenian Fund's account at the Banque Nationale de Paris, which Mrs. Elbis Kovanian Ferahian donated to the Fund. We salute her memory which will forever be a reflection of the noble aim of serving the homeland, and we thank you for your assistance in realizing her intention. We ask that you convey our gratitude to Mr. Ara Vruyr as well for his patriotic efforts in this regard.

The Diocesan Assembly approved a motion to use the proceeds from the sale of Mrs. Ferahian's home to build a kindergarten in Narmak and to name it after her, but that project never got off the ground because of a pre-existing dispute between the owner of the intended site and the neighbors. Then one day in 1997, at a meeting of the Diocesan Assembly, there was an announcement that the Diocesan Council had sold Mrs. Ferahian's house for 14 million tomans, converted the money into US dollars and deposited it in the bank. I was incredulous and very, very angry. The house was worth at least 70 million tomans by the standards of the day. Moreover, as the executor of Mrs. Ferahian's will, I was supposed to be informed if the property was going to be sold or its status altered in any way. As a result, an unpleasant dispute arose between the Council and myself. I protested the sale several times and the Council responded that they had consulted with two expert appraisers before selling the house and they had sold it for the price the appraisers had set. That was completely unacceptable to me and I protested once again. Finally, the Assembly delegated me and a group of Representatives to investigate the matter and report back. Upon visiting the house, we all agreed that the sale price was too low. Oksen Alexanian, a shrewd and experienced businessman, whispered in my ear that it wouldn't even cover the cost of the bricks in the building!

Over the next few years, I took every opportunity to remind the Diocesan Council that the kindergarten in Narmak had yet to be built in accordance with Mrs. Ferahian's will, but the Council gave it a very low priority and eventually dropped it altogether. Finally, when Aida Hovhannisian was elected to chair a new Council, she told me they had decided to rename the Koushesh-Davidian Kindergarten the Elbis Ferahian Kindergarten. That was their way of resolving the issue. Clearly, with the passage of time and the rising cost of construction, it was no longer possible to build a new kindergarten with the proceeds of Mrs. Ferahian's estate. I had no choice but to sign off, in writing, on the Council's decision.

Mrs. Ferahian had entrusted my wife Bella with a pearl ring, a gift from her husband, and asked her to see that it was given to her brother's granddaughter, a violinist living in St. Petersburg, Russia. Bella often traveled to Paris, so she took the ring and left it with her sister Jacqueline for safekeeping. Then she contacted the violinist and let her know that the ring was there waiting for her to come and pick it up. When the rightful heiress took possession of the heirloom, the story of Mrs. Ferahian's will came to a close.

The Gabrielian Building

The five-story Gabrielian Building on Motahhari Avenue was one of a number of properties we had acquired on behalf of the Prelacy when I was chairman of the Diocesan Council. An Iranian Armenian millionaire had built it as a commercial venture, using top-quality materials, but because it was located in what was then a residential area, he was unable to commercialize the building and it remained empty. After the Revolution, Gabrielian left Iran and settled in Switzerland, but in order to save the building from being expropriated, he turned it over to the Diocesan Council. We promptly put it to good use, allocating office space to the Armenian Professional Association and the Armenian Research Center (HOOSK), among other groups, as mentioned earlier.

Toward the end of my term on the Diocesan Council, the government changed the way it administered so-called abandoned property and we were ordered to vacate the Gabrielian Building preliminary to its expropriation, which was truly alarming since every floor was occupied. I contacted an old university friend whose son-in-law was in charge of expropriations. He came to my office and I explained the situation. A few days later, he told me that a solution was in the works and we should hold off on vacating the building. A week after that, he told me the building was about to be sold for 15 million tomans. At that point, Ruben Karapetian and I met with him and asked him to see if the price could be lowered. Two days later, he called and said we could buy the building for 12 million tomans (approximately $100,000). We secured the approval of the Diocesan Assembly, though not without difficulty, and after the Council's term came to an end in July 1986, the new Council followed up and completed the purchase.

When I chaired the property committee in 1998, we leased the Gabrielian Building to a government research center for 12 million tomans a year, which was the original purchase price. The lease allowed for a 10-percent annual increase, and thus the building became one of the community's highest income-generating properties.

The Property Committee

One of our tasks on the property committee was to take stock of community-owned real estate and authenticate the titles. We were unable to complete that task during my tenure on the committee but the succeeding committee finished the job. The inventory provided a comprehensive picture of the status of each and every property and formed a rational basis for managing them. For instance, the Armenian population in the old Sheikh Hadi neighborhood downtown had decreased to the point where it was no longer practical to continue using the Mariamian School for its original purpose, so the Diocesan Council decided to sell the property and build a new school in Majidiyeh which had a large Armenian population.

Likewise, the Koushesh School hadn't been used as a school for years. There were fourteen shops and businesses on the ground floor but the rental income was insignificant in comparison with the value of the property. We needed to either sell it or rationalize its use. If the building were to be sold, the renters would have to be evicted and the Diocesan Council would be forced to spend millions of tomans in key money, especially considering that one of the renters was a bank. The Council decided to renovate the disused classrooms on the upper floors and rent them out as well. We put the project out for tender and the winning bid promised to transform the classrooms into seven large office suites with the appropriate amenities. After receiving permission from the municipality, we presented the Council with a tentative budget of 20 million tomans. According to our calculations, if all the space were rented, we would be able to repay the loan in two years. Unfortunately, the Council delayed presenting the project to the Assembly, which ultimately approved it, but the Council's term was coming to an end. As chairman of the property committee, I was proud to have played a key role in the success of that project, but sadly, the new Council postponed the necessary decisions and as a result, the start of the renovation was delayed by a year and it ultimately cost three times the original budget.

The vice-chairman of the new Diocesan Council presented himself as an economist but the economy was one subject he knew nothing about! I knew him well since he had worked at Sati for a few months. One day, he presented the Diocesan Assembly with a "master plan" that enraged me. He proposed to sell off all the community-owned real estate and put the proceeds in the bank, which was offering 18-percent interest on five-year deposits. He said the arrangement would spare us a great deal of headache and the interest income would easily sustain us. In my view, that would be a grave mistake. According to published figures, the annual rate of inflation was 24 percent, and if we were to follow his advice, the money would be losing 6 percent a year when real estate prices were going up. Of course, he didn't originate the plan because he lacked the capacity to come up with such an idea. Knowing our community as I do, I was certain that others who were very well informed about the economy had put the idea into his head for their own ulterior motives.

The Shishmanian Property

Gevorg Shishmanian was a Western Armenian survivor of the Genocide who had settled in Iran. He started out driving trucks, then he developed a business importing parts for big rigs, and later he represented British Leyland. In time, he became one of the richest Armenians in Tehran and he donated large sums of money to the Prelacy. He was also a patriot with a strong attachment to the homeland. For example, he donated $500,000 worth of state-of-the-art magnetic resonance imaging equipment to Soviet Armenia. His wife Asdghik was a philanthropist too. She served as president of the local branch of the Armenian General Benevolent Union for many years.

Baron Shishmanian was a hunter and I had the honor of hunting with him a couple times. I had met him and his wife through her brother, Hrand Shadikian. Hrand and his wife were a very kind and gracious couple who lived next door to André Shop. It was through Hrand that my father had first met Archbishop Manoukian. The Shadikians had no children and they transferred their love to our Vahe and Annette. The Shishmanians were not blessed with children either, but Asdghik had adopted an Armenian orphan named Arsiné. She raised her daughter with love and care and sent her to college in Switzerland. When Arsiné returned to Tehran, she married our good friend Grisha Der Hagopian whom we called Gougoush. Unfortunately, their marriage was not blessed with children either, but that did not interfere with the family's happiness. Both Gougoush and Hrand worked for Shishmanian, and as his business grew, Gougoush and another friend opened a Leyland auto parts shop which also flourished.

Shishmanian's primary business occupied nearly an acre of land on Shah Reza Street between Vali Asr and Tehran University. When he decided to retire, he was inclined to hold on to all of his properties. I was aware of this and I proposed via Gougoush that Shishmanian donate the property on Shah Reza to the Diocese. Toward the end of his life, he expressed his wish to convey it to the Prelacy in a short letter to me.

After the Revolution, a group of squatters occupied the property. When I was elected chairman of the Diocesan Council, one of the first items on our agenda was to initiate legal proceedings to establish the Diocese as the owner. According to Shishmanian's will, Arsiné and Gougoush retained an interest in the property, but they graciously donated their interest to the Prelacy, and our lawyers successfully cleared the title based on the testimony of Archbishop Manoukian and other Armenian clerics as well as myself as Council chairman.

It took nearly two decades to evict the last squatter, and when the land was finally "liberated" in 2002, a Council member who was well known for his cavalier approach to community-owned properties suggested that Shishmanian's lot be sold for 400 million tomans. He was unaware of the fact that a respected contractor had estimated its value at twice that figure. In fact, two years later, it was sold for one billion tomans (roughly $2 million). If the Council hadn't called for caution when it did and the property had been sold for 400 million tomans, who would have borne the loss, or rather, who would have gained on the resale?

Chapter 29

The Armenian Business Forum

The first Diaspora business conference in Yerevan, held in May 1991, evolved into the Armenian Business Forum, an annual meeting of business professionals sponsored by Armenia's Ministry of the Economy. The Forum's main purpose was to help integrate Armenia into the international economy and promote its distinctive economic and cultural attributes, while raising awareness of international business standards within Armenia. Delegates to the Forum came from countries with large Armenian populations such as Argentina, Australia, Egypt, France, Greece, India, Iran, Syria and the USA, and especially from the American cities of Boston, Los Angeles, New York, San Francisco and Washington, DC.

The founders and members of the Armenian Business Forum were mostly members of the Iran-Armenia Chamber of Commerce (IACOC) which was well organized and very active, and because of that, the Forum's executive board was required to have two Iranian members. I was elected first vice-chairman and Vahe Jovakim was the other Iranian board member.

I always wrote a report for *Alik* on my return from the annual conference, and before we left for the 1993 conference, *Alik* interviewed me about the role of the IACOC:

> Our purpose is to acquaint Iranian business professionals with Armenia's commercial potential. We have members from various professions – engineers, architects, business owners, merchants, factory managers, etc. – all of whom are interested in different sectors of the Armenian economy. We are heartened by the interest our efforts have generated. When the formation of the IACOC was first announced in *Alik*, there were twenty people involved, but today we have fifty-five members and they're all going to Yerevan for the Armenian Business Forum.
>
> Another purpose of our work is to introduce Iran's huge manufacturing capacity to Armenia. I believe our efforts have been successful so far. When I attended the first Diaspora

business conference two years ago, almost nothing was said about Armenia's economically powerful southern neighbor. In fact, I was the only person who talked about the importance of Iran. Fortunately, things are different now.

The temporary Meghri Bridge is open and 10,000 tons of freight have crossed the border at that point. There's an almost equal exchange of goods in both directions. Fortunately, the exchange has intensified since the first of Farvardin [March 21].

I should add that we've signed contracts on an individual basis, outside the framework of the IACOC's activities. For instance, we're shipping merchandise to Armenia that comes into Iran through Bandar Abbas.

I continue to be hopeful that economic ties will be further strengthened, and with stronger economic ties, the relationship between our two nations will be consolidated.

We'll be meeting with government officials and business people in Yerevan and those meetings will contribute significantly to the work of the IACOC. A similar organization is in the process of formation in the Armenian capital. Its purpose will be comparable that of the Chamber of Commerce, Industry and Mining here in Tehran. We hope to see the Yerevan wing of our work become better organized during the upcoming conference.

The Third Annual Conference

We flew to Yerevan for the third annual conference of the Armenian Business Forum on Wednesday, May 26, 1993, and checked into the Armenia Hotel. The size of our delegation was noted with interest, especially in government circles. The next morning, several members of our delegation were interviewed at the hotel by a production crew from Armenian state TV's Channel 1. The interview was broadcast later that day on *Lraber* (Herald), a popular public affairs program, and after that we were contacted by scores of business people and other professionals.

Friday, May 28, was a free day in the best sense of the term. May 28 is First Republic Day, an Armenian national holiday that marks the founding of the First Republic in 1918. Some delegates spent the day visiting Yerevan's cultural sites and tourist attractions, and everyone joined in the festive celebration in Freedom Square which was attended by His Holiness Vazgen

I and President Ter-Petrosyan. It began with a parade of Armenia's newly constituted Army and its recently acquired equipment. The law and order prevailing in the square that day brought joy and satisfaction to all.

Later that night, some of our delegates enjoyed an evening at the theater and others attended a concert by the Armenian Philharmonic Orchestra. The latter was part of a fifteen-day program mounted by Loris Tjeknavorian to commemorate the ninetieth anniversary of the birth of composer and conductor Aram Khachaturian. Tjeknavorian prefaced each concert with inspiring words that made a powerful impression on the audience. He began every concert with the symbolically resonant *Mer Hayrenik* (Our Fatherland) and asked the audience to sing along, and every night he concluded with *Zeytountsiner*, all of which stamped the performances with a strong national quality. It was a deeply gratifying experience.

The conference itself opened at 3:00 PM on Saturday, May 29, in the old Parliament building. Armen Yeghiazaryan, the Minister of the Economy, delivered the opening speech. Then chairman Vahe Jazmadarian read the annual report, which was supplemented by a summary of future plans as well as members' opinions and recommendations. Next, financial officer Souren Sarkissian reported on the Forum's finances. That was followed by a series of speakers beginning with Armen Darbinyan, the Deputy Minister of the Economy and the government's official liaison to the Forum.

On Sunday, May 30, the Iranian delegation was invited to Holy Echmiadzin to attend the divine liturgy conducted by His Holiness Vazgen I. Afterwards, we met privately with the Holy Father and received his blessing. Then we presented him with a handmade silver tray. He thanked us for the gesture and for the dedication our community had shown toward the Mother See. He also remarked on the size of our delegation and our strong commitment to the Forum's mission of strengthening Armenia.

The conference resumed at 9:00 AM on Monday, May 31, and immediately proceeded to the presentation of reports by the directors of various enterprises. Telman Ter-Petrosyan, a member of the Forum's executive board and the general manager of Hrazdan-Mash, emphasized the importance of bilateral economic relations between Iran and Armenia and said that economic activity between the two countries was currently valued at one billion rubles. He also reported that components of the permanent

Meghri Bridge were being transported to the construction site and that the bridge would be completed within a year.

I spoke on behalf of the Iranian delegation and reported on a number of issues. I noted that work on the permanent Meghri Bridge had begun the previous September and that 10,000 tons of construction materials had been transported for the project thus far (6,500 tons from Iran, 3,500 tons from Armenia, and 1,000 tons from Russia). I described how support from the Iranian Armenian community was reaching Armenia through the Diocesan Council in Tehran, and I outlined some of the difficulties incurred, especially with respect to banking and customs. I observed that Armenia was suffering from an acute lack of management expertise in the areas of transport and tourism and I suggested that a group of young Armenians from Armenia be offered training consistent with international standards in those areas. Finally, I emphasized the crucial importance of the permanent Meghri Bridge and asked that this be noted in the Forum's final report.

Remarks by President Ter-Petrosyan

The general business meeting was brought to a close at noon in order to welcome President Ter-Petrosyan. His entrance into the hall was greeted with wild applause. He began by greeting everyone and thanking us for the warm welcome. He said he considered it his duty to keep abreast of our deliberations and therefore he followed them closely. Then he switched gears and started talking about current politics.

President Ter-Petrosyan was deeply unhappy with the attitude of the opposition press toward his government's policies. He said that Armenia had all the prerequisites to become a well developed and forward-looking country, but 90 percent of its economic and political energy was being diverted to the war in Gharabagh, and he blamed the shortage of fuel and electricity on the Azerbaijani and Turkish embargoes. He said that large sectors of the population were already benefiting from his government's reform program, and he cited the privatization and redistribution of agricultural land to the peasantry. If that had not already been achieved, he said, Armenia would now be facing famine. He said that his government was committed to fully carrying out the reform program, even though some large-scale projects had had to be temporarily suspended.

Next, he turned his attention to the war itself. He recalled that two years earlier, in the spring of 1991, the Azerbaijanis in collaboration with Soviet forces had occupied twenty-four Armenian villages in Artsakh (Gharabagh), but the dissolution of the Soviet Union had created propitious conditions for Armenia. The Azerbaijanis, bolstered by weapons that Soviet troops had left behind, thought the Armenian fighters would be unable to resist their military onslaught, but their calculations were proven wrong when Gharabagh's experienced and well-trained army succeeded in retaking twenty-two of those villages, in addition to Mardouni and Gedashen. After being resupplied by Russia, the Azerbaijanis were able to occupy Mardagert and Shahumyan. But that was reversed last winter when the Armenians retook Mardagert and launched an attack on Karavajar (Karvachar, Kelbajar) in the spring.

President Ter-Petrosyan explained that the capture of Karavajar was a tactic to force the Azerbaijanis to the negotiating table. He saw it as a bargaining chip and didn't anticipate that Gharabagh could hold on to the region. He said the time would come when it would be advantageous, through very delicate negotiations, to hand Karavajar back while making certain this would benefit rather than harm the Gharabagh Armenians.

Then he discussed the economic problems facing Gharabagh. He said things were better this year than last. Life was relatively inexpensive there and wages were very low. He observed that Armenians from Armenia had been buying property from Armenians in Gharabagh and he said that was why wages had been raised in Gharabagh and the "robbery" was halted. He concluded by saying that he hoped the Gharabagh Armenians would not reject Armenia's proposals for ending the conflict and that peace could be established in the region. When he finished speaking, there was a long ovation. Berj Msrlian thanked him for his remarks and said the Iranian Armenian community would like to offer him a memento, and he invited me to present the gift our delegation had brought. The President expressed his appreciation for the gesture and the meeting came to an end.

A Private Meeting

As people were leaving the hall, the members of the executive board stayed behind to discuss some pending issues, but before we could start, a government official came in and said the President wanted to see me. He led me through the building to an office in the back. Several Ministers were waiting outside but my escort ushered me in directly. President Ter-Petrosyan was sitting in an armchair, waiting for me. He shook my hand and invited me to sit down in the armchair next to his. We had a very animated conversation that lasted for an hour.

We started out discussing issues related to the Armenian Business Forum. Then he stunned me by asking why the Diocesan Council had condemned his gesture of placing flowers at the tomb of Turgut Özal (the Turkish President had died in April). Hadn't other heads of state done the same? Wasn't that an accepted convention all over the world? He said he had read about the Council's condemnation in the Paris daily *Haratch*. I assured him that the Council never interfered in politics. I said the story was obviously invented by the ARF and it probably came from the April 24 organizing committee. I looked into the matter when I got back to Tehran and confirmed that my hunch had been correct.

President Ter-Petrosyan also wanted to know why his Embassy in Tehran had failed to establish good relations with the Iranian Armenian community. Why couldn't his representatives change the community's negative attitude toward his government? I explained that the community was divided: those aligned with the ARF were opposed to his government but the left and the unaffiliated elements had very good relations with the Embassy. I assured him that the majority of Iranian Armenians supported his government. When I left his office, the Ministers were still waiting outside.

Remarks by Vice President Harutyunyan

On Tuesday, June 1, the executive board held a formal meeting and Minister Yeghiazaryan sat in on it. Afterwards, the Iranian delegation was invited to meet with Vice President Gagik Harutyunyan in his office. He began by expressing his satisfaction with the large number of Iranian participants in the Forum and with the strengthening of trade relations between Iran and Armenia. He was pleased to note that the Islamic Republic would soon host a trade fair in Yerevan (it took place the following year), and he expected it to boost bilateral trade. In this regard, he said, the improvement of telephone and postal communications was a key requirement. He announced that Armenia and Iran had agreed to increase cultural and parliamentary exchanges, and he remarked that Armenia had similar relations with China, Vietnam and several South American countries.

The Vice President said that Armenia's southern Zangezur Province used to be considered isolated, closed to the outside world, but now, thanks to the Meghri Bridge, it was becoming a gateway to the world. The new route would allow Armenia to make good use of Iranian ports on the Persian Gulf and the Caspian Sea. He said construction of the permanent bridge was proceeding apace and he expected it to be completed in another year. Zangezur would play an extremely important role in the development of trade, he said, but it would require a huge financial investment. As a start, $1.2 million had been allocated to road construction in the province and that work had already begun.

The Vice President then turned to the problem of securing a sufficient and reliable supply of natural gas. Armenia's sole supply at the time traversed more than 3,000 miles of pipeline through Turkmenistan, Uzbekistan, Kazakhstan, Russia and Georgia, each of which had its own unique problems. But negotiations were underway to build a new pipeline from Iran transiting Nakhichevan. It would deliver 700 million cubic meters of natural gas per year, in addition to the quantity delivered via the northern route, for a total supply of 1.3–1.4 billion cubic meters per year (bcmy). (The pipeline, completed some fifteen years later, passes through Zangezur, not Nakhichevan, and has a capacity of 1–2 bcmy.)

The Iranian Armenian delegation listened to the Vice President's remarks with great interest. When he finished speaking, we presented him with a sample of Iranian handicraft and then had some photographs taken. With that, the work of the Forum concluded.

Ashot Safaryan, the Ministry of Industry, arranged a tour of several factories for the Iranian delegation on Wednesday, June 2. We were particularly impressed by Hrazdan-Mash, the large-scale enterprise headed by Telman Ter-Petrosyan. Afterwards, the management of Hrazdan-Mash hosted a reception where we were joined by Minister Safaryan himself.

A Dinner Party

My younger brother George, a civil engineer by profession, attended the Forum with the Iranian delegation. He had become close friends with the singer Ruben Matevosyan when he was studying in America, and now Ruben invited us both to dinner at his home in Yerevan, along with my old friend Daniel (Dodig) Sahakian. While we were sitting around the table, the doorbell rang and Matevosyan's son went to open the door. Suddenly the subdued conversation of the adults was drowned out by the children's happy exclamations. A tall gentleman who appeared to be about sixty years old was introduced as the children's uncle and he joined us at the table. After dinner, he took out his business cards and handed one to each of us. Since it identified him as the ARF representative in Armenia, I asked him whether his party was the one we were all familiar with, or the KGB-created party. He was momentarily stunned, then he shot back that his party was the real ARF. It had all the official seals and historic documents from the First Republic of Armenia in its possession. According to him, Hrair Maroukhian represented the KGB-sponsored ARF and he said he knew for a fact that Maroukhian was in Moscow at that very moment, being briefed to take power in Armenia! I was obliged to set the record straight. Since I had met with Maroukhian in Tehran only a few days earlier, I knew he wasn't in Moscow. Otherwise, I might have believed what the gentleman was saying.

On Friday, June 4, a group of us visited the studios of Armenian state radio. Our visit was arranged by Digran Davidian, an Iranian émigré who had worked as an editor for *Alik* before he moved to Armenia to continue his education, and now he worked for the Voice of Yerevan. We met the station manager and talked at length with the staff. As Iranians, we were interested in the content of the programs and the quality of the signal transmission. They were surprised that we were so interested in their broadcasts and they promised to improve the programs and boost the signal, which left us all very hopeful.

Later that afternoon, we attended a tea reception at the Iranian Embassy which was still located in its temporary quarters at the Hrazdan Hotel. Chargé d'affaires Bahram Ghasemi and First Secretary Mohammad Farhad Koleyni welcomed us warmly and quickly established an amicable atmosphere. Koleyni gave an overview of bilateral relations between Iran and Armenia and Iran's position on the regional political and economic situation. Then he asked me to say a few words. I thanked the Embassy staff for their warm reception and then I described our delegation's mission and projects. I said that we Iranian Armenians loved Iran and were always working for the country's interests, but because we were also Armenians, we loved Armenia too. I said we were working to improve trade relations between the two countries we loved. I also mentioned the deep respect and amiability that Armenian officials had shown toward the Islamic Republic of Iran and its Armenian citizens. Then I offered the gift of an Iranian handicraft item which Mr. Koleyni graciously accepted.

On our last evening in Yerevan, we hosted a reception and dinner at the Armenia Hotel. We invited Mr. Ghasemi and Mr. Koleyni and their guests from the Iranian Embassy, and Energy Minister Sebouh Tashjiyan, Armen Darbinyan, Telman Ter-Petrosyan and Loris Tjeknavorian. The mood was enhanced by the house band that played Armenian melodies. A special performance by Ruben Matevosyan gave the evening an added allure. As a sign of respect for our Iranian Embassy guests, no alcohol was served. Mssrs. Tashjiyan, Darbinyan and Ter-Petrosyan all gave impromptu speeches at the dinner table and there were many expressions of friendship and goodwill. The atmosphere was exceptionally cordial.

The Iranian delegation left Yerevan on Saturday morning, June 5, taking the ninety-minute direct flight to Tehran. We returned home with the sweetest memories.

As in previous years, I prepared a report for *Alik* that was published on July 7, 10 and 11, 1993. In addition to covering our day-by-day activities in Yerevan and the remarks of the Armenian President and Vice President, I reported that the conference was productive and successful, although the shifting arrival and departure dates of our European colleagues had necessitated adjustments. More delegates had the opportunity to speak than the year before, but it would have been better if the themes of their remarks had been vetted beforehand. One positive change was the replacement of inactive board members with new people which we hoped would make the organization more dynamic and productive. Another positive change was lowering the membership fee from $1,000 to $200 which we hoped would encourage more people to join. Since we were acutely aware of the need to get the word out, the Forum had published a fifty-two–page report on Armenia, including its history, political structures, geography, and tourist attractions, as well as investment information and guidelines. The cover page was a photograph of President Ter-Petrosyan. The IACOC also put together an attractive booklet about its members and their professional work. We printed up 360 copies and they were all gone the first day. There was a noticeable decrease in the number of business professionals from Armenia, whereas their increasing presence was very important for the work of the Forum. We needed to do more advertising ahead of time, months before the conference. I noted the presence of a group of Armenian student-observers and said I thought it would be beneficial to meet with them in the future and hear their views. And finally, and on behalf of the Iranian Armenian delegation, I gratefully acknowledged the assistance of Transportation Minister Henrik Kochinyan who facilitated our travel arrangements.

The Armenian Business Forum Company

Following the conference, a new organization was created under the sponsorship of the Armenian government. Its first board of directors included three Armenian Ministers as well as Telman Ter-Petrosyan and a number of

Diaspora Armenians. The board elected Vahe Jazmadarian as its chairman. He had served as general manager of Crédit Suisse in Paris for many years. I was elected vice-chairman, Souren Sarkissian was elected financial officer, and Ruben Grigorian served as secretary. Ruben was immensely dedicated to Armenia. I had known him since the late 1960s when he was the general manager of Levant Express in Iran. He had settled in Paris after the Islamic Revolution. Berj Msrlian was elected as an alternate member of the board. He was a member of the ARF, and over the course of several Forum conferences, I had come to know him as a man of noble character and a great patriot. The board had very good relations with the membership and questions of political affiliation were irrelevant or non-existent. We were all united in our desire to serve the homeland.

After two years of work, the board of directors decided to move the central office to Paris. Souren Sarkissian, a native of Syria long resident in the French capital, provided a secretary and an office pro bono in one of the most prestigious areas of the city, on a side street off the Champs Élysées. The Armenian Business Forum had completed its original mission and the board decided to dissolve it and replace it with a commercial firm that would make loans to small start-up businesses in Armenia. We named it the Armenian Business Forum Company (ABFCo) and registered it in Yerevan, with the old Forum's Yerevan office serving as its local headquarters.

ABFCo developed very quickly and hundreds of Armenians from all over the world attended the first general meeting in May 1995. As with earlier Forum meetings, the largest contingent came from Iran, and they all wanted to buy shares in the new company. Some bought shares for family members too, so that the number of Iranian shareholders reached seventy-two and the Iranian contingent held the largest number of shares. ABFCo's capital investment rose to $430,000 which was a lot of money for Armenia in those days.

Once the company's internal bylaws were approved, loan guidelines and interest rates were determined. The prevailing rate of interest on US dollar loans was 25–30 percent, but we decided on 15 percent. We also decided to require collateral whose value exceeded that of the loan. We had many applicants and most of them offered real estate as collateral. Altogether, ABFCo made loans totaling $200,000.

Our first loan, in the amount of $40,000, went to a woman who planned to import fabric from Russia and make tents for the Ministry of Defense. As collateral, she offered a vineyard on the Ararat Plateau. A house on the property was supplied with water from a stream that flowed through the property. We approved the loan based on expert evaluation of the collateral, but this "most respected" woman never made a single payment toward the principal or the interest. We later learned that she had reached a "tacit understanding" with the expert evaluators. She simply took the money and moved to Russia.

Some time after that, the board of directors elected me chairman at a meeting from which I was absent. As chairman of the board, I decided to go and see this vineyard for myself. Only then did we realize the scale of the woman's deception. The so-called vineyard was worth only one-tenth the value of the loan, if that; there was no stream flowing through the property; what water there was only emerged when the subterranean water level rose; and whenever that occurred, the water collected in what could be called a stream that crossed the property. That was the first loss ABFCo suffered.

We made another loan of $35,000 to a rabbit breeding farm whose purpose was to manufacture vaccines for domestic animals from the spinal fluid of newborn rabbits. We thought the enterprise could potentially generate two income streams, since the vaccine was in great demand by the government of India, and rabbit meat is a very nutritious type of protein. But that project failed too. I wanted to get a better idea of the problem, so I went to the farm and met the two young entrepreneurs. They were both veterans of the Gharabagh liberation struggle and they were good people, but they lacked the expertise to carry out such a project.

A third loan went to a breeder who offered his stable as collateral, but instead of breeding his animals, he took them to market and sold them. Thus, ABFCo became the owner of a vineyard, a rabbitry and a stable.

One small company did manage to make good honest use of our loan. It manufactured surgical tools and equipment, and our dealings with the two young men who ran the company were mutually beneficial. Another young man, an Iranian Armenian immigrant named Vartan Kamalian, also used his loan wisely and made his payments on time. He was the ARF renegade who had challenged Hrair Khalatian for the northern Armenian parliamentary seat back in 1980. A few years after that, when the ARF launched a campaign to repopulate the historically Armenian villages in northwestern Iran, Kamalian was among those whom they helped to settle and take up farming in the region, but conditions were not propitious and the campaign was not crowned with success. Kamalian had subsequently moved to Gharabagh and become a farmer.

The Faucet Factory in Ghapan

There was a controversy in Tehran over funds raised to aid the victims of the Spitak earthquake. Out of $650,000 donated by the community, the Diocesan Council had given $100,000 to Catholicos Vazgen I, and had used the rest to set up a faucet factory in Ghapan, a small town in southern Zangezur Province. It seems that the equipment was still sitting up there in its original packaging and a large sum (I can't remember the exact figure) was still owed to the contractor. Meanwhile, the Council had set aside 120,000 tomans ($1,000) from its modest annual budget to pay for security guards at the factory. The whole project had become so complicated that the Council wanted to extricate itself at any cost.

Diocesan Council vice-chairman Ruben Karapetian contacted me to say that they were thinking of turning the factory over to ABFCo. I informed the board of directors and we asked our manager, Samvel Gouzigyan, to look into the matter and report back. He contacted a firm in Yerevan that specialized in assessing the investment potential of manufacturing firms. For a fee of $2,000, they would determine whether or not a product was competitive and likely to return a profit to investors. Gouzigyan went down to Ghapan with the appraisers in order to observe their investigation himself.

The firm reported that a minimum of $250,000 would be required to make the factory operational. Much of that cost was related to the process of nickel-plating the faucets which involved cyanide, a very dangerous chemical. Another problem was how to dispose of the highly toxic liquid waste-products. They could not be stored in a well or an artificial reservoir, and if they entered the water system, it would lead to hundreds of deaths. It was possible to import a chemical that would neutralize the toxicity, the cost of which would be over and above the already very large budget. But the most important consideration was whether the product was competitive. High-quality German and Italian faucets and middling-quality Chinese and Turkish faucets were already on the market in Armenia. If this factory was going to be profitable, retailers would first have to become familiar with the product. We would have to give them a certain quantity on credit, and only after they believed in its quality could we anticipate any income. Such a credit arrangement would require an additional investment of $200,000.

Based on that report, we categorically declined to accept this wondrous gift! I informed the Diocesan Council of our decision, and in a separate letter to Archbishop Manoukian, I proposed that the factory be turned over to the Echmiadzin Catholicosate as the best solution to a thorny problem, which is what happened. As far as I know, the rusty equipment is still sitting in boxes in Ghapan.

An important issue was at stake here: by what right had a group of unknown individuals decided to take $500,000 from an earthquake relief fund and spend it on a half-baked project when so many Armenians had died in the quake and the whole country was in dire need of basic necessities? The Iranian Armenian community had donated money to that fund with the utmost faith in its purpose, yet today not a single structure in the earthquake zone bears our name. A shadowy group of unprincipled individuals exploited the community's good will to do whatever they pleased, then refused to take responsibility and derided the community for its naïveté. Their machinations cast serious doubt on the integrity of the Diocesan Council and the Diocesan Assembly.

ABFCo and the Privatization of Armenian State Enterprises

When the Armenian government launched its industrial privatization program, it did so on the principle that the factories belonged to the people. It therefore decided to distribute one-third of the total book value of those holdings to the people in the form of "privatization certificates," i.e. vouchers that could be used to purchase shares when the factories were sold. Over 3 million vouchers were issued to the people beginning in October 1994, but many people needed cash, so they sold their vouchers on the open market at a fraction of their face value. ABFCo decided to buy some of those vouchers, and later, when the government began selling off the factories one by one, ABFCo used its vouchers to buy a 3-percent interest in a tobacco factory and an 8-percent interest in a medical supply company, both located in Yerevan. We deposited the company's remaining capital in three different bank accounts at 24–26-percent interest as a hedge against losses.

I have always tried to be realistic, and I soon realized that it was impossible for me to direct ABFCo's work in Yerevan via fax and phone from Tehran, especially given that our employees, with a few exceptions, were either indifferent or nepotistic. For instance, one day our office manager called me to say that certain people were prepared to buy our share in the tobacco factory for $25,000. Based on past experience, I insisted that the board of directors vet the sale. A few months later, I learned to my surprise that the office manager had facilitated the sale for $60,000. That transaction caused of quite a bit of unpleasantness. Jazmadarian informed me from Paris that according to the buyer himself, he had bought the share at a price substantially below its real value because his brothers had bribed certain people with "gifts." Once I heard that, there were two options open to me. Either I had to give up my work in Tehran and settle in Yerevan, or else I had to ignore all the problems I was faced with. The appropriate course was to resign from the chairmanship of the board of directors, and so I tendered my resignation.

The new chairman was a very patriotic Armenian who had never occupied such a position of authority before. He somehow managed to withdraw $25,000 from one of ABFCo's bank accounts without the cosignature of the financial officer, which was absolutely illegal, and he spent $3,000 to cover a hotel bill in Istanbul. Since ABFCo was no longer making loans and was not involved in any projects in Istanbul, it was clear to me that the new chairman was misappropriating company funds. I flew to Yerevan and told him he had two choices: he could either return 75 percent of the money or we would sue him. He took the first option. I went straight back to Tehran and called a meeting of my investor-colleagues and briefed them on the situation. They contacted the board of directors and demanded a refund of their investments, which they had a right to do according to the company's bylaws, and after a short time, their capital was returned to them. That was how I ended my involvement in ABFCo and also preserved my reputation among my colleagues.

I don't think it would be arrogant of me to say that I played a significant role in carrying out the Forum's mission. Forty or fifty Iranian business professionals attended the conference every year, and in those days, it wasn't as easy to get a visa as it is today. Not only did I do all the visa applications and post the financial guarantees, but I made the arrangements for air travel, hotel accommodations and tours of historic sites. Before every trip, I organized a fundraiser to buy commemorative gifts for the President and the Holy Father. President Ter-Petrosyan usually dropped in on the conference, and after closing the hall to the press, he would brief us on the situation in Gharabagh and economic and political developments in Armenia. During some of our conferences, he even hosted a reception where the delegates could converse with him at length. I did all this organizing without any expectation of financial gain. Of course, a number of dedicated community members helped me with everything.

Famous Armenians I Have Known

One of the positive outcomes of Armenian independence was that now its people could travel abroad and foreigners could visit the country free of Soviet-era constraints. Strong relations developed between Armenians in Armenia and Armenians in the Diaspora. Perhaps the Iranian Armenians were the most fortunate, for even though Iran and Armenia share a border, they had been quite far apart politically prior to independence. Once the political obstacles were removed, we had many opportunities to mix and I constantly made new friends in Armenia, including politicians, industrialists and artists.

Telman Ter-Petrosyan introduced me to Garen (Karen) Demirchyan, the former chairman of the Supreme Soviet of the Armenian Soviet Socialist Republic; Fadey Sargsyan, the president of the Armenian National Academy of Sciences; Robert Yengoyan, the manager of the Kanaz aluminum foil plant in Yerevan; and the artists Zulum Grigoryan and his son Mushegh. We enjoyed meeting at the home-studio shared by Zulum and his son – it was like an Armenian Club in Yerevan.

The most pleasant pastime was *nardi* (backgammon). I had the good fortune to play with Demirchyan several times. He played hard and he always won. Zulum was his best friend and the only person who dared to needle the former Communist Party chief during a game of nardi. Demirchyan had a direct, no-nonsense personality that inspired respect. Unlike many former Communist officials, he didn't tolerate any attack on Armenia's post-Soviet government.

In all the years I knew him, I never heard anyone address him by his full name. As a sign of respect, people always called him Karen Seropitch, the Russified variant of his father's name (the Armenian version would have been Seropi). On one occasion when he visited Iran at the head of an Armenian political and economic delegation, I had the honor of escorting them around town and I invited them to my home for dinner. We spent a very pleasant evening together.

Karen Demirchyan was a true patriot in every sense of the word. He had a deep love – not to say admiration – for his people. After he reentered politics, we no longer met at Zulum's place because he was so busy with public commitments. In 1998, he founded the People's Party of Armenia (*Hayastani Zhoghovrdakan Kusaktsutyun* or HZhK) and made a run for the presidency (which he lost to Robert Kocharyan). The following year, he won a seat in the National Assembly and was elected Speaker. The last time I saw him was when Robert Yengoyan invited us both to dinner at his home. Afterwards, Demirchyan took me to see the headquarters of the HZhK. Only a few months later, he was assassinated. When his widow set about building his tomb, I sent the granite from Iran, and in that way I was able to share in the noble task of perpetuating the memory of a great Armenian who was loved and respected by many.

The Ani String Quartet

Arriving in Yerevan on October 13, 1997, I heard that the Armenian Philharmonic Orchestra was giving a concert that very night. I rushed to Aram Khachaturian Hall and got a seat. I didn't know it was Loris Tjeknavorian's sixtieth birthday, but after the concert he invited me to a party in his private quarters. His guests included some of Armenia's best-known artists, musicians and intellectuals. After the crowd thinned out, I apologized to him for not bringing him a birthday present. He proposed an alternative. He said there were four very talented young musicians who wanted to start a quartet but they lacked the means to fully devote themselves to the project. If I could finance their effort for one year, they would become one of the best female quartets in the country. I immediately agreed to do so on behalf of my wife Bella and myself, and we supported the Ani String Quartet for three years.

The quartet's first concert series outside Armenia took place in Tehran at the invitation of the Armenian Club, and all four performances were sold out. We had forgotten to tell them that they had to wear headscarves in Iran, and when they arrived at the airport bareheaded, the authorities insisted they cover their heads. We were outside waiting for them when they suddenly emerged carrying their instruments, their heads covered with black trash bags. The crowd began to titter and we were aghast. A man approached us and asked if they were our guests. When I said they were, he asked me to apologize to our guests on behalf of the Iranian people for putting them in such an awkward position.

Sati transporting a 450 ton load for Lordegan Petrochemical Complex *(top)* and 1250 ton load to Bandar Dayyer *(below)*.

Former Armenian president Kocharyan at Iranian Trade Fair.

Dr. Ghasemi *(center right)* and Armenian Minister of Economy
Mr. Jshmaritian *(center left)* at Trade Fair.

Author receives certificate of appreciation from the Armenian Trade Palace.

With the maestro Loris Tjeknavorian in Armenia.

Chapter 30

Diplomatic Overtures and Contretemps

When the new Republic of Armenia began to establish its diplomatic missions in foreign capitals, a decision was made with respect to those countries where there were large Armenian communities to request their assistance in housing the chancelleries. The Tehran Diocese had come into possession of a two-story, 4300-square–foot residence on Razi Street in the Park-e Shahr (City Park) neighborhood. It had been willed to the Prelacy by the famous Iranian carpet merchant Vahram Avakian and his wife Roza, who had no children, and after her husband died, Mrs. Avakian had transferred it to the Diocesan Council. The Council decided to renovate the property to serve as the Armenian Embassy. The Diocesan Assembly approved a generous budget and the Council spared no expense in refurbishing the building and its courtyard. Once it was ready, the Council handed it over to the Republic of Armenia.

The Embassy opened on December 22, 1992. Ambassador Vahan Bayburdyan had arrived in Tehran a few days earlier, accompanied by Vice President Gagik Harutyunyan and two Foreign Ministry officials, both of whom would later serve as Ambassador to Iran: Deputy Foreign Minister Arman Navasardyan and Grigor Arakelyan (the latter is a native of Tabriz whose family emigrated in the postwar "repatriation" to Soviet Armenia).

Given the modest size of the new Embassy, only a limited number of guests were invited to the opening ceremony. Iran was represented by Deputy Foreign Minister Mahmoud Vaezi and Ambassador Sobhani, who had not yet taken up his post in Yerevan. The three community religious leaders, the members of the Diocesan Council and the Diocesan Assembly, both Armenian MPs and the staff of *Alik* were all invited. Bella and I were invited too. We had attended many official events over the years, but the opening of the Armenian Embassy had a very special meaning for us.

The ceremony began with the Iranian national anthem, after which Ambassador Bayburdyan respectfully evoked the names of the late Emam Khomeini, Supreme Leader Ayatollah Khamenei and President Hashemi-Rafsanjani. He marked the day as a milestone and expressed the hope that cultural, political, economic and commercial relations between the two countries would develop to a level desirable for both nations. Then Vice President Harutyunyan spoke:

> This moment is full of historic symbolism. The cooperative friendship between our two nations, whose history goes back thousands of years, is in the midst of a revival and this occasion makes it a reality. Our relationship is now liberating itself from the awkwardness and illogic of the past decades and developing along a clear path.

The Armenian Vice President concluded by expressing his gratitude to the leadership of the Islamic Republic of Iran for their goodwill and energetic efforts in the new direction. "Every step must be taken to ensure more contacts, more exchanges and more agreements between our two peoples."

Deputy Foreign Minister Vaezi then spoke to the gathering. He said his government's foreign policy was based on the creation of strong relationships with its neighbors, which was why Iran had been one of the first to recognize Armenian independence and to initiate political, commercial and cultural exchanges with the new Republic. He said the relationship had thus far not developed as satisfactorily as it should. It must be improved and strengthened. A land link had already been established with the temporary bridge over the Arax River and goods were being exchanged between the two countries. There were direct flights between Mehrabad and Zvartnots Airports, and plans were underway to open a branch of Bank Mellat (Nation's Bank) in Yerevan. Vaezi concluded by congratulating the Armenian people on the opening of the Embassy and wishing them a prosperous New Year and a joyous Christmas.

Archbishop Manoukian then blessed the proceedings and Vice President Harutyunyan and Ambassador Bayburdyan went outside to raise the flag. Everyone began to sing the Armenian national anthem, including the hundreds of young Armenians who had gathered outside to see this part of the ceremony. When the flag of independent Armenia unfurled to fly free atop the building, they broke into applause and a flash of indescribable joy and festivity overtook the entire assembly.

Ambassador Bayburdyan began his tenure as Chargé d'affaires, perhaps in parallel to Bahram Ghasemi's status at the Iranian Embassy in Yerevan. Bayburdyan's appointment as Ambassador Extraordinary and Plenipotentiary was confirmed on November 9, 1994, and he presented his credentials to President Hashemi-Rafsanjani on December 20. The President received him very warmly and expressed his hope that the conflict between Armenia and Azerbaijan would soon be resolved so that the two neighbors could live in peace. The Ambassador responded in fluent Persian which impressed the President. Referring to Iran's strategic location and the centuries-old friendship between their two peoples, he said he hoped this friendship would continue and be strengthened.

Ambassador Bayburdyan's tenure coincided with the mounting crisis between President Ter-Petrosyan and the ARF, and that had a direct bearing on our community's attitude toward Bayburdyan himself. He was disrespected by ARF partisans and supported by the party's opponents. Broadly speaking, the community was split in two, which complicated the Ambassador's work. Nevertheless, he tried to bring Armenia and the Diaspora closer to each other, within the limits of the policies set by his government. Thanks to his intelligence and foresight, he was generally able to carry out his duties and to rebuild relations that had been severely damaged over the seventy-year period of Soviet rule.

Commercial and Cultural Exchanges

One of the most urgent requirements for bilateral trade was banking services, and on January 14, 1995, Bank Mellat opened a branch in Yerevan. Iranian Finance Minister Morteza Mohammadkhan and a group of Ministry officials attended the ribbon-cutting ceremony. The Iran-Armenia Chamber of Commerce was invited too, and I was there as a member of the IACOC delegation. When President Ter-Petrosyan arrived to cut the ribbon, he was surrounded by a huge entourage, but when he saw me, he stretched out his hand in greeting and asked me how I was. It was only a brief encounter, but he said something very wise:

"Maintaining good relations with Iran is very important to Armenia."

A few hours later, Vahan Papazyan came to see me at the Armenia Hotel. Previously an advisor to the President, he was now the Foreign Minister. Since our families were close and we knew each other well, he was able to speak frankly. Without any preliminaries, he asked me what impact the President's attack on the ARF was having on the Iranian Armenian community. I should note that President Ter-Petrosyan had gone on national television two weeks earlier and accused the ARF of a host of crimes, shut down its daily *Yerkir* (Country) and other periodicals, and suspended the party altogether. Some thirty activists had been arrested, including an Iranian émigré named Hrand Markarian. I told Vahan that he already knew how influential the party was in Iran, given its long history of political activity and propaganda. The Iranian Armenian community had come to know the ARF for its commitment to the nation and its struggle for national preservation. The President's action had clearly made a negative impression on the community. Our discussion lasted for almost an hour. Afterwards, I realized that the President must have sent him on this urgent errand after our fortuitous encounter that morning.

I had been working with Bahram Ghasemi to try and get permission from the Iranian government for Loris Tjeknavorian to bring the Armenian Philharmonic Orchestra (APO) to Tehran, and Minister Mohammadkhan's presence in Yerevan offered the perfect opportunity. He met the conductor and heard about the APO's amazing artistry, and Tjeknavorian agreed to give a command performance in honor of the Iranian delegation. A few nights later, Tjeknavorian mounted the conductor's podium in Khachaturian Hall and announced the orchestral suite from one of his own compositions, *Rostam and Sohrab*, a tragic opera based on one of the most moving stories in Ferdowsi's immense *Shahnameh*, the Iranian national epic.

Tjeknavorian has said that he based this composition on the traditional modes and rhythms of Iranian mourning rituals for the martyrdom of Emam Hossein which is the saddest and most painful chapter in the history of the Shia. The one-hour performance deeply touched everyone in attendance. Minister Mohammadkhan was sitting two seats away from me and I saw him crying like a baby. His entire delegation was on the verge of tears, and when the concert ended, they were all discreetly wiping their eyes. When it became obvious that they all felt the same way, their reticence gave way to an outpouring of authentic emotion that was as natural as it was appropriate to the occasion.

After the concert, Tjeknavorian invited us to a reception in his large and impressively furnished private quarters. When tea, coffee and pastries had been served, he approached Minister Mohammadkhan who was sitting on a large couch. He called me over to join the conversation, saying that I was one of his closest friends, "a true brother" as he put it. Mohammadkhan asked Tjeknavorian why the APO had never performed in Tehran, and the conductor replied that there were two reasons. One was that dark forces wanted to spoil such a project. The other was a question of funding: he was not sure he could raise the money for 200 performers, their travel expenses, accommodations and fees. Mohammadkhan replied,

"Maestro, with this composition, you have taken Ferdowsi far beyond the realm of literature. Even if it means a minor adjustment to the state's budget, we must bring you to Tehran!"

The Minister was as good as his word, and a few years later, Tjeknavorian and the APO gave a series of concerts in Tehran's thousand-seat Vahdat Hall (the former Roudaki Hall), and a female soloist sang for an Iranian audience for the first time since the Islamic Revolution. Every performance was sold out and hundreds were turned away. After that initial series, performances by the Armenian Philharmonic Orchestra became an annual feature of Iranian cultural life. This tradition has brought great prestige and honor to our community.

Economic and Political Exchanges

In April 1995, the Armenian Embassy in Tehran called me to say that two Embassy officials would like to meet with me. I said they were welcome to come to my office whenever they liked. Azad Manukyan came to my office with Armen Darbinyan, who had previously served as his government's liaison to the Armenian Business Forum. After the usual greetings and chitchat, they delivered a message from Foreign Minister Papazyan: Prime Minister Hrant Bagratyan would be leading a delegation to Iran in May in order to finalize a number of trade and technology agreements and he wanted to meet with members of the Armenian community while he was in Iran. I was asked to contact Archbishop Manoukian and the ARF about organizing a meeting and I promised to deliver the message.

The next day, I phoned a representative of the ARF Central Committee and asked for a meeting. He invited me over to his office the same day, and when I delivered the message, he was somewhat offended. Why hadn't the Embassy contacted him directly? I explained that they wanted to avoid embarrassment in case their request was rebuffed. He calmed down and said he would get back to me. The next day, I delivered the same message to the Prelate. Without putting it in so many words, he indicated that it was up to the Diocesan Council to organize such a meeting. Two days later, I met with the ARF representative again. He was upset that I had gone around him and asked the Prelate to handle the matter. I explained that I had delivered the same message to both the ARF and the Prelate at the Embassy's explicit request.

Two weeks went by and neither the ARF nor the Prelate got back to me. In the meantime, Vahan Papazyan came to town to prepare the way for the Prime Minister's visit. Rubina Papazian, the wife of Vahan's cousin, hosted a dinner for him at her home and I was one of the guests. At one point during the evening, he took me aside and said never mind about the ARF and the Prelate. Instead, he asked me to organize a meeting with Iranian business professionals.

I went to work on it immediately. I called an extraordinary meeting of the board of the Iran-Armenia Chamber of Commerce and we decided to ask the Iranian Chamber of Commerce, Industry and Mining to make its great hall available for the reception. Once that was confirmed, we invited hundreds of business professionals, both members and non-members of either chamber, and the Iranian Foreign Ministry promised to send some of its officials.

The great hall, which seats 500, was filled to capacity when Prime Minister Bagratyan arrived with Minister of Industry Ashot Safaryan, Minister of Food and Agriculture Ashot Voskanyan, Telman Ter-Petrosyan and other members of the delegation. The reception was of the highest caliber and a number of media outlets covered it. After the IACOC and the Foreign Ministry officials formally welcomed the delegation, Prime Minister Bagratyan delivered a speech to the gathering. He is an economist by training and he provided extremely valuable information about Armenia's economy and the prospects for bilateral trade.

Incident in Isfahan

The Iranian government arranged for Prime Minister Bagratyan and his delegation to tour Isfahan and meet with the Armenian community in New Julfa. They took a morning flight out of Tehran, and that same night at 10:00 PM, I got a call from Ashot Voskanyan. He told me that something terrible had happened at All-Savior's Cathedral. Apparently, someone had introduced a feral dog into the walled courtyard and they were prevented from going in. And while they were standing there outside the wall, they were confronted by an elderly man who identified himself as the father of Hrand Markarian and handed Prime Minister Bagratyan a letter demanding his son's release. There was a moment of indecision, and as the delegation tried to leave, a group of demonstrators ran up and started shouting ARF slogans and cursing President Ter-Petrosyan.

The next day, I met with members of the Armenian delegation and found them terribly hurt and offended. Telman Ter-Petrosyan blamed the new

Iranian Ambassador to Armenia who happened to be a former mayor of Isfahan. At the very least, he said, the incident wouldn't have happened without his benign indifference. I knew the Armenians of Isfahan to be a patriotic people and I found the whole incident shocking. What was most shocking was that the Prelate of Isfahan had allowed himself to be used as a pawn in a partisan struggle against the Armenian government.

That night, Ambassador Bayburdyan held a reception for Prime Minister Bagratyan at the Embassy. He had invited religious leaders, the heads of various community organizations and members of the Diocesan Council and the Diocesan Assembly, including a large number of political independents. Not a single member of the Council or the Assembly turned up, nor did the Prelate of Tehran. The only clerics who came to meet the Armenian Prime Minister were Bishop Tekeyan and the V. Rev. Father Tossounian from the Armenian Catholic Church.

News of the Isfahan incident spread quickly. People were shocked and scandalized. How could the Iranian Armenian community treat the Prime Minister of Armenia like that? Armenians had been deprived of an independent state for centuries, and now that their dream had come true, how was it possible that an Armenian government delegation could be met by a wild dog in New Julfa? The incident was first and foremost a blow against the Church. It proved that the See of Cilicia was a tool in the hands of the ARF. I was so upset that when the Diocesan Assembly nominated me to attend the consecration of Catholicos Aram I at Antelias in June, I withdrew my name without a second thought.

I discussed the incident with Albert Bernardi and Vigen Gevorkian. We agreed that silence was no longer an option. The ARF had no right to speak on behalf of a community that didn't support it, nor should it exhibit such open-faced bias. Something similar had happened back in 1984 when the ARF had backed Ardavazd Baghoumian against the leftist candidate in the contest for the southern Armenian parliamentary seat. Baghoumian had won thanks to hundreds of party members bussed down from Tehran to vote in Isfahan.

We decided to write to the Prelates and the Diocesan Councils of both Tehran and Isfahan to protest their stance against the Armenian government. We noted that many people whom they were supposed to represent did not share that stance. We pointed out that such treatment as that meted out to the Armenian Prime Minister weakened the position of the Republic of

Armenia and thus harmed the Armenian nation. We informed them that some Iranian officials had expressed surprise and regret at the lack of respect shown to a guest of the Islamic Republic. Our letters emphasized the need to preserve the traditional impartiality of the Church, and when we solicited the endorsement of other community leaders, some thirty signed on, including members of the ARF who were critical of their party's actions.

A week later, Bernardi, Gevorkian and I were invited to meet with the Tehran Diocesan Council. Each of us was individually questioned by the Council and we each unequivocally condemned the abhorrent treatment of Prime Minister Bagratyan and his delegation. One Council member remarked that if he didn't know me better, he might have thought our letter was written by the Iranian-Armenian National and Cultural Association (IAMM), an old antagonist of both the Council and the ARF.

"You are mistaken," I replied. "Not only did I sign that letter, I helped write it."

Media Campaign

Now the ARF cranked up its campaign against President Ter-Petrosyan and the Armenian National Movement (ANM). *Alik* started printing any scrap of news that was critical of Ter-Petrosyan's administration, so much so that the uninformed reader might get the impression that Armenia was under enemy occupation. For example, *Alik* published an editorial on May 31 under the headline, "The 'Levonian Project' to Weaken the Diaspora." Here is an excerpt:

> We are all familiar with recent events in Armenia where the ANM under the leadership of Levon Ter-Petrosyan, in an attempt to satisfy its authoritarian tendencies, has targeted not only the internal opposition but the Diaspora as well, knowing that events in the Diaspora have repercussions in the homeland.
>
> The ANM and its leader know full well that by weakening the Diaspora, they weaken Armenia's diverse political parties and factions, especially the nationalist elements. The deepening chasm between Armenia and the Diaspora allows the Armenian authorities to contain nationalist aspirations just as the Communists did, to change the character of the Diaspora and erase the last traces of its long-held national profile, and to divide and conquer the Diaspora which has done so much to preserve national values. They want to control the Diaspora by

sowing disunity. Divide and conquer is the centerpiece of their project, which is characterized by the absence of national concerns, patriotism and state interests, and by the domination of petty interests, greed and hunger for glory....

When they call the ARF a secret organization with a terrorist agenda, when they relentlessly pursue individuals who have been alienated or expelled from the ARF and use those individuals to create parallel organizations that falsely use the party's name, when they publicize fake documents cooked up in the presidential palace to support their allegations, their aim is to foment distrust in the leadership of the ARF, to divide the people from the party and to raise suspicions in the minds of foreign leaders....

When I ran out of patience, I wrote a letter pointing out the absurdity of such charges and sent it to the editors of *Alik*. Even if President Ter-Petrosyan had wanted to divide the Diaspora and crush the internal opposition, I wrote, such a destructive campaign would have required tremendous expertise and huge capital, whereas the government of Armenia was barely able to maintain its Embassies abroad. Besides, the government had its hands full with the war in Gharabagh, high unemployment and the shortage of food and energy. I honored the ARF for its struggle against the Ottoman yoke, Russian tsarism and Bolshevik rule, but the President symbolized the Republic and it was impossible to separate them, and therefore the anti-Levon campaign was effectively anti-Armenia. Of course, *Alik* refused to publish my letter.

One day, I happened to be sitting next to Seroj Soukiassian on a flight to Yerevan. Two women from Armenia were sitting in the row ahead of us and we overheard one say to the other,

"Have you read *Alik*? They print such terrible lies about Armenia!"

As a member of the ARF, Soukiassian felt obliged to lean forward and apologize.

The New Iranian Ambassador to Armenia

Iranian Chargé d'affaires Bahram Ghasemi was a very kind and capable person. He was instrumental in putting relations between Iran and Armenia on the path of unprecedented development. It was during his tenure that Iran purchased its permanent Embassy building in Yerevan and he and his staff of three organized a number of events that helped push things in the right direction. After he was appointed as Ambassador to Spain, Ambassador

Sobhani served in Yerevan for a period during which there was little improvement in bilateral relations. Toward the end of his term, I heard from a Foreign Ministry official that Sobhani was being replaced by Hamid-Reza Nikkar-Esfahani.

When Ambassador Nikkar-Esfahani's appointment was made public, Ambassador Bayburdyan hosted a reception for him at the Esteqlal Hotel. I was among those invited, along with the Prelate, the members of the Diocesan Council, *Alik*'s editor-in-chief and other community leaders. Speaking in Persian, Ambassador Bayburdyan offered an elaborate introduction to the Iranian Ambassador, and everyone was surprised and deeply impressed that an Armenian from Armenia could be so fluent in Persian.

Six months after Nikkar-Esfahani was posted to Yerevan, the Deputy Director of the Caucasus desk in the Iranian Foreign Ministry invited me to pay him a call. Since he knew me well, he felt comfortable asking for my advice on how to quietly halt the illicit transshipment of Turkish goods to Armenia via Iran. I explained how transport companies – of which Sati was one – could alter the paperwork to show Iran as the country of origin, and I advised him to submit a confidential complaint to FIATA, the International Federation of Freight Forwarders Associations. He followed up with FIATA and that practice came to an end.

Not long afterwards, the same official asked me to come in again. This time, he was concerned about Ambassador Nikkar-Esfahani. He said the Iranian Ambassador was practically isolated in Yerevan and he was becoming increasingly apathetic. He asked me to use my contacts in Armenian government circles to help improve the situation. I promised to do my best.

I immediately flew to Yerevan and contacted Telman Ter-Petrosyan, the President's elder brother. I asked him to meet with the Iranian Ambassador, and I also requested that Ashot Safaryan sit in on the meeting. As the Minister of Industry, Ashot had important responsibilities that were affected by diplomatic relations between Armenia and Iran. I suggested the meeting take place in the intimate atmosphere of a private dinner and Telman agreed. Then I took my proposal to Ambassador Nikkar-Esfahani. He agreed to the meeting and said he would leave the time and place up to Ter-Petrosyan. Then I met with the manager of the Armenia Hotel and asked him to make the arrangements for a private dinner for four. He showed me a tastefully appointed suite off the main hall on the second floor that was perfect. I confirmed the time and place with both sides.

At the appointed time, I was there to receive my guests at the entrance to the main hall, and I showed them to the private suite reserved for our meeting. I made the introductions, interpreting for both sides, and we began with a few minutes of pleasantries, but Telman soon cut to the chase. He said he wanted to speak frankly about what had led to the cooling of relations between our two countries. Ambassador Nikkar-Esfahani welcomed this approach. At that moment, the waiter came in and took our orders.

Telman resumed as soon as the waiter left. He said there were two problems the Iranian government needed to address. The first was its connivance with the ARF against the Armenian government. He said the Iranian Foreign Ministry knew what the ARF was up to and yet it continued to support the party, both openly and covertly. He mentioned a recent reception at the Iranian Embassy and said that far more ARF partisans had been invited than Armenian government officials. Ambassador Nikkar-Esfahani expressed surprise. Surely it was unintentional, he said. His staff must have used the previous Ambassador's guest list.

Telman then moved on to the second problem. He said that a certain individual on the Ambassador's staff was interfering in Armenia's internal affairs. This individual had been seen meeting with certain people and frequenting certain places that cast doubt on his judgment. If necessary, a detailed report on the man's contacts could be provided. Telman could barely contain his anger when he said this individual could not possibly be carrying on as he was if he were not an Iranian intelligence officer. Nikkar-Esfahani promised to take care of it, and in fact, the man was sent back to Iran. (Two years later, after President Ter-Petrosyan had resigned, the same individual returned to the Iranian Embassy in a higher position.)

As the evening continued, our conversation turned to purely Armenian issues, and when we were finally ready to leave, Telman urged the Ambassador to contact him should any problem arise. He emphasized that he would spare no effort to resolve it. On that note, he and Safaryan left. Safaryan hadn't said a word throughout the entire evening.

Ambassador Nikkar-Esfahani thanked me for arranging the meeting. He also said that he would like to meet Foreign Minister Papazyan. He knew Vahan played tennis and suggested they might meet on the court. I relayed the message to Vahan the next day and he told me when and where he played and said he would be happy to play a set with the Ambassador. I communicated that information to Nikkar-Esfahani and considered my mission accomplished.

It was clear to me that the Armenian government had been deliberately isolating the Iranian Ambassador ever since the incident in Isfahan, and apparently waiting for the right opportunity to express its dissatisfaction.

Persistent Partisan Sniping

I was out of the country when my secretary called to say that Catholicos Aram I was scheduled to visit the Aharonian Kindergarten the next day. I had already booked my return flight and when I landed in Tehran at 5:00 AM, I barely managed to drive home, shower, change, and race to the kindergarten. All the students were standing at attention with their teachers, awaiting the new Cilician Catholicos. He arrived at exactly 9:00 AM and spent more than an hour at the kindergarten. Then he went next door to Soukerian Hall where several hundred residents of Majidiyeh were awaiting him. He was met with tremendous joy and enthusiasm. He delivered a rousing speech, and at one point he said something about the Republic of Armenia that made a powerful impression on the crowd. I was standing next to MP Vartan Vartanian, and when Archbishop Aram finished speaking, I told Vartan that the Holy Father's attitude toward Armenia was similar to that of people like me. Vartan heard me but said nothing.

When the meeting was over, we all left Majidiyeh in a three-car convoy and drove to the Ararat Center where Loris Tjeknavorian was conducting a special performance by the Armenian Philharmonic Orchestra as part of the festivities organized to celebrate the visit of the Cilician Catholicos to Iran. Sassountsi David Hall was filled to capacity, and when the Holy Father made his entrance, 2,000 people stood up to welcome him. As I looked around for a seat, I saw Ambassador Bayburdyan and his staff sitting in the fourth row. Then I noticed several ordinary citizens sitting in the first row with the guest of honor and various community leaders. That being the case, why should the Ambassador be sitting in the fourth row? Whether or not one agreed with the policies of the Armenian government, he was its official representative and he should have been seated in the front row.

The concert lasted two hours and it was a total nightmare for me, devoid of any pleasure. After it was over, I approached the Ambassador. He confided that he and his staff had considered leaving before the concert began but decided to remain in their assigned seats so that everyone could see how they were treated. He went on to say that if I invited him to my house and, God forbid, made him sit under the table with my dog, that would be an affront attributable to a lack of grace and understanding, but when the same treatment was meted out by a so-called community organization, that was another matter altogether. While we were talking, a member of the Ararat Association approached and invited us to the post-concert dinner. The Ambassador excused himself, saying he had a prior commitment. Of course, none of this passed unnoticed and people were talking about it the next day.

As a member of the Ararat Armenian Sports and Cultural Association, I considered that incident unacceptable. As its full name indicates, the association's mandate is primarily the promotion of sports and culture. Its leadership had no right to take a position on a political issue. This was all the more imperative when the issue was the government of the Republic of Armenia. If the ARF had a dispute with the Armenian government, it should not have saddled the Ararat Association with it, especially when 80 percent of its members did not belong to the ARF. In the final analysis, the incident brought no honor to a political party that had contributed to the mission of national preservation. Such incidents, which were engineered by certain party leaders, were more injurious to the ARF than anything else. They left indelible black marks on the party's body politic. The Ararat Association had always preached patriotism to its members. How could it now permit such an open affront to the government of independent Armenia?

Such narrow-mindedness and immaturity, which the party described as part of a "struggle," persisted until the end of Ambassador Bayburdyan's tenure. In fact, his Embassy was under double-barreled attack the whole time, vulnerable to the hostility of local Azeris on the one hand, targeted by the ARF on the other. The ARF was always criticizing President Ter-Petrosyan for his "unjust" policy but it passed over the reasons why he expelled Hrair Maroukhian and banned the party in Armenia. It never published the texts of his televised speeches of June 29, 1992 and December 28, 1994, or his speech to the National Assembly on May 18, 1995. Some day an unbiased historian or an objective political analyst will explain what really happened.

Alik's Role

When *Alik* inaugurated its new media center on June 22, 1997, Catholicos Aram came to Tehran to deliver the benediction, with all three Iranian diocesan leaders in attendance. The reception was hosted by publisher Albert Ajemian along with ARF Bureau member Mgrditch Mgrditchian. There was wild applause when the Holy Father cut the ribbon and proceeded to enter the building. He led the invited guests up to the large room on the second floor where editor-in-chief Seda Grigorian (Davitian) congratulated everyone and Mgrditchian thanked them for their support. His Holiness then lauded *Alik*'s essential role in the life of the Iranian Armenian community and spoke of the paper's noble mission of service to Armenians, not only in Iran but throughout the Diaspora. The party lasted for some three hours and everyone left in high spirits.

It would be unfair if I failed to discuss *Alik*'s place in the life of the Iranian Armenian community, and such disregard is not in keeping with my character. *Alik* has been the hope and support of the community and the Diocesan Council. The paper has always stood with us and with the Armenian nation and has unconditionally supported Armenian rights. It has kept its readers abreast of the state of our schools, and in particular the status of religious education in our schools. It tries cover the many different Armenian communities in Iran, especially their organizations and schools, including the kindergartens. In so doing, *Alik* helps to spread the idea that the community is not alone, that intellectuals, community leaders and elected representatives stand together in one united front. The paper pays special attention to young artists, intellectuals, poets and athletes. Its sports page highlights the achievements of Armenian athletes in Iran and Armenia and in other Diasporan communities. One of *Alik*'s most noteworthy services has been its participation in and coverage of the annual April 24 commemorative activities.

Alik started out as a weekly in 1931 and became a daily in 1941. Although its masthead makes no reference to its political affiliation, even a cursory reading will show that it belongs to the ARF. The paper's editors have always been ARF intellectuals and activists, such as Dajad Boghosian (who originated the "Raffi" calendar), André Amourian, Norair Pahlavouni, Edvart Yeritsian, Norair Elsaian, Seda Grigorian and Derenik Melikian. Dr. Rostom Stepanian was the publisher of record for many years until he was succeeded by Albert Ajemian.

Unfortunately, no other newspaper has enjoyed continuous publication over the same period. Of course, others were published from time to time but they were all short-lived. *Alik* remains the go-to source for community news, announcements, press releases and ARF-approved articles.

Alik's Publisher Arrested

One morning, my close friend Lemuel Avedian came to my office looking very downcast. Albert Ajemian was his brother-in-law and he told me that Albert had been kidnapped: last night, when he left his architectural office at 5:00 PM, he was surrounded by a group of men and taken away. At that point, Lemuel broke down in tears.

I immediately called my friend General X on his direct line. The number was known to only a few people and he always picked up. He recognized my voice and I told him what had happened. I said Ajemian was an important community leader. If he were to disappear, it would have very negative repercussions. I asked the General to use every means at his disposal to find him. He told me to call back in an hour.

When I called back, General X told me that Ajemian was safely in custody and he promised to arrange for him to speak with his wife by phone, which he did. The next day, Vartan Vartanian and I called on Albert's wife and explained that his detention was politically motivated and that he would soon be released. In fact, he was held for twenty days. Afterwards, he and I never discussed the incident, but from that point on, *Alik* often featured the Supreme Leader, the President and other government officials in front-page stories.

Chapter 31

An Unexpected Request

A disagreement with a business partner whose relatives enjoyed the support of certain prominent officials brought me to the attention of the Iranian Ministry of Intelligence and Security (MOIS). I was called in for questioning several times and accused of monopolizing freight shipment between Iran and Armenia. My interrogators said I was "crushing the competition." They piled on more charges in order to make things more difficult for me, yet in the end they simply told me to settle the matter with my competition. But those sessions gave us the opportunity to get to know each other better, and eventually they proposed that I spy for them. That I categorically refused to do. Then they asked if they could consult with me in their effort to understand a number of issues related to Armenia. To this I agreed.

One day in 1995, they invited me to meet with them in a private room at the Homa Hotel (the former Sheraton) in Vanak. When I knocked on the door at the appointed time, they welcomed me warmly and offered me tea and pastry. As the conversation progressed, they proposed that we do business together. Huge consignments of bottled soft drinks were being shipped from Dubai to Armenia in those days and we happened to have such an order from a Russian company whose manager was an Armenian. I told them about it and Mr. Kashani – they all used aliases and Kashani had introduced himself by that name – said we could buy the merchandise from one of their associates in Dubai. He put me in touch with the vendor and we negotiated a price of $200,000 and shipped the freight to Sochi in ten containers.

Our agreement with the buyer was that we would receive payment upon delivery, but before we even received payment, which was a bit late, our new business associates invited me back to the Homa Hotel and asked for their commission. Despite the fact that in such arrangements, the vendor ordinarily pays the commission, I promised they would have it in two days. Two days later, I put $2,000 in an envelope and went to the Homa Hotel. I spotted Kashani in the lobby, sitting around a table with several other men. I went in and sat down at another table. As soon as Kashani saw me, he came over and sat down across from me. The first thing he said was,

"Have you got the money with you?"

I said I did and he signaled for me to hand it over. Based on bitter experience, I slipped the envelope under the table. He coldly placed it on top of the table and asked,

"How much is it?"

When I told him, his face lit up with a satisfied smile and he thanked me. I said I had another meeting and quickly left the hotel.

The Asia Hotel

In August 1996, I was summoned to the Homa Hotel again to meet with the same MOIS officers. As usual, our conversation drifted from one topic to another and my responses were always cautious and measured. I knew they were sophisticated and skillful interrogators and they could create big problems for me if they wanted to. This time, they surprised me by asking whether I had recently started any new projects. I replied no, but the senior officer repeated the question. That made me think more carefully and I thought of the Asia Hotel in Julfa.

It all began in 1992 when the national liberation struggle in Gharabagh was approaching a climactic point. Armenia was suffering a severe shortage of heating oil and Transportation Minister Henrik Kochinyan told me that his government had reached a barter agreement whereby Armenia would commission the shipment of heating oil from Russia's Caspian port of Makhachkala to Iran at Bandar Enzeli, in exchange for which Iran would make an equivalent supply of heating oil available to Armenia via the land route. Kochinyan asked me to contribute to this effort in any way I could. Even though Armenia was getting a bad press over the war, I knew how seriously it was threatened so I agreed to help.

We began trucking heating oil from a refinery in Tabriz to Julfa. There it was transferred to a fleet of Armenian tanker trucks that delivered it directly to front-line villages in Gharabagh. Garen Galoustian (Karen Galstian, who became the Minister of Energy some years later) came down to Sati's office in Julfa to oversee the operation. The Armenian drivers would go shopping in town while their tankers were being loaded, but eventually, with tensions rising due to the war, the authorities told us they could no longer be responsible for the drivers' safety. So, in order to give them a safe place to stay, we bought the dilapidated Asia Hotel at auction for 100 million tomans and took out a private loan to fix it up. Then the delivery operation ceased, for reasons unknown to us, so we sold the hotel, paid off the loan and that was the end of it. But the whole affair hadn't been completely liquidated at the time of this interview.

After listening to the saga of the Asia Hotel, my interrogators said that wasn't what they had in mind. They were thinking of a more immediate situation in which I was facing financial difficulties. Suddenly I realized they were alluding to the situation I was dealing with on my elder brother's account. I explained that it wasn't my own affair but that I had assumed financial responsibility in order to preserve the honor of a member of my family. Here I should say that my brother's financial collapse is one of my bitterest memories.

Family Financial Crisis

In 1990, my elder brother Henrik was still managing André Shop and had started producing *yershig* (sausage) in a small facility across the street. Since my younger brother and I were generally not involved in the business, we decided to leave all the income to Henrik so that he could finance the education of his children in the USA. We were all encouraging our children to come back to Iran after they finished school and carry on the enterprises we had built. When Henrik's elder son came home, he started working with his father at André Shop but he soon grew bored and lost interest. Nor were any of our children interested in the shop. Since the economy was finally beginning to recover from the war, we decided to set up a full-scale meat-processing plant. Henrik took the initiative and founded a new company named after our late father, secured a license from the government, got a bank loan and built the factory on a five-acre lot we owned near Karaj. We made his son the plant manager and gave him a 10-percent share in the company.

Around that time, the Emam Khomeini Economic Fund tried to expropriate André Shop and the land on which it was built. We owned the shop but the land itself belonged to a man of the Baha'i faith. (Before the Revolution, the Baha'i were a significant religious minority with considerable political power, but the Islamic government had banned the Baha'i as apostates and punished those who continued to practice their religion.) According to the law, we had a right to compensation for the shop, but the government denied us that right. We were forced to either buy the land or give up the shop, so I sold my house in Farmaniyeh and bought the land.

The factory soon began to meet our production goals and turn a profit. Unfortunately, an undercurrent of conflict arose and rumors began to circulate among my extended family. I sensed that my nephew was the source of the conflict. He was unfamiliar with how business was done in Iran and I was afraid that his missteps could jeopardize our venture. As chairman of the company as well as a shareholder, I couldn't remain silent, but he was avoiding me so I tried to warn his parents, both in writing and in private conversation, but my efforts had no effect. I decided not to interfere for a while. But then I heard from here and there that Henrik was borrowing money at rates so scandalous that people were pulling money out of term accounts to lend it to him. Of course, they trusted him and relied on our late father's impeccable reputation.

I remember a telling exchange that took place when the plant was under construction. My nephew went to buy some rebar and found that he was 20,000 tomans short (about $60). When he said he would go home and get the money, the vendor asked him what the rebar was for. At the mention of his grandfather's name, the vendor said he could take what he needed and pay whenever he liked. My nephew was amazed. In the USA, he said, if a customer was even a penny short, the vendor wouldn't let him take the merchandise. I explained to him that the vendor was relying on our family's reputation. It would not even occur to him that a member of our family would not pay what he owed.

Unfortunately, our relations deteriorated and things got so bad that I was kept completely in the dark about the factory's financial situation. Finally, I went to the Ministry of Finance and looked up its annual report. I was shocked by what I read. Not only did it show no profit, but the company was 70 million tomans in the red (roughly $200,000). That frightened me because it pointed to massive embezzlement. I also heard from various people that Henrik was facing serious financial difficulties, and meanwhile, his son was buying the latest model cars on credit.

In March 1996, six months before this particular interview with the MOIS officers, I had just returned from a trip to Yerevan when my secretary said that my brother had called twice, saying he had urgent matters to discuss with me. I called Henrik the next day and he said he wanted to meet with me, alone. Although he had a home in one of the best areas of northwest Tehran, we met in our late mother's small apartment across the street from the shop. He quickly came to the point. The factory was bankrupt and he was in serious debt. I asked how serious and he said his total debt was 50 million tomans ($150,000). He was in no position to repay it or even to pay the interest. On top of that, he had applied for a loan of 17 million tomans ($50,000) in order to save his son from total ruin, but the bank required my cosignature. I told him to send me the note and I would sign it. At the same time, I asked him to turn over all the factory's account books to me. That night I called George and explained the situation. We decided that he and our nephew would go over the accounts together. Less than two days later, I was told that our nephew had tried to commit suicide but he survived.

This was just before Nowruz and I and some friends and family, including George, were planning to spend the two-week holiday at our summer home in Darya Kenar. George only spent the first five days with us before he returned to Tehran to review the accounts with our nephew. When we came back at the end of the holiday, George was still analyzing the accounts and he told me it looked like the total debt was more than ten times 50 million tomans. When he finished his analysis, he said the bottom line was that Henrik, his son and the factory owed a combined total of 1.6 *billion* tomans ($4.7 million). When I heard that, I almost went mad. It meant that all of our assets could evaporate in a second.

When my own family asked me what I intended to do, I explained that even though what happened was done without my knowledge, I had legal responsibilities as chairman of the company. There was another consideration. If Henrik and his son went to jail, the magnitude of the debt and the creditors' allegations would keep them locked up for years and they might not survive. Most important was that the whole affair would tarnish our family's honor which could never be restored at any price. My parents had built their reputation through hard work and good character. They had commanded trust and respect through their immutable humanity and undeviating probity. No one had the right to besmirch their good name. I decided to face up to the creditors – some 500 individuals, including everyone who worked at the factory, from security guards to supervisors, and scores of others unknown to me.

Meanwhile, my nephew quietly left the country, claiming he was psychologically exhausted. In due course, it was revealed that he had forged papers, post-dated checks and used other deceptions to collect the equivalent of $2 million before he fled. And since some of those checks were written on joint accounts he shared with his father, Henrik was still liable to be thrown in jail at any time. He went into hiding with friends and family for three years until I was able to pay off all the loans.

I was threatened with death by his creditors many times. They even attacked Sati's offices. One day, they brought along a cameraman who filmed the action while they destroyed furniture and equipment, and those scenes were shown on TV. I was surrounded by creditors everywhere I went, but we kept André Shop and the sausage factory running and George managed them both until they were sold.

I asked an old and trusted friend to help me organize a repayment scheme. He divided the creditors into three categories: those who were owed less than 500,000 tomans, those who were owed no more than 2 million, and those who were owed more than 2 million. We repaid those in the first category first, which significantly reduced the number of creditors. Then we began to repay the larger debts. In time, as the creditors saw that they were slowly but steadily being repaid, they softened their stance and began to wait their turn. Through the mediation of a lawyer, we were able to negotiate a reduction of the accrued interest, given that usury is generally forbidden in Islamic law.

Ultimately, we cleared the astronomical debt over three years of tortuous work. We sold the shop and the factory, as mentioned, as well as four new buildings that Henrik had built, cars, land and other assets. I paid the equivalent of $1.5 million, money that I had worked hard for, money that was supposed to secure my family's future. Henrik too had worked all his life to guarantee his children a good future, but this debacle destroyed his zest for life and he remained depressed to the end of his days.

Thus I recounted the saga of my family's ongoing financial crisis. My interrogators seemed to be satisfied with my explanation. Not long afterwards, however, I was invited to meet with a new group of intelligence officers at the Tehran Grand Hotel (*Bozorg-e Tehran*) in Behjatabad. I knew one of them but this was my first encounter with the other three. They wanted to discuss a letter they had received alleging that I was involved in a plot to overthrow the government. I knew who had written the letter, a retired colonel who was attempting to exploit my brother's financial embarrassment, so I explained the whole story all over again. After hearing me out, they were convinced of my innocence, and for the first time, one of them gave me his phone number and said I could call him if I needed anything.

Henrik was acquainted with a lawyer named Khalili who was actively spreading rumors about our family. This lawyer held himself out to be a decent man and a devout Muslim but he was the exact opposite. He had lent my brother 10 million tomans (approximately $30,000) and now he was demanding 110 million tomans in repayment. In other words, the interest was ten times the original loan! Khalili's rationale was that it was permissible to charge interest to a non-Muslim. Henrik owned a beautiful one-and-a-half–acre lot that was mortgaged by the note he had given Khalili, and Khalili was scheming to force an auction so that he could seize the property. I wanted to preserve the lot as security for Henrik's future, so I decided to pre-empt this conspiracy. I called the intelligence officer and he succeeded in having the auction postponed. At the suggestion of our lawyer, we had a backdated contract drawn up for the sale of the property to a close friend of ours and we submitted this fictitious document to the court, which saved the property. Khalili was persuaded to accept half of what he was owed and I wrote him a series of sequentially postdated checks, as per agreement, and within a few months he was paid the full amount we had agreed upon.

Armenia's 1996 Presidential Election

Throughout this period, I continued to meet with MOIS officers every month or so, and in early September, they invited me to the Homa Hotel and asked for my views on Armenia's upcoming presidential election which was scheduled for September 22. I told them that President Ter-Petrosyan's reelection was a foregone conclusion. Everybody liked him: civil servants, factory workers, teachers and professors, the military rank and file, the political parties and the new parliamentary "factions" all supported him. That was the nationwide trend in urban and rural areas alike. His most serious challenger, former Prime Minister Vazgen Manukyan, wasn't nearly as popular. When they asked me about the role of the ARF, I said bluntly that the ARF had no political influence in Armenia, especially not in this election. Nevertheless, my interrogators had a high opinion of the party and thought it could still play an important role in Armenia.

There was a lot of horse-trading in the run-up to the election and an old family friend asked me to deliver a message from Vazgen Manukyan to Albert Ajemian who was a member of the ARF Bureau. Since the ARF was still banned in Armenia and prevented from running a candidate of its own, Manukyan wanted the party to support his candidacy. When I gave Albert the message, he laughed derisively and ridiculed the contender. What was even funnier was that the party subsequently endorsed him. Ten days before the election, the ARF and three other parties threw their support to Manukyan, but he still lost with 41 percent of the vote to Ter-Petrosyan's 51.75 percent, according to published returns.

A few weeks after the election, the same intelligence officers invited me to another meeting at the Homa Hotel. They started out by discussing Armenia's "real" election returns and they showed me district-level data, even for rural districts. According their information, Manukyan had actually outpolled Ter-Petrosyan. They expressed satisfaction with the ARF, saying the party had operated much more efficiently than they had expected. Well-informed friends in Armenia later told me that the numbers they cited were pretty close to the truth.

The Two Holy Sees

My interrogators were very interested in the two Holy Sees of Echmiadzin and Cilicia. The long-serving Supreme Patriarch and Catholicos of All Armenians, Vazgen I, had died at Echmiadzin in August 1994, and Catholicos Garegin II of the See of Cilicia was elected to succeed the Supreme Patriarch in April 1995. Upon his election, he took the name Garegin I. Two months later, Archbishop Aram was elected at Antelias to succeed him as Catholicos of the See of Cilicia. When my interrogators asked me how the two Holy Sees differed, I said they had radically different hierarchies, missions and policies. In my view, His Holiness Garegin I was wholeheartedly carrying out his mission to preserve and protect the Armenian religion, language and culture as the pillars of our nation. As for the See of Cilicia, 95 percent of Iranian Armenians didn't know where Antelias was, but I respected both Sees because they were both staunch defenders of our nation.

My interrogators often asked me about the relationship between Catholicos Aram and the ARF and I always answered truthfully. I said the See of Cilicia and its leader were completely under the influence of the party. They appeared satisfied with my unequivocal response. In fact, that was the purpose of these interrogations: they wanted my unvarnished views. The senior officer said that Catholicos Aram's visits to Iran were organized by the ARF in collaboration with the Iranian government and they scheduled all his meetings, adding that their support extended to Beirut and to any other capital where they had the necessary resources. Of course, I was well aware of that, having observed throughout my years of community service and leadership how the three major Armenian Churches in Iran (Echmiadzin, Cilicia and the Armenian Catholic Patriarchate) obeyed the dictates of the ARF.

After Armenia's 1996 presidential election, my interrogators asked me to take a message to His Holiness Garegin I. They wanted to know what he thought of Iran and its policies, and to that end, they asked me to arrange a confidential meeting. They were adamant about keeping it secret from the Armenian government. At some later date, they said, the Holy Father would be formally invited to Iran by the Ministry of Foreign Affairs or the Ministry of Culture and Islamic Guidance. When that happened, they assured me, he would be received with the utmost pomp and circumstance, which would be in marked contrast to his reception in Turkey (there had been a bomb scare during his recent visit to an Armenian church in Istanbul). To further illustrate the point, they mentioned Prime Minister Bagratyan's reception in Isfahan the year before. They also said the Iranian government was preparing to receive an emissary from Alexy II, the Primate of the Russian Orthodox Church.

Then the discussion turned to the bilateral relationship between Iran and Armenia. They said the Iranian government was unhappy with Armenia's policy toward the Islamic Republic and they wanted to see a rapid and comprehensive development of bilateral relations, because the USA was busy sowing confusion in the region. As examples, the senior officer cited the American role in the protracted negotiations around Caspian Sea hydrocarbon resources; the D'Amato Act (i.e. the Iran and Libya Sanctions Act signed into law in August 1996); and Armenia's fraudulent presidential election and the rioting and repression that followed (a mass rally in Yerevan demanded a recount, demonstrators occupied the National Assembly and beat up the Speaker, and several hundred were arrested). The senior officer said the Americans had lost in Afghanistan and failed in Iraq, and now Turkey was poised to further its interests and expand its borders. Iran and Armenia needed to exercise the utmost caution. A direct channel for the confidential and expeditious exchange of political and military information was urgently needed. Speaking on behalf of the Iranian government, he proposed that the Armenian government appoint a trusted liaison to Iran's Supreme National Security Council (*Showra-ye Ali-ye Amniyat-e Melli*). He emphasized that this must be kept absolutely confidential: neither country's Embassy must know a thing about it.

Then he asked how I might contact President Ter-Petrosyan and communicate their proposal. I suggested three possibilities. One was through Berj Msrlian, a respected former member of the ARF whom I had met during my work on the Armenian Business Forum. He had broken ranks with Hrair Maroukhian and sided with President Ter-Petrosyan, and for that he had been expelled from the party. Another alternative was through the President's brother, Telman Ter-Petrosyan, a very close friend of mine who was familiar with my activities in Armenia and had the utmost respect for me. The third alternative was direct contact. I could simply request an appointment with the President. My interrogators rejected the first alternative and opted for the second, reasoning that it wouldn't be easy to get an appointment with the President but his brother could visit him any time and deliver the message.

Chapter 32

Dual Mission to Armenia

On Sunday, October 27, 1996, I took an Armenian Airlines flight to Yerevan in pursuit of my dual mission on behalf of the Iranian government. Norair Melkonian, Sati's director of operations in Armenia, and his deputy Makar Arakelyan met me at Zvartnots Airport and took me straight to the Armenia Hotel. There in the lobby, I saw Ashot Safaryan, the Minister of Industry, chatting with group of Iranians. When I approached them, MP Ardavazd Baghoumian shook my hand and introduced me to Governor Eshagh (Eshaq) Jahangiri of Isfahan Province. Then I turned to Safaryan, and after the usual courtesies, I asked him if we might have a glass of beer together in the hotel restaurant. He joined me there shortly afterwards and we spent a pleasant hour in private conversation, during the course of which I gathered that he was worried about a change in leadership that might leave him out office. Indeed, he kept his position in the cabinet shuffle announced the following week, but when Robert Kocharyan was named Prime Minister in March, Safaryan was not reappointed.

Mission to Echmiadzin

After leaving Safaryan, I went to my room to rest. I was exhausted. Later, I called Telman Ter-Petrosyan and told him I needed to see him on a very important matter. He said we could meet at 4:00 PM the next day. Then I went down to the restaurant and had a delicious meal of chicken khorovats. In the evening, I called Professor Hagop Papazyan and asked him for the private number of Catholicos Garegin I because I needed to make an appointment with him. Professor Papazyan said that wasn't necessary, he was taking some Iranian guests to meet His Holiness the next day at 1:00 PM and I was welcome to join them.

On Monday, we drove to Echmiadzin in a car provided by Sati. When we got there, I told Professor Papazyan that I needed fifteen minutes alone with His Holiness and he graciously offered to create the opportunity. Catholicos Garegin I welcomed us warmly, and after the introductions, the first thing he did was to ask me about Archbishop Manoukian's health (the Prelate had been diagnosed with a diabetic condition). Then he engaged the Iranian visitors in conversation, and at the opportune moment, Professor Papazyan asked whether they might see the museum on the second floor. His Holiness took out his keys, handed them to an assistant and asked him to take his guests upstairs.

After they left, we chatted about sundry subjects until I brought up the purpose of my visit. I told him that the Iranian Ministry of Intelligence and Security wanted to know his views on the policies of the Iranian government. He said he had always viewed the Iranian regime in a positive and optimistic light and he was surprised the authorities didn't already know that. Then I told him about my conversations with the intelligence officers and said they wanted to meet with him in person. He accepted the proposal and suggested they meet in Copenhagen. Then he changed his mind and said Paris or Geneva would be preferable. He said he would fax me once he had decided.

At that moment, the door opened and in walked Catholicos Aram I. He said he had come to Armenia for the annual meeting of the All-Armenian Fund, but before anything else, he had come to pay a visit to the Supreme Patriarch and Catholicos of All Armenians. Thus I was present at a meeting of the two Catholicoses of the Armenian Apostolic Church. I soon bid them goodbye and rejoined Professor Papazyan and his guests who were waiting outside, and we drove back to Yerevan.

Mission to Yerevan

I barely had time for a quick bite before taking the company car to Telman's office in the Avan district. He was there waiting for me with two assistants. We chatted for a few minutes before he dismissed them so that we could speak privately. First, he asked about my family and especially my wife Bella. Then he started talking about the terrible shortages of food and fuel and said he wondered how Armenia would ever get out of this crisis. Yet the country was becoming more stable by the day, he said, and he could see progress overall. He was about to cite an example when I interrupted him and brought up my mission. I gave a succinct account of the Iranian proposal and asked for the President's response by the following Sunday. Telman was very pleased with this démarche and he was sure that his brother would be too. He said the President was busy with a full agenda of meetings, but he promised to get back to me by Friday.

On Friday, I was busy all day with the biannual meeting of the Armenian Business Forum Company. Telman called me at around 7:00 PM to say the

President had dismissed his cabinet and was extremely busy forming a new one. He had been with his brother all day but hadn't had a chance to deliver my message, but he assured me he would do so at the first opportunity.

Saturday passed without any news. In the afternoon, I left the hotel on some personal errands, and when I returned at 8:00 PM, the floor attendant told me that Telman had called several times and left the message that I was to stay put and wait for his call. At 9:00 PM, someone rang to say that Telman would be at the hotel at midnight. Two hours later, the same person called again and said that Telman would be delayed by half an hour. At 12:30 AM, the main desk rang and told me some gentlemen were waiting for me in the lobby. I went down and saw Telman sitting around a table in the company of four or five men. My first impression was that they were military men, not personal friends. He introduced me as a good friend of the Diaspora, particularly the Iranian Armenian community. Then he excused himself for a moment and we sat down at another table. He said he had delivered the message as well as my congratulations on the President's re-election, for which the latter had asked him to thank me. He said the President was seriously considering the proposal and would respond very soon. Our conversation lasted no more than ten minutes, after which we rejoined the others and said goodnight.

On the way out, Telman confided in a low voice that Armen Sargsyan had been appointed Prime Minister. He told me I was the first person outside the President's inner circle to hear the news. I grabbed a few hours' sleep before my driver arrived at 6:00 AM and took me to Zvartnots Airport for the Sunday shuttle to Tehran. As soon as we landed, I went straight home to rest and didn't go to work at all that day.

Back in Tehran

Almost as soon as I walked into the office on Monday, November 4, an intelligence officer called me. We agreed to meet at the Homa Hotel on Tuesday. The group included two new faces, one of whom outranked all the others. I briefed them on my meetings with the Supreme Patriarch and the President's brother and delivered the President's message. I also told them about the new Prime Minister but they already knew about that. When I finished my presentation, the senior official thanked me and said both targets of my dual mission were of the highest importance to them.

On Wednesday, Ambassador Bayburdyan called and asked if I would be in town over the next few days. Somewhat mystified, I told him I had no travel plans.

On Thursday, the Ambassador called me at 5:00 PM and said that President Ter-Petrosyan's chief of staff had just arrived in Tehran and wished to speak with me. He passed the phone to Shahen Karamanukyan, and after the initial greetings and questions about my family's well-being, Karamanukyan said he wanted to meet with me as soon as possible. I was quite surprised since I had agreed to keep this whole thing secret and the Embassy wasn't supposed to know about it. I was also surprised that the President had dispatched Karamanukyan on a roundabout European flight rather than wait for the weekend shuttle. That told me that he too considered it a matter of the highest importance. Karamanukyan was staying at the Esteqlal Hotel, so we agreed to meet there for breakfast at 9:00 the next morning.

At breakfast, Karamanukyan said he wanted to meet with the Iranians that very day, if possible, so that he could catch the return flight to Amsterdam and get back to Yerevan as soon as possible. I explained that because it was Friday, it would be difficult to reach them – they wouldn't even be answering their cellphones – but I promised to do my best to arrange the meeting. I spent the rest of the day trying to reach my contact, without result.

He finally he picked up my call on Saturday at 9:00 AM. He was surprised and pleased that President Ter-Petrosyan had responded so quickly. He said he would call me back in an hour with the time and place of our meeting. Two hours later, he called and said we would meet for dinner at 7:00 PM in a private room at the Homa Hotel, but they wanted to meet with me separately beforehand.

I immediately called Karamanukyan and arranged to pick him up at 6:30 PM. He suggested that Azad Manukyan take part as the interpreter. He said Azad was trusted by the President and had served as his interpreter when he met with President Hashemi-Rafsanjani. I told him it wasn't up to me, I would have to check with the Iranian group. When I met with them at 5:00 PM and told them what Karamanukyan had suggested, the senior official rejected any role for Azad Manukyan. He said Manukyan was in charge of security at the Embassy (which was news to me) and if he were to take part in the discussion, he would be obligated to report the details to the Ambassador which was contrary to the conditions both sides had agreed upon.

"Information is like a pyramid," he said. "The smallest leak from the top inevitably filters down and spreads out on the lowest level."

Instead, he asked me to serve as interpreter, saying I was the most trustworthy person for them. Then he asked about Karamanukyan's background and his relationship with the Armenian President. I said that, as far as I knew, he was born in Aleppo, like the President, and he had repatriated to Armenia and received his education in Yerevan. He was the President's chief of staff and they had a close relationship.

I left them and drove over to the Esteqlal to pick up Karamanukyan. He was waiting at the entrance with Azad Manukyan. When he greeted me and said they were ready to go, I had to take him aside and explain the situation, which he accepted without demur. We said goodbye to Manukyan and headed back to the Homa.

A Meeting with President Ter-Petrosyan's Emissary

When we entered the lobby a few minutes before 7:00 PM, we were approached by a young man who greeted me and escorted us to an elevator. We got out on the seventh floor and he led us to a room where three Iranians welcomed us so amicably that an outsider might have taken the scene for a family reunion. After the initial greetings, Karamanukyan described his position and said that he had come with specific instructions from the President of Armenia. The leader of the Iranian group thanked him for coming and introduced himself as the Deputy Director of the USA–Europe–Caucasus Division in the Ministry of Foreign Affairs, a specialist in the Diaspora, and presently heading the Armenia desk at the Supreme National Security Council.

"Iran is governed according to Islamic principles and I myself am a pious man," he said. "Armenia's independence is important to Iran, and my country will do whatever it is asked to do in order to safeguard your country's independence."

Karamanukyan interjected to thank him for these words and for his warm welcome. The Iranian noted that they had chosen me to take a message to the Armenian government because they considered me an honorable citizen and the most reliable person for the mission. Karamanukyan seconded him on that:

"Baron Aharonian is well respected and much trusted by Armenia."

"Iran and Armenia appear to have a strong relationship, but things are not what they seem," the senior official resumed. "Our relationship is not strong enough to benefit either country, nor is it contributing enough to achieve Iran's goals. That is why Iran is proposing to develop new avenues toward improving our relationship. Specifically, we are proposing a core bilateral group to examine shared concerns, exchange views and take prompt decisions, because certain issues have become obstacles to the improvement of our relationship."

When Karamanukyan asked for an example, the senior Iranian cited a speech by President Ter-Petrosyan in which he had advocated unifying the two Holy Sees under the worldwide jurisdiction of Echmiadzin.

"Given its relevance to Armenians in Iran and to Iranian Armenians outside the country, he should have discussed it with the Iranian government before he ever made such a statement. Sensitive issues like that can get out of hand."

He reiterated his point that the two countries had common interests that could only be achieved through cooperation. Karamanukyan took his point but said the President had merely expressed his opinion and had not translated it into action.

The senior Iranian brought up another example. At the height of the Gharabagh war, when a group of local Azeris had attacked the Armenian Embassy in Tehran, the Ambassador had fled the building, yet the police had arrived immediately and stopped the attack.

"The Ambassador should have remained at his post," he said. "His flight showed that he acted out of fear. That was contrary to the spirit of our struggle and our relationship. Our embassies have been attacked and occupied at least forty times, but our government has never strayed from its chosen path."

Karamanukyan was rapidly taking notes. I noticed that when the Iranian touched on matters concerning the Embassy, he switched to another sheet of paper.

Next, the Iranian mentioned Ambassador Nikkar-Esfahani:

"Our government had specific reasons for appointing him to head the mission in Yerevan, but the Armenian government failed to understand that. And there were other unpleasant incidents that President Hashemi-Rafsanjani chose to ignore. He kept the relationship on an even keel because of his deep love for Armenia."

Karamanukyan said he didn't know what the gentleman was referring to and asked for clarification. Without hesitating, the Iranian reeled off a list of complaints. He said the first mistake was liberating Shushi when the Armenian President was visiting Iran in May 1992. The second mistake was capturing Kelbajar in April 1993 without giving Iran a heads up. The third mistake was downing an Iranian Air Force C-130 over Gharabagh on March 17, 1994. En route from Moscow to Tehran, the pilots experienced technical difficulties and requested permission to land in Azerbaijan, but Azerbaijani air control at Kantsag (Ganja) misdirected them to Stepanakert and Gharabagh's self-targeting air-defense system locked onto the plane and shot it down, killing all thirty-two on board. Among the passengers were members of Iran's Moscow Embassy staff and a number of Iranian students. They were heading home for Nowruz.

Karamanukyan made no response but merely listened and took notes.

Now the senior Iranian official turned to multilateral relations. He said Iran was disappointed that Armenia had failed to insist on Iran's inclusion in the Minsk Group. (Established by the Organization for Security and Cooperation in Europe to resolve the conflict in Nagorno Gharabagh, the Minsk Group had sanctioned the Russian-brokered ceasefire agreement in May 1994.)

Karamanukyan pointed out that Armenia had never backed away from its policy of maintaining good relations with Iran, despite all the pressures from the West, and especially from the USA. He said the good relationship between our two countries was proof of Armenia's staunch resistance to such pressures. The Iranian replied that his government was likewise unbending in the face of similar pressures, and he cited the example of Saddam Hussein who was seeking support from Eastern leaders, in exchange for which he was promising to do his utmost to sabotage Iran.

The senior Iranian official was a skillful diplomat, alternately attacking and conciliating his interlocutor. Having thus laid out a list of "unpleasant incidents," he expressed his government's appreciation of Armenia's recent abstention in a UN vote to investigate human rights abuses in Iran. Then he said that Iran was aware of the close cooperation between Armenia and Greece and would like to be part of that cooperative relationship. Karamanukyan countered that Armenia had established close relations with France too and would like to see Iran do the same. The Iranians responded positively to that suggestion and repeated that Iran's foreign policy was based on friendly relations with its neighbors.

As an example, the senior Iranian official brought up the situation in Afghanistan. He said Iran, Saudi Arabia and the USA had reached an understanding a year ago to cooperate in resolving the conflict there, and the Russian Federation and four Central Asian Republics had signed a joint declaration only a month ago (in October 1996), urging the UN Security Council to seek a comprehensive settlement of the conflict, and now these two international constellations were starting to coordinate their work. According to him, Iranian diplomacy had forced the USA to cooperate with Iran on Afghanistan, even though they had no diplomatic relations, and he cited press reports that Foreign Minister Dr. Velayati had confirmed the exchange of messages between Iran and the USA via the US Interests Section in the Swiss Embassy.

The senior Iranian official restated his main contention that Iran and Armenia had parallel interests in the Caucasus that could only be safeguarded through cooperation. (A few days after this meeting, foreign media reported that the USA was providing Azerbaijan with military training, despite Congressional restrictions on aid to Baku. In fact, Azerbaijan was being drawn into NATO through its Partnership for Peace program and American military advisors were operating under NATO's aegis).

At this point, Karamanukyan sought to redirect the conversation to North/South issues, and he mentioned a proposed natural gas pipeline from Russia to the Mediterranean that would supply Israel. It was obvious that the Iranians knew nothing about this plan and its revelation was a coup for Armenia.

The Iranians then raised the issue of Kurdistan, although I didn't understand what it had to do with Armenia. The senior official said foreign powers seemed to be creating tensions in the Kurdish areas, but neither side wished to delve too deeply into the issue and that discussion soon came to a close.

The senior Iranian official then brought up the commercial relationship between the two countries and insisted that it must be strengthened. According to him, $50 million in annual trade would be a realistic and respectable goal. He said that Armenia should have no fear that importing natural gas from Iran would compromise her independence or freedom of action, and he alluded to the comments of an Armenian government official.

Karamanukyan asked for the man's name, but the Iranian said his identity was immaterial since he had already been relieved of his duties. (I knew for a fact that he was referring to Foreign Minister Papazyan who had been replaced by Alexander Arzoumanyan in the new cabinet announced earlier in the week.)

Finally, the senior Iranian official said that Iran was ready to cooperate with Armenia in all spheres and welcomed the frank exchange of views. As topics of common interest, he mentioned the activities of the ARF, the work of the Armenian Church, the resolution of various political issues, and of course, problems related to bilateral trade. In conclusion, the two sides agreed to present proposals around five major categories: politics, national security, information, trade and development.

Unauthorized Fundraising

Once that plan was agreed, the formal discussion concluded and the conversation turned to other issues. But even then, the senior Iranian official sought to enlighten and caution Mr. Karamanukyan. He mentioned the name of a certain "Mrs. Manougian" and asked how she was connected to the Armenian government. Karamanukyan said he knew of no one by that name who might have contacts with his government. The Iranian countered that, according to his information, she had worked in the office of the President and she was in charge of an Armenian charity. I interjected to say that must be Mrs. Manoushag Petrossian – her husband was an Iranian Armenian who had repatriated to Armenia many years ago. I knew him as the executive director of the All-Armenian Fund. Karamanukyan said Petrossian had just been appointed to an important position in the Ministry of Science. I said Mrs. Petrossian had visited Iran two years ago, looking for her husband's uncle, and I had assisted her. She found him working in a shoe factory in the Molavi Bazaar in southeast Tehran and talked to him for two hours.

The senior Iranian official confirmed that she was indeed the woman he had in mind. She had sought help from the Armenian Prelacy and various community organizations in raising funds for Armenia, but she went home empty-handed because the Armenian Embassy had failed to inform the Iranian government in advance. He said no one had the right to raise funds in Iran for any outside entity without permission from the government. To emphasize his point, he said no one had the right to drink a glass of water in Iran without informing the national security apparatus, and when it came to raising money, Armenia must inform the Foreign Ministry so that the

Interior Ministry could make the necessary arrangements. I noticed that Karamanukyan was taking notes as fast as he could.

I should mention that the failure of Mrs. Petrossian's mission was related to the struggle between the ARF and President Ter-Petrosyan. Some people thought the ARF had ordered its members not to donate to the All-Armenian Fund because of its vendetta against the Armenian President, and I had protested to Archbishop Manoukian at the time. When I faulted him for the community's failure to contribute, he made no reply. Now I understood why. The Iranian government had quashed the campaign.

After the farewells, I drove Karamanukyan back to the Esteqlal Hotel. He told me he was satisfied with the meeting and he thanked me for carrying out my national duty so well. He said he couldn't remember a more frank and transparent discussion between representatives of Iran and Armenia and he considered it a turning point in their relationship.

Chapter 33

A Series of Historic Meetings

In late December 1996, Iranian Vice President Hassan Habibi headed a 120-member delegation to Yerevan. The delegation included the Deputy Ministers of Industry and Communications, the director of the Customs Service, bankers, merchants and members of the Iranian Chamber of Commerce, Industry and Mining. I and several other members of the Iran-Armenia Chamber of Commerce (IACOC) were also invited to join the delegation.

We split up into various groups dealing with trade, industry, banking and social issues. I and my colleagues Meline Piroomian and Razmik Tomas from the IACOC took part in meetings with representatives of the Armenian Ministry of Trade. We spent two full days in negotiations. At one point, I suggested that the IACOC organize an exhibition of Iranian products in Yerevan next year. Both sides liked the idea and we decided to add it to the draft articles of agreement.

At the end of the second day, the Iranians hosted a banquet where President Ter-Petrosyan and several Ministers were the guests of honor. As the affair was winding down and the Iranians were saying goodbye to the Armenian dignitaries, the President made eye contact with me and shook my hand. He came back a little later and we struck up a conversation. He thanked me for my patriotism and said these meetings were facilitating a rapprochement between our two countries. I told him that while some may oppose his policies, I had the utmost respect for him and the office he served. I wanted him to know that I believed in him and the work he was doing for Armenia and its people. Standing by while we conversed were Vice President Gagik Harutyunyan, Prime Minister Armen Sargsyan, Transportation Minister Henrik Kochinyan, Minister of Industry Ashot Safaryan and Health Minister Ara Babloyan. They were impressed that I was the focus of his attention. When I took my leave, they each shook my hand and wished me success in my endeavors, which made me feel that I had accomplished my patriotic duty.

On Sunday morning, I accompanied several members of the delegation to meet His Holiness Garegin I at Echmiadzin. He was pleased to receive us and he reminisced about the two wonderful years he had spent as the Prelate of

Isfahan in the early 1970s. After a photo op with the Holy Father, one of his assistants gave us a tour of the museum.

At some point when we found ourselves alone, the Holy Father told me that he had just returned from a visit with Pope John Paul II, and while he was in Rome, he said, the Iranian Ambassador to the Vatican had invited him to a banquet. He felt flattered by the invitation. He also remarked that he was surprised the Iranian Vice President hadn't scheduled a visit to Echmiadzin while he was in Armenia. I was not privy to the details of Mr. Habibi's itinerary but I suggested two possible reasons, the first being the delegation's focus on purely economic issues, and secondly, it might have been thought that a visit to Echmiadzin could cause tension since the Iranian dioceses were under the jurisdiction of Antelias.

His Holiness then asked me if I had received his message regarding the meeting with the Iranian intelligence officers, but before I could answer, he told me that he planned to be in Paris during the first week of February and they were welcome to meet him there if they wished. As for his message, it was a handwritten note detailing his upcoming tour of France and the Far East. I had already conveyed that information to the Iranians and they had told me they would pass it on to the Foreign Ministry, adding that I could join them for the meeting if I liked. But I still hadn't heard anything definite from them.

The Iranian delegation returned to Tehran the next day. Both sides were pleased with the outcome. They had signed several agreements that became the cornerstone of bilateral relations between Iran and Armenia.

Foreign Minister Arzoumanyan Visits Iran

In late January 1997, Armenian Foreign Minister Alexander Arzoumanyan led a five-member delegation to Iran. They were welcomed at the airport by a group of high-level officials from the Iranian Foreign Ministry. Their itinerary called for two days of political negotiations in the capital, followed by a one-day trip to Isfahan. This time, Archbishop Papian organized a proper welcome, unlike the last time an Armenian Minister had visited New Julfa. Apparently there was now some support for rapprochement. However, the ARF activist Hrand Markarian was still in prison in Yerevan, and there was his father again, handing a letter to another Armenian Minister, demanding his son's release. Arzoumanyan responded positively, promising the elder Markarian that he would work toward that goal. When he got back to Tehran, he told me he was pleased with his visit to Isfahan. (Hrand

Markarian was finally released a year later, a week after President Ter-Petrosyan resigned from office.)

The Tehran Diocesan Council hosted a reception at the Prelacy for Mr. Arzoumanyan on January 25. Ambassador Nikkar-Esfahani and several other Iranian officials attended, as did Ambassador Bayburdyan and Consul General Armen Darbinyan. Apparently this was the first time the two Ambassadors actually met. Archbishop Manoukian and MP Vartanian were in Rome visiting the Pope, which accounted for their absence, but MP Baghoumian was present, along with the editor of *Alik*.

After words of welcome from his Diocesan Council hosts, Mr. Arzoumanyan spoke to the gathering about the relationship between Armenia and Iran and extolled the success of Vice President Habibi's recent visit to Yerevan. He added that his own visit was a continuation of that bilateral exchange and expressed his hope for its further development. Ambassador Bayburdyan followed up with similar remarks, and then he said that he hoped the Armenian Church would one day be unified under a single leadership. Judging from the looks on some people's faces, that particular comment was not well received. Next, Ambassador Nikkar-Esfahani spoke to the gathering. He said that successful bilateral relations depended upon the continuing engagement of both sides. On the domestic front, he described Iran as one of the most democratic countries in the world. As evidence of this, he said there were many functioning churches in Iran but in Armenia there were only three.

During the question-and-answer session that followed, most of the questions addressed to Mr. Arzoumanyan concerned the ongoing dispute between the ARF and President Ter-Petrosyan. He said he was confident that the dispute could be resolved through consultation and negotiation. He also said the unified stance of Armenians worldwide was vital for the Republic of Armenia, especially now that Artsakh (Nagorno Gharabagh) was approaching a critical juncture.

After the formal program concluded, Ambassador Nikkar-Esfahani approached me and said he was not pleased with Ambassador Bayburdyan's reference to the issue of Church reunification: it was an inappropriate subject for discussion at the ambassadorial level. At that point, Ardavazd Baghoumian and the editor of *Alik* joined us and started bashing the Armenian government. Nikkar-Esfahani calmly responded by upholding his government's policy toward Armenia. Then he turned back to me and told me that a few weeks earlier, when Vice President Habibi's delegation was in

Yerevan, he was present when Telman Ter-Petrosyan gave the Vice President a copy of *How the Meghri Bridge Was Built*, which includes a photograph of myself. Leafing through the book, Habibi pointed to the photo and asked who it was, and Telman identified me as an Iranian Armenian who had played an important role in building the Meghri Bridge, which Mr. Habibi was happy to hear.

The heated atmosphere of a few minutes earlier cooled off as our conversation continued in this vein, but then Baghoumian and his colleague turned up the heat again, interjecting that President Ter-Petrosyan's government was politically inept. For a moment, I was almost ashamed to be an Armenian. It was inconceivable to me that those two university-educated individuals would vilify the Armenian government in front of Iran's first fully accredited Ambassador to Armenia.

The next day I flew to Yerevan, and as it happened, I was seated next to Mr. Arzoumanyan and Shahen Avakian, a French-educated Iranian lawyer who worked with him in the Armenian Foreign Ministry. We had a very candid conversation during which I mentioned the previous night's unpleasant exchange between the Iranian Ambassador, the Armenian MP and the editor of *Alik*. I told Mr. Arzoumanyan that the Ambassador had suggested that *Alik* publish the bilateral agreements recently signed by Iran and Armenia, but the editor had declined, saying the paper had no access to those documents. Now I asked Mr. Arzoumanyan to provide me with a copy of the agreements. He seemed pleased by my request and he asked Mr. Avakian to see that I got it.

"There are no secret codicils," he added, "there is nothing to hide."

As promised, I got a copy of the agreements and I sent it to *Alik*.

I was impressed by Mr. Arzoumanyan. Despite his youth – he was thirty-eight years old at the time – I thought he was doing an admirable job as Foreign Minister.

Speaker Araktsyan Visits Tehran

Practically on the heels of the Foreign Minister's visit, the Speaker of the Armenian National Assembly, Babken Araktsyan, arrived in Tehran on February 1, 1997, at the head of a fifteen-member delegation. Mr. Araktsyan met with President Hashemi-Rafsanjani, Speaker Ali-Akbar Nateq-Nuri and other officials.

A few months earlier, at the request of a number of Japanese companies doing business in Iran, the IACOC had hosted an event at the Armenian Club where I made a presentation on the economic situation in Armenia. Afterwards, the Japanese Commercial Development Board wrote to enlist our help in organizing a visit to Armenia. We worked with the Ministry of Industry to set up a tour for executives from some twenty corporations, including JGC, Marubeni, Mitsubishi, Panasonic, Sony and Sumitomo. IACOC members Souren Shahbazian and Rafik Der Petrossian led the tour, and they spent a week visiting various factories, most of which were unfortunately no longer functioning. Some of their proprietors had asked what the Japanese investors could do for them, and after being told that this was purely a fact-finding mission, they didn't even bother to show up when the Japanese executives visited their establishments.

The Japanese were most impressed by Mars Electronics & Robotics LLC, whose general manager, Stepan Demirchyan (the son of Karen Demirchyan), showed them around the entire plant and provided detailed information about its operations. Thanks in part to his succinct and intelligent remarks which he delivered in English, the JGC Corporation, an international engineering and construction company based in Yokohama, decided to invest in Armenia.

Toward this end, when Speaker Araktsyan and his delegation came to Tehran in February, the manager of JGC's Tehran office, Keiichi Yanagita, asked me to set up a meeting with the Armenian Minister of Industry, which I was happy to do. He met Ashot Safaryan at the Esteqlal Hotel on February 4 and told him that JGC was prepared to build a petroleum refinery in Armenia with a capacity of 25–30,000 barrels per day, and that thirty-year financing could also be arranged. Safaryan liked the idea and suggested that the raw material could come from Iran. Yanagita then asked me to set up a meeting with Ardavazd Baghoumian who was a member of the parliamentary petroleum committee. Baghoumian assured Yanagita that Iran would be more than happy to supply the refinery. Yanagita had another proposal related to Armenian coal: he said that with the latest technology, 99 percent of the raw material could be converted into electricity without emitting noxious fumes. He and I later collected samples from mines around Alaverdi and sent them to Japan for laboratory analysis.

While Araktsyan's delegation was in Tehran, I invited them to my home for dinner. Araktsyan himself was meeting with Iranian officials that night, but I was pleased to host Ashot Safaryan, Telman Ter-Petrosyan, Robert

Yengoyan, Karen Demirchyan and others. Safaryan thanked me for facilitating his meeting with Yanagita. We were all thrilled by these trilateral trade prospects, but the Armenian government rejected Yanagita's proposals and the excitement was quickly forgotten.

Logistics for a Meeting with the Supreme Patriarch

I knew that Catholicos Garegin was now in Paris, but I still didn't know whether the Iranian intelligence officers were amenable to meeting him there as he had suggested. We had a meeting at the Homa Hotel and they told me their boss preferred to meet in Geneva. I surmised they were worried about getting visas for France because of a dispute between France and Algeria in which Iran had taken sides with the latter.

I called His Holiness at the Hôtel de la Trémoille and gave him the message. He said his itinerary was now set. After visiting the Armenian communities in Nice and Lyon, he was leaving for the Far East on February 9 and he would be based at a hotel in Singapore. He gave me his phone number at the hotel and suggested the Iranians could meet him there, but if they insisted, he said, he would be back in Paris by February 27 and he could make a one-day trip to Geneva.

I took a short holiday in Darya Kenar, and as soon as I returned to Tehran, I set about finalizing the arrangements. When I tried to reach the officer in charge of logistics, I was told that he was in Isfahan for a few days. I wondered what he was doing there, but that was cleared up on February 14 by *Alik*'s front-page coverage of Vazgen Manukyan's visit to Isfahan as the guest of the Southern Diocesan Council. The story emphasized that Manukyan had been invited by the local Armenian community, not the Iranian government, and noted that he had been welcomed in New Julfa by Archbishop Papian, MP Baghoumian and ARF Bureau member Tatool Ohanian.

That same day, I was invited to a reception for Vazgen Manukyan at the Prelacy in Tehran. I recalled the Prelacy's low-key reception for Babken Araktsyan barely two weeks earlier, when the only people who came to meet the Speaker of the Armenian National Assembly were the Prelate and four priests. But the reception for Mr. Manukyan was a community-wide affair. It dawned on me that Iran was playing both sides against the middle, negotiating with the Armenian government in a series of high-profile diplomatic exchanges while facilitating the Iranian tour of Armenia's most prominent opposition leader. Iran was using the ARF as leverage to pressure the Armenian government, while the ARF was using the Church to advance its political aims and discrediting the authority of the Church in the process. I was disappointed at such political gamesmanship.

That night, I met with the Iranian intelligence officers at the Homa Hotel and told them that Catholicos Garegin would be in Paris on February 27 and he planned to return to Yerevan from there, so they needed to decide when and where they were going to meet with him. They immediately settled for Geneva on February 27 and asked me to join them. Being under tremendous pressure on the business front at the time, I reluctantly accepted.

Once that was settled, we fell into casual conversation and the senior officer asked me if I had read *The Clash of Civilizations* by Samuel Huntington. He said the author seemed to think that Islam was the greatest threat to world peace. I said I hadn't read the book. Then he started talking about a Carnegie Foundation study that saw the unification of Orthodox Christianity as the greatest potential threat. If the Orthodox Churches of Europe, Russia, Greece, Georgia and Armenia were to join forces with Iran, it would be a formidable constellation of power that could even disrupt the flow of oil from the Persian Gulf. He said the study predicted that a decade from now, Azerbaijan would have sufficient military strength to lay claim to Iranian Azarbayjan, and if that happened, Russia and Iran would lay claim to Baku, then the USA would get involved and the whole world would be on the brink of disaster, but other powers would intervene and impose peace.

I began to wonder whether this wild prediction wasn't actually part of Iran's grand strategy. These intelligence officers had already told me they were negotiating with a deputy to Patriarch Alexy II, the head of the Russian Orthodox Church. Now the senior officer said that Iran was planning to invite the Russian and the Armenian Patriarchs to visit Tehran at the same time. He said it had to be done that way in order not to offend Catholicos Aram of Cilicia. He added that he hoped some of the differences between Cilicia and Echmiadzin could be ironed out in Geneva, and he insisted once more on my presence at the meeting.

I flew out of Tehran on February 26. At the airport, I spotted three familiar intelligence officers and we pretended not to see each other, but now I was certain that the meeting was really on. As soon as I landed in Paris, I picked up my Swiss visa. Then I called Catholicos Garegin at La Trémoille. He told me he was flying to Geneva that evening and would check into the Intercontinental Hotel. He proposed to meet with the Iranians there at 11:00

the next morning. After reconfirming the arrangements, I went to my hotel and waited for the Iranian group to contact me.

Someone eventually rang and gave me a number to call. I dialed it and the head of the Iranian group picked up. He said he was in Geneva and asked whether the Catholicos was there yet. I confirmed that he was and told him the time and place of the meeting. Then I flew to Geneva and went straight to the Intercontinental where I rang the Catholicos. He welcomed me and asked if the Iranians had arrived and I confirmed that they had. I felt satisfaction at having successfully arranged such an important meeting abroad.

The next morning, I was waiting in the lobby of the Intercontinental when the senior Iranian intelligence officer came in with another man whom I hadn't met before. We sat down around a table and the senior officer cautioned me to be alert and objective in my role as interpreter. He said that Iran had good relations with the ARF and he wanted my assurance that I wouldn't disparage the party during the meeting. His concern stemmed from the fact that he had known me to criticize the ARF and its policies in previous conversations. I assured him that I was there as an Iranian citizen and would carry out my role with the utmost objectivity.

At 11:00 AM, I called His Holiness and told him the Iranians were here. Ten minutes later, Berj Msrlian stepped out of the elevator and gave me a big hug. I was taken aback, since my presence in Geneva was supposed to be strictly confidential. Moments later, I was even more surprised to see Archbishop Gyut of France. As it turned out, neither one knew about the meeting.

The Meeting in Geneva

The meeting took place in a private room on the second floor of the Intercontinental Hotel. Catholicos Garegin took the initiative and said that he wanted to explain Echmiadzin's historic role, after which he would be more than willing to answer any questions. He spoke of Bishop Drambian and Bishop Kostanian whom Echmiadzin had sent to Tehran and Isfahan, respectively, in 1943–44. In fact, he said, they were sent by the NKGB and their real mission was inimical to the Church. After they left (or were expelled) in the early 1950s, the Armenian communities in Iran were without pastoral guidance until they asked the See of Cilicia to assume responsibility, and in 1959, Antelias sent Father Ardak Manoukian to serve as the Prelate of Tehran. Of course, his presence was sanctioned by the Iranian authorities, and when the objection was raised in certain quarters that he was not an

Iranian citizen, they simply granted him citizenship. All this took place during a time of political crisis in Iran. The Shah was determined to crush the Iranian Communists and any attempt by Echmiadzin to send a pastor to Iran would have been seen as a direct threat. But now that the Cold War was over, said His Holiness, it no longer made sense for the Church to have two heads. He himself always spoke highly of Iran in his sermons and in his instructions to the followers of Echmiadzin, and many people wondered why Iran didn't recognize Echmiadzin as the official head of the Church.

The Holy Father said that his knowledge of Iran didn't come solely from books. He had personally experienced Iranian culture when he had served as the Prelate of Isfahan from 1971 to 1973. He knew perfectly well that the Shah's regime had privileged a small sector of Iranian society, just as he knew that the present regime treated everyone equally.

He evoked the efforts of his predecessor, Catholicos Vazgen I, to rekindle the people's spirituality, and he said that he himself was continuing on the same path. There were now two seminaries in Armenia with eighty-six students, he said, twenty of whom were on the path to ordination as priests.

He went on to explain that immediately after the 1988 earthquake, when he (as Catholicos Garegin II of the See of Cilicia) met with Catholicos Vazgen I, they discussed the possibility of returning the Dioceses of Greece and Iran to the jurisdiction of Echmiadzin. In the case of Greece, which had likewise been absorbed by Antelias during the Cold War, Catholicos Vazgen accepted the condition that the Prelate of Athens would retain his office. But, said Catholicos Garegin, Vazgen's death had put the whole issue on the backburner. Little did His Holiness know how well informed we Iranian Armenians were on such issues, perhaps even more so than he was.

The senior Iranian officer thanked the Holy Father for this background information. Then he said that he would like to offer a different perspective. Certain statements had been made in Tehran that were unacceptable to his government. For example, during the reception for Foreign Minister Arzoumanyan in January, Ambassador Bayburdyan had advocated the unification of the Armenian Church without first checking with the Iranian government. Many people were opposed to unification and had criticized the government for allowing such a tactless statement to be made. That was why the authorities had advised the Armenian community not to organize a big reception for Mr. Araktsyan when he came to Tehran not long after Mr. Arzoumanyan. Of course, the government couldn't control everything, he said, and he cited the incident in Isfahan two years earlier, when Prime Minister Bagratyan had been met by a wild dog and a crowd of demonstrators. He said both sides needed to cooperate and coordinate their efforts in order to prevent such unpleasant incidents.

At that point, His Holiness interjected and said frankly that those "demonstrators" were members of the ARF and the party was using the Church as leverage for political gain in Armenia because it had failed to gain a foothold there. This was a very dangerous game, he said. For his part, he went on, he couldn't fathom how the Church could take a stand on political issues in Iran, such as backing one candidate over another for the Armenian seats in the Majles, nor could he imagine intervening from Echmiadzin on behalf of someone incarcerated in Iran. Such actions would be damaging not only to the Church and its servants but to the Armenian community as a whole. Speaking for himself, he said, he neither shared the views nor approved of the actions of any political group.

The implication of his remarks was obvious: no Iranian Armenian group could act without the knowledge and approval of the Iranian government, and the Iranian government was backing the ARF against the Armenian government. At the beginning of their conversation, it seemed to me that the senior Iranian officer had been trying to back the Catholicos into a corner, but as their talk continued, I realized that, thanks to his calm demeanor, the latter had forced the former to be more cautious and restrained.

His Holiness returned to the issue of the Cilician See and said that he was well aware of Catholicos Aram's abilities. After all, he said, the younger man had been his student – implying that the Iranians should not overrate the Cilician Patriarch nor attempt to manipulate him for political gain. He noted that the ARF had organized a world tour for Catholicos Aram with the intention of undermining the influence and authority of Echmiadzin, and added that he was unaware if the Armenian Foreign Ministry provided support for his own international travels and that, in any case, Armenia's Ambassadors never discussed Church issues.

Now the senior Iranian officer tried to undercut the Holy Father by relating a story which he said was a state secret that had never been shared with an outsider. During a celebration of Lebanese Independence Day in Beirut last fall, he said, the Armenian Ambassador to Lebanon had told his Iranian counterpart that Yerevan was well aware of the close relationship between Antelias and Tehran, and that his government was hoping to undermine that relationship and strengthen the relationship between Echmiadzin and Tehran, with the ultimate goal of unifying the two Sees. As the Iranian intelligence officer saw it, the President of Armenia had delivered a message on behalf of the Supreme Patriarch and Catholicos of All Armenians.

"It's too bad your name was used without your knowledge," he added.

The look on the Holy Father's face briefly betrayed his surprise and dismay, but he retorted that he was always candid and he never needed a messenger to convey his views.

"Had I wished to send a message to the Iranian Foreign Ministry," he added, "I would have spoken to Ambassador Nikkar-Esfahani myself. In fact, I never conveyed such a message, but thank you for disclosing a state secret."

With that, the Iranian dropped the issue and began to laud Armenia for its services to Iran, especially its "patriotic support" during the Iran-Iraq War. As an amicable atmosphere was now restored, the Catholicos placed a call to Archbishop Gyut and asked him to reserve a table for four at a nearby restaurant.

While we were walking to the restaurant, I asked the senior Iranian intelligence officer if he was satisfied with the discussion. He replied that the main issue had yet to be raised and he would reserve judgment until then.

Over lunch, His Holiness spoke of his influence in the World Council of Churches, which he said was related to a project to build a school and a hospital in the Manjil-Rudbar district of northwestern Iran, where a +7 magnitude earthquake had taken some 50,000 lives in 1990. He said he had proposed this project and the WCC was helping to fund it, and he had appointed the Tehran Diocesan Council to oversee it. I admired his tactful diplomacy and the Iranians were clearly impressed too.

He went on to describe his meetings with Pope John Paul II at the Vatican in December, with President Clinton at the White House in January, and with President Chirac at the Élysée Palace earlier in February, at which point he handed the senior Iranian officer the latest issue of *Nouvelles d'Arménie* with a photograph of himself and the French President on the cover. He was obviously trying to suggest a level of influence and clout that was beyond the reach of Catholicos Aram, and I thought it was working since the two Iranians listened in awed silence.

Then he mentioned his recent meeting with Patriarch Alexy II, and the sense he had gained that there was friction among the Russian, Ukrainian and Belorussian Orthodox Churches. The senior Iranian officer commented that since the Western powers considered the potential solidarity of the Orthodox Churches a threat to their interests, that friction could well be the result of their machinations.

After lunch, we returned to our private room at the Intercontinental Hotel and the senior Iranian officer finally got to the point. He said that his government was prepared to invite Catholicos Garegin to visit Iran, on condition that the status of the Armenian dioceses in Iran would never be brought up for discussion. The theme of the proposed visit would be "peace and solidarity among the peoples of the Caucasus." His Holiness then asked specifically which government office would extend the invitation. Rather indirectly, the Iranian responded that Catholicos Aram had been invited by the Islamic Culture and Relations Organization (ICRO) which was a unit of the Supreme Leader's Office of International Relations. Catholicos Garegin said nothing, implying that an invitation from that quarter would not be sufficiently prestigious for him to accept.

He then asked whether he would be allowed to visit local churches and meet their congregations. The Iranian replied that if the ICRO were to issue the invitation, the details could be negotiated. But if the Office of the President were to invite him, then his visit would be governed by diplomatic protocol and he might not be able to visit any church or congregation. His Holiness then asked how he would meet with the three Prelates. Would they be representing their prelacies? Or would they be representing Catholicos Aram? And would the Armenian newspaper (meaning *Alik*) formally identify him as the Supreme Patriarch and Catholicos of All Armenians?

"These are internal questions the Armenians must decide for themselves," replied the senior Iranian officer. "As for the question of who will extend the invitation, that will be determined in Tehran and the decision will be relayed through a cleric."

"Perhaps you yourself could communicate the decision to me at Echmiadzin."

The senior Iranian intelligence officer ruled that out, citing security considerations. His Holiness then hinted that he would like to visit Isfahan too.

"Only a visit to Tehran is contemplated," said the Iranian.

The Holy Father countered that if he were to visit one diocese and not the others, it might cause needless tension and speculation. Perhaps as an enticement, the senior Iranian officer said that his itinerary would include a visit to St. Thaddeus Monastery and that he would be flown there from Tehran.

"It looks like you don't want me to go to Tabriz," His Holiness replied. "Somehow I can understand that, but I cannot understand why I shouldn't go to Isfahan. After all, they say 'Isfahan is half of the world'!"

The senior Iranian officer smiled at that and promised to think about it. As the meeting was drawing to a close, he and his colleague presented the Holy Father with a hand-carved wooden memento from Mashhad. The Holy Father thanked them and apologized for the fact that he had been unable to bring an appropriate gift, having come directly from Australia, but he promised to reciprocate at their next meeting. The senior Iranian officer thanked him for the meeting and I accompanied him and his colleague out of the room. I wished them a safe return and they both thanked me again for facilitating the meeting. The senior officer said it was more successful than he had expected and he might require my intermediation in the future.

I rejoined the Holy Father and told him the Iranians were quite satisfied with the meeting. He thanked me and asked me how well I knew them and why they had approached me to arrange the meeting. I told him that I had been chairman of the Diocesan Council for six years and in that capacity I had developed contacts with several highly placed government officials. Aside from that, my company was a transport firm and I had been the president of Iran's International Transport Companies Syndicate for four years. In both capacities, I had had contacts with Iranian intelligence officers. I also told him that the Foreign Ministry's Deputy Director for the Caucasus had consulted with me on more than one occasion. Furthermore, I was fully cognizant of the need for confidentiality, and no one, not even my wife, knew that I was in Geneva.

The Holy Father said that he too was satisfied with the meeting and acknowledged my input, adding that he would like me to take part in any follow-on meeting. This invitation was political, not religious, he said, at which point I told him about my earlier conversation with the senior Iranian intelligence officer and his concept of a rapprochement between Iran and the Orthodox Churches based on his reading of the Carnegie study and Samuel Huntington's "clash of civilizations" theory.

His Holiness said that he had learned a great deal during the meeting. For instance, it was news to him that Ambassador Bayburdyan had brought up the issue of Church unification, something that clearly exceeded his brief, and he said he would raise the matter with President Ter-Petrosyan and ask him to instruct the Foreign Ministry to steer clear of the issue. He considered such mistakes unavoidable and certainly unintentional. When Armenia became independent, he said, not a single politician or diplomat had any experience in international affairs because Moscow had always decided everything. Even the ARF lacked such expertise, since its experience was largely gained in the Diaspora and had nothing to do with running a country or managing a government.

He said that he himself came from a family steeped in ARF ideals, but the party was no longer what it used to be and the direction it was taking now could only have a negative impact on Armenia. As an example, he cited the recent visit to Iran of a prominent Armenian opposition figure (an allusion to Vazgen Manukyan) who had been invited by the ARF and given a platform from which to attack the Armenian government. That was a major cause of discord among Armenians at a time when the fate of Artsakh was still in the balance and they should be mobilizing every resource to meet this and other challenges facing the Republic.

Our meeting lasted half an hour. I left Geneva for Paris at 6:30 PM, and from there I flew back to Tehran. After three days of travel and six hours of intensive interpreting, I was exhausted, but I was satisfied with the results.

Second Meeting with President's Ter-Petrosyan's Emissary

During the third week of October 1997, the Armenian Embassy notified me that Shahen Karamanukyan was in Tehran and wanted to meet with me. Of course, it wasn't me he wasn't interested in meeting. Rather, he wanted me to arrange another meeting with the Iranian officials he had met at the Homa Hotel the previous November.

The meeting took place in my office at 10:00 AM on October 24, 1997. The Iranians arrived first, and Karamanukyan came in with Azad Manukyan a few minutes later. After a brief introduction, Karamanukyan said that he was pleased the meeting had been arranged so promptly and asked if it were acceptable for Mr. Manukyan to serve as interpreter. This time the Iranians made no objection.

The Iranians immediately proceeded to the main topic which was developing the bilateral relationship between Iran and Armenia. They were pleased with the diplomatic exchanges and with the way they had been presented to the public by the leaders on both sides, but they complained that the pace was still too slow. Karamanukyan pointed out that a new Prime

Minister (Robert Kocharyan) had taken office and his administration needed time to come up to speed on foreign policy issues. He also reminded his interlocutors that he had asked them to send a qualified representative to Yerevan for further talks, which the senior Iranian official conceded was true. The two sides then agreed that annual meetings were insufficient to produce a thorough analysis and understanding of important security issues.

Karamanukyan brought up the issue of Azerbaijan and observed that the USA was making substantial investments in Baku. The Iranian team replied that the USA was investing in Yerevan too. Indeed, Iran was concerned that Armenia might fall under American influence. Karamanukyan responded that Armenia was under heavy pressure from the World Bank and other international lending institutions and that those pressures, in combination with Baku's economic progress, were tilting the regional balance of power in a direction that was unacceptable to Yerevan. He mentioned Azerbaijan's recent purchase of four Boeing aircraft, but the senior Iranian official argued that such things had more public relations value than real impact, which Karamanukyan conceded.

Broaching the subject of Nagorno Gharabagh, the senior Iranian official complained that Armenia was putting out contradictory statements about negotiations with Azerbaijan. Karamanukyan replied that there had always been disagreements between the leaders of the Republic of Armenia (ROA) and the leaders of the Republic of Nagorno Gharabagh (NKR), something that only occasionally came to the attention of the public as a result of leaks to the press. He added that Russia was well aware of this internal discord but the USA was not. In any case, he said, the disagreements were over strategy more than anything else. He added that Arkady Ghukasyan (recently elected President of the NKR) was politically inexperienced but he would gain experience in due time and the discord between the ROA and the NKR would dissipate. The senior Iranian official countered that NKR Defense Minister Samvel Babayan was making public statements on issues outside his area of expertise. Karamanukyan replied that in due time he too would gain more awareness of his specific responsibilities and refrain from publicly commenting on extraneous matters.

The Iranian side was dissatisfied with these explanations and asked whether the ROA had any clear strategy to resolve the conflict. Karamanukyan replied that his government had clear goals in negotiating with Azerbaijan and he offered a specific example. The ROA had been trying to introduce the prospect of a railway linking Armenia and Iran via the Azerbaijani exclave of Nakhichevan. In the event that gambit failed, the ROA was prepared to invest in an alternative route through the province of Zangezur. That project would cost at least $3 billion and take at least three years to complete. If Tehran approved of the project, Yerevan would be willing to sign an agreement immediately, on condition that construction begin no later than the year 2000.

Then Karamanukyan mentioned that his government had decided to build a new nuclear power plant. (The two-unit Metsamor plant, located some twenty miles west of Yerevan, had been shut down since the Spitak earthquake, but given the energy crisis, the second unit had been restarted in 1995.) Karamanukyan acknowledged that many countries opposed the new project, including the USA, but he said it was supported by Russia, France and Germany. It was still under study and the projected cost was $5 billion.

The Iranian side returned to the issue of Nagorno Gharabagh. They said that statements President Ter-Petrosyan had made during his 1992 visit to Tehran did not comport with his subsequent actions and that was incomprehensible to them. When Karamanukyan asked them to specify the statements they were referring to, they cited the Armenian President's undertakings to bring about a ceasefire and pursue negotiations for a lasting solution to the conflict. Karamanukyan replied that Armenia had fulfilled both promises and that Iran's view of the negotiations was at odds with reality. Armenia was conducting high-level negotiations with Azerbaijan under the auspices of the European Council, Russia and the USA in the context of the Minsk Group. The Iranian side suggested that Armenia should also make use of the Diaspora lobby.

It was obvious to me that Iran sided with Armenia on the issue of Artsakh, since her negotiators never criticized Armenia's use of force, but they needed assurances that the ROA was not backpedaling and was on course with negotiations. Karamanukyan assured them that this was the case and the Iranians seemed content with that. But they were still concerned about the harsh criticism of President Ter-Petrosyan that they were hearing both in the ROA and in the Diaspora, especially on the question of Artsakh. (Of course, I myself heard such opinions expressed whenever I visited Yerevan.) Karamanukyan assured them that the peace process was still on track but that it would be at least another eight to fifteen years before the conflict was finally resolved. Then he said that if there were only three people in the room, he could divulge additional information. Taking the cue, I got up and left the room, followed by all the Iranians except the senior official.

His private meeting with Karamanukyan and their interpreter lasted fifteen minutes, after which they came out and joined the rest of us. Karamanukyan thanked me for hosting the meeting, then turned to the Iranian officials and said that Armenia and Iran were friendly neighbors and must maintain open and honest communication for the sake of their security and their mutual interests. Apropos, he mentioned that, prior to this meeting, he had met with other officials in the Iranian Foreign Ministry (whose positions he did not know), but he had been disappointed with the results. The Iranians commiserated with him and said the issues were much clearer now. Judging from their facial expressions, I felt they were satisfied with the meeting.

After the Armenian team left, the Iranians stayed behind for a moment and thanked me for my patriotic role. They looked at the framed photographs on the walls of my office and asked me about one in particular, that of myself with Supreme Leader Ayatollah Khamenei which had been taken some fifteen years earlier when he was the President of the Islamic Republic. It was on that occasion that I, along with Archbishop Manoukian and the late Hrair Khalatian, had presented him with the funds collected by the Iranian Armenian community for the families of soldiers martyred in the Iran-Iraq War.

On November 2, I hosted Mr. Karamanukyan and his entourage for dinner at my home. While discussing politics over dinner, my wife Bella candidly mentioned the negative feelings in the community toward President Ter-Petrosyan. Karamanukyan said the rumors of his selling out Artsakh were pure fiction, cooked up by his opponents. He advised us to ignore the rumors and read the transcript of the President's September 26 press conference.

Chapter 34

Reflections on Politics and Diplomacy

In March 1998, my wife and I flew to the USA to spend some time with our children over the Nowruz holiday. During the long flight from Paris to Los Angeles, I finally had time to go over my notes and reflect on the high-level meetings I had attended and consider the larger regional geopolitical issues.

The contrast between the newborn Armenian state and the mindset and diplomatic experience of the 3000-year–old Persian state was striking. It was obvious during the two meetings I had attended with Karamanukyan and the Iranian officials that the latter had access to a vast store of information about regional developments which they were able to manipulate to their advantage. When they referred to the "Diaspora lobby," they meant the Armenian National Committee of America, and when they evoked the power of the Diaspora, they had the ARF in mind. They knew Karamanukyan was aware of this but they emphasized their familiarity with internal Armenian politics and their close ties with Diaspora organizations in order to provoke him into stating his government's true position on various issues. Nevertheless, Karamanukyan successfully ignored such provocations and managed to suggest creative solutions to some complex issues.

The key question for me was the role of Armenia and the Armenian Diaspora – including the Armenian political parties operating in the Diaspora – and how Iran was able to manipulate them. When the Islamic government first came to power, it saw the ARF as being pro-American, and consequently it allowed the emergence of dissident Armenian groups in order to weaken the party's hold over the community. Nevertheless, the ARF continued to dominate the Iranian diocesan structures which were all under the jurisdiction of Antelias.

When Armenia declared its independence in 1991, Iran was one of the first states to recognize the new Republic. Its diplomatic mission consisting of Chargé d'affaires Ghasemi, First Secretary Koleyni and two intelligence officers immediately established temporary quarters at the Hrazdan Hotel in Yerevan, and after the mission established a permanent Embassy and expanded its staff, it developed a useful relationship with the ARF.

At the time, Iran had little information about Armenia's internal politics, but the ARF was propagandizing and recruiting all over the country and it soon emerged as a faction in the so-called First Convocation of the Supreme Council, the Republic's transitional parliamentary body. Iran needed a reliable political party through which to establish solid relations with the new government of Armenia. Iranian strategists were also aware of the fact that the ARF was politically active in Lebanon and other countries in the region and they sought to develop relations with those countries through the ARF.

Revolutionary Iran had forged strong relations with President Hafez al-Assad of Syria. In fact, the Islamic Republic developed a trilateral relationship with Syria and the Lebanese Hezbollah who were considered "family" or at least "close friends." But Iran needed to establish relations with non-Muslim countries too, and it seems that its strategists had determined that it could do this through the ARF, which had developed useful connections with Armenians in key countries in order to achieve its own ends. At the same time, Iran was trying to expand its international influence through religious centers and their leaders, and of course, the ARF controlled the See of Cilicia based in Lebanon.

When ARF Bureau chief Hrair Maroukhian visited Tehran in April 1993, he met with officials in the Foreign Affairs Ministry and the Ministry of Intelligence and Security, and the upshot of those meetings was that the ARF agreed to support Iran in its international lobbying efforts, while Iran agreed to cooperate with the ARF in Lebanon and Armenia and to allow the party more freedom to operate in Iran. Domestically, this was a replay of the post-coup arrangement forty years earlier, when the young Shah, restored to his throne, recognized the ARF as the sole representative of the Iranian Armenian community and thereby sought to neutralize the community's radical leftist elements.

In Armenia, however, relations between the ARF and the government of President Ter-Petrosyan deteriorated to the point where the President banned the party altogether in 1994. It was then that the Iranian government, no longer able to rely on the ARF but still intent on developing political and economic relations with Armenia, began to cultivate me as an intermediary through the Ministry of Intelligence and Security.

Iranian strategists saw Armenia as a gateway to Europe. When they compared the international standing and influence of the two Catholicosates, it was clear that Echmiadzin cast a longer shadow than Antelias, so they began to hedge their bets. While Antelias could develop relations with Christian Churches in the Middle East and Europe, and to a lesser extent, the USA, it had little or no influence with the Eastern Orthodox establishments in Russia, Ukraine and Belarus, especially when these latter had close relations with Echmiadzin dating back to the Soviet era, hence Iran's motivation to meet with Catholicos Garegin I. And because the ARF and the Armenian government remained at loggerheads, both were kept in the dark about Iranian contacts with the Supreme Patriarch. The potential advantage to the latter was that if he were to visit Iran at the invitation of the government, the Iranian Armenian community would be persuaded that Echmiadzin was the legitimate seat of their spiritual leadership, and Antelias would be definitively relegated to a subordinate role.

On New Year's Eve in 1997, the Iranian intelligence officers whose meeting with the Supreme Patriarch I had facilitated invited me to lunch at the Laleh Hotel (the former Intercontinental) on Dr. Hossein Fatemi Street. They wanted to thank me and present me with a gift. Three months later, at the start of Nowruz, I called their chief and asked for another meeting. I wanted to reciprocate their gesture and make sure they knew that everything I had done was my patriotic duty as an Iranian. That was our last meeting. Years have passed and I have neither seen nor heard from them again, because Armenia had a regime change in 1998 and President Kocharyan, in contrast to his predecessor, had very good relations with both the ARF and the Iranian government, and consequently, there was no longer any need for intermediaries like me.

Ambassador Bayburdyan

Despite the difficulties Ambassador Bayburdyan faced due to the conflict between the ARF and the government he represented, non-affiliated community members (and there were many such people) spared no effort to support him and facilitate the smooth and efficient operation of the Embassy. Yet ARF influence over the Iranian dioceses was such that when the Ambassador's tenure was coming to an end in the summer of 1998, one of those dioceses refused to cooperate in organizing a farewell event. A group of fifty politically unaffiliated private citizens therefore hosted a farewell dinner for him at the Armenian Club. As a token of our sincere appreciation for his services, we presented him with a beautiful carpet which we had purchased solely through our personal contributions.

Ambassador Vahan Arak'eli Bayburdyan (b. 1933) was an Orientalist, an accomplished linguist and a historian who was very well informed about the history of Iran, and especially the history of its relations with Armenia. His first book was a study of the early history of the Armenian community of New Julfa which he wrote in Russian. He was a professor of Persian at Yerevan State University when he was drafted to serve as Ambassador, and during his tenure, he completed a book on the role of Iranian Armenian merchants in international commerce in the seventeenth century, which was published in two editions in Tehran in 1996, one in Armenian and the other in Persian translation by Edic Baghdasarian. After Ambassador Bayburdyan left office, he headed the Iranian Department at the Institute of Oriental Studies in Yerevan and he subsequently founded the Faculty of International Relations at Yerevan State University.

Ambassador Gharibjanyan

Ambassador Gegham Dirani Gharibjanyan (b. 1951) succeeded Ambassador Bayburdyan in February 1999 and served until December 2004. I had met him in September 1998 during the celebration of Armenian Independence Day at the Sports Complex in Yerevan. I was with a group of government officials and intellectuals gathered around Karen Demirchyan when Gharibjanyan approached us and Demirchyan introduced him as Armenia's next Ambassador to Iran.

Gharibjanyan was a born diplomat. His family was well known in Armenia. His paternal uncle had served as Minister of Education during the Soviet period, and he himself had served on the staff of the Soviet Embassy in Tehran for many years. He spoke Persian very well.

When Ambassador Gharibjanyan took up his post in Tehran, a year had passed since President Ter-Petrosyan had resigned and Robert Kocharyan was elected to replace him. The ARF had no disagreement with Kocharyan and therefore relations between the party and the Embassy improved. That had a positive influence on the community, since the conflicts and tension disappeared, and Ambassador Gharibjanyan played a significant role in that development. He was quick to realize that the community was not a monolith, and he began to "play on two strings," as they say, aiming to please the ARF and its opposition as well as the politically unaffiliated. For example, he never mentioned the prospect of unifying the Armenian Apostolic Church under a single catholicosate at Echmiadzin. On the contrary, he developed excellent relations with Archbishop Sebouh Sarkissian who succeeded Archbishop Manoukian as the Prelate of Tehran in 2000. And he hosted a lavish annual celebration of Armenian Independence Day at the Embassy, inviting members of the ARF and other Iranian Armenian community leaders, high-level Iranian government officials and foreign diplomats stationed in Tehran.

President Kocharyan's first state visit at the invitation of President Khatami in 2001 helped strengthen relations between the two countries. In addition to his official reception and high-level meetings, he met with the community at St. Sarkis Church and the Ararat Center, where he delivered a speech to a packed Sassountsi David Hall. I well remember his words: "Artsakh is ours and will never be separated from Armenia." His presentation generated a great deal of enthusiasm in the audience.

An extremely important development during Ambassador Gharibjanyan's term was the finalization of an agreement to deliver natural gas from Iran to Armenia, in exchange for which Armenia would deliver electricity to Iran. This was confirmed by President Khatami's first state visit to Armenia in 2004. Construction of the pipeline began that year and it was inaugurated by President Kocharyan and President Ahmadinejad in 2007.

In late 2004, as Ambassador Gharibjanyan's term was coming to an end, the three Armenian Prelates co-sponsored a lavish farewell event at the Ararat Center's Vachik Gharabegian Hall. Ambassador Gharibjanyan was subsequently appointed Deputy Foreign Minister for the Middle East and he later served as Ambassador to Qatar and Abu Dhabi in the United Arab Emirates.

Ambassador Nazaryan

Ambassador Garen (Karen) Arshagi Nazaryan (b. 1966) succeeded Ambassador Gharibjanyan. After earning a Master's degree in Oriental Studies at Yerevan State University, Nazaryan continued his education at the Diplomatic Academy of Moscow. He joined the new Republic's Ministry of Foreign Affairs in 1991 and served as Armenia's Permanent Representative to the United Nations, both before and after his term as Ambassador to Iran. He presented his credentials to President Khatami on February 23, 2005.

Ambassador Nazaryan quickly gained the trust and respect of the Iranian Armenian community, in large part because of his modesty, his measured conduct and his diplomatic experience. I first became aware of his capabilities at a reception for Catholicos Aram, where more than thirty diplomats from various countries were present. The Ambassador delivered a speech in fluent English that left a very positive impression on me. (For his part, Catholicos Aram responded in English, continued in French, switched to Arabic, and concluded his remarks in Armenian.) I and other members of the Iran-Armenia Chamber of Commerce subsequently met with the Ambassador numerous times for the purpose of helping Armenia's progress and development.

On September 21, 2005, Ambassador Nazaryan organized a two-part celebration of Armenian Independence Day. He invited Iranian officials and other Muslim guests to the first part, and Armenian community leaders and non-Muslim diplomats to the second part which featured an extraordinary performance by a musical group brought in from Gharabagh. The Ambassador addressed his guests in Armenian, Persian and English, and the Iranian officials were impressed by his command of Persian which they took as evidence of his government's respect for the Iranian nation.

It is worth noting that Ambassador Nazaryan's grandmother was born in Isfahan and that his grandfather is buried in New Julfa. He was able to find his grandfather's gravesite with the assistance of local Armenians.

Chapter 35

Business and Philanthropy in Armenia

Following up on a suggestion I had made during trade talks in December 1996, the Iran-Armenia Chamber of Commerce (IACOC) arranged with the government to sponsor an exhibition of Iranian products in Yerevan the following May. Three Iranian trade fairs had already been held in Yerevan, but this was the first one organized by the IACOC. The ten-day fair was held in Armenia's largest indoor arena, the Sports Complex overlooking the Hrazdan River gorge west of the city center. One hundred and ten exhibitors took part.

Prime Minister Robert Kocharyan presided over the opening ceremony. It began with the Iranian and the Armenian national anthems performed by the Armenian Philharmonic Orchestra under the baton of Loris Tjeknavorian. After a short welcoming speech, I invited Iranian Ambassador Nikkar-Esfahani to the podium. Armenia's Deputy Minister of Industry and Trade also spoke. Each speech was punctuated with a flourish from the orchestra. Prime Minister Kocharyan then ascended to the second-floor exhibition space where he cut the ribbon at each booth and engaged the attendants with technical questions about their products.

Our trade fair received wide coverage in both the Armenian and the Iranian press. The Armenian weekly *Gortsarar* (Executive) published an article extolling the advantages of bilateral relations in an international context, casting Iran as "the most credible counterforce" to Turkey's "pan-national ambitions" in the Caucasus and Central Asia. *Gortsarar* suggested that Armenia could help Iran circumvent the "D'Amato principle," a reference to America's Iran and Libya Sanctions Act which imposed sanctions on firms doing business with either country. The journal also suggested that Iran could benefit from Armenian scientific and technological expertise in its twenty-five–year plan for a future "economy without oil." It urged Armenia to become "a bridge between the East and the West," as Iran was attempting to do, and commended business professionals from both countries for taking steps in that direction. It concluded with a recommendation that politicians in both countries recognize their common interests and open the way to bilateral free trade.

Second IACOC Trade Fair, 1998

With the IACOC's second trade fair, which opened at the Sports Complex on November 19, 1998, the exhibition became an annual event. After President Ter-Petrosyan had resigned in February, Prime Minister Kocharyan had briefly served as Acting President, and in March, he was elected President of Armenia. He sent his representative, David Zadoyan, to preside over the fair's opening ceremony. Six days later, President Kocharyan himself toured the exhibition with a party of government officials and businessmen, including Hayk Gevorgyan, the Minister of Industry and Trade, and Aram Vardanyan, the chairman of the Union of Manufacturers and Businessmen of Armenia (UMBA, founded by Telman Ter-Petrosyan in 1995). Iran's incoming Ambassador Mohammad Farhad Koleyni headed the welcoming party and I served as interpreter while the President toured the exhibits.

The first display that caught his eye was that of the Ministry of Culture and Islamic Guidance which featured scenic paintings and photographs and traditional miniatures. I translated the captions on the photos and the inscriptions in the miniatures for him, and Ershad's representative presented him with some beautifully designed books.

Moving along from one display to the next, I was struck by President Kocharyan's powers of recall. He compared a lathe on display to one he had seen the previous year and pointed out the improvements in its design. Another pleasant surprise occurred at the Bank Mellat booth hosted by the manager of the Yerevan branch. He had been studying Armenian and he welcomed the President in his own language and followed up with a lively sales pitch.

Touring the section devoted to Iranian teas, President Kocharyan was offered a sample of Gilani tea. He accepted a glass and drank it, and said he liked it very much. Iranians pay particular attention to the quality of their tea. They prefer the loose-leaf kind, which involves seeping the leaves in a kettle atop a samovar. It takes about fifteen minutes for the tea to infuse the water with its distinctive coloring. Then a small amount of the brew is poured into tea glasses and twice as much boiling water is added from the samovar. There is a Persian saying, *Chayi bayad labsouz, labriz ve labdouz bashad* (Tea must overflow from the cup, must inflame and burn the lips), which means that tea must be served in abundance, very hot, and so delicious that one purses one's lips as if they were sewn together.

At the end of his tour, President Kocharyan told the press that he was very impressed.

"Last year, the exhibitors were thinking in terms of cooperation, but this year they have moved beyond that and they're thinking in terms of joint ventures."

Third IACOC Trade Fair, 1999

Our third trade fair (November 26 – December 6, 1999) took place in unusual circumstances. Only a month earlier, on October 27, Armenia had been shaken by the tragic assassination of Speaker Karen Demirchyan and Prime Minister Vazgen Sargsyan and six others in the National Assembly chamber. We considered cancelling the event but we decided to go ahead with it. Our reasoning was that it would raise people's spirits.

The exhibition showcased the products of some forty companies. Acting Prime Minister Aram Sargsyan (brother of the late Prime Minister) opened the fair at the Sports Complex, and afterwards, we invited him and his Ministers, along with Ambassador Koleyni and MP Vartan Vartanian, to a reception in the VIP lounge. There I was honored with a gold medal from the Union of Manufacturers and Businessmen, a gesture inspired by UMBA chairman Aram Vardanyan. As Prime Minister Sargsyan presented the award, he said,

"I always enjoy handing out awards, but since this one comes from UMBA, it comes from me too, and therefore I offer it with great pleasure."

I in turn presented him with my book of Armenian translations, *Live a Healthy Life*. He said he was surprised to learn that I was an author, but he must have known about my book because I had already given copies to his Ministers.

The day's events were covered by the Armenian media. Under the headline, "A Close Neighbor Is Better Than a Distant Friend," *Gortsarar* emphasized the importance of joint ventures and reported that trade between the Republic of Armenia, with a population of 3 million, and the Islamic Republic of Iran, with a population of 64 million, had reached $100 million in 1998, 60 percent of which consisted of Iranian imports.

School No. 136 Destroyed by Fire

Earlier in November, my wife and I had seen a TV news report from Armenia that made a huge impression on both of us. School No. 136, located in the middle-class Yerevan neighborhood of Kanaker-Zeitoun, had been completely gutted by fire. Given the serious economic crisis in Armenia, it was clear that the school would not reopen any time soon.

While I was in Yerevan for the trade fair, I visited the school with Norair Melkonian, the manager of Sati operations in Armenia. We met the principal, Miss Greta Tounyan, in the ruins of the main building, and we surveyed the damage together. It was devastating. Miss Tounyan was extremely sad. She told us the students had all been reassigned to other schools.

After the fair was over, I went back to the site with some friends in the construction business. The four-story main building had a footprint of 8,000 square feet and a total area of 32,000 square feet. In addition to classrooms and offices, the building had housed a 1600-square-foot gym, a cafeteria about the same size, and an auditorium with a capacity of 250. My friends estimated that it would cost approximately $200,000 to completely rebuild it. Miss Tounyan was delighted when I told her that I was willing to undertake the task. She told me that a local business had already donated $15,000 to rebuild the first-floor staircase.

Since the schools were under the jurisdiction of the municipality of Yerevan, I went to see Mayor Albert Bazeyan. I put forward four conditions for rebuilding School No. 136: the reconstruction must be completed according to the municipal architects' plans and with their oversight; imported construction materials must be duty-free; the municipality must supply the job site with water and electricity on a timely basis; and once the school was reopened, Persian would be added to the curriculum as a required language. When Mayor Bazeyan accepted my conditions without reservation, I decided to take full financial responsibility for rebuilding the school and the work began immediately. I was committed to bringing the students back in time for the 2001 academic year.

Fourth IACOC Trade Fair, 2000

For its fourth trade fair (November 18–27, 2000), the IACOC decided to seek a more convenient location. A delegation made several visits to Yerevan and finally settled on the 8,000-square-foot hall of the centrally located Goom Department Store (so-called after Moscow's famous GUM and later replaced by the Tashir Shopping Mall). Once the contract was finalized, an organizing committee consisting of myself, Fereydoun Asgarian (CEO of Tavanza) and two trade fair specialists from Iran's National Productivity Organization went to Yerevan to do the preparatory work. Meanwhile in Tehran, promotional materials were prepared for the participating companies and the products to be exhibited were collected for shipment to Yerevan. Forty-seven Iranian companies took part, and because of the convenient location, there were more visitors than ever.

Rebuilding School No. 136

Meanwhile, the reconstruction of School No. 136 was underway. I have always been lucky in having good friends, and during the planning stage, I met an old friend of mine, Seroj Soukiassian, an Iranian architect who was already involved in the construction business in Yerevan. He introduced me to Hayk Barseghyan, a local architect whom I enlisted to supervise the accounting, while Sati manager Norair Melkonian saw that the bills were paid.

I was authorized to import up to $300,000 worth of construction materials and furnishings free of tariffs and customs duties. I sent tiles, doors, cabinets, desks, chairs and power cables from Iran. Over seventy workers were employed at the site. The renovation included fire sprinklers and separate restrooms for teachers and students on each floor. The gym was provided with modern equipment, the auditorium was furnished with seating for 250, the stage was finished with high-quality wood flooring, and the entire school was fenced and gated.

As the project neared completion in August 2001, a problem arose which gave me concern that the reopening might be delayed. Five-hundred disassembled desks and chairs had arrived from Tabriz, and Hayk told me it could take at least three months to put them together. I flew to Yerevan and took along my friend Ashot Perker and his wife Annik. We arrived on August 22, and as soon as we got there, we formed four working groups to assemble the desks and chairs, polish the welds, polish the floor tiles, and paint the walls.

In the final stretch, the workdays were twelve to thirteen hours long. I promised the workers they would get paid at the end of each day and that really gave them a boost. There was extraordinary cooperation among the workers, teachers and students, and as a result of their collective efforts, the job was finished on August 30. All that remained was to pave the playground and that was done in a day. Then we raised the Armenian flag at the entrance.

Even though the project cost me twice the initial estimate, I was satisfied. The important thing for me was that the students could return to their school on time.

Before the school could reopen, the question arose as to what to rename it. Since the schools in Armenia were public property, it was the state's prerogative to name them, but from my experience in Iran, when a school was built or renovated with private funds, its name was chosen in consultation with the benefactor. The kindergarten I built in Majidiyeh, for example, is named after my parents. The staff at School No. 136 wanted to rename it after me, but others wanted to honor a warrior who had fallen in Nagorno Gharabagh. I proposed to name it "Raffi" after the great Armenian novelist, but there was already a Raffi School in Yerevan. The Mayor proposed to name it after the late Karen Demirchyan. I was against that and I met with him to explain why. I had known Demirchyan personally, but he had been First Secretary of the Armenian Communist Party during the Soviet era and I was ideologically opposed to communism. Furthermore, if the school were to be named after him, the Iranian authorities would inquire about my connection to a communist leader and demand an explanation. The Mayor found my arguments persuasive and School No. 136 retained its original name.

Reopening School No. 136

The reopening of School No. 136 meant a lot to Bella and me. Despite the fact that she had breast cancer and was undergoing chemotherapy in Paris, she and her sister Jacqueline flew to Yerevan for the occasion.

September 1, 2001, fell on a Saturday and the students arrived in high spirits, accompanied by their parents and other community members who brought flowers. Miss Tounyan gave a short speech and then invited me to speak. The crowd cheered, "Thank you! Thank you!" I was very moved. I could only wish them well in their studies and ask them to serve their nation and fatherland. I also urged them to take good care of their school so that future generations could be educated there too.

A more formal ceremony was held on Tuesday, September 4. In addition to the students and their parents, a representative of Prime Minister Andranik Markaryan attended, as well as officials from the municipality and several Ministries. Also present at my invitation were Archbishop Sebouh Sarkissian from Tehran and Bishop Navasard Kjoyan, Vicar of the Araratian Patriarchal Diocese of Yerevan. A military band played the national anthem and TV personality Karen Mirzoyan served as Master of Ceremonies. Robert

Nazaryan, the new Mayor of Yerevan, spoke in praise of our service to the community. The two religious leaders followed in turn with similar remarks. Miss Tounyan, speaking on behalf of the student body and their parents and teachers, thanked us again for our good work.

When I was invited to the podium, I said that School No. 136 had a vital role to play in educating future politicians, ministers, scientists and artists. I concluded by again advising the students to take good care of their school. The older generation was doing its utmost and we expected the new generation to be dedicated citizens and help develop the fatherland.

Just as I had earlier given President Ter-Petrosyan a hand-made carpet from Tabriz with his image woven into the design, I had commissioned one for President Kocharyan. It had taken almost a year to make, and now I presented it to Mayor Nazaryan and asked that he give it to the President. I also gave Miss Tounyan a sculpture for the school and distributed gifts to everyone who had taken part in the reconstruction, including Hayk Barseghian, Norair Melkonian and Ashot Perker. We in turn received gifts from the students and their parents. Bella was presented with the coat of arms of the city of Yerevan and I was made an honorary member of the community.

After the speeches and the exchange of gifts, the students performed some songs and dances. Then Mayor Nazaryan and I cut the ribbon and School No. 136 was officially declared open. The crowd dispersed throughout the building and regathered for the reception in the auditorium, where everyone tried to thank us personally. It is impossible to describe my feelings. I had realized one of my fondest dreams and I was ecstatic, happy beyond words.

A week later, I received a message at my office on Mashtots Avenue that Catholicos Garegin II wished to meet me (Catholicos Garegin I had passed away in 1999). I went to Echmiadzin the following afternoon and found His Holiness sitting on a couch in the courtyard. He bade me sit down with him and commended me for doing my patriotic duty with respect to School No. 136. Coffee and fruits were served and we spent an hour in conversation. Before I left, he gave me his blessing.

Construction Boom in Yerevan

The turn of the century witnessed the start of a construction boom in Yerevan, stimulated by the development of Northern Avenue, a pedestrian mall that cuts through the urban grid from the Opera House toward Republic Square and opened to the public in 2007. After the route was finalized, the properties flanking it were auctioned off through the city council, and over a period of two years, sale prices shot up to fifteen times their originally assessed value, and elsewhere in the capital, real estate prices multiplied by ten. The new buyers were primarily Russian Armenians and secondarily Iranian Armenians. All this had a gentrification effect and there was a great demand for renovation and restoration services. Seroj Soukiassian and Albert Ajemian were the first Iranian Armenian architects to work in this field in independent Armenia.

Given these developments, the IACOC decided to focus its 2002 and 2003 exhibitions on construction, a strategy that proved successful. Armenian architects, engineers and contractors had the opportunity to learn practically all there was to know about construction tools and materials manufactured in Iran. More than thirty-five Iranian firms exhibited in May 2003, and the fair was moved back to the Sports Complex in order to accommodate the products on show.

Jointly presiding over the opening ceremony were Iranian Ambassador Koleyni and Artashes Tumanyan, President Kocharyan's chief of staff and a specialist on Iran who would be appointed Ambassador to Iran in 2015. Ambassador Koleyni presented Mr. Tumanyan with a beautiful gift whose design was inspired by ancient Persepolis. He also presented me with a beautiful example of Iranian handicraft and a letter of appreciation which I quote:

> In saluting you, I would like to express my appreciation for the role you have played in the development and strengthening of relations between the Islamic Republic of Iran and the Republic of Armenia. No doubt, the Iran-Armenia Chamber of Commerce will continue its unique role in the development of economic and trade relations between the two countries, as well as in national and people-to-people contacts. I ask the Almighty to grant you prosperity and success.

I thanked the Ambassador for his gift and expressed satisfaction with my modest contribution to the growth of relations between Iran and Armenia.

Alinaghi (Ali-Naqi) Khamoushi, the long-time chairman of the Iranian Chamber of Commerce, Industry and Mining, headed the Iranian delegation to the fair, and Shahrokh Zahiri, my fellow IACOC board member, was a member of the delegation. He knew that I had renovated School No. 136 and he proposed that we go see it. So I arranged a visit with the principal and we took Mr. Khamoushi and several other Iranians along. Miss Tounyan introduced us to a third-grade classroom where Persian was part of the curriculum. It was my condition for the renovation that the school should teach Persian. The students greeted us in Persian and then presented a program of Persian poetry, song and dance. Mr. Khamoushi was moved. As we left, he told me the visit had special meaning for him and he commended me for a job well done.

After 2003, the IACOC organizing committee decided to suspend the fair for a year in order to consider how to make it more productive and attract more visitors. Thereafter, we continued to sponsor exhibitions at two year intervals.

The Armenia School Foundation

Once I began renovating School No. 136, I learned a lot about the deplorable condition of Armenia's schools. Almost two-thirds of them – nearly a thousand schools – were in need of repair or renovation. That made me sad. How could children build the future if they were deprived of a normal education? The concept of private schools lacked currency in Armenia, the Ministry of Education lacked sufficient funding and the government had other vital preoccupations. On the other hand, I believe that not everything should be done by the state, so I decided to address the situation myself.

I made a number of proposals at the Second Armenia-Diaspora Conference in 2002 and I discussed them with Levon Mkrtchyan, the Minister of Education and Science. I had known him since 1995 when I sponsored the publication of his history of *The Zeytoun Uprising* (in Armenian) and he really impressed me. After hearing me out, he made a commitment to help. We met with several other officials and decided to set up a fund called *Hay Dbrotz Himnadram* (Armenia School Foundation). We would focus on providing new classroom furniture: desks, chairs, blackboards and map displays. Our attorney Nazeli Vartanian filed the necessary paperwork and we were legally registered in Armenia.

Over the following year, I traveled to various countries and spent a lot of time explaining the project. In Los Angeles, I met with Hovhannes Balayan, the owner and editor of a magazine named *Katch Nazar* (Nazar the Brave) and the host of a local cable TV show. He had me on as a guest and I was able to get across the dire situation of Armenian schools. A lot of people called in, many of whom knew me from Iran. Several community activists joined the cause, including Anahid Sarian, Jeannette Mirzaian, Seroj Mirbegian and Caro Minas.

I returned to Yerevan to discuss the formation of a governing board with Minister Mkrtchyan. I wanted to recruit members on the basis of their dedication to the cause, irrespective of party affiliation. For example, I recruited an old friend, now an immigrant to the USA, who had been a known leftist in Iran. Mkrtchyan was an ARF party stalwart himself but he suggested adding members from the Ramgavar (Ramkavar) and the Hnchak parties, which showed his open-mindedness. After he won a seat in the National Assembly, he resigned from his ministerial position, but Sergo Yeritzyan, who replaced him, continued the Ministry's support of the project and assigned Hrach Tadevossian as liaison.

In Los Angeles, attorneys Armen Janian and Nik Nshanian registered the ASF as a non-profit, charitable, tax-exempt 501(c)(3) organization. Caro Minas was elected chairman of the board. Nshanian allocated an office and a secretary to the foundation. We soon received the first large donation of $10,000 from Gagik Galustian.

In Yerevan, we asked the Ministry of Education and Science to provide us with an office, but since nothing they proposed was suitable, we set up an office at Masisavan, the construction company I cofounded with Vazgen Amirkhanian, and we hired Zarouhi Zanjirchyan as executive director of ASF-Yerevan. The Armenia School Foundation was officially launched with a special event at the Armenia Hotel on September 26, 2003.

Next, we organized a town hall meeting in Tehran on December 22, 2003. We invited around a hundred people from Iranian Armenian organizations and asked for their support. Silva Markarian and my business partner, Varouj Sourenian, were a great help in this effort. We received contributions from many friends, including Loris Tjeknavorian who dedicated the proceeds of one of his concerts, some $12,000, to ASF. We raised enough to purchase eighty tons of steel elements and six tons of paint and ship them to Yerevan.

In Los Angeles, the board launched the foundation on April 2, 2004. Miss Anahid Sarian served as Mistress of Ceremonies. The event was a great success. The attendees were impressed by video footage from various Armenian schools and we raised $55,000.

The Ministry of Education and Science had given us a list of the schools in need of furniture, but the board discovered that the list was inaccurate. Ara Karapetyan was given the task of rectifying the information and he, along with two other volunteers, visited 300 villages and collected data on the number of schools, the number and ethnicity of students and teachers in each school, the supply of water and power to each school, the socio-economic conditions of the village, and the proximity of any monuments or historic sites. This was a tremendous contribution because it allowed the ASF to meet specific local requirements.

Our plan was to assemble the furniture in Armenia. My friend Ashot Perker, with whom I had such a great experience during the renovation of School No. 136, sent the necessary equipment to Yerevan and followed up in person to organize the assembly and painting of 3,000 desks and 6,000 chairs.

The village school in Oshakan received the first delivery on March 15, 2005. Oshakan was chosen because the tomb of St. Mesrop Mashtots, creator of the Armenian alphabet, is located in a crypt under the altar of the village church, and 2005 was the 1600th anniversary of his invention. The villagers organized a reception that received wide media coverage. The guests included school principal Raihan Sargsyan, Minister Yeritzyan, Aragatsotn Provincial Governor Gabriel Geozalyan, and myself as President of the ASF.

My Personal Investments in Armenia

As noted before, my ties with Armenia increased exponentially after it gained its independence. Armenia needed the assistance of its Diaspora, though not all Diaspora Armenian ventures were successful. After extensive consultation with friends, I decided to open a Sati affiliate in Yerevan. I bought an apartment on Mashtots Avenue to serve as an office, and in 1993, Sati-Armenia began operating in the areas of international transport, freight forwarding, airline ticket sales and tourism. It soon became clear that the ticket sales effort was premature, so that was suspended and the company focused on transport and tourism. It was in the red for years and only after a decade did it start making a small profit, but it provided employment for a dozen people.

I met many businessmen and politicians in Armenia, one of whom was Robert Yengoyan, the manager of Kanaz, the aluminum plant in Yerevan's Kanaker district. The foil production line was sold to a Russian company and Kanaz started producing aluminum profiles (industrial billets). Two Iranian Armenian businessmen, Norair and Souren (Hrair) Shahbazian, bought one-third of the operation, and in 2003, when Yengoyan and I heard that the government was planning to privatize the rest of it, we decided to each bid for a one-third share. The section we obtained was called Ar-Al. It was in a shambles and it took us eighteen months to refurbish it. Once it became operational, it employed thirty people, with the potential for further growth. According to market research, sixty to seventy tons of aluminum profiles were used in Armenia every month and we planned to produce the bulk of that in our factory.

During the Soviet period, Kanaz had built several recreational and educational facilities for its workforce, and after the company was fully privatized, the Ministry of Industry decided to auction off those subsidiary holdings. My partner and I bought two buildings, one of which was a former kindergarten in the Kanaker-Zeitoun district. We planned to build a thirty-room hotel on the site. We also bought a campground in the village of Pyunik, upriver from Hrazdan. The site comprised five dormitories, each with a capacity for eighty children, a large dining hall, an all-purpose hall and several playgrounds. It hadn't been maintained for years and it was in rather poor shape. The engineers we consulted advised against restoring the existing facilities. Instead, I bought out my partner and built three new buildings on the site. I intended it to be a place where children from Armenia and the Diaspora could interact and get to know each other, and I completed the project in 2010.

The Masisavan Condominium Complex

In the summer of 2003, I was in Yerevan for a week when a friend asked me why I was focusing solely on philanthropy and not investing in the construction business. I told him that I simply wasn't interested in construction. He took me to the neighborhood known as Monument which overlooks the city center, and he showed me a three-and-a-half–acre lot the municipality was trying to sell. I thought it had potential as the site of a grand hotel, and not long afterwards, I bought it at auction. Some people showed interest in forming a development partnership, but that was short-lived. People kept telling me the season for tourism in Armenia only lasted three or four months a year and hotels were therefore unprofitable. The cost of building a hotel would have been $10–12 million. That was beyond my means so I abandoned the idea.

One day, Vazgen Amirkhanian visited me at my office. He was an old friend of mine from Tamaddon School days when he was a champion athlete. He became an engineer, left Iran after the Revolution and was now living in Los Angeles with his family. The issue of this lot came up and he proposed to buy a quarter-acre of the property and build a residential complex on it.

Initially I disliked the idea, but after further discussion, we agreed to form a partnership to develop the entire lot.

We established a company called Masisavan, and while developing the project, we set up an office in the venerable Architects Union Building on Baghramyan Avenue, close to the construction site. The building was in a shambles and Vazgen proposed that the owners grant us the use of the first and second floors rent-free, in return for which we would renovate the entire building. The renovation went quickly and we moved in. We secured the permits and approvals to construct five five-story buildings with three modern apartments of various sizes on each floor. The first building also contained a shopping mall. Additionally, we planned to build a number of free-standing two-story homes, a sports facility, and a club with all the amenities. This project, which provided jobs for architects, engineers and construction workers, broke ground in March 2005 and was completed four years later. It was the first development of its kind in Armenia. The high quality of the apartments was attractive to Diasporan Armenians and home ownership strengthened their ties with the homeland.

Chapter 36

The Last Day of Archbishop Ardak Manoukian

During Archbishop Manoukian's last years, a conflict arose between him and the Diocesan Council that deeply disturbed him. The outgoing Council had ordered a Peugeot sedan for his use, but the incoming Council decided that its members should have the use of it too. Then, at the end of its term, having no further rights or duties, the Council sold the car just to spite the Holy Father.

I last saw him in May 1999 in the passenger lounge at Mehrabad Airport. He was on his way to a conference in Yerevan at the head of a delegation of ARF members and prominent community figures. He was terribly sad and upset and he simply couldn't control himself. He spoke in terms I had never heard him use in all the years I had known him. He cursed the Council members and said he would never forgive them for what they did.

I felt terrible inside. How could they so carelessly offend this noble man of religion who had risked his life for the community? Of course, it would be absurd to attribute their attitude to the issue of a mere automobile. That was dictated from higher levels. I felt great unease when I saw that the Cilician Catholicosate did nothing to defend its own representative in Iran.

Nevertheless, when Archbishop Manoukian died on October 16, 1999, the community buried its devout and devoted religious leader with the highest and purest emotions and the most somber ceremony.

When Ardak Manoukian came to Tehran in 1959, he was a mere youth of twenty-eight, but he established himself and maintained his stature all throughout the monarchy, the Islamic Revolution and the aftermath. He was always on the front line, defending the community's interests. He protected and maintained our schools and our language. When others felt hopeless and demoralized, he inspired hope and refused to countenance hopelessness. He would never have survived that cauldron had he not been such a strong personality.

Archbishop Manoukian was well-versed in psychology and diplomacy. He understood that the Iranian Armenian community was not a monolith. Every move he made was measured and well considered. His intelligence and graciousness earned respect from every layer of the community. When Armenian leftists attacked the ARF in their weekly *Pyunik* and called the Cilician Catholicosate a foreign imposition, they never said a word against Archbishop Manoukian. I was told by a reliable source that President Ter-Petrosyan had proposed to President Hashemi-Rafsanjani that the Iranian dioceses be returned to the jurisdiction of Echmiadzin, but that Rafsanjani had rejected the proposal because Iranians and especially Iranian Armenians loved Archbishop Manoukian too much.

The Prelate always maintained his independence in religious affairs. Souren's wedding is one example. Earlier I related how Souren and his "Sourenagans" held the Diocesan Council hostage in 1979. When it came time for Souren to marry, the Council tried to prevent him from marrying in the church, but Archbishop Manoukian said it was his decision and he decided to allow it.

Archbishop Manoukian wrote in a rich but accessible style. His literary output has been published in thirty-four volumes of prose, poetry and commentary on national religious themes and Armenian folk traditions. Some of these volumes have been translated into English and Persian.

Archbishop Sebouh Sarkissian

After Archbishop Manoukian passed away, the Cilician Catholicosate put forward the names of two or three possible successors, but the supporting documents they sent to the Diocesan Assembly clearly showed that Archbishop Sebouh Sarkissian had the best credentials, and I thought he was their preferred candidate. When Assembly chair Dr. Harmik Davitian laid out the candidates' qualifications, I said the Assembly was wasting its time because it was clear which one Antelias preferred. But the Assembly had to go through the motions, and after listening to various views, the Representatives unanimously elected Archbishop Sarkissian as Prelate of Tehran in June 2000.

With his dynamism and hard work, Archbishop Sarkissian did not allow the community to feel the absence of his predecessor. He has shown that he is worthy of his position. Born in Syria and educated at Antelias, he was, whether he liked it or not, in the sphere of the ARF. But he quickly realized that the community was not monolithic, and because of that he was able to prove that he was a leader for the entire community.

Very early in Archbishop Sarkissian's tenure, the chair of the Diocesan Council informed the Diocesan Assembly that the living quarters formerly occupied by Archbishop Manoukian would now serve as guest quarters, and that the new Prelate, as a man of religion, should live in a cell. When Archbishop Sarkissian took office, however, he had those quarters renovated and made them his place of residence. He also arranged for the purchase of another Peugeot. He made it clear that, as the community's spiritual leader, his way of life must reflect his position. I wish Archbishop Sarkissian great success in his mission.

The following is excerpted from the autobiographical sketch he provided me with.

> I was born on October 26, 1946, in the Armenian village of Jukha, near Qamishli in northeastern Syria, where I received my elementary education. I enrolled in the Theological Seminary of the Cilician Catholicosate at Antelias in 1961, and I was ordained as a Deacon in 1965. On June 16, 1968, I was ordained as a Celibate Priest by Archbishop Dajad Ourfalian, Primate of the Prelacy of Lebanon, and given the name Sebouh. From 1969 to 1970, I studied Arabic literature and Islamic philosophy at St. Joseph University in Beirut. On February 14, 1971, I was ordained Doctor of the Church by Catholicos Khoren I. In addition to carrying out my religious duties during that period, I taught Armenian language, literature and religion.
>
> From 1974 to 1977, I was a lecturer in religious studies and Armenian literature at the Karen Jeppe Armenian College in Aleppo. I also directed the Armenian Nursing Home in Aleppo and served as Deputy Prelate of Beirut. I returned to Antelias toward the end of 1977, and the following year, I was appointed supervisor of Armenian Sunday Schools.
>
> I studied at the University of Birmingham in the United Kingdom between 1979 and 1981 and I received the title of Senior Doctor of the Church on June 2, 1985. At the invitation of Vazken I, Catholicos of All Armenians, I served as supervisor of Armenian Sunday Schools in Armenia in 1990–91, for the purpose of promoting Christian education in Armenia.
>
> From 1992 to 1998, I was Pontifical Delegate to the Damascus Prelacy, and in 1998, Deputy Catholicos of Kuwait and the Gulf. On June 22, 1997, I was ordained Archbishop by Catholicos Aram I.

I have been a member of the Unit on Faith and Unity in the Middle East Council of Churches since 1984 and a member of the MECC's executive body since 1991. I participated in the general meeting of the World Council of Churches in 1998. I am a member of the WCC's Advisory Committee on Interfaith Dialogue.

I am the author of five books on religion and two religious education textbooks. From 1984 to 1999, I was the editor of *Nor Aztag* monthly, the official publication of the Sunday Schools of the Armenian Church.

1700th Anniversary Celebrations

The year 2001 was one of immense significance for Armenia and for Armenians throughout the world. It marked the 1700th anniversary of Armenia's adoption of Christianity as a state religion in 301 CE. It was also the Year of Dialogue Among Civilizations which Iran had proposed to the UN based on President Khatami's concept of interfaith dialogue. Encouraged to promote this theme as widely as possible, the Diocesan Council set up a committee to organize a program of events, one of which was an extended visit of Catholicos Aram I of Antelias.

His Holiness arrived in Tehran on Wednesday, July 12, 2000, accompanied by his Scepter Bearer, the V. Rev. Father Mashdots Chobanian, and Bishop Khajag Hagopian, the future first Cilician Prelate of Canada. They were met at the airport by Hojjatoleslam Nomani representing Ershad's Islamic Culture and Communication Organization (ICCO), Armenian Ambassador Gharibjanyan, Archbishop Sarkissian of Tehran, Archbishop Papian of Isfahan, the V. Rev. Father Topouzian of Tabriz, MPs Dr. Levon Davidian and George Abrahamian, members of the Diocesan Council and other community leaders.

Catholicos Aram and his entourage proceeded to St. Sarkis Church where, following the holy mass, he delivered a sermon, and afterwards he laid a wreath at the Martyrs Monument in the courtyard. In the evening, a welcome banquet was held in his honor.

On Thursday, July 13, he visited the shrine of Emam Khomeini, and that evening he attended a truncated session of the Eleventh Diocesan Assembly. He blessed the gathering and took a few questions from the floor, after which Dr. Harmik Davitian brought the meeting to a close. I was sitting near the entrance and the Holy Father approached me on his way out. He said he would like to meet with me and he asked Archbishop Sarkissian, who was standing beside him, to make the arrangements. We met privately the following week.

On Friday, July 14, Catholicos Aram paid a visit to the Holy Translators Church in Narmak, where he conducted the holy mass and then delivered the sermon. That evening, he visited an exhibition of religious-themed paintings by Iranian Armenian artists at the Ararat Center.

On Saturday, July 15, he visited St. Vartanants Church in Heshmatiyeh. In the afternoon, he met with Dr. Ataollah Mohajerani, the Minister Culture and Islamic Guidance, at the Ministry. Later that day, he met with the Syrian Ambassador to Iran and visited *Alik*'s office complex.

On Sunday, July 16, he attended the holy mass at St. Mary's Church in the old Sheikh Hadi neighborhood. He also visited the Armenian Embassy and met with Ambassador Gharibjanyan and his staff, and took part in a seminar on peaceful coexistence between Muslims and Armenian Christians sponsored by the ICCO.

On Monday, July 17, in the company of Archbishop Sarkissian and MPs Davidian and Abrahamian, Catholicos Aram met with President Khatami at the Saadabad Palace complex in north Tehran. The President welcomed them very warmly and said the Armenian community had always stood side by side with the Muslims of Iran.

The Catholicos then flew to Isfahan. On Thursday, July 20, he presided over the holy mass at All-Savior's Cathedral in New Julfa, and the following day, he went to nearby Shahin Shahr where he prayed at St. Vartanants Church and delivered a sermon.

Returning to Tehran, he attended a community event on Saturday, July 22, in Sassountsi David Hall at the Ararat Center. It began with a choral performance, after which Archbishop Sarkissian called forth twenty-one individuals "who have served Armenian culture by giving their time and energy to the community for thirty, forty, or even fifty years," as he said, and he asked Catholicos Aram to bestow medals upon the honored individuals. Six were awarded the St. Mesrop Mashtots Medal and fifteen the Knight of Cilicia Medal. The former were all members of the ARF and none but two had done a fraction of the work that others had done for our community, which demonstrated the House of Cilicia's subservience to the party. The faithful expect the Church to be fair, but in this case it was not, and it is because of such preferential attitudes and actions that the ranks of those who oppose the Cilician Catholicosate are constantly increasing.

Catholicos Aram sensed the community's dissatisfaction, and the next day, when he visited an exhibition of traditional Armenian costumes at the Armenian Club sponsored by the Armenian Women's Association (*Hay Geen*), he remarked on the awarding of the medals, saying he had had no say in selecting the recipients. Nevertheless, the controversy continued for months afterward in the pages of *Alik* and *Louys*.

The Holy Father also met with Hojjatoleslam Mehdi Karroubi that day. Recently elected Speaker of the Majles, Hojatoleslam Karroubi had long been a staunch defender of the Armenians. He received His Holiness with the utmost warmth and respect and he again expressed his admiration for our community and his appreciation of our contributions to progress and development in Iran.

Pilgrimage to St. Thaddeus Monastery

A few days later, Bella and I joined the forty-sixth annual pilgrimage to St. Thaddeus Monastery in Iran's far northwest province. Mrs. Rita Cherchian, the director of Sati's tourism section and a member of the Diocesan Council's organizing committee, had facilitated the visas and travel arrangements for a group of twenty American Armenians who also joined the pilgrimage.

When Catholicos Aram arrived at the monastery's massive fortified walls, he was met by local Armenians with the traditional bread and salt. After blessing the offering, he entered the holy precinct and blessed the congregation, and then he delivered a rousing sermon.

On Saturday, July 29, His Holiness led the pilgrims to the Chapel of Dzordzor, a few miles downstream from St. Thaddeus. Situated on a mountainside overlooking the Aghtcha (Barun) River, the chapel had been threatened by the construction of the Maku-Barun reservoir, but thanks to Varoujan Arakelian, it had been relocated and restored in time for the 1700th anniversary celebrations. Together with St. Thaddeus and the Monastery of St. Stepanos near Julfa, the Chapel of Dzordzor was listed as a UNESCO World Heritage Site in 2008.

Catholicos Aram consecrated the chapel in the presence of Ambassador Gharibjanyan and his staff, a number of high-ranking local provincial officials and a large number of Armenians from Tabriz, Tehran and elsewhere. My wife and I were present, along with a friend of Bella's who had come with the

American group. Afterwards, everyone joined His Holiness for dinner outdoors under tents, all of which was organized by Varoujan Arakelian.

In the evening, back at St. Thaddeus, Vartan Vahramian conducted a performance by the Komitas Choir of Tabriz. The next morning, the holy mass was performed in the presence of Catholicos Aram and hundreds of pilgrims. One of those pilgrims was an American woman who spoke the purest Isfahani dialect, even though she had never been to Isfahan. Bella introduced her to my colleague Ardashes Zomorodian and his wife Lucig, and the two women eventually figured out that they were blood relatives.

Touring Salmas with Raffi Hovannisian

Also taking part in the pilgrimage was Raffi Hovannisian, President Ter-Petrosyan's first Foreign Minister (1991–92), and he told me that he would like to see the historic villages of Salmas. I had planned to return to Tehran that night, but not wishing to disappoint him, I left Bella with her American friend and prepared for the journey. I warned Hovannisian that if he wanted to see the real Salmas, he should forget about eating in restaurants, but I had the car's mini-fridge filled with sausages and other delectables. I drove down toward Salmas (Dilman), a distance of about 125 miles, while my driver, Madteos, sat in the back seat with his university-educated son and made little sandwiches which we ate as we drove. We stopped at Khoy and visited St. Sarkis Church where we saw ancient clay jars said to be children's burial urns. The church had recently been renovated by Iran's volunteer Reconstruction Crusade (*Jihad-e Sazandegi*).

In my natal village of Haftvan, we looked up Baron Ardavazd, the sole remaining Armenian and the elected chief of the Kurdish and Azeri residents. He showed us the local church which had also been renovated by the Reconstruction Crusade, but there was no trace of our old home, nor that of my late Uncle Mnatsakan. From Haftvan, we drove to my maternal grandmother's natal village of Mahlam, now inhabited almost entirely by Kurds. The doors of the Armenian church were locked and had apparently been locked for years. We found the village cemetery, the final resting place of Armenian fedayeen who had sacrificed themselves in national liberation struggles. Their graves were marked by monumental tombstones. Then we drove west to the mountains bordering Turkey and visited the bee hives of Baron Ishkhan, a resident of Salmas, but unfortunately he wasn't there that day.

Turning back to the main Salmas-Urumia road, we stopped at Payajuk, the birthplace of Raffi, the great Armenian novelist. Fifteen years earlier, on the sesquicentennial anniversary of the novelist's birth, the Diocesan Council of Tehran, in collaboration with the Diocesan Council of Azarbayjan and the Salmas local council, had built a wall around the site of Raffi's ancestral home and planted over 200 trees on the property. The plan was to protect it until the local St. Sarkis Church, which had been destroyed in the 1930 earthquake, could be rebuilt there. All this was part of a drive to restore Armenian churches and monuments in Salmas and to demonstrate that these villages were historically Armenian. It was hoped that they would eventually attract both foreign and domestic tourists. Now, Raffi's wall was still standing and the trees had grown, but there was no further development. The caretaker, Baron Ararat, was the only Armenian resident. We spent a half-hour with him and then drove up to the old cemetery at the top of the hill on the outskirts of the village, where I located the gravestone of the novelist's mother.

Then we headed for Tabriz by way of the road that runs along the shore of beautiful Lake Urumia. My esteemed guest wanted to soak his feet in its therapeutic mud, so I stopped the car and we walked to the shore where he immersed his feet for a few minutes. Back at the car, Madteos offered him some water to rinse his feet. We reached Tabriz at 9:00 in the evening and stopped at the home of Varoujan Arakelian where he and his family were waiting for us. I didn't stay long because I was very tired. I went back to my hotel for a good night's sleep and flew to Tehran the next morning.

Chapter 37

Louys, *Houys*, and the Diocesan Assembly Elections

I had always wanted to publish a magazine. After the Islamic Revolution, I tried to start a monthly journal called *Arax*. I was acquainted with Colonel Emil Hagopian of Tabriz who had worked with the editorial board of *Hoor* (Flame), the prerevolutionary bilingual literary journal founded by Dr. Gaguik Hovakimian. Colonel Hagopian helped me get started by recruiting several collaborators. I applied for a permit to publish, but I was told that it would take a year or two or even longer for the Ministry of National Guidance to review the application and issue a permit. In the meantime, I was elected president of the Transport Syndicate, and then I was elected to the Tenth Diocesan Assembly of Representatives, and then a member and finally chair of the Diocesan Council. All those positions meant ceaseless and ever increasing work, so I gave up the idea and withdrew my application.

Years passed and things changed in our community. After Armenia regained its independence, the sorry state of the Iranian Armenian press became all the more glaring as *Alik*'s coverage of events unfolding in the new Republic was so clearly dictated by the ARF. That led me to reconsider the idea of publishing an independent journal. I discussed it with a number of politically independent friends and they promised to help. I had it in mind to let the editors set up an office in my late parents' four-room apartment at Vali Asr and Enqelab, and Henrik instantly agreed. I brought together some prominent community figures, including philanthropists Babig Tomassian and Rubina Papazian, the poet Ruben Hovanissian, the engineer Njdeh Aslanian, and engineers Rouzas Markarian and my brother George. Over the course of a year, we held a series of meetings in my office to discuss editorial policy and work out the financing. Ultimately, we realized that we lacked the professional expertise to produce a magazine.

At that time, I subscribed to *Apaga* (*Abaka*, Future), the Tehran-based monthly journal of Armenian and Iranian studies edited by Edic Baghdasarian. I didn't know Edic personally but I knew and respected his work. His Persian translation of *The History of the Armenian People* had been reprinted several times, and he had translated the study by Ambassador

Bayburdyan mentioned earlier. He had also written a booklet in Persian titled *Let's Learn Armenian*. He had a solid presence in literary circles, but being a left-leaning intellectual, he was little known in the larger community.

A mutual friend introduced us and I invited Edic to meet with my collaborators. We presented him with two alternative proposals: either he publish our new four-color, bimonthly journal to be called *Louys* (Light), along with *Apaga*, or he stop publishing *Apaga* and instead become the publisher and editor of *Louys*, and we would take care of all financial matters. As a counter-proposal, he suggested that we also assume financial responsibility for *Apaga* for one year. We agreed to that and five of our group promised to contribute 250,000 tomans each toward the continuation of *Apaga*. Edic went ahead and applied for a permit to publish *Louys*, in the expectation that it would take at least a year, but it was granted much sooner than anticipated and thus we were in a position to launch almost immediately. I decided to finance *Louys* on my own and Rubina Papazian chipped in 500,000 tomans. The cost of setting up the office with desks, chairs, computers, phones, utilities and so forth amounted to $10,000.

Edic was named the owner and editor of *Louys* and he appointed the editorial board: Ruben Keshishian, Andranik Khechoumian, Dr. Ruben Sardarian, Garo Sarksian, Vachik Vartanian and myself. I had met Vartanian in the Tenth Diocesan Assembly where he represented the electoral district of Heshmatiyeh, and I knew Keshishian was an Armenian language teacher, but I didn't know the others nor did I know what their political views were, but I assumed they aligned with those of Baghdasarian since they were all friends of his. But that wasn't very important because we decided to be objective and work without bias toward any political ideology. My dream was that *Louys* would satisfy the community's need for cultural, civic and national information, and on that basis it was categorized as a "cultural and civic bimonthly."

Launching *Louys*

The first issue of *Louys* came out on March 15, 2000, with a print run of 1,000. We allocated 300 copies of the first issue to complimentary distribution in the community, and we sent 200 copies to Diaspora organizations working in Armenia. Rubina Papazian was instrumental in introducing *Louys* to Diaspora communities and signing up subscribers. Soon *Louys* was available in Armenia, the USA, Canada, the UK, France, Austria, Sweden, Lebanon, Syria, Australia, Argentina and even Brazil. The cover price in Iran was 300 tomans, and outside the country a subscription cost $30 per year (twenty-four issues).

The cover of the first issue was a reproduction of *Surp Tarkmanchats* (The Holy Translators), Grigor Khanjian's illustration of a tapestry at Echmiadzin commissioned by Catholicos Vazgen I. It shows King Trdad (Tiridates) and Saint Mesrop with his miraculous invention, the Armenian alphabet, in gold lettering. Herewith is the inaugural editorial, prefaced with a verse by the poet Paruyr Sevak:

> *I am tired of cold diminished words*
> *Better an ironsmith than a jeweler*
>
> The press is the mirror of a community, as they say – the true expression of its authentic passions and experiences – that is, if the press is honest and straightforward. For many years now, the Iranian Armenian community has needed a new "mirror," but only now have conditions allowed us to realize our dream of publishing an independent journal that is not drowning in factionalism but truly mirrors our community.
>
> The monthly *Apaga* recently injected new hope and energy into the ranks of those who follow culture and public affairs. Only the reader can judge its value, but *Apaga* has thus far benefited from the indifference of "community leaders" and the appreciation of enlightened minds in our community, in the Diaspora and in the homeland.
>
> Now *Louys* is being launched to spread light and raise national cultural awareness to a higher level. Obviously, it is not the sole privilege of anyone to be a good Armenian, a good human being. Today our community needs a united effort to safeguard our interests. Therefore, the editors of *Louys* aim to:
>
> 1. Reflect the cultural, literary, artistic, scientific, athletic and public life of the Iranian Armenian community within the press guidelines of the Islamic Republic of Iran.
>
> 2. Focus on the most important events and issues facing Iran as well as the Armenian world.
>
> 3. Be independent and avoid the sectarian interests of those groups that do not reflect the community.

4. Create an important forum where our youth can express their ideas.

5. Promote the cultural and spiritual values of the Iranian Armenian world.

6. Defend the national and human rights of the Armenian people within the limits of possibility.

7. Include the views of all community members, sectors and groups in resolving community issues, and challenge one-sided solutions to those issues.

8. Strive to fulfill our national and community obligations as members of the Iranian and Armenian press corps.

9. Publish one-third of the journal's content in Persian, given the need to introduce our culture to the Iranian people.

10. Employ classical orthography, considering the readers' and especially the younger readers' familiarity with the form, and based on the recommendations of other Diaspora communities, while also respecting the values of the new style.

In order to accomplish these goals, *Louys* will include sections on public affairs, health, science, culture, art, literature, sports and current events, as well as a section for young readers. All of its pages are dedicated to satisfying the spiritual needs of our noble people.

The editorial board of *Louys* is always ready to receive serious comments and recommendations from our readers and they will be taken into consideration in future issues.

The first issue reported on the results of the first round of elections for the Sixth Islamic Majles (in which Dr. Levon Davidian and George Abrahamian succeeded Vartan Vartanian and Ardavazd Baghoumian as the Armenian MPs for northern and southern Iran, respectively); the Iranian premiere of the concert version of Loris Tjeknavorian's opera, *Rostam and Sohrab*, conducted by the composer at the Fifteenth Fajr International Music Festival; Archbishop Sarkissian's visit to St. Vartanants Church in Heshmatiyeh; a meeting between Iranian Vice President Hassan Habibi and Armenia's Acting Prime Minister Aram Sargsyan; and the announcement that President Robert Kocharyan had named the late Vazgen Sargsyan and Karen Demirchyan as National Heros of Armenia, the Republic's highest title.

An item headed "In Anticipation of Cultural Vitality" welcomed Archbishop Sarkissian and wished him success in his religious and national mission as the new Prelate of Tehran.

Under the rubric of "Iranian Armenian Philanthropists," there was an appreciation of Rubina Papazian and her daughters Meliné and Christine for their noble and patriotic endeavor to fund the renovation of the neonatal intensive care unit at Yerevan Children's Hospital.

The "Heroic Tales" section featured an article about Saint Vartan in which the writer summarized the turbulent history and future mission of the Armenian people.

Other features included an interview with the director of an Armenian theater group that took part in the Fajr Festival, an article on natural ways of lowering cholesterol, and finally, an article on the soccer tournament sponsored by the Raffi Association and an interview with soccer star Edmond Bezik (Bezikian).

The Persian-language section included an editorial, an article about the role of Armenians in Iranian theater titled "Salty Tears on Marble," a short story titled "Voyage" and an article about the Armenian Genocide in the context of documents from the trials of the Young Turks.

And so it began. Vachik Vartanian served as managing editor, coordinating the work of three staff members who were paid very modestly. *Louys* provided unbiased coverage of all public, national and cultural community events. One of our criteria was that our coverage should do nothing to impair the community's unity. Its positive impact was soon felt not only in the Iranian Armenian community but also among émigrés and intellectuals in Armenia.

But certain individuals with partisan agendas were displeased with how we covered events in Armenia, and they prepared the ground for a struggle against *Louys*, beginning with a campaign of lies and hurtful comments about me. They said I had separated myself from "community leaders" and joined the left, which made me a pariah in their eyes. One day, a former editor of *Alik* said to me,

"Poor Mr. Aharonian, you don't know what kind of people you're dealing with."

Such comments didn't phase me at all.

Assessment of the Eleventh Diocesan Assembly

After many years of trying, the Diocesan Council finally secured Interior Ministry permission to hold elections for a new Diocesan Assembly of Representatives. As mentioned earlier, when Catholicos Aram came to Iran for the 1700th anniversary celebrations, he saw me at a meeting of the Eleventh Diocesan Assembly and said he would like to meet with me. A few days later, Archbishop Sarkissian arranged for us to meet at the Prelacy, and there I found the Holy Father waiting for me in a private room. We talked about various subjects, but when the Diocesan Assembly came up, he fell silent and looked at me thoughtfully.

"Holy Father," I asked, "how do you rate the competence of the Representatives?"

"Very weak," he replied.

"Now that the election of a new Assembly has finally been sanctioned," I said, "I hope to see some new people elected with higher standards and better behavior."

He responded that he had been talking with a certain person and my name came up (I soon realized he was referring to the leader of the ARF Central Committee in Iran). He told me that he had advised this person to give independents like myself a chance to be elected. That upset me.

"Holy Father, for twenty years, my friends and I, under the leadership of the late Archbishop Manoukian, defended the community's rights and interests in the most difficult conditions, and now this person is supposed to decide who gets elected?"

He replied that the man in question had told him that I was publishing a journal that was working against the community's interests. That really hurt, and I responded with great determination.

"Holy Father, for many years, I have placed every resource at my disposal in the service of the nation. I even put my health and life at risk. Where were those people after the Islamic Revolution, when the community itself was in danger? They fled the country! Who knows what they were doing abroad? And now they want to make decisions on my behalf?"

I also told him about how they had treated the late Prelate in the last months of his life. He fell silent, as though deep in thought. After a while, he broke his silence to say that he would be pleased if I were to make a financial contribution to the See of Cilicia. I replied that I had already undertaken to rebuild School No. 136 in Yerevan and that I lacked the means to support another project at this time.

Campaign for the Twelfth Diocesan Assembly, 2000

As the community gradually got caught up in electoral politics, a great rift emerged among the ARF rank and file and quite a few members were expelled from the party. As the field shaped up, the contestants fell into four categories: those running as independents, the old left (that is, to the left of the ARF), the ARF itself, and finally, those expelled from the ARF. Some of the latter ran as independents and some joined the old left. The Union of Iranian-Armenian Engineers and Architects (the Garni Society) nominated a list of six candidates and I was one of them. I decided to run again because I had been involved in the community for more than twenty years and I wanted to continue my work. Given my wide experience and my good health and stamina, I believed I could be of great service to my people.

The Garni Society pasted its campaign posters on walls and hoardings in Armenian neighborhoods, but they were all torn down, ripped up and left in the street. Not even the ones posted in the Ararat Center, which had been put up by friends of mine who were members of the ARF, stayed up for more than a day. *Louys* was attacked in schools and community meetings.

A number of candidates who had been expelled from the ARF asked if they could use our editorial office as their campaign headquarters. We turned them all down, but we offered to profile any candidate who asked to be interviewed. Our reporters covered all the community meetings related to the election and we received numerous letters of appreciation and support for our coverage. Vachik Vartanian and Dr. Ruben Sardarian, along with several reporters, organized community forums to clarify the issues. The forums were hosted by well-known figures such as the architects Armen Hakhnazarian and Seroj Soukiassian, the attorneys Albert Bernardi and Aida Hovhannisian, Diocesan Assembly chair Dr. Harmik Davitian, Assembly Representatives Hratch Khosrovian and Oksen Alexanian, and tennis pro Ashot Avedissian (Ashot Black).

In July, the ARF leadership in the Eleventh Diocesan Assembly moved to lower the voting age from eighteen to sixteen years. Their logic was that the party held sway over most of the teachers in Armenian schools and those teachers would tell their students to vote for the ARF candidates. The measure failed with twenty-seven votes against (including mine), five in favor, and one abstention. *Louys* covered the debate in several issues, and I myself penned an article titled "Welcome News" in the July 31ˢᵗ issue, explaining the legal basis and the rightness of the Assembly's decision. I concluded as follows:

> The decision was taken through a democratic process, the process was legal, the motion was rejected by the majority, and the decision must therefore be respected. Otherwise, there will be negative consequences for our community life. The future is yours, dear youth, and the work is endless. You will participate in future elections and choose your community Representatives. Today, our community has an intelligent and energetic spiritual guide who foresees hopeful changes. Of course, change is necessary for our people, especially for the younger generation. We must support our Holy Father in his efforts to carry out his plans.

The Controversy over Aid to Armenia

On September 30, 2000, three weeks before the election, *Louys* published an extended interview titled "An Interview with Community Leader and Philanthropist Levon Aharonian." The pull-quote was, "I hope those people will apologize some day for their rash decision."

The editors started out by asking me about my background, education, involvement in community affairs and service in the Eleventh Diocesan Assembly. Then they asked what happened to the funds the community had raised for the victims of the Spitak earthquake. Twelve years after the quake, people still didn't know how or where their donations had been used. I thought they had a right to know whether their generosity had achieved its purpose. Of course, I knew it hadn't and it was my responsibility to shed some light on the matter.

> *Aharonian:* After the 1988 earthquake in Armenia, aid started arriving from all over the world. The Iranian Armenian community likewise spared no effort to provide aid. The Diocesan Council appointed me to chair the committee that was set up to deal with it. People were calling the Prelacy day and night to offer donations. The various subcommittees had no trouble raising money. Around 70 million tomans was collected [approximately $650,000 in 1988]. But the Council never disclosed that fact, either to the community or to the Diocesan Assembly. It decided to use the funds to build a

faucet factory [in Ghapan] and allocate part of the income from the factory to the earthquake survivors.... That was a mistake. The community had donated funds to build homes, schools and clinics for their compatriots in Armenia, and while Armenians from all over the world were going to Spitak and Gyumri and other towns in Armenia to start construction projects, the money raised by Iranian Armenians was just sitting in baskets.

According to an announcement made at the last meeting of the Diocesan Assembly, the amount was 450 million tomans [approximately $562,000 in 2000], which is different from the original 70 million tomans, but that is due to the rise in the toman-dollar exchange rate during the twelve intervening years. In addition, the Diocesan Council incurs a monthly expense of $1,000 just to maintain that sum.

This is a clear indication of a lack of respect for the people's wishes, especially since the decision to build the faucet factory was never announced by the Diocesan Council or ratified by the Diocesan Assembly. The community donated money to help the victims, not to build factories. If they had known about the faucet factory project, that sum would never have been raised. In short, their donations have not served their purpose. I hope those people will apologize to the community some day for their rash decision.

Louys: Is it true that MP Vartan Vartanian entrusted Catholicos Vazgen I with an advance of $100,000?

Aharonian: That I don't know. If he did, it would have been made public in the Diocesan Assembly, but it was not disclosed and has never been discussed.

Louys: What other campaigns were initiated to raise funds for Armenia?

Aharonian: In 1993, in response to a recommendation from the Diocesan Assembly, the Diocesan Council appointed a committee to raise funds for Armenia, and that committee was under my responsibility. A total of 30 million tomans was raised, provisions were purchased, and Vartan Vartanian facilitated their delivery to Armenia on two C-130 transport planes made available by the Red Crescent Society. Norair

Melkonian was in charge of a second aid project. He collected 6 million tomans and that was used to buy food staples and the Diocesan Council sponsored the distribution of those staples in Meghri, Agarag and Zangezur.

The editors then brought up the community's real estate holdings and observed that the issue was never discussed with the community at large.

Louys: Are all of our Diocesan Assembly Representatives informed about this? Or is such information the privilege of only a few?

Aharonian: The community's holdings are well protected. Some small dwellings may have been sold without the Assembly's prior approval, but all such transactions were ultimately approved by the Assembly.

Louys: Are all these properties serving their intended purposes?

Aharonian: We have different types of properties. There is some real estate in cities and towns with large Armenian populations such as Rasht, Enzeli, Sari, Qazvin and Mashhad. The Diocesan Council assists in safeguarding those properties. We still own real estate in towns and cities where there are no longer any Armenian residents, such as Kermanshah, Hamadan, Gorgan and elsewhere. The Diocesan Council has proposed selling those properties and the Diocesan Assembly has approved that proposal. There are also large income-generating buildings, some vacant lots, and the schools, as well as some small dilapidated houses that it doesn't pay to maintain. The Assembly has approved a proposal to sell the latter on condition that the income be used to build a new structure or be invested in a community-related project.

Louys: How transparent is the work of the Diocesan Assembly? What effect does it have on community issues?

Aharonian: As you know, the Diocesan Assembly is the supreme council for community affairs and the Diocesan Council is the executive body. The Eleventh Assembly has carried out its mission in the best way possible. The Council carries out the Assembly's decisions, and those decisions undoubtedly have an impact on community affairs.

Louys: What is your advice for the Twelfth Diocesan Assembly?

Aharonian: As someone well informed on community matters,

I propose that our bylaws be thoroughly re-examined at the first opportunity because they do not correspond to present realities. The Council cannot assume financial responsibility for the huge expenses of the Diocese solely with the income from weddings, baptisms and funerals. The Assembly should examine this issue and come to some important decisions. And in order to make that happen, the Iranian Armenian community must carry out its local and national role by voting in the elections for the Twelfth Diocesan Assembly.

Finally, after inquiring about my work building the Aharonian Kindergarten in Majidiyeh and renovating School No. 136 in Yerevan, the editors asked whether I thought our community was united. After considering the question from various angles, I concluded with the following words:

In the twenty-first century, the peoples of the world are moving in the direction of democracy, which means that the people have the last word. Only then can we have real unity.

I felt much less burdened after this interview was published, but it seemed to have the effect of a bomb going off. It was a huge blow to the committee that was dealing with the issue of the Ghapan faucet factory. Up to that point, no one had ever dared to express similar opinions or offer such explanations. And it was daring of *Louys* to publish the interview.

Louys soon received a letter from the diocesan public relations committee which sent a copy of the letter to *Alik* and asked that it be published immediately. *Alik* published the committee's letter on October 14 (page 2), but without publishing any part of the interview in *Louys* to which the letter made reference:

Diocesan Public Relations Committee Demands Immediate Correction

Dear Editorial Board of *Louys*:

The September 18 [*sic*] issue of your publication featured an interview with Mr. Levon Aharonian under the heading, "I hope those people will apologize some day for their rash decision." The interview dealt with issues related to donations made by the Iranian Armenian community and the National Authority in the wake of the earthquake in Armenia. It included some comments that have resulted in a series of misunderstandings that will be clarified in due course.

Moreover, in response to a question about Vartan Vartanian having advanced $100,000 to Catholicos Vazgen, Mr. Aharonian replied, "That I don't know. If he did, it would have been made public in the Diocesan Assembly but it was not disclosed and has never been discussed."

This is an issue of grave importance. The response to the journal's deliberate question by someone who has been a member of the Diocesan Assembly for fourteen [sic] years accuses the Diocesan Council and Mr. Vartanian, a [former] member of the Iranian Islamic Majles, and in so doing sows the seeds of mistrust regarding the National Authority. We therefore demand that you publish the following report by the public relations committee, as well as the attached letter from the late Catholicos, at the earliest opportunity:

"*On December 15, 1988, Iranian Armenians sent an airplane carrying aid from the community to the victims of the earthquake. Mr. Ardavazd Baghoumian accompanied the flight. On December 21, Mr. Vartan Vartanian went to Armenia, taking a check in the amount of $100,000 to be presented to the Catholicos of All Armenians, Vazgen I. On December 23, the sum of $100,000 was presented to Catholicos Vazgen by Vartan Vartanian and Ardavazd Baghoumian. The Catholicos confirmed receipt of the sum in a letter dated December 26, 1988.*"

The flight and the donation of $100,000 were covered in reports published in *Alik* on December 15 and 21, 1988, and January 3, 1989. The Diocesan Council informed the Diocesan Assembly about the donations in a detailed report dated November 29, 1989. If Mr. Levon Aharonian, who is a member of the Eleventh Diocesan Assembly, is unaware of these events, that is his problem.

The Public Relations Committee of the Tehran Diocese

I responded to *Alik* immediately and my letter was published in *Louys* on October 15, along with the diocesan public relations committee's original letter:

Regarding the Letter from the Diocesan Public Relations Committee

Dear Editorial Board of *Alik*:

In response to the letter from the diocesan public relations committee that was published in *Alik* on October 14, I find it necessary to present the following explanation and request that you publish this in your paper too.

The donations collected for the victims of the earthquake in Armenia constituted a general sum whose distribution was the task of the Diocesan Assembly of Representatives.

Article 41 of the diocesan bylaws states, "The Assembly of Representatives is the legal and supreme authority of the Diocese of Tehran. The Representatives are directly elected by the community. The Assembly governs the public, religious, educational, financial and administrative affairs of the Diocese according to the bylaws and pursuant to its decisions."

The second clause of Article 41 states, "In each term, the Assembly of Representatives determines the maximum expenditure which the Diocesan Council may make on the above-referenced affairs without the Assembly's prior approval."

During the relevant term, the allocation was 2 million tomans (currently, the allocation is 5 million tomans). Article 41 makes it clear that sums dispensed over and above the limit set by the Assembly require the Assembly's approval. That did not happen.

Representatives get their information from the minutes and reports of the Assembly's meetings, not from the media. The Council's ex post facto report of November 29, 1989, is no substitute for the Assembly's prior approval.

My interview of September 30, whose basic theme was issues related to the Diocesan Assembly, should have been understood in general terms. If I discussed the lack of information on how $100,000 was dispensed, it was because that information was not reported to the Assembly. It had nothing to do with being uninformed.

The Diocesan Council's public relations committee has not taken into consideration my twenty years of community service and the fact that I have always stood by the Diocese and will continue to do so in the future.

The purpose of such interviews is to prevent the repetition of such mistakes in the future.

Considering the activities of the Armenian press in Tehran

as well as those of the electoral committee over the past few months, we hope that a stable and independent Diocesan Assembly of Representatives, one that will protect the community's interests, will come into being.

Respectfully,

Levon Aharonian

Alik published my letter a week after the election in the back of the paper under a very small-font headline. But all throughout the week preceding the election, it published a series of offensive made-up letters and announcements under the rubric, "Comments from Our Readers." And on October 16 and 19, nearly twelve years after Spitak, *Alik* published a two-part interview with Ruben Karapetian about the funds raised for the earthquake victims under the headline, "One Question, One Answer."

There was nothing new in this interview. Karapetian had been a member of the Diocesan Council at the time and he was knowingly misleading the readers of *Alik*. Obviously, the funds were allocated to a useless project that wasn't properly vetted. Anywhere else in the world, if funds collected for one purpose were used for another purpose, legal considerations would arise and the responsible individuals would be punished. Karapetian repeated the story that Vartan Vartanian, who was a member of the Diocesan Assembly at the time, delivered a check for $100,000 to Catholicos Vazgen I, that the remaining funds were spent on heaters, blankets and food staples worth $20,000, and that those goods were flown to Armenia in five cargo planes, but that the operation was halted when they were told that the supplies were not achieving their intended purpose.

After reading this made-up interview, I had a few questions to contend with. First, were the funds that were spent on earthquake relief approved by the Diocesan Assembly, and if so, why did the Assembly, the most culpable party in this matter, not inform the public? Why did I, as committee chairman, not see those purchases? And why did I, as a member of the Assembly and chairman of the committee, have to learn about it from my friends in the Assembly? The real question is how did the Diocesan Assembly, of which Karapetian was also a member, learn that the relief supplies were not achieving their intended purpose? And how was it that supplies from other countries reached their intended destination but supplies sent from Iran did not?

In fact, the earthquake relief sent to Armenia consisted of supplies purchased by the Iranian government along with provisions purchased directly by the Armenian community (clothing, blankets, heaters, etc.). Food staples were sent in 1992 when Armenian radio broadcast the message that the people of Abovian were on the verge of starvation. That very same day, the Diocesan Assembly created a committee which I chaired, and its members included Souren Shahbazian, Azad Abcarian and a number of others whose names I have unfortunately forgotten. The committee quickly raised 30 million tomans, purchased various food staples and sent them to Armenia. One quarter of the floor space in Soukerian Hall, which is big enough to hold 500 people, was covered with provisions purchased with the donations of the Armenians of Tehran. The Red Crescent Society flew everything to Armenia. Unfortunately, illness prevented me from being on that flight.

In his interview, Karapetian mentioned the Iran-Armen Company which he said had tried to help Armenia, but he failed to name the company's investors or explain how it was set up or even say what it actually did. Wasn't that company's capital the property of the community which had donated funds for a single, sacred purpose? In fact, they used the good name of the Diocesan Assembly to spread their own ideology and start a new factory in Armenia when scores of factories were sitting idle! Karapetian repeated several times that they decided to turn the factory over to Echmiadzin. Since when has Echmiadzin ever run a factory? How can people like this face the community?

In fact, a group of irresponsible persons who are not held in high esteem by the community sit behind closed doors and make decisions, and people like Karapetian carry out their orders and arrangements. The reader will forgive me for trying his or her patience, but I write about this not out of vengeance or to punish the guilty, but rather in the hope that such individuals will come to their senses and cease their harmful activities. Karapetian's interview in *Alik* was designed to muddy the waters and he only did it because *Louys* had already exposed the truth.

Election of the Twelfth Diocesan Assembly

On election day, Bella and I cast our votes at St. Minas Church in Vanak. Candidates were not supposed to linger at any one polling station, so we left St. Minas and briefly toured a few other stations. At St. Sarkis Church, I saw an ARF party member who happened to be an old friend of mine taking sheets of pink paper from his pocket and handing them to everyone who went inside to vote, which was a gross violation of the election rules. My brother Henrik told me that when he and his wife went to vote, a poll worker gave them one of those pink sheets and said it was a list of all the candidates.

Henrik quickly scanned it and saw that my name wasn't on it. When he asked the poll worker why my name was missing, the man replied,

"Didn't you read that article in *Alik*? Don't you know what kind of person he is?"

After the polls closed, the election committee counted the ballots late into the night, in the presence of observers from the Interior Ministry. The next day, a friend of mine who was on that committee called to congratulate me. He said my name had been checked on almost all the ballots he had seen. But when I got my copy of *Alik*, I was surprised to see that I was not listed among the winning candidates.

Louys subsequently published a detailed analysis of election irregularities, citing evidence of voter impersonation, ballot stuffing, illegal campaigning at polling stations, misleading and illegal campaign literature inside and outside polling stations, and irregular procedures at the count which increased the possibility of falsifying the results.

Although I wasn't elected, everyone I spoke with, including people I didn't even know, thought I was prevented from winning a seat. Overall, the results produced a deep sense of mistrust in the community. But in Narmak, at least, the opposition carried the day when ARF expellees and non-members joined forces to defeat the party's candidates. Most interesting was the fact that Ruben Sardarian, a member of *Louys*'s editorial board, received the highest number of votes in Narmak.

The day after the election of the Twelfth Diocesan Assembly, Gidoush Arzouian, a well-known intellectual and theater director, a member of the ARF, and a member of the Eleventh Diocesan Assembly, sent *Louys* a speech that he had delivered on September 21, during the last meeting of the last session of that body. He asked that we publish it *in toto*, which we did:

> **Holy Father, Members of the Eleventh Diocesan Assembly of Representatives,**
>
> Fifteen [*sic*] years have passed in the life of this body, and I have attended fifteen sessions as a Representative of the community, but very few steps were taken for the benefit of the community. For fifteen years, all I heard from skilled workers, teachers, salaried employees and other sectors of the community was this:
>
>> "You talk about emigration, you talk about our schools, you talk about funds raised for earthquake victims in Armenia, you talk about never-ending plumbing budgets, you talk about

all the schools you built with your legacies and bequests, but what have you done for us?

"Our students are leaving our schools and going to state-run schools. Their parents are deserting their birthplace. Only the price of textbooks goes up. Are all your efforts serving to enrich Armenian education, or to fatten your wallets? Why can't you find a way to hire good teachers and increase the salaries of experienced teachers? How many years will it take to complete the copula of St. Sarkis Church? Of all the buildings under your jurisdiction, have you provided housing for even one needy family? Or do you profit from your real estate holdings by having your employees rent those buildings out?

"You talk about culture, but you yourselves talk on your cellphones during concerts."

For fifteen years, I felt like part of the community, not like one of the Representatives who could ease the community's burdens.

Today I ask myself, "Have we really thought about why our community meeting halls are empty when we want to explain to our community what the Assembly has done?"

Now that only a month remains before this Assembly concludes its work, allow me to say that fifteen years is long enough to play the role of scarecrow. In this final month, I resign from that role and I will not attend another meeting.

Finally, I recommend that the Twelfth Diocesan Assembly of Representatives adopt a more open-minded approach and place the interests of the community above their own.

The ARF was so shocked by the election results that it perpetrated some cruel attacks. One night at midnight, three party members went to the home of an expelled member and attempted to abduct him. When the man's father-in-law, who was a party member himself, tried to intervene, they stabbed their intended captive. The commotion woke up the neighbors and they all came running. Two of the attackers fled, but the neighbors caught the third one and gave him a good beating. Someone phoned MP Davidian but he refused to get involved, saying that if the party ordered the action, he couldn't do anything about it because he was a party member first and an MP second. Then the neighbors called Vagrig Manoukian, a long-time community activist and a veteran party member, and recently retired MP Baghoumian.

They both came to the rescue and resolved the situation by sunrise. *Louys* was asked not to write about the incident and acceded in the interest of unity.

During a meeting of the Twelfth Diocesan Assembly, the police came to arrest the vice-chairman, but they didn't know what he looked like and he was able to flee the scene. After that, he didn't attend another meeting for a whole year. According to the bylaws, if a Representative absents himself for a prolonged period of time for no good reason, he is automatically relieved of office, in which case the highest-ranking losing candidate from the same district is invited to take his place. According to the election results, I was that candidate, but I was not invited to join the Twelfth Diocesan Assembly, which was yet another infraction of the bylaws. Had I been invited, I would have refused, but the fact remains that the bylaws were broken.

Election of the Thirteenth Diocesan Assembly, 2004

The marginalization of people like me made the community deeply mistrustful of the ARF, and the irregularities in 2000 affected turnout for the election of the Thirteenth Diocesan Assembly in 2004. Less than two weeks before it took place, the chairman of the Ararat Association asked me for a meeting. He came to my office with a representative of the ARF Central Committee. After the usual greetings and some casual chitchat, they invited me to run for a seat in the Thirteenth Assembly. They even offered me the chairmanship. I thanked them for their "consideration" but told them that at my age, I couldn't take on any more responsibilities. They were quite befuddled. Apparently they had assumed that I was a man without principles. It only goes to show how the party tries to manipulate our people without considering their individual needs and aspirations.

As it happened, there was an overall decline of 45 percent in the number of voters as compared with the turnout four years earlier:

District	2000	2004	Less Votes	Percent Less
St. Sarkis Church and Vanak	2,788	1,007	-1,781	64%
St. Mary's Church	298	141	-157	53%
Heshmatiyeh	466	300	-166	36%
Majidiyeh	2,301	1,300	-1,001	44%
Narmak	3,133	2,150	-983	31%
Total Votes Cast	**8,986**	**4,898**	**-4,088**	**45%**

I asked a few of my friends if they had voted and they all answered the same way: What difference does it make whether I vote or not? They'll elect whoever they want. Why should I take part in a phony exercise whose outcome is preordained? Nevertheless, significant numbers of ex-ARF party members and non-members were elected to the Thirteenth Diocesan Assembly.

The End of *Louys*

Louys was making great progress, with rising circulation both inside and outside Iran. People who had regularly been exposed to distorted news in the past liked what they read in *Louys* and had confidence in what they were reading. Relations among the members of the editorial board were harmonious and uncomplicated. Sometimes we argued, of course. Apart from myself, the others were negatively predisposed toward community structures and upset by positions the Diocese took. I tried to convince them that the National Authority had a positive track record, that it had worked tirelessly and energetically for our schools, our community rights and other collective concerns. Two board members quit because of an irreconcilable difference with the editor, but that didn't affect the quality of the magazine.

At one point, someone sent me a caricature of a fat lady in a dress with the letters G and M, reading a book titled *Diary*. The message was that Germanik (Edic Baghdasarian's pen name) had sold himself to a rich man who was none other than myself! I ignored it because, as I said, I had an open and honest relationship with the editorial board. I had the same rights as every other board member. I was financing *Louys* because I believe in serving Armenian culture, which could never be a reason to impose my will on others. I also have the utmost respect for Edic's work and his service to Armenian culture. When he told me he had written a *History of the Armenian Church* (in Persian) but couldn't find a sponsor, I said I would finance the book and it was published in 2001.

Then one day, Edic told me that he was taking his family to Canada. He said he planned to return in two months at the latest, but he remained abroad and tried to carry on by email. *Louys* continued publication for a few more months, but there were miscommunications and production delays, and there was also the risk that the Ministry of Culture and Islamic Guidance (Ershad) would shut it down because of the editor's extended absence, so the board decided to cease publication. It was a great disappointment for us.

Launching *Houys*

In an attempt to make up for the loss, I applied to Ershad for a permit to publish *Houys* (Hope), which I described as a bilingual biweekly journal with 70 percent of the material in Armenian and 30 percent in Persian. Ershad invited me to come in and answer some questions, and an Interior Ministry official who seemed to know me sat in on the interview. He told me that his Ministry was aware of the fact that the election of the Twelfth Diocesan Assembly had been rigged to prevent me from being reelected, and he said they had been waiting for me to lodge a complaint so they could nullify the election. I replied that the Ministry had denied us the right to elect a new Assembly for more than a decade. And furthermore, I said,

"If I had contested the results, there's a good chance you would have denied us that right again, in which case the real losers would have been our community. They weren't responsible for what happened. And besides, what would they think of me?"

A few years passed and there was no further response regarding my application to publish a new journal. Then Ershad organized a reception in honor of religious minorities which the Minister himself was supposed to attend. I was advised to write him a personal letter, which I did, and I personally handed it to him at the reception. Less than a week later, I was notified that my file would be considered when my turn came. I waited a few months before writing to Ershad again. Not long after that, the Executive Director of the Press and Publications Department invited me to a meeting. He told me that a permit could be granted right away if *Houys* were to be published solely in Armenian.

My friend and business partner Varouj Sourenian helped me form the editorial board which included Robert Safarian, Lea Khachikian and Vachik Vartanian. We started holding weekly editorial meetings, and on June 19, 2007, we hosted a reception to introduce *Houys* to the community. In my remarks, I stressed the new journal's significance and thanked the government for granting permission to publish it. Ambassador Karen Nazaryan, MP Robert Beglarian, *Alik* editor-in-chief Derenik Melikian and other prominent figures also addressed the gathering.

I wrote the first editorial in the first issue, as follows:

> For years, I have thought about the need for diversity in our community's periodical press. I previously cooperated with *Louys* biweekly, but that did not go as far as I had hoped. I plan

to make this new journal a reflection of community life, especially in the areas of culture and literature. I want to acquaint the younger generation with both Armenian and Iranian culture and folklore. Another task of the new journal will be to analyze the emigration problem and find solutions. Politically, *Houys* will tend to provide space for diverse views from the Armenian community. It will be supportive of its senior partner, *Alik Daily*. It will also promote cooperation between Iran and Armenia.

I should add that we regularly distributed 500 copies in Armenia. Before long, the Ministry indicated its appreciation of *Houys* by allowing me to add a Persian section.

Chapter 38

Sati's Fiftieth Anniversary

With the triumph of the Islamic Revolution and then the eight-year war with Iraq, Iran was on a war footing for a full decade, and aside from oil and energy–related projects, economic activity virtually came to a standstill, but Sati never stopped working. In truth, we had no competition. The owners and managers of scores of transport firms emigrated, leaving hundreds of people out of work. But from the very first days of the Revolution, I decided to stay and keep running the company in which I had invested so much time and energy. I also knew that at my age – I turned fifty in 1980 – it would have been difficult if not impossible for me to find other employment befitting my expertise and experience in a new country.

Once I made that decision, I put all my energy and resources into developing Sati. I expanded the scope of the business, modernized the systems and equipment and hired more staff. We never had less than 200 employees and they too worked with energy and dedication. Even though I was chairman of the Diocesan Council and president of Iran's International Transport Companies Syndicate, Sati was always my main focus.

Our company played a significant role in the energy sector and earned the trust and respect of an administration that was very demanding. After the war, we won the contract to transport construction materials and equipment for the new petrochemical complex in Arak. Our highest-profile project was moving an Air Force F-14 fighter jet from its airbase to the site of a public exhibition, and afterwards moving it back to the airbase. We were new at that kind of operation and we carried it out with the utmost care and under conditions of extraordinary control, and we won high praise for our work.

Sati would be fifty years old in September 2001. We decided to celebrate that milestone but we were swamped with work, so we scheduled the event for March 18, 2002, and we had quite a lot of preparations to make.

We produced a booklet presenting an overview of the company's multifarious activities, its special projects and its five major divisions: Finance, which covers accounting, banking, personnel and secretarial services; Transport (with branch offices in several cities), covering domestic shipping, packaging, maintenance and repair; International Travel, covering airline ticket sales, tourism, transit services, airfreight shipping, and freight export and import; Transoceanic Shipping; and Trade. The booklet included a short biography of myself with a photograph, and similar information and photos of my three business partners, Alfred Barzegar Mehrabi (Mehrabian), Varouj Sourenian and Ardashes Zomorodian. We also included biographical sketches of the eleven employees (in addition to Mehrabian and Zomorodian) who had been with the company for more than a quarter of a century.

Alfred Mehrabian has the equivalent of an MBA from the Petroleum Ministry's School of Accounting and Finance. He started as a summer intern in Sati's accounting department when he was still a high school student. As soon as he was admitted to university, he was put on the payroll and he has worked for no other firm since then. Alfred is an extremely kind and hard-working individual. Given my advanced age, he has taken on a great deal of responsibility for Sati's projects in recent years. Varouj Sourenian has an MBA in finance and more than twenty years' experience in international transport, and he is in charge of Sati's international transport projects. Ardashes Zomorodian has a graduate degree in linguistics. He too began his professional life at Sati and he is in charge of all domestic transport projects. My three partners are all share-holders in the company.

Mehrabian and I also have an export-import company named Tavanza which has strong commercial relations with business professionals in Armenia and with European companies. Tavanza has been operating for some thirty years now.

The booklet featured a table showing constant growth in the monetary value of the freight shipped by Sati from 1962 to 2000. The peak year was 2000, when we shipped 140,000 tons. The last section of the booklet consisted of testimonials from various government agencies, all of which acknowledged Sati's high standards. We also received a testimonial from Archbishop Sarkissian and a similar tribute from the Diocesan Council.

The celebration was held on a Monday evening in the banqueting hall of the Laleh Hotel. We invited some 300 people and the hall was completely full, with guests sitting around beautifully decorated tables. Unfortunately, because it was a Muslim day of mourning, we were unable to incorporate a musical program. Our special guest speakers, the president of Iran's International Transport Companies Association (previously the Syndicate) and the head of the Department of Heavy and Special Freight in the Ministry of Transportation, were each introduced in turn by the Master of Ceremonies. Then the MC called me up to the stage to honor Sati's eleven most senior employees, from mailroom workers to managers. As I presented each of them with their award, I embraced and kissed them warmly, except for the one female honoree, since, according to Islamic law, I had to refrain from even the most fleeting physical contact with her.

I recalled the days when these now middle-aged individuals first began working at Sati. They were bright-eyed and energetic young people who had gone on to experience life's trials and become mature adults. They all had secure lives and loving families who were present that evening to see them receive this well-deserved acknowledgment of their years of service. Their happy faces and proud demeanors made me happy and full of contentment.

I have always treated my workers with honor and respect. I made it a policy not to allow any of them to face salary-related difficulties and I always tried to resolve any such problem that came up. I have never been late in paying their salaries, nor have I allowed any insurance problem to remain unresolved. I believe that all workers contribute their time, at the very least, and if they work diligently within the limits of their abilities and their knowledge, what right does an employer have to pressure them or deny them their rights?

The ceremony revived memories stretching back some forty years. I recalled the heated discussions I had had with our drivers and the sage advice one driver gave me. They were submitting fuel expense claims that were far higher than expected. When I did the math and figured out what was going on, I became nervous and angry, not only because of the unpleasantness of the situation, but also because I was spending my precious time dealing with a seemingly intractable problem. Then this particular driver told me frankly that even if I gave them all a bonus or a raise, I would still have the same problem because the padding in their fuel expense claims had a different "taste" (*mazeh*). I thought long and hard about that and I realized he was right. I decided to raise our transport fees by 5 percent to cover the loss, and to this day, I have had no further problems in that area.

The celebration brought Sati's fifty years of activity into focus: the vehicles, equipment and real estate we purchased over the years and their constant increase in value; the development of our staff and the increasing responsibilities they took on; our relations with government agencies, banks and other financial institutions; the reputation and respect we earned from those agencies and institutions; and finally, the major projects all over Iran that we completed with the utmost degree of professionalism and competence. Because the results have invariably been excellent, Sati is ranked as one of Iran's best transport companies.

In 2000, we created Kimia Kish in collaboration with Bourbon Offshore of France to serve the oil and gas industry in the Persian Gulf, ferrying workers from Kish Island to offshore drilling platforms. More recently, in a joint venture with Italy's Fagioli Group, we established Fasan Qeshm Services Co. Ltd., which specializes in the transportation of over-size and extra-heavy loads (up to 350 tons) by rail. And in 2003, Sati purchased a new three-story building on Tehran's prestigious Motahhari Street. We added two floors and now we have a five-story building with over 20,000 square feet of floor space which is more than adequate for our needs.

All this tells me that my life has not been devoid of meaning or consequence. Without boasting, I can say that my life has been full of energy and significance and I am proud of that.

Chapter 39

Three Deaths in the Family

In his last years, my elder brother Henrik lived a life of relative comfort. He was a professional philatelist who amassed a large collection of stamps. He was a photographer and he collected family photographs and scanned them to CD. He shot many of those photos himself on a trip to Armenia and Artsakh in 2001. He was a collector who amassed over a decade's worth of *Alik Daily*. He was also a talented cartoonist and miniaturist who sketched and painted from imagination rather than life, and he preserved his cartoons on film.

Henrik owned a 30-percent share of our family's sausage factory near Karaj and he visited the plant three days a week. After a trip to the plant on July 7, 2004, he came home, had dinner and went to bed. He woke up in the middle of the night complaining of nausea, but he refused to go to the hospital, thinking he would bother me. His wife called at 6:00 AM and told me Henrik was in very bad shape. I came straightaway and persuaded him to go to the hospital, but as we were going down in the elevator, he passed away in my arms.

Archbishop Sarkissian conducted Henrik's funeral service. It was a solemn gathering marked by the highest honors. His remains were buried at Nor Bourastan, the Armenian cemetery in Tehran.

A few days later, his wife sent me a package of his miniature paintings on paper, each approximately one inch by two inches in size. I showed them to a number of experts, including the respected art critic, Armand Ayvazian, and I was surprised to be told they were works of great quality. Armand showed them to the director of the Artist's House Gallery in Tehran. He was completely taken by them and he mounted a week-long exhibition in March 2005. I published a catalogue that was distributed to the guests on opening night. Several thousand people saw the show and it was widely covered in the Iranian media and greatly appreciated in artistic circles.

I had written an article about Henrik that was published in *Alik* and it served as the preface to the catalogue of his paintings:

> We were three brothers. Henrik was a unique and peculiar character. He was always humble, even as a child, but his vision was wide-ranging. He never talked about his personal

endeavors or his achievements.

As a teenager, Henrik was highly disciplined, unlike myself and our younger brother George. He kept to himself and lived in his own world.

He was a brilliant student who always completed his assignments perfectly. He never took part in team sports or the games we played in the street.

Henrik spent most of his time reading and drawing maps. He loved *Sovetakan Hayastan* (Soviet Armenia), an Armenian-language journal published in Yerevan. He read it from cover to cover. It was hard to find and my father went out of his way to get it for him.

In 1946, Henrik asked my father for permission to go to school in Armenia, but he never fulfilled that wish. After finishing high school, he was drafted into the Army. He served in Tehran for six months and then he was posted to the Iran–USSR border where he served as a third lieutenant and was twice commended by his commander.

We three brothers shared a single bedroom in those days. One day, while Henrik was away on duty, I looked through his books and papers and came upon his writings and sketches. His artistic talent was obvious. He had translated *Kalileh ve Dimneh* into Armenian and illustrated the ancient fairy tale with some beautiful drawings. When I showed my parents his work, they were amazed. I kept in touch with Henrik through letters and I wrote him that our parents were aware of his secret.

Henrik had my mother's artistic nature. One of her hobbies was embroidery, even before she was married. Like her, he enjoyed practicing his art throughout his entire life.

After finishing his military service, my brother studied economics at Tehran University, and upon graduation, he worked at Bank Melli Iran (Iranian National Bank) for five years. Then he found a similar job at Bank Etebarat, a branch of Crédit Lyonnais, and he worked in the foreign currency department for nine years. After our father passed away, Henrik resigned from his job at the bank to manage our father's grocery business. Upon his resignation, the management gave him a handmade silver memento.

Henrik decided to expand our father's business and he founded a family sausage factory and named it after our father. He called his elder son back from the USA and we gave him a 10-percent share and appointed him director of the factory. Unfortunately, due to his son's mismanagement, Henrik sank into debt. It took me three years to pay off the debts. During those years, Henrik stayed home and spent much of his time on his art. It was during that period that he painted most of the miniatures that baffle many art connoisseurs today.

Henrik often painted in secret. For example, he made a painting of me in my hunting outfit and we only found it after he died.

Henrik never attended art school or received any professional training as an artist. It is interesting to note that his younger son has inherited his talent. He too, though likewise untrained as an artist, paints marvelous pictures.

My colleague and friend Vachik Vartanian, who often saw Henrik during his last years, shared these reflections on my brother:

> Sadly, it was only during the last few years that I had a chance to get to know this artist, but even during those few years, I had the pleasure of a lifetime. Henrik Aharonian conquered hearts with his sweet nature. His presence generated high spirits whenever he came to the editorial offices of *Louys*, and when he left, an inexplicable silence remained. People would say what a nice person he was, how knowledgeable he was, but they were most impressed by his humility.
>
> Henrik was indeed a very humble person, and his humility kept him in the shadows. Very few people were aware of his artistic talent. Without the efforts of his brother Levon, his art might have been forgotten.
>
> Henrik Aharonian was an ardent reader with wide intellectual horizons. Whenever we met and the topic of *Louys* came up, I sensed that he had read it from cover to cover. He would discuss every detail of every article as though he had written them himself.
>
> I was one of the few who got to see his paintings, but when I asked him to allow me to publish them in *Louys*, he refused, saying he would let me know when the time came.

One could see Henrik's patriotic spirit in his paintings. As a teenager, he begged his father to let him go to university in Soviet Armenia, but immigration was already becoming very difficult and he was never able to go. Who knows? Had he gone to art school in Yerevan, he might have become a renowned artist....

Far Away in Fars Province

When the first petrochemical plant was built in Kermanshah, Sati was contracted to transport heavy equipment from Bandar Abbas to the construction site. The equipment was unusually large – the biggest piece weighed 460 metric tons and could not have passed through tunnels or tree-lined roads – so we had to find secondary routes, and in some places we had to widen and pave the road. The route we plotted was 1700 miles long.

I don't like sitting at my desk and managing things from afar and I have always tried to visit our work sites. On June 19, 2005, I flew to Shiraz with my business partner, Ardashes Zomorodian, to observe the progress of a seven-vehicle convoy and spend a few days with the crew. Our company driver had taken a car down the day before and he met us at the airport. We caught up with the crew in the vicinity of Neyriz and then checked into the hotel where they were staying. When they came back at the end of the day, we all had dinner together. I was impressed by their hard work and endurance.

After dinner, I wandered around the hotel grounds, admiring the fountains, pools and streams. My heart was filled with fondness for the people of Fars, for their creativity, taste and refinement. The majority of the people in Fars are ethnic Persians, unmixed with any other Iranian ethnic group. Fars was the birthplace of the poets Hafez and Saadi. I was deep in thought, musing about how the Persians had preserved their language, culture and traditions and their patriotic passion through all the eras when the country was ruled by Mongols, Turks and Arabs, and about the role of the people of Fars in all that.

Around 8:00 PM, I stumbled out of my reverie, bid my colleagues good evening and retired for the night. Fifteen minutes later, Ardashes came into my room and handed me his cellphone. My friend Dr. Razmik Sirakian was on the line. He told me I had to go to Yerevan right away. Something had happened to my daughter Annette. He wouldn't elaborate, only repeating that I had to go immediately.

I felt like I had been hit by an earthquake. Only a few minutes earlier, I was in a dream-like state, and now I was stricken by calamity, lost and uncertain. I quickly gathered my things and told Ardashes we had to return to Tehran immediately. He reserved seats on the last flight out that night. Our driver got behind the wheel and we said goodbye to our colleagues. We made the 150-mile trip to the airport in three hours of complete silence. Knowing Dr. Sirakian as I do, and the fact that he had called, I concluded that what was awaiting me could not be anything good.

We reached the airport ten minutes before flight time. No sooner were we seated than the plane taxied out to the runway and took off. We landed in Tehran an hour and a half later. I picked up my car, drove to Ardashes's house and dropped him off, and then drove to Sati to pick up my passport. It was 2:00 AM when I reached home. Bella was sitting on the veranda. She burst into tears when she saw me. She knew no more than I did, but she was expecting the worst. We didn't sleep until sunrise. We just kept praying for the safety of our daughter, without knowing what had actually happened.

At 7:00 AM, my friend Robert Yengoyan called from Yerevan and offered his condolences. Now I knew that truly the worst had happened. After I hung up, I didn't want to break the terrible news to my wife. I started sobbing uncontrollably and protesting to God. Annette was the meaning of our life, the guardian of our lives. When Annette had a headache, we shared her pain. When she was happy, we were happy. We were always asking each other, Have you talked to Annette today?

From that moment on, our world turned dark. Friends met us at the airport in Yerevan and told Bella the whole story. She asked to be taken straight to the hospital. She wanted to see Annette one last time but our friends advised against it. They said the doctors were conducting an autopsy even as we spoke, and we should wait a few days to arrange for a viewing.

The cause of Annette's death was an embolism. A few months earlier, she had suffered a lung infection and was treated for it in Tehran. The infection returned several times, but each time she underwent treatment and seemed to recover. The day before she died, she felt a pain at her waist. She asked her housekeeper, Vartouhi, to massage her waist, but the pain continued. When Vartouhi came to the apartment the next day, she found Annette in bed. Annette said she wanted to sleep some more and asked Vartouhi to take her dog Bonbon out for a walk. When Vartouhi returned, Annette was still in bed, utterly still, her mouth covered in blood. Vartouhi called the doctor immediately, he came, examined Annette, and said she had left our world.

Funerary Rites

According to Armenian tradition, Annette's body lay in repose for several hours at the Architects and Engineers Association Hall in Yerevan. In the hour of her departure, she looked like an angel. Hundreds of people came to pay their last respects and offer us their condolences. Among them were Artashes Tumanyan, President Kocharyan's chief of staff, Ministers of State and members of the National Assembly, poets, artists and intellectuals, and Annette's close women friends.

Annette's body was flown to Tehran on June 23 and her funeral was held at St. Sarkis Church on June 26. It was a somber event, officiated by Archbishop Sarkissian who was attended by the Prelates of Isfahan and Tabriz. Among the hundreds of mourners were Annette's women friends from Armenia and Belgium. The funeral concluded with memorial speeches by her friends. Afterwards, most of the mourners followed Archbishop Sarkissian to Nor Bourastan where Annette's body was returned to the earth. That was the most painful moment of my life. My only consolation was that death is the end of us all and thus part of life. On the other hand, I was the oldest member of the family and it was my duty to console the others. We had lost two in a single year, first my elder brother and now my beloved daughter.

That evening, the mourners gathered at the Armenian Club to share a supper for the dead. I had asked that donations be made to the Armenia School Foundation in lieu of flowers and many responded to my wish, but there were many wreaths and bouquets at our gathering.

And so, once again, I was the beneficiary of our community's kindness and spiritual nobility. That is why I bow to them all and express my deep gratitude. I will never forget their support in my hour of sorrow and need. On the day of my daughter's funeral, I felt that we were not only a community but the sons and daughters of one family whose members understand and support one another.

My good friend Loris Tjeknavorian suggested that we organize a series of memorial events to mark Annette's *karasounk*, the forty-day mourning period. He collected, arranged and conducted the *sharagans* (hymns) to be sung by a choir of sixteen from Armenia. With Archbishop Sarkissian's blessing, the performances took place at six venues, beginning with the Church of St. Gregory the Illuminator in Majidiyeh on Thursday, July 28.

The most interesting performance took place on Friday at Surp Khatch Chapel in the Ararat Center. It was patterned on the *Arevagal*, a traditional Armenian Lenten service which the Archbishop said had never before been performed in Iran, but which he intended to incorporate into future Lenten ceremonies. The chapel was crowded with the faithful. The performance lasted for about an hour and left a deep impression on those in attendance, including Dr. Levon Davidian, the chairman of the Thirteenth Diocesan Assembly, and MP Gevorg Vardan. Afterwards, a memorial dinner was offered for the soul of the deceased. Later that same evening, a concert titled "The Life of Christ" took place at St. Sarkis Church. A number of diplomats and community leaders attended, including the Chargé d'affaires at the Armenian Embassy in Tehran, Garnik Badalian, the Ambassadors of Iraq, Georgia and the Czech Republic, the chairman of the Diocesan Council, Norair Armanian, and MP Vardan. After the performance, Archbishop Sarkissian addressed the gathering in Armenian and English:

> This concert was in essence the life of Christ, culled from the Acts of the Apostles, all of which have reached us through our hymns and religious music. Every word, every line, every hymn is complete in itself, an idea, a life – the life of our Lord Jesus Christ. The more we know our religious treasures, our religious music, the more we grow to love them because knowledge brings forth love. When we acquire knowledge about our church and our religious treasures, we are better able to be proud of our heritage.

The performance of "The Life of Christ" was repeated over the weekend at the Church of the Holy Translators in Narmak and the Ararat Center. The final performance for Annette's karasounk took place at St. Sarkis Church on Sunday, July 31. That same day, a memorial service was held at the Ararat Center, and on that sad occasion, there was a reading of letters from Annette's friends.

All these events consoled us greatly. We remain in debt to our community for the nobility of spirit, the generosity and the love expressed to us. We bow our heads in gratitude for the kind and forgiving attitude of our compatriots.

Remembering Annette

What is important is not how many years one has lived but rather what one has done with the life one has lived. Annette Aharonian's forty-eight years constitute a fuller life than what many people could never achieve in a hundred years.

Annette was born on May 2, 1957. She was educated at the Koushesh Kindergarten, the Alishan Elementary School and the Hadaf School in Tehran. She studied art history at the Free University in Brussels. Her chosen field was Armenian art in the Islamic world, and she closely followed developments in Armenian and international art. She was fluent in Persian, Armenian, English and French.

Annette spent many years working in museums and collaborating on films with her colleagues in Belgium. Later, because of her love for Armenia and its culture, she settled in Yerevan. During the cold, dark years of the 1990s, she spent hours in line for heating oil which she then distributed to the elderly and the indigent. She was also involved in providing free meals to needy families. She worked closely with Sati-Armenia, and after I invested in Ar-Al, she joined me and my partner in founding the Alumtek Corporation which she ran while continuing to work with Sati-Armenia. When her mother and I established the Armenia School Foundation, she shared in its work and chaired its board of directors.

Because of Annette's deep love for Armenian art, she was able to gather a circle of artists, musicians, actors and directors around her in Yerevan. During the last two years of her life, she sponsored talented children who needed financial support and she recruited other sponsors abroad, which allowed these blossoming talents to continue their studies at Armenia's Open University. Annette also taught Persian and French at School No. 136 which her mother and I had rebuilt.

Those who knew Annette were deeply shaken by her death. Greta Tounyan, the principal of School No. 136, described Annette as "an ambassador of peace, a white dove soaring into the cloudless blue sky." Mary (Zarouhi) Zanjirchyan, who directed the Yerevan office of the Armenia School Foundation, said,

> Annette was like the mild spring breeze in her optimism and willingness to help others. She had the capacity to very quickly turn that willingness into reality. While others were thinking

about how to go about things, she would already have lent her assistance.

Samvel Baghdasaryan, the director of Ceramics at the National Center of Aesthetics (NCA) and the founder of the Fine Arts Department at the Open University, said,

> I cannot but speak about the love and care that Annette had toward people involved in the arts, especially talented children. She liked being around children, asking them seemingly naïve questions about their work. In reality, she was trying to understand their psychology, to enter into a conversation with children who would take our place in the mission of forging a country and a nation. Annette's enthusiasm swelled when she saw their bold ideas and ventures. She believed it was essential to support them so that they would move forward without hesitation. Within the limits of her capability, she helped everyone, in both humanitarian and financial terms. So many students were spared the worry of paying tuition at the NCA, all because of Annette's generosity.

Marianna Hovanissyan, a student at the Open University who had been sponsored by Annette, recalled that "when she liked something someone had created, she would buy it through someone else, thus helping her students indirectly." Arminé Hovhannisyan, a painting and ceramics instructor at NCA, shared this touching recollection:

> Annette had the most interesting artistic taste. Her paintings were unusual and she avoided showing them to people. She loved working in clay. One day not long before her death, she called and said she wanted to come over and make something. She arrived, took some clay and began to work with it. She decided to make a bowl for her dog whom she loved very much. She finished the bowl but she was upset when she saw that it retained an imprint of her finger. She left the bowl to dry and we agreed to meet again the next Monday, but we did not. Still, she is always, her soul is alive.

After Annette passed away, our family life changed fundamentally. I tried to distract myself with my business in order to control my sorrow. The same was true of my wife Bella. We both did our best to minimize the pain of our loss.

African Safari

One day, Bella suggested we take a trip to Africa with our son and his family and Bella's sister Jacqueline and her husband Yves Levard. Since I had seen *The Snows of Kilimanjaro* and read the story by Ernest Hemingway when I was young, I had always wanted to travel to Africa and see its wildlife and unbounded nature, but I never had the opportunity nor a friend to accompany me on such a long journey. We Iranians think of two things when traveling – pilgrimage and shopping – otherwise we don't think much about traveling and exploring other civilizations. Now I could see Africa with my family and spend time with my grandchildren who were six and nine years old. I immediately began to make the travel arrangements and Yves designed the tour and made the in-country reservations.

On December 24, 2005, Bella and I flew to Dubai and from there to Nairobi where the others joined us from Paris and Los Angeles. We all checked into an English-style hotel that was built during the British colonial period. Taking advantage of the lovely weather, we went sightseeing that day, and the high point of the day was seeing giraffes in the zoo. We celebrated Christmas in Nairobi and enjoyed the hotel's holiday banquet. The next morning, we flew to a small airport at the Tanzanian border named after Mount Kilimanjaro. It was a thrill to see the beautiful mountain as we descended. Since Tanzania didn't have an embassy in Tehran, we got our visas at the border check-point. The border guards were surprised when they saw our passports. They had never seen any Iranian tourists entering Tanzania at that crossing.

We continued on to Arusha and from there we took another flight for Lake Manyara where we met Mr. Gibson, our guide and driver for the next two weeks. He drove an open Toyota Land Cruiser that allowed us to see everything and take photos. First we visited the Ngorongoro Conservation Area and spent six days there. Then we went to Serengeti National Park which was not in the best condition due to the drought. The Maasai and Samburu people led very humble lives and their customs were very interesting for us. Back in Kenya, on the last day of our trip, we took a one-hour hot air balloon tour starting at 5:00 AM, which was a thrilling experience. Sunrise in Africa is unforgettable, especially seeing the herds of zebras, buffalos and wildebeests on the horizon and the packs of jackals running and playing at the same time. I wrote a story about our trip that was published in the Iranian monthly *Safar* in March 2006, and a translation was published in *Alik*.

Our Fiftieth Wedding Anniversary

On June 19, 2006, we held a memorial service for Annette. It was a sad occasion for us. I therefore suggested to Bella that we celebrate the fiftieth anniversary of our wedding on July 11 in Yerevan. We invited a hundred guests to join us and Bella was very happy that day.

While we were in Armenia, my grandchild was baptized at Echmiadzin. We met with Catholicos Garegin II and he told me that the Holy See was going to honor me with the Medal of Surp Grigor Lusavorich during a special ceremony on September 22. When that day came, His Holiness conducted the award ceremony and spoke of my dedication and my achievements, among which he mentioned my school renovation projects. Bella and I were both very happy that day. We made plans to celebrate New Year's Eve with our son and his family in America. And as a New Year's present, I decided to take her on a ten-day vacation in Hawaii. We had a great time.

Bella had complained of fatigue several times. On February 22, 2007, she joined me to celebrate the twenty-second anniversary of the Garni Society. The next morning, she awoke before dawn and held my hand. She told me she was having severe pain in her chest. She could only mutter,

"My God, what kind of pain are you giving me? You are taking me away, but why the pain?"

I was lost. I called for an ambulance but she was in her last moments. Ten minutes later, she was gone. My whole life turned upside down when my friend of fifty-five years and my wife of fifty-one years passed away before my eyes.

Bella's funeral service was held on February 27. Archbishop Sarkissian presided. The church was filled with friends and relatives, community leaders and government officials. Although I had asked my friends to make donations in Bella's name to the Armenia School Foundation and to needy students in Armenia in lieu of sending flowers, her grave and Annette's grave were completely covered with flowers. Afterwards, we had a memorial luncheon at the Armenian Club.

Bella was high-spirited, humble and extremely friendly. She was a member of Hay Geen and she devoted her time to charitable work. She was a devout Christian who was educated at the Jeanne d'Arc School for Girls and she respected the sisters who taught there. She was exceptionally caring toward children. She was a friend to our kids. Above all, she was a devoted mother.

That is why Annette's death was such a heavy blow to her, hence her sadness and fatigue during the last year of her life.

Many condolences were published in *Alik* over the following weeks. Once more, I sincerely thank all those who supported me during those days.

Chapter 40

The Iran-Armenia Friendship Society

I had been invited to the Strategic Studies Office of the President of Iran on February 20, 2007, which was quite unusual for me. I met a few people there whom I already knew, former officials from the Iranian Embassy in Yerevan. They introduced me as an "unofficial ambassador of Iran" who always promoted Iranian interests abroad. A senior official told me that Iran wanted to promote relations with Armenia through non-official channels, hence they were planning to create an Iran-Armenia Friendship Society and they asked for my input. I agreed that such an association was needed. After some discussion, I was offered the presidency of the association, in order to get things organized. I was shocked. How could I bear the responsibility of such a task at my age? Nevertheless, the officials persuaded me to accept the position.

Two days later, Bella passed away and everything was postponed. After a couple of months had gone by, I returned to the project with the assistance of a lawyer named Dr. Momeni. We had at least ten meetings in my office to set up committees for culture, sports, financing, etc. Dr. Momeni prepared the paperwork and registered the association the following year.

Presently, the Iran-Armenia Friendship Society is an officially registered organization and we hope to promote friendly relations between our two peoples.

Chapter 41

The Establishment of the "Hay Dbrotz" (Armenian School) Foundation

In 1999, when I decided to renovate School Number 136, then the Gojoian school bathrooms and the museum of natural history, and learning a lot about the desperate situation of the school buildings in general, I decided to create a special fund to address this dire situation. I was well aware that the Ministry of Education lacked the necessary funds. The government had other vital preoccupations, socio-economic problems and national defense.

According to data, there were 1,560 schools in Armenia at that time, 960 of which were in a bad state of repair. These made me sad and led me to ponder whether the young generation of Armenia, living in poverty and deprived of normal education, would be in a position to build the future of the country. I was also convinced that not everything should be done by the state to address the situation. In developed countries, many schools belonged to the private sector. This concept was absent in Armenia.

When I decided to renovate schools, I already had the experience of the School Number 136. I was convinced that the task was not going to be an easy one. Therefore, I started consulting some friends and specialists who thought my idea was a great one and that it would have a very positive impact.

In May 2002, the Armenia-Diaspora conference was held in Yerevan, where I had submitted my proposals regarding education (see the previous pages). During that conference, I met with the Minister of Education Mr. Leon Mgrtichian and discussed my proposals. I had known him since 1995, when I sponsored the publication of his book, *The Uprising of Zeitoon*. He had impressed me a lot.

After listening to me, the minister told me that he was committed to help me. Later, we had some meetings with several other officials and decided to establish a special fund, which was called *Hay Dbrotz Himnadram* (Armenian School Foundation). A Board of Trustees was created along with an executive director. We asked Nazeli Vartanian, a lawyer, to proceed with the necessary legal paperwork and the fund was legally registered. But in 2003, there were new elections in Armenia and Minister Leon Mgrtichian was elected as a member of parliament, on his party's (ARF) list. As minister, he was replaced by Sergo Yeritzyan, who continued the ministry's support of the project.

The new minister was a former journalist, MP, and known for his interest in agrarian issues. He assigned one of his officials, Mr. Hrach Tadevossian as a liaison with our Board. On September 26, 2003, the Foundation was officially announced at a special event at Hotel Armenia. In his remarks, the minister referred to the poor condition of schools and the benefits that the foundation was going to bring.

After this event, we asked the Minister to provide us an office. They proposed several buildings but none was suitable. I was obliged to take an office on our Massisavan company headquarters. Soon we hired Miss. Zaruhi Zinjirjian as executive director, who was fully committed to her job.

Now it was the turn of fundraising. I dedicated a lot of time in explaining the task of the Foundation in different countries. Many agreed with me. A year before the launching of the Foundation, I had visited Los Angeles and had met with the owner-editor of *Kaj Nazar*, Mr. Hovhannes Balayan. He knew about my activities in Armenia. I felt at ease with him. He invited me to an interview on his TV program. The interview went very well and I underscored the dire situation of Armenian schools. I also elaborated about the need to create a special fund for this task. It was a call-in program, so a lot of people called, and many knew me from Iran.

Later on, during my several visits to Los Angeles in following year, I had several occasions to explain my ideas about the schools in Armenia. There I met with lawyers, Armen Janian and Nik Nshanian and together we decided to create a support group. While in Los Angeles, I also met with several community activists and one of them, Miss. Anahid Sarian, soon became a dedicated supporter of the cause. Other people also became supporters, like Mrs. Jeannette Mirzaian, Seroj Mirbegian (businessman) and Caro Minas. The latter was elected as Chairman of our Los Angeles board. Nik Nshanian allocated an office, along with a secretary, to the Foundation.

During this time, I went back to Armenia and discussed our Los Angeles activities with the Minister, Mr. Leon Mgrtichian. While presenting our members in Los Angeles, I stressed the fact that they were chosen on the basis of their dedication to our Foundation and not their party affiliation. While speaking about Varooj Gyureghian, I presented him not only as an ideologically committed person (he was a known leftist in Iran), but also someone with a strong sense of patriotism. Then, the minister proposed to add individuals who belonged to the Ramgavar and Hunchakian parties to my list. I was impressed by this proposal as it showed that the Minister was very open minded.

Since Mr. Gyureghian used to travel between Los Angeles and Yerevan, we assigned him as the liaison between the two committees, in both cities.

Then we started the fundraising. In the US, donations are tax deductible, but since we did not have that legal status yet, we confronted some difficulties. Our lawyer eventually managed to register the Foundation as a charitable trust and the Foundation became a legal entity in the state of California. Soon after that, the Foundation received its first large donation from Knarik and Gagik Galstian, for the amount of $10,000.

In early 2004, my wife and I once more visited Los Angeles and had a chance to make our case through the local Armenian TV channels. Our local committee decided to organize a fundraising event on April 2, a few months later.

I was getting ready to go on vacation in late March, when I received a call from Los Angeles, asking me to be there for that special event. I flew to Los Angeles. The event was a success. There, we watched footage from different schools in Armenia on the screen, and the audience was impressed. The MC was Miss. Anahid Sarian. During my remarks, I stressed the need of refurbishing schools in Armenia, so that the younger generation could receive quality education.

The success of the event was mostly because of the efforts of Board members, along with their family members. We succeeded in raising $55,000 for the Foundation. Raffle tickets were also sold with the potential of raising a further $20,000.

After the initial fundraising, the Foundation's attention focused on getting new furniture for the schools. We were to import raw material and needed exemption from import duties. For that reason, we presented our project to the corresponding governmental office on December 9, 2003 and cleared that hurdle. The furniture was to be assembled in Armenia, according to local standards. Therefore, this time our Board applied to the Institute of Measurements and Quality of Armenia, in order to get the necessary permits and guidelines. After a few months, we got the permits, which were based upon European standards. But we still had not received the funds from the United States. The furniture required iron rods which were to be imported either from Iran or Ukraine. Our Board decided to buy the material from Iran, using the funds which were raised there.

I had received large donations from my friends in Tehran, including the former conductor of the Armenian Philharmonic, Mr. Loris Tjeknavorian, the proceeds of one of his concerts, which was close to $12,000. The money was transferred to our Foundation.

In Tehran I had great support from Mr. Varouj Sourenian, who was also one of my business partners. Also, Miss. Silva Markarian rendered a great deal of support, along with several other people.

On December 22, 2003, we organized a town-hall meeting and invited around 100 people from Iranian-Armenian organizations, to ask for their support. With the funds raised through this effort, we bought 80 tons of raw iron and six tons of paint and sent them to Yerevan.

The following year the price of the iron ore had doubled but that did not deter us from our work. The renovation job was contracted to my friend Ashod Perker, with whom I had a great experience during the renovation of School Number 136. Ashod sent the necessary tools to Yerevan and he too followed suit, to organize the job there. We were to build 6,000 chairs and 3,000 desks. It was a huge task. The woodwork (MDF) was contracted to a Swiss company named Caritas. We searched for the necessary raw materials and ordered them from China. In early 2005, the iron works was ready, but the pain job was delayed since the temperatures in Armenia were at a record low and the painting needed moderate temperature to be applied.

The Ministry of Education had submitted us the list of schools which needed furniture. When the Board studied those lists, it noticed that they were not correct. Thus, Mr. Ara Karapetyan was given the task of collecting the exact data. He, along with two other volunteers, visited 300 villages and collected data on 333 schools, based upon a specially prepared questionnaire. The questionnaire tried to gather information on the socio-economic conditions of the villages, whether or not there were any cultural and historic sites or monuments near that location, the number of schools in each village, the supply of water and electricity in the schools, and other information related to the number and ethnic makeup of the students and teachers in each school.

This information was a huge contribution to the Foundation's work, since the distribution of furniture, chairs and desks could be more appropriate.

The First Delivery

It was the Oshakan village school which got the first delivery of the furniture. On the specified date of delivery, the Minister of Education was present and during highly praised the Foundation's achievements.

The reason why the first donation was in Oshakan was that St. Mesrob Mashtots, the creator of the Armenian Alphabet, was buried there. The locals had prepared a reception for the guests, during which, I made some remarks as President of the Foundation. The event got wide coverage both in print and broadcast media. Below are two articles from Armenian newspapers *Avanguard* and *Horizon* covering the event:

The Armenian School Becomes the Center of Attention

Iranian-Armenian philanthropist Leon Aharonian, realized his promises by donating school chairs and desks to the eight years old school in Oshakan. Attending the official ceremony were Armenia's Minister of Education and Science, Sergo Yeritzyan, the governor of Aragatsotn region, Gabriel Geozalyan, many intellectuals and guest.

The First Donation of Hay Dbrotz (Armenian School) Foundation

Iranian-Armenian philanthropist Leon Aharonian's important contribution to Armenian education.

It's not unusual for the villagers of Oshakan to witness events and ceremonies at their village as many such occasions occur in the village where Mesrob Mashtots has been buried. However on March 15, the focal point of a ceremony was not the church where Mashtots was buried but a small wooden structured eight-year old school at the edge of the village.

It has to be mentioned that in couple of weeks the term "wooden and simple structured" will be obsolete as there is a new building under construction next to the school. According to officials, students in the next academic year will start their classes in this new building. The event on March 15 designated the launching of the activities of Hay Dbrotz Foundation, which aims at updating the school furniture in Armenia. More details about the foundation will appear in our subsequent issues. For now it is enough to mention that the Foundation has already prepared 3,000 chairs and desks which will be donated to schools in the country which have enrollment at or less than 120. The first recipient of the donation is the eight-year old school in Oshakan which bears the name of a former teacher and a martyr of the war, Paylak Babgenian. The choice of this school to become the first recipient is because of the 1,600 anniversary of the invention of the Armenian alphabet and the choice of the village is homage to Mesrob Mashtots.

All the classrooms in the school have already been equipped with high quality desks and chairs. The next stage will be the updating of the blackboards and maps. Receiving the gratitude of the principal of the school, Rehan Sarkissian; the Minister of Education and Science, Sergo Yeritzyan; and the governor of Aragatsotn region, Gabriel Geozalyan, the president of Hay Dbrotz Foundation and philanthropist, Leon Aharonian delivered the following words:

"Years ago when I was first informed about the dire conditions of Armenian schools I was extremely moved. It is not suitable for a nation which has made many contributions to world culture to have its children sit at desks and on chairs which are in shambles. Our people have always been pursuing education and each one of us has a responsibility to alleviate the burden of providing assistance to our schools. Today we witness the realization of the work we started a couple of years ago. I have not done this work on my own. We worked with a large group, whom I want to thank individually. Today we put up the first sign of Hay Dbrotz Foundation at the entrance of this school and I am certain that in the coming years dozens of such signs will be posted at school entrances all over Armenia."

And just as Mr. Aharonian thanked and honored Armenian teachers "especially women who, even with their low salaries, support the children," the audience thanked and honored the great philanthropist Leon Aharonian and the members of the Hay Dbrotz Foundation.

Lia Ivanyan

My Investments in Armenia

As noted before, my ties with Armenia have increased exponentially after the country's independence. Armenia needed all the potential and assistance of its Diaspora. Not all ventures from the Diaspora Armenians were successful. After long consultations with friends, I decided to open an affiliate of my transportation company Sati in Yerevan. I bought an apartment on Mashtots Street to use as an office and, starting from 1993, the company began its operations in the fields of international transport, air travel and tourism. It soon became clear that the travel agency aspect of the company (selling airline tickets) did not yet have potential, so those activities were suspended and the company focused on international transport and tourism.

For years the company was in the red and it was only during the past several years that it started to make a profit which, although was not sizeable, provided jobs for 12 employees. It has always been my hope that Sati's operations will one day develop further and create more employment.

Personal Investments in Armenia

In Armenia I met several businessmen and political figures. One of them was Robert Yengoyan, the director of Ganantz factory, which produced aluminum foils. It had a large demand. Soon it started producing aluminum profiles too. The foil production line was sold to a Russian company.

The name was changed into Armenal and later, a German company, Offenbach, refurbished it with modern technology with an investment of $100 million.

One third of the factory Ganantz was bought by two Iranian Armenian businessmen, Norair and Hrair Shahbazian. When we heard that the Ministry of Industry was planning to privatize 66% of the company, Yengoian and I decided to bid for 33% ownership each of the company. The section of the factory that we obtained was called Ar-Al and it was in shambles. It took us 18 months to refurbish it, and once it was done and operational, it provided employment for 30 individuals with the potential to grow.

According to market research and analysis, every month 60-70 tons of aluminum profiles were used in Armenia, and we planned to produce the bulk of that demand in our factory.

During Soviet years, Ganantz factory had several buildings for social, educational and cultural needs of its employees. After the privatization of the factory, the Ministry decided to sell those buildings too. My partner and I bought two of these buildings through an auction. One of the buildings used to be a kindergarten during Soviet times in Kanaker-Zeitoon district. After the privatization documents were completed, our goal was to build a 30-room hotel.

Along with my partner, we had bought a camp ground, near the city of Hrazdan, in the village of Pyunik. It was designed as a camping site for the children of Ganantz employees. The site was comprised of five buildings, each of which had a capacity for 80 children, a function hall, a large dining hall and several playgrounds. Lacking maintenance for years, the site was not in a great shape. The construction engineers did not recommend refurbishing. Instead, I bought the shares of my partner and planned the construction of three new buildings which were completed in 2010. The plan was to host hundreds of children from Armenia and the Diaspora and provide an opportunity for them to interact and get to know each other

Large Construction Plans in Armenia

In the summer of 2003, I was in Yerevan for a week. One day a friend asked me why I just focused on philanthropy and did not invest in the construction business. My response was that I was not interested in construction.

We went to a neighborhood known as "Monument", which was located on a hill overlooking Yerevan. There he showed me a parcel of land, which belonged to the municipality. It was up for sale. I thought that it was possible to build a Hilton, or a Sheraton or a Hyatt hotel on that parcel of land. I was convinced that the project could boost the tourist industry in Armenia. Soon I got in touch with a realtor. She informed me that the Municipality had tried twice to sell the land, but there were no buyers. A short while later, the Municipality once again put that land (14,400 sq. meters) up for auction. I was successful in my bid and bought it. The news spread not only in Armenia, but also in Iran. Some people showed interest in partnership for a future development, but that short-loved enthusiasm soon passed and no one expressed any interest in pursuing it. The main argument that was mentioned repeatedly was that tourism in Armenia lasts only for three or four months; therefore a hotel was not profitable. The cost of building a hotel would have been in around $10-12 million, something which was beyond my capacity, hence I abandoned the idea.

One day, an old friend of mine Mr. Vazgen Amirkhanian – who was an engineer and had left Iran after the revolution to live in LA with his family –

visited me in my office and in our conversation the issue of the property came up. He proposed to buy 1,000 sq. meters of my land, something which I had not thought of. Then he proposed to develop that land and build a residential complex. Initially I disliked the idea but after thinking about it, I agreed. We established a company and named it Massisavan. Soon we prepared the necessary plans through engineers in Yerevan and Los Angeles and we presented them to the Municipality for approval and a permit. We got the permit to construct five buildings on the whole lot, each comprising of five stories, and each floor having three modern apartments of various sizes. The first building contained a shopping mall. We also planned to build two storey houses, a sports facility, and a club with all the necessary amenities.

The project started in March, 2005 and was to be delivered in May of 2007. But due to some difficulties, it was delayed until 2009.

At the time, our project was quite unique in Armenia and the quality of the apartment actually encouraged many Diasporan Armenians to buy them, thus strengthening their ties with the homeland. Moreover, the added value of this project was that it provided jobs for many engineers and construction workers for 30 months.

While developing the land, we looked for an office for Massisavan company and found one on Baghramian Street which was conveniently located close to the land that we were developing. It was an office in a building known as "The Building of the Architects' Union" which was quite famous since Soviet times. When we first entered the building we were disappointed, since it was in shambles. My friend Vazgen proposed to the owners that they provide us the first and second floors rent-free and in return we would take on the responsibility of the complete renovation of the building. The renovation was quite quick and we soon moved there.

Chapter 42

The Role of Iranian Armenian Organizations After the Islamic Revolution

After the Iranian revolution, local Armenian organizations and schools came under the strict control of the Islamic government. That development was not peculiar to the Armenian community alone. The new authorities were trying to impose Islamic laws everywhere. There were instances where during family parties, the Revolutionary guards would come and arrest the participants for organizing mixed-gender gatherings and playing live music. The young men and women who were arrested were usually released after paying huge fines or being lashed physically.

The 16 year old daughter of a Muslim friend was arrested because she was at the birthday party of a friend, alongside other male guests. All of the young people who were arrested were punished by 70 lashes each. My friend's daughter's lashing took place in public at the Shahre Farang Molavi square.

One day, during the Iranian New Year (Nowrooz) holiday, we went to Dariakenar, a sea resort. After a couple of days, news reached us that a 16 year old granddaughter of an Armenian friend of mine was arrested for talking to a teenage boy. Both teenagers were held in custody all evening and only after the mediation of a Muslim friend of my friend did the Pasdaran (the Revolutionary Guard) release his granddaughter. Before her release, the local commander had forced the girl to sign a paper, whereby she had promised not to engage in prostitution any more.

The Board of Trustees of the "A. Avedissian" medical clinic used to meet each Sunday at 7 pm. The meetings lasted at least 3-4 hours. On Sundays, my wife Bella used to walk to the house of a friend of ours, waiting for me to finish the meeting, and then back home.

One Sunday, after my meeting, I walked over to my friend's house and knocked on the door to accompany my wife home. The landlady, in astonishment told me that Bella did not show up that day. I called home, but nobody answered. Our neighbors told me that they hadn't seen her either. I went to another friend's home and met Bella there. She told me that, while she was walking in the street, a woman in chadors (body covering veils) ordered her to take a bus which was waiting at a distance. When Bella asked her the reason, the woman told her that her socks were colorful, and that women are only allowed to wear black socks. Bella tried to explain that her socks were actually black but to no avail. The bus she went on took all the women to a center of the Pasdaran. While there, they found out that Bella was Christian, so they took her to another room and then let her go. During that time, a younger Muslim woman gave Bella a Golden cross and asked her to hide it since, if the authorities found out that she was carrying a cross, they would have accused her of converting to Christianity and she would have been heavily punished. This was the general mood in Iran at that time.

In order to avoid these unpleasant surprises, the community started to gather around Armenian organizations. The leadership, in its turn, tried hard not to provoke the authorities, while trying to involve the students of the Armenian schools in the activities of the community organizations. These organizations worked hard to keep the national culture alive through special events. They organized Genocide commemoration day on April 24, Armenian Independence day on May 28, Vardanants day, Christmas, Easter and other national holidays.

Many choirs, theater groups and dance groups were formed, which contributed a lot to the community's cultural and collective life.

During these difficult days, when I was in Glendale (California), I learned that a poetry recital evening was organized for Mrs. Marie Rose Abousefian, from Armenia. I was extremely impressed by her performance. I bought the tapes of the event and took them with me to Tehran. There we watched the tape and all of my friends were also impressed. Somebody proposed to copy the tape and disseminate the copies in the community, something which I did.

Hereby I wish to inform the readers about the cultural organizations of the Iranian Armenian community. These organizations played a paramount role in not only preserving Armenian culture but also enriching and developing it to keep the cultural life of the community alive.

In order not to make mistakes, I asked the following organizations to provide me with information for my descriptions below.

Ararat Armenian Cultural and Sport Organization (AACO)

If we didn't have AACO, I wonder what our community life would look like. AACO was established in 1945. Soon after, the AACO built an auditorium for 500 people. The land on which the auditorium was built belonged to the royal family. After the revolution, the new authorities ordered the community to either buy the land or to vacate it. The organization did not have the necessary amount to buy it and didn't even know what they would do if they vacated the center.

I met with the Iranian official in charge of these affairs, Mr. Karbassi, whom I knew when he was vice minister of transportation. I met him in his office and explained the important role that AACO played in our community. He agreed to lower the sum requested by the government and that allowed the AACO to buy the property and build a cultural and sports complex on the land.

AACO has four major departments: sports, arts, scouts and seniors. It was an all encompassing organization. It had four chapters in Urumia, Gerdabad, Tabriz and Shiraz. I have to also mention that the Homenetmen chapter of Glendale was founded by former AACO members and called Ararat, but it is not under the jurisdiction of AACO.

The AACO has its own governing structure and is run mostly by volunteers.

After the Iranian revolution, difficulties arose regarding the teaching of Armenian in our schools, and all Armenian organizations were impacted. But the membership of AACO did not hesitate to pursue their volunteer work to preserve the Armenian language and culture with greater passion.

When the AACO realized that the complex that they operated was running out of space, they decided to expand it by building a new building next to the current one, and began fundraising. For this purpose I donated $15,000.

In 2004, the AACO marked its 60th jubilee with a special event. I was a member of the organizing committee. We had planned a whole year of activities. One of our alpinist teams decided to climb Mt. Ararat, naming the project "From Ararat to Ararat". But due to the difficulties raised by the Turkish government, the project was scrapped. Instead, it was decided to climb Mt. Aragats in Armenia. The event was a success. Later, a member of AACO alpinist team, Suren Stepanian and his wife Kathrin succeeded in climbing Ararat and both were bestowed by a special medal by AACO.

That same year, many activities took place in different cities of Iran. The AACO organized its 39th Pan-Armenian sports games, which gathered athletes from Armenia, Javakhk and France. The official banquette was memorable too. Guests were invited from Armenia. The closing ceremonies took place in November, after which every committee member was honored by the governing body of AACO.

The AACO operates under auspices of the ARF.

The Armenian Association of Tehran Senior Citizens

This is the only community organization which is under auspices of the Municipality of Tehran. The main organization was founded in 2003, when an Armenian chapter was also created. Today the organization has 400 members and they organize sightseeing activities for its members to various regions in Iran.

I got acquainted with the members in 2004, when they invited me to give them a lecture about a book which I had published (Live Healthy) five years earlier. Although it was a weekday, I was surprised to see an audience of over 200 people. It was a pleasant evening for me and I wished they would organize more evens like that to expose their audience to new ideas and new lecturers.

The Tehran Chapter of the Armenian General Benevolent Union (AGBU)

The AGBU (Tehran) chapter is part of the broader AGBU organization, which was founded in 1908 in Cairo for benevolent purposes. In Tehran, its most active departments are its scouts and the ladies auxiliaries. In 2005, the ladies' section marked its 70th jubilee, during which, its chairwoman, Astghik Babaian outlined the activities of the group during those years, focusing on their cultural, educational and benevolent activities.

According to a report prepared by the AGBU, the organization was founded by Boghos Noubar Pasha, along with several supporters. The organization had a political vision as well. It currently has chapters in 34 countries with the following goals:

(1) To support the moral, spiritual and cultural development of Armenia and the Armenian people.

(2) To support the economic development of Armenians in general.

(3) To organize events and publications to reach these goals.

The bylaws of the organization has three major principles. First, the AGBU is a humanitarian organization and does not engage in political or party activities. Second, the main capital of the organization must remain untouched, and third, any change in the bylaws has to go through a General Membership Meeting.

The Iranian association was founded in 1931 through the efforts of Janik Chaker and Movses Khan Khachatourian. Until 1946, the AGBU devoted its efforts to the relief of Armenian villagers who were struck by natural calamities. That same year, relief was granted to those Armenians who were immigrating to Armenia during the repatriation movement. Between 1951 and 1973, AGBU contributed a great deal to the cultural and educational life of the Iranian Armenians by establishing schools and cultural centers.

In 1933, a group of women established a relief organization which, two years later, was incorporated into the AGBU local chapter. This Ladies' Auxiliary has devoted itself to the relief of needy families, along with social work. During the years of immigration to Armenia (ca. 1946) they did a great job in helping those families who arrived in Tehran, prior to their departure for Armenia.

They, along with other women's organizations, undertook yearly fundraising to support community schools. They organized a three day embroidery exposition, supporting local cultural and relief initiatives. During the last years, the organization has organized lecture series to promote cultural and national awareness. They also sent financial support to families stricken by the earthquake in Armenia.

AGBU (Tehran) has also organized Armenian language classes.

Iranian Armenian National and Cultural Union (IANCU)

The Iranian Armenian National and Cultural Union was founded in September of 1979. Its foundation was triggered by the desire of some community members who had opposed the established National Community Council. The Islamic government let this organization operate under certain restrictions, with the goal of providing an alternative to the ARF dominated Iranian Armenian community.

After the fall of the USSR, IANCU started cultivating relations with the Diocese Council and began publishing a journal titled *Dziadzan Monthly*. Currently they have a four-page publication titled *Khosnak*.

Apart from Tehran, the organization has chapters in two other cities. They oppose the ARF and the Cilician Catholicosate. It is my belief that any organization which manages to congregate Armenian youth around it and engage in cultural and educational programs should be supported regardless of what political outlook it might have.

Below are excerpts from a report that the group provided me.

> The general assembly of the IANCU elects a board of 7-11 people. The organization supports the Armenian Cause, the recognition of the Armenian Genocide and land reparations.
>
> The organization works to enhance the national identity of the community and defends its national, religious and cultural rights. The IANCU recognizes Echmiadzin as the sole and supreme authority of the Armenian Church.
>
> The first chairman of the board of IANCU was Galust Khanentz. The organization partakes in community life and activities, and it has participated both in the parliamentary and Diocesan Council elections.
>
> IANCU has a women's, sports, youth and children's sections, and each section has its own set of activities.
>
> All Armenian traditional feasts have been commemorated with community events in order to enhance the national identity of IANCU members and the community at large.

Iranian-Armenian Craftsmen's Association

This organization was founded in 1983 in order to educate the youth in craftsmanship in different fields. Some of the members who were specialists rendered a great service to Iran during the Iran-Iraq war by repairing machinery damaged in the war, as well as repairing aircrafts and vehicles damaged by mines. In recent years, this organization participated in expositions showcasing some of its products. Its showcases attract the attention of many individuals and government officials

Recently, the Association marked its 20th anniversary, and it continues to function.

Iranian-Armenian Writers' Union

The Iranian-Armenian Writers Union was founded in 1961, in Tehran. The founding congress took place at the Ararat Union's center. Writers like Aram Garone, Manuel Marootian, André Amoorian (Der Ohanian), Grish Davtian, Arsen Mamian, Souren Asatrian, Dr. Alfred Danielian and George Mardirossian have served as its chairmen. The present chairman is Varand Kurkjian.

Some of the Union's members have received the Gevork Melitinetsi Literary Prize, while others the Nerses Shnorhali medals. The Union has published several works of Iranian Armenian writers; it has organized literary events and anniversaries dedicated to prominent writers; and it has taken part in community organized events. The Union has also invited and hosted several prominent writers from Armenia on various occasions, such as the celebration of the 75th anniversary of the birth of the Armenian poet Paruyr Sevak, or the 90th anniversary of another poet, Hovannes Shiraz.

In 2001, the Union celebrated its 40th anniversary and had the Provost of Khachatur Abovyan University (from Armenia) deliver the keynote speech.

Being a specialized and professional group, the Union does not have a large membership, which currently numbers about 30 people.

Iranian-Armenian Engineers' and Architects' Union

During the last several hundred years, Armenian architects have had a considerable input in the development of Iran by building mosques, churches, bridges and other structures.

During the reign of the last Shah of Iran, several Iranian-Armenian architects took part in the construction of community and public buildings, such as St. Sarkis Cathedral and the Armenian Catholic church, along with the medical university of Qom, the Central Post office and the foreign ministry building.

Many hotels, royal palaces, grain silos, the Ararat Sports center, Hay Agoomb's (Armenian Club) auditorium and scores of others edifices were designed and built by Armenian-Iranian architects. This fact has encouraged many young people in the community to enter the state architectural universities.

There were several architectural firms, like Garni, Garniran, and Garnitech, which were founded and operated by a prominent architect, Tovmas Tovmassian. In 1965, he also founded the Iranian-Armenian Engineers' and Architects' Union which continues to function until now. The author of this book is a member of this Union.

This Union was officially established in March 27, 1985, when a founding meeting took place and several months later, a board was elected. The Union's main aim was to gather all the engineers and architects under a single umbrella.

In 2003, due to an agreement with the Diocesan Council, an office space was provided to five different Unions, including the IAEAU, in the Vatche Hovsepian Cultural complex.

Today, the Union has 81 members and operates according to its own by-laws.

Armenian Women's Benevolent Union of Tehran

This Union was founded in 1905 and has made a great contribution to the social development of the Iranian Armenian community. Prior to that date, several consultative meetings took place, led by a prominent community activist, Leon Babaian. Eventually, in October 1905, the first founding congress took place at the Armenian school of Hassanabad with the participation of a few dozen women activists. The by-laws and program of the organisation were set at this meeting. The meeting also elected a Board, comprising of seven women, which in its turn, elected Mrs. Katharine Davitkhanian as chairwoman, Mrs. Mariam B. Gevorkian as treasurer, and Miss. H. Medzbaian as secretary.

According to their bylaws, the goal of the union was to assist the needy individuals in the community by:

(1) Providing financial assistance to the unemployed.

(2) Providing medical assistance and medicine to those who need them.

(3) Finding employment opportunities for unemployed individuals.

(4) Assisting orphans by providing them with food, clothing, school-stationary and other assistance as needed.

Any woman over 18 years of age could be a member of this union.

The Union still raises its funds through membership dues and different fundraising activities. Also, it has several committees which pursue different tasks within the framework of the organizations' program and by-laws.

Hay Agoomb (Armenian Club)

It is a rare phenomenon that in an oriental setting a religious minority is able to establish and sustain a center for its activities. Over 85 years ago, a group of Armenian architects, engineers, professionals and industrialists decided to build a center where they could gather to celebrate weddings, baptisms and national holidays. They bought a building on Naderi (presently Jomhoori) Street. After several years, they sold it and bought the former building of the Swedish embassy on Khark Street. This new building was renovated by

Rostom Voskanian, an architect, and included an auditorium for functions. Over the years, this center changed locations and by the time of the Islamic revolution it – along with the Armenian Club – became one of the few locations in Iran where entrance to non-Christians was forbidden. Women entering the Armenian Club could do so without the need to keep their head scarves or veils on.

According to its minutes, the Executive Board of the Club is elected for two years. The Club is a social and apolitical gathering place for professionals of the community, where they organize lectures, theatre performances, art expositions, and concerts by prominent artists and community activists.

In the 1940s, several cultural and sports organizations were founded in Iran, thus the significance of the Armenian Club was diminished.

During recent years, the Armenian Club has invited several artists and prominent figures from Armenia and elsewhere. The doors remain open and the Club has become a sort of a family, a home for all.

Difficulties arose during WWII and the Islamic Revolution years, and later during the Iran-Iraq war. But eventually the difficulties were sorted out. Presently the Board has appointed a committee, in order to compile all the archives of the Club.

On March 1998, the Club organized a series of events, on the occasion of its 80th anniversary. Thus, artists were invited from Armenia, concerts were organized for the community, and other art expositions, theatrical performances and additional events took place under the auspices of the Prelate, Archbishop Ardak Manoukian.

Church Ladies' Union of Tehran

The oldest Armenian church of Tehran is St. Gevork, built in 1790-95. This was followed by the construction of St. Thadeus and St. Bartholomew church in 1908. St. Mary's church was built in 1938–45. Meanwhile, the Armenian population of Tehran reached 110,000, and the need for new churches arose. Subsequently, to help with these needs, the Ladies' Union was founded.

The union was founded in 1928, to support the Board of Trustees of St. Mary's church, and it dealt with the promotion and well being of church property. The membership was dedicated to the promotion of traditional Christian family values, as well as cultural and educational activities.

When Armenian schools were shut down in 1936 by government decree, the Ladies' Guild founded "clandestine" classes. They also provided material and moral relief to those Armenian families who became homeless during the Emigration to Armenia (*Nergaght*) in 1946. It was through their efforts that the Diocese building was constructed in the 1950s. They renovated many schools and provided the churches with religious artefacts.

To finance its activities, the Guild organized fundraising events, bazaars, art expositions and cultural events.

The first members of the Board have been Victoria Patmagrian (chair), Mariana Amirkhanian (vice chair), Victoria Aghaian (secretary), and Sofia Pilossian (treasurer), along with Shooshanik Hovakimian, Berasbe Hovhannissian and Noonia Hordananian.

The first woman elected as a member of the Diocesan Council was been Satenik Asrian, who was the Chair of the Guild for 25 years.

Hay Geen (Armenian Woman) Organization

This is one of the main organizations of the Tehran Armenian community, founded in 1938. It is dedicated to the promotion of Armenian culture, assisting the school system, and supporting other community organizations. It provided scholarships to scores of Armenian students in different universities, and generally supported educational efforts through several chapters.

Hay Geen organized an exposition of traditional Armenian costumes and even received Queen Farah as a visitor. Below, I have included an excerpt from a brochure that Hay Geen produced celebrating its 60th anniversary.

How and Why was Hay Geen Founded?

The period 1934–1942 was a turbulent time for all Iranian Armenians. When Reza Shah returned from Turkey, in 1934, he ordered the closure of all Armenian schools in Iran – possibly as a result of his negotiations with Mustafa Kemal. This decision had profound repercussions in the community and it weighed heavily on everyone. Thus, at the beginning of the school year in 1936, when students were anxiously waiting to start their academic year, the changes and initial plans to shut down the schools were already felt. It was in this context that the Hay Geen organization was founded. The community tried to cope with this harsh decision in an instinctive self-defense mode. Thus, Armenian language classes started in private homes. This passive reaction led to the idea of founding the Hay Geen organization, in order to fill the vacuum in the field of national education and preserving the national identity of the youth. Many active Hay Geen members have written vivid descriptions of these years in their memoirs.

After six years of the government decree, the Shah abdicated and the schools were reopened, but the Hay Geen organization continued its task, this time as a supporting mechanism for the cultural and educational efforts of the community.

Founding Member
Hasmik Sahakian
June 1999, Tehran

Nairi Armenian Cultural Association

This organization was founded in 1981 in the Majidiyeh (Zeitoon) neighborhood of Tehran and was dedicated to sports and cultural activities. They have a center which includes a basketball court and a function hall.

The organization has four divisions, namely sports, seniors, arts and scouts, and also organizes summer camps. It has close ties with local schools and churches.

The sports division promotes chess, basketball, football and table tennis for the youth, but due to lack of facilities, it can not engage all the youth in its neighborhood. The teams take part in all-community sports games with 120 players.

The seniors' division deals with organizing religious and other activities, including dinners on various occasions. It tries to involve the youth in these events.

The arts' division is active in cultural events, including a theatrical group. There are even attempts to create a theatrical group for children.

The scouts' division has approximately 150 members who are divided into six divisions based on age and gender.

"Charmahal" Armenian Sport and Educational Association

Before talking about this association, several clarifications need to be made. The Armenian community of Charmahal has been one of the most active and prolific communities. It has produced countless Armenian scientists, engineers, architects, doctors, government officials, teachers and lecturers. Charmahal – which in Farsi means four regions – neighbors one of the richest provinces, Khuzestan, and is located southwest of the city of Isfahan in a region where the Bakhtiyari tribe plays a prominent role. Up until the coming of Reza Shah, the Bakhtiyari were considered to be one of the strongest and most influential feudal communities in Iran. At the time, whenever there was a political issue that concerned them, the Bakhtiyari would play an important role in supporting or opposing the government by mobilizing their thousands of warriors to protect their feudal rights. During the Qajar period, when the British were extracting oil in Khuzestan province, British Petroleum used to share some of the oil revenues with the Bakhtiyari to appease them. With the coming of Reza Shah to power that situation changed.

Since Charmahal was adjacent to Khuzestan, Armenians living in the region managed to obtain a high level of education and, having the advantage of learning English because of British presence in the region, managed to occupy important positions in British Petroleum Company. Soon afterwards, these Armenians managed to establish cultural and educational centers in Abadan, Ahvaz and Masjed Soleyman (all of which are cities in Khuzestan Province). Moreover, when Armenians from other provinces started moving to these cities, the high concentration of Armenians along with their high standards of education and job opportunities made it possible for the rise of many prominent individuals who became active in Armenian intellectual life.

The Armenian Revolutionary Federation (ARF) had a strong presence in Charmahal. Most of the Armenians in higher level management positions in British Petroleum were ARF members. In the 1930s the need to establish a community association in Abadan became important. Below, I have included excerpts from the association's activity reports provided by Yessayi Abrahamian.

In 1908, there were many Charmahal Armenians working and living in Abadan and Masjed Soleyman. There were many graduates of the Armenian school of Calcutta who had returned to Iran and held important positions in the community. These young and educated masses were fully aware of the dire conditions of people living in rural areas who were subjected to the oppressive feudal system of leadership. It was in such an environment that there arose a need for an organization that could address the cultural and educational needs of the rural population. On October 12, 1930, in the city of Abadan, a group of people came together and founded an association named "Aror". The founding members of the group included: Mnatzakan Madatian, Simon

Avedissian, Mardiros Megerdumian, Melkon Israyelian, Simon Israyelian and Sarkis Madatian. Soon after its foundation, the organization managed to coalesce a large number of Charmahal Armenian and it was renamed "Armenian Educational Association of Charmahal". The name of the association later changed to "Charmahal Armenian Educational Association". The group later established chapters in many cities in the province of Khuzestan and Nor Jugha (Isfahan).

In 1964, the headquarters of the Association, along with all the archives, moved from Abadan to Tehran. Between 1930 and 1965, the organization helped the local Armenian villagers, and sent teachers and textbooks to the local schools. It also founded a medical clinic, which operated until 1946. Later, the organization even helped the Lebanese Armenian community during the civil war of Lebanon.

By 1966, the region's demographic changed significantly, since most Armenians from the region had migrated to other urban areas. This provided the organization with a new challenge which, instead of dissolving the association, expanded its realm of activities to include all Armenian communities of Iran.

The principal aim of the organization has since been the enhancement of Armenian cultural and educational life among the youth, including through literature and sports.

The "Cultural House" of the Association

In the minutes of the meeting of the executive body of the organization dating back to April 1962, several issues were raised concerning the activities of the association. These included:

(1) To protect and preserve the archives of the organization.

(2) Create a gathering space for the youth where they could focus on cultural and athletic activities.

(3) To have a center where community events could be held.

(4) To have a location conducive of an environment where intellectual exchange takes place with visitors from Armenia and other Diaspora communities.

In the 1960s, Tehran had become the center of the Armenian community as many Armenians from other provinces (including Khuzestan) had migrated to the city. Consequently the organization decided to build a center in Tehran and acquired a 1,200 square meter plot. The construction of the center was concluded in 1968 and it had three auditoriums and a few office rooms, along with a library and a gym. In the following years, the building was renovated to accommodate the growing needs of the community.

This center, which came to be known as "The Cultural House of Charmahal Armenian Educational Association" was built exclusively by donations from the members of that association.

The Youth Section

The organization created its long awaited youth sector in 1968, in Tehran, with its own bylaws, which anticipated a structure composed of administrative, literary, sports and arts departments. In the early 1970s the youth wing of the organization had a membership of about 150 individuals, who took part in pan-Armenian games and had the unequivocal support of the executive body of the organization. The youth section currently has about 80 members.

Women's Auxiliary

The women's auxiliary had existed and operated side by side the executive body of the organization since its inception. The women's auxiliary organizes lectures on various occasions, as well as various cultural and social events.

Literary-Artistic Section

This division started its activities in 1979 and its main task has been to promote national cultural heritage, through commemorative events, with the assistance of the organization's theater group and choir.

Library and Publications

The organization has its own library which was established in 1969 and was named after a prominent ARF leader, Arshak Jamalian. The library has over 2,000 titles in various languages and on different themes.

In 1982, the organization published *The History of Charmahal Armenians*, by A. Sarian, which is an ethnographic study of that particular community in Iran.

Choir

The formation of the organization's choir has gone through several stages. Prior to 1975, any artistic interlude during community events were handled by the two local Tehran choirs, "Anoosh" and "Komitas". In 1975, the organization's choir was founded and was named "Araz", with Alec Bazukian as conductor. In 1981, a new and more successful choir was founded by Jora

Minassian, and was named "Urartu". This choir has performed in nearly every city in Iran and has continued to partake in many community events. By 1983 the choir already had over 120 members and was quite popular for its professional recitals. In 1996, Mr. Minassian resigned his position as conductor as he was leaving the country, and his position was offered to Mrs. Ani Hakobian who has been the choir's conductor up until the present.

Theater

The theatre group of the association was formed in 1981 under the directorship of Mr. Tony Amatouni and it was named "Geghard". The group offered many performances and plays and was quite popular with the community. Mr. Edik Aslanian, who had replaced Mr. Amatooni as director, took the group to new heights and after his passing, Mr. Souren Mnatzakanian took over the directorship of the group. Currently the group has three main sections:

(1) Youth Theater group directed by Mr. Hayrik Aghanian.

(2) "Araz" children's choir under the leadership of Ms. Teni Hakobian.

(3) Youth-Literary group under the leadership of Mr. Misha Hayrabedian.

Pilgrimage

Every summer, the association organizes a pilgrimage to Charmahal to visit the villages and locations which once included a large number of Armenians. According to tradition, the pilgrims would visit their ancestral cemeteries and place wreaths on the tombstones. This pilgrimage is usually organized by the organization's Isfahan chapter.

Currently the organization has about 500 members in three geographic locations: Tehran, Isfahan and Ahwaz.

"Sipan" Armenian Sport and Cultural Organization

In previous chapters, I have already mentioned the beginning and the termination of immigration of Armenians from the Diaspora to Armenia in 1945. After the border with Soviet Armenia was closed, a large number of Armenian villagers who had moved to Tehran in anticipation of their repatriation to Armenia were left stranded in the northwestern part of the capital in a neighborhood known as Behjatabad. The local government under the leadership of a general Khosrovani ordered the relocation of these villagers to the northeastern suburb of the capital which was sparsely populated. After the relocation, those who had financial means started constricting buildings and houses and eventually the Armenian neighborhood of Heshamtiyeh was created. Soon after, other neighborhoods such as Majidiyeh, Vahidiyeh and Narmak-Zarkesh developed. The community leadership eventually stared building churches and schools for these Armenians.

Because of their talents and hard work, most of these new urban dwellers found jobs in the country's growing industries and their children were given opportunities to enroll in universities and obtain higher education. With the growing educated masses, there was a need to organize cultural organizations. In 1963, a group of ARF members, led by Norair Elsaian, founded the "Sipan" Cultural organization in the Narmak quarter of the city. Soon the organization had hundreds of members and had vibrant cultural activities. Teenagers in the organization were involved in many activities and formed groups focusing on music, theater, painting, dancing and athletics. In time, "Sipan" athletes became quite active in national sports either individually or in team sports.

Below I have included some highlights taken from the organization's report that focuses on their various activities.

The Founding of the Organization

"Sipan" Armenian Cultural Organization was founded to address a need to gather the youth in the neighborhood and provide them with moral, ethical and national guidance. The organization was founded in December 1963 under the auspices of "Alik" foundation. At first, the central executive of the organization had its office and headquarters in "Nayiri" then "Toonyan" Armenians schools, organizing various branches to deal with performing arts, theater, library, language and literature. The athletic division of the organization had its volleyball, basketball and soccer teams.

The Building of a Headquarter

In time, the leadership of the organization succeeded in raising funds for the construction of a center. With community efforts, the fundraising activities included donations from "Alik" and the "Gulbenkian" foundations and purchased a lot on which a one story building was built in 1967. In subsequent years, a basement and two more stories were added to the building. In 1989, the executive of the organization purchased a two story building attached to the center. With the building of a physical center, the organizational life flourished, and soon after Boy Scout and Girl Scout chapters were created.

Snapshots of the Organization's Cultural Activities

(1) Since its foundation, the theatrical division of the organization presented many plays. Ms. Aroosyak Tashchian, Mr. Vardkes Bashian and Mr. Nazar Nazarian, were very instrumental in the activities of the theatrical group in the early years.

(2) In 1974, the "Sipan" choir was founded under the guidance and leadership of Mr. Heros Gabrelian. A few years later, another choir group, "Komitas", was founded under the direction of Mr. Digran Soukiassian.

(3) In 1980, Mr. Souren Mnatzakanian was invited to become the director of the newly created theatrical group, "Megrerdich Tashchian". Over the next two decades, the group performed many plays all over the country.

"Paruyr Sevak" Library

As part of the literary subdivision, the library became a focal point for many cultural activities. Thus there were regular screenings of movies, poetry reading and lectures organized at the library. The literary subdivision even started publishing a new quarterly titled *Aybooben* in 1981.

Scouting and Student activities

The boy and girl scout movements were quite active in the organization. There are now about 250 active scouts at various levels and the organization's scouts partake in pan-Armenian activities.

In 1987, the central executive of the organization felt that there was a need to create a student union to help coalesce the university students from the same neighborhood. This student association became active in organizing lectures on a myriad of topics ranging from sciences to health to social sciences and humanities.

"Raffi" Sports and Cultural Organization

After the Islamic revolution in Iran, certain community groups which opposed the ARF came together and founded the "Raffi" Sports and Cultural Organization in 1979. At first the organization had limited financial resources and they only had a soccer field for practice. However, when I witnessed the athletes at pan-Armenian games, I was pleasantly surprised by their discipline, organization and drive. I got to know more about this organization when I read an interview with the organizations' leadership published in *Looys* newspaper (July 15, 2001). I have included below a part of the interview.

Introducing "Raffi" Organization

"Raffi" is one of those Iranian-Armenian organizations that has done a tremendous amount of work. In particular, it has had an undeniable role in developing the sports life of Armenians in Iran. Looking through the list of famous sportsmen, one can easily notice that most of them were the students of "Raffi" union. Leading such a huge complex requires great strength and energy.

Armenian "Raffi" sport and cultural union was established in 1979 by community efforts. At first, it only had a football field, which later developed to become a multi-purpose complex. The complex spans over 6,000 m^2, 2,000 of which is occupied by the events hall and its neighboring buildings. The remaining section is the football field. The complex has a dual focus, sport and culture.

Iranian-Armenian Physicians' Association

In 1979, during a meeting organized by the Armenian Students Association of Tehran, a proposal was made to establish an association of Armenian physicians. An organizing committee was created which put together a roster of more than 100 doctors. Soon after, the group had a meeting attended by 28 doctors who decided to create an association separate from the student association. Organizational by-laws were adopted and an executive board was elected during that meeting. The aim of the Association was to create a network of Armenian doctors, organize public events on medical and public health issues, and to serve the community.

Soon the membership increased to 44. Upon the request of the Diocese Council, the Association drafted a plan to address community needs. By purchasing medical equipments and opening medical centers in various parts of the city, the association managed to provide medical assistance to various segments of society. During the Iran-Iraq war, the association was active in helping the casualties of war.

The Association has had close ties with medical institutions in Armenia and Artsakh (The Armenian name of Nagorno-Karabagh), by assisting survivors of the 1988 earthquake in Armenia, as well as hosting over 250 children from Armenia who needed medical attention. In the context of cooperating with medical institutions in Armenia, the association donated medical equipments to various clinics in Armenia and Artsakh as well as hosting visiting physicians from Armenia.

The Iranian-Armenian physicians' association has also been an active member of the Armenian Medical International Committee (AMIC) and the Armenian International Dental Association. A number of members of the association have also participated in AMIC's and AIDA's world congresses. The Association has also offered its help to the Armenian community through the media – by having a medical column in Armenia newspapers – and it also organized special events educating the public about various health related issues.

As of 2007, the Association has 66 members and its headquarters is located at the Vatche Hovespian Center.

"Sardarabad" Armenian Cultural and Sport Organization

When the immigration to Armenia stopped in the mid 1940s, some of those who were left behind resettled in different neighborhoods of Tehran. Soon, schools were opened and cultural organizations were formed to serve these newly formed communities. One such community was Heshmatiyeh, which had a large Armenian community. The community managed to lease an area where they established a school called "Shahaziz", and along with it, "Masis" Association. After a while and with the generous assistance of the Sahakian family, a new school was built and named after its benefactor, "Sahakian" School, which at its zenith had over 1,500 students.

When the school moved to the Sahakian building, the Association continued using the old space for cultural and athletic activities. At some point, a small church was built and consecrated. After the Islamic Revolution in Iran, the landlord of the space reclaimed the land through legal action, thus forcing the association to move its activities to the major hall of "Sahakian" School. Soon afterwards, the association was renamed "Ani". Later on the hall was consecrated as a church by the late Prelate, Archbishop Ardak Manoukian, and was known as St. Vardanants Armenia church.

In 1983, a group of young people established the "Sardarabad: association in the same community and the neighborhood was renamed (by the community) as Sardarabad neighborhood. At first, the executive council meetings of the association used to take place at the homes of executive members. A couple of years later, with the help of Minas Hovannissian and *Alik* daily, a property was bought and the activities of the association moved there. Soon the Diocesan Council helped the association to expand the property and made it possible for the community to have a vibrant cultural and athletic life. This organization has around 100 members and promotes cultural and sports activities.

"Sosse Mayrik" Seniors' Home

In 1977, with the donation of late Mrs. Shooshanik Hordananian, the Tehran Women's Benevolent Organization bought a property to establish a home for seniors. After renovations and the blessing of the new structure, the facility, which was named "Sosse Mayrik", started its operations.

The seniors' home accommodated 14 permanent residents and has all the necessary utilities to accommodate the residents. The managers of the facility have included Mrs. Genof Aghabegian, Arusyak Hacobian, Bella Petrosian and it is currently headed by Mrs. Varsik Baghdasarian. The funds of the home are raised through rent collected from the residents as well as funding provided by municipal and government agencies. The facility boasts a superb quality as testified by government officials.

The resident seniors enjoy the benefits of a high quality social service, as well as vibrant cultural and religious events which are organized for them on a regular basis

A Brief Glance at the Hay Dad (Armenian Cause) Committee of Tehran

After the 50th anniversary of the Armenian Genocide in 1965, the ARF formed Hye Dad (Armenian Cause) Committees across the Armenian Diaspora. One was formed in Tehran too, which tried to promote awareness regarding the Armenian Genocide and to promote the interests of the Iranian-Armenian community. It tried to gather Iranian friends of the Armenian Cause.

In 1982 this Committee was officially registered under the name of Research Center on Armenian Issues (HOOSK by its Armenian acronym) and soon had its own offices.

The Center has its newsletter titled "Baregam" and organizes lectures to inform its membership and the community about issues related to Armenia and Armenians. It gathers materials regarding the Armenian Cause and the role of Armenians in Iranian cultural life and promotes them through public events.

Iranian Friends of the Armenian Cause

The Center has done a significant job among the Iranian public at large and especially among the intelligentsia. It has established contacts with Iranian official circles, press and academia, and has published materials about the Armenian Cause in Persian. It has a remarkable reference center for academic researchers and helps non-Armenian researchers, sometimes even translating documents and books into Farsi. One of the main activities of this group is to organize lectures for Iranian intellectuals and to invite non-Armenian specialists to give talks. The group has also organized cultural expositions promoting Armenian culture.

The Committee cooperates closely with the two Armenian deputies in the Iranian Parliament to promote awareness of the Armenian Genocide.

"Bayman" Quarterly

Bayman is the quarterly newsletter of the Committee, published in Farsi, since 1996. It is a strong publicity tool for the Armenian Cause in Iran. Many prominent public intellectuals and academics have contributed, and continue to contribute and support the quarterly, making it a well respected journal.

The quarterly has a circulation of 1,500 and it is sent to key government offices, MPs, universities, research centers, as well as foreign embassies. It also has its own website.

Publications and Related Events

One of the Committee's tasks is to undertake translations into Persian and publish works related to the Armenian Cause. 10 books and six booklets were published between 2003 and 2007.

This committee also spends a lot of time and resources in organizing special events for the Iranian public and political figures. Sometimes prominent political figures have been invited as keynote speakers. Along with this, at each commemoration of the Armenian Genocide, memoranda are sent to the UN offices and embassies in Tehran highlighting the issue of the Genocide as an unpunished tragedy.

Focusing on the issue of the Armenian Genocide, several documentaries have been prepared for Iranian and Armenian audiences. Moreover, special classes have been organized to introduce young students to the topic of the Genocide, and these classes are presented by specialists and academics.

Since 2003, the Committee has organized annual seminars on the theme, "The Armenian Cause Today". During these seminars, many Hye Dad activists and historians from Armenia and Europe have made presentations analyzing the current situation in Armenia, Turkey, Artsakh, Javakht and elsewhere within the context of the Armenian Cause. The proceedings of all these conferences and seminars have been published.

The Van-Vaspoorakan Historical Research Center

In April-May of 1996, on the encouragement of Mr. Lemuel Avedian, a group of Armenians who traced their ancestry to the city of Van in Western Armenia, decided to found a center, dedicated to the history of Van. Soon, Mr. Avedian dedicated an apartment to this center, and after a few meetings, the newly-born organization was called Van-Vaspoorakan Historical Research Center with a set of its by-laws. Vaspoorakan is the name of a province in which the old city of Van was located.

This center's task was to organize excursions to Van (which they did seven times) and to other Western Armenian historic sites. They also presented several photographic exhibitions regarding these places. Each year, the Center recognizes survivors of the Armenian Genocide. Other activities include special gatherings and lecture series related to Van and the monuments of Western Armenia. The lecturers are usually prominent figures, specialists and academics from Armenia, as well as young researchers and Iranian historians specializing on Urartian history.

All these events have been filmed and documented.

Mr. Lemuel Avedian has been a close friend of mine. He was a goldsmith who catered to the bourgeoisie of Iran. He was so highly regarded as a specialist in his craft that the new Islamic government gave him the task of sorting out the jewelry in the state's possession. He even published in his specialty.

General Union of Armenian University Students

This Union was founded in 1943 in order to promote higher education among the youth and to serve the community at large. At that time, they had only a single room as their office, but in 1971, they bought a property, which later included an auditorium.

The goal of this union was to create a network of university alumni, promote the idea of getting higher education, and later become active members of their community. This idea arose in 1936, when the Armenian schools were closed on the order of the government.

Thus it was decided to create contacts with similar organizations in the Diaspora, more cooperation with students in local Armenian schools, support Armenia-Iran cultural and scientific cooperation, and encourage the membership to be more active in the community.

Presently, this Union operates mainly in the fields of education, humanities, sports and arts. They also organize language classes.

My grandchildren, Andrei and Badrik.

Happy days in Africa.

With my family.

Gomidas Institute
42 Blythe Rd.
London W14 0HA
England
www.gomidas.org

INDEX

A

Abadan, Iran 46, 59, 72, 90, 139, 165, 205, 207, 208, 556
Abbasabad, Iran 71
Abcarian, Azad 512
Abcarian, Petros 191
Aboulian, Hrair 339
Aboulian, Shahen 181
Abousefian, Marie Rose 546
Abrahamian, Hovannes 309
Abrahamian, Leon 370
Abrahamian, MP George 281, 282, 286, 493, 501
Abrahamian, Robert 370
Abrahamian, Yessayi 556
Afshar, Mohammad (Farrokh) 330, 332, 333, 335, 337
Aftandalian, Shora (Alexander) 115
Agarag (Agarak), Armenia 348, 372, 507
Agassi, André 48
Aghabegian, Genof 564
Aghaian, Victoria 554
Aghamalian, Henrik 339
Aghanian, Hayrik 559
Aghassi, Emmanuel (Manuel "Mike" Agassi) 48
Aghayan, MP Felix 113
Aghazarian, Georgik 279
Aharonian, Almast Babloyan 13, 14
Aharonian, André 14, 18–21, 24, 25, 37, 39, 42, 43, 51, 52, 69, 72, 73, 77, 86, 87, 305, 398, 524
Aharonian, George 19, 498
Aharonian, Henrik 14, 20, 50, 72, 73, 305, 370
Aharonian, Levon 181
Aharonian, Vahe 73
Ahmadinejad, President Mahmoud 475
Ahvaz, Iran 95, 100, 102, 105, 106, 132, 165, 205, 207, 211, 220, 250, 556
Ajemian, Albert 266, 310, 327, 355, 392, 431–433, 440, 484
Akhavi, General Hassan 61, 76
Ala, Prime Minister Hossein 60, 76
Al-Assad, President Hafez 472
Alaverdi, Armenia 458
Aleppo, Syria 448, 492
Alexanian, Oksen 395, 504
Alexy II, Primate of the Russian Orthodox Church (1990–2008) 442, 460, 464
Ali, Yousef 303
Allahverdian, Ashot 14
Allahyari, Souren 371
Aloumian, Vardan 191
Alyokhin, Mr. 103, 104
Amatouni, Tony 47, 559
Amirkhanian, Mariana 554
Amirkhanian, Sebouh 309
Amirkhanian, Vazgen 48, 486, 488, 543
Amourian, André 432, 550
Amouzegar, Prime Minister Jamshid 137, 139
Ananyan, Vakhtang 99
Andimeshk 18
Andonian, Yeprem Der 370

Antelias, Lebanon 109, 181, 264, 297, 299, 425, 441, 455, 461–463, 471, 473, 491–493
Aragatsotn, Armenia 487, 540
Arak (Sultanabad), Iran 291
Arakelian, Berjouhi 288
Arakelyan, Grigor 419
Arakelyan, Makar 444
Araktsyan, Speaker Babken 457–459, 462
Aram I, Catholicos of the See of Cilicia (1995–) 425, 430, 445, 492, 493
Ardalan, Mr. 96
Armanian, Norair 529
Artchounian, Hratch 371
Artsakh (Nagorno Gharabagh) 403, 456, 467, 469, 470, 475, 523
Arzouian, Gidoush 513
Arzoumanian, Golia 288, 371
Arzoumanyan, Alexander 452, 455–457, 462
Asatorian, Jean 28, 41
Asatourian, Artoush 47
Asatrian, Souren 550
Asgarian, Fereydoun 481
Asgar-Oladi, Asadollah 370
Aslanian, Edik 559
Aslanian, Njdeh 498
Aslikhan Mayrik 13, 17, 34
Asrian, Satenik 22, 554
Atabaki, General Esmail 101, 102, 141, 142, 145, 147, 148
Atabegian, Mr. 346–349
Atayan, Arshak 15
Avakian, Grigor Tadevos 371
Avakian, Khosrow 18
Avakian, Roza 419
Avakian, Shahen 457
Avakian, Vahram 419
Avakian, Voski Babloyan 18
Avedian, Lemuel 368, 371, 433, 566

Avedissian, Ashot (Black) 47, 504
Avedissian, Avedis 16
Avedissian, Babken 46
Avedissian, Gevorg 16, 293
Avedissian, Simon 557
Ayat, Hassan 227
Aysseh, Alfred 92, 159
Ayvazian, Abraham 371
Ayvazian, Armand 523
Azhari, General Gholam-Reza 140
Azizian, Heros 209

B
Babaian, Astghik 548
Babaian, Leon 552
Babakhanian, Edward 187
Babakhanian, Vachik 371
Babayan, Sako 67, 116
Babayan, Samvel 468
Babgenian, Paylak 541
Babloyan, Abraham (Mghdsi Abro) 13
Babloyan, Agnes 45
Babloyan, Ara 454
Babloyan, Ashot 303
Babloyan, Hayganoush Avakian 13, 14, 17
Babloyan, Mnatsakan 13, 14, 17, 18, 44, 303, 496
Babolsar, Iran 112, 118, 126, 289, 290, 292
Badalian, Garnik 529
Badalian, Hovannes 191
Badrei, General Abdol-Ali 148
Baghdanian, Jahangir 67
Baghdasarian, Edic (Germanik) 242, 474, 498, 499, 516
Baghdasarian, Varsik 564
Baghdasaryan, Samvel 531
Baghdassarian, Annette 340
Baghdikian, Alexander 284
Baghi (Baqi), Emadeddin 336

Baghoumian, Andranik 181, 208, 228
Baghoumian, MP Ardavazd 279, 281, 286, 376, 380, 388, 392, 425, 444, 456, 458, 459, 501, 509, 514
Baghramyan, Marshal Ivan (Hovhannes) 107
Bagratyan, Hrant 423–426, 442, 463
Bahonar, Ayatollah Dr. Mohammad Javad 153, 154, 187, 188, 227, 229, 238
Bakhtiar, General Teymour 64, 66, 67
Bakhtiar, Prime Minister Shapour 137, 141, 142, 145, 147
Baku, Azerbaijan 348, 451, 460, 468
Balayan, Hovhannes 485, 537
Baliozian, Bishop Aghan 387
Bandar Abbas (Bandar Shahid Rajai), Iran 209, 311, 385, 401, 526
Bandar Emam Khomeini (formerly Bandar Shahpur) 95, 100
Bandar Enzeli (formerly Pahlavi), Iran 49, 73, 289, 435
Bani-Sadr, President Abolhassan 153, 154, 165, 183, 187, 188, 206, 226
Barkhan, Rozig 371
Barkhoudarian, Shavarsh 270
Barseghian, Salman 371, 483
Barseghyan, Hayk 481
Bashian, Vardkes 561
Basra, Iraq 311
Bastani, Shapour 170, 172, 175
Bayburdyan, Ambassador Vahan Arak'eli 340, 392, 419–421, 425, 428, 430, 431, 447, 456, 462, 466, 473, 474, 499
Bazargan, Prime Minister Mehdi 134, 145, 152–156, 176, 335
Bazeyan, Albert 480
Bazukian, Alec 558
Bedesta, Rima 349–352, 361
Beglarian, MP Robert 283, 286, 517
Behbahani, Mr. 96

Beheshti, Ayatollah Dr. Mohammad Hossein 153, 165, 185, 186, 223–227, 238, 241, 245, 278, 292
Behjatabad, Tehran 50, 110, 208, 293, 300, 439, 559
Beirut, Lebanon 109, 271, 298, 317, 357, 389, 441, 463, 492
Berberian, Arzrouni 350
Berberian, Lida 350
Bernardi, Dr. Albert 168, 196, 232, 240, 244, 256, 311, 370, 425, 426, 504
Bezik (Bezikian), Edmond 502
Bikfaya, Lebanon 109
Bleda, Ambassador Tanşuğ 215–217
Boghosian, Dajad 432
Boghosian, Razmik 116
Bojolyan, Edward 366, 368
Bokov, Stanislav 342–344
Borujerdi, Ayatollah Mohammad Hossein 143
Boukhanian, Mihran 371
Brussels, Belgium 141, 284, 303, 326, 394, 530
Budaghian, Budagh 14
Budaghian, Mahi Babloyan 14
Bushehr, Iran 83, 132

C
Capucci, Archbishop Hilarion 177
Carter, President Jimmy 137, 138, 176, 177
Chahar Mahall (Charmahal), Iran 50, 234, 279, 306, 556, 558
Chaker, Janik 549
Chalus, Iran 48
Cherchian, Rita 495
Chirac, President Jacques 464
Chobanian, V. Rev. Father Mashdots 493
Clinton, President William (Bill) 464

D
Danielian, Dr. Alfred 550
Darbinyan, Armen 386, 402, 407, 408, 423, 456
Darya Kenar, Iran 112, 125, 155, 183, 307, 315, 316, 318, 326, 438, 459
Dastgheib, Ayatollah Seyyed Abdol-Hossein 227
Dastgheib, Seyyed Abdollah 368–373, 382, 383
Davidian, Digran 407
Davidian, MP Dr. Levon 281, 282, 286, 340, 391, 392, 493, 494, 501, 514, 529
Davitian, Dr. Haroutiun (Harmik) 240, 309, 310, 491, 493, 504
Davitian, Edward 370
Davitkhanian, Katharine 552
Davtian, Grish 550
Demirchyan, Garen (Karen) 414, 415, 458, 459, 474, 479, 482, 501
Demirchyan, Stepan 458
Der Hagopian, Torgom 181
Derderian, Bishop Varazdad 232, 242, 392
Derderian, Isahak 288
Dilman (Salmas), Iran 14, 496
Divan, Dr. 74
Drambian, Bishop Vahan 461
Dubai, United Arab Emirates 311, 385, 434, 532

E
East Azarbayjan, Iran 166
Echmiadzin, Armenia 99, 109, 180, 299, 313, 352, 356, 360, 369, 402, 412, 441, 444, 449, 454, 455, 460–465, 473, 475, 483, 491, 500, 512, 533, 550
Edelmann, Dr. 74
Elchibey, Abulfaz 360
Elsaian, Norair 190, 240, 279, 311, 366, 385, 432, 560
Emami, Saeed 336

Eqbal, Dr. Manucher 284
Eskandari, Parvaneh Majd 335
Eskandarian, Eskandar 181, 208, 289

F
Farmaniyeh, Tehran 86, 87, 113, 147, 194, 436
Fatemi, Dr. Hossein 61, 65, 473
Fave, Iraq 210
Fazeli, General Mohammad 104
Ferahian, Elbis Kovanian 129, 288, 392–395
Firuz Kuh, Iran 118, 123, 124
Fitisov, Mr. 24
Ford, President Gerald 137
Forouhar, Dariush 137, 335, 336

G
Gabrelian, Heros 561
Gabrielian, Mr. 396
Gabrielov, Mr. 96–98, 342, 343
Gachsar, Iran 49
Gaduk, Iran 124
Galoustian, Bishop Aharon 222, 274, 290, 392
Galoustian, Garen 435
Galstian, Dr. Galoust 311
Galstian, Knarik and Gagik 486, 538
Gamsakhurdia, President Zviad 360
Ganji, Akbar 336
Garabedian, Bagour 303
Garegin I, Catholicos of All Armenians (1995–99) 441, 444, 454, 483
Garegin I, Catholicos of the See of Cilicia (1945–52) 473
Garegin II, Catholicos of All Armenians (1999–) 483, 533
Garegin II, Catholicos of the See of Cilicia (1983–95) 264, 298, 299, 339, 340, 441, 462
Garone, Aram 550
Gasparian, Rafik 355, 390
Gedashen, Nagorno Gharabagh 404

Geneva, Switzerland 326, 445, 459–461, 466, 467
George, Dr. 293, 294
Geozalyan, Gabriel 487, 540, 541
Gerdabad, Iran 547
Gevorgyan, Hayk 478
Gevorkian, Mariam B. 552
Gevorkian, Vigen 179, 370, 425, 426
Ghaffar, Seyyed Mehdi 366, 368
Ghapan, Armenia 314, 347, 349, 411, 412, 506, 508
Gharabegian, Grigor (Gougoush) 114, 194
Gharabegian, Vachik 114, 194, 195, 475
Gharanei, General Valiollah 155
Gharibian, Jerair 111, 226
Gharibjanyan, Ambassador Gegham Dirani 474, 475, 493–495
Ghasemi, Bahram 382, 407, 420, 422, 427, 471
Ghavam ol-Saltaneh, Prime Minister Ahmad 42
Ghoddousi, Ayatollah Ali 227
Gholi, Mirza 124, 125
Ghorogh, Iran 289, 290
Ghotbzadeh, Sadegh 135
Ghukasyan, President Arkady 468
Giveian, Mr. 193, 274
Gonbad-e Kavous, Iran 167, 208
Gorbachev, President Mikhail 313, 350, 353, 366, 367
Gorgan, Iran 118, 127, 289, 290, 507
Goris, Armenia 347, 349, 382, 383
Gouzigyan, Samvel 411
Goya, Mr. 160, 161, 333
Gracey, Dr. 74
Grigorian, Mardiros 370
Grigorian, Ruben 91, 409
Grigorian, Seda (Davitian) 432
Grigorian, Vachik 371
Grigoryan, Mushegh 414
Grigoryan, Zulum 414

Guilleau, Mr. 89
Gyumri (formerly Leninakan), Armenia 313, 506
Gyureghian, Varooj 537
Gyut, Archbishop 461, 464

H
Habibi, Vice President Hassan 455–457, 501
Hacobian, Arusyak 564
Haddad-Adel, Dr. Gholam-Ali 268
Haddad-Adel, Haj Agha 268
Haeri, Ayatollah Abdol-Karim 142, 143
Hafez 526
Haftvan, Iran 14–19, 44, 52, 303, 496
Hagopian, Bishop Khajag 493
Hagopian, Colonel Emil 498
Hagopian, Dr. Oshin 208, 343
Hagopian, Grisha (Gougoush) Der 398
Hagopian, Torgom Der 192, 252
Haiser, General Robert 142
Hajian, Father Hovhannes 109
Hakhnazarian, Dr. Armen 180, 181, 244, 299, 301, 302, 373, 504
Hakobian, Ani 559
Hakobian, Teni 559
Halabche, Iraq 210
Hamadan, Iran 281, 289, 291, 507
Hamidi, Mehdi 26
Haroutunian, Hovik 181, 302
Haroutunian, Onnik 371
Haroutunian, Shahen 115, 176
Harriman, Averell 60
Harutiun, Melik 13
Harutyunyan, Gagik 385, 387, 394, 405, 419, 420, 454
Harutyunyan, Khosrov 350, 352, 374
Hashemi-Rafsanjani, President Ali-Akbar 155, 166, 240, 244, 246, 256, 278, 311, 336, 373, 374, 376–382, 419, 421, 447, 449, 457, 491
Hayrabedian, Jorgig 371

Hayrabedian, Misha 310, 311, 392, 559
Heelsum, The Netherlands 75
Heshmatiyeh, Tehran 51, 189, 195, 258, 285, 293, 301, 308, 494, 499, 501, 515
Heydari, Mr. 329
Hordananian, Noonia 554
Hordananian, Shushanik 289, 564
Hormozgan, Iran 209
Hovakimian, MP Dr. Gaguik 113, 284, 285, 498
Hovakimian, Shooshanik 554
Hovanissian, Arpik 290
Hovanissian, Felix 118, 290
Hovanissian, Gagik 228
Hovanissian, Hagob 22
Hovanissian, MP Ardashes 284
Hovanissian, Ruben (R) 345, 498
Hovanissyan, Marianna 531
Hovannes, Baron 50
Hovannisian, Raffi 374, 496
Hovannissian, Minas 189
Hovenissian, Haikaz 136
Hoveyda, Prime Minister Amir-Abbas 113, 137–140, 148, 153
Hovhannisian, Aida 182, 187, 240, 256, 295, 299, 303, 395, 504
Hovhannisian, Bayar 187
Hovhannissian, Berasbe 554
Hovhannisyan, Arminé 531
Hovhannisyan, Gevorg 374
Hovian, Anoush 259
Hovnatanian, Vahig 226
Hovsepian, Bishop Haik Mehr 335
Hovsepian, Mardik 115
Hovsepian, Vatche 552
Hovsepyan, Ruben 344, 345, 352
Hrazdan, Armenia 543
Hussein, President Saddam 206, 450

I

Illichivs'k, Russia 106
Injirgholli, Vahe 371

Irevani, Rahim 101
Isfahan, Iran 37, 50, 85, 122, 132, 142, 143, 160, 165, 174, 185, 209, 220–222, 254, 279, 281–284, 299, 334, 342, 375, 380, 392, 424, 425, 430, 442, 444, 455, 459, 461, 462, 465, 476, 493, 494, 496, 528, 557
Israyelian, Melkon 557
Israyelian, Simon 557

J

Jafari, General Fazlollah 277
Jaghabegian, Golia 196, 309
Jahangiri, Governor Eshagh (Eshaq) 444
Jamalian, Arshak 558
Janian, Armen 486, 537
Jannati, Ayatollah Ahmad 256
Jazmadarian, Vahe 402, 409, 413
Jimmy 122–124
Jovakim, Vahe 371, 400
Jukha, Syria 492
Julfa, Iran 15, 91, 100–105, 107, 221, 223, 279, 281, 283, 331, 372, 380, 383, 424, 425, 435, 455, 459, 474, 476, 494, 495

K

Kajaran, Armenia 347, 349
Kalava, Iran 291
Kamalian, Vartan 195, 410, 411
Kanaker-Zeitoun, Yerevan 480, 488
Kanon, Gabriel (Joseph) 116
Kantsag (Ganja), Azerbaijan 450
Karaj, Iran 39, 48, 49, 85, 118, 125, 127, 436, 523
Karamanukyan, Shahen 447–453, 467, 468, 470, 471
Karapetian, Dr. Tadevos 180
Karapetian, Ruben 353, 355, 371, 396, 411, 511, 512
Karapetyan, Ara 486, 539
Karavajar (Karvachar, Kelbajar), Nagorno Gharabagh 404
Karbassi, Mr. 547

Karroubi, Hojatoleslam Mehdi 495
Karroubi, Hojjatoleslam Mehdi 211
Kashani, Mr. 434
Kelardasht, Iran 62
Kermanshah, Iran 289, 291, 312, 507, 526
Keshishian, Father Varazdad 332
Keshishian, Levon 301
Keshishian, Mardiros 132, 205
Keshishian, Mihran 106
Keshishian, Ruben 499
Khachatourian, Movses Khan 549
Khachaturian, Aram 402, 415
Khachaturian, Edic 101
Khachaturian, MP Dr. Hratch 165, 185, 228, 240, 279
Khachaturian, Sanasar 46, 101
Khachaturian, Vachik 180, 194
Khachaturian, Vahik 188, 194, 232, 244, 264, 297
Khachikian, Lea 517
Khachikian, Samvel 46
Khalafabad, Iran 106
Khalatian, MP Hrair 163, 165, 181, 185, 189, 195, 214, 222, 234, 240, 242, 244, 249–252, 256, 259, 264, 279, 286, 299, 410, 470
Khalili, Mr. 440
Khalkhali, Hojjatoleslam Sadegh (Sadeq) 153, 154, 167
Khamenei, Supreme Leader Seyyed Ali 152–154, 167, 223, 226, 229, 240, 249, 252, 275, 278, 312, 336, 382, 419, 470
Khamoushi, Alinaghi (Ali-Naqi) 485
Khanentz, Galust 550
Khanjian, Grigor 500
Khanlari, MP Karen 286
Khark-Island, Iran 66
Khatami, President Mohammad 272, 336, 475, 494
Khatchadrian, MP Hratch 286
Khayyatzadeh, Mr. 289
Khechoumian, Andranik 499
Khodabakhshian, Manook 115
Kholian, Grigor 16
Khomein, Iran 142
Khomeini, Ayatollah Seyyed Ruhollah Mousavi 134, 138, 140, 143–145, 148–155, 163, 164, 166, 167, 169, 173, 175, 176, 206, 221, 225, 227, 230, 249, 255, 260, 261, 263, 265, 311, 312, 324, 419, 436, 493
Khomeini, Hojjatoleslam Seyyed Ahmad 106, 213, 261, 324, 376
Khorasan, Iran 135, 290
Khoren I, Catholicos of the See of Cilicia (1963–83) 264, 298, 492
Khorramshahr, Iran 60, 83, 84, 89, 90, 132, 205, 209, 311
Khosh Yelagh, Iran 127
Khoshnevisan, Mr. 183–186, 190, 238, 278
Khosrova, Iran 52
Khosrovian, Hratch 504
Khosrowdad, General Manuchehr 101, 148
Khoudabakhshian, Razmik 371
Khoy, Iran 13, 15, 23, 496
Khuzestan, Iran 59, 86, 95, 160, 167, 207, 291, 556, 557
Kianuri, Dr. Nureddin 227
Kjoyan, Bishop Navasard 482
Kocharyan, President Robert 415, 444, 468, 473–478, 483, 501, 528
Kochinyan, Henrik 388, 408, 435, 454
Koleyni, Ambassador Mohammad Farhad 407, 471, 478, 479, 484
Koloushani, Mr. 209
Kostanian, Bishop Vahan 461
Krasnodar, Russia 13, 14
Kurkjian, Hakob (Yasha) 48
Kurkjian, Levon (Leon Kurukchian) 48

Kurkjian, Varand 550
Kuznetsov, Valentin 344

L

Lachin, Nagorno Gharabagh 373
Laghi, Francesca 126
Lahijan, Iran 48
Lazar, Rudolf 48
Lazarian, Janet 191
Levard, Jacqueline and Yves 532
Limontian, Arax 290
Loukinov, Mr. 101, 105
Louvard, Dr. Yves 307

M

MacArthur II, Ambassador Douglas 136
Madani, Admiral Ahmad 167
Madani, Ayatollah Asadollah 227
Madani, Mr. 274, 278
Madatian, Mnatzakan 556
Madatian, Sarkis 557
Madteosian, Dilbar 14, 18
Madteosian, Gaspar (Gago) 19
Madteosian, Gevorg 14, 18, 19
Mahabad, Iran 166
Mahdavi-Kani, Ayatollah Mohammad-Reza 153, 154, 229, 321
Mahlam, Iran 13, 16, 496
Majidiyeh, Tehran 51, 183, 185, 189, 190, 194, 195, 257, 293, 300, 308, 316, 338, 339, 397, 430, 482, 508, 515, 528, 555, 560
Maklakov, Alexander Sergeyevich 98
Maleki, Khalil 40
Mamian, Arsen 550
Manjil, Iran 49, 88, 89, 464
Manoukian, Archbishop Ardak 87, 109, 111, 114, 163, 167, 169, 179, 181, 183, 185, 188, 189, 193, 207, 211–214, 221, 224, 226, 229, 240, 242, 249, 252, 255–259, 263, 268, 270, 273, 276, 277, 289, 291, 292, 293, 297–302, 307, 313, 315, 338, 340, 352, 355, 360, 368, 392, 398, 412, 420, 423, 444, 453, 456, 461, 470, 475, 490, 491, 503, 553, 563
Manoukian, Mary 273
Manoukian, Vagrig 181, 193, 214, 244, 257, 264, 278, 297, 299, 514
Mansourian, Vahik 371
Mansourian, Vazrig 226
Manukyan, Azad 423, 447, 467
Manukyan, Prime Minister Vazgen 344, 346, 347, 352, 353, 357, 359, 361, 440, 441, 459, 467
Maragheh, Iran 24, 39, 42
Marakan, Iran 119, 120
Mardagert, Nagorno Gharabagh 404
Mardirossian, George 550
Mardouni, Nagorno Gharabagh 404
Maremati, Vahid 15
Markarian, Emil 48, 50
Markarian, George 47
Markarian, Hrand 422, 424, 455, 456
Markarian, Rouzas 371, 498
Markarian, Silva 340, 486, 539
Markaryan, Prime Minister Andranik 388, 482
Markaryan, Samuel 367, 368
Marootian, Manuel 550
Maroukhian, Hrair 47, 297, 298, 353, 359, 389, 390, 407, 431, 442, 472
Mashhad, Iran 66, 122, 135, 142, 143, 289, 290, 466, 507
Masjed Soleyman, Iran 556
Matevosyan, Ruben 406, 407
Matian, Azad 279
Medvedev, General Vladimir Alekseyevich 107
Medzbaian, H. 552
Megerdumian, Mardiros 557
Meghri, Armenia 345–351, 354, 359, 373, 374, 383, 386–388, 401, 403, 405, 457, 507
Mehrabian, Alfred Barzegar 159, 160, 327, 520

Mehrabian, Garnik 47
Melikian, Derenik 432, 517
Melikian, Dr. Ardavazd 181, 182
Melikian, Grigor 301
Melikian, Hrachouhi 301
Melkonian, Avres 48
Melkonian, Norair 196, 355, 444, 480, 481, 483, 507
Melkonian, V. Rev. Father Bagrad 254, 270, 299
Memmedov, Acting President Yakub 381
Mesropian, Ohanik 52
Mesropian, Perino 47
Mgrdichian, Babken 47
Mgrditchian, Mgrditch 431
Mgrtichian, Leon 536, 537
Mianeh, Iran 24
Mikaelian, Reverend Tadevos 271, 272, 335, 392
Minas, Caro 486, 537
Minassian, Jora 559
Minassian, Norair 48
Mirbegian, Seroj 486, 537
Mir-Salim, Mostafa 275
Mirzabegian, Jora 351, 371, 373, 387, 388
Mirzaian, Jeannette 486, 537
Mirzoyan, Karen 482
Mkrtchyan, Levon 485
Mnatsakanian, Felix 48
Mnatzakanian, Souren 559, 561
Moayed, Mohammad-Ali 371
Moazzemi, Colonel 258, 259
Mofatteh, Hojjatoleslam Dr. Mohammad 153, 155
Moghaddam, Fatemeh 272, 273
Mohajerani, Dr. Ataollah 494
Mohammadkhan, Morteza 387, 421, 422
Mohtashamipour, Hojjatoleslam Ali-Akbar 317
Momeni, Dr. 535

Montazeri, Ayatollah Hossein-Ali 147, 153, 221, 263, 278, 279
Montazeri, Sheikh Mohammad 147, 221, 226, 342
Mortazavi, Mr. 242, 267
Mortazi, Mr. 25, 26
Mosadegh, Ahmad 77
Mosadegh, Dr. Gholam Hossein 77
Mosadegh, Mohammed 40, 42, 59–65, 77, 110, 134, 137, 176
Moscow, Russia 42, 95–97, 100, 102, 105, 107, 227, 313, 342–344, 351, 353, 355, 366, 367, 407, 450, 467, 475, 480
Motahhari, Ayatollah Morteza 135, 153, 155
Mouradian, Tadevos 370
Mouradian, Vigen 370
Mousavi, Prime Minister Mir-Hossein 264
Mousavi-Ardebili, Ayatollah Seyyed Abdol-Karim 153, 240–246
Mousavi-Khoeiniha, Hojjatoleslam Seyyed Mohammad 153, 166
Mousavi-Tabrizi, Mollah Hossein 166
Moutafian, Armen 355, 361, 370
Movsisian, Hrand 115
Movsissian, Gurgen 303
Mozaffar, Mr. 238, 240, 244, 253, 256, 273, 274, 278, 366
Msrian, Hratch 113
Msrlian, Berj 384, 404, 409, 442, 461

N

Nagorno Gharabagh (Karabagh) *See* Artsakh
Naghavi, Agha Ali 122, 123
Nahabedian, Dr. Vartkes 163, 179, 194, 240
Najaf, Iraq 134, 139, 144
Nakhichevan, Azerbaijan 346, 348, 406, 469
Nalbandian, Garnik 48

Narmak, Tehran 51, 110, 190, 195, 222, 274, 279, 292–296, 300, 308, 395, 494, 513, 515, 529, 560
Nasiri, General Nematollah 62, 64, 139, 140, 148
Nateghi, Haj Agha 128
Nategh-Nuri, Hojjatoleslam Ali-Akbar 153
Navasardyan, Arman 419
Nazarian, Nazar 561
Nazaryan, Ambassador Garen (Karen) Arshagi 476, 517
Nazaryan, Mayor Robert 483
Nazih, Dr. Hassan 154
Neauphle-le-Château, France 144, 213
Nersissian, Dr. Zaven 293, 294
Nersissian, Goriun 93, 159
Neyshabour, Iran 291
Nikkar-Esfahani, Ambassador Hamid-Reza 428–430, 449, 456, 464, 477
Nikpay, Mayor Gholam-Reza 140
Nixon, President Richard 66, 137
Nomani, Hojjatoleslam 493
Nor Jugha (New Julfa), Isfahan 221, 557
Nourdouz, Iran 348, 371
Novikov, Dr. 19, 20
Nowruzi, Mohammad (Haj Agha Younesi) 330, 333, 335
Nshanian, Nik 486, 537
Nshanian, Yuri 344, 345, 349, 350

O

Ohanian (Oganiants), Ovanes 46
Ohanian, Deacon Zareh 302
Ohanian, Tatool 459
Oshakan, Armenia 487, 540
Ourfalian, Archbishop Dajad 492
Özal, President Turgut 405

P

Pahlavi, Ali Reza 118, 119
Pahlavi, Farah Diba 76, 113, 126, 554
Pahlavi, Mohammad Reza Shah 21, 37, 41, 76, 336
Pahlavi, Reza Shah 17, 38, 40, 85, 143, 154, 336, 389, 554
Pahlavi, Soraya Esfandiary-Bakhtiari 62
Pahlavouni, Norair 47, 111, 116, 432
Papanian, Boris 120, 121
Papazian, Meliné 502
Papazian, Rubina 424, 499, 502
Papazian, Vantsig 368
Papazian, Yervand 99, 100
Papazyan, Hagop 99, 340, 345, 347, 351, 352, 384, 444, 445
Papazyan, Vahan 374, 382, 421–424, 429, 452
Papian, Archbishop Goriun 185, 221, 254, 299, 355, 360, 375, 376, 380, 392, 455, 459, 493
Parvaresh, Ali-Akbar 238, 240, 244, 246, 252–256, 260, 266, 273, 338
Pasghaleh, Iran 47
Patmagrian, Victoria 554
Payajuk, Iran 16, 303, 497
Perker, Annik 481
Perker, Ashot 481, 483, 487, 539
Petrosian, Bella 564
Petrossian, Dr. Vazrig Der 307, 345, 347, 348, 349
Petrossian, Manoushag 395, 452, 453
Petrossian, Rafik Der 181, 301, 370, 458
Pezeshkian, Vachik 370
Pilossian, Sofia 554
Piroomian, Mehran Boghos 370
Piroomian, Meline 454
Pishevari, Jafar 42
Poladian, Father Emmanuel 22, 112, 271, 375
Pyunik, Armenia 488, 543

Q

Qaleh Boland, Iran 122, 123
Qamishli, Syria 492

Qazvin, Iran 18, 38, 49, 118, 289, 316, 507
Qom, Iran 138, 143, 144, 166, 167, 222, 279

R

Raffi (Hakob Melik Hakobian) 16, 303, 497
Rafigh-Doust, Mohsen 145, 344, 345, 353, 354
Rahmani, Mr. 85, 155
Rajai, President Mohammad Ali 154, 187, 227
Rajavi, Masoud 165
Rajkov, Zdravko 115, 292
Ramsar, Iran 48
Rasht, Iran 48, 49, 67, 118, 289, 507
Reagan, President Ronald 178
Reza Shah 17
Roosevelt, Kermit (Kim) 63
Roudaki, Commander Haj Abdollah 371, 373
Roumestan, Jacqueline 70
Roumestan, Mr. 70, 72, 75, 83, 84, 89, 91, 93
Roumestan, Regine 70
Roustamian, Hrair 116
Rubina, Rubina 498
Rudbar, Iran 49, 123, 464

S

Saadabad, Tehran 38, 494
Saadi 526
Sabzevar, Iran 291
Saddoughi (Sadduqi), Ayatollah Ali-Mohammad 227
Sadeghi, Morteza 371
Sadr ol-Hefazi, Mr. 324
Saeedi Sirjani, Ali-Akbar 335
Safai, Hojjatoleslam Gholam-Reza 212
Safarian, André 126, 127, 142
Safarian, Robert 517
Safarian, Seroj 48

Safaryan, Ashot 369, 406, 424, 428, 429, 444, 454, 458
Safizadeh, Mr. 267, 268, 274
Saginian, MP Sevag 47, 113, 284
Sahakian, Anahid 16
Sahakian, Daniel (Dodig) 16, 155, 406
Sahakian, Edward 115
Sahakian, Hasmik 555
Sahakian, Henrik 16
Sahakian, Israel 16
Sahakian, Onnik 370
Sahakyan, Ara 374
Sajjadi, Mr. 230, 232
Salakhanian, Vartan 67
Salehi, Major 66
Salmast (Salmas), Iran 14–17, 44, 194, 279, 303, 496, 497
Sanandaj, Iran 166
Sanjabi, Dr. Karim 137, 154
Sarakhs, Iran 158
Sardarian, Dr. Ruben 499, 504, 513
Sargsyan, Acting Prime Minister Aram 479, 501
Sargsyan, Fadey 414
Sargsyan, Prime Minister Armen 446, 454
Sargsyan, Prime Minister Vazgen 479, 501
Sargsyan, Raihan 487
Sarhadian, Leon 371
Sari, Iran 289, 290, 507
Sarian, Anahid 486, 537, 538
Sarkissian, Archbishop Sebouh 296, 341, 475, 482, 492–494, 501–503, 520, 523, 528, 529, 533
Sarkissian, Gurgen 16
Sarkissian, Markar 16
Sarkissian, Rehan 541
Sarkissian, Sos 367
Sarkissian, Souren 402, 409

Sarkissian, Vazgen 16
Sarkissian-Maroukhian, Anahid 298, 389
Sarksian, Garo 499
Sarna, Iran 16
Saroukhanian, Tomas 355
Sassoun (Vahidiyeh, Zarkesh and Narmak), Tehran 308
Savad Kuh, Iran 72, 123
Saveh, Iran 52, 86
Sayenkov, Mr. 160, 161, 344
Schalamche (Iran) 205
Semnan, Iran 118
Sergeyev, Mr. (Sergei) 97, 343
Sevak, Paruyr 16, 190, 500, 551
Shabanian, Fariborz 344, 345, 353
Shadikian, Hrand 398
Shahbazi, Mr. 102, 141
Shahbazian, Edward 371
Shahbazian, Norair 371, 487, 542
Shahbazian, Souren (Hrair) 371, 458, 487, 512, 542
Shahbazian, Yeznik 181, 289, 301, 371
Shahen, Shahen 370
Shahin Shahr, Iran 165, 279, 494
Shahnazarian, Vahik 371
Shahoumian, Grish 48
Shahpur 17
Shahrud, Iran 88, 89, 118
Shahsavar (Tonekabon), Iran 14
Shahumyan, Nagorno Gharabagh 404
Shahverdian (Begoumian), Rubina 115
Shambayati, Dr. Jaleh 162, 182, 325
Shamlu, Ahmad 67
Shariati, Dr. Ali 135, 225, 329
Shariatmadari, Ayatollah Seyyed Mohammad Kazem 144, 152, 166
Sharif-Emami, Prime Minister Jafar 139, 140
Shazand, Iran 70–72, 291

Sheikh Hadi, Tehran 21, 185, 302, 397, 494
Shemiran, Tehran 135, 324, 385
Shiraz, Iran 26, 83, 142, 143, 165, 227, 526, 547
Shirazi, Karimpour 65
Shirvanian, Father Mesrop 109
Shishmanian, Arsiné 398
Shishmanian, Asdghik 398
Shishmanian, Gevorg 398
Shushi, Nagorno Gharabagh 373, 381, 382, 450
Siahkal, Iran 136
Simonian, Jean Marie 393
Simonian, Jirair 300
Sirakian, Dr. Razmik 310, 316, 527
Sisian, Armenia 349
Sistan-ve-Baluchestan, Iran 167
Sobhani, Ambassador 419, 428
Sochi, Russia 386, 434
Soukiassian, Digran 561
Soukiassian, Seroj 180, 193, 196, 481
Sourenian, Varouj 486, 517, 520, 539
Spitak, Armenia 351, 411, 469, 505, 506, 511
Stepanakert, Nagorno Gharabagh 381, 450
Stepanian, Dr. Rostom 432
Stepanian, Dr. Sampson 194
Stepanian, Hovsep 47
Stepanian, Stepan 371
Stepanian, Suren and Kathrin 547
Stepanyan, Yesayi 355, 357, 361
Syunik (Zangezur), Armenia 347

T

Tabatabai, Judge 230, 232
Tabriz, Iran 16, 18, 24, 41, 46, 50, 67, 110, 138, 142, 143, 166, 220, 227, 254, 270, 299, 303, 371, 373, 383–385, 392, 419, 435, 466, 481, 483, 493–498, 528, 547
Tadevossian, Hrach 486, 537
Taghavi, Colonel 372, 373

Tajbakhsh 27
Taleghani, Ayatollah Seyyed Mahmoud 139, 167
Tashchian, Aroosyak 561
Tashjiyan, Sebouh 374, 407, 408
Tbilisi (formerly Tiflis), Georgia 354, 387
Tehran, passim 15
Tekeyan, Bishop Vartan 257, 425
Ter Minassov, Mr. 107
Ter-Petrosyan, President Levon 352, 357, 359, 361, 367, 371–382, 387, 389, 390, 394, 402–405, 408, 413, 421, 426–431, 440–442, 447, 449, 453–457, 467, 469, 470, 472, 474, 478, 483, 491, 496
Ter-Petrosyan, Telman 356, 388, 402, 406–408, 414, 424, 428, 443, 444, 457, 458, 478
Terzian, Petros 369
Tilimian, Seroj 260
Tjeknavorian, Loris 351, 386, 402, 407, 415, 422, 423, 430, 477, 486, 501, 528, 539
Tolyatti, Russia 105
Tomas, Razmik 454
Tomassian, Babig 498
Tomassian, Jenik 337
Tomassian, Tomas (Babig) 191, 230, 274, 322, 325, 334, 337, 371, 498
Topouzian, V. Rev. Father Nshan 375, 392, 493
Tossounian, V. Rev. Father 425
Tounayan, Angelle 340
Tounyan, Greta 480, 482, 483, 485, 530
Tovmassian, Tovmas 551
Truman, President Harry 59
Tumanyan, Artashes 47, 484, 528

U
Urumia, Iran 13, 15, 121, 497, 547
Ushan, Iran 50

V
Vaezi, Mahmoud 419, 420
Vaezian, Joseph 46
Vaghefi, Governor 380
Vahidi, Dr. Iraj 77
Vahidiyeh, Tehran 51, 189, 195, 308, 560
Vahramian, Vartan 496
Valangerud, Iran 127
Van Skarenburg, Dr. 74
Vanak, Tehran 113, 180, 191, 195, 284, 302, 308, 434, 512
Varand (Soukias Hakob Kurkjian) 48
Vardan, Gevorg 282
Vardan, MP Gevorg 283, 286, 511, 529
Vardanyan, Aram 478, 479
Vartanian, Ara 126, 128
Vartanian, MP Vartan 181, 234, 274, 279, 280, 286, 313, 321, 325, 327, 338–340, 368, 376, 380, 388, 392, 430, 433, 456, 479, 501, 506, 509
Vartanian, Nazeli 485
Vartanian, Sebouh 126
Vartanian, Vachik 499, 502, 504, 517, 525
Varvash (Varavasht), Iran 118
Vayk, Armenia 346, 347
Vazgen I, Catholicos of All Armenians (1955–94) 351, 360, 369, 394, 401, 402, 411, 441, 462, 500, 506, 511
Velayati, Dr. Ali-Akbar 374, 451
Verneuil, Henri (Ashot Malakian) 352
Vesali, Mr. 25, 26
Vis (Veys), Iran 100
Vosdanik 22
Voskanian, Rostom 113, 114, 302, 553
Voskanian, Rubik 113
Voskanian, Souren 288
Voskanyan, Ashot 424
Vrouyrian, Khoren Der 181
Vruyr, Ara 394, 395

W

Wageningen, The Netherlands 74
West Azarbayjan, Iran 13, 119, 166, 300
Wilber, Donald 63

X

X, General 318, 327, 330, 337, 433

Y

Yanagita, Keiichi 458, 459
Yazdi, Dr. Ebrahim 135, 153, 154
Yeghiazaryan, Armen 402, 405
Yengoyan, Robert 414, 415, 459, 487, 527, 542
Yenokyan, Gohar 350, 352, 361
Yerevan, Armenia 468, 471, 474–478, 480–490, 502, 504, 508, 524, 526–528, 530, 533, 535
Yeritsian, Edvart 432
Yeritsyan, Mr. 366, 367
Yeritzyan, Sergo 486, 537, 540, 541
Younesi, Haj Agha 320
Younesi, Hojatoleslam Ali 319–321, 325–327, 330, 334

Z

Zadoyan, David 478
Zafaraniyeh, Tehran 324
Zahedi, Ambassador Ardeshir 61, 64
Zahedi, General Fazlollah 61, 62
Zahiri, Shahrokh 370, 371, 484
Zandi, Mr. 160–162, 316
Zangezur (Syunik), Armenia 385, 406, 411, 469, 507
Zanjan, Iran 42, 121
Zanjan, Mr. 188
Zanjirchyan, Zarouhi (Mary) 486, 530
Zargarian, Dr. Vigen 279
Zarkesh, Tehran 51, 308, 560
Zinjirjian, Zaruhi 537
Zohrabekian, Leon 28
Zohrabian, MP Vahram Khan 284
Zolfaghari 42, 121
Zomorodian, Ardashes 158, 373, 496, 520, 526

www.ingramcontent.com/pod-product-compliance
Lightning Source LLC
Chambersburg PA
CBHW021713300426
44114CB00009B/127